PROFESSIONAL
SQL SERVER® 2014 ADMINISTRATION

PROFESSIONAL

SQL Server® 2014
Administration

PROFESSIONAL

SQL Server® 2014
Administration

Adam Jorgensen
Bradley Ball
Steven Wort
Ross LoForte
Brian Knight

wrox™
A Wiley Brand

Professional SQL Server® 2014 Administration

Published by
John Wiley & Sons, Inc.
10475 Crosspoint Boulevard
Indianapolis, IN 46256
www.wiley.com

Copyright © 2014 by John Wiley & Sons, Inc., Indianapolis, Indiana

Published simultaneously in Canada

ISBN: 978-1-118-85913-1
ISBN: 978-1-118-85926-1 (ebk)
ISBN: 978-1-118-85919-3 (ebk)

Manufactured in the United States of America

10 9 8 7 6 5 4 3

For general information on our other products and services please contact our Customer Care Department within the United States at (877) 762-2974, outside the United States at (317) 572-3993 or fax (317) 572-4002.

Wiley publishes in a variety of print and electronic formats and by print-on-demand. Some material included with standard print versions of this book may not be included in e-books or in print-on-demand. If this book refers to media such as a CD or DVD that is not included in the version you purchased, you may download this material at http://book-support.wiley.com. For more information about Wiley products, visit www.wiley.com.

Library of Congress Control Number: 2014930416

This book is dedicated to my wife (the first time I get to call her that in a book). I love you sweetheart!

—Adam Jorgensen

For Colton, I hope you find your inner-geek.

—BRIAN KNIGHT

I want to dedicate this book to my Dad, Robert Ball. Throughout my life, you have been a constant inspiration. Your handiwork, dedication to family, ethics, and integrity amaze me, and my appreciation continues to grow as I get older. The random moments in life with you have always been some of my most treasured—sitting in your squad car getting to blow the siren as a child, climbing the hill/mountain on the Pacific Coast to see the lighthouse, being introduced to the back of the house at your restaurant, eating Fruity Pebbles on the beach, or posing for a picture outside of the White House before going to work. Every victory I achieve, you achieve with me. This book is one of those achievements. I love you, Dad.

—BRADLEY BALL

ABOUT THE AUTHORS

 ADAM JORGENSEN is an award-winning and globally recognized leader with success in growth-focused and global organizations. His current focus is on helping clients build a data culture where they are identifying, analyzing, and driving their business opportunities through proper analytic solutions. Jorgensen's current focus is directing strategic and operational aspects of Pragmatic Works, and serving the community as the Executive Vice President and Director of PASS (the world's largest organization of data professionals). Both organizations drive professionals to new and powerful ways of being better at what they do through a data-driven lens.

 BRADLEY BALL is a Microsoft Certified IT Professional (MCITP) 2005 and 2008 DBA with more than 15 years of experience. Bradley spent eight years working as a Department of Defense contractor for clients such as the U.S. Army, The Executive Office of the President of the United States, and Publix Supermarkets. Currently, he is the Data Platform Management Lead with Pragmatic Works, specializing in Data Platform solutions, and a Microsoft Virtual Technology Solution Professional (VTSP), assisting Microsoft in delivering technical solutions, troubleshooting problems, and evangelizing SQL Server for Microsoft. He has presented at many SQL Saturdays, for PASS SQL Server User Groups (SSUGs) across the United States from California to Florida to New Hampshire, SQL Rally, DevConnections, SQL Live 360, and the PASS Summit 2011, 2012, and 2013. He currently resides in central Florida, and can be found blogging about SQL Server or anything else that interests him at http://www.sqlballs.com.

 STEVEN WORT has been working with SQL Server since 1993, starting with version 4.2 running on OS2. He has more than 30 years of experience developing applications in the IT industry. Wort joined Microsoft in 2000 as an escalation engineer in the Systems Integration Engineering (SIE) team, where he co-authored multiple workshops on debugging Windows and .NET. In 2004, he moved to the SQL Server team to work on scalability for SQL Server 2005. After a short spell in the Windows group spent working on scaling large database systems, he moved back to the SQL Server group to build SQL Server appliances. He is now working as an architect in the CRM Service Engineering team, focusing on performance and scalability of SQL Server. Wort has co-authored several books on SQL Server administration, troubleshooting, and performance tuning.

ROSS LOFORTE is a Technology Architect at the Microsoft Technology Center Chicago, focused on Microsoft SQL Server solutions. LoForte has more than 20 years experience with business development, project management, and SQL architecture solutions. For the past 13 years, he has been working with the Microsoft Technology Centers, and has led architecture design and proof-of-concept engagements for Microsoft's largest and most strategic customers to design enterprise, mission-critical SQL Server solutions. LoForte is a SQL Server instructor at DePaul University in Chicago, and regularly presents at SQL Saturday, TechEd, SQL PASS, Gartner, TDWI, and Microsoft internal conferences. He is a published author, and has been active for many years with the Professional Association for SQL Server, the Chicago SQL Server Users Group, and the SQL Server community.

BRIAN KNIGHT is the co-owner and founder of Pragmatic Works, and is a serial entrepreneur, starting up other companies. Knight has been a contributing columnist at several technical magazines and does regular webcasts. He is the author of more than a 15 technical books. Knight has spoken at dozens of conferences like PASS, SQL Connections, and TechEd, and at many Code Camps. He has received a number of awards from the state, governor, and press, including the Business Ambassador Award (Governor) and Top CEO (*Jacksonville Magazine*). His blog can be found at http://www.bidn.com.

ABOUT THE CONTRIBUTORS

CHAD CHURCHWELL is a seasoned database professional with more than 10 years of experience working with SQL Server. He currently is a Premier Field Engineer with Microsoft, and has also served as a SQL Server consultant, as well as managed a team of enterprise DBAs in an operations management capacity. He is very involved in the SQL Server community, including donating his time to speak at various SQL Saturday's around the Southeast, as well as SQL Live 360. In his spare time, he can be found around Jacksonville Beach enjoying the nice Florida weather.

DAN CLARK is a senior BI consultant/programmer specializing in Microsoft technologies. He enjoys learning new technologies and training others how to best implement the technology. Clark has written several books on .NET and database programming. He is also regular speaker at developer/database conferences, as well as at user group meetings.

KIM HATHAWAY is a senior database consultant with 27 years of experience across several database management systems platforms. She specializes in troubleshooting errors and performance, managing multiple clients in database services, provisioning SQL health assessments, developing project plans, upgrading SQL platforms, recommending and implementing high-availability solutions, and developing SQL solutions for business needs. She also has hands-on experience with multiple aspects of the Microsoft Business Intelligence stack. She is committed to providing quality end-to-end solutions to each and every business problem. She is continually expanding her skillset with new technologies and gives back to the community through speaking at events.

BRADLEY SCHACHT is a senior consultant and trainer at Pragmatic Works in Jacksonville, Florida. He has co-authored three books on SharePoint and SQL Server. His experience includes SharePoint 2010, SharePoint 2013, data warehousing, and extensive work on the Microsoft BI platform. He has helped numerous companies in successfully developing and implementing new BI solutions into their organizations. Schacht frequently presents at community events around the country. He is a contributor to sites such as SQLServerCentral.com and an active member of the Jacksonville SQL Server User Group (JSSUG).

JORGE SEGARRA (also known as "SQLChicken") is a SQL Server Most Valuable Professional (MVP), author, blogger, and presenter. Jorge is based out of Tampa, Florida, and is currently a Senior Data Platform consultant for Pragmatic Works. He specializes in virtualization, Parallel Data Warehouse (PDW), performance tuning, and writing about himself in the third person.

KATHY VICK is a Senior BI Consultant with Pragmatic Works. She spent 12 years working for Microsoft in IT and Consulting, as well as two years at Expedia.com. She has been supporting SQL Server since 1994, and has spent her career focusing on data. She has enjoyed the consulting life, working with many large Fortune 100 companies while working for both Microsoft and Pragmatic

Works. Vick blogs at `http://mskathy.com`, and can be found on Twitter at `@MsKathyV`. When she is not working, she has a passion for photography, and loves to travel. She lives in the Seattle area with her husband, kids, and grandchildren.

ROGER WOLTER has more than 25 years of experience in databases and distributed systems. He has extensive experience developing and delivering large, complex applications on Windows environments with emphasis on databases, transaction processing, client server, reliable messaging, communications interfaces, and Master Data Management. During his 12 years with Microsoft, he served as a program manager for SQL Server, and as architect for a variety of product teams. His SQL Server projects include Service Broker, SQLXML, and SQL Express. Since leaving Microsoft in 2010, Wolter has been a database architect specializing in performance, consolidation, Parallel Data Warehouse (PDW), and Master Data Services (MDS).

ABOUT THE TECHNICAL EDITORS

KATHI KELLENBERGER is a BI consultant and former DBA. She is also a SQL Server MVP. Kellenberger enjoys teaching, presenting, and writing about SQL Server, and is the author or co-author of several SQL Server books. When she is not working, she enjoys time with family and friends. If you have heard of #sqlkaraoke, you can blame Kellenberger. She organized the first karaoke event at PASS Summit in 2006 with three of her friends.

JASON STRATE is Solution Architect with Pragmatic Works. He has been working with SQL Server for more 15 years. His experiences include architecting and implementing transactional and data warehousing solutions on Microsoft Data Platform technologies, including SQL Server and Analytics Platform System. Strate has been a recipient of the Microsoft Most Valuable Professional (MVP) award for SQL Server since 2009, and is also a Microsoft Certified Master for SQL Server. He blogs at www.jasonstrate.com and tweets as @StrateSQL.

DANIEL TAYLOR started his technical career as a QA at the Nielsen Media Research Company. He moved into the ranks of programming and began working with Sybase ASE 11 thru 12.5, Sybase IQ, eventually moving to SQL Server. Taylor has worked with SQL Server versions from 7.0 through 2014. He also worked for Publix as Senior DBA, Technical Specialist, and was the SQL Server Team Lead that supported more than 2,000 instances of SQL Server. Currently, he is a Senior SQL Database Specialist at New York Life, Tampa Division, where he is part of a support team that administers the BI environment and SQL Server backend databases. You can find him on Twitter as @DBABullDog, blogging at http://dbabulldog.wordpress.com and LinkedIn http://www.linkedin.com/pub/daniel-taylor/5/B1/A96.

CREDITS

ACKNOWLEDGMENTS

I would like to thank the incredible team at Wiley who have helped us keep this book moving forward, as well as Bradley Ball for his time and dedication to this title and our community. A special thanks to the SQL Server community, and those who make it amazing --this book is for you. Another special thanks to Dan Taylor, who was instrumental in getting this book finished and keeping all of us honest!

—ADAM JORGENSEN

I want to acknowledge and thank many people. First, I want to thank Wiley's editorial staff—Kevin Shafer, Mary Beth Wakefield, and Robert Elliott. Thank you for keeping us on track, task, and together. To Adam Jorgensen, thank you for giving me a shot! Thanks to my Sigma Nu brother, Tim Pickles, who convinced me to change my major from Art to Computers (best sober college decision ever)! Thanks to my buddy, Daniel Taylor, who has been my technical sounding board for almost five years. Thanks to my fellow authors—amazing work from a great talented crew that I'm proud to be associated with. Most importantly, I want to say thank you to my children—Chesney, Zachary, William, and Serenity—for putting up with the days when I couldn't go and play, or had to stay inside. The greatest thing I've ever done is be your father. I love you all—no matter what!

—BRADLEY BALL

I would like to acknowledge my wonderful wife, Tracy, and my daughters, Eleanor and Caitlin, who have to endure me while I am writing. Thanks also to everyone in the SQL Program Group at Microsoft for your help in answering my questions.

—STEVEN WORT

I'd like to thank my wife, Anna, and my daughter, Jennifer, for the support and dedication while writing this book. I'd like to thank the Microsoft Technology Center's staff for their support, and for making the Microsoft Technology Center Chicago a great facility to learn and experience. Additionally (and foremost), I'd like to thank the SQL Server development team for delivering another excellent release, full of features in SQL Server 2014. Last, but not least, thanks to the Technical Editors, Project Editor (Kevin Shafer), and several folks at Wiley (including Robert Elliott) for getting these words into print to enable our readers to share my passion for SQL Server.

—ROSS LOFORTE

ACKNOWLEDGMENTS

Thanks to everyone who made this book possible. As always, I owe a huge debt to my wife, Jenn, for putting up with my late nights, and to my children, Colton, Liam, Camille, and, John, for being so patient with their tired dad who has always overextended. Thanks to the makers of Guinness for providing my special juice that helped me power through the book. Thanks for all the user group leaders out there who work so hard to help others become proficient in technology. You make a huge difference!

—BRIAN KNIGHT

CONTENTS

CHAPTER 12: MONITORING YOUR SQL SERVER

INTRODUCTION

SQL Server 2014 represents the largest jump forward in scalability, performance, and usability for the database administrator (DBA), developer, and business intelligence (BI) developer of any SQL Server release. SQL Server 2014 has already broken two world records in the TCP-H benchmark in the 3TB and 10TB configurations, breaking records previously held by Oracle/SPARC, as well as outperforming Oracle in both categories. The power and performance of SQL Server 2014 bring capabilities previously only available in the Parallel Data Warehouse (PDW) and Analytic Platform System (APS) appliances, and deliver them to regular SQL Server users and businesses large and small. Understanding the features and when to apply them is one small part of your job. Once a system is built, it must still be maintained.

It is no longer unheard of to have 40TB databases running on a SQL Server. SQL Server administration used to be just the job of a DBA. But as SQL Server proliferates throughout smaller companies, many developers have begun to act as administrators and BI developers as well. Poor configuration of features can result in poor performance. SQL Server now enables all roles through significantly improved developer tools experiences, better security integration, and drastic improvements in data integration, administration, availability, and usability.

Professional Microsoft SQL Server 2014 Administration is a comprehensive, tutorial-based book to get you over the learning curve of how to configure and administer SQL Server 2014.

WHO THIS BOOK IS FOR

Whether you're an administrator or developer using SQL Server, you can't avoid wearing a DBA hat at some point. Developers often have SQL Server on their own workstations, and must provide guidance to the administrator about how they'd like the production configured. Oftentimes, they're responsible for creating the database tables and indexes. Administrators or DBAs support the production servers and often inherit the database from the developer.

This book is intended for developers, DBAs, and casual users who hope to administer or may already be administering a SQL Server 2014 system and its BI features (such as SQL Server Integration Services, or SSIS). This book is a *professional* book, meaning the authors assume that you know the basics about how to query a SQL Server, and have some rudimentary concepts of SQL Server. For example, this book does not show you how to create a database, or walk you through the installation of SQL Server using the wizard. Instead, the author of the installation chapter provides insight into how to use some of the more advanced concepts of the installation. Although this book does not cover how to query a SQL Server database, it does cover how to tune the queries you've already written.

HOW THIS BOOK IS STRUCTURED

This edition of the book covers almost all the same great information covered in the previous edition, *Professional SQL Server 2012 Administration*. There is a new chapter covering in-memory online transaction processing (OLTP), a new feature within SQL Server 2014. The authors—SQL Server MVP's, Microsoft employees, former Microsoft employees, and top speakers at international conferences—leveraged their knowledge to deliver a thorough update, with loads of new content added for SQL Server 2014.

Numerous new features to improve the performance and scalability of SQL Server needed to be addressed, while tried-and-true performance tuning techniques have been updated with new techniques and configurations to deliver optimal performance of SQL Server 2014. In short, the new version of SQL Server focuses on improving your efficiency, the scale of your server, and the performance of your environment, so you can do more in much less time, and with fewer resources and people.

Following is a brief description of each chapter:

➤ **Chapter 1, "SQL Server 2014 Architecture"**—The book starts with a review of the new architecture changes, and focuses on the overall components that make up SQL Server 2014.

➤ **Chapter 2, "Installing SQL Server 2014 Best Practices"**—This chapter reviews the different ways to install SQL Server 2014, and covers best practices for the process.

➤ **Chapter 3, "Upgrading SQL Server 2014 Best Practices"**—This chapter covers upgrading to SQL Server 2014, as well as best practices to keep in mind while upgrading. Choosing the best upgrade method, requirements, and benefits of upgrading are also covered.

➤ **Chapter 4, "Managing and Troubleshooting the Database Engine"**—This chapter focuses on the setup and configuration of the Database Engine, and working through challenges as they arise. It also covers management and tools appropriate for the task.

➤ **Chapter 5, "Automating SQL Server"**—This chapter focuses on automation throughout the SQL Server 2014 world, including jobs, PowerShell, and other ways to automate.

➤ **Chapter 6, "Service Broker in SQL Server 2014"**—Service Broker is a great tool to handle messaging inside the database. This chapter covers processing data asynchronously, setup, sending messages, and receiving messages using Service Broker.

➤ **Chapter 7, "SQL Server CLR Integration"**—SQL Server and .NET work together inside the Common Language Runtime (CLR). This chapter focuses on integrating .NET and the CLR with SQL Server, including assemblies and other options.

➤ **Chapter 8, "Securing the Database Instance"**—Security is critical in the Database Engine. This chapter helps you outline and implement your security plan, and understand the new security settings in SQL Server 2014.

➤ **Chapter 9, "In-Memory OLTP"**—In-memory OLTP is the largest architectural change for SQL Server in more than a decade. This chapter reviews the new in-memory OLTP technology, and covers how to assess your current tables, size your hardware, and implement new in-memory structures.

➤ **Chapter 10, "Configuring the Server for Optimal Performance"**—Configuring and setting up your server properly is important for maximizing application and database performance. This chapter discusses storage, server options, and other settings critical to system performance.

➤ **Chapter 11, "Optimizing SQL Server 2014"**—This chapter covers topics that help the reader review and analyze performance. It also focuses on settings and configuration items that improve SQL Server performance.

➤ **Chapter 12, "Monitoring Your SQL Server"**—Monitoring SQL Server is critically important to ensure that you keep performance where it needs to be. This chapter covers the important aspects and tools used to monitor SQL Server 2014.

➤ **Chapter 13, "Performance Tuning T-SQL"**—Writing efficient and effective T-SQL is important to having good application performance and scalability. This chapter explains how to optimize your T-SQL to make it more efficient. It focuses on how SQL Server's engine and internals read and execute your queries. You also learn how to take advantage of areas where this process can be tweaked, and where best practices can be leveraged.

➤ **Chapter 14, "Indexing Your Database"**—Indexing is critical to successful database performance. This chapter discusses considerations and strategies for effectively indexing your database, and covers the new indexing features of SQL Server 2014.

➤ **Chapter 15, "Replication"**—Replication is a key feature in SQL Server for keeping tables and databases in sync, as well as supporting applications. This chapter covers the different types of replication, how to set them up, and the pros and cons of each.

➤ **Chapter 16, "Clustering SQL Server 2014"**—This chapter takes you through the setup, configuration, and testing of your clustered configuration of SQL Server 2014.

➤ **Chapter 17, "Backup and Recovery"**—Backup and recovery is critical to the success of a continuity plan and operational achievement. This chapter outlines the options in SQL Server for backups and recoveries, provides recommendations to make the most of these features, and covers new backup options available in SQL Server 2014.

➤ **Chapter 18, "SQL Server 2014 Log Shipping"**—This chapter goes through setup, configuration, and administration of log shipping.

➤ **Chapter 19, "Database Mirroring"**—Database mirroring was a deprecated feature in SQL Server 2012, but is still available in SQL Server 2014. However, it is the only truly robust high-availability/disaster-recovery feature that prevents data loss available in Standard Edition. This chapter thoroughly reviews mirroring for those using the technology.

➤ **Chapter 20, "Integration Services Administration and Performance Tuning"**—Integration is the key to ensuring that systems stay in sync. This chapter focuses on administering and tuning this great feature in SQL Server.

➤ Chapter 21, "Analysis Services Administration and Performance Tuning"—Analysis Services is the online analytical processing (OLAP) product of choice, and cannot be ignored by data administrators. This chapter helps you get prepared.

➤ Chapter 22, "SQL Server Reporting Services Administration"—Reporting Services is often administered by the DBA, and this chapter prepares you to handle those Reporting Services challenges, no matter what your role.

➤ Chapter 23, "SQL Server 2014 SharePoint 2013 Integration"—SharePoint now is a bigger part of SQL Server than ever before. This chapter covers what you need to know about how SharePoint 2013 integrates with SQL Server so that you can be prepared to interact with that team, or take on some SharePoint database administration responsibilities yourself.

➤ Chapter 24, "SQL Database Administration and Configuration"—This chapter introduces you to SQL Database platform as a service (PaaS) in Azure, and gets you up and running on the cloud.

➤ Chapter 25, "AlwaysOn Availability Groups"—This chapter focuses on the Availability Group feature in Always-On. These groups allow you to control instances and servers as groups, and to assign prioritization and additional flexibility to how failover and high availability are handled in your environment.

WHAT YOU NEED TO USE THIS BOOK

To follow the examples in this book, you need to have SQL Server 2014 installed. If you want to learn how to administer the BI features, you must have Analysis Services and the SQL Server Integration Services (SSIS) components installed. You need a machine that can support the minimum hardware requirements to run SQL Server 2014, and you also need the AdventureWorks2012 and AdventureWorksDW2012 databases installed. When code references the AdventureWorks database, rest assured that this is the 2012 database. You can find instructions for accessing these databases in the Readme file on this book's website at www.wrox.com.

Some features in this book (especially in the high-availability part) require the Enterprise or Developer Edition of SQL Server. If you do not have either of these editions, you can still follow through some of the examples in the chapter with the Standard Edition.

CONVENTIONS

To help you get the most from the text and keep track of what's happening, you see a number of conventions throughout the book.

> **WARNING** *Boxes like this one hold important, not-to-be forgotten information that is directly relevant to the surrounding text.*

> **NOTE** *Notes, tips, hints, tricks, and asides to the current discussion are offset and placed in italics like this.*

As for styles in the text:

- ➤ We *highlight* new terms and important words when we introduce them.
- ➤ We show keyboard strokes like this: Ctrl+A.
- ➤ We show filenames, URLs, and code within the text like so: `persistence.properties`.
- ➤ We present code in two different ways:

```
We use a monofont type with no highlighting for most code examples.
We use bold to emphasize code that's particularly important in the context of
    the chapter.
```

SOURCE CODE

As you work through the examples in this book, you may choose either to type in all the code manually, or to use the source code files that accompany the book. All the source code used in this book is available for download at `www.wrox.com`. You will find the code snippets from the source code are accompanied by a download icon and note indicating the name of the program so that you know it's available for download, and can easily locate it in the download file. Once at the site, simply locate the book's title (either by using the Search box or by using one of the title lists) and click the Download Code link on the book's detail page to obtain all the source code for the book.

> **NOTE** *Because many books have similar titles, you may find it easiest to search by ISBN; this book's ISBN is 978-1-118-85913-1.*

After you download the code, just decompress it with your favorite compression tool. Alternatively, you can go to the main Wrox code download page at `www.wrox.com/dynamic/books/download .aspx` to see the code available for this book and all other Wrox books.

ERRATA

Every effort is made to ensure that there are no errors in the text or in the code. However, no one is perfect, and mistakes do occur. If you find an error in one of our books, such as a spelling mistake or a faulty piece of code, we would be grateful for your feedback. By sending in errata, you may save another reader hours of frustration, and, at the same time, you can help us provide even higher quality information.

To find the errata page for this book, go to www.wrox.com and locate the title using the Search box or one of the title lists. Then, on the book details page, click the Book Errata link. On this page, you can view all errata that has been submitted for this book and posted by Wrox editors. A complete book list, including links to each book's errata, is also available at www.wrox.com/misc-pages/booklist.shtml.

If you don't spot "your" error on the Book Errata page, go to www.wrox.com/contact/techsupport.shtml and complete the form there to send us the error you have found. The information will be checked and, if appropriate, a message will be posted to the book's errata page, and the problem will be fixed in subsequent editions of the book.

P2P.WROX.COM

For author and peer discussion, join the P2P forums at p2p.wrox.com. The forums are a Web-based system for you to post messages relating to Wrox books and related technologies, as well as interact with other readers and technology users. The forums offer a subscription feature to e-mail you topics of interest of your choosing when new posts are made to the forums. Wrox authors, editors, other industry experts, and your fellow readers are present on these forums.

At http://p2p.wrox.com you can find a number of different forums to help you not only as you read this book, but also as you develop your own applications. To join the forums, follow these steps:

1. Go to p2p.wrox.com and click the Register link.

2. Read the terms of use and click Agree.

3. Complete the required information to join as well as any optional information you want to provide, and click Submit.

4. You will receive an e-mail with information describing how to verify your account and complete the joining process.

> **NOTE** *You can read messages in the forums without joining P2P, but to post your own messages, you must join.*

When you join, you can post new messages and respond to messages other users post. You can read messages at any time on the Web. If you want to have new messages from a particular forum e-mailed to you, click the Subscribe to this Forum icon by the forum name in the forum listing.

For more information about how to use the Wrox P2P, read the P2P FAQs for answers to questions about how the forum software works as well as many common questions specific to P2P and Wrox books. To read the FAQs, click the FAQ link on any P2P page.

1

SQL Server 2014 Architecture

WHAT'S IN THIS CHAPTER?

➤ Getting to know the new important features in SQL Server 2014

➤ Understanding how new features relate to data professionals based on their roles

➤ Understanding SQL Server architecture

➤ Getting to know the editions of SQL Server and how they affect the data professional

SQL Server 2012 offered a fresh look at how organizations and their developers, information workers, and executives use and integrate data. SQL Server 2014 continues that story and pushes forward into the future with the integration of cloud and in-memory technologies. Exciting new features and improvements provide breakthrough performance, availability, and manageability for mission-critical workloads on premises or in the cloud. This chapter provides enough information to give you an understanding of how SQL Server operates.

SQL SERVER 2014 ECOSYSTEM

The SQL Server data platform has become quite large over the past few releases. This first section provides a review of the overall SQL Server ecosystem, which is now referred to as less of a product and more of a data platform, because many interactions with other products and features drive increased performance, scale, and usability. SQL Server 2014 focuses on the following areas:

➤ **Mission-critical performance**—New In-Memory Online Transaction Processing (OLTP) features that allow faster performance with no application changes, updatable columnstore indexes, buffer pool extensions using solid-state drives (SSDs), and AlwaysOn enhancements (including support of up to eight replicas) make this the most powerful, available release of SQL Server.

➤ **Faster insights**—With new Office-based Business Intelligence (BI) tools such as Power Query and Power Map, as well as enhancements on Power View and PowerPivot, getting insights on your data has never been easier. Also, enterprise options such as Parallel Data Warehouse with Polybase allow an organization to easily explore its Big Data and gain never-before-seen insights on its data by leveraging the full power of the Microsoft BI stack.

➤ **Platform for hybrid cloud**—Whether your environment is pure on-premises, virtualized, or all in the cloud, SQL Server 2014 has options for you. New features such as the Microsoft SQL Server Backup to Windows Azure Tool enables backup to Windows Azure Blob Storage, and encrypts and compresses SQL Server backups stored locally or in the cloud. You can also now choose a Windows Azure virtual machine (VM) as a replica in an AlwaysOn Availability Group configuration.

NEW IMPORTANT FEATURES IN 2014

You will be excited about a number of new things, depending on your role and how you use SQL Server. This section touches on the features you should be checking out and getting your hands on. Many of these features are quick to get up and running, which is exciting for those readers who want to begin delivering impact right away.

Production DBA

Production database administrators (DBAs) are a company's insurance policy that the production database won't go down. If the database does go down, the company cashes in its insurance policy in exchange for a recovered database. The Production DBA also ensures that the server performs optimally, and promotes database changes from development to quality assurance (QA) to production. New features include the following:

➤ **In-Memory OLTP**—This release offers a new memory-optimized OLTP database engine for SQL Server. Experience significant performance and scalability gains to your application with little to no code changes.

➤ **AlwaysOn Availability Groups**—Availability functionality includes Availability Groups and the ability to fail over databases in groups that mimic applications. Though not a new feature in 2014, enhancements in this release include support of up to eight secondaries (up from four in the 2012 release), as well as performance and management improvements.

➤ **SQL Server Backup to Windows Azure tool**—This free tool enables backing up to Windows Azure Blob Storage. It encrypts and compresses backups stored locally or in the cloud. This tool supports SQL Server 2005 and later.

➤ **SQL Server Backup to URL**—Originally released in SQL Server 2012 SP1 CU2, this feature is now fully integrated into the Management Studio interface so that you can back up or restore from the Windows Azure Blob Storage service.

➤ **SQL Server Managed Backup to Windows Azure**—This new feature fully automates SQL Server backups (full and transaction log) to the Windows Azure Blob Storage service based on retention period and transaction workload on the database.

➤ **Columnstore indexes**—The 2014 release includes updatable clustered columnstore indexes for optimizing large data volumes.

➤ **Encrypted backups**—Support is now included for encrypted backups, including algorithm support for Advanced Encryption Standard (AES) 128, AES 192, AES 256, and Triple Data Encryption Standard (DES). You must use either a certificate or an asymmetric key to perform encryption during backup.

➤ **Delayed durability**—This includes the ability to reduce latency by designating some or all transactions as delayed durable. This asynchronous process reports a COMMIT as successful before log records are written to disk. Delayed durable transactions become durable when the transaction log entries are flushed to disk in chunks. This feature is available for In-Memory OLTP only.

➤ **Compression and partitioning**—Improved compression and partitioning include the capability to rebuild single partitions.

➤ **Resource Governor**—This now enables you to specify limits on physical I/O within a resource pool.

Development DBA

Since the release of SQL Server 2000, there has been a trend away from full-time Production DBAs, and the role has merged with that of the *Development DBA*. The trend may have slowed, though, with laws such as Sarbanes-Oxley, which require a separation of power between the person developing the change and the person implementing the change. In a large organization, a Production DBA may fall into the operations department, which consists of the network of administrators and Windows-support administrators. In other instances, a Production DBA may be placed in a development group. This removes the separation of power that is sometimes needed for regulatory reasons.

Development DBAs play a traditional role in an organization. They wear more of a developer's hat, and serve as the development staff's database experts and representatives. This administrator ensures that all stored procedures are optimally written and that the database is modeled correctly, both physically and logically. The Development DBA also may be the person who writes the migration processes to upgrade the database from one release to the next. The Development DBA typically does not receive calls at 2:00 A.M like the Production DBA might for failed backups or similar problems. Following are some of the things Development DBAs should be excited about in this new release:

➤ Transact SQL (T-SQL) enhancements include features such as the inline specification of indexes for disk-based tables. The SELECT…INTO statement can now operate in parallel with databases, in compatibility mode set to at least 110.

➤ Updates for SQL Server Data Tools for Business Intelligence (SSDT-BI) include support for creating Power View reports against multidimensional models. Additional improvements to SSDT-BI include support to create projects for older versions (2005+) of Analysis Services and Reporting Services. Backward compatibility for Integration Services projects is not yet supported.

The Development DBA typically reports to the development group, and receives requests from a business analyst or another developer. In a traditional sense, Development DBAs should never have modification access to a production database. However, they should have read-only access to the production database to debug in a time of escalation.

Business Intelligence DBA and Developer

The *BI DBA* is a role that has evolved as a result of the increased capabilities of SQL Server. In SQL Server 2012, BI grew to be an incredibly important feature set that many businesses could not live without. The BI DBA (or developer) is an expert at these features. SQL Server 2014 improves upon the end-user BI experience started in SQL Server 2012, with all new extensibility through the Power BI solution with Office365, as well as the existing BI offerings.

Development BI DBAs specialize in the best practices, optimization, and use of the BI toolset. In a small organization, a Development BI DBA may create your SQL Server Integration Services (SSIS) packages to perform extract, transform, and load (ETL) processes or reports for users. In a large organization, developers create the SSIS packages and SQL Server Reporting Services (SSRS) reports. The Development BI DBA is consulted regarding the physical implementation of the SSIS packages and SQL Server Analysis Services (SSAS) cubes, or SSAS tabular models.

Development BI DBAs may be responsible for the following types of functions:

➤ Modeling/consulting regarding Analysis Services cubes/tabular models and solutions

➤ Creating reports using Reporting Services

➤ Creating/consulting around ETL using SSIS

➤ Developing deployment packages to be sent to the Production DBA

These responsibilities, coupled with the following new features, make for an exciting time for the BI-oriented folks:

➤ Rapid data discovery with Power View and PowerPivot

➤ Lightning-fast query response time with use of columnstore indexes

➤ Users can easily discover, access, and combine various data sources themselves using Power Query

➤ Users can create powerful geospatial visualizations using Power Map

➤ Managed Self-Service BI with SharePoint and BI Semantic Model

➤ Credible, consistent data with Data Quality Services and Master Data Management capabilities

➤ Robust data warehousing solutions with Parallel Data Warehouse and Reference Architectures

SQL SERVER ARCHITECTURE

SQL Server 2014 brings many enhancements to your data platform solution. These not only give you a whole new level of breakthrough performance and scalability, but also provide exciting Self-Service BI opportunities that enable end users to explore and analyze their data faster and easier than ever before. New features such as in-memory OLTP provide massive performance gains to your applications with little to no schema changes for the application. Other features such as AlwaysOn Availability Groups allow you to quickly and easily scale out your database application.

To know how to best leverage all of these exciting features and functionality, it's important to understand the basic architecture of SQL Server. This section covers the primary file types in SQL Server 2014, file management, SQL Client, and system databases. It also covers an overview of schemas, synonyms, and Dynamic Management Objects. Finally, it also goes into the data types, editions, and licensing options.

Database Files and Transaction Log

The architecture of database and transaction log files remains relatively unchanged from prior releases. Database files serve two primary purposes, depending on their type. *Data files* hold the data, indexes, and other data support structure within the database. *Log files* hold the data from committed transactions to ensure consistency in the database.

Database Files

A database may consist of multiple *filegroups*. Each filegroup must contain one or more physical data files. Filegroups ease administrative tasks for a collection of files. Data files are divided into 8KB data pages, which are part of 64KB extents. You can specify how full each data page should be with the fill factor option of the `create/alter index` T-SQL command. In SQL Server 2014, you continue to have the capability to bring your database partially online if a single file is corrupted. In this instance, the DBA can bring the remaining files online for reading and writing, and users receive an error if they try to access the other parts of the database that are offline.

In SQL 2000 and before, the largest row you could write was 8,060 bytes. The exceptions to this limit are `text`, `ntext`, `image`, `varchar(max)`, `varbinary(max)`, and `nvarchar(max)` columns, which may each be up to 2GB, and are managed separately. Beginning with SQL 2005, the 8KB limit applies only to those columns of fixed length. The sum of fixed-length columns and pointers for other column types must still be less than 8,060 bytes per row. However, each variable-length column may be up to 8KB in size, allowing for a total row size of well more than 8,060 bytes. If your actual row size exceeds 8,060 bytes, you may experience some performance degradation because the logical row must now be split across multiple physical 8,060-byte rows.

Transaction Log

The purpose of the *transaction log* is to ensure that all committed transactions are persisted in the database and can be recovered, either through rollback or point-in-time recovery. The transaction log is a *write-ahead log*. As you make changes to a database in SQL Server, the data is written to the log, and then the pages that need to be changed are loaded into memory. The pages are then "dirtied" by having the changes written to them. Upon checkpoint, the dirty pages are written to disk, making them now clean pages that no longer need to be part of the write buffer. This is why you may see your transaction log grow significantly in the middle of a long-running transaction even if your recovery model is set to simple. (Chapter 17, "Backup and Recovery," covers this in much more detail.)

SQL Server Native Client

The SQL Server Native Client (SNAC) is a data-access method that shipped with SQL Server 2005 and was enhanced in 2012. It is used by both an online object linking and embedding (OLE) database and Open Database Connectivity (ODBC) for accessing SQL Server. The SQL Server Native Client simplifies access to SQL Server by combining the OLE DB and ODBC libraries into a single access method. The access type exposes the following features in SQL Server:

- ➤ Database mirroring
- ➤ AlwaysOn readable secondary routing
- ➤ Multiple Active Result sets (MARS)
- ➤ Native client support for LocalDB
- ➤ FILESTREAM support
- ➤ Snapshot isolation
- ➤ Query notification
- ➤ XML data type support
- ➤ User-defined data types (UDTs)
- ➤ Encryption
- ➤ Performing asynchronous operations
- ➤ Using large value types
- ➤ Performing bulk copy operations
- ➤ Table-value parameters
- ➤ Large Common Language Runtime (CLR) user-defined types
- ➤ Password expiration
- ➤ Service Principal Name (SPN) support in client connections

With these features, you can use the feature in other data layers such as Microsoft Data Access Components (MDAC), but it takes more work. MDAC still exists, and you can use it if you don't need some of the new functionality of SQL Server 2008/2012. If you develop a COM-based application, you should use SQL Native Client; and if you develop a managed code application (such as in C#), you should consider using the .NET Framework Data Provider for SQL Server, which is robust and includes the SQL Server 2008/2012 features as well.

SQL Server 2014 actually installs SQL Server 2012 Native Client because there is no SQL Server 2014 Native Client. Other major changes include the deprecation of the ODBC driver in SQL Server Native Client. Because of this deprecation, there will be no more updates to the ODBC driver in SQL Server Native Client. The successor of the ODBC driver in SQL Server Native Client is called the Microsoft ODBC Driver 11 for SQL Server on Windows, which is installed with SQL Server 2014 by default.

Standard System Databases

The system databases in SQL Server are crucial, and you should leave them alone most of the time. The only exceptions to that rule are the `model` database (which enables you to deploy a change such as a stored procedure to any new database created) and `tempdb` (which will probably need to be altered to help with scaling your workload). The following sections go through the standard system databases in detail.

> **WARNING** *If certain system databases are tampered with or corrupted, you run the risk that SQL Server will not start. The* `master` *database contains all the stored procedures and tables needed for SQL Server to remain online.*

The resource Database

SQL Server 2005 added the `resource` database. This database contains all the read-only critical system tables, metadata, and stored procedures that SQL Server needs to run. It does not contain any information about your instance or your databases because it is written to only during an installation of a new service pack. The `Resource` database contains all the physical tables and stored procedures referenced logically by other databases. You can find the database in a default installation at `C:\Program Files\Microsoft SQL Server\MSSQL14.MSSQLSERVER\MSSQL\Binn`, and there is only one `Resource` database per instance.

> **NOTE** *The use of drive C: in the path assumes a standard setup. If your machine is set up differently, you may need to change the path to match your setup. In addition, the* `.MSSQLSERVER` *is the instance name. If your instance name is different, use your instance name in the path.*

In SQL Server 2000, when you upgraded to a new service pack, you needed to run many long scripts to drop and re-create system objects. This process took a long time to run, and created an environment that couldn't be rolled back to the previous release after the service pack. Since SQL Server 2012, when you upgrade to a new service pack or hot fix, a copy of the `resource` database overwrites the old database. This enables you to both quickly upgrade your SQL Server catalog and roll back a release.

The `resource` database cannot be seen through Management Studio and should never be altered unless you're under instruction to do so by Microsoft Product Support Services (PSS). You can connect to the database under certain single-user mode conditions by typing the command **USE MSSQLSystemResource**. Typically, a DBA runs simple queries against it while connected to any database, instead of having to connect to the `resource` database directly. Microsoft provides some functions that enable this access. For example, if you were to run this query while connected to any database, it would return your `resource` database's version and the last time it was upgraded:

```
SELECT serverproperty('resourceversion') ResourceDBVersion,
    serverproperty('resourcelastupdatedatetime') LastUpdateDate;
```

> **NOTE** *Do not place the* `resource` *database on an encrypted or compressed drive. Doing this may cause upgrade or performance issues.*

The master Database

The `master` database contains the metadata about your databases (database configuration and file location), logins, and configuration information about the instance. You can see some of the metadata stored in `master` by running the following query, which returns information about the databases that exist on the server:

```
SELECT * FROM sys.databases;
```

The main difference between the `resource` and `master` databases is that the `master` database holds data specific to your instance, whereas the `resource` database just holds the schema and stored procedures needed to run your instance but does not contain any data specific to your instance.

> **WARNING** *You should rarely create objects in the* `master` *database. If you create objects here, you may need to make more frequent* `master` *database backups.*

The tempdb Database

The `tempdb` database is similar to the operating system paging file. It's used to hold temporary objects created by users, temporary objects needed by the database engine, and for row-version information. The `tempdb` database is created each time you restart SQL Server. The database will be re-created to its original database size when the SQL Server is started. Because the database is re-created each time, you cannot back it up. Data changes made to objects in the `tempdb` database benefit from reduced logging. You must have enough space allocated to your `tempdb` database because many operations that you use in your database applications use `tempdb`. Generally speaking, you should set `tempdb` to autogrow as it needs space. Typically, your `tempdb` size varies, but you should understand how much temp space your application will use at peak, and ensure that there is enough space with 15–20 percent overhead for growth. If there is not enough space, the user may receive one of the following errors:

➤ **1101 or 1105**—The session connecting to SQL Server must allocate space in `tempdb`.

➤ **3959**—The version store is full.

➤ **3967**—The version store must shrink because `tempdb` is full.

The model Database

`model` is a system database that serves as a template when SQL Server creates a new database. As each database is created, SQL Server copies the `model` database as the new database. The only time this does not apply is when you restore or attach a database from a different server.

If a table, stored procedure, or database option should be included in each new database that you create on a server, you may simplify the process by creating the object in `model`. When the new database is created, `model` is copied as the new database, including the special objects or database settings you have added to the `model` database. If you add your own objects to `model`, it should be included in your backups, or you should maintain a script that includes the changes.

The msdb Database

`msdb` is a system database that contains information used by SQL Server Agent, log shipping, SSIS, and the backup-and-restore system for the relational database engine. The database stores all the information about jobs, operators, alerts, policies, and job history. Because it contains this important system-level data, you should back up this database regularly.

Schemas

Schemas enable you to group database objects together. You may want to do this for ease of administration because you can apply security to all objects within a schema. Another reason to use schemas is to organize objects so that the users may find the objects they need easily. For example, you may create a schema called `HumanResource` and place all your employee tables and stored procedures into it. You could then apply security policies on the schema to allow appropriate access to the objects contained within it.

When you refer to an object, you should always use the two-part name. The `dbo` schema is the default schema for a database. An `Employee` table in the `dbo` schema is referred to as `dbo.Employee`. Table names must be unique within a schema. You could create another table called `Employee` in the `HumanResources` schema. It would be referred to as `HumanResources.Employee`. This table actually exists in the `AdventureWorks` sample database for SQL Server 2014. (All SQL Server 2014 samples must be downloaded and installed separately from `wrox.com`.) A sample query using the two-part name follows:

```
USE AdventureWorks2014
GO
SELECT BusinessEntityID, JobTitle
FROM HumanResources.Employee;
```

Prior to SQL 2005, the first part of the two-part name was the username of the object owner. The problem with that implementation was related to maintenance. If a user who owned objects were to leave the company, you could not remove that user login from SQL Server until you ensured that all the objects owned by the user were changed to a different owner. All the code that referred to the objects had to be changed to refer to the new owner. By separating ownership from the schema name, SQL 2005 and later versions remove this maintenance problem.

Synonyms

A *synonym* is an alias, or alternative name, for an object. This creates an abstraction layer between the database object and the user. This abstraction layer enables you to change some of the physical implementation and isolate those changes from the consumer. The following example is related to the use of linked servers. You may have tables on a different server that need to be joined to tables on a local server. You refer to objects on another server using the four-part name, as shown in the following code:

```
SELECT Column1, Column2
FROM LinkedServerName.DatabaseName.SchemaName.TableName;
```

For example, you might create a synonym for `LinkedServerName.DatabaseName.SchemaName`
`.Tablename` called `SchemaName.SynonymName`. Data consumers would refer to the object using the following query:

```
SELECT Column1, Column2
FROM SchemaName.SynonymName;
```

This abstraction layer now enables you to change the location of the table to another server, using a different linked server name, or even to replicate the data to the local server for better performance without requiring any changes to the code that refers to the table.

> **NOTE** *A synonym cannot reference another synonym. The* `object_id` *function returns the* id *of the synonym, not the* id *of the related base object. If you need column-level abstraction, use a view instead.*

Dynamic Management Objects

Dynamic Management Objects (DMOs) and functions return information about your SQL Server instance and the operating system. DMOs are grouped into two different classes: *Dynamic Management Views (DMVs)* and *Dynamic Management Functions (DMFs)*. DMVs and DMFs simplify access to data and expose new information that was not available in versions of SQL Server prior to 2005. DMOs can provide you with various types of information, from data about the I/O subsystem and RAM to information about Service Broker.

Whenever you start an instance, SQL Server begins saving server-state and diagnostic information in memory, which DMVs and DMFs can access. When you stop and start the instance, the information is flushed from the views and fresh data begins to be collected. You can query the views just like any other table in SQL Server with the two-part qualifier. For example, the following query uses the `sys.dm_exec_sessions` DMV to retrieve the number of sessions connected to the instance, grouped by login name:

```
SELECT login_name, COUNT(session_id) as NumberSessions
FROM sys.dm_exec_sessions GROUP BY login_name;
```

Some DMFs are functions that accept parameters. For example, the following code uses the `sys.dm_io_virtual_file_stats` dynamic management function to retrieve the I/O statistics for the `AdventureWorks` data file:

```
USE AdventureWorks
GO
SELECT * FROM
sys.dm_io_virtual_file_stats(DB_ID('AdventureWorks2014'),
FILE_ID('AdventureWorks_Data'));
```

Many new DMVs and DMFs were introduced in SQL Server 2012. These views focus on improved insight into new and existing areas of functionality and include the following:

➤ AlwaysOn Availability Groups

➤ Change Data Capture–Related

➤ Change Tracking–Related

➤ Common Language Runtime–Related

➤ Database Mirroring–Related

➤ Database-Related

➤ Execution-Related

➤ SQL Server Extended Events

➤ FileStream and FileTable

➤ Full-Text Search and Semantic Search

➤ Index-Related

➤ I/O-Related

➤ Object-Related

➤ Query Notifications–Related

➤ Replication-Related

➤ Resource Governor–Related

➤ Security-Related

➤ Server-Related

➤ Service Broker–Related

➤ Spatial Data–Related

➤ SQL Server Operating System–Related

➤ Transaction-Related

SQL Server 2014 introduced the following new DMVs and DMFs:

➤ Cluster Shared Volume (CSV)–Related

➤ Buffer Pool Extension–Related

➤ In-Memory OLTP–Related

SQL Server 2014 Data Types

Data types are the foundation of table creation in SQL Server. As you create a table, you must assign a data type for each column. This section covers some of the more commonly used data types in SQL Server. Even if you create a custom data type, it must be based on a standard SQL Server data type. For example, you can create a custom data type (Address) by using the following syntax, but notice that it is based on the SQL Server standard varchar data type:

```
CREATE TYPE Address
FROM varchar(35) NOT NULL;
```

If you change the data type of a column in a large table in SQL Server Management Studio's table designer interface, the operation may take a long time. You can observe the reason for this by scripting the change from the Management Studio interface. Management Studio creates a secondary temporary table with a name such as tmpTableName and then copies the data into the table. Finally, the interface deletes the old table and renames the new table with the new data type. Other steps along the way, of course, handle indexes and any relationships in the table.

If you have a large table with millions of records, this process can take more than 10 minutes, and, in some cases, more than 1 hour. To avoid this, you can use a simple one-line T-SQL statement in the query window to change the column's data type. For example, to change the data type of the JobTitle column in the Employees table to a varchar(70), you could use the following syntax:

```
ALTER TABLE HumanResources.Employee ALTER COLUMN JobTitle Varchar(70);
```

> **WARNING** *When you convert to a data type that may be incompatible with your data, you may lose important data. For example, if you convert from a numeric data type that has data, such as 15.415, to an integer, the number 15.415 would be rounded to a whole number.*

You may want to write a report against your SQL Server tables that displays the data type of each column inside the table. You can do this dozens of ways, but a popular method shown in the following example joins the sys.objects table with the sys.columns table. You may not be familiar with two functions in the following code. The TYPE_NAME() function translates the data type ID into its proper name. To go the opposite direction, you could use the TYPE_ID() function. The other function of note is SCHEMA_ID(), which is used to return the identity value for the schema. This is useful primarily when you want to write reports against the SQL Server metadata.

```
USE AdventureWorks2014;
GO
SELECT o.name AS ObjectName,
       c.name AS ColumnName,
       TYPE_NAME(c.user_type_id) as DataType
FROM sys.objects o
JOIN sys.columns c
ON o.object_id = c.object_id
WHERE  o.name ='Department'
and o.Schema_ID = SCHEMA_ID('HumanResources');
```

This code returns the following results (the *Name* data type is a user-defined type):

```
ObjectName          ColumnName       DataType
------------------------------------------------------

Department          DepartmentID     smallint
Department          Name             Name
Department          GroupName        Name
Department          ModifiedDate     datetime
```

Character Data Types

Character data types include varchar, char, and text. This set of data types stores character data. The primary difference between the varchar and char types is data padding. If you have a column called FirstName that is a varchar(20) data type and you store the value of "Brian" in the column, only 5 bytes are physically stored, plus a little overhead. If you store the same value in a char(20) data type, all 20 bytes would be used. SQL inserts trailing spaces to fill the 20 characters.

> **NOTE** *You might ask yourself, if you want to conserve space, why would you ever use a* char *data type? There is a slight overhead to using a* varchar *data type. For example, if you store a two-letter state abbreviation, you're better off using a* char(2) *column. Although some DBAs have opinions about this that border on religious conviction, generally speaking, it's good to find a threshold in your organization, and specify that anything below this size becomes a* char *versus a* varchar. *In general, a good guideline is that any column less than or equal to 5 bytes should be stored as a* char *data type instead of a* varchar *data type, depending on your application needs. Beyond that point, the benefit of using a* varchar *begins to outweigh the cost of the overhead.*

The nvarchar and nchar data types operate the same way as their varchar and char counterparts, except these data types can handle international Unicode characters. This comes at a cost, though. Data stored as Unicode consumes 2 bytes per character. If you were to store the value of "Brian" in an nvarchar column, it would use 10 bytes, and storing it as an nchar(20) would use 40 bytes. Because of this overhead and added space, you should not use Unicode columns unless you have a business or language need for them. Think ahead to the future and consider instances in which you might need them. If there is no future business need, avoid them.

Table 1-1 shows the data types with short descriptions and the amount of storage required.

TABLE 1-1: SQL Server Data Types

DATA TYPE	DESCRIPTION	STORAGE SPACE
Char(n)	N between 1 and 8,000 characters	n bytes
Nchar(n)	N between 1 and 4,000 Unicode characters	(2 × n bytes)
Nvarchar(max)	Up to ((2 to the 30th power) – 1) (1,073,741,823) Unicode characters	2 × characters stored + 2 bytes overhead
Text	Up to ((2 to the 31st power) – 1) (2,147,483,647) characters	1 byte per character stored + 2 bytes overhead
Varchar(n)	N between 1 and 8,000 characters	1 byte per character stored + 2 bytes overhead
Varchar(max)	Up to ((2 to the 31st power) – 1) (2,147,483,647) characters	1 byte per character stored + 2 bytes overhead

Exact Numeric Data Types

Numeric data types consist of bit, tinyint, smallint, int, bigint, numeric, decimal, small-money, and money. Each of these data types stores different types of numeric values. The first data type, bit, stores only a null, 0, or a 1, which in most applications translates into true or false. Using the bit data type is perfect for on and off flags, and it occupies only a single byte of space. Table 1-2 shows other common numeric data types.

TABLE 1-2: Exact Numeric Data Types

DATA TYPE	DESCRIPTION	STORAGE SPACE
Bit	0, 1, or null	1 byte for each 8 columns of this data type
tinyint	Whole numbers from 0 to 255	1 byte
smallint	Whole numbers from −32,768 to 32,767	2 bytes
Int	Whole numbers from −2,147,483,648 to 2,147,483,647	4 bytes
bigint	Whole numbers from −9,223,372,036,854,775,808 to 9,223,372,036,854,775,807	8 bytes

DATA TYPE	DESCRIPTION	STORAGE SPACE
numeric(p,s) or decimal(p,s)	Numbers from −1,038 + 1 through 1,038 −1	Up to 17 bytes
money	−922,337,203,685,477.5808 to 922,337,203,685,477.5807	8 bytes
smallmoney	−214,748.3648 to 214,748.3647	4 bytes

Numeric data types, such as decimal and numeric, can store a variable number of digits to the right and left of the decimal place. *Scale* refers to the number of digits to the right of the decimal. *Precision* defines the total number of digits, including the digits to the right of the decimal place. For example, 14.88531 would be a numeric(7,5) or decimal(7,5). If you were to insert 14.25 into a numeric(5,1) column, it would be rounded to 14.3.

Approximate Numeric Data Types

The data types float and real are included in this group. They should be used when floating-point data must be represented. However, because they are approximate, not all values can be represented exactly.

The n in the float(n) is the number of bits used to store the mantissa of the number. SQL Server uses only two values for this field. If you specify between 1 and 24, SQL uses 24. If you specify between 25 and 53, SQL uses 53. The default is 53 when you specify float(), with nothing in parentheses.

Table 1-3 shows the approximate numeric data types with a short description and the amount of storage required.

TABLE 1-3: Approximate Numeric Data Types

DATA TYPE	DESCRIPTION	STORAGE SPACE
float[(n)]	−1.79E + 308 to −2.23E-308,0, 2.23E-308 to 1.79E + 308	N <= 24 − 4 bytes N> 24 − 8 bytes
real()	−3.40E + 38 to −1.18E-38,0, 1.18E-38 to 3.40E + 38	4 bytes

> **NOTE** *The synonym for* real *is* float(24).

Binary Data Types

Binary data types such as varbinary, binary, and varbinary(max) store binary data such as graphic files, Word documents, or MP3 files. The values are hexadecimal 0x0 to 0xf. The image data type stores up to 2GB outside the data page. The preferred alternative to an `image` data type is `varbinary(max)`, which can hold more than 8KB of binary data and generally performs slightly better than an `image` data type. Introduced in SQL Server 2012 was the capability to store `varbinary(max)` objects in operating system files via FileStream storage options. This option stores the data as files and is not subject to the 2GB size limit of `varbinary(max)`.

Table 1-4 shows the binary data types with a short description and the amount of storage required.

TABLE 1-4: Binary Data Types

DATA TYPE	DESCRIPTION	STORAGE SPACE
Binary(n)	N between 1 and 8,000 hex digits	n bytes
Varbinary(n)	N between 1 and 8,000 hex digits	1 byte per character stored + 2 bytes overhead
Varbinary(max)	Up to 231 – 1 (2,147,483,647) characters	1 byte per character stored + 2 bytes overhead

Date and Time Data Types

The `datetime` and `smalldatetime` types both store date and time data. The `smalldatetime` is 4 bytes and stores from January 1, 1900, through June 6, 2079, and is accurate to the nearest minute.

The `datetime` data type is 8 bytes and stores from January 1, 1753, through December 31, 9999, to the nearest 3.33 millisecond.

SQL Server 2012 introduced four new date-related data types: `datetime2`, `dateoffset`, `date`, and `time`. You can find examples using these data types in SQL Server Books Online.

The `datetime2` data type is an extension of the `datetime` data type, with a wider range of dates. Time is always stored with hours, minutes, and seconds. You can define the `datetime2` data type with a variable parameter at the end—for example, `datetime2(3)`. The 3 in the preceding expression means to store fractions of seconds to three digits of precision, or 0.999. Valid values are between 0 and 7, with a default of 3.

The `datetimeoffset` data type is just like the `datetime2` data type, with the addition of the time offset. The time offset is + or – up to 14 hours, and contains the UTC offset so that you can rationalize times captured in different time zones.

The `date` data type stores the date only, a long-requested piece of functionality. Alternatively, the `time` data type stores the time only. The `time` data type also supports the `time(n)` declaration, so you can control granularity of the fractional seconds. As with `datetime2` and `datetimeoffset`, n can be between 0 and 7.

Table 1-5 shows the date/time data types with a short description and the amount of storage required.

TABLE 1-5: Date and Time Data Types

DATA TYPE	DESCRIPTION	STORAGE SPACE
Date	January 1, 1 to December 31, 9999	3 bytes
Datetime	January 1, 1753 to December 31, 9999, Accurate to nearest 3.33 millisecond	8 bytes
Datetime2(n)	January 1, 1 to December 31, 9999 N between 0 and 7 specifies fractional seconds	6 to 8 bytes
Datetimeoffset(n)	January 1, 1 to December 31, 9999 N between 0 and 7 specifies fractional seconds +- offset	8 to 10 bytes
SmalldateTime	January 1, 1900 to June 6, 2079, Accurate to 1 minute	4 bytes
Time(n)	Hours:minutes:seconds. 9999999 N between 0 and 7 specifies fractional seconds	3 to 5 bytes

Other System Data Types

Table 1-6 shows several other data types, which you have not yet seen.

TABLE 1-6: Other System Data Types

DATA TYPE	DESCRIPTION	STORAGE SPACE
Cursor	This contains a reference to a cursor, and may be used only as a variable or stored procedure parameter.	Not applicable
Hierarchyid	Contains a reference to a location in a hierarchy.	1 to 892 bytes + 2 bytes overhead
SQL_Variant	May contain the value of any system data type except text, ntext, image, timestamp, xml, varchar(max), nvarchar(max), varbinary(max), and user-defined data types. The maximum size allowed is 8,000 bytes of data + 16 bytes of metadata.	8,016 bytes
Table	Used to store a data set for further processing. The definition is like a Create Table. Primarily used to return the result set of a table-valued function; they can also be used in stored procedures and batches.	Dependent on table definition and number of rows stored
Timestamp or Rowversion	Unique per table, automatically stored value. Generally used for version stamping; the value is automatically changed on insert and with each update.	8 bytes

continues

TABLE 1-6 *(continued)*

DATA TYPE	DESCRIPTION	STORAGE SPACE
Uniqueidentifier	Can contain Globally Unique Identifier (GUID). guid values may be obtained from the Newsequentialid() function. This function returns values that are unique across all computers. Although stored as a binary 16, it is displayed as a char(36).	16 bytes
XML	This is Unicode by definition.	Up to 2GB

> **NOTE** *A* cursor *data type may not be used in a* Create Table *statement.*

The XML data type stores an XML document or fragment. It is stored like an nvarchar(max) in size depending on the use of UTF-16 or UTF-8 in the document. The XML data type enables the use of special constructs for searching and indexing. (This is covered in more detail in Chapter 15, "Replication.")

CLR Integration

In SQL Server, you can also create your own data types, functions, and stored procedures using the portion of the Common Language Runtime (CLR) referred to as SQLCLR. This enables you to write more complex data types to meet your business needs in Visual Basic or C#, for example. These types are defined as a class structure in the base CLR language.

EDITIONS OF SQL SERVER

SQL Server 2014 is available in several editions, and the features available to you in each edition vary widely. The editions you can install on your workstation or server also vary based on the operating system. The editions of SQL Server range from SQL Express on the lowest end to Enterprise Edition on the highest.

Edition Overview

Three major editions of SQL Server 2014 are available. Additional, smaller editions are intended for select use cases, so they are not covered here. For more details on these, see www.microsoft.com/sqlserver. As shown in Table 1-7, SQL Server 2014 offers three principal SKUs:

➤ **Enterprise Edition**—This contains all the new SQL Server 2014 capabilities, including high availability and performance updates and features that make this a mission critical–ready database. This edition contains all the BI functionality as well.

➤ **Business Intelligence Edition**—The BI Server Edition offers the full suite of powerful BI capabilities in SQL Server 2014, including PowerPivot, Power View, Data Quality Services, and Master Data Services. One major focus of this edition is empowering end users with BI functionality.

This is ideal for projects that need advanced BI capabilities, but don't require the full OLTP performance and scalability of Enterprise Edition. The new BI Edition is inclusive of the standard edition and still contains the basic OLTP offerings.

➤ **Standard Edition**—This remains as it is today, designed for departmental use with limited scale. It has basic database functionality and basic BI functionality. New features are now included in the Standard Edition, such as compression.

TABLE 1-7: SQL Server 2014 Editions

ENTERPRISE EDITION (INCLUSIVE OF BUSINESS INTELLIGENCE EDITION)	BUSINESS INTELLIGENCE EDITION (INCLUSIVE OF STANDARD EDITION)	STANDARD EDITION
Mission-critical and Tier 1 applications	Corporate and scalable reporting of analytics	Departmental databases
Data warehousing	Power View and PowerPivot enable self-service analytics	Limited business intelligence project
Private cloud and highly virtualized environments		
Large, centralized, or external-facing business intelligence		

Note: Web Edition will only be available via Service Provider License Agreement (SPLA)

Table 1-8 provides you with an at-a-glance view of some of the key features in SQL Server 2014 by edition.

TABLE 1-8: SQL Server 2014 Capabilities by Edition

SQL SERVER CAPABILITIES		SQL SERVER EDITIONS	
	STANDARD	BUSINESS INTELLIGENCE	ENTERPRISE
Maximum number of cores	16 cores	16 cores (database; operating system maximum for business intelligence)	Operating system maximum
Supported Memory	128GB	128GB	Operating system maximum
Basic OLTP	X	X	X

continues

TABLE 1-8 *(continued)*

SQL SERVER CAPABILITIES		SQL SERVER EDITIONS	
	STANDARD	BUSINESS INTELLIGENCE	ENTERPRISE
In-memory OLTP			X
Basic reporting and analytics	X	X	X
Programmability and developer's tools	X	X	X
Manageability (SSMS, policy-based management)	X	X	X
Enterprise data management (data quality, master data services)		X	X
Self-service BI (Power View, PowerPivot for SPS)		X	X
Corporate BI (semantic model, advanced analytics)		X	X
Advanced security (advanced auditing, transparent data encryption)			X
Data warehousing (ColumnStore index, compression, partitioning)			X
Maximum scalability and performance			X
High availability	Limited	Basic	X
ColumnStore index			X
AlwaysOn			X
Buffer Pool Extension	X	X	X
Virtualization licensing	1 virtual machine	1 virtual machine	Unlimited

The basic functionality is kept in the Standard Edition. Key enterprise BI features are included in the Business Intelligence SKU. When you need to go to high-end data warehousing and enterprise-level high availability, the Enterprise Edition is the right edition for you.

As you can see in Table 1-8, for the Standard Edition, there is a 16-core maximum compute capacity for the Database Engine. For the Business Intelligence Edition, there is a 16-core maximum for database use and up to the OS Maximum for BI features (Analysis Services, Reporting Services). The Enterprise Edition can be used up to the maximum number of cores in the operating system.

Both the Business Intelligence Edition and Enterprise Edition offer the full premium BI capabilities of SQL Server 2014, including Enterprise Data Management, Self-Service BI, and Corporate BI features. The Enterprise Edition adds mission-critical and Tier-1 database functionality with the maximum scalability, performance, and high availability. With the Enterprise Edition under Software Assurance, customers also get unlimited virtualization, with the ability to license unlimited virtual machines, as well as full mobility of those licenses.

Licensing

Starting with SQL Server 2012, licensing has changed significantly. This new licensing scheme can impact your environment if you do not run Software Assurance on those licenses. This section is an overview of the changes, not an exhaustive licensing discussion. See your Microsoft account manager for more details on these changes.

SQL Server pricing and licensing better aligns to the way customers purchase database and BI products. The new pricing and licensing offers a range of benefits for customers, including the following:

➤ **SQL Server offers market leading Total Cost of Ownership (TCO):**

   ➤ SQL Server continues to be the clear high-value leader among major vendors. This is exemplified through the pricing model, features included in non-Enterprise editions, and world-class support, no matter the edition.

   ➤ Customers with Software Assurance get significant benefits and ways to help ease the transition to new licensing models. These benefits include access to upgrades and enhanced support options during your license term.

   ➤ Customers with Enterprise Agreements have the easiest transition to the latest versions of SQL Server and realize the greatest cost-savings.

➤ **SQL Server 2014 is cloud-optimized:**

   ➤ SQL Server 2014 is the most virtualization-friendly database platform with expanded virtualization licensing, the flexibility to license per VM, and excellent support for Hyper-V.

   ➤ Hybrid on-premises and cloud-based solutions are fully supported with features such as support for SQL Server Data Files in Windows Azure, SQL Server Managed Backup to Windows Azure, ability to deploy a database from an on-premises instance directly to an instance in a Windows Azure Virtual Machine, support for backing up databases to Windows Azure BLOB Storage, and ability to add a replica to your AlwaysOn Availability Group in a Windows Azure Virtual Machine.

➤ **SQL Server pricing and licensing is designed to enable customers to pay as they grow:**

   ➤ The new streamlined editions are aligned to database and BI needs.

   ➤ For data center scenarios, licensing is better aligned to hardware capacity.

   ➤ For BI, licensing is aligned to user-based access, which is the way most customers are accustomed to purchasing BI.

CPU Core (Not Processor) Licenses

With the release of SQL Server 2012, Microsoft switched to a per-core processing model. The CPU Core licenses (available only for the Standard and Enterprise Edition) are sold in two core "packs." So, a quad-core CPU needs two of these packs per socket. These license packs cost half of what a SQL Server 2008 R2 CPU license costs. The catch here is that you must purchase at least four cores per CPU.

Following are some examples:

> ➤ Two sockets with 2 cores each, you need four license "packs" (eight core licenses).

> ➤ Two sockets with 4 cores each, you need four license "packs" (eight core licenses).

> ➤ Two sockets with 6 cores each, you need six license "packs" (12 core licenses).

> ➤ Two sockets with 8 cores each, you need eight license "packs" (16 core licenses).

Virtualized SQL Server and Host-Based Licensing

When you run a virtualized SQL Server, you must license at least four cores for the VM. If you have more than four virtual CPUs on the VM, you must have a CPU Core license for each virtual CPU that you have assigned to the VM.

SQL Server 2014 still includes host-based licensing for those customers with Software Assurance and an Enterprise Agreement. The host-based licensing works just like it did before: you purchase enough Enterprise Edition CPU Core licenses for the host, and you can run as many VMs running SQL Server as you want. This will likely be the preferred way for many of you. Those customers not running with Software Assurance or an Enterprise Agreement will want to contact their Microsoft Representative or reseller, because host-based licensing is not available for those customers.

As you can see, this is a lot of change. The pricing has changed, too, but is not discussed here because of the wide variations depending on your individual agreements with Microsoft. Microsoft has tried hard to ensure that the cost does not go up dramatically for many of you, so don't fret, but be judicious and check this out with your Microsoft Account teams.

SUMMARY

The architecture for SQL Server 2014 has advancements under the covers that will improve performance, increase developer efficiency and system availability, and decrease overall operating cost. SQL Server 2014 also delivers exciting new features that allow your system to scale and offer greater performance than ever before. It is important to focus on your current and future roles, and understand the types of features and editions that will apply to your situation and organizational needs.

In Chapter 2, you learn about best practices for upgrading to SQL Server 2014.

2

Installing SQL Server 2014 Best Practices

WHAT'S IN THIS CHAPTER

> ➤ Planning and executing a successful SQL Server 2014 installation

> ➤ Understanding the necessary post-installation configurations

> ➤ Troubleshooting common installation issues

WROX.COM CODE DOWNLOADS FOR THIS CHAPTER

The wrox.com code downloads for this chapter are found at www.wrox.com/go/prosql2014admin on the Download Code tab. The code is in the Chapter 2 download and individually named according to the names throughout the chapter.

The installation process of SQL Server 2014 can be as easy as executing the Setup Wizard from the installation media and following the prompts in each of the setup screens. The Setup Wizard makes several important decisions for you during this process. Throughout this chapter, you learn about those decisions, as well as the appropriate configurations for a secure, stable, and scalable installation.

The core installation process follows these general steps:

1. Plan the system.

2. Prepare hardware and software.

3. Install the operating system and service packs.

4. Set up the I/O subsystem.

5. Install SQL Server and service packs.

6. Burn in the system.

7.   Do post-install configurations, if necessary.

8.   Clean up for deployment and go!

This chapter focuses on the plan and the actual install.

PLANNING THE SYSTEM

The first step before initiating a SQL Server installation involves proper planning. A successful SQL Server installation starts with a good game plan. As the old saying goes: "Failing to plan is planning to fail."

Some of the necessary planning includes the following tasks and considerations:

➤   Baseline of current workload

➤   Estimated growth in workload

➤   Minimum hardware and software requirements

➤   Proper storage system sizing and I/O requirements

➤   SQL Server Edition

➤   SQL Server collation, file locations, and `tempdb` sizing

➤   Service account selection

➤   Database maintenance and backup plans

➤   Minimum uptime and response-time service levels

➤   Disaster-recovery strategy

This list provides just a few of the things to keep in mind when deploying, upgrading, or migrating a SQL Server 2014 instance. The next sections cover some of these considerations and best practices in more detail.

Hardware Options

Choosing the right hardware configuration may not always be straightforward. Microsoft provides minimum hardware requirements to support a SQL Server 2014 installation, but as the word *minimum* implies, these are only the minimum requirements, but not necessarily the most appropriate. Ideally, you want to provision hardware that exceeds the minimum requirements to meet current and future resource requirements.

This is the reason why you must create a baseline of current resource requirements, and also estimate future needs. Having the necessary hardware to meet future requirements can not only save you money, but also avoid downtime required to carry out hardware upgrades.

To guarantee a smooth installation process and predictable performance, become familiar with the minimum hardware requirements provided by Microsoft, as listed in Table 2-1.

TABLE 2-1: SQL Server 2014 Minimum Hardware Requirements

COMPONENT	REQUIREMENT
Processor	For 64-bit installations (with a speed of 1.4GHz or higher), AMD Opteron, Athlon 64, Intel Pentium IV with Intel EM64T support, Xeon with Intel EM64T support
	Note: Although Books Online describes 32-bit requirements, the installation produces an error stating 32-bit installations are not supported
Memory	1GB (512MB Express Edition): Recommended 4GB
Storage	Database Engine and data files, Replication, Full-text Search, and Data Quality Services: 811MB
	Analysis Services and data files: 345MB
	Reporting Services and Report Manager: 304MB
	Integration Services: 591MB
	Master Data Services: 243MB
	Client Components (other than SQL Server Books Online components and Integration Services tools): 1,823MB
	SQL Server Books Online Components to view and manage help content: 375KB

Processors

SQL Server 2014 instances that experience a high number of transactions and a high number of concurrent connections benefit from as much processing power as there is available. Processing power comes in the form of high-clock-speed processors and a large number of available processors. Multiple slightly slower processors perform better than a single fast processor. For example, two 1.6GHz processors perform faster than a single 3.2GHz processor.

Newer processor models offer multiple cores in a single physical socket. These multicore processors have many advantages, including space and power consumption savings. Multicore processors enable you to run more than one instance of SQL Server 2014 within the same physical server, either as named instances or as virtual machines. In other words, you can run as many SQL Server 2014 servers as your hardware and licensing allows with a single physical server. Space is drastically reduced in your data center because multiple physical servers can be consolidated into a single physical server. This consolidation enables you to reduce your power bill because you have fewer servers physically connected to the power grid.

Core-Based Licensing was introduced in SQL Server 2012, and continues for SQL Server 2014. In the SQL Server 2014 Core-Based Licensing model, each core in a multicore processor is now required to be licensed. This model applies both to physical servers and virtual machines. For more details on SQL Server 2014 Licensing, refer to Chapter 1.

Memory

Memory is an important resource for optimal performance of SQL Server 2014. Well-designed database systems make proper use of available memory by reading as much as possible from cached data pages in memory buffers.

Memory must be allocated both for the SQL Server instance and the operating system. As much as possible, you should avoid installing memory-intensive applications in the same Windows server as your SQL Server instance.

A good starting point for deciding how much memory you need is to factor the number of data pages of each of the databases hosted on the SQL Server instance, along with query execution statistics such as minimum, maximum, and average memory utilization for a typical workload. The goal is to allow SQL Server to cache as many data pages and execution plans in memory as possible to avoid costly data page reads from disk and execution plan compilations.

You must also be aware of memory limitations imposed by specific SQL Server editions. For example, SQL Server 2014 Enterprise Edition supports up to 2TB of RAM; Standard Edition and Business Intelligence Edition supports up to 128GB of RAM; and Express Edition supports up to 1GB of RAM.

A new feature introduced with SQL 2014 is the built-in in-memory online transaction processing (OLTP) capability. This in-memory feature (code-named *Hekaton*) is available in the Enterprise Edition only. Data can now live entirely in memory, reducing the I/O overhead associated with accessing data on disk. Hekaton is discussed in detail in Chapter 9.

Storage

The storage system of a SQL Server 2014 instance requires special consideration, because slow-performing storage can bring database performance to a halt. When planning for storage for your SQL Server 2014 databases, consider your availability, reliability, throughput, and scalability requirements.

To test and validate your storage system's performance, you must gather important metrics such as maximum number of I/O requests per second (IOps), throughput (MBps), and I/O latency. Table 2-2 provides a brief description of these three key metrics.

TABLE 2-2: Key Storage Metrics

METRIC	DESCRIPTION
I/O requests per second (IOPS)	Number of concurrent requests the storage system can handle in one second. You want this number to be high, usually between 150 and 250 IOPS for a single 15K RPM SAS drive, and between 1,000 and 1,000,000 IOPs for enterprise SSDs and SANs (depending on configuration and manufacturer).
Throughput (MBps)	Size of data the storage system can read or write in one second. You want this number to be high.
I/O latency (ms)	Time delay between I/O operations. You want this number to be zero, or close to zero.

You can gather these key metrics by using free tools such as SQLIO, SQLIOSim, IOMeter, and CrystalDiskMark. The explanation on how to use these tools is beyond the scope of this chapter, but you can find good documentation about them at `http://msdn.microsoft.com/en-us/library/cc966412.aspx`.

Two main types of storage are used in SQL Server installations: DAS and SAN. The following sections explain these types in detail.

Direct-Attached Storage (DAS)

Direct-Attached Storage (DAS) is the simplest storage option to understand. In this type of storage, the disk drives are located within the server box enclosure, and attached directly to a disk controller. Alternatively, they can also be located in an external enclosure attached directly through a cable to a Host Bus Adapter (HBA). No additional equipment is required such as switches.

The main advantage of DAS is that it is easier to implement and maintain at a lower cost. The main disadvantage is limited scalability. Although, in recent years, DAS storage systems have been catching up with features found only in higher-end SAN units, they are still bound by limitations such as the number of disk drives and volume size they can scale up to and manage, the number of servers they can be attached to, and the distance between the storage unit and a server.

In particular, server connectivity and distance are the biggest differentiators, because DAS requires direct physical links between the storage unit and the servers, limiting the number of servers that can be attached simultaneously and the distance separating the storage unit and a server, usually just a couple feet long.

Storage Area Network (SAN)

Storage area networks (SANs) are specialized networks that interconnect storage devices made available to servers as DAS volumes. This network of storage devices is interconnected through high-speed dedicated Fibre Channel (FC) devices known as *fabric switches*, or through the iSCSI protocol using regular Ethernet switches.

One of the great advantages of SANs is the capability to span them over a large geographical area, typically through TCP/IP routing using dedicated wide area network (WAN) connections. This enables organizations to implement features such as storage replication between distant data centers in their disaster-recovery efforts.

In addition, SANs offer the best reliability and scalability features for mission-critical database systems. Well-architected SANs offer much better throughput and reduced I/O latency than DAS. SANs can also scale up to handle many more disk arrays than DAS.

The main disadvantages of SANs are the higher cost and complexity to implement and maintain them.

Choosing the Right Type of Storage

The type of storage for your SQL Server installation depends on your specific needs. As you learned from the preceding comparison, DAS is a lot less expensive and easier to configure and maintain than a SAN. However, SANs offer many performance, availability, and scalability benefits.

A key element to take into consideration when choosing a storage system is the disk drive technology used in your storage system, and how these disk drives are pooled together. Both DAS and SANs use an array of disk drives that are usually configured to create a storage pool that can then be presented to a server as a single entity.

In the next section, you learn about the different disk drive technologies and how they can be pooled together through RAID levels.

Disk Drives

As previously discussed, an important consideration involves the amount of throughput necessary to support your I/O requirements. To satisfy large throughput requirements, you often need to spread reads and writes over a large number of fast-spinning disk drives.

Spreading these I/O operations means storing small chunks of the data on each of the disk drives that are lumped together. In this type of distributed storage, no single disk drive contains the complete data. Therefore, a failure on one disk means total data loss. This is the reason you should always consider reliability with any decision for storage systems. To avoid data loss caused by a disk failure, special arrangements of disks called *disk arrays* or RAID can be configured to satisfy both throughput and reliability. Choosing the right disk RAID level is a key decision that can impact overall server performance. Table 2-3 describes the most common disk RAID levels used for SQL Server environments.

TABLE 2-3: Commonly Used RAID Levels

RAID LEVEL	DESCRIPTION
RAID 0	Also known as a *stripe set* or *striped volume*. Two or more disks lumped together to form a larger volume. No fault tolerance. Fast read/writes.
RAID 1	Also known as *mirrored drives*. Data written identically to two drives. One drive can fail with no data loss. Slower writes. Only half of total raw storage available.
RAID 1+0	Also known as RAID 10. Mirrored sets in a striped set. Better write performance and fault tolerance. Only half of total raw storage available.
RAID 0+1	Striped sets in a mirrored set. Less fault tolerant than RAID 1+0. Good write performance.
RAID 5	Tolerates one drive-failure. Writes are distributed among drives. Faster reads, slow writes. Some raw storage space lost.
RAID 6	Tolerates two drive-failures. Faster reads, slower writes than RAID 5 because of added overhead of parity calculations. Similar raw storage loss to RAID 5.

Solid State Drive (SSD) technology has become more and more popular as it has become more affordable and reliable. SSDs offer as much as 100 times better read-and-write throughput than spinning disk drives. SQL Server can reap the benefits of faster read-and-write operations, especially for databases with high I/O demand.

Adoption of SSDs continues to increase partly because of improved reliability and cost reduction. Several SAN storage system vendors also offer SSD arrays.

> **NOTE** *Even with the added reliability that SSDs offer by eliminating spinning disks, they should still be protected by RAID. SSDs are still susceptible to electronic component failures and corruption.*

Another key element to consider when selecting your storage system, (particularly if you are leaning toward DAS) is the disk controller. In the following section, you learn about specific features of disk controllers that improve DAS performance and reliability.

Disk Controllers

Disk controllers are a critical piece of hardware that you must select with special care when using direct-attached disk drives. Disk controllers can be the source of major I/O bottlenecks because they have throughput limits as well.

Fast drives are not enough to ensure a fast storage system. Disk controllers can add an additional layer of overhead if not correctly configured. Most disk controllers provide settings that you can customize to your specific workloads. For example, you can configure a disk controller to be optimized for a higher percentage of write operations for high-transaction systems. You can optimize disk controllers dedicated to reporting database systems such as data warehouses and operational data stores for heavy read operations.

Another important consideration about disk controllers is write caching. Although this feature is handy to improve write operation performance, unexpected consequences can also occur, such as data loss and database corruption.

Disk controllers improve write operations by temporarily storing data in their cache and eventually flushing it to disk in batches. When the data is saved in the disk controller's cache, SQL Server acknowledges this as a committed transaction. In reality, the data has not been committed to disk and exists only in memory space. If a server is unexpectedly shut down without waiting for disk controllers to commit their cached data to disk, this data does not make it to the database transaction log, resulting in data loss.

Critical database environments should consider using enterprise-level disk controllers with redundant sources of power such as UPS and internal disk controller batteries to avoid potential data loss.

Software and Install Options

The next step is to ensure that several important configuration options are set up correctly, such as proper database file location and setting up the right service accounts.

Collation

SQL Server *collation* specifies a set of rules that stores, sorts, and compares characters. Collation is important because it specifies the code page used. Different code pages support different characters and behave differently when sorting or comparing strings. Setting the wrong collation may force you to reinstall your SQL Server instance because changing the collation of an instance can be complex.

You must understand the locale requirements, sorting, case, and accent sensitivity of the data in your organization and your customers to determine which collation to use. You can find the code page that a Windows Server uses under Control Panel ➪ Regional Settings. The code page selected for the Windows Server may not always be the code page required for your SQL Server instance.

Following are two types of collations: SQL Server and Windows.

SQL Server Collation

SQL Server collations affect the code page used to store data in char, nchar, nvarchar, varchar, and text columns. They affect how comparisons and sorting are done on these data types. For example, if you were to create a SELECT statement such as the following against a case-sensitive collation database, it would not return the employee named Jose stored in proper case as shown here:

```
 SELECT FROM Employees
WHERE EmployeeFirstName='JOSE'
Results: <none>
SELECT FROM Employees
WHERE EmployeeFirstName='Jose'
Results: Jose
```

Windows Collation

Windows collations use rules based on the chosen Windows locale for the operating system. The default behavior is that comparisons and sorting follow the rules used for a dictionary in the associated language. You can specify binary, case, accent, Kana, and width sensitivity. The key point is that Windows collations ensure that single-byte and double-byte character sets behave the same way in sorts and comparisons.

Case-Sensitivity

Your collation is either case-sensitive or not. *Case-sensitive* means that "U" is different from "u." This is true for everything in the region to which the collation applies (in this case, master, model, resource, tempdb, and msdb). This is true for all the data in those databases. Here is the gotcha: Think about what the data in those databases actually is; it includes data in all the system tables, which means object names are also case-sensitive.

Sort Order

The collation you choose also affects sorting. Binary orders (Latin1_General_BIN, for example) sort based on the bit value of the character; they are case-sensitive. Consider the SELECT statement shown in Figure 2-1 for a table that contains employee names for Mary, Tom, mary, and tom. If you choose a dictionary sort order (`Latin1_General_CS_AI`, for example), that statement would yield the result set shown in Figure 2-2.

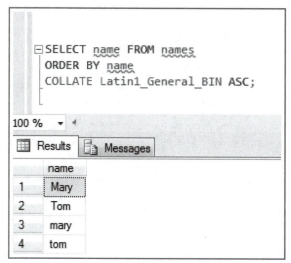

```
SELECT name FROM names
ORDER BY name
COLLATE Latin1_General_BIN ASC;
```

100 %

Results | Messages

	name
1	Mary
2	Tom
3	mary
4	tom

FIGURE 2-1

```
--Apply an typical collation
SELECT name FROM names
ORDER BY name
COLLATE Latin1_General_CS_AI ASC;
```

.00 %

Results | Messages

	name
1	mary
2	Mary
3	tom
4	Tom

FIGURE 2-2

Service Accounts

Service accounts are an important part of your security model. When choosing service accounts, consider the principle of *least privilege*. Service accounts should only have the minimum required permissions to operate. Separate service accounts should be used for each service to track what each service is doing individually. Service accounts should always be assigned strong passwords.

You can choose from several service account options:

➤ **Windows or Domain account**—This Active Directory or Windows account that you create is the preferred account type for SQL Server services needing network access.

➤ **Local System account**—This highly privileged account should not be used for services because it acts as the computer on the network, and has no password. A compromised process using the Local System account can also compromise your database system.

➤ **Local Service account**—This special, preconfigured account has the same permissions as members of the Users group. Network access is done as a null session with no credentials. This account is unsupported.

➤ **Network Service account**—The same as the Local Service account, except that network access is allowed, credentialed as the computer account. Do not use this account for SQL Server or SQL Agent Service accounts.

➤ **Local Server account**—This local Windows account that you create is the most secure method you can use for services that do not need network access.

You should use dedicated Windows or domain accounts for production systems. Some organizations choose to create a single domain account for all their SQL Server instances, whereas others choose to create individual domain accounts for each service.

Using one service for all of your SQL Servers is a recipe for disaster. If one account were to be compromised or locked out, then all of your SQL Servers would be locked out. If the SQL Server Service account is locked out, then SQL Server will not be able to start upon reboot or service restart. In clustering, this could cause a failed health check, and could lead to the cluster going offline. Best practices are to have a separate SQL Server Service account per instance.

INSTALLING SQL SERVER

In this section, you learn about the different types of installations: new installs, side-by-side installs, and upgrades. You also learn how to perform unattended and attended installs using the graphical user interface (GUI), the Command Prompt, configuration files, and Windows PowerShell scripts. More details about upgrades are covered in Chapter 3, "Upgrading SQL Server 2014 Best Practices."

New Installs

A new install occurs when you have a clean slate and no other SQL Server components are on the server. Check the directories and the registry to ensure that you have a clean system, and that you have no remnants of previous SQL installs.

Side-by-Side Installs

SQL Server also supports a side-by-side install. A *side-by-side install* occurs when you have multiple instances of SQL Server on a single server. SQL Server 2014 supports multiple instances of the

Database Engine, Reporting Services, and Analysis Services on the same box. It also runs side by side with previous versions of SQL Server. If the existing instance is a default instance, your new install must be a named instance, because only one default instance can exist on each server.

The biggest issue with side-by-side installs is memory contention. Make sure you set up your memory so that each instance does not try to acquire the entire physical memory. I/O contention can also become an issue if database files from the different instances share the same storage resources.

Upgrades

If SQL Server components exist on the box, you can upgrade the existing instance. In this case, you install SQL Server on top of the existing instance, also known as *in-place upgrade*. To upgrade to SQL Server 2014 from a previous version of SQL Server, you launch the Upgrade Wizard from the SQL Server Installation Center using the Upgrade from SQL Server 2005, 2008, SQL Server 2008 R2, or SQL Server 2012 shortcut under the Installation tab.

Attended Installations

The simplest and most common way SQL Server is deployed is through attended installs using the GUI that the Setup Wizard provides. Attended installs require frequent user interaction to provide the information and parameter values required to complete a SQL Server 2014 installation.

To initiate an attended SQL Server 2014 install, follow these steps:

1. Launch `Setup.exe` from your SQL Server 2014 installation media. The Installation Center opens, as shown in Figure 2-3.

2. Click the Installation tab on the left, and then click the first option on the right titled "New SQL Server Stand-alone Installation" or "Add Feature to an Existing Installation." The SQL Server 2014 Setup Wizard launches.

> **NOTE** *You will see a pop-up stating that the installation is in process, and asking you to please wait.*

3. It will take a few moments to initialize the installation operation.

4. Depending on the installation media and your license agreement, you may be prompted to select the SQL Server Edition and to enter a Product Key on the next screen. Click Next to continue.

5. The License Terms screen opens. Accept the terms and click Next.

6. The Global Roles screen opens and progresses to the next screen.

7. The Microsoft Update Screen Appears. Your organization should establish a minimum build version. Do not check this box. Click Next. Apply updates to SQL Server per your organization's guidelines.

8. The Product Updates screen opens. Click Next to continue.

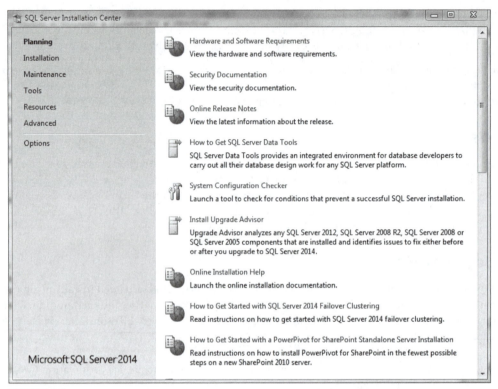

FIGURE 2-3

9. The Install Setup Files screen opens and progresses to the next screen.

10. The Install Rules screen identifies problems that may occur during the Setup Support Files installation. When this step finishes, click Next if all statuses have passed.

11. The Setup Role screen opens. Select the SQL Server Feature Installation option and click Next.

12. The Feature Selection screen opens. Select Database Engine Services and Management Tools - Basic and click Next. Figure 2-4 shows the list of features available to install in SQL Server 2014.

13. The Feature Rules screen opens if anything can cause the installation process to lock. Click Next.

14. The Instance Configuration screen opens. In this screen, you can decide to install the instance as a default instance, or as a named instance. You can also provide an instance ID and change the default root directory. Click Next.

15. The Server Configuration screen shown in Figure 2-5 opens. Provide the service accounts under which SQL Server Database Engine, SQL Server Agent, and SQL Server Browser run, and the collation to be used by SQL Server 2014. Click Next.

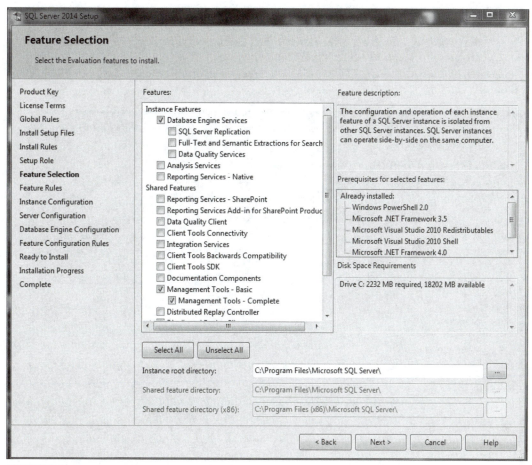

FIGURE 2-4

> **NOTE** *As a security best practice, always consider choosing Service Accounts following the principle of least privilege. Whenever possible, avoid assigning Service Accounts that have elevated privileges in the domain or server.*

---

16. The Database Engine Configuration screen opens. Specify the Authentication Mode, SQL Server Administrators, and default Data Directories, and enable FILESTREAM. It is important to assign at least one account that has SQL Server Administrator privileges on this screen. Also, the Authentication Mode must be defined on this screen either as Windows Authentication or Mixed Mode. If Windows Authentication Mode is chosen, only authenticated Windows accounts can log in. If Mixed Mode is chosen, both Windows accounts and SQL Server accounts can log in. Click Next.

> **NOTE** *Do not leave the* SysAdmin *(SA) password blank. Always assign a strong password, and disable it after installation completes to avoid security attacks targeting this well-known account.*

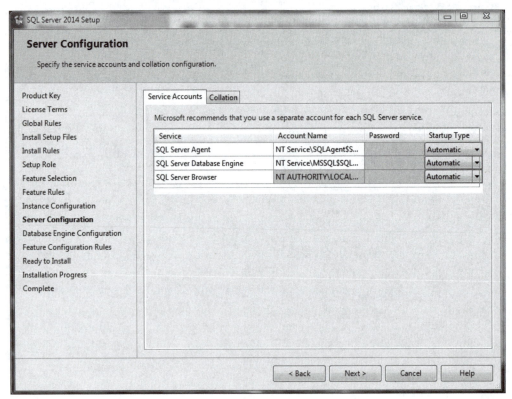

FIGURE 2-5

17. The "Ready to Install" screen opens. At this point, all required information has been gathered by the Setup Wizard, and displays for review before initiating the installation process. Click Install to start the installation.

This finalizes the attended installation process of SQL Server 2014.

> **NOTE** *Microsoft makes available sample databases for download specifically for SQL Server 2014. You can download these sample databases (along with sample project files) for free from Codeplex.com at* http://msftdbprodsamples.codeplex.com/.

Unattended Installs

SQL Server 2014 enables you to perform unattended installations via command-line parameters or a configuration file. Unattended installations enable you to install SQL Server with the exact same configuration on multiple servers with little or no user interaction during the setup process. All screen entries and dialog responses are made automatically using stored information in the configuration file, or by passing them as command-line parameters.

Unattended Installation from the Command Line

To perform a new SQL Server 2014 installation from the command line, follow these steps.

1. Launch the Command Prompt window with elevated Administrator privileges by right-clicking the Command Prompt executable and selecting "Run as Administrator." The Command Prompt window opens.

2. In the command line, type the following command and press Enter:

```
D:\setup.exe /ACTION=install /QS /INSTANCENAME="MSSQLSERVER"
/IACCEPTSQLSERVERLICENSETERMS=1
/FEATURES=SQLENGINE,SSMS
/AGTSVCACCOUNT="YourDomain\Administrators"
/AGTSVPASSWORD="YourPassword"
/SQLSYSADMINACCOUNTS="YourDomain\Administrators"
```

> **NOTE** *Your installation path may differ depending on your installation media. Parameters may vary depending on desired features to be installed. Also, you need to change the value for* /SQLSYSADMINACCOUNTS *to a valid domain name and user account.*

This command-line script performs an unattended installation of SQL Server Database Engine and SQL Server Management Tools - Basic. Table 2-4 describes each command-line parameter used in the preceding script.

TABLE 2-4: Command-Line Parameters

PARAMETER	DESCRIPTION
/ACTION	Specifies the action to be performed—in this case, a new installation.
/QS	Specifies that Setup runs and shows the installation progress, but no input is accepted, and no error messages are displayed.
/INSTANCENAME	Specifies a required instance name.

continues

TABLE 2-4 *(continued)*

PARAMETER	DESCRIPTION
/IACCEPTSQLSERVERLICENSETERMS	Required to acknowledge acceptance of the license terms when using /Q or /QS.
/FEATURES	Required parameter to specify features to install.
/SQLSYSADMINACCOUNTS	Required to provide members of the sysadmin role.
/AGTSVACCOUNT	Required to specify the account for the SQL Server Agent.
/AGTSVCPASSWORD	Required to specify the password for the SQL Server Agent Service.

> **NOTE** *For a complete list of command-line parameters, visit* http://msdn
> .microsoft.com/en-us/library/ms144259(v=sql.120).aspx.

Unattended Installation from a Configuration File

By default, SQL Server 2014 Setup creates a configuration file that logs the options and parameter values specified during an installation. This configuration file is useful for validation and auditing purposes. It is especially useful to deploy additional SQL Server installations using the same configurations.

To create a configuration file, follow these steps:

1. Launch Setup.exe from your SQL Server 2014 installation media. SQL Server Setup launches.

2. Specify the options and parameters for your SQL Server 2014 installation. All options and values specified are recorded in the configuration file as you go through the Setup Wizard.

3. Follow the Setup Wizard until the "Ready to Install" screen displays.

> **NOTE** *At this point, the configuration file has been created, and all options and parameter values specified in previous screens have been recorded in the* ConfigurationFile.ini *file.*

4. Open Windows Explorer, and navigate to the folder where the configuration file has been created. Typically, this will be in the C:\Program Files\Microsoft SQL Server\120\

`Setup Bootstrap\Log`, and then a folder with the date and time will be created. Inside the folder with the date and time, you will find the `ConfigurationFile.ini` file. Click the Cancel button to stop the SQL Server 2014 Setup Wizard.

5. Locate `ConfigurationFile.ini` and copy it to a folder that can be referenced for unattended installs. For example, use a shared folder such as `\\fileserver\myshare`.

6. Open `ConfigurationFile.ini` to modify it. Make the following changes to prepare the file for unattended installs:

➤ Set `QUIET = "True"`

➤ Set `SQLSYSADMINACCOUNTS = "YourDomain\Administrators"`

➤ Set `IACCEPTSQLSERVERLICENSETERMS = "True"`

➤ Remove `ADDCURRENTUSERASSQLADMIN`

➤ Remove `UIMODE`

After you have customized the configuration file for unattended installations, use the Command Prompt to execute `Setup.exe` and specify the path to the configuration file. The following command-line script exemplifies the syntax:

```
D:\Setup.exe /ConfigurationFile=\\fileserver\myshare\ConfigurationFile.ini
```

Scripted Installation with Windows PowerShell

You can also use Windows PowerShell to perform unattended installs. Simple Windows PowerShell scripts can be written to execute SQL Server 2014 Setup through its command-line interface. For example, you can execute the command-line script used in the previous section from the command line as follows:

```
$cmd = "d:\setup.exe /ACTION=install /Q /INSTANCENAME="MSSQLSERVER"
/IACCEPTSQLSERVERLICENSETERMS=1
/FEATURES=SQLENGINE,SSMS
/SQLSYSADMINACCOUNTS="YourDomain\Administrators"
/AGTSVCACCOUNT="YourDomain\Administrators"
/AGTSVPASSWORD="YourPassword";
Invoke-Expression -command $cmd | out-null;
```

More complex Windows PowerShell scripts can be written for larger SQL Server 2014 deployments. A common approach is the use of Windows PowerShell functions that accept the setup parameters necessary to perform unattended installations. These Windows PowerShell functions are then executed in batches or inside a process that loops through a list of server names with corresponding parameters.

For example, a Windows PowerShell function can be saved in a Windows PowerShell script file and called along with setup parameters to perform a large-scale unattended deployment of SQL Server 2014. Listing 2-1 (code file: `Install-Sql2014.ps1`) provides an example of a Windows PowerShell function that can be used for SQL Server 2014 unattended installations.

LISTING 2-1: Install-Sql2014.ps1

```
Function Install-Sql2014
{
 param
 (
  [Parameter(Position=0,Mandatory=$false)][string] $Path,
  [Parameter(Position=1,Mandatory=$false)][string] $InstanceName =
   "MSSQLSERVER",
  [Parameter(Position=2,Mandatory=$false)][string] $ServiceAccount,
  [Parameter(Position=3,Mandatory=$false)][string] $ServicePassword,
  [Parameter(Position=4,Mandatory=$false)][string] $SaPassword,
  [Parameter(Position=5,Mandatory=$false)][string] $LicenseKey,
  [Parameter(Position=6,Mandatory=$false)][string] $SqlCollation =
  "SQL_Latin1_General_CP1_CI_AS",
  [Parameter(Position=7,Mandatory=$false)][switch] $NoTcp,
  [Parameter(Position=8,Mandatory=$false)][switch] $NoNamedPipes
)
#Build the setup command using the install mode
if ($Path -eq $null -or $Path -eq "")
{
#No path means that the setup is in the same folder
$command = 'setup.exe /Action="Install"'
}
else
{
#Ensure that the path ends with a backslash
if(!$Path.EndsWith("\"))
{
$Path += "\"
}
$command = $path + 'setup.exe /Action="Install"'
}
#Accept the license agreement - required for command line installs
$command += ' /IACCEPTSQLSERVERLICENSETERMS'
#Use the QuietSimple mode (progress bar, but not interactive)
$command += ' /QS'
#Set the features to be installed
$command += ' /FEATURES=SQLENGINE,CONN,BC,SSMS,ADV_SSMS'
#Set the Instance Name
$command += (' /INSTANCENAME="{0}"' -f $InstanceName)
#Set License Key only if a value was provided,
#else install Evaluation edition
if ($LicenseKey -ne $null -and $LicenseKey -ne "")
{
$command += (' /PID="{0}"' -f $LicenseKey)
}
#Check to see if a service account was specified
if ($ServiceAccount -ne $null -and $ServiceAccount -ne "")
{
#Set the database engine service account
$command += (' /SQLSVCACCOUNT="{0}" /SQLSVCPASSWORD="{1}"
```

```
/SQLSVCSTARTUPTYPE="Automatic"' -f
$ServiceAccount, $ServicePassword)
#Set the SQL Agent service account
$command += (' /AGTSVCACCOUNT="{0}" /AGTSVCPASSWORD="{1}"
 /AGTSVCSTARTUPTYPE="Automatic"' -f
$ServiceAccount, $ServicePassword)
}
else
{
#Set the database engine service account to Local System
$command += ' /SQLSVCACCOUNT="NT AUTHORITY\SYSTEM"
/SQLSVCSTARTUPTYPE="Automatic"'
#Set the SQL Agent service account to Local System
$command += ' /AGTSVCACCOUNT="NT AUTHORITY\SYSTEM"
 /AGTSVCSTARTUPTYPE="Automatic"'
}
#Set the server in SQL authentication mode if SA password was provided
if ($SaPassword -ne $null -and $SaPassword -ne "")
{
$command += (' /SECURITYMODE="SQL" /SAPWD="{0}"' -f $SaPassword)
}
#Add current user as SysAdmin
$command += (' /SQLSYSADMINACCOUNTS="{0}"' -f
 [Security.Principal.WindowsIdentity]::GetCurrent().Name)
#Set the database collation
$command += (' /SQLCOLLATION="{0}"' -f $SqlCollation)
#Enable/Disable the TCP Protocol
if ($NoTcp)
{
$command += ' /TCPENABLED="0"'
}
else
{
$command += ' /TCPENABLED="1"'
}
#Enable/Disable the Named Pipes Protocol
if ($NoNamedPipes)
{
$command += ' /NPENABLED="0"'
}
else
{
$command += ' /NPENABLED="1"'
}
if ($PSBoundParameters['Debug'])
{
Write-Output $command
}
else
{
Invoke-Expression $command
}
}
```

After you download Listing 2-1 from the Wrox companion website, save it to a folder (for example, `c:\scripts`). Because this is a file that you download from the Internet, you may be required to right-click the file and unblock it. When downloaded, execute this function by following these steps:

1. Launch the Windows PowerShell command line with elevated Administrator privileges by right-clicking the Windows PowerShell executable and selecting "Run as Administrator." The Windows PowerShell command line opens.

2. Verify that you can run and load unsigned Windows PowerShell scripts and files. In the Windows PowerShell command line, type **get-executionpolicy** to verify the current execution policy. If it is not set to RemoteSigned you must change it to this value by executing the following command:

   ```
   Set-ExecutionPolicy RemoteSigned
   ```

3. Next, load the Windows PowerShell function in the script file by executing the following command:

   ```
   . c:\scripts\Install-Sql2014.ps1
   ```

   Notice the . and blank space before the script file path. The . and blank space is a required character to dot-source the script file.

4. Verify that the function has been loaded by issuing the following command:

   ```
   get-command Install-Sql2014
   ```

   A single row is returned showing CommandType Function and Name Install-Sql2014.

5. At this point, you are ready to invoke the Windows PowerShell function you just loaded. Invoke Install-Sql2014 as follows:

   ```
   Install-Sql2014 -Param1 Param1Value -Param2 Param2Value ..
   ```

   For example, the following command invokes the Install-Sql2014 function and sets the SQL Server service account and password along with the InstanceName, and initiates a SQL Server 2014 installation:

   ```
   Install-Sql2014 -Path d:\ -ServiceAccount "winserver\Administrator"
   -ServicePassword "P@ssword"
   -SaPassword "P@ssword"
   -InstanceName "MyInstanceName"
   ```

> **NOTE** *The SQL Server 2014 installation path may differ depending on your installation media.*

> **NOTE** *A community-based project called SPADE that automates SQL Server installations using Windows PowerShell is available for download at Codeplex.com. For more information about this project, visit* `http://sqlspade.codeplex.com/.`

INSTALLING ANALYSIS SERVICES

SQL Server Analysis Services is a straightforward installation. You can include it with other SQL Server 2014 features and services (as shown in Figure 2-6), or install it separately (as shown in Figure 2-7).

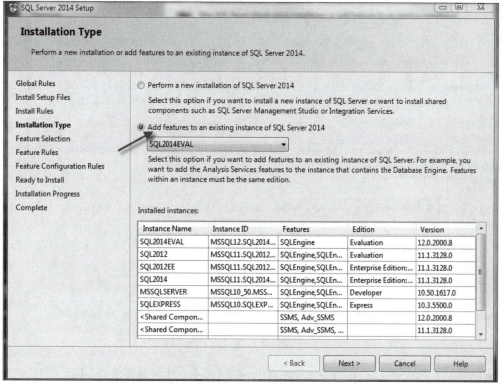

FIGURE 2-6

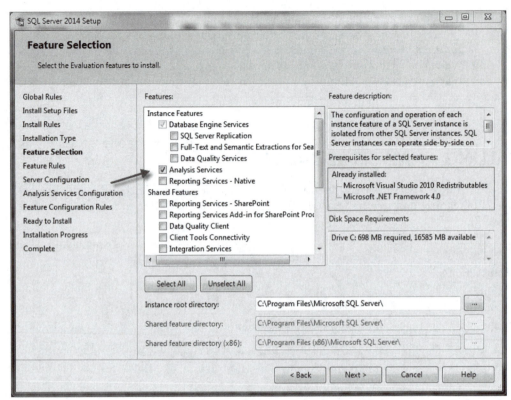

FIGURE 2-7

Starting with SQL Server 2012, you now have the option to install Analysis Services in either of two modes:

➤ Multidimensional and Data Mining Mode (UDM mode)

➤ Tabular Mode

You choose between these two modes in the Analysis Services Configuration screen in SQL Server 2014 Setup, as shown in Figure 2-8.

In the next sections, both Analysis Services modes are described briefly.

Multidimensional and Data Mining Mode (UDM Mode)

Analysis Services Multidimensional and Data Mining mode (UDM mode) installs the traditional Analysis Services engine available since SQL Server 2005. This engine is based on the Unified Dimensional Model (UDM).

The UDM serves as an intermediate layer between one or more data sources, and consolidates all the business rules. UDM acts as the hub of the multidimensional model, enabling users to query, aggregate, drill down, and slice and dice large Analysis Services databases with blink-of-an-eye response times.

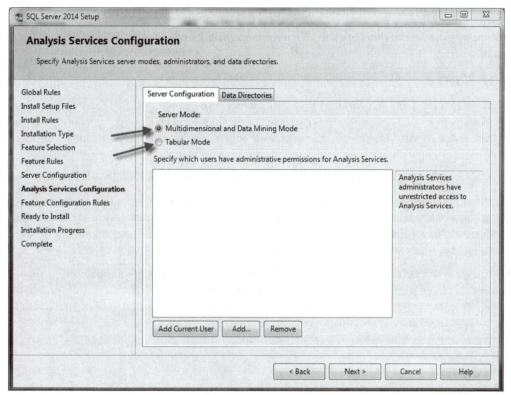

FIGURE 2-8

The Analysis Services UDM mode supports multidimensional online analytical processing (MOLAP), relational online analytical processing (ROLAP), and hybrid online analytical processing (HOLAP) storage and processing modes described in the next sections.

MOLAP

In MOLAP storage mode, data is stored and aggregated in one or more partitions of the multidimensional database. This storage mode is designed to maximize query performance. Data stored in MOLAP storage mode is current as of the last processing time.

ROLAP

In ROLAP storage mode, data is not stored within the Analysis Services database. If queries cannot be satisfied from the query cache, it uses internal indexed views to retrieve data from the relational data source. Query times can be much slower than MOLAP. Data is more real time as its sourced from the transactional system.

HOLAP

In HOLAP storage mode, some portions of the multidimensional database are stored in MOLAP, and some portions are retrieved directly from its relational source. Queries that access more aggregated data are satisfied from its multidimensional store as in MOLAP. Drill-down queries are retrieved directly from their relational data sources as in ROLAP.

Tabular Mode

The Analysis Services Tabular Mode is based on a new database engine called the Vertipaq engine. The *Vertipaq engine* is a column-based database that enables high levels of compression because of the reduced need to store discrete values along with advanced compression algorithms.

The capability to compress large amounts of data enables the Vertipaq engine to store, retrieve, and manipulate data from RAM much faster than the traditional disk-based Analysis Services engine.

Tabular Mode supports the new Semantic Model called Business Intelligence Semantic Model (BISM). The development environment is similar to that of the PowerPivot add-in for Excel. The PowerPivot add-in for Excel runs a scaled-down version of the same Vertipaq engine that Analysis Services Tabular Mode uses.

Similar to the traditional Analysis Services UDM engine, Analysis Services Tabular Mode supports querying from its in-memory storage, or directly from the relational data source, or a hybrid of both. These query mode options are available in the BISM model properties. The four available query mode options include the following:

➤ InMemory

➤ DirectQuery

➤ InMemoryWithDirectQuery

➤ DirectQueryWithInMemory

These four query mode options are described in the next sections.

InMemory Query Mode

In InMemory Query Mode, data is stored and queried from in-memory stored data sets. Little or no latency is involved because disk I/O latency costs are minimized or eliminated. Because of its in-memory data set access, complex calculations and sorting operations are almost instantaneous.

InMemory Query Mode is similar to MOLAP storage in the traditional Analysis Services engine in that it holds point-in-time (PIT) data. If data changes in its relation data source, its in-memory storage must be refreshed with the new data sets.

DirectQuery Mode

In DirectQuery Mode (also known as *pass-through mode*), queries are processed by its data source, in most cases a relational database. The Direct Query Mode advantage over Vertipaq Query Mode resides on it is capability to provide real-time data sets over larger data volumes that cannot fit in-memory.

Similar to ROLAP in the traditional Analysis Services engine, Direct Query Mode is designed for real-time access requirements of the data source.

InMemoryWithDirectQuery Mode

In this query mode, unless otherwise specified by the connection strings from the client, queries use the data set stored in cache by default. It supports the capability for the client to switch to real-time data.

DirectQueryWithInMemory Mode

Opposite to DirectQueryWithinMemory Mode, unless otherwise specified by the connection strings from the client, queries use the relational data source by default. It supports the capability for the client to switch to cached data.

INSTALLING POWERPIVOT FOR SHAREPOINT

PowerPivot for SharePoint Mode is a feature role option that has been available since SQL Server 2008 R2. The PowerPivot for SharePoint option installs a version of the new Analysis Services Vertipaq engine to support server-side processing and management of PowerPivot workbooks that you publish to SharePoint 2010–2013.

PowerPivot for SharePoint must be installed in a server joined to a domain, SharePoint 2010 Enterprise with Service Pack 1, or SharePoint 2013 RTM, and the instance name PowerPivot must be available on the server where it is installed.

To install PowerPivot for SharePoint, follow these steps:

1. Launch `setup.exe` from your SQL Server 2014 installation media. The Installation Center opens.

2. Click the Installation tab on the left, and then click the first option on the right titled "New SQL Server Standard Installation" or "Add Feature to an Existing Installation." The SQL Server 2014 Setup Wizard launches.

3. The Setup Support Rules runs to identify problems that may occur during the setup support files installation. When this step finishes, click OK. The Install Setup Files process initiates.

4. When the Install Setup Files process completes, a second set of Setup Support Rules must be checked. Click OK to continue.

5. Depending on the installation media and your license agreement, you may be prompted to select the SQL Server Edition and to enter a Product Key on the next screen. Click OK to continue.

6. The License Agreement screen opens. Accept the terms and click Next.

7.   The Setup Role screen opens. Select the PowerPivot for SharePoint option. You can also install an instance of SQL Server Database Services with this installation by checking the check box. Click Next. The Feature Selection screen opens. The options are preselected and displayed for informational purposes.

9.   Click Next. The Installation Rules screen opens to determine if anything can cause the installation process to fail. Click Next.

10. The Instance Configuration screen opens. You cannot change the instance name because it must be PowerPivot. Only the instance ID can be modified. Click Next.

11. The Disk Space Requirements screen opens and displays a summary of space to be used by the features selected. Click Next.

12. The Server Configuration screen opens. In this screen, you provide the service account under which the Analysis Services Engine runs. A domain account is required. Click Next.

13. The Analysis Services Configuration screen opens. Add domain accounts that require administrative permissions of the Analysis Services instance.

14. Click Next until you reach the "Ready to Install" screen. Review the installation summary page, and click Install.

This finalizes the installation steps for PowerPivot for SharePoint.

BURNING IN THE SYSTEM

Before you move a system into common use, you should "burn it in." This means that you should stress the server. It is not unusual for a server to work in production for months or years with a hardware problem that existed at the time the server was deployed. Many of these failures do not show up when the server is under a light load, but become immediately evident when you push the server hard.

You can use several free tools to burn in and stress-test a database server to ensure that the storage system is ready to handle required I/O workloads, memory pressure, and CPU processing power demand. Some of these tools include the following:

➤ **SQLIOSim**—This is a free tool from Microsoft that is designed to generate similar SQL Server I/O read and write patterns. This tool is great to test I/O-intensive operations such as DBCC CHECKDB and Bulk insert, delete, and update operations. SQLIOSim replaces SQLIOStress. You can download SQLIOSim at http://support.microsoft.com/kb/231619.

➤ **IOMeter**—This is another free tool great for running a stress test with capability to simulate concurrent application workloads.

➤ **Prime95**—This free tool was designed to find Mersenne Prime numbers and is CPU and RAM memory-intensive. It can be customized to stress test CPU and memory workloads for sustained periods of time.

You can search online for several other free and paid applications that can perform an initial burn-in and stress test. Some server and server component manufacturers also provide tools to benchmark and stress test your equipment.

POST-INSTALL CONFIGURATION

After you install SQL Server 2014, you must configure additional settings and complete the tasks necessary to have a production-ready server. Some of these settings (including max server memory, parallelism threshold, and network packet size) are meant for fine-tuning the SQL Server instance for optimal performance. Other settings and tasks (typically changing default port, login auditing, and disabling an SA account) are geared toward securing, auditing, and monitoring a SQL Server instance.

Configuring SQL Server Settings for Performance

SQL Server 2014 provides system settings that can be optimized to your particular environment and workload patterns. Some of the most important performance settings are discussed in the following sections.

Memory

Two important server property settings include maximum and minimum server memory. By default, SQL Server is configured with a minimum memory of 0MB and a maximum memory of 2,147,483647MB (2TB), as shown in Figure 2-9.

The consequences of leaving the default values for these two settings are sometimes misunderstood and often overlooked. The minimum server memory setting specifies the amount of memory that is not released back to the operating system by SQL Server when allocated. In other words, SQL Server holds on to this minimum amount of memory, even if it is no longer needed.

> **NOTE** *A common misconception is that SQL Server immediately allocates up to this minimum amount of memory upon startup. Actually, SQL Server allocates memory only as it is required, and may or may not reach the minimum server memory value specified.*

The minimum server memory setting does not need to be changed unless the operating system constantly requests memory resources for other applications sharing the same memory space. You want to avoid releasing too much memory to the operating system because that could potentially starve a SQL Server instance from memory.

On the other hand, the maximum server memory sets limits for the maximum amount of memory a SQL Server instance can allocate. A value set too high can potentially starve an operating system from memory resources. The maximum server memory value should not equal or exceed the total amount of available server memory. This value should be at least 4GB less than the total server memory.

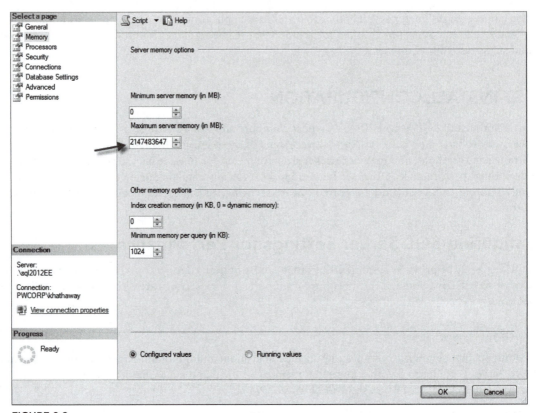

FIGURE 2-9

Network Packet Size

The default network packet size for SQL Server 2014 is 4,096 bytes. Setting a packet size larger than the default size can improve performance for SQL Server instances that experience a large number of bulk operations, or that transfer large volumes of data.

If Jumbo Frames are supported and enabled by the server's hardware and the network infrastructure, increase the network packet size to 8,192 bytes.

Instant File Initialization

Each time a database file is created or needs to grow, it is first zero-filled by the operating system before the new space is made available for writing. This operation can be costly because all write operations are blocked until the zero-fill completes. To avoid these types of blocks and waits, you can enable instant file initialization by adding the SQL Server service account to the list of users in the Perform Volume Maintenance Tasks policy under User Rights Assignment in the Local Policies of the server's Security Settings.

tempdb

One of the most important system databases that require special consideration and planning is tempdb. Over the years, tempdb has taken on more responsibility than it had in the past. Historically, tempdb has been used for internal processes such as some index builds and table variable storage, as well as temporary storage space by programmers. The following is a partial list of some of the uses for tempdb:

- ➤ Bulk load operations with triggers
- ➤ Common table expressions
- ➤ Database Console Command (DBCC) operations
- ➤ Event notifications
- ➤ Index rebuilds, including SORT_IN_TEMPDB, partitioned index sorts, and online index operations
- ➤ Large object (LOB) type variables and parameters
- ➤ Multiple active result set operations
- ➤ Query notifications
- ➤ Row versioning
- ➤ Table variables
- ➤ Sort operators
- ➤ Spill operations

Creating additional tempdb files can dramatically improve performance in environments in which tempdb is used heavily. Depending on your workload, consider creating a number of tempdb files proportional to each logical CPU to enable SQL Server scheduler workers to loosely align to a file. Generally accepted ratios of tempdb files to logical CPUs vary between 1:2 and 1:4. In extreme cases, you may want to create one tempdb file per logical CPU (1:1 ratio). The only way to know how many tempdb files you should create is by testing.

An important consideration is the placement of tempdb. The tempdb file or files should be isolated from database and log files to avoid I/O contention. If you use multiple tempdb files, consider isolating each tempdb file in its own Logical Unit Number (LUN) and physical disks.

Properly sizing tempdb is crucial to optimizing overall performance. Consider setting the initial size of tempdb to something other than the default to avoid expensive file growths. The space to be preallocated depends on the expected workload and features enabled in your SQL Server instance.

A good methodology to estimate the initial size of tempdb is to analyze the query plan of the queries executed during a typical workload. In the query plan, query operators such as sort, hash match, and spool can provide important information to calculate size requirements. To estimate the space required by each operator, look at the number of rows and the row size reported by the operator. To calculate the space required, multiply the actual (or estimated) number of rows by the estimated row size. Although this method is not precise, it gives you a good reference point. Only experience and testing will guarantee more accurate sizing.

Model and User Databases

The model database is the most often overlooked system database. It serves as a template for all user databases. In other words, all database settings of the model database are inherited by each new database created in the SQL Server database instance.

Setting the model database's initial size, autogrowth, and recovery model settings ensures that all user databases created are configured properly to optimize performance.

Set the initial database size to a size large enough to handle the expected volume of transactions in a large enough period of time. The key is to avoid constantly increasing the size of the database. When the database requires more space than originally allocated, you can allow it to automatically increase its size by enabling the *autogrowth* database setting. Even though you should enable auto-grow, autogrow operations are expensive and time-consuming. Think of autogrow as an emergency growth operation. When you enable autogrow, choose a file-growth increment large enough so that autogrow operations do not frequently occur.

> **WARNING** *You should never turn on the auto shrink database setting or schedule shrink operations on your database. Database shrinking operations can cause extensive waits and blocks, consume a lot of CPU, memory, and I/O resources, and increase fragmentation.*

Configuring SQL Server Settings for Security

SQL Server 2014 provides system settings that can be optimized for a more controlled and secure environment. Some of the most important security settings are discussed in the following sections.

SA Account

The sysAdmin (SA) account is a default system account with top-level privileges in SQL Server. Because it is a well-known account, it is the target of a large number of exploit attacks. To eliminate exposure to these types of attacks, always assign a strong password that only you know and never gets used. Secure the password in a vault, and disable the SA account.

TCP/IP Ports

SQL Server uses the default TCP/IP port 1433 to communicate with clients. On the other hand, named SQL Server instances are dynamically assigned TCP/IP ports upon service startup. For hacking prevention and firewall configuration purposes, you may need to change default ports and control the port numbers over which named SQL Server instances communicate.

SQL Server 2014 includes a tool called SQL Server Configuration Manager (discussed in more detail later in this section) to manage SQL Server services and their related network configurations. You can find the SQL Server Configuration Manager under the `Microsoft SQL Server 2014\ Configuration Tools` folder in the Start menu. Figure 2-10 shows the TCP/IP Properties dialog box in SQL Server Configuration Manager where you can change the default 1433 port.

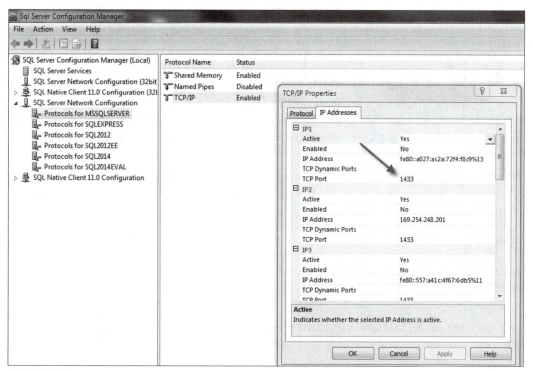

FIGURE 2-10

Service Packs and Updates

After a freshly installed SQL Server instance, you must review available updates. SQL Server updates may be available in the form of hotfixes, cumulative updates, and service packs. Carefully review all updates before applying them to avoid negatively impacting your applications. You absolutely want to install security fixes marked as critical to protect your database systems against known threats, worms, and vulnerabilities. Do not enable automatic updates on production SQL Server instances. Test all updates in a controlled testing environment before you apply them in production.

Additional SQL Server Settings

Additional SQL Server settings and properties are available through SQL Server Management Studio and the `sp_configure` System Stored Procedure.

> **NOTE** *For a complete list and description of all SQL Server configuration options available through the* `sp_configure` *System Stored Procedure, visit* `http://msdn.microsoft.com/en-us/library/ms188787(v=sql.110).aspx.`

Chapter 4, "Managing and Troubleshooting the Database Engine," covers SQL Server configurations in more detail.

SQL Server Configuration Manager

The SQL Server Configuration Manager tool enables you to specify SQL Server Services options, and whether these services are automatically or manually started after Windows starts. SQL Server Configuration Manager enables you to configure services settings such as service accounts, network protocols, and ports SQL Server listens on.

You can access the SQL Server Configuration Manager under Configuration Tools in the Microsoft SQL Server 2014 `Program Menu` folder. It is also available under Services and Applications in Computer Management Console.

Back It Up

Backup plans should be on your checklist after completing a SQL Server installation. You must define backup schedules and backup storage locations for system and user databases. In addition, if using encryption, you need to back up the encryption key.

Always create your backup files in a shared network drive or backup device, and never on the same server being backed up. Consider keeping redundant copies of your backups, and ensure that backups are secured and immediately available in case of a disaster.

Databases should be backed up in full or incrementally. Depending on the database recovery mode log, backups should also be part of your backup schedule to restore from the log if necessary. Refer to Chapter 17, "Backup and Recovery" for more details.

Define your backup retention policy to avoid storing unnecessary historical backups. Routinely restore backups to ensure that they successfully restore at any given time to avoid surprises when facing a disaster. Remember, a good backup is as good as its last restore.

UNINSTALLING SQL SERVER

In some circumstances, you may need to uninstall a SQL Server instance completely because of problems such as incompatibility issues with a newer version, or for licensing consolidation purposes. You can uninstall SQL Server using Programs and Features under Control Panel. During the uninstall process, you can choose to remove all or some of the features installed for a specific instance. If more than one instance is installed, the uninstall process prompts you to select the instance you want to remove.

Additional components and requirements installed during Setup may not be uninstalled, and must be uninstalled separately.

Uninstalling Reporting Services

When you uninstall Reporting Services, you must perform manual cleanup on some items, as described in this section. Before the uninstall, though, you must gather some information. Make sure you know which databases are used by this instance of Reporting Services. You can obtain this information using the Reporting Services Configuration tool. Discover which directory this instance of Reporting Services is installed in by running SQL Server Configuration Manager. You also need to discover which directory the Reporting Services usage and log files use.

Uninstalling Reporting Services does not delete the `ReportServer` databases. You must manually delete these, or a new Reporting Services instance can reuse them.

Uninstalling Analysis Services

Uninstalling Analysis Services also requires some manual cleanup. You should always gather some information prior to the uninstall. Discover which directory this instance of Analysis Services is installed in by running SQL Server Configuration Manager.

Although the normal uninstall does not leave any databases behind, it does leave all the Analysis Services log files. The default location is the Analysis Services install directory or the alternative location you previously discovered. To delete them, simply delete the appropriate directories.

Uninstalling the SQL Server Database Engine

As with other services, log files are not deleted when you uninstall the SQL Server Database Engine. To delete them, simply delete the appropriate directories. You may need to separately remove the MS SQL Server Native Client, and you may find that some directories remain and must be manually removed as well.

If you have no other instances of SQL Server on your machine, instead of deleting only the `120` directory, under Program Files you can delete the entire MS SQL server directory. The .NET Framework is also left on the machine. If you want to remove it, do so from the Programs and Features in Control Panel, but make sure no other applications use it.

TROUBLESHOOTING A FAILED INSTALL

Failed installations may occur most commonly because of failed setup support and installation rules. During setup, a series of rules are checked to identify issues that may prevent a successful SQL Server installation. When a rule failure is detected, it must be corrected before continuing. A rules error report link and description is always provided during attended installs, and error log files are generated for later review.

A detailed report is always available when a failure occurs. These reports provide valuable information to help you identify the root of the problem. In many cases, you can fix these failures by installing missing features or applications.

You can retrieve error reports from the `%Program Files%\Microsoft SQL Server\120\Setup Bootstrap\Log` folder. Each installation attempt generates a time-stamped folder with detailed information stored in a log file that can help you troubleshoot any errors.

> **NOTE** *For a complete list and description of the log files generated during Setup, visit* `http://msdn.microsoft.com/en-us/library/ms143702(v=sql.120).aspx.`

SUMMARY

As you may conclude, installing SQL Server 2014 is generally quite simple, and can be performed with little or no user interaction. Planning before you initiate an installation is key to a successful deployment. A successful SQL Server 2014 install starts with a good plan and a good definition of requirements. These requirements should define hardware and software requirements, prerequisites, authentication, collation, service accounts, file locations, and so on.

A successful SQL Server 2014 install does not conclude after the Setup Wizard completes. Several post-installation tasks require multiple default configuration settings to be modified, such as max memory, parallelism thresholds, TCP/IP ports, patches, and more. You can use SQL Server Management Studio and SQL Server Configuration Manager to change these default configuration options. Database servers must be burned in and stress tested to avoid unexpected behavior under heavy load.

If you plan to upgrade, Chapter 3 offers some good advice in that area.

3

Upgrading SQL Server 2014 Best Practices

WHAT'S IN THIS CHAPTER?

➤ Planning an upgrade

➤ Understanding discontinued and deprecated features

➤ Choosing an upgrade method

➤ Knowing what to watch for after the upgrade

Chapter 2, "SQL Server 2014 Installation Best Practices," covers performing a new installation of SQL Server 2014. This chapter discusses upgrading SQL Server from a previous version. The best strategy for a successful upgrade is planning and preparation. First, you learn reasons for upgrading to SQL Server 2014. You then consider the pros and cons of various upgrade strategies, and you learn about the various tools available to help mitigate risk during the upgrade process. Then you learn about SQL Server 2014 behavior changes, and discontinued features that you need to know about before upgrading. To wrap up, this chapter explores unexpected issues you might encounter after the upgrade. By the end of the chapter, you will have learned everything you need to know to perform a successful upgrade to SQL Server 2014.

WHY UPGRADE TO SQL SERVER 2014?

This book introduces significant enhancements throughout the product. During the development cycle, consider the three pillars of focus for the product: mission-critical confidence, breakthrough insight, and cloud on your terms. With the release of SQL Server 2014,

Microsoft enhanced numerous features in the areas of scalability, reliability, availability, and security. Following are many benefits that these new features and capabilities provide:

- ➤ Mission-critical performance enhancements:
  - ➤ In-Memory OLTP features built into the core database for online transaction processing (OLTP) and data warehousing
  - ➤ Updatable in-memory columnstore indexes with archival compression
  - ➤ Extend the SQL Server Buffer Pool to solid-state drives (SSDs) using Buffer Pool Extensions
  - ➤ Delayed Durability that allows write-ahead logging to be delayed, regardless of recovery model
  - ➤ Query Optimizer improvements with changes to the cardinality estimator
  - ➤ Backup encryption without the requirement of Transparent Data Encryption
  - ➤ New security roles for increased separation of duties
  - ➤ Automated backups and direct backup to Windows Azure
  - ➤ Greater high availability with enhanced AlwaysOn to eight secondaries, plus a replication wizard
- ➤ Faster insights from any data:
  - ➤ Easy access to Big and Small Data with Power Query, Windows Azure MarketPlace, and Parallel Data Warehouse (PDW) with Polybase
  - ➤ Faster and richer insights with Excel, PowerPivot, Power View, data mining add-ins, and mobile business intelligence (BI) applications
  - ➤ Complete BI solution with near real-time Access streaming data, Data Quality Service, Master Data Services, Analysis Services, and BI Semantic Model
- ➤ Platform for hybrid cloud:
  - ➤ Reduce capital expenditures (CAPEX) and operating expenses (OPEX) to improve business continuity
  - ➤ Fully functional SQL Server to Windows Azure
  - ➤ Quick development of variable-demand cloud applications

Risk Mitigation—the Microsoft Contribution

As with all previous versions of SQL Server, the SQL team took extraordinary steps to ensure that the quality of SQL Server 2014 is as high-grade as possible. The specific steps of the software engineering cycle are beyond the scope of this book, but a few points are highlighted here, considering public knowledge about the daily build process.

Today, a daily process produces x86 and x64 versions of SQL Server 2014 code (called *builds*) that have gone through a battery of tests. This process is utilized for both the development of new releases, and the development of service packs for SQL Server 2014. These tests are a convergence of in-house build tests, customer-captured workloads, and Trustworthy Computing processes. Microsoft Research worked on bringing innovations to Microsoft's products. In the areas of software development, the Microsoft Research team is an essential contributor to the software engineering and testing processes. It improves the test harness with enhancements in several areas, including threat modeling, testing efficiencies, and penetration analysis.

In addition, many customer-captured workloads are also part of the software testing harness. These workloads are acquired through an assortment of programs such as the Customer Playback program and various lab engagements, including SQL Server 2014 compatibility labs.

The daily builds are tested against this gathered information, and out of this process come performance metrics, security metrics, and bugs. Bugs are subsequently filed, assigned, prioritized, and tracked until resolution. After a bug is fixed, its code goes through security testing as part of the software engineering process. This happens before the code is checked back into the software tree for the next testing cycle.

This rigorous development and quality assurance process helps ensure that the shipped product is reliable and ready for production environments. The bottom line is that the adage, "Wait until the first service pack to upgrade," is no longer true for SQL Server 2014.

Independent Software Vendors and SQL Community Contributions

Starting with SQL Server 2005 and continuing with SQL Server 2014, the concept of community technology preview (CTP) was adopted. The June 2013 CTP1 and October 2013 CTP2 were the first of several such releases, in addition to Release Candidate (RC) releases. The decision to adopt this snapshot in time of code (or build) resulted in hundreds of thousands of CTP and RC downloads, providing unprecedented access to updated code to both independent software vendor (ISV) and SQL community testing. This type of access to beta code was leveraged as a means to identify additional bugs, conduct additional testing of software fixes, and drive additional improvements based on community feedback.

UPGRADING TO SQL SERVER 2014

Chapter 2 covers the installation guidelines, so this section mainly focuses on upgrade strategies and considerations for the SQL Server 2014 database component. A smooth upgrade requires a good plan. When you devise an upgrade plan, you must break down the upgrade process into individual tasks. This plan should have sections for pre-upgrade tasks, upgrade tasks, and post-upgrade tasks.

➤ Your *pre-upgrade tasks* consider SQL Server 2014 minimum hardware and software requirements, as well as SQL version compatibility. Create an inventory of applications that access the server, database-collation requirements, server dependencies (including connection strings), and legacy-systems requirements such as data-access methods. The checklist should include database consistency checks and a backup of all databases. Plans should be in place for establishing benchmark testing of the upgrade process and applications. Identify all backward-compatibility issues, and document workarounds or fixes. Use the SQL Server 2014 Upgrade Advisor (as described later in this chapter) to assist in identifying and resolving these issues. Review discontinued SQL Server 2014 Features on the Microsoft Developers Network (MSDN).

➤ The *upgrade execution process* is a smooth execution of your well-documented and rehearsed plan. To reiterate the importance of this step, ensure that you make a backup of all the databases before you execute the upgrade process. The more environments that can take place, the more detailed the plan for upgrading will become.

➤ *Post-upgrade tasks* consist of reviewing the upgrade process, bringing the systems back online, monitoring, and testing the system. You must perform specific database maintenance before releasing the system to the user community. These and other recommended steps are outlined later in this chapter. Run your database in backward-compatibility mode after the upgrade to minimize the amount of change to your environment. Update the database-compatibility if there are features from prior releases that have been deprecated in SQL Server 2014 features.

As part of deciding on your upgrade strategy, consider both in-place (upgrade) and side-by-side migration methods for upgrading.

In-Place Upgrading

The in-place server upgrade is the easier, but riskier, of the two options. This is an all-or-nothing approach to upgrading, meaning that after you initiate the upgrade, there is no simple rollback procedure. This type of upgrade has the added requirement of greater upfront testing to avoid using a complex back-out plan. The benefit of this approach is that you don't need to worry about users and logins remaining in sync, and database connectivity changes are not required for applications. In addition, SQL Server Agent jobs migrate during the upgrade process.

Following is a high-level, step-by-step scenario of an in-place upgrade based on Figure 3-1.

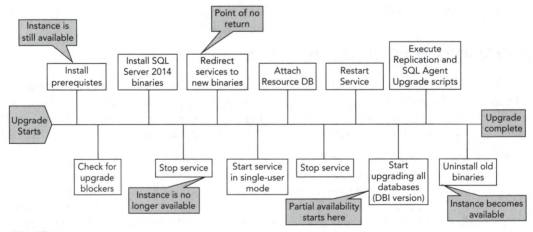

FIGURE 3-1

1. Install the prerequisite files on your system. Before upgrading to SQL Server 2014, your server needs (at a minimum) the following:

   ➤ .NET 3.5 with Service Pack 1

   ➤ .NET Framework 4.0 will be installed with the SQL Server 2014 Setup

   ➤ Windows PowerShell 2.0

   ➤ A current instance of SQL Server 2005 SP4, SQL Server 2008 SP3, SQL Server 2008 R2 SP2, or SQL Server 2012 SP1

2. Download and run the SQL Server 2014 Upgrade Advisor, which will analyze installed components from earlier versions of SQL Server, and then generate a report that identifies issues to fix either before or after you upgrade.

3. Run the System Configuration Checker (SCC). The SCC examines the destination computer for conditions that would prevent an upgrade from completing (such as not meeting the minimum hardware or software requirements). If such a condition is found, setup aborts and the SQL Server 2014 components uninstall.

4. Once verified, the SQL Server setup program can lay the 2014 bits and backward-compatibility support files on a disk while SQL Server 2012, 2008 R2, 2008, or 2005 SP4 is still available to users. However, don't plan to upgrade a server while users are online. The setup program takes the server offline by stopping the existing SQL Server services. The 2014-based services assume control of the master database and the server identity. At this point, the SQL Server service takes over the databases and begins to update them while not allowing users back into the environment.

5. Finally, kick off the uninstall procedure for the old binaries. This step occurs only if no remaining SQL Server instances are on the server. SQL Server Agent jobs are now migrated.

Following are the advantages of an in-place upgrade:

➤ It is fast, easy, and automated (best for small systems).

➤ No additional hardware is required.

➤ Applications retain the same instance name.

➤ It preserves SQL Server 2012, 2008R2, 2008, or 2005 functionality automatically.

The disadvantages of an in-place upgrade are as follows:

➤ Downtime is incurred because the entire SQL Server instance is offline during upgrade.

➤ There is no support for component-level upgrades.

➤ It entails a complex and manual rollback strategy.

➤ Backward-compatibility issues must be addressed for that SQL instance.

➤ In-place upgrade is not supported for all SQL Server components.

➤ Large databases require substantial rollback time.

Additionally, if you would like to change editions as a part of your upgrade, you must be aware of some limitations. There are specific upgrade paths to SQL 2014 for each release/version. If this is of interest to you, see SQL Server 2014 Books Online (BOL), "Version and Edition Upgrades," under the section "Upgrading to SQL Server 2014," or access the link `http://msdn.microsoft.com/en-us/library/ms143393(v=sql.120).aspx`.

Side-by-Side Upgrade

In a side-by-side upgrade, SQL Server 2014 installs either along with SQL Server 2012, 2008 R2, 2008, or 2005 SP4 as a separate instance, or on a different server. This process is essentially a new installation followed by a database migration. Because of the backup and restore times involved in a back-out scenario, if you have a sizable database, this is definitely the option to use.

As part of this method, you can simply back up the databases from the original server, and then restore them to the SQL Server 2014 instance. Other options are to detach your database manually from the old instance and reattach it to the new instance, use log shipping, or database mirroring. You can also leverage the Copy Database Wizard to migrate your databases to the new server. Although this approach provides for a good recovery scenario, it has additional requirements beyond those of the in-place upgrade, such as maintaining the original server name, caring for application connectivity, and keeping users and their logins in sync.

Following are the arguments in favor of a side-by-side upgrade:

➤ You have more granular control over the upgrade component-level process (database, Analysis Services, and others).

➤ You can run SQL Servers side-by-side for testing and verification.

➤ You have a rollback strategy because the original server is still intact.

➤ It is best for large databases because restore time could be sizable.

The arguments against a side-by-side upgrade are as follows:

➤ You have the issue of instance name changing for connecting applications.

➤ Two licenses for SQL Server must be purchased for the machine. Currently you must license at least one instance per version.

In-Place Upgrade versus Side-by-Side Upgrade Considerations

Consider numerous factors before selecting an upgrade strategy. Your strategy should include the need for a component-level upgrade, the ability to roll back in case of failure, the size of your databases, and the need for partial upgrade. Your top priorities might depend upon whether you can upgrade to new hardware, facilitate a change of strategy such as a server consolidation, and manage a small server outage window for the upgrade. Table 3-1 shows a summary of the two upgrade methods.

TABLE 3-1: In-Place and Side-by-Side Upgrade Comparison

PROCESS	IN-PLACE UPGRADE	SIDE-BY-SIDE UPGRADE
Number of resulting instances	One	Two
Data file transfer	Automatic	Manual
SQL Server instance configuration	Automatic	Manual
Supporting upgrade utility	SQL Server setup	Various migration and data transfer methods

PRE-UPGRADE STEPS AND TOOLS

Now that you understand the reasons and options for upgrading to SQL Server 2014, you can move on to choosing your upgrade tools to assist in the upgrade process and performing pre-upgrade steps. Prior to the upgrade process, you can take preventative measures to avoid common upgrade issues, such as running out of disk space or executing startup stored procedures during the upgrade. A number of tools also can help identify potential upgrade issues in your environment. The two most useful tools to aid in this process are the SQL Server Upgrade Advisor and the SQL Server Upgrade Assistant. These tools both provide pre-upgrade analysis, and help you gain confidence that your upgrade will run successfully. Upgrade Assistant uses workload testing to test post-upgrade application behavior, and Upgrade Advisor performs in-place analysis of your databases for potential compatibility issues.

Pre-Upgrade Steps

You have a number of steps to take prior to performing the upgrade process. These precautions and preventative measures help eliminate surprises during an upgrade.

- ➤ Set your data and log files to autogrow during the upgrade process.
- ➤ Disable all startup stored procedures because the upgrade process stops and starts services on the SQL Server instance being upgraded.
- ➤ Allocate additional space or have plenty of space for tempdb to grow during the upgrade process. tempdb is the central database used for managing temporary objects, row versioning, and online index rebuilds.
- ➤ Disable all trace flags before upgrading to SQL Server 2014. The possibility exists that the trace-flag functionality is either different in SQL Server 2014, or does not exist. After the upgrade process, test to determine which (if any) of your trace flags are still required.
- ➤ Migrate to Database Mail. SQL Mail was discontinued in SQL Server 2012.

Pre-Upgrade Tools

Performing an upgrade can be a daunting task. Mitigate the risk of a failed upgrade or unexpected post-upgrade behavior by examining your instances prior to performing the upgrade process. Two tools to consider as you begin preparing for an upgrade are SQL Server Upgrade Advisor (SSUA) and Upgrade Assistant for SQL Server 2014 (UAFS).

SQL Server Upgrade Advisor

The rules checked by Upgrade Advisor represent conditions, situations, or known errors that might affect your upgrade to SQL Server 2014. If you want to take advantage of the lessons other SQL Server users have learned about upgrading, the SQL Server 2014 Upgrade Advisor is the tool for you.

This tool is based on feedback from early adopters and internal lab-testing feedback. The SQL Server 2014 Upgrade Advisor is a free download available as part of the Microsoft SQL Server 2014 Feature Pack, and is also available as part of the SQL Server 2014 installation media for all editions.

The purpose of this tool is to identify known upgrade issues, and provide guidance for workarounds or fixes for the identified issues on a per-server components' basis. Microsoft worked hard on this tool as a risk-mitigation effort to empower SQL Server 2005, SQL Server 2008, and SQL Server 2012 users to upgrade to SQL Server 2014. So, whether you run Analysis Services, Integration Services, Reporting Services components, or a combination of components, the Upgrade Advisor tool can assist.

Installing the SQL Server 2014 Upgrade Advisor

The Upgrade Advisor is a relatively simple tool install and use. You can find installation for the Upgrade Advisor in the "Planning" section of the default screen of the installation media. It can also be found under Microsoft Downloads.

Navigate to the Upgrade Advisor from the Programs menu, after installation. A Welcome screen for the Upgrade Advisor (as shown in Figure 3-2) is the initial flash page. Select "Check for Updates" because upgraded versions of this tool are available online.

The tool is constantly updated to reflect the lessons learned by the DBAs who upgraded before you. The tool requires .NET 4.0, which you can download through the Windows Update service or from MSDN. Alternatively, you can choose to install a single instance and version of the tool to test servers across your enterprise. This option supports a zero-footprint interrogation with read-only access to servers.

> **NOTE** *This tool is read-intensive and should be tested on a test server to evaluate the potential impact on your systems.*

The installation process is straightforward. The only option is to select the location where you would like to install the tool. The default install path is `C:\Program Files (x86)\Microsoft SQL Server Upgrade Advisor`.

Using the Upgrade Advisor

When installed, the Upgrade Advisor presents you with two choices: Upgrade Advisor Analysis Wizard and Upgrade Advisor Report Viewer. Launch the Upgrade Advisor Analysis Wizard to run the tool. As shown in Figure 3-3, select a server and the components to analyze for upgrade, or click the Detect button, which starts the inspection process that selects the components installed on your system.

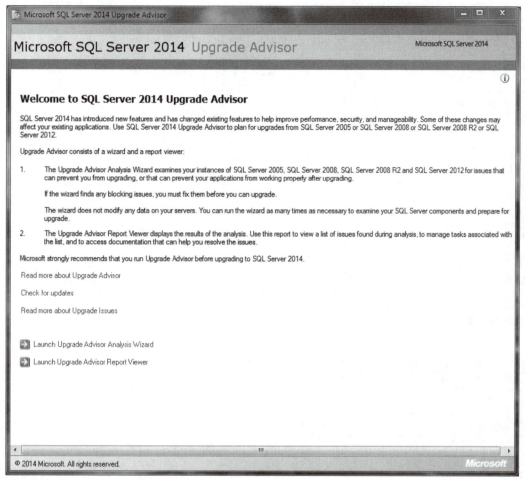

FIGURE 3-2

After you select the components for testing, the next decision is to select the databases that you would like to have evaluated for upgrade, as shown in Figure 3-4. The best part of this process is that you have the option to analyze SQL Profiler trace and SQL batch files to help make this a comprehensive analysis. That is, by adding these files to the evaluation process, Upgrade Advisor evaluates not only the database, but its trace workload and SQL scripts as well. By evaluating this additional information, Upgrade Advisor evaluates not only the database as it exists right now, but also information about past database usage and behavior contained in the trace and batch files. All you need to do is select the path to the directory where your trace files or your batch files are located.

After you complete configuration of the components that you want to evaluate, you will be prompted to begin the analysis. If you have any questions during the configuration steps, the Help button brings up an Upgrade Advisor-specific Book Online (UABOL) that is rich in information and guides you through the options. As the component-level analysis completes, a green, yellow, or red dialog box indicates the outcome of the test.

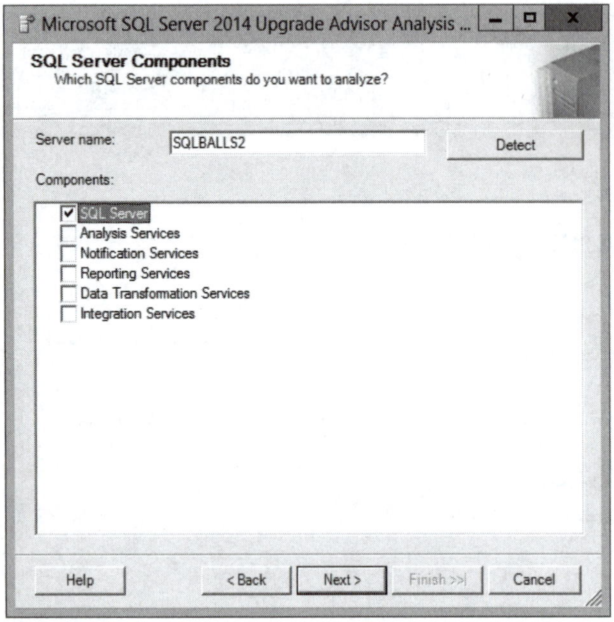

FIGURE 3-3

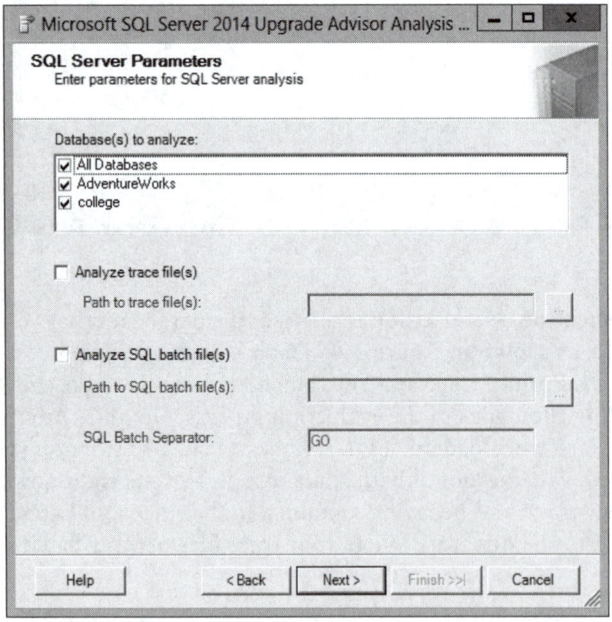

FIGURE 3-4

When the test completes, you can view the discovered issues via the Upgrade Advisor Report Viewer. As shown in Figure 3-5, the reports are presented in an interface similar to a web browser.

You can analyze the information by filtering the report presented by server, instance, or component, or issue type. You learn how to interpret the results of this report later in this chapter.

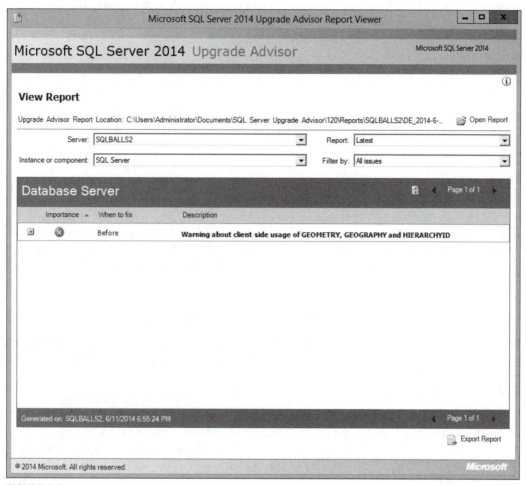

FIGURE 3-5

Scripting the Upgrade Advisor

If you have a server farm or just prefer scripting, a command-line capability is also available. With the UpgradeAdvisorWizardCmd utility, you can configure the tool via an XML configuration file and receive results as XML files. The following parameters can be passed to the UpgradeAdvisorWizardCmd utility:

➤ Command-line help

➤ The configuration path and filename

➤ The SQL Server login and password for SQL Server (if SQL Server authentication is used, rather than Windows authentication)

➤ An optional flag to indicate whether to output reports in a comma-separated value (CSV) format

The configuration file exposes all capabilities and parameters discussed in the wizard section. You can still view the results from a command-line execution in the Report Viewer, via XML documents or Excel if you use the CSV option. For example, the following XML document from Upgrade Advisor reflects the choices of analyzing all databases, Analysis Services, and SSIS packages on a server named SQL14Demo and an instance named SQL2014:

```
<Configuration>
   <Server>SQL14Demo</Server>
   <Instance>SQL2014</Instance>
 <Components>
    <SQLServer>
       <Databases>
          <Database>*</Database>
       </Databases>
    </SQLServer>
 </Components>
</Configuration>
```

You can modify the file in an XML editor (such as Visual Studio) and save the file with a new file-name. Then, you can use the new file as input to the command line of Upgrade Advisor. For example, the following code snippet displays the command prompt entry required to run the command line of Upgrade Advisor using Windows authentication. The configuration file already contains names for a remote server named SQL2014 and an instance named SQL2014, and the PATH environment variable contains the path to the Upgrade Wizard.

```
C:\>UpgradeAdvisorWizardCmd -ConfigFile "SQL2014Config.xml"
```

From the command prompt, you can also install or remove the Upgrade Advisor application. From there you can control the install process with or without the UI. You can also configure the install path and process-logging options.

> **NOTE** *For more information on the Upgrade Advisor's configuration files, see the Upgrade Advisor Help section, "UpgradeAdvisorWizardCmd Utility."*

Resolving Upgrade Issues

The Upgrade Advisor's report contains a wealth of information. The key is to understand how this information appears, what you need to resolve, and when. As shown previously in Figure 3-6, the first column indicates the importance of a finding or a recommendation, the second column tells you when you need to address it, and the Description column tells you about the issue. Approach this analysis by first categorizing the information by "Importance" and "When to Fix" the items. Specifically, the sum of the indicators should dictate whether you need to address issues before or after the upgrade process. Table 3-2 provides recommendations of when to address these issues.

TABLE 3-2: When to Address Upgrade Issues

IMPORTANCE	WHEN TO FIX	RECOMMENDATION
Red	Before	Resolve before upgrade
Red	Any Time	Resolve before upgrade

IMPORTANCE	WHEN TO FIX	RECOMMENDATION
Red	After	Resolve after upgrade
Yellow	Any Time	Resolve after upgrade
Yellow	After	Resolve after upgrade
Yellow	Advisory	Resolve after upgrade

Issues that have been flagged with an "Importance" of Red, and a "When to Fix" of "Before" or "Any Time" should be addressed before starting an upgrade process. Typically, these issues require remediation because of SQL Server 2014 functionality changes (such as discontinued features). You can usually resolve the remaining issues after the upgrade process because they either have a work-around within the upgrade process, or do not affect it at all. If you expand the error in question, additional information appears, as shown in Figure 3-6.

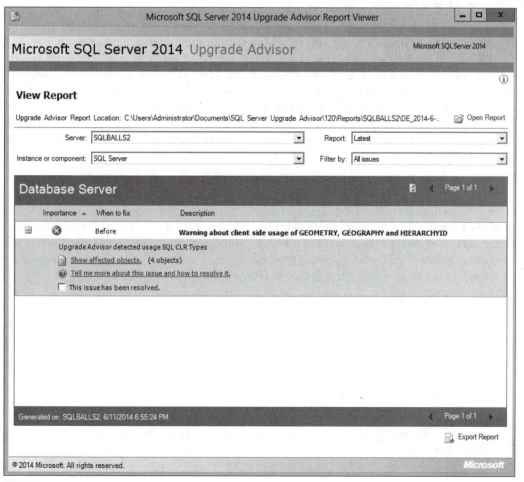

FIGURE 3-6

The "Show affected objects" link shows the exact objects flagged by the Upgrade Advisor process as affected, whereas the "Tell me more about this issue and how to resolve it" link takes you to the corresponding section of the Upgrade Advisor Books Online (UABOL). The UABOL describes the conditions and provides guidance about corrective action to address the issue. The UABOL provides guidance for problem resolution in areas beyond the scope of the tools (such as replication, SQL Server Agent, and Full-Text Search).

The "This issue has been resolved" check mark is for your personal tracking of resolved issues. This metadata check mark is in place to support remediation processes by enabling the report to be viewed by the filtered status of resolved issues or pre-upgrade (unresolved) issues.

If you prefer command-line scripting, the viewer is nothing more than an XSLT transformation applied to the XML result file located in your `My Documents\SQL Server 2014 Upgrade Advisor Reports\` directory. You can find individual component results and configuration files in each server's name-based directories. You can even export viewer-based reports to other output formats such as CSV or text.

Capturing the Environment

You should establish your baseline by backing up all SQL Server 2008 (or 2005) systems and user databases from your server. Following this step, you need to start capturing your trace file to avoid gaps in the process. When you capture a trace file, it needs to be a good representation of the workloads that characterize your environment. To do this, you might need to create an artificial workload that better represents the workloads of the application over time. While capturing the trace file, it's a good idea to avoid multiserver operations such as linked server calls or bulk-copy operation dependencies. Be aware that there is a performance cost while tracing. The sum of the trace files and database backups represent a repeatable and reusable workload called a *playback*.

When migrating from SQL Server 2012 to SQL Server 2014, you can use the Distributed Replay Utility (DRU) to assess the impact of a SQL Upgrade. DRU is a tool that was introduced in SQL Server 2012 to replace the deprecated SQL Profiler Trace replay component. DRU adds to Profiler's functionality, and is able to replay workloads from multiple machines, which will better simulate mission-critical workloads. You can use Extended Events capturing to capture a workload by capturing the `sqlserver.sql_batch_completed` and `sqlserver.sql_statement_completed` events and the action `sqlserver.sql_text` for use in DRU as well.

DRU runs in the following two different modes:

➤ *Synchronization mode* will run the trace workload exactly as it has been defined including waits between commands, and so on.

➤ *Stress mode* will just run the workload and beat up your target server.

Following are some important DRU concepts:

➤ **DRU administration tool**—A console application, `DReplay.exe`, is used to communicate with the distributed replay controller. Use the administration tool to control the distributed replay.

➤ **DRU controller**—This is a computer running the Windows service named "SQL Server Distributed Replay controller." The DRU controller orchestrates the actions of the distributed replay clients. There can only be one controller instance in each DRU environment.

➤ **DRU clients**—This is one or more computers (physical or virtual) running the Windows service named "SQL Server Distributed Replay client." The DRU clients work together to simulate workloads against an instance of SQL Server. There can be up to 16 clients in each DRU environment, each running up to 255 threads.

➤ **Target server**—This is an instance of SQL Server that the DRU clients can use to replay trace data. It is recommended that the target server be located in a test environment.

Setting Up the Baseline Server

Now that you have captured the playback using SQL Profiler or Extended Events, you can set up the baseline system to use for the remainder of the test. Load this server with SQL Server 2008 R2 SP1, 2008 SP2, or SQL Server 2005 SP2, with the minimum requirement for upgrading to 2014. In reality, it should be identical to the source system in collation and patching level.

The tool then checks your server for this matching. If necessary, you are prompted to patch or rebuild the master database. It then restores your databases in the correct order so that your database IDs match to production. (This also includes padding the database creation process to accomplish this.) Finally, SSUA re-creates your logins and ensures that the IDs match production because all this is necessary to run the trace file. The next step in the process is to run the Upgrade Advisor as described earlier. When the environment has been remediated, you can then proceed to the next step to replay the trace.

Running the DRU

When you run the trace, first the statistics update on all databases. The replay tool then uses the API and runs all the queries within the trace file in order. This tool is a single-threaded replay, but blocking can occur. If the trace appears to run slowly or stop, you may want to check SQL Server blocking; and if it does not clear up by itself, you must kill the blocking processes. The output from this step generates a trace-output file for comparison in the final analysis.

Upgrading to SQL Server 2014

Now you are ready to upgrade to SQL Server 2014. You have two options. You can use SSUA to restore the state of the SQL Server 2005, 2008, 2008 R2, or 2012 to its baseline and then upgrade in-place to SQL Server 2014, or you can migrate to an existing SQL Server 2014 instance.

As discussed earlier in this chapter, the decision to perform an in-place or side-by-side upgrade is based on a number of factors specific to your environment. You do not measure performance metrics, so these servers don't need to be identical. You measure workload behavior between two versions of SQL Server.

After restoring the baseline on a SQL Server 2014 platform, go through the Running the DRU step again, but this time on SQL Server 2014. The output from this step generates the other trace-output file for comparison in the final analysis.

Final Analysis

After completing all these processes, you will reach the final steps to compare the output files by filtering and comparing all batches in both trace files for discrepancies. The Report Viewer shows one error condition at a time by showing the last correct step, the error step, and the next correct sequences of the batch files. When a condition has been identified, it can be filtered from the error-reviewing process to enable the DBA to focus on identifying new error conditions. After the SQL Server 2014 upgrade completes, change the database compatibility mode to 120, and run your application to validate that it works in SQL Server 2014 compatibility mode. This ensures that no application behavior differences exist when your application runs on the database compatibility level of 120.

BACKWARD COMPATIBILITY

This section covers major product changes to SQL Server 2014 classified in one of three categories: unsupported, discontinued, or affecting the way prior releases of SQL Server behave today. Although the Upgrade Advisor tool highlights these conditions if they are relevant to your environment, you should read this section to learn about these changes.

Unsupported and Discontinued Features in SQL Server 2014

From time to time, to move a technology forward, trade-offs must be made. As shown in Table 3-3, several features have been discontinued from SQL 2008 to SQL Server 2014.

TABLE 3-3: Discontinued Features

CATEGORY	DEPRECATED FEATURE	REPLACEMENT	FEATURE NAME
Backup and restore	`RESTORE { DATABASE | LOG } WITH [MEDIA] PASSWORD` continues to be deprecated. `BACKUP { DATABASE | LOG } WITH PASSWORD` and `BACKUP { DATABASE | LOG } WITH MEDIAPASSWORD` are discontinued.	None.	`BACKUP DATABASE` or `LOG WITH PASSWORD`
			`BACKUP DATABASE` or `LOG WITH MEDIAPASSWORD`
Compatibility levels	Upgrade from version 90 (SQL Server 2005 Database Engine).	Compatibility levels are only available for the last two versions.	Database compatibility level 90.

CATEGORY	DEPRECATED FEATURE	REPLACEMENT	FEATURE NAME
		In SQL Server 2014, you can upgrade a SQL Server 2005 database, but the compatibility level is updated from 90 to 100 during the upgrade operation.	
Database objects	Capability to return result sets from triggers.	None.	Returning results from trigger.
Encryption	Encryption using RC4 or RC4_128 is deprecated, and is scheduled to be removed in the next version. Decrypting RC4 and RC4_128 is not deprecated.	Use another encryption algorithm such as AES.	Deprecated encryption algorithm.
Remote servers	sp_addremotelogin	Replace remote servers by using linked servers. sp_addserver can only be used with the local option.	sp_addremotelogin
	sp_addserver		sp_addserver
	sp_dropremotelogin		sp_dropremotelogin
	sp_helpremotelogin		sp_helpremotelogin
	sp_remoteoption		sp_remoteoption
Remote servers	@@remserver	Replace remote servers by using linked servers.	None.
Remote servers	SET REMOTE_PROC_TRANSACTIONS	Replace remote servers by using linked servers.	SET REMOTE_PROC_TRANSACTIONS
Set options	SET ROWCOUNT for INSERT, UPDATE, and DELETE statements.	TOP keyword.	SET ROWCOUNT

continues

TABLE 3-3 *(continued)*

CATEGORY	DEPRECATED FEATURE	REPLACEMENT	FEATURE NAME
Table hints	`HOLDLOCK` table hint without parenthesis.	Use `HOLDLOCK` with parenthesis.	`HOLDLOCK` table hint without parenthesis.
Tools	`sqlmaint` utility.	Use the SQL Server maintenance plan feature.	None.

> **NOTE** *This is a limited list of discontinued features. For a complete list of discontinued and deprecated features, go to* `http://msdn.microsoft.com/en-us/library/ms144262.aspx`.

SQL Server 2014 Deprecated Database Features

These features are no longer available as of the SQL Server 2014 release or the next scheduled release of the product. Following are some of the features scheduled for deprecation. Try to replace these features over time with the recommended items.

➤   SOAP/HTTP endpoints created with `CREATE ENDPOINT` and `ALTER ENDPOINT`. (They have been replaced with Windows Communication Framework (WCF) or ASP.NET.)

➤   The compatibility level 90 will not be available after SQL Server 2012.

➤   Encryption using RC4 or RC4_128, is scheduled to be removed in the next version. Consider moving to another encryption algorithm such as AES.

➤   Not ending T-SQL statements with a semicolon will no longer be supported in a future version of SQL Server.

Other SQL Server 2014 Changes Affecting Behavior

The behavior changes in the following features could adversely affect migration to SQL Server 2014:

➤   If you create a new job by copying the script from an existing job, the new job might inadvertently affect the existing job. This is because the parameter `@schedule_uid` should not be duplicated. Manually delete it in the script for the new job.

➤   Deterministic scalar-valued CLR user-defined functions and deterministic methods of CLR user-defined types are now foldable. This seeks to enhance performance when these functions or methods are called more than once with the same arguments. However, if a nondeterministic function or method has been marked deterministic in error, it can create unexpected results.

➤ When a database with a partitioned index upgrades, there may be a difference in the histogram data for these indexes. This is because SQL Server 2014 uses the default sampling algorithm to generate statistics rather than a full scan.

➤ Using `sqlcmd.exe` with XML Mode behaves differently in SQL Server 2014.

> **NOTE** *For additional behavior changes, see SQL Server 2014 Books Online or go to* `http://msdn.microsoft.com/en-us/library/ms143359%28v=sql.120%29`.

Behavior changes in some features could adversely affect migration to SQL Server 2014. For example, in earlier versions of SQL Server, queries against an XML document that contains strings over a certain length (more than 4,020 characters) can return incorrect results. In SQL Server 2014, such queries return the correct results.

SQL SERVER COMPONENT CONSIDERATIONS

This section discusses individual components, along with any respective considerations that you should evaluate during an upgrade process. Components not covered here are covered later in the book in their respective chapters.

Upgrading Full-Text Catalog

During the upgrade process, all databases with Full-Text Catalog are marked Full-Text Disabled. This is because of the potential time involved in rebuilding the catalog. Before you upgrade your Full-Text Search environment, you should familiarize yourself with some of the enhancements. The database attach and detach processes also result in the Full-Text Catalog being marked as Full-Text Disabled. You can read SQL Server 2014 Books Online to learn about additional behavior.

Upgrading Reporting Services

Reporting Services 2008 and Reporting Services 2005 support upgrading to Reporting Services 2014. Prior to upgrading, run the SQL Server 2014 Upgrade Advisor and follow its recommendations, guidance on possible mitigation options, and steps. Then, before executing the upgrade, back up the database, applications, configurations files, and the encryption key.

Following are two ways to upgrade Reporting Services:

➤ **In-place upgrade**—You can accomplish this by executing the SQL Server 2014 `setup.exe`; select the older Reporting Services to upgrade with Reporting Services 2014. This has the same advantages and disadvantages described earlier with the in-place upgrade. The risk with this is that it is an all-or-nothing approach; it's difficult to roll back except by reinstalling it again.

➤ **Side-by-side upgrade**—With this option, the Reporting Services 2014 instance installs in the same physical server along with the older version of Reporting Services or on a separate physical server. After the Reporting Services 2014 instance installs, the report content migrates either individually or in bulk, using one of the following options:

> ➤ Redeploy the reports using SQL Server Data Tools (SSDT)
>
> ➤ Use rs.exe to extract and deploy the reports
>
> ➤ Use Report Manager

Published reports and snapshot reports are upgraded. After upgrading Reporting Services 2014, redeploy any custom extensions and assemblies, test the applications on Reporting Services 2014 after it is fully operational, and then remove any unused applications and tools from the previous version.

> **NOTE** *When upgrading to SQL Server 2014, the default Compatibility Level of the database will be preserved. You must manually change this from 90 (2005), 100 (2008(r2)), or 110 (2012), to 120 (2014) in order to utilize the new Query Optimizer and its improvements.*

Upgrading to 64-Bit

Upgrading from a SQL Server 2005 32-bit platform or SQL 2008 32-bit platform to SQL Server 2008 x64-bit platform is not supported. Although running a SQL Server 2005 32-bit platform with Service Pack 2 or SQL Server 2008 32-bit platform on a Windows x64-bit subsystem is supported, upgrading this configuration to a SQL Server 2014 x64-bit environment is not supported. Side-by-side migration is the only supported upgrade path for migrating databases from a 32-bit to x64-bit platform.

POST-UPGRADE CHECKS

The information presented here is about product behaviors that have surprised a lot of people after upgrading. There is nothing worse than successfully upgrading your environment and then having end users blame the upgrade for poor query performance. Proactive attention to post-upgrade issues lessens the risk that your careful planning and hard work will be tainted by post-upgrade problems.

A possible reason for poor query performance after upgrading to SQL Server 2014 is that the old statistics are considered outdated and cannot be used by the query optimizer. For most situations, this should not be an issue, as long as you have enabled the auto-update statistics and auto-create statistics options. This enables statistics to be automatically updated by default when needed for query compilation.

The statistics built from these features are built only from a data sampling. Therefore, they can be less accurate than statistics built from the entire data set. In databases with large tables, or in tables where previous statistics were created with `fullscan`, the difference in quality may cause the SQL Server 2014 query optimizer to produce a suboptimal query plan.

> **NOTE** *With SQL Server 2014, when you create an index, the statistics use the query optimizer's default sampling algorithm.*

To mitigate this issue, you should immediately update the statistics after upgrading to SQL Server 2014. Using `sp_updatestats` with the `resample` argument rebuilds statistics based on an inherited sampling ratio for all existing statistics. Typically, that is a full sample for index-based statistics and sampled statistics for the rest of the columns. An additional benefit that you could gain from this process is that if the data is less than 8MB (the minimum sampling size), the statistics are also built with `fullscan`.

SUMMARY

Many compelling reasons exist for upgrading to SQL Server 2014. Some strategies and tools for doing so include the Upgrade Assistant for SQL Server 2014 and the SQL Server 2014 Upgrade Advisor, which can be leveraged during the upgrade. The upgrade process includes the pre-upgrade, the actual upgrade, and the post-upgrade steps for a successful upgrade.

You should watch out for several discontinued features (including database compatibility level 90 and SQL Mail), along with features whose behavior changes could also affect your upgrade (such as partitioned index histograms post-upgrade and `sqlcmd.exe` with XML mode). Now that you have done the groundwork for a successful upgrade, it's time to jump into SQL Server 2014.

In Chapter 4, you learn how to manage and troubleshoot SQL Server's Database Engine.

4

Managing and Troubleshooting the Database Engine

WHAT'S IN THIS CHAPTER?

➤ Configuring your instance using SQL Server Management Studio

➤ Using a dedicated administrator connection to access an unresponsive server

➤ Monitoring processes using Dynamic Management Objects (DMOs)

WROX.COM CODE DOWNLOADS FOR THIS CHAPTER

The wrox.com code downloads for this chapter are found at www.wrox.com/go/ prosql2014admin on the Download Code tab. The code is in the Chapter 4 download and individually named according to the names throughout the chapter.

In this chapter, you learn how to configure and monitor your SQL Server instance. This is the key to a smooth-running database—proper configuration and active monitoring. In addition, you learn some troubleshooting methods that help you identify what is happening when the instance is not performing as expected. This chapter assumes you already know the basics of SQL Server Management Studio navigation, and focuses on what you need to know as a database administrator (DBA). Many other chapters in this book cover various aspects of SQL Server Management Studio, so those points are not duplicated here (backing up your database, for example, is covered in Chapter 17, "Backup and Recovery").

CONFIGURATION AND ADMINISTRATION TOOLS

After you install SQL Server or upgrade to SQL Server 2014, you will likely need to configure it for your needs. In SQL Server 2014, Microsoft maintained its policy to increase out-of-the-box security established with SQL Server 2008 by turning off features after installation, thereby reducing the software footprint. The features turned off vary based on the edition of SQL Server. For example, TCP/IP is disabled in Developer Edition by default, and every edition has Common Language Runtime (CLR) integration turned off. This makes the environment more usable for you as an administrator because features you don't care about are not crowding your administration screen. It also reduces the options that a hacker or, more likely, a malicious user can use to penetrate your system. As a result of these security measures, there is even more reason to invest time in configuring SQL Server 2014 toward your specific needs. In this section, you learn how to configure SQL Server for your specific environment and security needs in a few ways: by using SQL Server Configuration Manager, startup parameters, startup stored procedures, and partially contained databases. SQL Server Configuration Manager is the best place to start.

SQL Server Configuration Manager

The SQL Server Configuration Manager configures the SQL Server services much like the Services applet in the Control Panel, but it has much more functionality than the applet. For example, the program can also change what ports SQL Server listens on and what protocols each instance uses.

To start configuring SQL Server to fit your environment's needs, follow these steps:

1. Go to the top-left corner (Windows 8, Windows 2012, and up) and get the spyglass icon. Type **SQL Server Configuration Manager,** and click the icon for SQL Server Configuration Manager. The screen shown in Figure 4-1 appears.

FIGURE 4-1

2. To configure an individual service such as SQL Server, double-click the service name to open the service Properties page. In the Log On tab, you can configure which account starts SQL Server. You should start SQL Server with a regular domain user account with minimal rights. The account should not have the privilege to "Log on Locally," for example. There is no reason for the account to be a local or domain administrator in SQL Server 2014.

3. Next, create a non-expiring password so your SQL Server doesn't fail to start when the password expires. If the SQL Server services do not need to communicate outside the instance's machine, you could start the service with the Local System account, but the account may have more local rights than you want. (This is discussed more in Chapter 8, "Securing the Database Instance.")

NOTE *Use Configuration Manager to change Services attributes instead of the Windows Services dialog boxes in the Administrative Tools area. In SQL Server 2005, the way that the SQL service account's password is encrypted was changed. If you attempt to change the password with the Services Window instead of SQL Server Configuration Manager, the service will fail to start the next time the SQL service is restarted.*

4. On the Service tab, specify whether you'd like the service to start automatically, manually, or be disabled.

The rest is optional, but highly recommended. For example, if you go to the Advanced tab for each service, you can configure the more interesting options. Here you can turn off Customer Feedback Reporting. This feature enables Microsoft to receive utilization reports from your SQL Server. Even if you wanted to do this, in most production environments, your SQL Server may not send the report because of a lack of Internet access from production servers.

You can also check the Error Reporting option in the Advanced tab to e-mail Microsoft whenever a critical error has occurred. The minimal and anonymous information is sent over a secure HTTPS protocol.

Additionally, by accessing the SQL Server 2014 Network Configuration page in the Configuration Manager (see Figure 4-2), you can see a list of network protocols that SQL Server is listening on by instance. If you want to turn a protocol on or off, you can do so by right-clicking the protocol and selecting Enable or Disable. By enabling only the Shared Memory protocol, only clients that run on the same computer can connect to your instance of SQL Server.

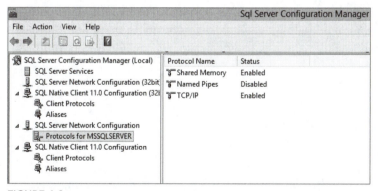

FIGURE 4-2

NOTE *The VIA protocol was discontinued in SQL Server 2012. It is no longer available in SQL Server 2014.*

Startup Parameters

SQL Server has an array of switches you can use to enable advanced settings for the Database Engine or help with troubleshooting. You have two ways to set these configuration options: from SQL Server Configuration Manager or via a command prompt. You enable these switches via the SQL Server Configuration Manager by altering the SQL Server service's startup parameters. Configuring settings through Configuration Manager causes SQL Server to use the configured startup parameter every time it starts. Or, you can temporarily set the switches by running SQL Server from a command prompt. To enable a particular switch from a manual startup, perform the following steps:

1. In the SQL Server 2014 Services page, double-click SQL Server (MSSQLServer by default, but it may vary depending on your instance name).

2. Go to the Startup Parameters tab. Add any startup parameters (also known as *trace flags*) that you want to be enabled on startup of the SQL Server instance, as shown in Figure 4-3.

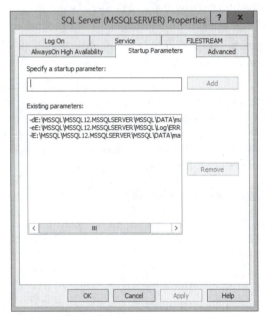

FIGURE 4-3

To enable a particular switch from a command prompt startup, perform the following steps:

1. Run `sqlservr.exe` from the command prompt. The file is located by default in the `C:\Program Files\Microsoft SQL Server\MSSQL12.MSSQLSERVER\MSSQL\Binn` directory.

2. Turn on any non-default parameters you want by adding the switch after `sqlservr.exe`. This is generally the preferred way to start your SQL Server in a one-off debug mode because you won't leave any settings intact that you may not want. You can stop SQL Server by using the Ctrl+C combination, or by closing the command prompt window.

> **WARNING** *Never start SQL Server with command prompt for normal use; after you log off the machine, your command prompt closes, stopping SQL Server.*

The syntax for the `sqlserver` runtime is as follows:

```
SQLServr.exe [-dmaster_file_path] [-lmaster_log_path]
      -eerror_log_path] [-sinstance_name][-c] [-f]
      [-gmemory_to_reserve] [-h] [-kcheckpoint Speed in MB/sec]
      [-m] [-n] [-Ttrace#] [-ttrace#] [-x]
      [-ystack dump on this error] [-B] [-K]
```

The startup options are useful in troubleshooting a problem, or for solving quick, one-off problems. Rather than describe every switch, only the ones you are likely to use most frequently are covered here:

➤ `-d` **and** `-l` **switches**—You can change which master database SQL Server uses by using the `-d` and `-l` switches:

```
SQLServr.exe -d C:\temp\TempMasterDB.mdf -l C:\temp\TempMasterLog.ldf
```

The `-d` switch specifies the database file, and the `-l` switch specifies the log file. This may be useful if you want to use a temporary configuration of the `master` database that may not be corrupt.

➤ `-T` **switch**—Another useful switch is `-T`, which enables you to start given trace flags for all the connections for a SQL Server instance. You can use this, for example, to turn on a trace flag to monitor deadlocks in your SQL Server instance (note that the "`T`" is uppercase):

```
SQLServr.exe -T1204
```

> **NOTE** *SQL Server also includes a lowercase trace flag option:* `SQLServr.exe -t1204`*. You should use this with caution, because using this flag sets other internal trace flags.*

> **WARNING** *If you try to start an instance of SQL Server while it is already running, you get errors. When SQL runs against a* `master` *file, it opens the file exclusively to prevent another instance from writing to the same file. One of the errors tells you that a file is in exclusive use or not available. No harm is done when this occurs.*

➤ -f **switch**—This switch places SQL Server in minimal mode and only enables a single connection. By placing SQL Server in minimal mode, SQL Server starts with a minimum configuration, and suspends the CHECKPOINT process, startup stored procedures, and remote connections.

> **NOTE** *Using SQL Server Configuration Manager, make sure you stop SQL Server Agent before placing SQL Server in single-user mode. Otherwise, SQL Server Agent takes the only available connection.*

➤ g **switch**—This switch reserves additional memory outside SQL Server's main memory pool for extended stored procedures.

➤ -m **switch**—This switch puts SQL Server in single-user mode (sometimes called *master recovery mode*) and suspends the CHECKPOINT process, which writes data from disk to the database device. This switch is useful when you want to recover the master database from a backup or perform other emergency maintenance procedures.

➤ -k **switch**—This switch is used to influence the CHECKPOINT frequency. It forces the regeneration of the system master key if one exists. Use this with extreme care, and only if directed by Microsoft Product Support Services (PSS).

➤ -s **switch**—This switch starts a named instance of SQL Server. When you start SQL Server from the command prompt, the default instance starts unless you switch to the appropriate BINN directory for the instance and provide the -s switch. For example, if your instance is named SQL2014, you should be in the C:\Program Files\Microsoft SQL Server\ MSSQL12.SQL2014\MSSQL\Binn directory and issue the following command:

```
sqlserver.exe -sSQL2014
```

➤ -c **switch**—This switch enables you to decrease startup time when starting SQL Server from a command prompt by taking advantage of the fact that the SQL Server Database Engine does not start as a service when starting from the command prompt. This switch bypasses the Service Control Manager, which is unnecessary in this situation.

You can obtain a complete list of switches by using the -? switch, as shown here (complete details appear in the SQL Server documentation):

```
sqlservr.exe -?
```

Startup Stored Procedures

Startup stored procedures work similarly to stored procedures, except that they execute whenever the SQL Server instance starts. For example, you may have a startup stored procedure that e-mails you when the instance starts. You can also use startup stored procedures to create objects in tempdb and load them with data when SQL Server starts. These stored procedures run under the sysadmin server role, and only a sysadmin can create a startup stored procedure. Errors written from a startup stored procedure are written to the SQL Server error log.

In the following steps, you enable startup stored procedures system-wide and create an example startup stored procedure.

> **WARNING** *Make sure that you do the examples in this section only against a development server until you're certain you want to do this in production.*

1. The stored procedure `sp_configure` enables startup stored procedures, but to set it, you must turn on the `show advanced options` setting, as in the following code snippet:

```
sp_configure 'show advanced options', 1;
GO
RECONFIGURE;
GO
```

2. By default, SQL Server does not scan for startup stored procedures. To allow it to do so, you must use `sp_configure`, as follows:

```
sp_configure 'scan for startup procs', 1;
GO
RECONFIGURE;
GO
```

3. After you run this, you must restart the SQL Server instance to commit the setting. Try a simple example. Create a table called `SQLStartupLog` in the `master` database that logs the time a SQL Server instance starts:

```
CREATE TABLE master.dbo.SQLStartupLog
(StartTime datetime);
GO
```

4. Create a stored procedure to log to the table. Be sure to create this stored procedure in the `master` database. The following stored procedure can do the trick, logging the current date to the table:

```
USE master
GO
CREATE PROC dbo.InsertSQLStartupLog
  as
  INSERT INTO master.dbo.SQLStartupLog
  SELECT GETDATE();
GO
```

5. Use the `sp_procoption` stored procedure to make the stored procedure a startup stored procedure. The `sp_procoption` stored procedure sets only one parameter. You must first specify the stored procedure you want to set; the only available option name is `startup`, with a

value of 1 (on) or 0 (off). Before running the following stored procedure, ensure that your SQL Server can scan for startup stored procedures, as shown here:

```
sp_procoption @ProcName = 'master.dbo.InsertSQLStartupLog',
  @OptionName= 'startup',
  @OptionValue = 1;
```

6. Stop and start your SQL Server instance, and query the `master.dbo.SQLStartupLog` to see if the record was written. Before you leave this section, make sure that you disable the setting by running the following query:

```
sp_procoption @ProcName = 'master.dbo.InsertSQLStartupLog',
  @OptionName= 'startup',
  @OptionValue = 0;

USE MASTER
GO
DROP TABLE master.dbo.SQLStartupLog;
DROP PROC dbo.InsertSQLStartupLog;
```

Partially Contained Databases

Partially contained databases were introduced as a new feature of SQL Server 2012. They provide an excellent configuration option for specific security scenarios. A full discussion of the security benefits is available in Chapter 8, "Securing the Database Instance." A *contained database* is a concept where all of the settings and metadata for that database have no configuration dependencies on the instance of SQL Server where the database resides. Users are able to connect to the database without authenticating a login at the instance level. This level of isolation makes a database with this configuration that is more portable from instance to instance, which can be quite beneficial when deploying a database to multiple instances (such as in a development environment).

In SQL Server 2014, fully contained databases are not implemented. Only partially contained databases are available for this release, meaning that objects or functions that cross the application boundary are allowed.

> **NOTE** *An* application boundary *is the boundary between the application model (database) and the instance. For example, the system table* `sys.endpoints` *is outside the application boundary, because it references instance-level objects. The system table* `sys.indexes` *is within the application boundary.*

By default, a SQL Server 2014 instance does not have contained databases enabled. Use `sp_config-ure` (shown in the following code snippet) to enable contained databases prior to migrating an existing database to this model:

```
sp_configure 'contained database authentication', 1;

GO
RECONFIGURE WITH OVERRIDE
GO
```

Before you migrate a database to a contained model, use the new Database Management Object (DMO) `sys.dm_db_uncontained_entities` to identify the containment level of your database. The output from the following query returns objects that can potentially cross the application boundary:

```
SELECT so.name, ue.*
FROM sys.dm_db_uncontained_entities ue
    LEFT JOIN sys.objects so
      ON ue.major_id = so.object_id;
```

> **NOTE** *An additional option to identify uncontained events in an application is the extended event* `database_uncontained_usage_event`. *This event fires whenever an uncontained event occurs in the application. See Chapter 12, "Monitoring Your SQL Server" for more information on Extended Events.*

If your database is a good candidate for partial containment and it is enabled, the CONTAINMENT option is used to convert a database to a partially contained database. Suitable candidates for partial containment include databases that do not use instance-level features, such as Service Broker. You can do this by issuing an ALTER DATABASE command, as shown in the following code snippet:

```
USE master
GO
ALTER DATABASE AdventureWorks SET CONTAINMENT = PARTIAL;
```

> **NOTE** *For more information on migrating to a partially contained database and the risks and limitations of this feature, go to* `http://msdn.microsoft.com/en-us/library/ff929139(v=sql.120).aspx`.

TROUBLESHOOTING TOOLS

Imagine you get a call informing you that a server is not responding. You go to SQL Server Management Studio to connect to the server to see what is going on. Your connection request waits, and waits, and then times out. You cannot connect, you cannot debug, and you cannot see anything. In this situation, you need tools in your arsenal to help you troubleshoot and repair core issues with your instance. The Dedicated Administrator Connection (DAC) is a very reliable tool for this type of situation. An alternative troubleshooting method that this section also covers is the process of rebuilding system databases in the event of a corruption or lost database.

Dedicated Administrator Connection

The DAC is a specialized diagnostic connection that can be used when standard connections to the server are not possible. When you need to connect to the server to diagnose and troubleshoot problems, the DAC is an invaluable administrative tool to have.

> **WARNING** *SQL Server attempts to make DAC connect in every situation, and most of the time it does. But in very severe situations, it cannot guarantee connection to an unresponsive server.*

SQL Server listens for the DAC connection on a dynamically assigned port. A connection can be made on this port only by sysadmin role members from SSMS or the `sqlcmd` tool. To connect to the DAC using SQL Server Management Studio, add a prefix to the server name. For example, if the server name is `SQL2014`, connect to server `admin:Prod`. You merely add the prefix `admin:` to the server name.

To connect using `sqlcmd`, use the `-A` option as follows:

```
sqlcmd -sSQL2014 -E -A -d master
```

By default, DAC is only allowed on a client running on the local server. However, by using `sp_configure`, you can enable remote admin connections by executing the following:

```
sp_configure 'remote admin connection', 1;
GO
RECONFIGURE WITH OVERRIDE
GO
```

You should enable a remote admin connection on instances where your security team and procedures allow you to. In some cases, you may need to connect using the TCP address and DAC port number found in the error log, particularly on clustered instances, as shown here:

```
Sqlcmd -S<serveraddress>,<DacPort>
```

If you connect locally using the IP address, use the Loopback Adapter address, as in the following example:

```
Sqlcmd -S127.0.0.1,1434
```

> **NOTE** *The* Loopback Adapter Address *is the Address of localhost (the local computer), and, on most systems, this translates to the IPv4 address* `127.0.0.1`. *Connecting to the Loopback Adapter Address is functionally the same as connecting to localhost.*

When connecting remotely, you need to know the port that DAC has been assigned. Port 1434 is the default, but the instance might be assigned something different if the connection to the default port failed during startup. Additionally, if remote administration connections are enabled, the DAC must be started with an explicit port number. Windows PowerShell is a good option for finding the port number, because it enables you to see assigned DAC ports across multiple instances at one time. The following Windows PowerShell example enables you to see which port has been assigned for DAC on each instance listed in the `$instances` variable:

```
$instances = "PRODUCTION", "PRODUCTION\R2", "PRODUCTION\SQL2012"
foreach($instance in $instances)
```

```
{
get-SQLErrorlog -SQLServer $instance |
where {($_.Text -match "Dedicated admin connection")} |
format-table  $DisplayResults -AutoSize
}
```

Rebuilding the System Databases

If one of your system databases becomes corrupted and your backups cannot be found, your last resort may be to rebuild the system databases. This can essentially reinstall the system databases and rid your system of anything that may be causing it to act unpredictably. The repercussion of this is that you must reinstall any service packs, and all your user-defined databases (including the Reporting Services support database) will disappear. Additionally, any logins or server configurations must be redone.

> **WARNING** *Rebuilding your system databases should not be taken lightly. It is a high-impact technical decision that you make when no other good option exists.*

To rebuild your system databases, follow these steps:

1. Go to a command prompt.

2. From the command prompt, run `setup.exe` as if you were installing SQL Server, but pass in a few switches, as shown here:

```
setup.exe /QUIET /ACTION=REBUILDDATABASE /INSTANCENAME=instance_name
        /SQLSYSADMINACCOUNTS=accounts /SAPWD=sa password
```

The switches indicate the following:

- ➤ `/QUIET` suppresses the errors and warnings while the rebuild runs. You see a blank screen while the process completes. Errors will still be logged to the error log.

- ➤ `/ACTION` indicates that the action is to rebuild the database, by providing the `REBUILDDATABASE` parameter.

- ➤ `/INSTANCENAME` provides the name of the instance where system databases should be rebuilt. Use `MSSQLSERVER` for a default instance.

- ➤ `/SQLSYSADMINACCOUNTS` provides Windows groups or individual accounts that should be provisioned as sysadmin. Use this option when SQL Server is configured for Windows Authentication mode.

- ➤ `/SAPWD` specifies the SA password. Use this option when SQL Server is configured for Mixed Authentication mode.

> **NOTE** *Prior to SQL Server 2008, the original installation media was required to rebuild system databases. Now, the system database and log files are copied to* `C:\Program Files\Microsoft SQL Server\MSSQL12.MSSQLSERVER\MSSQL\ Binn\Templates` *as part of installation. When you rebuild,* `setup.exe` *uses the files located here.*

3.   After the databases are rebuilt, return to your default configuration and databases. You need to restore the `master` database (more on this in Chapter 17) or reattach each user-defined database and re-create the logins. The preferable option, of course, is to recover the `master` database from a backup rather than rebuilding. Then your logins and databases automatically appear.

> **NOTE** *When you rebuild the system databases, the databases may appear to have disappeared, but the files are still in the operating system and can be reattached or restored. Reattaching the databases is generally the lowest-impact action.*

SQL SERVER MANAGEMENT STUDIO

DBAs spend a lot of time in SQL Server Management Studio. This tool enables you to perform most of your management tasks and to run queries. SQL Server 2014 uses a version of Visual Studio 2010 as its shell. Because this is a professional-level book, it won't go into every aspect of SQL Server Management Studio, but instead covers some of the more common and advanced features that you might like to use for administration.

Reports

One of the most impressive features of the SQL Server management environment is the integrated reports available in each area of administration. These standard reports are provided for the server instances, databases, logins, and `Management` tree item. Each runs as a Reporting Services report inside of SQL Server Management Studio. Server-level reports give you information about the instance of SQL Server and the operating system. Database-level reports drill into information about each database. You must have access to each database you want to report on, or your login must have enough rights to run the server-level report. You also have the capability to write custom reports and attach them to many other nodes in the Object Explorer window.

Server Reports

You can access server-level reports from the Object Explorer window in SQL Server Management Studio by right-clicking an instance of SQL Server and selecting Reports from the menu. A report favorite at the server level is the Server Dashboard, which is shown in Figure 4-4. The Server Dashboard report gives you a wealth of information about your SQL Server 2014 instance, including the following:

- ➤ The edition and version of SQL Server you run
- ➤ Anything for that instance not configured to the default SQL Server settings
- ➤ The I/O and CPU statistics by type of activity (for example, ad hoc queries, Reporting Services, and so on)
- ➤ High-level configuration information such as whether the instance is clustered

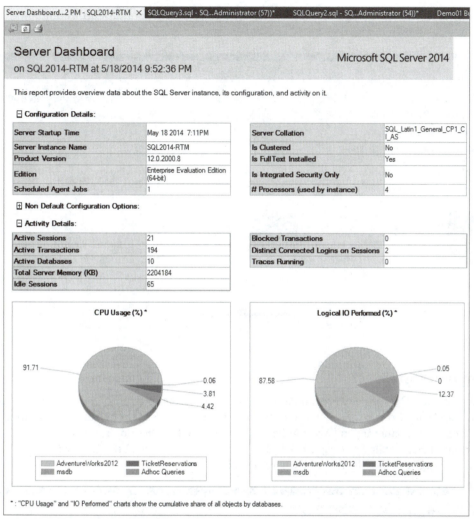

FIGURE 4-4

Most of the statistical information includes only data gathered since the last time you started SQL Server. For example, the Server Dashboard provides a few graphs that show CPU usage by type of query. This graph is not historical; it shows you the CPU usage only for the period of time that SQL Server has been online. Use caution when extrapolating information from this aspect of the Server Dashboard. Always keep in mind that what you see is a time-sensitive snapshot of server performance, not its entire history.

Database Reports

Database reports operate much like server-level reports. Select them by right-clicking the database name in the Object Explorer window in SQL Server Management Studio. With these reports, you can see information that pertains to the database you selected. For example, you can see all the transactions currently running against a database, users being blocked, or disk utilization for a given database, as shown in Figure 4-5.

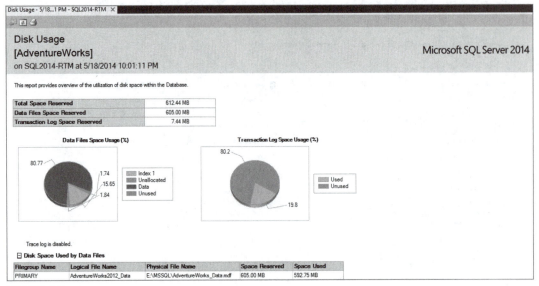

FIGURE 4-5

Object Explorer Details

The Object Explorer Details pane provides a wealth of information in a consolidated GUI. You can access this feature in two ways. From the View menu, select Object Explorer Details. Alternatively, pressing F7 opens the pane. If you have highlighted a node in Object Explorer, pressing F7 opens the details for that object, as shown in Figure 4-6. The Synchronize button on the Object Explorer pane synchronizes Object Explorer to Object Explorer Details.

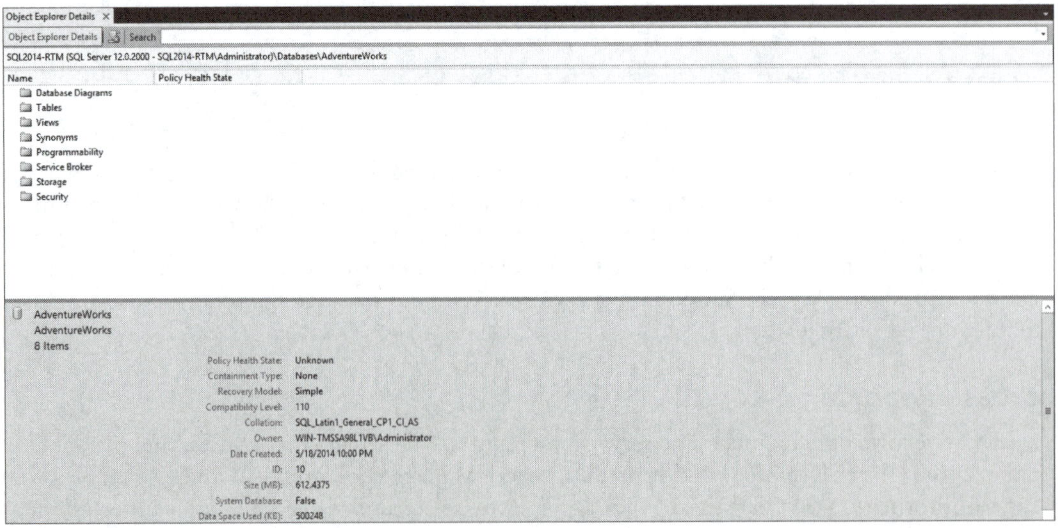

FIGURE 4-6

You can filter and customize the pane to your precise needs. Clicking a column header sorts by that column, and right-clicking the column header area gives you the opportunity to filter which details display.

Configuring SQL Server in SQL Server Management Studio

You have a few ways to configure your SQL Server. Earlier, you used SQL Configuration Manager. This tool helps you turn on various features and services. Let's look at other configuration options and take a more detailed look at `sp_configure`. For the Database Engine, you have two main methods to configure the instance: the `sp_configure` stored procedure or the Server Properties screen. To access the Server Properties screen, right-click the Database Engine you want to configure in SQL Server Management Studio and select Properties. Be careful before altering the configuration of your instance. Adjusting some of these settings could affect your instance's performance or security. This section describes a few of the more important settings, but more are covered throughout the book.

Using the Server Properties Screen

Using the Server Properties screen is much more user-friendly than `sp_configure`, but it doesn't provide all the options available to you through `sp_configure`. The following sections go through each screen in detail.

General

The General tab in the Server Properties screen shows you information about your SQL Server instance that cannot be altered, such as the version of SQL Server you currently have installed, and whether your instance is clustered. It also provides server information, such as the number of processors and amount of memory on the machine, as shown in Figure 4-7.

> **WARNING** *Although your server may have 128GB of RAM available, that doesn't mean that all that RAM is available to SQL Server. Overhead from the operating system and other processes running on the server also use this available memory.*

Memory

On the Memory page of the Server Properties screen, you can see how much memory SQL Server is configured to use. By default, SQL Server is configured to use as much memory as the operating system and the edition of SQL Server enables it to consume. Typically, it is a good idea to set the minimum and maximum amount of memory that your instances use in your environment.

Processors

In the Processors page, you can restrict the SQL Server Engine to use named processors, and assign some or all those processors to I/O or threading operations. This is useful typically if you have multiple CPUs and more than one instance of SQL Server. You may have one instance that uses four processors and the other instance use the other four processors, if you configure the instances to use CPU affinity. In some cases, when you have a large number of concurrent connections to your SQL Server, you may want to set the Maximum Worker Threads option. Configure this to 0 (the default) to enable SQL Server to automatically and dynamically find the best number of threads to enable on the processor. These threads can manage connections and other system functions, such as performing CHECKPOINTs. Generally, leaving this setting alone gives you optimal performance.

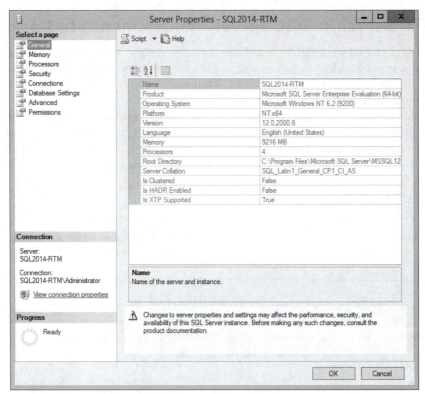

FIGURE 4-7

You can select the SQL Server Priority option to force Windows to assign a higher priority to the SQL Server process. Tweaking this setting may be tempting, but you should adjust it only after thorough testing because it may starve other system threads. Use of this option is not generally recommended unless directed by PSS.

Use the Lightweight Pooling option only on the rare occasion when the processor is highly utilized and context switching is extreme. Chapter 12, "Monitoring Your SQL Server," contains more information on lightweight pooling and how it works.

Note the "Configured values" and "Running values" radio buttons at the bottom of the Properties screens, as shown in Figure 4-8. When you select "Running values," you see the values that SQL Server currently uses. When you select "Configured values," you see the values that SQL Server will use the next time it restarts. This is necessary because some values do not take effect until after a restart.

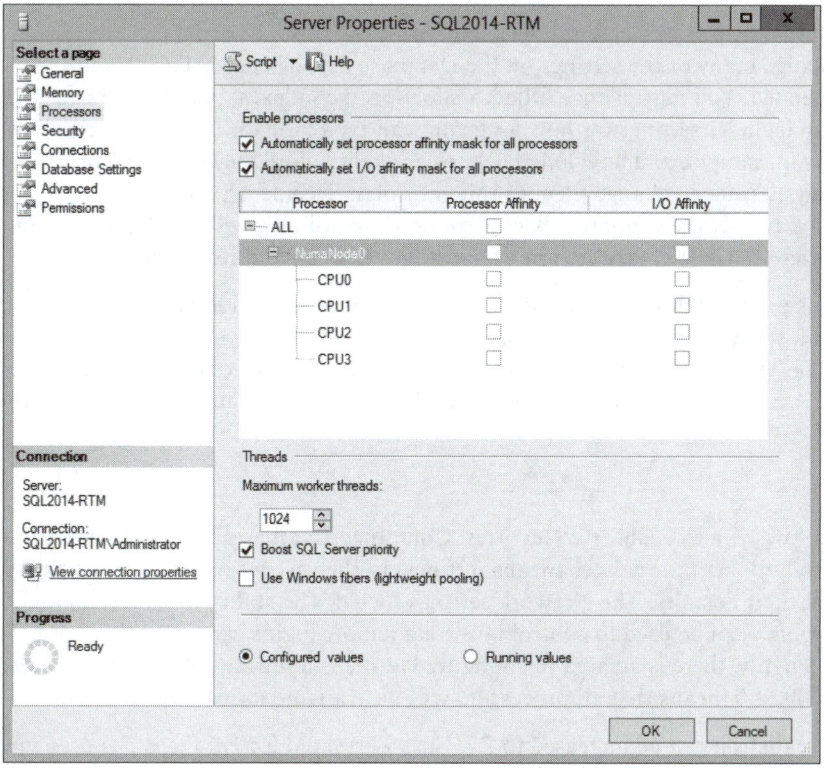

FIGURE 4-8

Security

On the Security page, you can adjust whether your SQL Server accepts connections through both SQL Server and Windows Authentication or Windows Authentication only. This same question is asked during setup of the instance, and this screen gives you another opportunity to change the setting. Under the Login Auditing section, you should always have at least Failed Logins Only selected. This enables SQL Server to audit when someone mistypes a password or is trying to force their way into the instance. (Chapter 8 talks much more about the other security settings on this page.)

Connections

On the Connections page, you can adjust the default connection properties. One possible option you may want to set here would be NO COUNT. This setting can prevent the (8 Rows Affected) message from being sent to the client if they do not request it. Often in stored procedures or queries, you can use the SET NOCOUNT T-SQL command to get the same effect. There is a small performance enhancement by doing this because this message is an additional record set sent from SQL Server and may be unneeded traffic.

Database Settings

You will not likely change many of the settings on the Database Settings page. The default index fill factor of 0 is recommended. You may change fillfactors for specific indexes, but probably not the default. This page also includes settings for how long you wait on a tape for backup (specify how long SQL Server waits for a tape), and how long backups are kept before they expire (default backup media retention, in days). You can change them to suit your plan. Decide whether you plan to compress database backups and set the Compress Backup option accordingly, which is highly recommended. Details for these settings are covered in Chapter 17, "Backup and Recovery."

The last setting on this page enables you to choose the default database and log file locations. The installation default setting places the log and data files on the same drive under the `%System Drive%\Program Files\Microsoft SQL Server\MSSQL12.MSSQLSERVER\Data` and `Log` directories. Unless this SQL Server install is for playing around, do not put your data and log files on the C:\ drive.

Advanced

The Advanced page allows you to enable two features: Contained Databases and `FILESTREAM`. In addition, there is a catch-all area for Miscellaneous settings. In the vast majority of cases, these settings should remain at their defaults. The Network settings include the ability to set a Remote Login Timeout in seconds, which can be used to control how long remote logins can attempt to connect before they time out. Finally, there is an area to configure Parallelism settings. A Max Degree of Parallelism (MAXDOP) of 0 means that all processors will be available for parallel queries.

Cost Threshold for Parallelism can be increased to 20. Cost Threshold for Parallelism is used when determining if the Query Optimizer should utilize a parallel plan. Its original value is 5, and has been since SQL Server 7.0. It was the value of the query score on a team member of the Query Optimizer team. When the member's desktop scored a 5, the plan needed to be parallel. The optimizer will use a parallel plan if MAXDOP <> 1, the cost of a parallel plan plus the cost of exchange iterators is less than the cost of a serial plan, and the cost of the plan exceeds the cost threshold for parallelism.

Permissions

The Permissions page shows each of the logins and roles available on the instance. From here, you can explicitly grant or deny very granular permissions for each login or role from the Explicit tab. In addition, the Effective tab shows you which of these permissions are currently granted to the login or role.

Using sp_configure

`sp_configure` is a stored procedure that enables you to change many of the configuration options in SQL Server. Following are some of the more commonly adjusted settings:

➤ **Max degree of parallelism**—For OLTP environments, this is usually set to the number of available sockets.

➤ **CLR enabled**—Enables CLR procedures to execute.

➤ **Blocked processes threshold**—Use to set time threshold before blocked process reports are generated.

When you run the stored procedure with no parameters, it shows you the options and their current settings. By default, only the basic, or commonly used, settings are returned, of which there are 15. To see additional options, you must configure the instance to display advanced options. You can do so by running sp_configure, as shown here:

```
sp_configure 'show advanced options', 1;
RECONFIGURE;
```

The change does not take effect until the RECONFIGURE command is issued. SQL Server does a check for invalid or not recommended settings when you use sp_configure. If you have provided a value that fails any of these checks, SQL Server warns you with the following message:

```
Msg 5807, Level 16, State 1, Line 1
Recovery intervals above 60 minutes not recommended. Use the RECONFIGURE WITH
OVERRIDE statement to force this configuration.
```

> **WARNING** *Issuing the* RECONFIGURE *command results in a complete flush of the plan cache. This means that nothing remains in the cache, and all batches are recompiled when submitted for the first time afterward. Be cautious of using* sp_configure *in a production environment, and make sure that you understand the impact of the cache flush on your database.*

This gives you an opportunity to reconsider what may have been a bad choice, such as setting a memory option to more memory than exists on the box. The following code shows you how to issue the override for the setting:

```
EXEC sp_configure 'recovery interval', 90;
RECONFIGURE WITH OVERRIDE;
GO
```

Filtering Objects

You can also filter objects in SQL Server Management Studio by following a few easy steps, which is useful when you begin to have dozens of objects:

1. Select the node of the tree that you want to filter, and click the Filter icon in the Object Explorer.

2. The Object Explorer Filter Settings dialog box (shown in Figure 4-9) opens. Here you can filter by name, schema, or when the object was created.

3. Use the Operator drop-down box to select how you want to filter, and then type the name in the Value column.

Error Logs

As you probably have already experienced, when something goes wrong with an application, one of the factors that you must consider is the database. It is up to the DBA to support the troubleshooting effort and to confirm that the database isn't the source of the problem. The first thing the DBA typically does is connect to the server and look at the SQL Server instance error logs and then the Windows event logs.

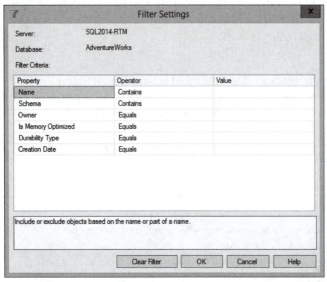

FIGURE 4-9

In SQL Server 2014, you can quickly look through the logs in a consolidated manner using SQL Server Management Studio. To view the logs, right-click SQL Server Logs under the Management tree, and select View ➪ SQL Server and Windows Log. This opens the Log File Viewer screen. From this screen, you can check and uncheck log files that you want to bring into the view. You can consolidate logs from SQL Server, Agent, and the Windows Event Files, as shown in Figure 4-10.

In some situations, you may want to merge the logs from several machines into a single view to determine what's causing an application problem. To do this, click the Load Log button at the top of the screen, and browse to your .log file. That file could be a Windows error log that has been output to .log format or a SQL log from a different instance. For example, you can use this to consolidate all the SQL logs from every instance on a single server to give you a holistic view of all the physical machines' problems.

Activity Monitor

The Activity Monitor gives you a view of current connections on an instance. You can use the monitor to determine whether you have any processes blocking other processes. To open the Activity Monitor in SQL Server Management Studio, right-click the Server in the Object Explorer, and then select Activity Monitor.

The tool is a comprehensive way to view who connects to your machine and what they do. The top section shows four graphs (Show Processor Time, Waiting Tasks, Database I/O, and Batch Requests/Sec) that are commonly used performance counters for the server. Under the graphs are four lists: Processes, Resource Waits, Data File I/O, and Recent Expensive Queries. In all these lists, you can also apply filters to show only certain hosts, logins, or connections using greater than a given number of resources. You can also sort by a given column by clicking the column header.

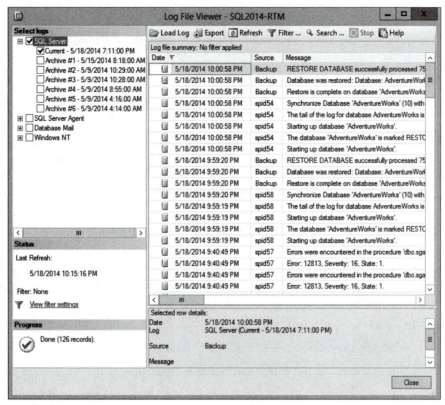

FIGURE 4-10

On the Process Info page (shown in Figure 4-11), you can see each login connecting to your machine (also called a Server Process ID, or SPID). It's easy to miss how much information is in this window. You can slide left to right to see loads of important data about each connection.

When debugging, most of the following columns are useful:

➤ **Session ID**—The unique number assigned to a process connected to SQL Server. This is also called a SPID. An icon next to the number represents what happens in the connection. If you see an hourglass, you can quickly tell that the process is waiting on or is being blocked by another connection.

➤ **User Process Flag**—Indicates whether internal SQL Server processes are connected. These processes are filtered out by default. You can change the value to see the SQL Server internal processes by clicking the drop-down and selecting the appropriate value.

➤ **Login**—The login to which the process is tied.

➤ **Database**—The current database context for the connection.

➤ **Task State**—Indicates whether the user is active or sleeping:

➤ **Done**—Completed.

➤ **Pending**—The process is waiting for a worker thread.

➤ **Runnable**—The process has previously been active, has a connection, but has no work to do.

➤ **Running**—The process is currently performing work.

➤ **Suspended**—The process has work to do, but it has been stopped. You can find additional information about why the process is suspended in the Wait Type column.

➤ **Command**—Shows the type of command currently being executed. For example, you may see SELECT, DBCC, INSERT, or AWAITING COMMAND here, to name a few. This won't show you the actual query that the user executes, but it does highlight what type of activity is being run on your server. To see the actual command, select a row in this table, right-click, and choose Details.

➤ **Application**—The application that is connecting to your instance. This can be set by the developer in the connection string.

➤ **Wait Time (ms)**—If the process is blocked or waiting for another process to complete, this indicates how long the process has been waiting (in milliseconds). It can have a value of 0 if the process is not waiting.

➤ **Wait Type**—Indicates the event you are waiting on.

➤ **Wait Resource**—The text representation of the resource you are waiting on.

➤ **Blocked By**—The Session ID (SPID) that is blocking this connection.

➤ **Head Blocker**—A value of 1 means the Blocked By Session ID is the head of the blocking chain; otherwise it's 0.

➤ **Memory Use (KB)**—The current amount of memory used by this connection, represented by the number of kilobytes in the Procedure cache attributed to this connection. This was reported in pages prior to SQL Server 2008.

➤ **Host**—The login's workstation or server name. This is a useful item, but in some cases you may have a web server connecting to your SQL Server, which may make this less important.

➤ **Workload Group**—The name of the Resource Governor workload group for this query.

> **NOTE** *By right-clicking any process, you can see the last query run with the connection, trace the process using Profiler, or kill the connection. You can also right-click over the graph area and select Refresh to manually refresh the data, or click Refresh Interval to set how often Activity Monitor refreshes. The default refresh rate is 10 seconds. Don't set the refresh to anything too frequent, because it can affect system performance, constantly running queries against the server.*

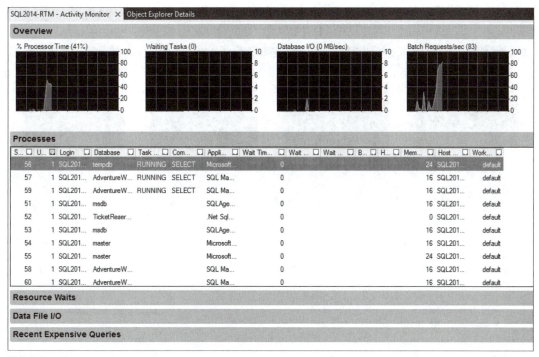

FIGURE 4-11

Another important function you can perform with the help of Activity Monitor is identifying a locking condition. The following steps explain how to set up a blocked transaction and how to use Activity Monitor to resolve this issue:

1. Run the following query in one query window while connected to the AdventureWorks database, and ensure you back up the AdventureWorks database before performing these steps:

```
BEGIN TRAN
DELETE FROM Production.ProductCostHistory
WHERE ProductID = 707;
```

This query was intentionally not committed. In other words, there is a BEGIN TRAN command but no ROLLBACK or COMMIT command. This means that the rows deleted from Production.ProductCostHistory are still locked exclusively.

2. Next, without closing the first window, open a new query window, and run the following query:

```
SELECT * FROM Production.ProductCostHistory;
```

This query should hang up and wait on the DELETE from Production .ProductCostHistory because the first transaction locks row one. Do not close either window. At the top of each query window, your session ID displays in parentheses, and at the bottom your login displays. If you cannot see the SPID in the tab at the top, hover your mouse over the tab, and a small window pops up showing the entire tab title, which includes the SPID. While the query windows are open, go ahead and explore the Activity Monitor to see what these connections look like (Figure 4-12).

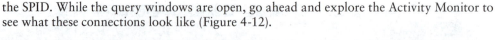

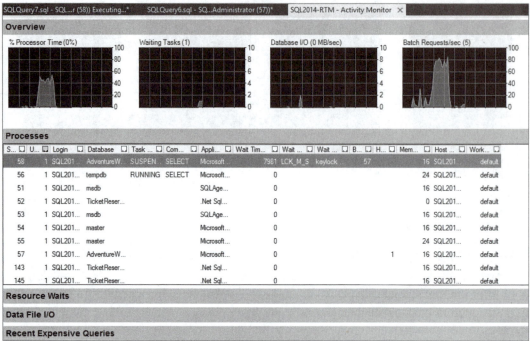

FIGURE 4-12

3. Open the Activity Monitor and note that one connection has a task state of Suspended. This is the query that is trying to do the SELECT. You can confirm this by comparing the session ID of the suspended session with the session ID of your query. Your wait type will be LCK_M_S, which means you are waiting on a shared lock for reading. If you hover the mouse over the Wait Resource column value, you can see more detailed information about the locks, including the object_IDs of the resources. In the Blocked By column, you can also see the session ID of the process that blocks you, and it should match the SPID of your first query. You have the option to kill the blocking process. To do so, select the row for the blocking process, right-click, and choose Kill Process.

4. While the locks still exist, take a look at a standard blocking report that comes with SQL Server 2014. In Object Explorer, right-click your server name, select Reports, Standard Reports, and choose Activity - All Blocking Transactions. You can see the report shown in Figure 4-13.

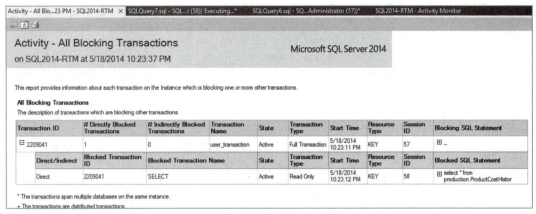

FIGURE 4-13

5. Now, back at the Activity Monitor, hover over the Wait Resource column to see the `mode=X`. This mode means that there is an exclusive lock on that resource. An *exclusive lock* means that no one else is allowed to read the data cleanly. If you see a request mode of `S`, then SQL Server has granted a shared lock, which, in most situations, is harmless, and others are allowed to see the same data. To request a dirty read of the uncommitted data, add a preceding statement to change the transaction isolation level to allow dirty reads. A *dirty read* enables you to read data in an inconsistent state because the transaction has neither been committed nor rolled back. You can do it like so:

```
SET TRANSACTION ISOLATION LEVEL READ UNCOMITTED

SELECT *
FROM Production.ProductCostHistory;
```

> **WARNING** *The* (NOLOCK) *query hint should rarely, if ever, be used in a production environment. The current way to achieve dirty reads is through changing the transaction isolation level. Your business use of the data will determine if there is tolerance for dirty reads. Another option to consider as an alternative to* (NOLOCK) *if dirty reads are necessary is to set the transaction isolation level to* SNAPSHOT *to allow versioning of records.*

6. The preceeding query returns the data. Before you leave this section, execute the following SQL in the query window that contains the DELETE statement:

```
ROLLBACK TRAN;
```

MONITORING PROCESSES IN T-SQL

You can also monitor the activity of your server via T-SQL. Generally, DBAs prefer this as a quick way to troubleshoot long-running queries or users who complain about slow performance. DBAs typically prefer T-SQL because the information you can retrieve is more flexible than the Activity Monitor.

sp_who and sp_who2

The `sp_who` stored procedure returns what is connecting to your instance, much like the Activity Monitor. You'll probably prefer the undocumented `sp_who2` stored procedure, though, which gives you more verbose information about each process. Whichever stored procedure you use, they both accept the same input parameters. For the purpose of this discussion, let's go into more detail about `sp_who2`. Just keep in mind that `sp_who` shows a subset of the information.

> **NOTE** *DBAs who are in the know have graduated from* `sp_who2` *to a tool called* `sp_whoisactive`. *This widely used procedure was developed by Adam Machanic, a SQL Server MVP and Boston-based independent consultant. If you're not familiar with it, download it, and read Adam's blog posts about what it can do to vastly improve your monitoring and troubleshooting efforts. A download file and installation instructions are available at* `http://tinyurl` `.com/WhoIsActive`. *While you're at it, check out Adam's blog series, "A Month of Activity Monitoring," which explains exactly why you should begin using* `sp_` `whoisactive` *straightaway at* `http://tinyurl.com/WhoIsActiveDocs`. *For the most part, this tool is freely offered to the community (with a few exceptions) at* `http://bit.ly/WhoIsActiveLicensing`.

To see all the connections to your server, run `sp_who2` without any parameters. This displays the same type of information in the Activity Monitor. You can also pass in the parameter of `'active'` to see only the active connections to your server, like so:

```
sp_who2 'active';
```

Additionally, you can pass in the SPID, as shown here, to see the details about an individual process:

```
sp_who2 55;
```

> **NOTE** *Although the example uses SPID 55, your process IDs may be different, and can be obtained from the Current Activity listing discussed earlier.*

sys.dm_exec_connections

The `sys.dm_exec_connections` Dynamic Management View (DMV) gives you even more information to help you troubleshoot the Database Engine of SQL Server. This DMV returns a row per session in SQL Server. Because it's a DMV, it displays as a table and enables you to write sophisticated queries against the view to filter out what you don't care about, as shown in the following query, which shows only user connections that have performed a write operation:

```
SELECT * FROM
   sys.dm_exec_sessions
WHERE is_user_process = 1
AND writes > 0;
```

In addition to the information shown in the methods described earlier to view processes, this DMV indicates how many rows the user has retrieved since opening the connection, and the number of reads, writes, and logical reads. You can also see this view in the settings for each connection, and what the last error was, if any.

sys.dm_exec_sql_text

You can use the `sys.dm_exec_sql_text` Dynamic Management Function (DMF) to retrieve the text of a particular query. This can be used in conjunction with the `sys.dm_exec_query_stats` DMV to retrieve the top 10 most poorly performing queries across all databases. Listing 4-1 (code file: `Top10WorstPerformingQueries.sql`) retrieves the number of times a query has executed, the average runtime by CPU and duration, and the text for the query.

LISTING 4-1: Top10WorstPerformingQueries.sql

```
SELECT TOP 10 execution_count as [Number of Executions],
   total_worker_time/execution_count as [Average CPU Time],
   Total_Elapsed_Time/execution_count as [Average Elapsed Time],
   (
     SELECT SUBSTRING(text,statement_start_offset/2,
       (CASE WHEN statement_end_offset = -1
             THEN LEN(CONVERT(nvarchar(max), [text])) * 2
       ELSE statement_end_offset END - statement_start_offset) /2)
     FROM sys.dm_exec_sql_text(sql_handle)
   ) as query_text
FROM sys.dm_exec_query_stats
ORDER BY [Average CPU Time] DESC;
```

The `sys.dm_exec_query_stats` DMV also shows a great deal of other information that you can use. It shows you a line for each query plan that has been run. You can take the `sql_handle` column from this DMV and use it in the `sys.dm_exec_sql_text` function. Because this view is at a plan level, when someone changes some of the query's text, it shows the new query as a new line.

These are just a few examples of how processes can be monitored in T-SQL. With the introduction and widespread adoption of DMOs, you have more options than ever to pinpoint database issues using T-SQL.

MULTISERVER MANAGEMENT

In this age of expanding data, the number of databases that need to be managed is proliferating as well. SQL Server DBAs often must administer a large number of instances and databases. Something as simple as adding a new login or setting a server option can become quite an endeavor if it must be done on dozens of servers. Luckily, Microsoft has provided a few tools to ease the DBA's life.

> **NOTE** *If you are one of the growing number of DBAs who manages multiple servers, make some time to learn Windows PowerShell. This language is a powerful tool that you can leverage to create reusable scripts that can consistently perform tasks across multiple servers, instances, or databases.*

Central Management Servers and Server Groups

SQL Server 2008 introduced a feature intended to ease your life: central management servers and server groups. This feature enables you to run T-SQL scripts and apply policy-based management (PBM) policies to a group of servers at the same time. You can execute T-SQL on a group of servers and aggregate the results into a single result set or keep each result set separate. When you aggregate the result sets, you have the option to include an extra column that indicates from which server each row is returned. You can use this tool to do any multiserver administration and much more. If you have common error tables on each server, you can query them all in a single statement.

These capabilities are part of SQL Server Management Studio, but before you start using them all, you must first register a central management server. In the Registered Servers dialog box of SQL Server Management Studio, right-click and select Register Central Management Server. You can choose a configuration server from the resulting dialog box. This server keeps metadata and does some of the background work for you.

After you create a central management server, you can create server groups and add server registrations to groups under the registration server. After you set up your servers, you can right-click anything—from the registration server to server groups or individual servers in groups—and select New Query, Object Explorer, or Run Policy. Then choose New Query, add T-SQL, and run the query against all the servers in the group.

> **NOTE** *Create groups of servers based on common management needs. A couple of options are to organize them by environment, such as development, QA, and production or to organize them by subject area, such as Human Resources, Accounting, and Operations. Carefully consider what management tasks are generally performed together, and use that as your grouping criteria.*

Following are a few items about your registration server:

➤ It cannot be a registered group under itself.

➤ All queries are executed using trusted connections.

➤ If your servers cross domains, you must have trusted relationships between them.

➤ You can configure multiple central management servers.

> **NOTE** *To set options for multiserver result sets, select Tools ⇨ Options ⇨ Query Results ⇨ SQL Server ⇨ Multi-server results.*

TRACE FLAGS

Trace flags provide advanced mechanisms to tap into hidden SQL Server features and troubleshooting tactics. In some cases, they enable you to override the recommended behavior of SQL Server to turn on features such as network-drive support for database files. In other cases, you can use trace flags to turn on additional monitoring. There is a set of flags that helps you diagnose deadlocks, including trace flag 1204. To turn on a trace flag, use the DBCC TRACEON command, followed by the trace you'd like to turn on, as shown here:

```
DBCC TRACEON (1204)
```

To turn off the trace, use the DBCC TRACEOFF command. This command is followed by which traces you'd like to turn off (multiple traces can be separated by commas), as shown here:

```
DBCC TRACEOFF (1204, 3625)
```

> **NOTE** *Trace flag 3625 used in the previous code snippet limits the amount of information returned to users who are not members of the sysadmin server role by masking the parameters of some error messages. This can be enabled as a security measure.*

When you turn on a trace, you are turning it on for a single connection by default. For example, if you turn on trace flag 1224 (which disables lock escalation based on the number of locks), lock escalation is disabled only in the scope of the connection that issued the DBCC TRACEON command. You can also turn on the trace at a server level by issuing the command followed by the -1 switch, as in the following:

```
DBCC TRACEON (1224, -1)
```

After you turn on the traces, you're probably going to want to determine whether the trace is actually running. To do this, you can issue the DBCC TRACESTATUS command. One method to issue the command is to interrogate whether a given trace is running, like so:

```
DBCC TRACESTATUS (3635)
```

This command would return the following results if the trace is not turned on:

```
TraceFlag Status Global Session
--------- ------ ------ -------
3625      0      0      0

(1 row(s) affected)
```

If you want to see all traces that apply to the connection, run the following command with the -1 parameter:

```
DBCC TRACESTATUS (-1)
```

As shown in the following results of this query, two traces are turned on. Trace flag 1224 is turned on globally for every connection into the SQL Server, and trace flag 3625 is turned on for this session:

```
TraceFlag Status Global Session
--------- ------ ------ -------
1224      1      1      0
3625      1      0      1

(2 row(s) affected)
```

If no traces are turned on, you would receive only the following message:

```
DBCC execution completed. If DBCC printed error messages, contact your system
administrator.
```

Your instance of SQL Server should not have trace flags turned on indefinitely, unless you have been instructed by Microsoft Product Support to do so. When left to run all the time, trace flags may cause your instance to behave abnormally. Moreover, the flag you use today may not be available in a future release or service pack of SQL Server. If you are in debug mode, you can turn on a trace flag from the command prompt when starting SQL Server. As mentioned earlier in this chapter, you can also start a trace when SQL Server starts at the command prompt by calling the sqlservr.exe program and passing the -T switch after it. Trace flags are discussed further in Chapter 11 "Optimizing SQL Server 2014."

There is a lot to say about trace flags, even though only a few are mentioned here, but as you proceed through this book, you see a number of other trace flags in practice.

> **NOTE** *Some functionality provided by trace flags (such as deadlock monitoring) can be more efficiently implemented by using Extended Events. See Chapter 12, "Monitoring Your SQL Server," for a complete discussion of implementing Extended Events in your environment.*

GETTING HELP FROM SUPPORT

Whenever you get stuck on a SQL Server issue, generally you call the next layer of support. Whether that next layer is Microsoft or a vendor, a number of new tools are available to communicate with that next layer of support. Use the SQLDumper.exe and SQLDiag.exe programs to better communicate with support to give them an excellent picture of your environment and problem while you reproduce the error.

SQLDumper.exe

Beginning in SQL Server 2000 SP3, SQLDumper.exe was included to help your SQL Server perform a dump of its environment after an exception occurs. A support organization (such as Microsoft's PSS) may also request that you execute the program on demand while you have a problem such as a hung server.

If you want to create a dump file on demand, you need the Windows process ID for the SQL Server instance. You can obtain this ID in a few ways. You can either go to Task Manager and look in the SQL Server log, or go to SQL Server Configuration Manager, as discussed earlier in the chapter. On the SQL Server 2014 Services page of Configuration Manager, you can see each of the SQL Server services and the process ID.

By default, SQLDumper.exe is located in the C:\Program Files\Microsoft SQL Server\120\ Shared directory because it is shared across all the SQL Server instances installed on a server.

This directory may vary, though, based on where you installed the SQL Server tools. To create a dump file for support, go to a command prompt, and access the C:\Program Files\Microsoft SQL Server\120\Shared directory. As with many command-line utilities, you can see the options by running the following command, and get more details about them from the SQL Server documentation:

```
SQLdumper.exe -?
```

When you are at the command line, you can create a full dump or a minidump. If a minidump is less than a megabyte, a full dump may run 110MB on your system. To create a full dump, use the following command:

```
Sqldumper.exe <ProcessID> 0 0x1100
```

<ProcessID> is the Process ID of your SQL instance. This outputs the full dump to the same directory that you're in. The filename is SQLDmpr0001.mdmp if this is the first time you've run the SQLDumper.exe program. Filenames are sequentially named after each execution. You cannot open the dump file in a text editor such as Notepad. Instead, you need advanced troubleshooting tools such as Visual Studio or one of the PSS tools.

A more practical dump would be a minidump, which contains most of the essential information that product support needs. To create a minidump, use the following command:

```
Sqldumper.exe <ProcessID> 0 0x0120
```

You can view the SQLDUMPER_ERRORLOG.log file to determine whether there were any errors when you created the dump file, or whether a dump occurred. You need to be a local Windows administrator to run `SQLDumper.exe` or be logged in with the same account that starts the SQL Server service.

SQLDiag.exe

A tool that's slightly less of a black box than `SQLDumper.exe` is `SQLDiag.exe`. This tool consolidates and collects information about your system from several sources:

➤ Windows System Monitor (sysmon)

➤ Windows event logs

➤ SQL Server Profile traces

➤ SQL Server error logs

➤ Information about SQL Server blocking

➤ SQL Server configuration information

Because `SQLDiag.exe` gathers so much diagnostic information, you should run it only when you're requested to do so or when you prepare for a call with support. The SQL Server Profiler trace files alone can quickly grow large, so prepare to output these files to a drive that has a lot of space. The process also uses a sizable amount of processing power as it runs. You can execute the tool from a command prompt or as a service; you can use the `-?` switch to see available switches.

> **NOTE** *The SQL Nexus Tool (available from Codeplex at* `http://sqlnexus` *.* `codeplex.com`) *can help you read and analyze* `SQLDiag` *output more efficiently.*

`SQLDiag.exe` can take a configuration file as input. By default, this file is called `SQLDiag.Xml`, but you can pass in a different filename. If a configuration XML file does not exist, one will be created called `##SQLDiag.XML`. You can alter this file to your liking and then later distribute it as `SQLDiag.XML`.

Now that you know what `SQLDiag.exe` can do, follow this example to use the tool against a local development server. If you cannot get in front of the server, use a support tool such as Terminal Services to remote into a server, because you can't point `SQLDiag.exe` at a remote instance.

1. To run the tool, go to a command prompt.

2. Because the SQL install adds the appropriate directory to the `PATH` environment variable, you don't need to go to the individual directory where the file is located. Instead, go to the `C:\Temp` directory or something similar to that on a drive that has more than 100MB available.

3. The default location for the executable file is `C:\Program Files\Microsoft SQL Server\120\Tools\Binn\SQLDIAG.EXE`, but you can alter that to a new location with the `/O` switch.

4. Type the following command (note the lack of spaces after the + sign):

```
sqldiag /B +00:03:00 /E +00:02:00 /OC:\temp /C1
```

This command instructs `SQLDiag.exe` to begin capturing trace information in three minutes from when you press Enter, and run for two minutes. This is done with the `/B` and `/E` switches. You can also use these two switches to start and stop the diagnostic at a given 24-hour clock time. The command also tells `SQLDiag.exe` to output the results of the traces and logs to the `C:\Temp` directory, and the `/C` switch instructs the tool to compress the files using Windows compression. If you were running this in your environment, you would wait until you were instructed by `SQLDiag.exe` (in green text on your console) to attempt to reproduce the problem. In Figure 4-14, `SQLDiag` collects to the default directory. Press Ctrl+C if you want to terminate the collection of data early.

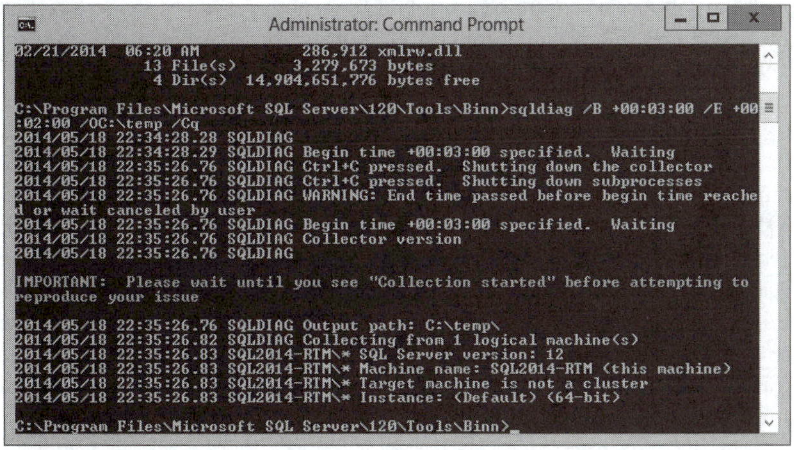

FIGURE 4-14

5. With the `SQLDiag.exe` now complete, go to the `C:\Temp` directory to zip up the contents and send them to Microsoft. In the directory, you can find a treasure chest of information for a support individual, including the following:

➤ `##files.txt`—A list of files in the `C:\Program Files\Microsoft SQL Server\120\Tools\binn` directory, with their creation date. Use this to determine whether you're running a patch that support has asked to be installed.

➤ `##envvars.txt`—A list of all the environment variables for the server.

➤ `SERVERNAME__sp_sqldiag_Shutdown.OUT`—A consolidation of the instance's SQL logs and the results from a number of queries.

➤ `log_XX.trc`—A series of Profiler trace files of granular SQL Server activities being performed.

➤ `SERVERNAME_MSINFO32.TXT`—A myriad of details about the server system and hardware.

These files are not only useful to support individuals; you also may want to consider running this on a regular basis to establish a baseline of your server during key times (before patches, monthly, or whatever your metric is). If you decided to do this, you wouldn't want the Profiler part of `SQLDiag` `.exe` to run for more than a few seconds.

You can gather useful baseline information if the tool periodically runs in snapshot mode. This mode performs the same functions just described, but exits immediately after it gathers the necessary information. The following command uses the `/X` switch to run `SQLDiag.exe` in snapshot mode and the `/N` switch (with 2 as the option) to create a new directory for each run of `SQLDiag.exe`:

```
sqldiag /OC:\temp\baseline /X /N 2
```

The first directory created is called `baseline_0000`, and each new one is named sequentially after that. Many corporations choose to run this through SQL Agent or Task Manager on the first of the month, or before key changes to have an automatic baseline of their server and instance.

SUMMARY

One of the most important things to remember when using SQL Server is your managing and troubleshooting of SQL Server. The key concepts for doing so are proper configuration, ongoing monitoring, and efficient troubleshooting. Methods for configuration include SQL Server Configuration Manager, startup parameters, and startup stored procedures. It is also important to use SQL Server Management Studio and T-SQL to actively monitor your databases. The DAC provides an excellent way to connect to your instance and troubleshoot when issues arise. When you've exhausted your troubleshooting options, know how to provide the information that product support needs by using `SQLDumper.exe` and `SQLDiag.exe`.

In Chapter 5, you learn ways to automate SQL Server.

5

Automating SQL Server

WHAT'S IN THIS CHAPTER?

➤ Automating common maintenance activities using Maintenance Tasks

➤ Scheduling jobs to perform maintenance activities using SQL Server Agent

➤ Securing the jobs you create using SQL Server Agent security

➤ Configuring SQL Server Agent to meet your needs

➤ Scheduling jobs across multiple servers using the multiserver admin capabilities

Much of the work that a database administrator (DBA) does is repetitive: backing up databases, rebuilding indexes, and checking for file sizes and disk-space availability. Responding to events such as a full transaction log being out of disk space may also be part of a DBA's daily life. The problems grow rapidly with the number of servers you must administer. Automating this work is more than a convenience; it is a requirement for enterprise systems.

Two features in SQL Server 2014 come to the rescue of the DBA: Maintenance Plans and SQL Server Agent. Maintenance Plans enable you to automate the routine maintenance activities for a database. Backups, database integrity checks, and index maintenance tasks can be automated with Maintenance Plans. The Maintenance Plan Wizard makes it easy to create Maintenance Plans. SQL Server Agent enables you to manually create a schedule of jobs to be run on a SQL Server, further enhancing the ability of the DBA to automate routine activities.

MAINTENANCE PLANS

Maintenance Plans are a quick-and-easy way to automate routine maintenance tasks in SQL Server. They are no more than a user interface on top of regular SQL Server Agent jobs. However, the tasks in a plan aren't equivalent to job steps because Maintenance Plans are built using SQL Server Integration Services (SSIS), and these are then run as a single SSIS job step in a job that maps to the Maintenance Plan name. For routine maintenance tasks, Maintenance Plans may be all that you need to automate on many SQL Servers.

You can create and maintain Maintenance Plans in two ways. The quick-and-easy way is to use the Maintenance Plan Wizard, and the manual way is to use the Maintenance Plan Designer.

> **WARNING** *If you use a fresh default install of SQL Server 2014, by default, the Agent XPs are disabled. This prevents you from starting the SQL Agent Service. If SQL Agent is not running, you see an error when you try to start the Maintenance Plan Wizard. To prevent this error, enable the Agent XPs using the following script, and then start the SQL Agent service (either from SQL Server Management Studio or SQL Server Configuration Manager):*
>
> ```
> sp_configure 'show advanced options', 1;
> GO
> RECONFIGURE;
> GO
> sp_configure 'Agent XPs', 1;
> GO
> RECONFIGURE
> GO
> ```
>
> *After you execute this script, the* SQL Server Agent *node in SQL Server Management Studio will no longer have the "Agent XPs disabled" tag appended.*

Maintenance Plan Wizard

This section walks you through the steps to create a backup using the Maintenance Plan Wizard:

1. First, launch the wizard, which lives on the context menu on the Maintenance Plans node in the Object Explorer in SQL Server Management Studio. Select the Maintenance Plan Wizard menu item to launch the first page of the wizard, as shown in Figure 5-1.

2. You can opt to not show this page again and then click Next. This brings up the Select Plan Properties page, where you can set some of the Plan options. As shown in Figure 5-2, on this page you specify a name and description for the plan, and select the scheduling options.

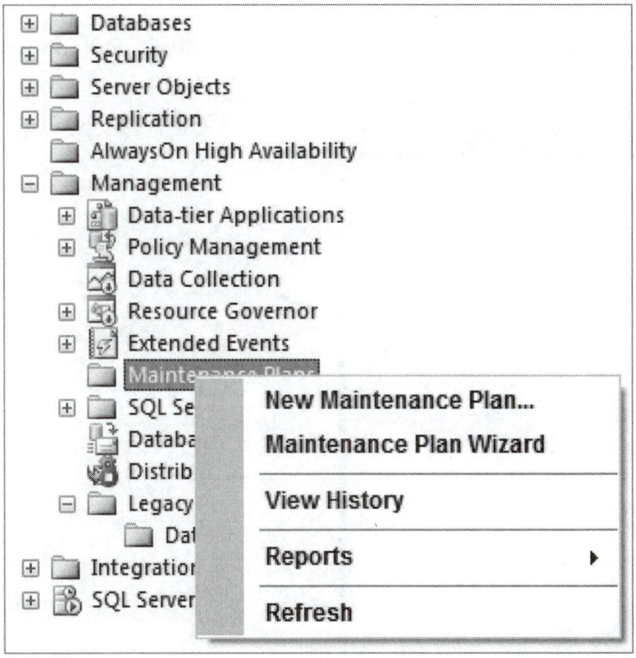

FIGURE 5-1

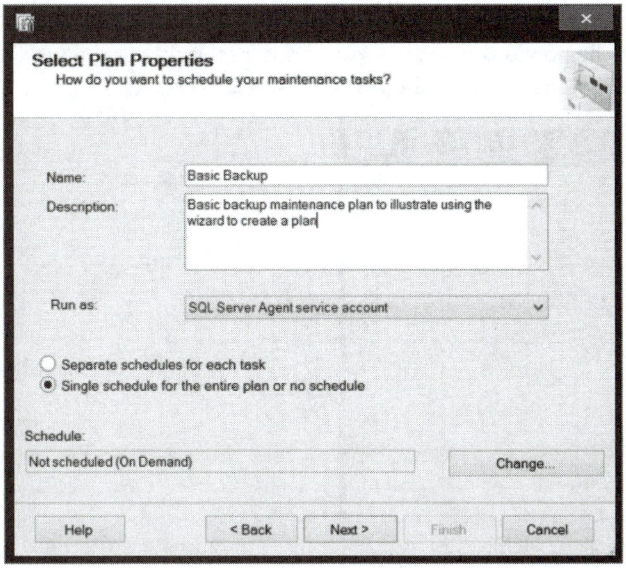

FIGURE 5-2

3. Click Next to move to the Select Maintenance Tasks screen, where you can choose the tasks you want the plan to perform. For this example, select the Back Up Database (Full) option, as shown in Figure 5-3.

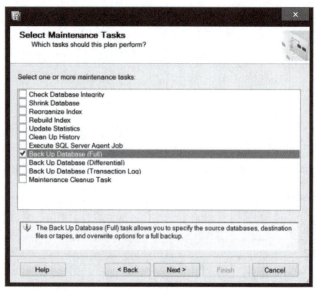

FIGURE 5-3

4. Click Next to move to the Select Maintenance Task Order screen, as shown in Figure 5-4. If you selected multiple tasks on the previous page, you can reorder them here to run in the order you want. In this example, you have only a single task, so click Next.

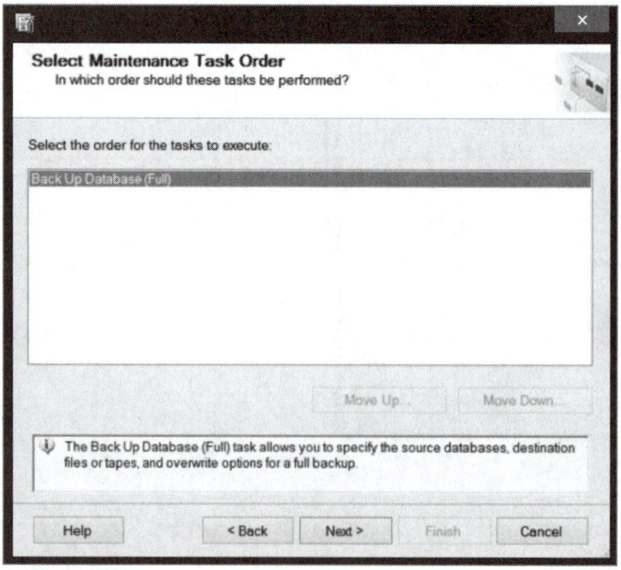

FIGURE 5-4

5. The next page is the Define Back Up Database (Full) Task screen, as shown in Figure 5-5. On this page, select the details for the backup task. If you selected a different task on the Select Maintenance Tasks screen, you must supply the details for that task. In the case of multiple tasks, this step presents a separate page for each task you selected in your plan.

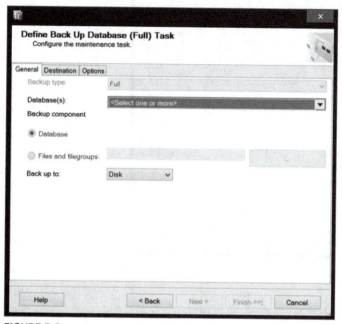

FIGURE 5-5

6. Figure 5-6 shows the dialog box where you can select the databases you want to back up. This figure shows just one database to back up. This dialog box has changed from SQL Server 2012, which was a single page. As shown in Figure 5-5, it now has three tabs: General, Destination, and Options.

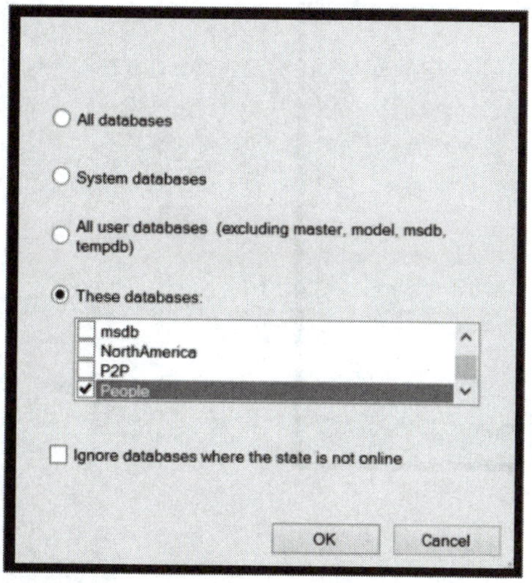

FIGURE 5-6

7. On the next page (shown in Figure 5-7), select the reporting options for the plan: "Write a report to a text file," "E-mail report," or both.

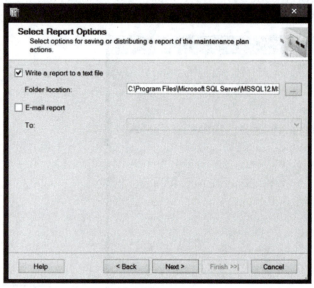

FIGURE 5-7

8. Click Next to go to the final page of the wizard, where you can confirm your selections, as shown in Figure 5-8.

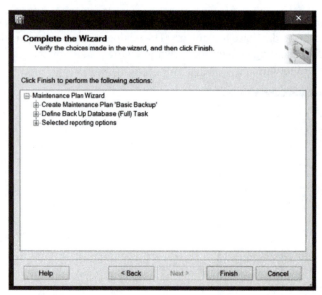

FIGURE 5-8

9. Click Finish to create your plan. While the plan is being created, a status page shows you the progress on each step of the plan's creation, as shown in Figure 5-9.

FIGURE 5-9

The new plan now displays in the Object Explorer under the Maintenance Plans node, and you can run it manually by using the menu from that node.

You should have noticed along the way that the Maintenance Plan Wizard can perform only a limited number of tasks, but these are some of the most important routine maintenance activities on the server. Using this wizard enables you to automate many of the essential tasks needed on a SQL Server.

To explore more details about the plan you just created, look at the job created for this plan in the SQL Server Agent node, under the Jobs node. The job will be named <*Your plan name*>.sub-plan_1, so, in this example, the job name is MaintenancePlan.Subplan_1.

Maintenance Plan Designer

Now that you've used the Maintenance Plan Wizard to create a basic backup job, it's time to learn how to use the Maintenance Plan Designer to achieve the same task. Follow these steps:

1. Expand the Management node in Object Explorer, then right-click the Maintenance Plans node. Now select the New Maintenance Plan item. This opens the New Maintenance Plan dialog box, which you can see in Figure 5-10. Enter a new plan name, **Basic Backup 2**, so you don't conflict with the plan created earlier using the Maintenance Plan Wizard. Click OK.

Figure 5-11 shows the Plan Designer dialog box that appears. You see two new windows inside Management Studio. The Plan Designer window appears in the center of the screen. The Properties window appears on the right of the screen. If the Properties window does not automatically display, you can see it by right-clicking the plan designer window, and selecting Properties from the menu.

The Maintenance Plan tasks Toolbox tab has been added to the left of the screen. To expand the toolbox, click the Toolbox tab along the left edge of the screen.

FIGURE 5-10

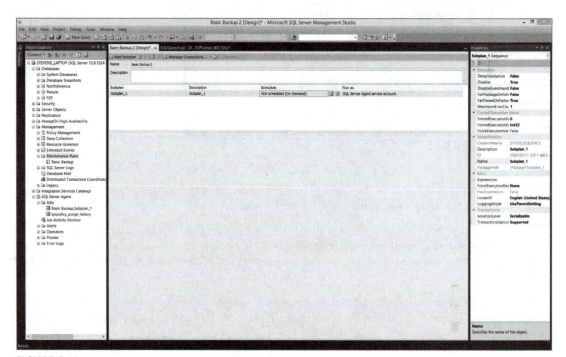

FIGURE 5-11

2. To create the Basic Backup task, click the Back Up Database Task in the toolbox and drag it onto the designer's surface. After doing this, your designer will look like Figure 5-12.

3. At this point, you have created the Basic Backup task, but haven't defined what the backup task needs to do. To specify the same parameters as you did when using the wizard, edit the properties of the Back Up Database Task by double-clicking the task on the designer. This opens the task properties screen, shown in Figure 5-13.

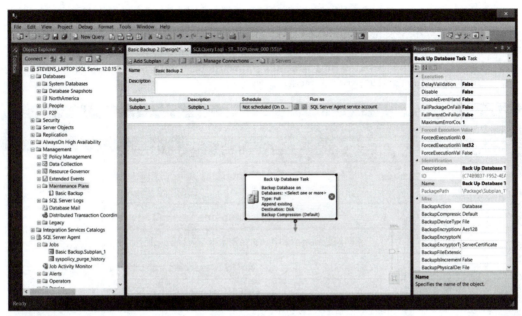

FIGURE 5-12

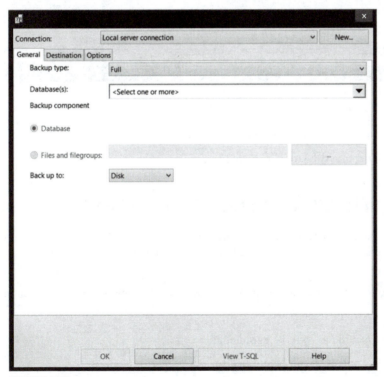

FIGURE 5-13

4. This is the same dialog box you completed using the wizard, so select the same database to back up, and the same options you selected when using the Maintenance Plan Wizard. When you have finished making these changes, click OK to return to the designer. This time the Back Up Database Task no longer has the red warning sign, but now looks like Figure 5-14 (indicating the database you selected).

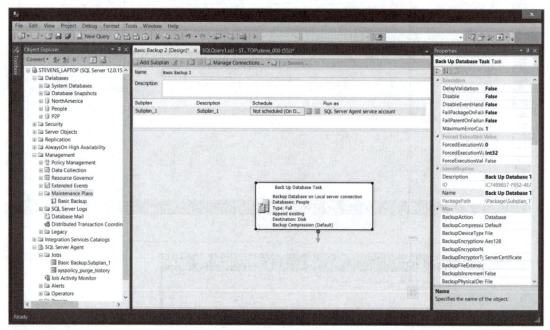

FIGURE 5-14

5. To create the plan you have just designed, merely save it. This creates the plan.

You can use the Plan Designer at any time to edit the plan's properties.

AUTOMATING SQL SERVER WITH SQL SERVER AGENT

When a Maintenance Plan does not cover all the automation you require on a SQL Server, or anytime you need to do more than you can with a Maintenance Plan, using SQL Server Agent directly is the way to go.

SQL Server Agent consists of four basic components, each of which the following sections discuss:

➤ **Jobs**—Defines the work to be done.

➤ **Schedules**—Defines when the job will be executed.

➤ **Operators**—Lists the people who can be notified for job statuses and alerts.

➤ **Alerts**—Enables you to set up an automatic response or notification when an event occurs.

Jobs

A great reason to use SQL Server Agent is to create tasks you can schedule to complete work automatically, such as backing up a database. A SQL Server Agent *job* contains the definition of the work to be done. The job itself doesn't do the work, but rather is a container for the job steps, which is where the work is done. A job has a name, a description, an owner, and a category, and a job can be enabled or disabled. Jobs can be run in several ways:

➤ By attaching the job to one or more schedules

➤ In response to one or more alerts

➤ By executing `sp_start_job`

➤ Manually via SQL Server Management Studio

Job Steps

A job consists of one or more *job steps*. The job steps are where the work is actually done. Each job step has a name and a type. Be sure to give your jobs and job steps good descriptive names that can be useful when they appear in error and logging messages. You can create a number of different types of job steps, including the following:

➤ **ActiveX Script**—Enables you to execute VBScript, JScript, or any other installable scripting language.

➤ **Operating System commands (CmdExec)**—Enables you to execute command prompt items. You can execute `.bat` files or any of the commands that would be contained in a `.bat` or `.cmd` file.

➤ **PowerShell job**—Enables you to execute Windows PowerShell scripts as part of a job.

➤ **SQL Server Analysis Services command**—Enables you to execute an XML for Analysis (XMLA) command. This must use the `Execute` method, which enables you to select data and administer and process Analysis Services objects.

➤ **SQL Server Analysis Services Query**—Enables you to execute a Multidimensional Expression (MDX) against a cube. MDX queries enable you to select data from a cube.

➤ **SQL Server Integration Services (SSIS) Package Execution**—Enables you to execute an SSIS package. You can assign variable values, configurations, and anything else you need to execute the package. This can save a great amount of time if you already have complex SSIS packages created, and want to execute them from a SQL Agent job step.

➤ **Transact-SQL Script (T-SQL)**—Enables you to execute T-SQL scripts. T-SQL scripts do not use SQL Server Agent Proxy accounts, described later in this chapter. If you are not a member of the `sysadmin` fixed-server role, the T-SQL step can run using your user credentials within the database. When members of the `sysadm` fixed-server role create T-SQL job steps, they may specify that the job step should run under the security context of a specific database user. If they specify a database user, the step executes as the specified user; otherwise, the step executes under the security context of the SQL Server Agent Service account.

> **NOTE** *The GUI for T-SQL security can be confusing. Although there is a Run As drop-down on the first page of the Job Step Properties dialog box where you set up job steps, this is not where you set the security for T-SQL steps. The Run As drop-down here is used to specify security contexts for other types of steps. To set security for your T-SQL step, click the Advanced tab. At the bottom of the dialog box is a Run As User drop-down. Set the T-SQL user security context here.*

Other job-step types exist that you do not usually create yourself, although it is possible to do so. These jobs, with their associated steps, are usually created by setting up replication. Each job step runs under a *security context*. The security contexts for other types of job steps are described later in this chapter. The process to set up replication defines jobs that use the following step types:

➤ Replication Distributor

➤ Replication Merge

➤ Replication Queue Reader

➤ Replication Snapshot

➤ Replication Transaction Log Reader

Some control of flow is related to job steps as well. You can specify an action for when the step succeeds and when the step fails. These actions can be one of the following:

➤ Quit the job, indicating success.

➤ Quit the job, with failure.

➤ Go to another job step.

You can also require that the job step be retried before it fails. You can specify the number of retry attempts and the retry interval (in minutes). Once you set these guidelines, a job step will then be retried the number of times you specify in the Retry Attempts field before it executes the On Failure control of flow. If the Retry Interval in Minutes field has been set, the step waits for the specified time period before retrying. This can be useful when dependencies exist between jobs. For example, you may have a job step that does a bulk insert from a text file. The text file is placed into the proper directory by some other process, which may run late.

When you create a job, you can place it into a job category. Each job can be in only one category. Several predefined job categories are available, including [Uncategorized (Local)] and Database Engine Tuning Advisor. You can also create your own job categories by following these steps:

1.   From the Object Explorer window of SQL Server Management Studio, open the SQL Server Agent item in the tree view, and right-click the Jobs node.

2.   From the menu, select Manage Job Categories. The dialog box shown in Figure 5-15 appears.

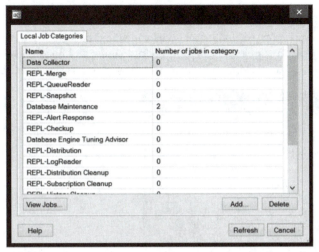

FIGURE 5-15

3. Click Add, and the dialog box shown in Figure 5-16 appears.

FIGURE 5-16

4. Enter the new job category name into the Name field, and click OK.

As trivial as it might seem, you should give some thought to organizing your jobs before creating your categories. You may be surprised how quickly the number of jobs on your server grows, making it difficult to find the correct job.

Job Step Logging

Each time a job is run, a *job history* is created. Job history tells you when the job started, when it completed, and if it was successful. You can configure each job step for logging and history as well. All the logging setup for a job step is on the Advanced tab of the job step properties, as shown in Figure 5-17.

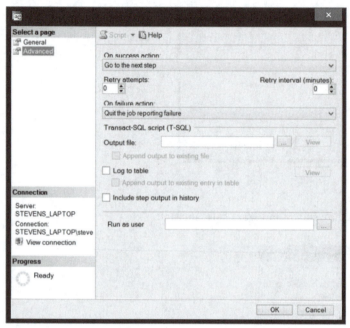

FIGURE 5-17

Following are the key options that affect logging:

➤ **Output file**—Job steps executed by `sysadmin` role members may also have the job-step history written to a file. To do so, enter the filename in the "Output file" text box. Check the "Append output to existing file" check box if you do not want to overwrite the file. Job steps executed by others can be logged only to `dbo.sysjobstepslogs` in the `msdb` database.

➤ **Log to table**—You can also choose to have the information logged to `dbo.sysjobstepslogs` in `msdb`. To log to this table, check the "Log to table" check box. To include step history from multiple job runs, also check the "Append output to existing entry in table." Otherwise, you see only the most recent history.

➤ **Include step output in history**—To append the job-step history to the job history, check the "Include the step output in history" check box.

> **NOTE** *Any time you refer to network resources such as operating system files, ensure that the appropriate proxy account has the correct permissions. Also, always use the UNC name for files, so the job or its steps are not dependent on directory maps. This is an easy place to get into trouble between the test and production environments if you are not careful.*

By default, SQL Server stores only 1,000 rows in its Job History Log, and a maximum of 100 for any one job. The Job History Log is a rolling log, so the oldest records are deleted to make room for newer job history. If you have a lot of jobs, or jobs that run frequently, the Job History log can soon become full, and start deleting old records. If you must to change the size of the log, you can do so under the SQL Server Agent properties, as shown in Figure 5-18.

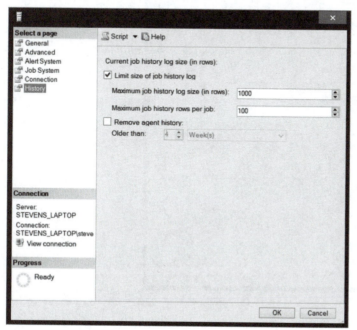

FIGURE 5-18

Job Notifications

You can configure SQL Server Agent to notify you when a job completes, succeeds, or fails. To do so, follow these steps:

1. In the Job Properties dialog box, choose Notifications to see the dialog box shown in Figure 5-19.

2. A job can send a notification via e-mail, pager, and Net Send. A job can also write to the Windows Application Event log. As Figure 5-19 shows, there is a line in the dialog box for each of these delivery methods. Place a check beside the delivery method you want. (You can choose multiple methods.)

3. Click the drop-down menu for each option and choose an operator to notify. An operator enables you to define the e-mail address for the delivery. (Operator setup is described later in this chapter.)

4. Choose the event that should trigger the notification. This can be when the job completes, when the job fails, or when the job succeeds. You may not want to be notified at all for some jobs (such as routine maintenance like Index Maintenance). However, for mission-critical

jobs, you might want to always be e-mailed when the job completes, and perhaps paged and notified through Net Send if the job fails, so that you can know immediately. Examples of more critical jobs where you do want notification might be Backups and DBCC CHECKDB.

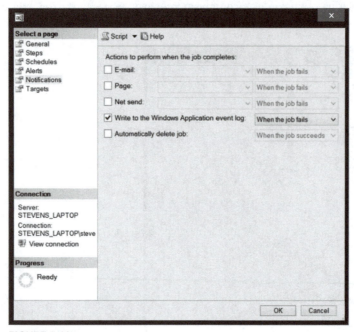

FIGURE 5-19

> **NOTE** *Windows Messenger Service must run on the server where SQL Server Agent runs to send notifications via Net Send. You can send a message to any workstation or user that can be seen from the SQL Server Agent server. The target workstation must also be running the Windows Messenger Service to enable it to receive the notification.*

Schedules

One of the advantages of SQL Server Agent is that you can schedule your jobs. You can schedule a job to run at any of these times:

➤ When SQL Server Agent starts

➤ Once, at a specified date and time

➤ On a recurring basis

➤ When the CPU utilization of your server is idle

To create a schedule in Management Studio, select the `SQL Server Agent` node, right-click Jobs, and choose Manage Schedules. The scheduler is particularly easy to use. For example, you can create a schedule that runs on the last weekday of every month. (It is convenient not to have to figure out which day is the last day of the month.) You can create a schedule when you create the job, or you can create it as an independent schedule, and later associate it with jobs.

After your schedule is created, you can associate it with one or more jobs. A job can also have multiple schedules. You may want to create a schedule for nightly batching and another for end-of-month processing. A single job can be associated with both schedules. If a scheduled job is triggered when the job is already running, that schedule is simply skipped.

Care and planning should be taken when naming schedules, or confusion can occur. The most common difficulty is deciding if the schedule name should reflect *when* the schedule runs or *what* kind of work it includes. You actually can use both time and type indications on the same schedule. An example of this might be Daily Backup Schedule, or Daily Index Maintenance Schedule. For business-related schedules, you might create a schedule named End of Month Accounts Payable or Biweekly Payroll Cycle. Including business names can be convenient for quickly finding a schedule associated with a specific action or process. Including when the work occurs may help if you want to change the frequency of a schedule.

Sometimes the CPU utilization of your server is idle, and these jobs can be worthwhile. You can define when the CPU is idle by setting up the Idle CPU Condition in SQL Server Agent Properties on the Advanced tab. You can define a minimum CPU utilization and a duration here. When the CPU utilization is less than your definition for the duration you specify, CPU idle schedules are triggered. If the CPU is not otherwise busy, you can get some batch-related work done. Be careful, however. If you have many jobs scheduled for CPU idle, they can begin to run quickly, and you can overpower your system. Be prudent with the number of jobs of this type that you schedule.

One item that is sorely lacking in SQL Server Agent's arsenal is the capability to link jobs together so that one begins as the other ends. You can still make this happen, though, by adding a final step in one job that executes the second job. You can do this using `sp_start_job`. However, using this approach puts all the navigation inside job steps. Navigation between jobs should not be happening at the job-step level; it should be outside at the job level. Some third-party tools do a good job of this. However, if you want to do it on your own, it is likely to be difficult to maintain.

Operators

An *operator* is a SQL Server Agent object that contains a friendly name and some contact information. Operators can be notified on completion of SQL Server Agent jobs and when alerts occur. (Alerts are covered in the next section.) You may want to notify operators who can fix problems related to jobs and alerts, so they can go about their business to support the business. You may also want to automatically notify management when mission-critical events occur, such as failure of the payroll cycle.

You should define operators before you begin defining alerts. This enables you to choose the operators you want to notify as you are defining the alert, saving you some time. To create a new operator, follow these steps:

1. Expand the SQL Server Agent node in the Object Explorer in SQL Server Management Studio.

2. From there, right-click Operators and select New Operator. The New Operator dialog box shown in Figure 5-20 appears, and here you can create a new operator. The operator name must be unique and fewer than 128 characters.

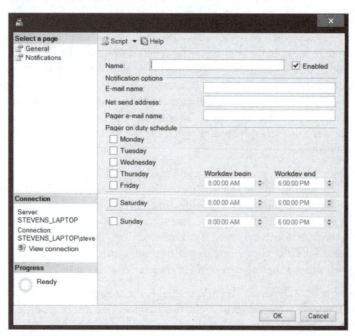

FIGURE 5-20

Operator Notifications

Jobs enable you to notify a single operator for three different send types:

➤ **E-mail**—To use e-mail or pager notifications, Database Mail must be set up and enabled, and SQL Server Agent must be configured. For e-mail notifications, you can provide an e-mail address. You can provide multiple e-mail addresses separated by semicolons. This could also be an e-mail group defined within your e-mail system. If you want to notify many people, it is better to define an e-mail group in your e-mail system. This enables you to change the list of people notified without having to change every job.

➤ **Pager**—For pager notifications, you also provide an e-mail address. SQL Server Agent does not come equipped with paging. You must purchase paging via e-mail capabilities from a third-party provider. SQL Server Agent merely sends the e-mail to the pager address, and your pager software does the rest. Some pager systems require additional configuration characters to be sent around the Subject, CC, or To line. You can set this up in SQL Server Agent Configuration (covered at the end of this chapter).

Notice that there is a "Pager on duty schedule" option associated with the "Pager e-mail name." This applies only to pagers. You can set up an on-duty schedule for paging this operator, and then set this operator to be notified regarding an alert or job completion. When the job completes or the alert occurs, the operator will be paged only during his or her pager on-duty schedule.

➤ **Net Send**—You can also use Net Send to notify an operator. To use Net Send, Windows Messaging Service must be running on the same server as SQL Agent. Additionally, you must provide the name of the workstation for this operator, and a Message dialog box pops up on his or her workstation. Out of these three send types, Net Send is the least reliable method of notification because the message is only available for a short period of time. If the operator is not at his or her desk at the time when the Net Send arrives, or the target server is offline or unavailable for any reason, the message will not be delivered.

Notifications from alerts can reach multiple operators. This provides you with several convenient options. For example, you can create an operator for each shift (First Shift Operators, Second Shift Operators, and Third Shift Operators), set up a group e-mail and a group page address for each of the shifts, set up the pager-duty schedule to match each shift's work schedule, and add all three operators to each alert. If an alert set up like this occurs at 2:00 A.M., then only the third-shift operators will be paged. If the alert occurs at 10:00 A.M., then only the first-shift operators will be paged.

Notice that the weekday schedule must be the same every day, although you can specify a different schedule for Saturday and Sunday. Additionally, there is nothing to indicate company holidays or vacations. You can disable operators (perhaps because they are on vacation), but you cannot schedule the disablement in advance.

Fail-safe Operator

What happens if an alert occurs and no operators are on duty, according to their pager on-duty schedule? Unless you specify a fail-safe operator, no one would be notified. The *fail-safe operator* is a security measure that enables an alert notification (not job notification) to be delivered for pager notifications (not e-mail or Net Send) that could not be sent. Failures to send pager notifications include the following:

➤ None of the specified operators are on duty.

➤ SQL Server Agent cannot access the appropriate tables in msdb.

> **NOTE** *The fail-safe operator option is disabled if no operators have been defined.*

To designate an operator as the fail-safe operator, perform the following steps:

1. Select the properties of SQL Server Agent.

2. Select the Alert System tab, as shown in Figure 5-21.

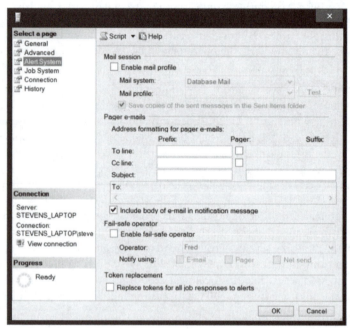

FIGURE 5-21

3. In the "Fail-safe operator" section, select "Enable fail-safe operator."

The fail-safe operator is used only when *none* of the specified pager notifications could be made, or `msdb` is not available. If you have three pager operators associated with a specific alert, and one of them is notified but two of them failed, the fail-safe operator will *not* be notified.

You can indicate whether the fail-safe operator will be notified using any or all of the three notification methods discussed in the previous section. However, a fail-safe operator can be notified only if a pager notification cannot be successfully delivered, in which case the fail-safe operator can be notified via e-mail, pager, Net Send, or a combination of these methods.

Because the fail-safe operator is a security mechanism, you cannot delete an operator identified as fail-safe. First, you must either disable the fail-safe setup for SQL Agent, or choose a different fail-safe operator. Then you can delete the operator. Disabling an operator defined as fail-safe can prevent any normal alerts or job notifications from being sent, but cannot restrict this operator's fail-safe notifications.

Alerts

An *alert* is an automated response to an event. An *event* can be any of the following:

➤ SQL Server event

➤ SQL Server performance condition

➤ Windows Management Instrumentation (WMI) event

You can create an alert as a response to any of the events of these types. The following responses can be triggered as the result of an event alert:

➤ Start a SQL Server Agent job

➤ Notify one or more operators

> **NOTE** *Although you can notify only one operator of each notification type for job completion, you can notify multiple operators for alerts.*

To create an alert, follow these steps:

1. Open the New Alert dialog box (shown in Figure 5-22) by selecting New Alert from the context menu on the `Alerts` node under the `SQL Server Agent` node in SQL Server Management Studio.

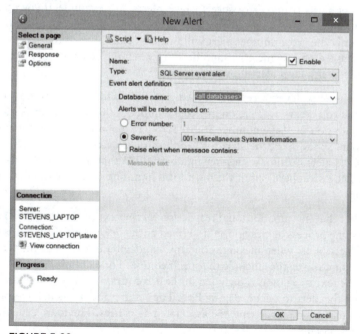

FIGURE 5-22

2. When you create an alert, you give it a name. Ensure that this name tells you something about what is going on; it will be included in all messages. Names such as Log Full Alert or Severity 18 Alert on Production might be useful.

3. Choose the event type on which the alert is based (refer to Figure 5-22). SQL Server events and SQL Server performance condition events are covered in this section. A complete discussion of WMI events is outside the scope of this book, and only addressed briefly here.

SQL Server Event Alerts

The SQL Server event alerts are based mainly on error messages. You can create an alert based on one of two things: a specific error number, or on an error's severity level.

For an alert based on a specific error number, you might create an alert on error number 9002 (log file full) or error number 1105 (out of disk space). An alert can be fired for any particular database or all databases. For example, you may care to get this alert only when the Production database transaction log is full, not when the other test and development databases run out of log space. In this case, choose the Production database in the "Database name" drop-down list. If you want to alert on two databases but not all of them, you must create two separate alerts. SQL Server doesn't currently support multiple database alerts.

Each error also has a severity level, and you can choose to create an alert based on this specific severity level. For example, severity 19 and above are fatal server errors, and you may want to receive an alert when any fatal SQL error occurs. If so, you would create alerts for each severity level from 19 through 25.

When using various combinations of error number and severity level alerts, it is important to remember that error number alerts trump error severity level alerts. For example, if you create an alert on one specific error number that has a severity level of 16, and then also create another alert for all severity-16 errors, only the error number alert will fire. You can think of the severity-level alert as a backup. Alerts defined on specific error numbers fire when the error occurs. For all other errors of that severity, the severity-level alert fires as needed.

If you create two of the same error-level or severity-level alerts in the same database, only one gets fired. For example, suppose you create an alert on message number 50001 in a database called Production and another alert on message number 50001 for <all databases>. In this case, when the error message occurs in Production, the alert for Production fires, not the <all databases> alert. The <all databases> alert fires for a message number 50001 that occurs in any database other than Production. The lesson here is that the most local handling of an event will trump a more general specification.

You can also create an alert that has an additional restriction on the text of the message. You can create an alert using the same process as previously described at the beginning of the "Alerts" section, but check the box "Raise alert when message contains," and enter a text string in the text box. The alert then fires only on messages that include the specified text. For example, you could create an event that fires when the text Page Bob is included in the error message. Then, applications could raise user errors that cause the alert to occur, paging Bob. The same principle as before applies here, though. If a message with matching text is sent, the associated alert fires. The more general alert fires only if there is no text match.

> **NOTE** *SQL Server alerts work by watching the operating system application event log. If the event is not logged, the alert does not fire. However, you can use the* sp_altermessage *system stored procedure and specify* @parameter = 'write_to_log' *to change the behavior such that the event is now logged.*

You can create error messages with the sp_addmessage stored procedure. You can specify whether the message is logged. For example, you can create a simple message using the following SQL:

```
sp_addmessage 50001,16 ,'MESSAGE', @with_log =  'TRUE'
```

The preceding message has a message number of 50001 and a severity level of 16. You can then create alerts to test your system. Set these alerts to use e-mail as the response. To test the alert, use the following code:

```
Raiserror(50001,16,1)with log
Select * from msdb.dbo.sysmail_allitems
```

Raiserror sends the error message. You can log an error message using the Raiserror command if you have the appropriate permissions.

Select displays all the mail items. Scroll to the bottom of the list to check for the mail notification that has been attached as a response to the alert.

SQL Server Performance Condition Alerts

When you install SQL Server, a collection of Windows Performance Monitor counters is also installed. The Windows Performance Monitor tool enables the operations staff to monitor the performance of the server, including CPU utilization, memory utilization, and much more. When SQL Server is installed, an additional collection of monitor counters is added to enable DBAs to monitor the performance and status of SQL Server instances. You can create an alert on a condition based on any SQL Server counter. For more information on monitoring SQL Server using Performance Counters, refer to Chapter 12, "Monitoring Your SQL Server." A SQL Server performance condition alert is shown in Figure 5-23.

> **NOTE** *You cannot create multicounter alerts. For example, you cannot create an alert that fires when Percent Log Used is greater than 80 and Transactions/sec is greater than 100. You must choose to alert on a single counter.*

Performance counters are grouped according to their objects. For example, the Databases object contains the counters associated with a specific database, such as Percent Log Used and Transactions/sec. The Buffer Manager object includes counters specific to buffer management.

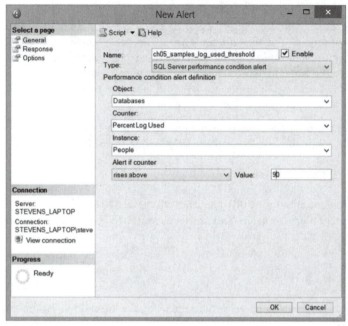

FIGURE 5-23

To begin creating an alert, follow these steps:

1. Choose the object and then the counter for which you want to create an alert.

> **NOTE** *You cannot create SQL Server alerts on counters that are not specifically for SQL Server, such as CPU utilization. However, the Performance Monitor tool enables you to set alerts for these other non-SQL Server counters.*

2. The next choice you make is in the Instance text box. When you choose Databases objects, the Instance text box contains the list of databases. Select the database on which to create the alert.

3. Next is the "Alert if Counter" box. You can alert if the counter falls below, becomes equal to, or rises above a value you specify. Specify the value in the Value text box.

Although you can still create an alert to notify you when the transaction log becomes full, this is not ideal because by then, it is a little too late. It would be better to know when it looks like the log may become full, but before it actually does. You can do this by creating a performance condition alert on the Percent Log Used counter for the Databases object for the database in which you are interested:

1. Choose when the counter rises above some safe limit, probably 80 to 95 percent. You can then be notified before the log is full.

2. Adjust this actual value so that you are not notified too quickly. If you have set up your log to be what you believe is large enough, you might instead want to notify on autogrow events.

WMI Event Alerts

Windows Management Instrumentation (WMI) is a tremendously powerful mechanism, but is also the least understood of all the alerting technologies.

SQL Server 2005 introduced the WMI Provider for Server Events, which translates WMI Query Language (WQL) queries for events into event notifications in a specific database. For more information on using event notifications see Chapter 12, "Monitoring your SQL Server."

To create a WMI event alert, select "WMI event alert" as the type for the alert, validate the namespace is correct, and enter your WQL query.

Alert Responses

As was previously discussed, you can respond to an alert by starting a SQL Server Agent job or notifying one or more operators. You set this up on the Response tab of the Create Alert dialog box. To execute this job, simply check the check box and choose an existing job or create a new job. To notify an operator, check the appropriate box, and select the operators you want to notify by choosing one or more of the notification methods. For alerts, it is nice to have an operator for each shift you must cover, with the pager on duty set up appropriately, as discussed in the "Operators" section earlier in the chapter.

As you think about how you might best use this in your enterprise, imagine a scenario such as the transaction log getting full. You could set up a performance alert to notify operators when the log is actually full, and run a job that grows the log. You could set up an alert that backs up the log when it becomes 80 percent full.

The scenario might play out as follows. You are having lunch and your pager goes off, notifying you that the log is 70 percent full. A job runs automatically that tries to back up the log to free space. In a couple of minutes you get a page telling you that the job completed successfully. After a few more potato chips, your pager goes off yet again—the log is now 80 percent full. The prior log backup did not free up any space. There might be a long-running transaction. The log backup job runs again, and you are notified upon its completion. You finish your lunch with no other pages. This means the last log backup freed up some space and you are now in good shape.

Your pager may have gone off again, telling you that the log is nearly full, and has either been extended with autogrow, or a job to extend the log has run and extended the transaction log onto an emergency log disk. It's probably time for you to get back to work, but the automation you have brought to the system has already been fighting this problem while you ate your lunch, notifying you of each step. With some thoughtful consideration, you might account for many planned responses such as this, making your life easier and operations tighter.

The Alert Options page in the Create Alert dialog box enables you to do several things:

➤ **Specify when to include more detailed information in the notification**—Sometimes the error text of the message might be long. Additionally, you may have a limit on the amount of data that can be presented on your devices. Some pagers limit you to as few as 32 characters. You should not include the error text for those message types that cannot handle the extra text, which are most commonly pagers.

➤ **Add information to the notification**—The dialog box includes a large text box labeled Additional Notification Message to Send. You can type any text here, and it will be included in the notification message. Perhaps something such as Get Up, Come In, and Fix This Problem Immediately might be appropriate.

➤ **Delay the time between responses**—At the bottom of the dialog box, you can set a delay between responses. The default value for this is 0. Imagine a scenario in which an alert goes off many times during a short period. Perhaps a program is repeatedly executing `Raiserror` or a performance condition alert is going wild. The performance condition alerts that run to alert of limited resources are especially vulnerable to this problem. You run low on memory, which causes an alert or job to run, which uses more memory. This causes the alert to fire again, using more memory, repeatedly. You are paged repeatedly as well.

You can right-click any of the SQL Server Agent objects and create a script that can drop or create the object. If you want the same object to exist on many servers, you can script it out, change the server name, and load it onto a different server. This means you would have to keep operators, jobs, alerts, and proxies in sync between multiple servers, which could be painful and error-prone. Event forwarding can also simplify your life when you administer many servers. Multiserver jobs and event forwarding are covered later in the section, "Multiserver Administration."

SQL SERVER AGENT SECURITY

SQL Server Agent security is more fine-grained than ever. This section covers not only the service account, but also security issues such as who can create, see, and run SQL Server Agent jobs. SQL Server 2014 enables multiple, separate proxy accounts to be affiliated with each job step. These proxy accounts are associated with SQL logins, which provide excellent control for each type of job step.

Service Account

The SQL Server Agent service account should be a domain account if you plan to take advantage of Database Mail or require any network connectivity. The account should map to a login that is also a member of the `sysadmin` fixed-server role.

Access to SQL Agent

After the installation, only members of the `sysadmin` fixed-server role have access to SQL Server Agent objects. Others cannot even see the SQL Server Agent object in the Object Explorer of Management Studio. To give other users access to SQL Agent, you must add them to one of three fixed database roles in the `msdb` database:

➤ `SQLAgentUserRole`

➤ `SQLAgentReaderRole`

➤ `SQLAgentOperatorRole`

The roles are listed in order of increased capability, with `SQLAgentOperatorRole` having the highest capability. Each higher role includes the permissions associated with the lower roles, so it is not necessary to assign a user to more than one role.

> **NOTE** *Members of the* sysadmin *fixed-server role have access to all the capabilities of SQL Server Agent and do not have to be added to any of these roles.*

SQLAgentUserRole

Members of the user role have the most restricted access to SQL Server Agent. They can see only the Jobs node under SQL Server Agent, and can access only local jobs and schedules that they own. They cannot use multiserver jobs, which are discussed later in this chapter. They can create, alter, delete, execute, start, and stop their own jobs and job schedules. They can view but not delete the job history for their own jobs. They can see and select operators to be notified on completion of their jobs, and choose from the available proxies for their job steps.

SQLAgentReaderRole

The reader role includes all the permissions of the user role. Members of this role can create and run the same things as a user, but can see the list of multiserver jobs, including their properties and history. They can also see all the jobs and schedules on the local server, not just the ones they own. They can see only the Jobs node under SQL Server Agent as well.

SQLAgentOperatorRole

The operator role is the least restricted role, and includes all the permissions of the reader role and the user role. This role has additional read capabilities and execute capabilities. Members of this role can view the properties of proxies and operators. They can list the available proxies and alerts on the server as well. Members of this role can also execute, start, or stop local jobs. They can enable or disable any job or operator; although they must use the sp_update_job and sp_update_schedule procedures to do so. They can delete job history for any job. The Jobs, Alerts, Operators, and Proxies nodes under SQL Server Agent are visible to this role. Only the Error Log node is hidden.

SQL Server Agent Proxies

A SQL Server Agent *proxy* defines the security context under which different job steps run. In the case where the user who creates a SQL Server Agent job does not have permissions to access the resources needed by the job, the job creator can specify a proxy. The proxy contains the credentials of a Windows user account that does have access to the resources needed by the job. For job steps that have a proxy specified, SQL Server Agent impersonates the proxy account and runs the job step while impersonating that user account.

SQL Server Agent Subsystems

SQL Server Agent *subsystems* are objects that group similar sets of functionality that can be used by SQL Server Agent proxies. These subsystems provide a security boundary that enables a more complex security model to SQL Agent proxies.

SQL Server Agent has 12 subsystems on which security can be placed. When you add a job step, the subsystems available appear in the following order as the type of new job step:

➤   ActiveX Script

➤   Operating System (CmdExec)

➤   PowerShell

➤   Replication Distributor

➤   Replication Merge

➤   Replication Queue Reader

➤   Replication Snapshot

➤   Replication Transaction Log Reader

➤   Analysis Services Command

➤   Analysis Services Query

➤   SSIS Package Execution

➤   Transact SQL

The permissions for Transact SQL are not governed by proxy. All users execute T-SQL under their own account. If you are a member of the sysadmin group, you can choose any SQL login as the Run As account. All the other subsystems use one or more proxies to determine permissions for the subsystem.

Subsystem Permissions

Each subsystem has its own permissions, but the proxy combines the permissions for the CmdExec step, as well as the users who may run under this proxy. Figure 5-24 shows the basic relationship among the parts.

Because the proxy combines these permissions, it is difficult to determine which operating-system permissions are used when someone executes a CmdExec job step. Issues may arise when setting permissions for proxies, so it is important to perform the setup correctly the first time. The following steps show the setup for permissions for the operating system (CmdExec) subsystem:

1.   First, you must create a credential. The easiest way to do this is in Management Studio. Expand Security, right-click Credentials, and choose New Credential. A dialog box like the one shown in Figure 5-25 displays.

2.   Give the credential a friendly name, and associate it with a Windows login or group. You must also provide the password to complete the creation. The permissions associated with this login or group will be the permissions applied to the CmdExec job step.

> **NOTE** *If your SMTP Server requires a login, you may want to set up a specific local account with minimum permissions specifically for sending SMTP mail. The sole purpose of this account is to follow the principle of least privileges; it should be used for nothing else.*

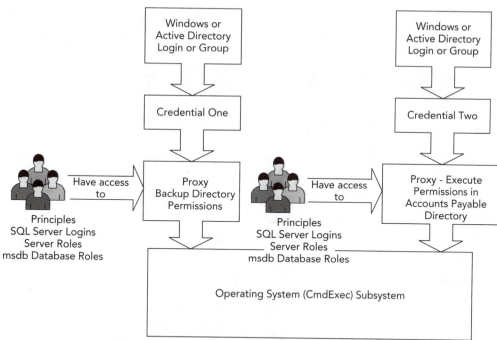

FIGURE 5-24

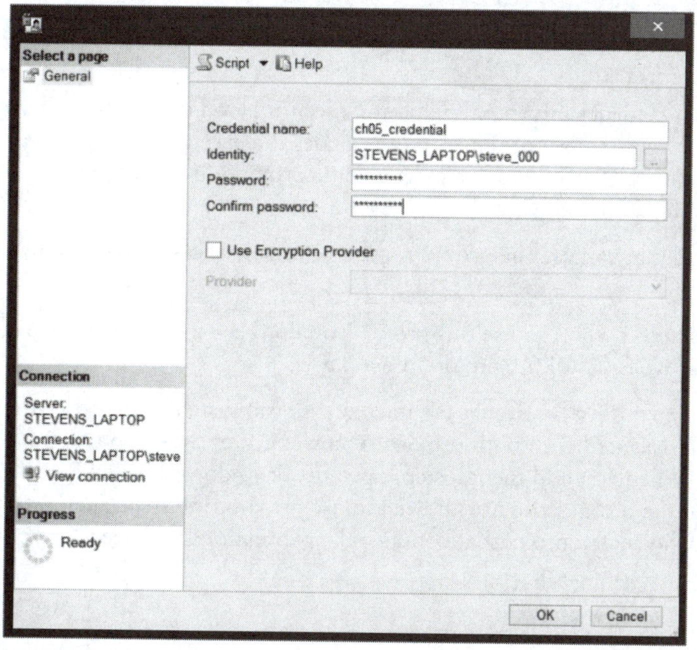

FIGURE 5-25

3. Now you can create your proxy. In Management Studio, expand SQL Server Agent, right-click Proxies, and choose New Proxy. You get a New Proxy Account dialog box, as shown in Figure 5-26.

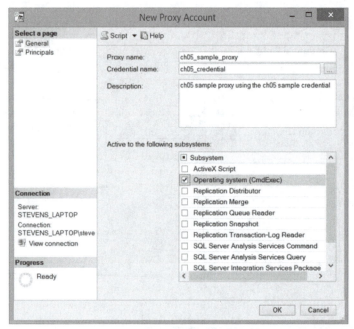

FIGURE 5-26

4. Give the proxy a name that provides information about its security level or its intended use. Then associate a credential with the proxy. The proxy provides the permissions associated with its credential when it is used. Provide a more detailed description of what the proxy enables and how it should be used and when.

5. Then, select the subsystems that can use the proxy. A proxy can be associated with many subsystems.

6. Create a list of users (principles) who can use this proxy. You do this on the Principles page. A principle can be a Server Role, a SQL Login, or an msdb role.

7. Now, assume you have created the two proxies for the CmdExec subsystem (refer to Figure 5-24). Your SQL login is associated with both proxies. You want to create a job that contains a CmdExec job step. When you add the job step, open the drop-down labeled Run As, which contains a list of all the proxies you are allowed to use for your job step. Each proxy has its own permissions. Choose the proxy that contains the permissions you need for your job step, and you should be ready to go.

CONFIGURING SQL SERVER AGENT

Now that you have learned how things work in SQL Agent, you can take on the configuration task. You already know about some of the configuration options, so now you can go through the different pages to configure the SQL Server Agent properties.

To start the configuration, right-click the `SQL Server Agent` node in Management Studio, and choose Properties.

General Properties

The General page appears, as shown in Figure 5-27.

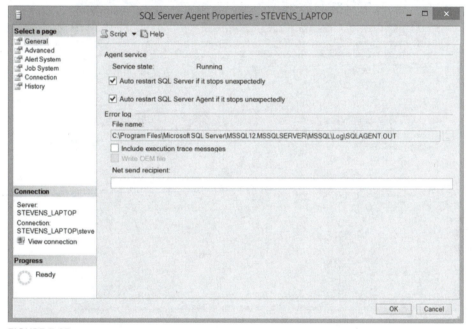

FIGURE 5-27

Review each section on this page and consider the following:

➤ Check the two top check boxes: "Auto restart SQL Server if it stops unexpectedly" and "Auto restart SQL Server Agent if it stops unexpectedly." The Service Control Manager watches both of these services and automatically restarts them if they fail.

➤ Usually you leave the error-log location at the default; however, you can change it if you want. If you need some additional logging, check "Include execution trace messages."

Execution trace messages provide detailed information on the SQL Agent operation, which is written to the SQL Agent Error Log. Enabling this option increases the space used in the SQL Agent Log, so Agent log size is something to consider when enabling this option.

➤ To get a Net Send when errors are logged, enter a workstation name in the "Net send recipient" text box. Of course, Windows Messaging Service must be running on the server for Net Sends to occur.

Advanced Properties

Choose the Advanced Page tab on the top left, which brings up the dialog box shown in Figure 5-28.

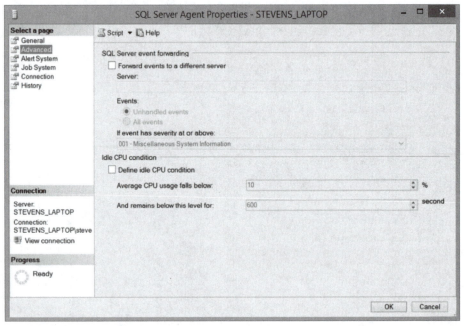

FIGURE 5-28

You have several options from which to choose on this page:

➤ The top section, "SQL Server event forwarding," enables you to forward your events from one server to another. You can set up operators and alerts on a single server, and then have the other servers forward their events to the single server. To use this capability, you also need to understand how to use SQL Server Agent tokens, which are covered in the section, "Using Token Replacement," later in this chapter. If you want to employ this capability, check the box labeled "Forward events to a different server." Then select the server name. You can forward all events or only unhandled events. An *unhandled event* is one that does not have an alert defined for it. You also select how severe the error must be before it can be forwarded. For example, you may not want anything less than a severity 16 error (Miscellaneous User Error) to be forwarded. Whether you forward severity 16 errors depends on whether you have application-defined errors that specify notifications. If you plan to use this capability, you must also understand how to use SQL Server Agent tokens, which are covered in the section, "Using Token Replacement," later in this chapter.

➤ The second section is "Idle CPU condition." Recall that you can create a schedule that runs when the CPU becomes idle. This is where you define what *idle* means. The default is CPU utilization at less than 10 percent for 10 minutes.

Alert System Properties

The next page is for the Alert System, as shown in Figure 5-29.

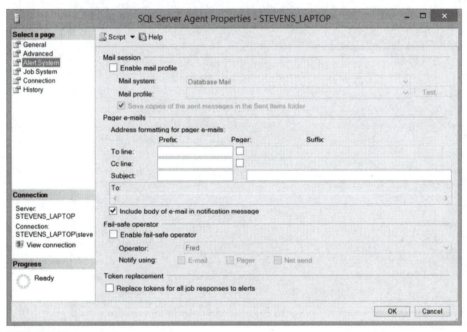

FIGURE 5-29

➤ If you plan to use Database Mail, you do the setup here. Although you may have many mail profiles in Database Mail, SQL Server Agent uses only one profile. Choose the mail system and profile.

➤ The second section is for pager e-mails. If your pager system requires special control characters in the To, CC, or Subject line, you can add those characters here in front of the item (prefix) or after the item (suffix). As you make changes, you can see the effect in the small box below your data-entry section. You can also choose to include or exclude the body of the e-mail for pagers by indicating your selection in the appropriate check box.

➤ The third section enables you to provide fail-safe operator information. Use this if you are doing any notifications. It is too easy to change a schedule in such a way that results in no one being notified, so don't get caught. Enable this section, choose an operator, and indicate how the fail-safe messages should be delivered (by e-mail, pager, Net Send, or some combination of these).

➤ The last check box enables you to specify whether you want to have tokens replaced in jobs run from alerts. Details of token replacement are covered in the section, "Multiserver Administration," later in this chapter.

Job System Properties

The Job System page is next, as shown in Figure 5-30.

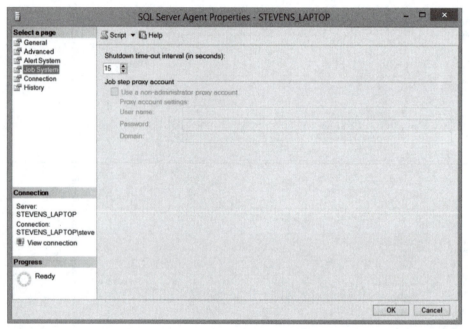

FIGURE 5-30

➤ In the first section, you can specify the shutdown period (in seconds) in the "Shutdown time-out interval" list. For example, suppose you are trying to shut down SQL Agent, and jobs are running. You can specify how long SQL Server Agent should wait for jobs to complete before killing them and shutting down.

➤ The second section is only available if you administer a SQL Server 2000 Agent. This enables you to set the backward-compatible, nonadministrator proxy. SQL 2000 allowed only one proxy. SQL Server 2005, 2008, 2012, and 2014 allow many proxies, so this is not necessary when administering SQL Server 2005, 2008, 2012, and 2014 Agents.

Connection Properties

The Connection page is one that most users do not need. SQL Server Agent connects to SQL Server, by default, using the server name, the default port, the SQL Server Agent Service account, and the highest-matching protocol between the client configuration and the protocols enabled for SQL Server. Following are several circumstances in which you may want to alter these defaults:

➤ Your server has multiple network cards, and you want to specify a particular IP or port.

➤ You want to connect using a specific protocol (IP, for example).

➤ You want SQL Server Agent to connect to the server using a login different from the service account login.

To create an alias for SQL Server, follow these steps:

1. Open Configuration Manager.

2. Expand SQL Native Client Configuration, right-click Aliases, and choose New Alias.

3. Set up the alias to suit your connectivity needs.

4. On the SQL Server Agent Connection page, enter the alias name and the connection information you want SQL Server Agent to use. Although SQL Server authentication is allowed, it is not recommended.

History Properties

The last page is the History page, shown previously in Figure 5-18. Here you can limit the size of the job history log to a fixed number of rows, and the "Maximum job history rows per job" option is a lifesaver. Imagine a job that runs repeatedly. It could be a job scheduled by a user to run every second, or it could be a job that runs from an alert that occurs repeatedly. In any case, the log entries from this job could fill up your entire job history, and you would have no history information for any other jobs. That could leave you in a tough spot if any other job needed debugging. This is exactly the situation that "Maximum job history rows per job" is intended to prevent. The default is 100 rows, but you can change it based on your needs.

MULTISERVER ADMINISTRATION

Several tactics within SQL Server 2014 enable you to easily administer multiple servers. The focus of these tactics is to centralize your administration. You can do this by forwarding events to a central event management server, which enables you to centralize alert handling. Another optimization is to use master and target servers to create jobs on a single master server and have the jobs run on multiple target servers.

Using Token Replacement

SQL Server 2014 has some nice capabilities related to SQL Server Agent job tokens. A *token* is a string literal that you use in your job steps (T-SQL scripts, CmdExec job steps, or Active Script). Before the job runs, SQL Server Agent does a string replacement of the token with its value. Tokens are usable only in SQL Server Agent jobs.

One of the tokens you can use is (STRTDT). For example, you might add the following in a T-SQL job step:

```
PRINT 'Job Start Date(YYYYMMDD): $ESCAPE_NONE(STRTDT))';
```

If you capture the output, it should look like this:

```
Job Start Date(YYYYMMDD):20141223
```

> **NOTE** *Tokens are case-sensitive.*

The following is a list of some of the tokens that you can use in any job:

➤ (DATE)—Current Date (YYYYMMDD).

➤ (INST)—Instance name of the SQL Server. This token is empty for the default instance.

➤ (JOBID)—SQL Server Agent job ID.

➤ (MACH)—Computer name where the job is run.

➤ (MSSA)—Master SQLServerAgent service name.

➤ (OSCMD)—Prefix for the program used to run CmdExec job steps.

➤ (SQLDIR)—SQL Server's install directory. The default install directory is C:\ Program Files\Microsoft SQL Server\MSSQL.

➤ (STEPCT)—The number of times this step has executed. You could use this in looping code to terminate the step after a specific number of iterations. This count does not include retries on failure. This is updated on each step run during the job (such as a real-time counter).

➤ (STEPID)—The job step ID.

➤ (SVR)—The server name of the computer running SQL Server, including the instance name.

➤ (TIME)—Current time (HHMMSS).

➤ (STRTTM)—The job's start time (HHMMSS).

➤ (STRTDT)—The job's start date (YYYYMMDD).

The following is a list of tokens that can be used only in a job that has been started from an alert. If these tokens are included in a job started any other way, the job throws an error:

➤ (A-DBN)—Database name where the alert occurred

➤ (A-SVR)—Server name where the alert occurred

➤ (A-ERR)—Error number associated with the alert

➤ (A-SEV)—Error severity associated with the alert

➤ (A-MSG)—Message text associated with the alert

The following token is available for use only on jobs run as the result of a WMI alert (see the "Using WMI" section later in the chapter).

➤ (WMI (property))—Provides the value for the WMI property named property. $(WMI(DatabaseName)) returns the value of the DatabaseName property for the WMI alert that caused the job to run.

All these tokens must be used with escape macros. The purpose of this change is to increase the security related to the use of tokens from unknown sources. Consider the following token, which you might have included in a T-SQL job step:

```
Print 'Error message: $(A-MSG)'
```

The T-SQL job step runs as the result of a user error (Raiserror). A malicious user could raise an error like this one:

```
Raiserror(''';Delete from dbo.Employee',16,1)
```

The error returned would be:

```
';Delete from dbo.Employee
```

The print message would be:

```
Print 'Error message:';Delete from dbo.Employee
```

If this happens, it means you have just been attacked with a SQL injection attack. The Delete statement runs if the T-SQL job step has permission.

To combat an attack such as this, you must add an escape macro. Because the print statement uses single quotes, a SQL injection attack closes out the single quote and then inserts its own SQL. To prevent this attack, you can double-quote any quote that comes in via the token. The escape macro ESCAPE_SQUOTE does exactly that. It is used like this:

```
Print 'Error message: $(ESCAPE_SQUOTE(A-MSG))'
```

Continuing the example, you end up with the following:

```
Print 'Error message:'';Delete from dbo.Employee
```

You then get an error because of the unmatched quote, and the step fails, keeping you safe.

The following is a list of escape macros:

➤ `$(ESCAPE_SQUOTE(token))`—Doubles single quotes (`'`) in the replacement string.

➤ `$(ESCAPE_DQUOTE(token))`—Doubles double quotes (`"`) in the replacement string.

➤ `$(ESCAPE_RBRACKET(token))`—Doubles right brackets (`]`) in the replacement string.

➤ `$(ESCAPE_NONE(token))`—The token replacement is made without changes. This is used for backward compatibility only.

You can also use these values directly if you ensure proper data types. The SQL script-looping job with tokens contains the following code that terminates a job step after it has executed five times. The top line converts the STEPCT token to an integer so it can be used in a comparison. Then the JOBID token for this job is converted to a binary 16 and passed to the sp_stop_job stored procedure, which can take the job ID of the job you want to stop:

```
IF Convert(int,$(ESCAPE_NONE(STEPCT))) >5
  BEGIN
  DECLARE @jobid binary(16)
  SELECT @jobid =Convert(Uniqueidentifier,$(ESCAPE_NONE(JOBID)))
  EXEC msdb.dbo.sp_stop_job @job_id = @jobid
  END
```

Imagine how you might use the alert-based tokens. You could create a SQL performance alert that fires when the `<any database>` transaction log becomes greater than 80-percent full. Create a job with a T-SQL step like this:

```
DECLARE @a varchar(100)
SELECT @a ='BACKUP LOG $(ESCAPE_SQUOTE(A-DBN))
  TO DISK = "\\UNCName\Share\$(ESCAPE_SQUOTE(A-DBN))\log.bak"'
SELECT @a
BACKUP LOG $(ESCAPE_SQUOTE(A-DBN))
  TO DISK = '\\UNCName\Share\\$(ESCAPE_SQUOTE(A-DBN))\log.bak'
```

Here UNCName is the name of the server where you want the backup to be stored and Share is the share on the server. Make sure the job runs when the alert occurs. If the alert fires for NorthAmerica, the backup command looks like this:

```
BACKUP LOG NorthAmerica TO DISK = \\UNCName\Share\\NorthAmerica\log.bak
```

You must create the directory first and grant appropriate permissions to the proxy you use. You could create a CmdExec step, which creates the directory on the fly. Now, a single log backup job can back up any transaction log. You might improve the name of the directory you create in the CmdExec step by adding the date and time to the filename.

Event Forwarding

Where events and alerts are concerned, you can create operators and alerts on a single system, and then have the other systems forward their events to your central alert-handling SQL Server, which responds to those alerts as necessary.

You designate a server to forward events on the Advanced Page of the SQL Server Agent properties dialog box (see Figure 5-28). Check "Forward events to a different server," and then you can specify the server to which you want to forward events.

You can configure which events will be forwarded by choosing from the options under Events. Here you can choose between "Unhandled events" and "All events." If you choose "All events," you can then add a filter on the severity level "If event has severity at or above." You can set up operators on your master event management system. Create the jobs that respond to the alerts. Then create alerts on the single master event management system to handle the event. The jobs you create can take advantage of SQL Server Agent tokens, and know on which server and database the original event occurred.

Using WMI

WMI is a set of functions embedded into the kernel of Microsoft operating systems and servers, including SQL Server. The purpose of WMI is to enable local and remote monitoring and management of servers. It is a standards-based implementation that incorporates the Distributed Management Task Force's (DMTF) Web-Based Enterprise Management (WBEM) and Common Information Model (CIM) specifications.

WMI is a big initiative, and probably warrants an entire book of its own. What you need to know most is that WMI has many events for SQL Server. Start with Books Online and search for WMI. You can discover the many, many events. You can create alerts on these events. Included are Data Definition Language (DDL) events that occur when databases are created or dropped, and when tables are created or dropped, for example.

WMI has a specific language to query these events called WMI Query Language (WQL). It is similar to T-SQL, and it is so easy that you should immediately feel comfortable with it.

Search Books Online for "WMI Provider for Server Events Classes and Properties." This material helps you navigate the many events available, and choose the specific event you want to monitor. Each event has a list of attributes, just like a table has a list of columns. Using WMI, you can select the attributes from the event in an alert.

To create an alert, use SQL Server Management Studio:

1. In Object Explorer, open the `SQL Server Agent` tree node, right-click `Alerts`, and choose New Alert. In the Alert Type drop-down box, choose WMI Event Alert. The namespace will be populated based on the server you connect to, and should look like this:

   ```
   \\.\root\Microsoft\SqlServer\ServerEvents\SQL2014
   ```

   The period (.) represents the server name, which you can change, such as `\\MYSQLSERVER\`. The last node should be `MSSQLSERVER` for a default instance and the *<instance name>* for named instances. In the preceding example, the instance was called `SQL2014`.

2. In the text box, you can enter your WQL query, as shown here:

   ```
   SELECT * FROM DDL_DATABASE_LEVEL_EVENTS
   ```

Or, to select only the `TSQLCommand` attribute, you can use this query:

```
Select TSQLCommand from DDL_DATABASE_LEVEL_EVENTS
```

3. Click OK and there will be a pause. If your namespace is incorrect, or the syntax or event/attribute names are incorrect, you get a message immediately.

4. Then, in your job, you can use the `WMI(attribute)` event token—in this case:

```
Print '$(ESCAPE_SQUOTE(WMI(TSQLCommand)))'
```

5. To get events from a database, Service Broker notifications must be turned on for that database. To turn on Service Broker notifications for `NorthAmerica`, use the following syntax:

```
ALTER DATABASE NorthAmerica SET ENABLE_BROKER;
```

If your alerts occur but the text replacement for the WMI token is not being done, you probably need to turn on the Service Broker for your database.

> **NOTE** *The service account that SQL Server Agent uses must have permission on the namespace and* ALTER ANY EVENT NOTIFICATION *permissions. This is done automatically if you use SQL Server Configuration Manager to set up accounts. However, to adjust these settings manually, from the Run prompt, type* **wmimgmt.msc.** *An administrative dialog box appears, allowing you to set up permissions.*

If you want to try WMI, there is a test program for WMI on your server. To run it from the command line, type **WBEMTest**. It is installed in the `WBEM` directory of your Windows system directory. To find out more, Microsoft has an entire subsection of its website devoted to WMI. Just search for WMI on `www.microsoft.com`.

Multiserver Administration—Using Master and Target Servers

SQL Server enables you to set up a master server (MSX). The master server can send jobs to be run on one or more target servers (TSX), but the master server may not also be a target server that receives jobs from another master server. The target servers receive and run jobs from a single master server, in addition to their own local jobs. You may have multiple master servers in your environment, but a target server is associated with a single master server. This is a simple two-level hierarchy; a server is a master server, a target server, or neither. The language used to describe the process is military in character: You *enlist* target servers to add them, and they *defect* to go away.

Setting up servers is easy. Simply follow these steps:

1. In SQL Server Management Studio, right-click the `SQL Server Agent` node, select Multi-Server Administration, and choose Make This a Master.

2. After the initial dialog box, you see a box where you can provide the e-mail address, pager address, and Net Send location to set up a *master server operator*. Fill in these fields appropriately. This operator will be set up on the master server and all target servers. This is the *only* operator who can be notified from multiserver jobs.

3. The next dialog box enables you to choose all the target servers. The list includes the servers that you have registered in SQL Server Management Studio. If you don't have any servers registered, open up the registered servers View, by selecting View and then Registered Servers. Then right-click on Local Servers Group, and select New Server Registration. This will bring up the New Server Registration dialog where you can specify the new server.

   Now that you have some registered servers, you can choose the servers that you want to be targets of this master, and click Next. You can add additional registrations by clicking the Add Connection button.

4. Close this dialog box. SQL checks to ensure that the SQL versions of the master and targets are compatible. If the versions are not compatible, drop the target from the list and then continue. Later, you can upgrade the target or master, so the versions are the same.

5. Go to the next dialog box and use the wizard to create a login on the target, if necessary, and grant it login rights to the master server. Target servers must connect to the master server to share job status information. After you complete the setup, refresh your SQL Server Agent nodes and see the change. There will be a note on the master server (MSX) and a note on the target server.

Now you can create jobs to be used at multiple target servers. Notice on the MSX that the Jobs node is divided into two sections: local jobs and multiserver jobs. To create a job, follow these steps:

1. Right-click Multi-Server Jobs, and select New Job to create a simple job.

2. Create a simple job on the MSX server and have it run at one or many TSX servers. While doing this, be sure to go to the notifications page. The only operator you can notify is MSXOperator.

Creating multiserver jobs is a nice way to manage a larger implementation without having to buy additional third-party products. No one on the TSX box can mess up your jobs. Use SQL Server Management Studio to connect to the target server as an administrator and look at the job properties for the job you just created and downloaded from the MSX. You can see the job, you can see the job history, and you can even run the job. You cannot delete the job, change the schedule, change the steps, or anything else. This job does not belong to you; it belongs to the MSX.

As you begin to think about how you might use this, be sure you consider the implications of a single job running on multiple servers. Any reference to directories, databases, and so on must be valid for all the TSXs where this job runs. You can create a single backup share that all the backups can use, for example.

Because a job can start another job, you could also create a master job that has a single step that starts another job. This other job is created on each TSX and is specific to each TSX. This enables you to perform some customization, if necessary. To create a master job, perform the following steps:

1. Back in SQL Server Management Studio, right-click the SQL Server Agent node on the master server.

2. Choose Multi-Server Administration. Here you can add target servers and manage target servers.

3. Choose Manage Target Servers. In this dialog box, you can monitor the status of everything. When you create a job for a target server, the job is automatically downloaded to the target server. If the unread instructions count does not go down to 0, poll the target server. This wakes it up to accept the instructions.

4. Click the relevant tab to see the details of downloaded instructions. This shows you details of when jobs are downloaded and updated.

5. Using the Post Instructions button in the Target Server Status dialog box, you can synchronize clocks between the servers, defect target servers, set polling intervals, and start jobs. You can also start the job directly from the Jobs node on the MSX or the TSX.

6. You can view job histories on the MSX for the job, just like any other job, but you cannot see job-step details. To get the step details, view the job history from the TSX.

7. You can defect TSXs from the TSX SQL Server Agent node, or from the Manage Target Servers dialog box on the MSX. When all the TSXs have been defected, the MSX is no longer an MSX.

SUMMARY

Automating SQL Server is one of the most important things you can learn to make your life and your business run smoothly and easily. Maintenance Plans take away a lot of the work of automating routine maintenance activities, and are a great way to get started with automating common maintenance tasks. Additionally, SQL Server Agent provides many features and services to make your life easier. Just creating a few simple backup jobs that notify operators can automate many normal tasks. If you want to be fancy, go ahead, but do some planning first, especially when considering multiserver jobs.

Using alerts is a great way to automate notifications about significant activities occurring on your database systems. You can use the pager notifications and the related on-duty schedules for regular e-mail or pagers. This is a good way to ensure that the correct people are notified. If you have many operators for alert notifications, consider creating e-mail groups and offloading some of the notification work to your e-mail server. Start small, and take your time. As you become more comfortable with Maintenance Plans and SQL Server Agent, you can spread your wings and fly.

In Chapter 6, "Service Broker in SQL Server 2014" you learn about the Service Broker in SQL Server 2014.

Service Broker in SQL Server 2014

WHAT'S IN THIS CHAPTER?

➤ Processing data asynchronously

➤ Configuring SQL Service Broker with T-SQL

➤ Sending and receiving messages with SQL Service Broker

WROX.COM CODE DOWNLOADS FOR THIS CHAPTER

The wrox.com code downloads for this chapter are found at www.wrox.com/go/prosql2014admin on the Download Code tab. The code is in the Chapter 6 download and individually named according to the names throughout the chapter.

This chapter reviews the various objects that make up the SQL Server Service Broker. As you move through the chapter, you look at the various object types and how to create the objects. Toward the end of the chapter, you learn about the T-SQL code to use the objects when sending and receiving messages within the SQL Server database, between databases on the same server, and to databases on different servers.

ASYNCHRONOUS MESSAGING

At the heart of most high-volume systems is a *queue* that stores requests until resources are available to process them. A queue allows a limited number of worker threads to service requests from thousands of clients. A worker thread takes a request off the queue, processes it, and returns the result. The thread then proceeds to the next request on the queue.

This is significantly more efficient than starting a new thread to process each request as it comes in because it saves the startup and shutdown costs for the thread. Queues also allow more efficient use of resources because when the rate of incoming requests exceeds the capacity of the system, the requests are left on the queue until processing resources are available. Two examples of systems that use queues to manage input are web servers and database servers. SQL Server requests from clients are not queued, but processing on worker threads uses asynchronous queuing to improve scalability.

The queues in web servers and SQL Server are *in-memory queues*. If the system loses power or crashes, the queue entries are lost. The user gets a timeout or error, and tries again.

In many applications, you can improve throughput by using a *persistent queue* to decouple parts of the application. For example, a stock trading application might do the actual trade interactively, and then put the trade on a queue so the back-office settlement work can be done as a background activity. In this case, the trade is complete before the background processing starts, so an in-memory queue won't work because losing the trade information isn't an option. A queue in the database is ideal in this case because the trade information can be put on the queue as part of the trade transaction, and removed from the queue as part of the backend processing transaction. The ACID (Atomicity, Consistency, Isolation, Durability) properties of transactions will guarantee that the trade isn't lost before it is completely processed.

Though the advantages of using a database table as a queue are obvious, it has significant disadvantages. In a highly parallel system, there may be hundreds of threads adding items to and removing items from the queue. This often leads to blocking and deadlocks. One of the main things the Service Broker does is to make the queue a first-class SQL Server object. Because Service Broker queues are part of the database engine, the Service Broker logic can access locks, latches, and caches directly, so Service Broker queues are significantly more efficient than just using a table as a queue.

Service Broker is more than just queues integrated into the database. It provides the infrastructure required to create reliable, asynchronous database services that you can use to assemble database applications that would be difficult to create without database services. That's where the name "Service Broker" comes from—a broker for reliable, asynchronous, database services.

As with any service-oriented application, Service Broker applications need to be distributed. To accomplish this without sacrificing the reliability of Service Broker queues, messages must be passed between queues with reliable messaging. Service Broker uses a Microsoft-designed reliable message protocol that takes advantage of Service Broker queues to ensure that messages are transferred reliably with transactional integrity.

The integration of the reliable messaging protocol into the SQL Server engine provides unprecedented transactional messaging performance. Many people think of Service Broker as a reliable messaging feature. Although it does do reliable messaging, it also provides a complete service-oriented database architecture environment. Keep this in mind as you learn about the Service Broker functions. Some parts of the Service Broker interface may seem strange to the developer who just wants to send messages reliably between servers, but these parts make sense if you look at the Service Broker as a development environment for reliable, asynchronous database services.

SQL Server Service Broker can fit the bill in a variety of scenarios. It has been deployed successfully in applications where it handles extract, transform, and load (ETL) between an online transaction protocol (OLTP) database and a data warehouse in real time, in banking applications where it handles nightly batch processing of transaction data, in social media that handles friend requests on

MySpace, as well as a variety of other applications where the command needs to be completed reliably, just not at the exact time that the command was issued.

SQL Service Broker Overview

As just discussed, Service Broker enables you to build reliable, asynchronous services in a SQL Server database. Service Broker services communicate by passing messages reliably and transactionally. For maximum flexibility, Service Broker doesn't impose structure on the messages it passes. They contain up to 2GB of binary data. You can associate an XML schema with a message, and Service Broker will validate the data in the message against the schema. But this isn't necessary, and the message can contain anything from a resume document to a JPG file.

Messages sent to a Service Broker service are put on the queue associated with the service. The service processing logic is implemented by a stored procedure or external application that removes messages from the queue, processes them, and returns a response to the Service Broker that sent the original message. This is similar to a .NET Windows Communication Foundation (WCF) Web Service. A web service receives a Simple Object Access Protocol (SOAP) message, processes it, and returns another SOAP message.

One of the issues with any service is that code must be running to process messages as they arrive. This issue is normally addressed by having one or more background processes running continuously to process messages as they arrive. This works well in many cases, but if message arrival rates vary greatly—large peaks when work starts in the morning and when everyone returns from lunch, for example—there will be times when there aren't enough resources available to handle the message load.

Service Broker addresses the resource load issue with a process known as *activation*. The activation process has a background process called the *activation monitor* that watches for messages on a queue. If a message arrives and no queue reader process is available to process it, the monitor will start one. If messages continue to arrive faster than the queue reader process is processing them, the monitor will start additional queue readers until enough queue readers are available to keep up. The queue readers are written so that if they detect that the queue is empty, they terminate. In this way, the number of queue readers increases as the load increases, and decreases as the load decreases. This ensures that enough resources are available to process the incoming message volume without wasting resources when the load decreases.

Services depend on the bidirectional exchange of messages. Requests are made of the service and the service returns responses. Service Broker uses persistent objects called *conversations* to track these exchanges. A Service Broker conversation is an object at each end of the message exchange that tracks what messages have been sent, what messages have been received, what messages have been acknowledged, and what acknowledgments have been received. The conversation *endpoints* also contain the address and security information required for the reliable and secure exchange of messages between services.

Conversations are stored as persistent database objects that survive database restarts. Conversations may last for many months if the interaction with the service lasts that long. For example, an order for something very complex like an airplane may take many months, and involve the exchange of thousands of messages. This complex interaction can be handled by a single Service Broker conversation. The conversation will ensure that all messages are delivered reliably and securely, even if one of the endpoints is offline for a while.

SQL Server Service Broker introduces three new commands that are used to send and receive messages, all of which are discussed in more detail later in this chapter. The first is the CREATE CONVERSATION command that creates the conversation on which messages are then sent. The second is the SEND command that is used to send messages on the previously created conversation. The third is the RECEIVE command that is used to remove messages from the queue for processing.

The beauty of SQL Server Service Broker is that messages are processed once, and only once, and in the order sent, provided that the messages are sent within the same conversation. In most other reliable messaging protocols, timeouts and retries can change the order in which messages are delivered, and there is no guarantee that a message won't be delivered multiple times. Exactly once, in-order message delivery greatly simplifies the writing of Service Broker services. Ordering of messages between different conversations is not preserved by the Service Broker protocols.

SQL Server Service Broker versus Other Message Queues

A variety of message queuing technologies are available. Microsoft makes two: SQL Server Service Broker and Microsoft Message Queue (MSMQ). You can also use several third-party technologies that function similarly to MSMQ.

The big difference between SQL Server Service Broker and other queuing technologies is that SQL Server Service Broker is built into the database, while other queuing technologies run as external processes. This makes transactional messaging (where the operations that receive and send messages are in the same transaction as where the database updates are done as a result of the queue operations) significantly more efficient and reliable. SQL Server Service Broker stores its messages within the database. This makes the queues transactionally consistent with the data that the queues back up and restore along with the database. The upside to this is that if the database is restored, the same messages will still be there when the database is backed up. If you use a message queue such as MSMQ, when the database is restored to an older point in time, any messages that were processed since the database was backed up are lost.

This doesn't necessarily mean that SQL Server Service Broker is always a superior queuing technology over other message queuing technologies. In some places, SQL Server Service Broker makes more sense as the solution, and in some places a message queue outside of the database makes more sense.

For example, if you have two Windows services (or applications) that need to send messages to each other and don't already have a need to access a database, using SQL Server Service Broker would not be a good fit. This is true because it adds a dependency to SQL Server that doesn't already exist, because SQL Server would require the database to be online for the applications to send messages to each other. This occurs because the database must be online and available for the application to send messages into a SQL Server Service Broker queue. There is no way to send a message to the SQL Server Service Broker without directly logging in to the database. In this situation, a message queue such as MSMQ would be a better solution because MSMQ enables you to send messages without being logged in to the database.

Most messaging systems like MSMQ or MQ Series can do transactional messaging, but the transaction spans two different data stores—the message store and the database—so the transaction must be a distributed transaction requiring a more complex two-phase commit. Non-transactional or non-reliable messaging systems are generally faster than Service Broker because they don't involve transaction commits. But if transactional messaging is required, SQL Server Service Broker is significantly faster than most available messaging systems.

On the other hand, if you have a situation in which you have a Windows service (or application) that needs to send messages to a database, and the database needs to process that message directly using T-SQL (or even SQL Server CLR, or SQLCLR, code), the SQL Server Service Broker might be a good choice. The reason SQL Server Service Broker is the better option is because the application needs to log in to the database to get the message to the database, and the SQL Server Service Broker can only be accessed via T-SQL. It makes sense to store the messages in a queue that can be accessed by T-SQL directly without any third-party, extended stored procedures.

CONFIGURING SQL SERVER SERVICE BROKER

Service Broker is considered an advanced SQL Server feature, so there is only minimal support for configuring Service Broker in the SQL Server Management Studio. The Service Broker state is a property of the database that you can set from the database properties dialog box in SQL Server Management Studio or with the ALTER DATABASE T-SQL command. You can create the Service Broker objects using templates in the Service Broker section of the Programmability menu for each database, or with T-SQL commands. This discussion emphasizes the T-SQL commands because they are used most often when creating a Service Broker application.

> **NOTE** *Configuring SQL Server Service Broker can be complex because it uses a lot of new terms, which can make the entire process confusing. If you are unsure of a term's definition initially, keep reading, because the term will likely be defined as the discussion evolves.*

Setting Broker State

To enable or disable SQL Server Service Broker using SQL Server Management Studio, connect to the database in question in the Object Explorer. Right-click the database, select Properties, and then select the Options page. Under Other Options, scroll down to the Service Broker section, as shown in Figure 6-1. The Broker Enabled setting is the only setting that you can configure by selecting either True or False.

You can also enable SQL Server Service Broker with T-SQL by using the ALTER DATABASE statement. You have several options for setting the Service Broker state in addition to enabling and disabling the Service Broker. These states are used to manage copies of databases that contain Service Broker queues.

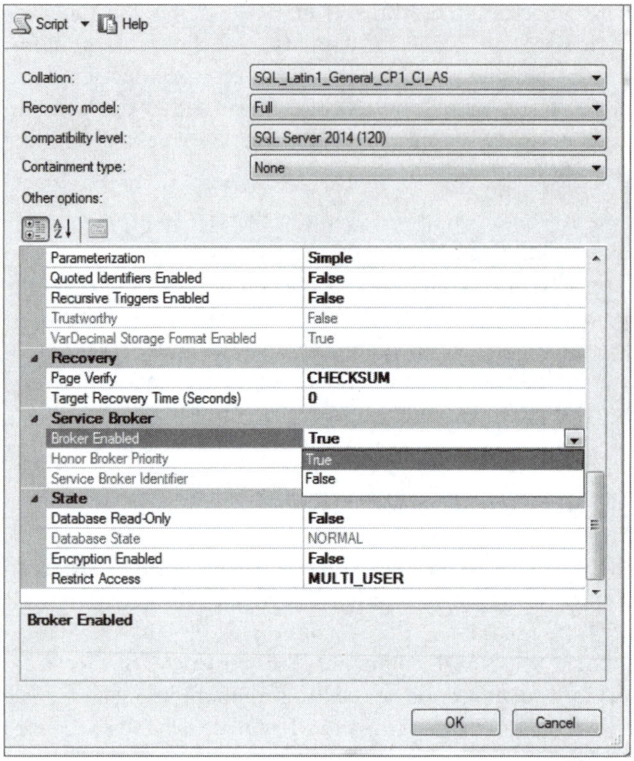

FIGURE 6-1

As mentioned previously, one of the advantages of Service Broker being built into the database is that the database can be backed up and restored (or detached and attached) without losing any messages. This feature allows a great deal of flexibility for disaster recovery or load-balancing situations where a database must be moved to a different server without losing undelivered or unprocessed messages. The downside of this feature is that if you use backup and restore (or attach) to create another copy of a database, you will now have two SQL Server databases trying to send and process the same messages.

To ensure that multiple databases don't try to send the same messages, Service Broker will be disabled by default when a database is restored or attached. If the database is being restored or attached to recover from an outage, there is an option in the RESTORE command to specify ENABLE_ BROKER so that Service Broker will be enabled when the restore finishes. If a database is restored without this option, you can use the ALTER DATABASE command to enable Service Broker. Following is an example:

```
ALTER DATABASE sample_database
SET ENABLE_BROKER
```

You can use several options to manage what happens to messages and conversations.

The first is the NEW_BROKER option that deletes all existing conversations and messages, and creates a new SERVICE_BROKER_GUID so that the database will look like a new Service Broker database configured exactly the same as the original database, but with a new identity. This is used for scaling out a Service Broker service by creating more copies of the database, or when creating a backup copy of a database for testing or development.

The second is the ERROR_BROKER_CONVERSATIONS option. In this case, the identity of Service Broker is unchanged, but any existing conversations are marked with an error status. This is done to clean up conversations in an orderly fashion so that both ends of the conversation are cleaned up and removed. The most common use for this would be after testing to ensure that the Service Broker environment is returned to a clean state.

You see if SQL Server Service Broker is enabled by looking at the value of the is_broker_enabled column of the sys.databases system catalog view. The is_broker_enabled column is a bit field with a value of either 0 or 1, where 1 indicates that Service Broker jobs are enabled for this database.

After SQL Server Service Broker has been enabled for a specific database, the SQL Server Service Broker objects can be created, and messages can be sent and received. When the Service Broker is enabled for a database, a few system tasks run to manage Service Broker objects in the database. If a database doesn't include any Service Broker objects, you should disable Service Broker to eliminate this unnecessary overhead. You can also disable Service Broker to prevent message processing as part of a maintenance process.

Message Types

The first object type that you need to create when configuring SQL Server Service Broker is a *message type*. The message type can be used by your service to determine what kind of data the message contains so that it knows how to process it. Message types optionally validate that the data within a message is in the expected format. You can use the following four different validation options:

➤ **NONE**—This means any data can be placed within the body of the message that is sent. When no value is specified for the VALIDATION option, the default value of NONE is used.

➤ **EMPTY**—This means only messages that are empty can be sent. Certain types of status messages don't need to have any data associated with them, so this type of message prevents the code that is calling the service from sending data that won't be processed.

➤ **WELL_FORMED_XML**—This means only messages consisting of well-formed XML documents can be sent. The message is parsed by an XML parser, and if the parser detects errors, the message is rejected by the service.

➤ **VALID_XML WITH SCHEMA COLLECTION**—This means only XML documents that fit with the specified XML schema can be used. The XML schema to use with the VALID_XML WITH SCHEMA COLLECTION option requires that the XML schema already exists within the database (which you accomplish by using the CREATE XML SCHEMA COLLECTION command).

The last two options are primarily used when a service can be called by any client that needs to use it. In many cases, a service is only called by a well-known set of clients, so the service can be sure that the incoming data is correct. In this case, you can improve performance by not validating the messages. Validation is expensive because the message must be loaded into an XML parser.

Beyond the validation option, the CREATE MESSAGE TYPE command has only two other options:

➤ The name of the message type, which must fit within the standard SQL Server object naming rules

➤ The AUTHORIZATION option, which sets the owner of the message type when it is created

When the person creating the message type is a member of the sysadmin fixed server role or the db_owner fixed database role, the value specified for AUTHORIZATION can be any valid database user or role. When the person creating the message type is not a member of the sysadmin fixed server role or the db_owner fixed database role, the value specified for AUTHORIZATION must be that user, or another user that the user in question has the rights to impersonate. If no value is specified for the AUTHORIZATION parameter, the message type belongs to the current user.

The following code snippet shows an example of the creation of a message type:

```
CREATE MESSAGE TYPE YourMessageType
AUTHORIZATION dbo
VALIDATION = WELL_FORMED_XML
```

Contracts

The second object type to create is a *contract*. Contracts define the message types that can be used within a conversation. A contract ensures that the code processing a conversation will not receive messages it doesn't know how to process. Similar to message types, contracts have a couple of parameters that must be specified when using the CREATE CONTRACT statement:

➤ The name of the contract, which must follow the standard SQL Server object naming rules

➤ The AUTHORIZATION value, which must be a user or role that exists within the database

The CREATE CONTRACT statement requires a specific list of message types that are bound to the contract, and each message type can only be used by a specific participant in the conversation. Following are the three options available for the service that can use each message type:

➤ **INITIATOR**—The SQL Server Service Broker SERVICE that initiated the conversation with the BEGIN DIALOG CONVERSATION command. (SERVICE is discussed in more detail later in this chapter.)

➤ **TARGET**—The SQL Server Service Broker SERVICE that INITIATOR targeted.

➤ **ANY**—Both the TARGET and the INITIATOR can use the message type. You can specify multiple message types with a comma-separated list, as shown in the following code examples:

```
CREATE CONTRACT MyContract
AUTHORIZATION dbo
(YourMessageType SENT BY ANY)
CREATE CONTRACT MyContract
AUTHORIZATION dbo
(YourMessageType SENT BY INITIATOR,
AnotherMessageType SENT BY TARGET)
```

Queues

The third object types you can create are *queues*. As discussed earlier in this chapter, queues are where the messages within the SQL Server Service Broker are stored in the time period between when they are received and when they are processed. Although the rest of the objects created are logical objects made up only of records in system tables, queues are physical objects that create physical tables under them that store the actual messages.

Because queues are physical tables, one of the many options available to the person creating the queue is the file group that will contain the queue. Note that queues are hidden tables that can't be accessed directly. You can SEND messages to queues and RECEIVE messages from queues, but you can't use INSERT, UPDATE, or DELETE statements with queues.

When creating the queue, you can specify several other options. All these choices are optional, with the exception of the name of the queue.

The first option is the STATUS of the queue, which can be ON or OFF. When a queue is ON, it is available to receive messages, and messages can be received from the queue. When a queue has a STATUS of OFF, and a stored procedure or other T-SQL code attempts to RECEIVE messages from the queue, the RECEIVE command returns an error message. The STATUS option defaults to ON.

The second option is RETENTION, which can be ON or OFF. When message retention is ON after messages are received, they are not removed from the queue; they are instead kept for auditing purposes. Although the messages cannot be received a second time, they can remain on disk, and you can view them later by selecting them with the SELECT statement with the queue name in the FROM clause. When message retention is OFF, the messages are removed from the queue as soon as they are received.

> **NOTE** *Although the retention option on the queues is great for auditing purposes, there is one downside: there is no way to easily purge some of the data from the queue. You can use the ALTER QUEUE command to change the RETENTION from ON to OFF, which would then purge all the data in the queue. However, if you wanted to purge only some data (for example, all data except for the last 90 days), there is no built-in way to do it. You would instead need to export the last 90 days' worth of data into a table and then purge all the data. The retention option makes most sense while developing applications. Retention can then be used to debug problems by retaining exactly what messages were received by the application. Retention should not be used in production.*

The third option is POISON_MESSAGE_HANDLING, which can be ON or OFF. When poison message handling is enabled on a queue (which is the default), it causes the queue to automatically disable after five consecutive transaction rollbacks. When poison message handling is disabled, the message handling must be handled within the application.

A poison message is a common problem in transactional messaging. While processing a message, an error causes the transaction to roll back, which puts the message back on the queue. This is a good thing if the error is caused by a transient condition like a deadlock, because the next time the message is read, it will be processed successfully. On the other hand, if the error is permanent—something like trying to insert a row into a table with a duplicate primary key—the message processing will loop indefinitely, thus preventing other messages from being processed. This is called a *poison message*.

Poison message handling should be built into the service. For example, an error that won't be corrected by a retry should be logged, and the transaction committed to get the poison message off the queue. If a poison message slips past the service logic, Service Broker will, by default, disable the queue if five transactions in a row are rolled back. This is a drastic solution, because the whole queue stops processing. But if your service is written correctly, it should never happen. If you are confident that your application handles poison messages correctly, and you want to avoid the call in the middle of the night that a queue has been disabled, feel free to turn off poison message handling for the queue.

The fourth option is the ACTIVATION stored procedure configuration, which is made up of four child settings:

➤ **STATUS**—Under the ACTIVATION setting, STATUS is used to enable or disable the activation procedure. When ACTIVATION is disabled, it stops only new threads of the activated stored procedure from being spawned; already running threads are left running.

➤ **PROCEDURE_NAME**—This parameter is the name of the stored procedure that should be activated.

➤ **MAX_QUEUE_READERS**—This is the maximum number of copies of the stored procedure that can be activated. Additional copies of the activation procedure are created as long as messages are arriving faster than the activation procedures are processing them. To keep a single queue from consuming too many resources, you can set a maximum number of procedures allowed for a queue. You can change the maximum dynamically while Service Broker is running if too many messages are accumulating on a queue.

➤ **EXECUTE AS**—This parameter specifies the username that the procedure should be run as. The values that you can specify are SELF, OWNER, or any valid user within the database. SELF means execute as the user calling the service. OWNER means execute as the user who created the queue.

The following code shows the various options that you can specify:

```
CREATE QUEUE YourQueue_Source
WITH STATUS=ON,
     RETENTION=OFF,
     ACTIVATION
         (STATUS=ON,
          PROCEDURE_NAME=dbo.MySourceActivationProcedure,
          MAX_QUEUE_READERS=10,
          EXECUTE AS OWNER),
     POISON_MESSAGE_HANDLING (STATUS = ON);
```

When creating a queue that has an activated stored procedure, you can configure the activated procedure when the queue is created, as shown in the preceding code snippet. However, the stored procedure must exist before the queue can be created using this method. Because of this, the queue is often created without configuring the ACTIVATION settings. Instead, the stored procedure is created and the queue is altered using the ALTER QUEUE command to set the activation settings. The end result of creating a queue while enabling the activation settings would be the same as if the queue were created without enabling the activation settings. In either case, the queue would call the stored procedure when messages were received in the queue.

Services

SQL Server Service Broker service objects define the interface a service exposes. Service Broker services are objects that you configure via the CREATE SERVICE statement in T-SQL. Services specify which contracts (and, therefore, which message types) can be used when sending messages to a specific queue. When messages are sent, they are sent to a specific service that then delivers the message into a specific queue. You send messages to a Service Broker service by using the name of the service as the destination. The actual name of the queue that receives the messages and the route that messages take to get to the queue are hidden behind the abstraction of the service name. This means that the physical implementation of a Service Broker service can change without requiring changes to the calling applications because the same service name is used.

CREATE SERVICE has only a few parameters that you can set:

➤ **Object name**—Like other objects, this setting follows the normal object-naming standards. Be sure to use capitalization that makes sense because, in some cases, the service name is case-sensitive.

➤ **AUTHORIZATION**—This works just like the AUTHORIZATION parameter when creating a message type or contract.

➤ **Queue name**—This is the name of the queue to which the messages sent to the service will be delivered.

➤ **Comma-separated list of contracts**—You can use this when creating conversations sent to this service.

Following is an example:

```
CREATE SERVICE YourService_Source
AUTHORIZATION dbo
ON QUEUE dbo.YourQueue_Source
(MyContract)
GO
```

When creating a queue for each side of the conversation, you must also create a service for each side of the conversation. Messages are sent from a service to a service. You specify these service names when using the BEGIN DIALOG CONVERSATION statement, which is explained in more detail later in this chapter.

> **NOTE** *When selecting the name for your services, do not select the name ANY. Within SQL Server Service Broker, the service name ANY is a reserved word that causes Service Broker priorities (discussed later in this chapter) to be applied to all services instead of to the specific service called ANY.*

Routes

Service Broker Route objects are used to define the network path that messages to a service follow. A route contains the name of the service that messages are being routed to, and the network address of the next SQL Server on the route. The route continues until a server is found where the address is set to "local," which means that this is the server where the service is located.

A route created in every database called AutoCreatedLocal is the default for all services that have no other routes specified. This route has no service name specified, which means it is used for any services that don't have a route specified. The address for this route is "local," which means that messages are routed to the local database server.

You can create routes in the database where the Service Broker is running, or in the MSDB database. The MSDB routes are used for forwarding messages. Forwarded messages come into the SQL Server instance and leave again without landing in any database.

Routes have a variety of parameters that you can configure via the CREATE ROUTE statement, including the following:

➤ **Name of the route**—This is the name of the route and follows the normal object naming rules.

➤ **Name of the service**—This is the name of the service to which the route should apply. You can either specify the name of the specific service, or you can omit the service name from the CREATE ROUTE statement, which causes the route to apply to all services. When specifying the service name as part of the CREATE ROUTE statement, the service name is always case-sensitive, ignoring the databases collation setting. The reason for this is that the SQL Server does a binary compare of the route's service setting and the service name within the database. Because uppercase and lowercase characters have different binary values, if a single character does not match, the route will not apply.

➤ **BROKER_INSTANCE**—This optional parameter indicates the route to which database on the server to send the messages. The BROKER_INSTANCE value can be queried from the service_ broker_guid column of the sys.databases catalog view on the instance that hosts the database to which the route is pointing. If the BROKER_INSTANCE value is not specified, SQL Server Service Broker attempts to identify the destination database on the instance based on matching the destination service name with the service names in the databases on the remote instance. If two or more routes with the same service name without database instances are specified, Service Broker assumes that the services are part of a scale-out set, so messages are routed to the available routes randomly.

➤ **LIFETIME**—This optional parameter indicates to SQL Server Service Broker for how many seconds the route should be active. When the lifetime of the route has expired, the route will be ignored. If the LIFETIME is omitted or a value of NULL is specified, the route will never expire. There aren't many use-cases for temporary routes, so LIFETIME is seldom specified.

➤ **ADDRESS**—This required parameter tells SQL Server Service Broker how to contact the remote database. This parameter can specify an IP address, a network name, or a fully qualified domain name followed by the TCP port number of the service broker endpoint that must be created on the remote instance. This is in the format of TCP://ServerName:PortNumber.

If the destination database is located on the same instance as the source database, you can specify the ADDRESS parameter as LOCAL. If the parameter is specified as TRANSPORT, Service Broker attempts to identify to which remote instance to connect, based on the name of the service. In this case, the service name is a URL. TRANSPORT routes are generally used for return addresses where hundreds of clients may send messages to the same service, so it doesn't make sense for the target service to maintain routes to hundreds of callers.

➤ **MIRROR_ADDRESS**—This optional parameter configures the route to support database mirroring if the destination database is configured for database mirroring. If the destination database is configured for database mirroring and the MIRROR_ADDRESS is not specified, and the database were to fail over to the mirror instance, the messages would not be delivered until the database failed back to the instance specified in the ADDRESS parameter. You should specify the value of the MIRROR_ADDRESS parameter in the same format at the ADDRESS parameter. When a MIRROR_ADDRESS is specified, Service Broker automatically sends messages to whichever server is currently the primary SQL Server in the mirror pair.

The following code snippet shows how to use various parameters when using the CREATE ROUTE statement:

```
CREATE ROUTE ExpenseRoute
    WITH SERVICE_NAME = 'MyService',
    BROKER_INSTANCE = '53FA2363-BF93-4EB6-A32D-F672339E08ED',
    ADDRESS = 'TCP://sql2:1234',
    MIRROR_ADDRESS = 'TCP://sql4:4567' ;
```

> **NOTE** *You will find that when remote service names are specified in Service Broker, they are always entered as case-sensitive strings. This is because the Service Broker architecture allows remote services to be non-Windows, non–SQL Server services that may not follow SQL Server naming rules. Although all Service Broker services are currently Windows SQL Server–based, the commands are structured to handle different service types in the future.*

Priorities

In many messaging applications, some messages are more important than others. Priorities are used to ensure that important messages are processed before unimportant messages. Messages in a Service Broker conversation are always processed in the order they were put into the conversation, so priorities on messages within a conversation are meaningless. Service Broker priorities are assigned to conversations.

SQL Server Service Broker priorities assign priorities to conversations to force higher-priority conversations to always be processed before lower-priority conversations. This can be important in high-load environments in which some messages must be processed before others. You assign the conversation priority by matching the name of the contract, the source service name, and the destination service name to what was configured in the Service Broker priority.

Because you don't specifically set a conversation's priority when the conversation is created, it is wise to create multiple contracts, all of which use the same message types, and are configured to be used for the specified services. You can use priorities to create a high-priority conversation and a lower-priority conversation by creating a contract with the name ContractLow and a second contract named ContractHigh. Then a priority could be named that triggers on the ContractHigh, which has a high-priority level assigned.

You create SQL Server Service Broker priorities via T-SQL using the CREATE BROKER PRIORITY statement. This statement accepts five different values:

➤   The first is the name of the priority.

➤   The next three values enable you to specify which conversations the priority will apply to. You can specify the conversation name, the local service name, and the remote service name to identify conversations. For any of these three parameters you can specify the special value of ANY, which means that parameter isn't considered in deciding which priority to assign to a conversation.

➤   The last parameter is the priority level that will be used for the conversations to which this priority will be applied. The priority can be any whole number from 1 through 10 with 10 being the highest priority. Conversations that do not have a specific priority applied to them are assigned the priority of 5.

The following code snippet shows how to use the CREATE BROKER PRIORITY statement. Here, a message sent to any service using the contract name MyHighPriority would be given the priority of 8 instead of the default of 5.

```
CREATE BROKER PRIORITY HighPriority
FOR CONVERSATION
SET ( CONTRACT_NAME = MyHighPriority ,
      LOCAL_SERVICE_NAME = ANY ,
      REMOTE_SERVICE_NAME = N'ANY' ,
      PRIORITY_LEVEL = 8
)
```

Messages are always received in priority order. Messages are sent in priority order if the Honor_Broker_Priority option is set to TRUE for the database.

Conversation Groups

One of the more difficult problems to deal with when building highly scalable queue-oriented applications is managing multiple threads reading the queue simultaneously. If the messages aren't related to each other, this works well. But if multiple messages are involved in the same operation, there is a possibility that messages being processed on different threads will conflict with each other.

For example, suppose an order-processing service sends out messages to an inventory service and a shipping service. When these services complete, they will send back result messages. When the order-processing service receives the results, it will update the order. If the two results return at the same time, and end up being processed on two separate threads, it's possible that the updates will conflict, and the order will be corrupted.

Messages within a conversation are not an issue because a message can't be received until the previous message has been processed. But this doesn't apply for different conversations created for the same operation. To resolve this issue, you can group related conversations into a *conversation group*. When a message in a conversation group is being processed, a conversation group lock is held that prevents other threads from processing messages from any conversation in the group. This means that although the queue processing can be massively parallel, the processing for messages in a conversation group is single-threaded—significantly simplifying the programming necessary to process messages.

By default, each conversation is put into its own conversation group unless a conversation group is specified when the conversation is created. You can specify the conversation group into which the new conversation should be placed in two ways:

➤ By specifying the conversation group that should be used

➤ By specifying the handle of the conversation with which the new conversation should be grouped

There is no specific command to create a new conversation group. When a new conversation is started, a new group is created automatically, and it is assigned a new GUID value as its identifier. To assign new conversations to a specific conversation group, you simply assign a new GUID value as the RELATED_CONVERSATION_GROUP parameter for the BEGIN DIALOG CONVERSATION statement, which is covered later in this chapter.

You can query the conversation group that the next message to be processed is a member of by using the GET CONVERSATION GROUP statement. To use this statement, specify a variable that the next conversation group will be placed into, as well as the name of the queue to get the conversation group from, as shown in the following code:

```
DECLARE @conversation_group_id AS UNIQUEIDENTIFIER;
GET CONVERSATION GROUP @conversation_group_id
FROM YourQueue;
```

USING SQL SERVER SERVICE BROKER

Sending and receiving messages through SQL Server Service Broker is a basic task. Instead of using INSERT to put messages into the queue (like you would do with a table) and SELECT to pull messages from the queue, you use the SEND statement to send messages and the RECEIVE statement to pull messages from the queue.

Sending Messages

You can send messages by using the SEND command. The SEND command accepts only two parameters: the conversation ID and the body of the message, as shown in the following code snippet. You can get the conversation ID from the BEGIN DIALOG CONVERSATION command, as shown in the previous code snippet used to assign priorities.

```
DECLARE @message_body AS XML, @dialog_handle as UNIQUEIDENTIFIER
SET @message_body = (SELECT *
    FROM sys.all_objects as object
```

```
      FOR XML AUTO, root('root'))
BEGIN DIALOG CONVERSATION @dialog_handle
    FROM SERVICE [YourSourceService]
    TO SERVICE 'YourDestinationService'
    ON CONTRACT [YourContract];
SEND ON CONVERSATION @dialog_handle
MESSAGE TYPE YourMessageType
(@message_body)
GO
```

As of the release of SQL Server 2012, the SEND command accepts a comma-separated list of conversation IDs. When more than one conversation ID is specified, a copy of the message is sent to each remote service specified by the conversation list. This is not only easier to code than doing multiple SENDs with a single conversation, but Service Broker also manages the conversations, so only one copy of the message is maintained on the sending side. This is considerably more efficient. This feature is called *multicasting*.

The BEGIN DIALOG CONVERSATION command accepts several parameters, some of which are required, and some of which are optional.

The first three parameters are required.

➤ Two parameters are the source and destination services that you use to send the message, as well as the contract from and to, respectively. Optionally, after the destination service name, you can specify the service broker GUID of the destination database, or CURRENT DATABASE. This parameter is required if there is more than one service with the same name.

➤ The third parameter is the contract that defines the message types used to send the messages.

The rest of the parameters are all optional:

➤ RELATED_CONVERSATION—This specifies a certain conversation group that relates the new conversation to another conversation. It accepts the conversation ID from another preexisting conversation.

➤ RELATED_CONVERSATION_GROUP—This also specifies a certain conversation group that relates the new conversation to another conversation. It accepts a specific conversation group ID of which the new conversation would then be a member.

➤ LIFETIME—This specifies the amount of time that the conversation remains open. The LIFETIME is the number of seconds until the conversation closes automatically. The LIFETIME value is expressed as an integer data type with the default being the maximum value of the INT data type, which is $2^{31}-1$ (2,147,483,647)—68 years.

➤ ENCRYPTION—This specifies whether the messages within the conversation should be encrypted while in transmission to another instance of SQL Server. This parameter accepts only ON or OFF, and encryption is ON by default. When sending messages between database instances, it is highly recommended that encryption be ON. When ENCRYPTION is ON and messages are sent within the same instance while the data isn't actually encrypted, the database master key and the certificates needed for the encryption are required for the conversation to successfully begin and to send the message.

The code shown earlier represents great start, but it isn't good for high-performance SQL Server Service Broker workloads. This is because the cost of creating a conversation for each message is expensive. When working with high-load systems that send hundreds of thousands or millions of messages per day, you want to reuse conversations sending multiple messages per conversation to reduce the overhead of sending messages. You can easily do this by logging the conversation handle (the value of the @dialog_handle value that is set in the BEGIN DIALOG CONVERSATION command) to a table so that it can be retrieved by future sessions. A table like this is shown in following code snippet:

```
CREATE TABLE dbo.SSB_Settings
([Source] sysname NOT NULL,
[Destination] sysname NOT NULL,
[Contract] sysname NOT NULL,
[dialog_handle] uniqueidentifier
CONSTRAINT PK_SSB_Setting PRIMARY KEY ([Source], [Destination], [Contract])
```

One key requirement for using multiple messages per conversation is that there must be a way for the sending side of the conversation to tell the receiving side of the conversation that there will be no more messages sent over that conversation. An easy way to do this is to have an additional message type within the database that is specifically used as a trigger on the destination side so that it knows when to end the conversation.

In a high-load environment, you could use a stored procedure to decide if a new conversation should be created, as well as storing the value as needed. Listing 6-1 (code file: Chapter6Code.sql) shows the send_sequence value from the sys.conversation_endpoints Dynamic Management View (DMV) to decide if it is time to end the conversation. Notice that a message type named EndOfConversation is used to trigger the remote side to close the conversation.

LISTING 6-1: Creating a Reusable Conversation.sql

```
CREATE PROCEDURE dbo.CreateConversation
     @Destination sysname,
     @Source sysname,
     @Contract sysname,
     @MessageType sysname,
     @MessageBody XML,
     @dialog_handle uniqueidentifier
AS
/*Get the conversation id.*/
SELECT @dialog_handle = dialog_handle
FROM dbo.SSB_Settings
WHERE [Source] = @Source
     AND [Destination] = @Destination
     AND [Contract] = @Contract;
/*If there is no current handle create a new conversation.*/
IF @dialog_handle IS NULL
BEGIN
     BEGIN TRANSACTION
     /*If there is a conversation dialog handle signal the destination
```

continues

LISTING 6-1 *(continued)*

```
    code that the old conversation is dead.*/
    IF @dialog_handle IS NOT NULL
    BEGIN
        UPDATE dbo.SSB_Settings
        SET dialog_handle = NULL
        WHERE [Source] = @Source
            AND [Destination] = @Destination
            AND [Contract] = @Contract;
        SEND ON CONVERSATION @dialog_handle
        MESSAGE TYPE EndOfConversation;
    END
    /*Setup the new conversation*/
    BEGIN DIALOG CONVERSATION @dialog_handle
    FROM SERVICE @Source
    TO SERVICE @Destination
    ON CONTRACT @Contract;
    /*Log the new conversation ID*/
    UPDATE dbo.SSB_Settings
        SET dialog_handle = @dialog_handle
    WHERE [Source] = @Source
        AND [Destination] = @Destination
        AND [Contract] = @Contract;
    IF @@ROWCOUNT = 0
        INSERT INTO dbo.SSB_Settings
          ([Source], [Destination], [Contract], [dialog_handle])
        VALUES
          (@Source, @Destination, @Contract, @dialog_handle);
END;
/*Send the message*/
SEND ON CONVERSATION @dialog_handle
MESSAGE TYPE @MessageType
(@XML);
/*Verify that the conversation handle is still the one logged in the table.
  If not then mark this conversation as done.*/
IF (SELECT dialog_handle
    FROM dbo.SSB_Settings
    WHERE [Source] = @Source
        AND [Destination] = @Destination
        AND [Contract] = @Contract) <> @dialog_handle
    SEND ON CONVERSATION @dialog_handle
        MESSAGE TYPE EndOfConversation;
GO
```

Receiving Messages

You receive messages by using the RECEIVE command. The RECEIVE command is written much like a SELECT statement. You can specify the columns that should be returned, and the queue is specified as a FROM statement, as shown in the following code snippet. After the data has been received into a variable, anything that needs to be done with it can be done.

```
DECLARE  @dialog_handle UNIQUEIDENTIFIER, @messagetype nvarchar(128),
     @message_body XML;

BEGIN TRANSACTION;
RECEIVE TOP (1) @dialog_handle = conversation_handle,
     @messagetype = [message_type_name],
     @message_body = CAST(message_body as XML)
FROM MyDestinationQueue
IF @@ROWCOUNT = 0
     BEGIN
          COMMIT TRANSACTION;
     END
ELSE IF @messagetype = N'http://schemas.microsoft.com/SQL/ServiceBroker/Error'
     BEGIN
          -- log the error in you application's log
          END CONVERSATION @dialog_handle;
          COMMIT TRANSACTION;
     END
ELSE IF @messagetype = N'http://schemas.microsoft.com/SQL/ServiceBroker/EndDialog'
     BEGIN
          END CONVERSATION @dialog_handle;
          COMMIT TRANSACTION;
     END
ELSE
     BEGIN
/*Do whatever needs to be done with your XML document*/
          COMMIT TRANSACTION;
     END
```

However, the basic code in this example is not the most efficient way to receive data. It is more efficient to receive multiple messages at once, and to receive the message body from the queue as the raw binary, and then convert it to XML (or whatever data type it was sent as) after it has been removed from the queue.

The following code shows how to receive multiple messages in a single statement:

```
DECLARE @dialog_handle UNIQUEIDENTIFIER, @message_body XML,
     @message_type nvarchar(128)
DECLARE @Messages TABLE
(conversation_handle uniqueidentifier,
message_type sysname,
message_body VARBINARY(MAX))
BEGIN TRANSACTION
WAITFOR (
     RECEIVE TOP (1000) conversation_handle, message_type_name, message_body
     FROM MyDestinationQueue
     INTO @Messages), TIMEOUT 5000;
     DECLARE cur CURSOR FOR select conversation_handle, message_type,
          CAST(message_body AS XML)
                    FROM @Messages
                    WHERE message_body IS NOT NULL
OPEN cur
FETCH NEXT FROM cur INTO @dialog_handle, @message_type, @message_body
```

```
WHILE @@FETCH_STATUS = 0
BEGIN
IF @message_type = N'http://schemas.microsoft.com/SQL/ServiceBroker/Error'
    BEGIN
            -- log the error in you application's log
            END CONVERSATION @dialog_handle;
    END
ELSE IF @message_type = N'http://schemas.microsoft.com/SQL/ServiceBroker/EndDialog'
    BEGIN
            END CONVERSATION @dialog_handle;
    END
ELSE
    BEGIN
/*Do whatever needs to be done with your XML document*/
            SELECT @message_body
    END
    FETCH NEXT FROM cur INTO @dialog_handle, @message_body
END
CLOSE cur
DEALLOCATE cur;
IF EXISTS (SELECT * FROM @Messages WHERE message_type = 'EndOfConversation')
    END CONVERSATION @dialog_handle
COMMIT TRANSACTION
GO
```

Sending Messages between Instances

One of the most powerful features of SQL Server Service Broker is its capability to send messages between databases on different instances, which run on different physical (or virtual) servers. Configuring Service Broker to send messages between instances is effectively the same as configuring Service Broker to send messages between databases on the same SQL Server instance. The major difference lies in the steps needed to configure the authorization of communications between the instances.

These steps are outlined here. You should perform them on both of the instances that will be exchanging SQL Service Broker messages.

1. Configure the database master key in the master database. This key will be used to encrypt the database master keys.

2. Configure the database master key in the application database. These keys will be used to protect certificates stored in databases.

3. Create a certificate in each database.

4. Exchange the certificates between the databases.

5. Create SQL Service Broker endpoints on each instance.

6. Configure routes to connect to the remote instance SQL Service Broker endpoint.

After you complete these steps, messages can route between the two databases.

Database Master Key

As just described, before you begin using Service Broker between instances, you must enable the database master key for both databases by using the CREATE MASTER KEY statement on both databases. If this has already been done, you do not need to do it again. Creating the master key is quite simple, as shown in the following code snippet, because the command accepts only a single parameter, which is the password used to secure the database master key.

```
CREATE MASTER KEY ENCRYPTION BY PASSWORD = 'YourSecurePassword1!'
```

The database master key is a symmetric key used to protect all the other keys within the database, including other symmetric keys, certificates, and asymmetric keys.

After you create the database master key, back it up using the BACKUP MASTER KEY statement so that the master key can be recovered if a database failure occurs. Store the backup of the database master key at a secure offsite location.

Creating Certificates

When using certificate authentication between the endpoints, you must create certificates in the master databases of the instances that exchange messages. You can create certificates using the CREATE CERTIFICATE statement within the master database, as shown in the following code snippet. When creating the certificates on each instance, assign a unique name to each one. The easiest way to do this is to include the server and instance name in the name of the certificate.

```
CREATE CERTIFICATE MyServiceBrokerCertificate
WITH SUBJECT = 'Service Broker Certificate',
     START_DATE = '1/1/2013',
     EXPIRY_DATE = '12/31/2099'
```

The certificates created with this command are called *self-signed certificates* because they are signed with internal keys. Certificates signed by a certificate authority are considered more secure, but self-signed certificates are generally adequate for Service Broker endpoint security.

Exchanging Certificates

Once you create the certificates, you must exchange them. You can exchange certificates between instances by backing up the certificate. On the machine that has the certificate, use the BACKUP CERTIFICATE statement, as shown in the following code. You must then restore the certificate to the remote instance using the CREATE CERTIFICATE statement, as shown in the second code snippet.

```
BACKUP CERTIFICATE MyServiceBrokerCertificate
    TO FILE='C:\MyServiceBrokerCertificate.cer'

CREATE CERTIFICATE MyServiceBrokerCertificate
FROM FILE='c:\MyServiceBrokerCertificate.cer'
```

SQL Service Broker Endpoints

Endpoints enable users or other SQL Servers to connect to the SQL Server instance on which the endpoint is created. For SQL Server instances to send messages to another instance, you must create endpoints on each SQL Server instance.

You can create endpoints using the CREATE ENDPOINT statement, as shown in the following code. Each SQL Server instance can have only one Service Broker endpoint; even if multiple instances send messages to a single server, all communication must be done through a single endpoint. Service Broker endpoints support a variety of authentication techniques including NTLM-, KERBEROS-, and CERTIFICATE-based authentication, as well as several combinations of those three authentication techniques. When doing cross-instance authentication for SQL Service Broker, messaging CERTIFICATE authentication is recommended because it removes the dependency on Active Directory.

```
USE master
GO
CREATE ENDPOINT ServiceBrokerEndpoint
STATE = STARTED
AS TCP (LISTENER_PORT = 1234, LISTENER_IP=ALL)
FOR SERVICE_BROKER
(AUTHENTICATION = CERTIFICATE MyServiceBrokerCertificate,
    ENCRYPTION = REQUIRED ALGORITHM AES);
GO
```

You can also configure encryption on the endpoint with the encryption being either DISABLED, SUPPORTED, or REQUIRED. Encryption is supported using both the RC4 or Advanced Encryption Standard (AES) algorithms, as well as combinations of both algorithms specified as AES RC4 and RC4 AES. RC4 isn't considered secure anymore, so you should use AES in all cases.

When configuring the SQL Server Service Broker endpoint, you must specify a specific TCP port (separate from the default SQL Server TCP port on which the instance is listening). You must also specify the IP address on which the endpoint should be listening. In the preceding code example, TCP port 1234 is used to listen on, and the endpoint can listen on all IP addresses that are configured on the server on which the instance runs. If the endpoint should listen only on a specific IP address, you should specify the IPv4 or IPv6 address where the LISTENER_IP setting is specified.

External Activation

External activation is different from the normal activated stored procedures, which are available via the CREATE QUEUE or the ALTER QUEUE statements. External activation runs as a separate Windows service (ssbea.exe), which monitors the SQL Server queue waiting for new messages to arrive in the queue.

When a new message arrives in the queue, the external activation service launches the Windows application that it is configured to run. The external activation service monitors the SQL Server Service Broker queue by having you configure an event notification on your queue, which then sends a message to a second monitoring queue. When a message arrives in the application queue, the event notification sends a message to the notification queue, which causes the external activation service to launch the application.

WHY USE EXTERNAL ACTIVATION?

Several cases exist in which people use an external activation service. The most common involves something happening outside of the SQL Server after something has happened within the SQL Server.

continued

For example, imagine files are stored on a file server and each file matches up to a row within a SQL Server table. You want to ensure that every time a row is deleted, the file is deleted as well, and the external activation process is a good way to accomplish this. To do so, you can set up a trigger on delete for the database table, and have that trigger send a message to a queue with the file information to delete. Then, the external activator would see that a message has arrived and launch the application that deletes the file from the file server. The application would then read the queue to which the trigger sent the message and delete the file based on the data within the message.

You could use another technique to perform this same action without using external activation, though. You could have the application that deletes the files run as a service looking into the queue every minute for messages to process. This, however, would be less efficient than using the external activation service, and, therefore, makes external activation the better option.

You could use the following sample code snippet to create the event notification. (You can download the external activation service from `http://filedir.com/windows/servers/microsoft-sql-server-2012-service-broker-external-activator-2586093.html`.)

```
CREATE QUEUE dbo.MyDestinationQueueEA
GO
CREATE SERVICE MyDestinationServiceEA
ON QUEUE dbo.MyDestinationQueueEA
(
    [http://schemas.microsoft.com/SQL/Notifications/PostEventNotification]
)
GO
CREATE EVENT NOTIFICATION MyDestinationNotificationEA
ON QUEUE MyDestinationQueue
FOR QUEUE_ACTIVATION
TO SERVICE 'MyDestinationServiceEA', 'current database'
GO
```

The code in this snippet assumes that the event notification and all the SQL Server Service Broker objects are created in the same database, which is why `'current database'` has been specified.

Log User Example

To put together all you have learned, this chapter concludes with a complete example of a simple Service Broker application. This application is based on one of the earliest production applications implemented with Service Broker.

A large software company had a number of remote desktop servers that employees use to access the network from outside the domain. The security rules required that each login be recorded in a central database before access to the network succeeds. This meant that if the database server was down, remote access was not available. The company did not use Service Broker conversations to send login records to the database server. When the logging server is not available, messages were queued for processing later, and logins continued.

The following script creates the Service Broker objects and stored procedure required to receive messages and insert them into a logging table (code file: LogUserReceiveSetup.sql):

```
CREATE DATABASE LogReceiveExample
GO
USE LogReceiveExample
GO
CREATE MASTER KEY ENCRYPTION BY PASSWORD = 'YourSecurePassword1!'
GO
ALTER DATABASE LogReceiveExample SET TRUSTWORTHY ON
GO
-- You may not need to do this. I do it so I can run the example on a laptop that's
-- not connected to a doamin.  The other alternative would be to create the
-- databases as a SQL Server authenticated user instead of as a Windows
-- authenticated user.
-- If you are running this on a server connected to a domain, then this
-- isn't required.
ALTER AUTHORIZATION ON DATABASE::LogReceiveExample TO SA
GO

-- Create the Service Broker obects that define the conversation
CREATE MESSAGE TYPE LoginMessage
AUTHORIZATION dbo
VALIDATION = NONE
GO

CREATE CONTRACT LoginContract
AUTHORIZATION dbo
(LoginMessage SENT BY ANY)
GO

-- This is the table that stores the records sent from the client
CREATE TABLE dbo.LoginRecords
(LoginEntry varchar(MAX))
GO

CREATE PROCEDURE dbo.ReceiveQueueHandler
AS
RETURN;
GO

ALTER PROCEDURE dbo.ReceiveQueueHandler
AS
BEGIN -- ReceiveQueueHandler
    DECLARE  @dialog_handle UNIQUEIDENTIFIER, @messagetype nvarchar(128);
    -- Create a table variable to hold received messages
    DECLARE @LoginMessage TABLE (
    [conversation_handle] uniqueidentifier,
    message_type_name nvarchar(128),
    [message_body] varchar(MAX)
    )
    -- Main receive loop
```

```
    WHILE (1 = 1)
        BEGIN
        BEGIN TRY
            BEGIN TRANSACTION;

            WAITFOR (
                RECEIVE TOP (1000) -- Receiving many messages at a
--time is more efficient
                    [conversation_handle],
                    [message_type_name],
                    CAST(message_body AS varchar(MAX)) AS LoginEntry
                FROM LoginReceiveQueue
                INTO @LoginMessage
            ), TIMEOUT 100;
            -- If no messages received, bail out
            IF @@ROWCOUNT = 0
                BEGIN
                    COMMIT TRANSACTION;
                    BREAK;
                END
            ELSE
                BEGIN
                    -- Check to see if system messages were received
                    SELECT TOP (1) @dialog_handle = [conversation_handle],
                        @messagetype = [message_type_name]
                    FROM @LoginMessage
                    WHERE [message_type_name] IN
(N'http://schemas.microsoft.com/SQL/ServiceBroker/Error',
    N'http://schemas.microsoft.com/SQL/ServiceBroker/EndDialog')
                    -- Handle system messages
                    IF @@ROWCOUNT > 0
                    BEGIN
IF @messagetype = N'http://schemas.microsoft.com/SQL/ServiceBroker/Error'
                        BEGIN
                            -- log the error in you application's log
                            END CONVERSATION @dialog_handle;
                        END
ELSE IF @messagetype = N'http://schemas.microsoft.com/SQL/ServiceBroker/EndDialog'
                        BEGIN
                            END CONVERSATION @dialog_handle;
                        END
                    END
                END
                -- Insert the received records into the log table
                INSERT INTO dbo.LoginRecords
                SELECT [message_body] AS LoginEntry FROM @LoginMessage

                COMMIT TRANSACTION

        END TRY
        Begin Catch
            Rollback Transaction;

            DECLARE @ErrorMessage NVARCHAR(4000);
            DECLARE @ErrorSeverity INT;
```

```
                DECLARE @ErrorState INT;
                DECLARE @ErrorNumber INT;
                DECLARE @ErrorLine INT;
                DECLARE @ErrorProcedure NVARCHAR(128);
                SET         @ErrorLine = ERROR_LINE();
                SET         @ErrorSeverity = ERROR_SEVERITY();
                SET         @ErrorState = ERROR_STATE();
                SET         @ErrorNumber = ERROR_NUMBER();
                SET         @ErrorMessage = ERROR_MESSAGE();
                SET         @ErrorProcedure = ISNULL(ERROR_PROCEDURE(), 'None');
                RAISERROR (99124, @ErrorSeverity, 1 , @ErrorNumber,
@ErrorSeverity, @ErrorState, @ErrorProcedure,
@ErrorLine, @ErrorMessage);
            End Catch;
        END -- WHILE
END -- ReceiveQueueHandler
GO


CREATE QUEUE LoginReceiveQueue
WITH STATUS=ON,
     RETENTION=OFF,
     ACTIVATION
         (STATUS=ON,
          PROCEDURE_NAME=dbo.ReceiveQueueHandler,
          MAX_QUEUE_READERS=10,
          EXECUTE AS OWNER),
     POISON_MESSAGE_HANDLING (STATUS = ON);
GO

CREATE SERVICE LoginReceiveSvc
AUTHORIZATION dbo
ON QUEUE dbo.LoginReceiveQueue
(LoginContract)
GO

-- SELECT * FROM LoginReceiveQueue
```

The example creates two databases in the same instance for simplicity. Separating the databases on different servers requires endpoint security and routing. The following code snippet sets up the logging server (code file: `LogUserExampleSetup.sql`):

```
--This script sets up the sending database for the remote login logging example.
--It uses the send logic from this chapter.

CREATE DATABASE LogSendExample
GO
USE LogSendExample
GO
-- Service Broker databases always need a database master key
CREATE MASTER KEY ENCRYPTION BY PASSWORD = 'YourSecurePassword1!'
GO
-- We're going to go between databases and for simplicity we're not going to
-- set up Service Broker
-- security with certificates so the databases have to be trusted
```

```
ALTER DATABASE LogSendExample SET TRUSTWORTHY ON
GO
-- You may not need this but it is required if you're not connected to your domain.
-- I used SA but any
-- SQL Server authenticated user will work.
ALTER AUTHORIZATION ON DATABASE::LogSendExample TO SA
GO


-- Create the objects required to establish a conversation with the server

CREATE MESSAGE TYPE LoginMessage
AUTHORIZATION dbo
VALIDATION = NONE
GO


CREATE CONTRACT LoginContract
AUTHORIZATION dbo
(LoginMessage SENT BY ANY)
GO


-- This is the procedure to handle the initiator queue.  In this case the server
-- doesn't send responses so the only message types we need to handle are
-- error and end conversation.
CREATE PROCEDURE dbo.SendQueueHandler
AS
BEGIN -- SendQueueHandler
     DECLARE  @dialog_handle UNIQUEIDENTIFIER, @messagetype nvarchar(128);
     WHILE (1 = 1)
           BEGIN
           BEGIN TRY
           BEGIN TRANSACTION;

                RECEIVE TOP (1) @dialog_handle = [conversation_handle],
                    @messagetype = [message_type_name]
                FROM LoginSendQueue
                IF @@ROWCOUNT = 0
                    BEGIN
                        COMMIT TRANSACTION;
                        BREAK;
                    END
                ELSE IF @messagetype = N'http://schemas.microsoft.com/
                        SQL/ServiceBroker/Error'
                    BEGIN
                        -- log the error in you application's log
                        END CONVERSATION @dialog_handle;
                        COMMIT TRANSACTION;
                        BREAK;
                    END
                ELSE IF @messagetype = N'http://schemas.microsoft.com/
                        SQL/ServiceBroker/EndDialog'
                    BEGIN
                        END CONVERSATION @dialog_handle;
                        COMMIT TRANSACTION;
                        BREAK;
                    END
```

```
            END TRY
            Begin Catch
                Rollback Transaction;
                DECLARE @ErrorMessage NVARCHAR(4000);
                DECLARE @ErrorSeverity INT;
                DECLARE @ErrorState INT;
                DECLARE @ErrorNumber INT;
                DECLARE @ErrorLine INT;
                DECLARE @ErrorProcedure NVARCHAR(128);
                SET         @ErrorLine = ERROR_LINE();
                SET         @ErrorSeverity = ERROR_SEVERITY();
                SET         @ErrorState = ERROR_STATE();
                SET         @ErrorNumber = ERROR_NUMBER();
                SET         @ErrorMessage = ERROR_MESSAGE();
                SET         @ErrorProcedure = ISNULL(ERROR_PROCEDURE(), 'None');
                RAISERROR (99123, @ErrorSeverity, 1 , @ErrorNumber,
@ErrorSeverity, @ErrorState, @ErrorProcedure,
@ErrorLine, @ErrorMessage);
            End Catch;
        END -- WHILE
END -- SendQueueHandler
GO


-- The initiator queue will only receive system messages
CREATE QUEUE LoginSendQueue
WITH STATUS=ON,
    RETENTION=OFF,
    ACTIVATION
        (STATUS=ON,
         PROCEDURE_NAME=dbo.SendQueueHandler,
         MAX_QUEUE_READERS=2,
         EXECUTE AS OWNER),
    POISON_MESSAGE_HANDLING (STATUS = ON);
GO

CREATE SERVICE LoginSendSvc
AUTHORIZATION dbo
ON QUEUE dbo.LoginSendQueue
(LoginContract)
GO

-- This is the table that holds the conversation handle for the conversation that
-- connects to the server.  Saving it here allows us to reuse it.
CREATE TABLE dbo.SSB_Settings
([Source] sysname NOT NULL,
[Destination] sysname NOT NULL,
[Contract] sysname NOT NULL,
[dialog_handle] uniqueidentifier
CONSTRAINT PK_SSB_Setting PRIMARY KEY ([Source], [Destination], [Contract]))
GO

-- This is the procedure that sends the login records to the server
CREATE PROCEDURE dbo.SendUserLog
    @Destination sysname,
```

```
        @Source sysname,
        @Contract sysname,
        @MessageType sysname,
        @MessageBody varchar(MAX)
AS
DECLARE        @dialog_handle uniqueidentifier

BEGIN TRANSACTION

/*Get the conversation id.*/
SELECT @dialog_handle = dialog_handle
FROM dbo.SSB_Settings
WHERE [Source] = @Source
    AND [Destination] = @Destination
    AND [Contract] = @Contract;
/*If there is no current handle create a new conversation.*/
IF @dialog_handle IS NULL
BEGIN
    /*If there is a conversation dialog handle signal the destination
    code that the old conversation is dead.*/
    IF @dialog_handle IS NOT NULL
    BEGIN
        UPDATE dbo.SSB_Settings
        SET dialog_handle = NULL
        WHERE [Source] = @Source
            AND [Destination] = @Destination
            AND [Contract] = @Contract;
        SEND ON CONVERSATION @dialog_handle
        MESSAGE TYPE EndOfConversation;
    END
    /*Setup the new conversation*/
    BEGIN DIALOG CONVERSATION @dialog_handle
    FROM SERVICE @Source
    TO SERVICE @Destination
    ON CONTRACT @Contract;
    /*Save the new conversation ID*/
    UPDATE dbo.SSB_Settings
        SET dialog_handle = @dialog_handle
    WHERE [Source] = @Source
        AND [Destination] = @Destination
        AND [Contract] = @Contract;
     -- If the update didn't find the record we need, insert it.
    IF @@ROWCOUNT = 0
        INSERT INTO dbo.SSB_Settings
          ([Source], [Destination], [Contract], [dialog_handle])
        VALUES
          (@Source, @Destination, @Contract, @dialog_handle);
END;
/*Send the message*/
SEND ON CONVERSATION @dialog_handle
MESSAGE TYPE @MessageType
(@MessageBody);

COMMIT TRANSACTION
GO
```

This code snippet creates a client application that sends messages to the server.

The following code snippet creates test code to demonstrate how a client application would call the application (code file: LogUserTest.sql). The real application implements this as a Windows service that manages remote logins.

```
USE LogSendExample
GO

--Execute this script to test the login record process.  In practice the
--procedure would be called from the security server

DECLARE @msg varchar(MAX)
SET @msg = 'Sam Smith - ' + CONVERT (varchar(100), GetDate(),109)


EXEC dbo.SendUserLog
    @Destination = 'LoginReceiveSvc',
    @Source = 'LoginSendSvc',
    @Contract = 'LoginContract',
    @MessageType = 'LoginMessage',
    @MessageBody = @msg

-- See if it worked
-- SELECT * FROM LogReceiveExample.dbo.LoginRecords
```

SUMMARY

Although SQL Server Service Broker is quite complex to set up, it is an extremely powerful tool to use when you require asynchronous messaging. SQL Server Service Broker is a flexible solution that can enable you to send messages within the database, from database to database within the same SQL Server instance, or from database to database between servers, even if the servers are located next to each other, or are half a world apart.

As you have seen throughout this chapter, you must configure a variety of objects. Although SQL Server Service Broker may at first appear to be quite complex, after some time working with it, you will find the system quite easy to use, and all the pieces begin to make sense.

7

SQL Server CLR Integration

WHAT'S IN THIS CHAPTER?

➤ Implementing CLR in SQL Server

➤ Creating and deploying SQLCLR assembly

➤ Securing SQLCLR assemblies

➤ Monitoring performance

WROX.COM CODE DOWNLOADS FOR THIS CHAPTER

The wrox.com code downloads for this chapter are found at `www.wrox.com/go/prosql2014admin` on the Download Code tab. The code is in the Chapter 7 download and individually named according to the names throughout the chapter.

SQL Server developers first saw the integration of the .NET Common Language Runtime (CLR) with the release of SQL Server 2005. As the .NET Framework has evolved through its versions, SQL Server has continued to support integration of CLR. CLR provides great benefits to developers and database administrators, and is a valuable tool to have in your arsenal.

Although a detailed discussion of writing managed code using a .NET programming language such as C# is beyond the scope of this chapter, you learn to create and deploy a simple .NET assembly and enable it for SQL integration. You then look at when a SQL Server CLR (SQLCLR) solution provides a better alternative to a traditional T-SQL solution. This chapter also discusses SQLCLR performance and security, which are critical issues to consider when deciding whether to use SQLCLR over traditional T-SQL.

INTRODUCTION TO CLR

With the integration of the .NET Framework CLR components in SQL Server, developers have the flexibility to write stored procedures, triggers, user-defined types and functions, and streaming table-valued functions using any CLR-compliant languages, the most common being C# and Visual Basic .NET. CLR supplies managed code capabilities with a plethora of services that the database engine is not able to provide, such as object lifetime management, code access security, and cross-language integration. And that is just the tip of the iceberg. If you take a good look at what the CLR extension provides the database engine, you'll discover many compelling benefits, including the following:

➤ **A rich programming model**—T-SQL is a data access and management language, whereas CLR-managed code is better suited for complex application logic. In addition, the .NET Framework exposes many pre-built classes that you can use. For example, it has classes for complex string manipulation, complex mathematical operations, and cryptography. Furthermore, CLR-managed code provides robust error handling and memory management.

➤ **Enhanced performance and scalability**—Because CLR-managed code is compiled code, it offers better performance when compared to complex aggregation, as well as when cursors are needed to perform similar calculations using T-SQL. Additionally, with SQLCLR integration, the SQL Server APIs control the memory management of CLR, and can effectively synchronize the scheduling of thread usage between CLR threads and SQL threads.

➤ **Enhanced security**—When uploading assemblies, you can indicate different permission sets under which the assembly will run. The SAFE permission set is the most secure, and restricts the assembly so that it can only have access to the local database, and is blocked from calling unmanaged code. The UNSAFE permission set is for highly trusted code that can call unmanaged code and access external resources. The CLR integration also uses the highly secure and reliable code access security to control permissions for the managed code.

➤ **Efficient development via a standardized environment**—The past few years have seen both the .NET development environment and the database development environment become more tightly integrated by using the Visual Studio Integrated Development Environment (IDE). Developers can use the same tools and development environment to write their database objects and scripts that they use to write their middle-tier and client components. This greatly enhances the capability to effectively debug and run automated tests against the code. You can also integrate with Team Foundation Server to manage the development life cycle.

As you can see, in certain situations, CLR is clearly the most reliable, scalable, and secure solution. But remember to use the right tool for the job at hand. You should never consider CLR as a replacement (except for extended stored procedures) for T-SQL. Rather, you should use CLR to quickly and efficiently solve the programming challenges that the T-SQL language cannot easily solve, such as string parsing, complex mathematics, CPU-centric workloads, and accessing external resources.

What makes the decision of which tool to use a little more difficult is that the T-SQL language continues to evolve, and many of the things that you couldn't easily do in T-SQL are now quite easy and efficient in newer versions of T-SQL. So, the answer to the question of which to use becomes, "It depends." Do some testing. Write the solution in both T-SQL and .NET to see which one performs better. The more you use it, the better feel you can get as to which method you should use for a given situation.

Let's now take a look at how CLR is integrated into the database engine.

SQL Server as a .NET Runtime Host

A *runtime host* is defined as any process that loads the .NET run time and runs code in a managed environment. With the CLR integration (also called the SQLCLR), SQL Server enables .NET programmers to write stored procedures, user-defined functions, triggers, user-defined types, and aggregates in any .NET-compatible language (usually C# or VB .NET).

One of the great benefits of SQLCLR is that any .NET code that SQL Server runs is completely isolated from SQL Server itself. .NET code runs within the SQL Server process space, but SQL Server uses a construct in .NET called the *application domain* (AppDomain) to completely isolate and separate all resources that the .NET code uses from the resources that SQL Server uses. The AppDomain, which is discussed shortly, protects SQL Server from all malicious use of system resources. It should be noted that SQL Server manages its own thread scheduling, synchronization and locking, and memory management, which adds to the security and performance of SQLCLR.

Application Domains

The primary design goal of placing assemblies in application domains is to achieve scalability and security, as well as isolation. Application domains have existed for quite a while to provide a form of isolation between applications. This is necessary to ensure that code running in one application cannot (and does not) affect other unrelated applications. You can see this type of isolation between operating systems and runtime environments.

The isolation boundaries created by the application domains also help with the security and reliability needed for application development, especially for isolating applications running on the same computer. When multiple applications exist on the same computer, each application is loaded into separate processes, accomplishing the needed isolation because memory addresses are process-related.

Similarly, SQL Server isolates code between databases by using application domains. As such, application domains exist for each database that allows you to create, load, and register an assembly, and call methods and functions within that database, independent of other assemblies registered in other databases.

You can have multiple assemblies per database, and one assembly can discover other assemblies at execution time using the .NET Framework reflection application programming interfaces (APIs).

T-SQL versus CLR

With the integration of CLR in SQL Server, the line that separates what is commonly known as the Business Logic Tier and the Data Tier just got a little fuzzier. That certainly is not meant to be taken in a negative tone; it just means that choosing where to put middle-tier logic and database access logic is not as cut-and-dried as it once was.

Best practices state that when doing data retrieval, T-SQL is the way to go. Leave the data manipulation and CPU-intensive functions and procedures to the managed code side of things, especially if complex logic is being processed on the returned data, such as complex mathematical calculations or string parsing.

Another thing to take into consideration is where the code will be executed. Is the client the best place to put certain logic, or will that same logic perform better on the server? Multi-tier applications typically have a data layer where much of the data logic is handled on a separate server, or on the client workstation. With SQLCLR integration, however, both T-SQL and managed code can be run on the database server. This brings the benefit of enhanced server processing power, and shortens the gap between data and code. On the other hand, the client may be a better choice because workstation computers are becoming increasingly powerful and can handle a lot of the application processing without drastic performance degradation. As a matter of fact, the processing capabilities of many client computers are severely underutilized. This means that a lot of the application processing can be offloaded to the client, freeing up the server for other tasks.

From a performance viewpoint, CLR is much faster at returning file information from the operating system than a T-SQL approach, simply because OLE automation has more overhead than the different methods used in CLR. However, raw speed shouldn't be the only consideration. You should also consider ease of development and ease of maintenance, which might take precedence over speed, depending on the situation.

As you can see, each method has many pros and cons. Keep in mind that managed code can run on either the client or the server; T-SQL can run only on the server.

Enabling CLR Integration

By default, CLR is disabled for users. (It is always enabled for internal system use). This means that you cannot execute any .NET code until you purposefully enable CLR. Not everyone can enable CLR; only members of the sysadmin and serveradmin server roles can do so, or any user granted the server-level permission ALTER SETTINGS.

Enabling CLR is as simple as running a query. A couple dozen "advanced" SQL Server settings can be changed or modified only via T-SQL. They are not found in any Properties dialog box; they are only accessible via the sp_configure option. Following is the syntax for enabling CLR:

```
EXEC sp_configure 'clr enabled', 1
GO
RECONFIGURE
GO
```

Don't enable CLR yet, though. You still have a few more things to consider.

There is another advanced setting called lightweight pooling that, when enabled, prevents CLR from executing. Per the MSDN documentation, CLR execution is not supported under lightweight pooling. The lightweight pooling option provides a means to reduce the system overhead associated with excessive context switching. Following is a description from Books Online (http://technet.microsoft.com/en-us/library/ms178074.aspx):

> *When excessive context switching is present, lightweight pooling can provide better throughput by performing the context switching inline, thus helping to reduce user/kernel ring transitions.*

BOL recommends that you disable one or the other (setting the value to 0). You cannot have both options enabled (option set to 1). Features that rely on CLR but do not work properly when `lightweight pooling` is enabled include the hierarchy data type, replication, and policy-based management.

Finally, enabling CLR is not an "enable it and leave it" option. When it is enabled, you should closely monitor SQL Server for several error messages in the error log, including the following:

➤   `Failed Virtual Allocate Bytes: FAIL_VIRTUAL_RESERVE <size>`

➤   `Failed Virtual Allocate Bytes: FAIL_VIRTUAL_COMMIT <size>`

Either of these errors might indicate that SQL Server is trying to free parts of the SQL Server memory pool to find space for items such as extended stored procedures, `.dll` files (CLR code files), or automation objects.

If you consistently see these errors in your error logs, there is a SQL Server startup option that can help with this. In the SQL Server Configuration Manager, use the `-g` startup option, which tells SQL Server to leave available memory for memory allocations within the SQL Server process, but outside of the SQL Server memory pool.

It is not a good idea to use the `-g` option and not monitor memory over a period of time, though. However, using the `-g` option is a good way to help fine-tune memory allocation, but only when physical memory exceeds the configured limit set by the operating system. Incorrect use of this option can lead to situations where SQL Server may encounter runtime errors or not start. If your CLR assemblies need a lot of memory, you should go back and look at what your CLR is doing, then make any necessary adjustments (such as breaking the assembly into smaller components).

CREATING CLR ASSEMBLIES

This section walks you through several examples to create, deploy, and register SQLCLR assemblies. These examples show you how to create and deploy the CLR assembly without using Visual Studio, then the examples follow that up by showing how to use SQL Server Data Tools in Visual Studio to create and deploy CLR assemblies.

The Non–Visual Studio Way

Creating assemblies to deploy to SQL Server 2014 is not any different from previous versions. For this example, follow these steps:

1. First, fire up an instance of your favorite text editor and add the script in Listing 7-1 (code file: `MyFirstSqlClr.cs`).

LISTING 7-1: MyFirstSqlClr.cs

```
using System;
using System.Data;
using Microsoft.SqlServer.Server;
using System.Data.SqlTypes;
public class FirstSQLCLRProc
```

continues

LISTING 7-1 *(continued)*

```
{
    [Microsoft.SqlServer.Server.SqlProcedure]
    public static void FirstSQLCLR(out string text)
    {
        SqlContext.Pipe.Send("Hello world!" + Environment.NewLine);
        text = "My First SQLCLR Assembly!";
    }
}
```

Listing 7-1 defines a public class that contains a single static method. The method uses the `SqlContext` and `SqlPipe` classes, which are used to create managed database objects to output a simple text message. The `SqlContext` object provides the environment in which the assembly code is activated and running. The managed code is executed from the server and, thus, runs as part of the user connection, or within the user *context*. At this point, the `SqlPipe` is accessible. `SQLPipe` is the SQL Server component that enables managed stored procedures to return results back to the caller. Results from a query execution are sent back to the client via the caller's *pipe*. This is really no different for CLR database objects, in that results are sent back to the client via the methods associated with the `SqlPipe` object (`send` and `ExecuteAndSend`).

2. After you add the preceding code, save the file as `MyFirstSqlClr.cs` in a directory of your choice. (However, remember where you saved this file.) In this example, the syntax is C#.

3. Next, compile the assembly. By default, SQL Server installs the .NET Framework distribution files, which include `csc.exe` and `vbc.exe`, the command-line compilers for C# and VB .NET. These exist in the following location (for .NET 4.0):

`C:\Windows\Microsoft.NET\Framework\v4.0.30319`

Open a command prompt and navigate to the directory where you previously saved your `.cs` file.

4. Use the following syntax to compile your code into an assembly:

```
C:\Windows\Microsoft.NET\Framework\v4.0.30319\csc /
    target:library myfirstsqlclr.cs
```

The `/target` option is the parameter that specifies to compile the code into an assembly.

5. After the program has been compiled into a library, you should see a new file in the directory with the same name, but with a `.dll` extension. This is the file that will be loaded into SQL Server.

6. Open up an instance of SQL Server Management Studio and open a new query window. Select the appropriate database in which you want to load the assembly, and type in the following T-SQL code. (This example assumes that you have a `temp` directory in the root of your C drive (`C:\temp`). If not, you must change the FROM location to where your assembly is located.)

```
CREATE ASSEMBLY myfirstsqlclr
FROM 'c:\temp\myfirstsqlclr.dll'
WITH PERMISSION_SET = SAFE
```

The preceding code loads the assembly into SQL Server and creates a SQL Server assembly reference using the location of the compiled assembly created in the previous step. Notice also the PERMISSION_SET option. This option sets the security level of the assembly. You learn more about these options shortly.

7. Next, create a T-SQL stored procedure called DoIt with a reference to the assembly created in step 6. Type the following T-SQL code in the query window and execute it:

```
CREATE PROCEDURE DoIt
@i nchar(50) OUTPUT
AS
EXTERNAL NAME myfirstsqlclr.FirstSQLCLRProc.FirstSQLCLR
```

After the procedure has been created, you can see your newly created assembly and stored procedure by looking in Object Explorer, as shown in Figure 7-1.

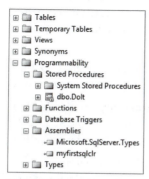

FIGURE 7-1

8. With your stored procedure created, you can run it like any other stored procedure by using standard T-SQL. In the query window, type the following T-SQL code and execute it. (If you have not enabled the CLR integration yet, make sure you do before executing.)

```
DECLARE @var nchar(50)
EXEC DoIt @var out
PRINT @var
```

You should see the following results in the Results window:

```
Hello world!
My First SQLCLR Assembly!
```

This isn't the only way to add assemblies. In the next exercise, you use Visual Studio and SQL Server Data Tools to create and deploy CLR assemblies.

Using Microsoft SQL Server Data Tools

Creating and deploying SQLCLR objects using SQL Server Data Tools (SSDT) is an easy way to create and edit database objects. This section shows a quick example of how to use SSDT to create and deploy a SQLCLR stored procedure. If you have not enabled the CLR integration yet, make sure you do so before performing the exercise.

1. Install SSDT by going to the following URL: `http://msdn.microsoft.com/en-us/data/tools.aspx`. Make sure you select the version that supports SQL Server 2014.

2. Once that is installed, open Visual Studio, and from the View menu, select SQL Server Object Explorer (SSOE), which opens the SQL Server Object Explorer window on the left of the Visual Studio IDE.

3. In SSOE, click the Add SQL Server button to register a new SQL Server instance in SSOE. In the Connect to Server dialog box, enter the server name and login credentials, and then click Connect. This registers a new SQL Server in SSOE.

4. With a new server registered, expand the server node. Then expand the databases node. Select the database to which you want to deploy the SQLCLR assembly, and then right-click that database. From the context menu, select Create New Project to open the Create New Project dialog box. In this dialog box, type in a project name and location for the new project. Then select the Create New Solution check box and the Create Directory for Solution check box. Click Start to create a new Database Project associated to the database selected in the SQL Server Object Explorer.

5. After you create the new project, in the Solution Explorer window, right-click the project node. From the context menu, select Properties to open the property pages for this project.

6. On the Project Settings tab, make sure the Target Platform is SQL Server 2014. You can also set the platform to several other versions of SQL Server. Notice on the SQLCLR tab you can set the permission level, as well as the target framework. Close the properties page.

7. Right-click the project again in Solution Explorer, and from the context menu, select Add ➪ New Item. In the Add New Item dialog box, select SQLCLR C# from the list of installed templates. (If you do not see the SQLCLR C# template, you will have to install it, or use the default VB template.) Then select the SQLCLR C# Stored Procedure item. Keep the default name, and click OK. A new C# SQLCLR class file will be added to the project and will be open, ready for you to add code to it.

   In the class, modify the method to return a string along with the code used in the non–Visual Studio example (C#):

   ```
   public static void SqlStoredProcedure1 (out string text)
   {
       SqlContext.Pipe.Send("Hello world!" + Environment.NewLine);
       text = "My Second SQLCLR Assembly!";
   }
   ```

8. Right-click the project in Solution Explorer, and from the context menu, select Build. With the project compiled, the next step is to deploy the new CLR stored procedure. Right-click the project in Solution Explorer, and from the context menu, select Publish to open the Publish Database dialog box.

9. In the Publish Database dialog box, click the Edit button to set the target server and database. When set, click the Publish button on the Publish Database dialog box. This packages the contents of the database project and deploys them to the selected database. In this case, all you have is a SQLCLR stored procedure, so that will be the only thing deployed to your database.

The output of the publish process displays in the Data Tools Operations window. Things such as the publish progress, messages, and errors are displayed in this window. The publishing of the CLR assembly should take only a minute, and when published, you should see it in the list of assemblies in SQL Server Object Explorer in Visual Studio.

You can execute the stored procedure by right-clicking it in the SQL Server Object Explorer. In the context menu, select Execute Procedure. You should see the message returned by the stored procedure.

As you can see, it is easier to use SSDT to create and publish SQLCLR assemblies because it provides a much easier and more efficient way to work with database objects, including CLR objects.

CLR INTEGRATION SECURITY

As with any code execution, you must take steps to ensure that SQLCLR integration is secure and isolated. To ensure a secure hosting environment for CLR, you should meet the following goals:

➤ Running managed code within SQL Server should not compromise the integrity, stability, and robustness of SQL Server.

➤ Managed code should not permit unauthorized access to user data or other user code.

➤ Mechanisms should be in place to restrict user code from accessing any resources outside of SQL Server.

➤ Managed code should not gain access to system resources just because it is running under the SQL Server process.

To assist in upholding these goals, CLR supports a security model called Control Access Security (CAS) for managed code. In this model, permissions are given to assemblies based on the identity of the code. The set of permissions that can be granted to the assemblies by the SQL Server host policy level are determined by the permission that is set and specified during the creation of the assembly in SQL Server. SQLCLR supports three permission sets:

➤ SAFE—Only local data access and internal computations are allowed. If no permission is specified during the assembly creation, SAFE permission is applied by default. No access to external system resources such as files or the registry exists.

➤ EXTERNAL_ACCESS—This is the same permission as SAFE, but with the added capability to access external resources such as the filesystem, registry, networks, and environment variables.

➤ UNSAFE—This means unrestricted access to all resources within SQL Server and outside SQL Server. This is the least secure and should rarely be used.

It is important that you set the correct level of security for the assemblies, and most assemblies should be set at the SAFE level. SQLCLR has the unwarranted reputation of being a security risk. In fact, it is quite secure and runs under tight restrictions.

PERFORMANCE MONITORING

As stated earlier, using CLR should not be considered an "enable it and leave it" option. When it's enabled, you must ensure that it performs as you expect, and does what you need it to do. To help with this monitoring, several tools and options are available to you, including Windows System Monitor, Extended Events, and Dynamic Management Views (DMVs).

Windows System Monitor

You can use Windows System Monitor (`PerfMon.exe`) to monitor CLR activities for SQL Server. Use the counter in the .NET CLR group in System Monitor, but select the `sqlserver` instance when you monitor CLR counters for SQL Server, as shown in Figure 7-2.

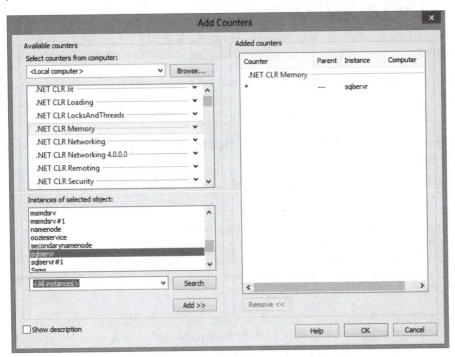

FIGURE 7-2

The following counters are extremely helpful in understanding the health and activity of the programs running in a SQL-hosted environment:

➤ **.NET CLR Memory**—This provides detailed information about the types of CLR heap memory and garbage collection. These counters can be used to monitor CLR memory usage, and to flag alerts if the memory used gets too large. If the code is copying a lot of data into memory, you may have to check the code and take a different approach to reduce memory consumption, or add more memory.

➤ **.NET CLR Loading**—SQL Server isolates code between databases by using `AppDomain`. This set of counters enables monitoring of the number of `AppDomains` and the number of assemblies loaded in the system. You can use this counter to determine loaded CLR assemblies.

➤ **.NET CLR Exceptions**—The Exceptions/Sec counter provides you with a good idea of how many exceptions the code generates. The values vary from application to application because sometimes developers use exceptions to test application functionality, so you should monitor over time to set the baseline and go from there. As this number increases, performance decreases.

Figure 7-3 shows the .NET CLR Memory:# Induced GC object, which displays the peak number of times garbage collection was performed because of an explicit call to `GC.Collect`. It is a good idea to let the garbage collection control the frequency of its collection. If you see activity for this counter, you should check to see if the CLR objects are explicitly calling the garbage collector, and make sure there is a good reason for this.

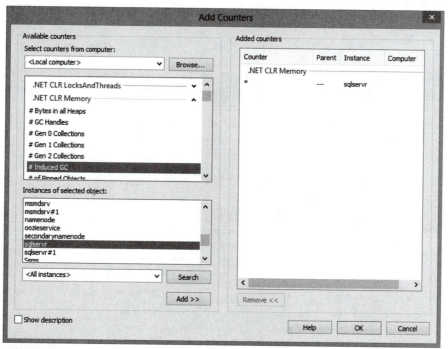

FIGURE 7-3

> **NOTE** *For more information on the different .NET counters, see* `http://msdn.microsoft.com/en-us/library/w8f5kw2e.aspx`.

Extended Events

Using extended events is an excellent way to monitor the health of your SQL Server. Figure 7-4 shows the Extended Events node under the Management folder in SQL Server Management Studio. If you right-click the `Sessions` folder, you can create a new session.

FIGURE 7-4

Two key extended events for monitoring CLR objects are `assembly_load` and the `clr_allocation_failure`. The `assembly_load` event occurs when a request to load an assembly occurs, and is used to monitor queries running CLR code. The `clr_allocation_failure` event occurs when managed code experiences a memory allocation failure. Figure 7-5 shows the event configuration options available for the `assembly_load` event.

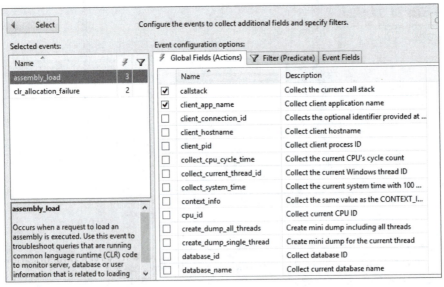

FIGURE 7-5

Dynamic Management Views (DMVs)

Dynamic Management Views (DMVs) return server state information that you can use to monitor the health of a server instance, diagnose problems, and tune performance. Following are four DMVs that pertain to SQLCLR:

- ➤ `sys.dm_clr_appdomains`—Returns a row for each application domain in the server.

- ➤ `sys.dm_clr_loaded_assemblies`—Returns a row for each managed user assembly loaded into the server address space.

- ➤ `sys.dm_clr_properties`—Returns a row for each property related to SQL Server CLR integration, including the version and the state of the hosted CLR.

- ➤ `sys.dm_clr_tasks`—Returns a row for all CLR tasks currently running.

Although these four DMVs provide great information, they don't provide the performance tuning information you need. To provide more insight into the operation and execution of CLR assemblies, you can use the following DMVs to give you that information for CLR assemblies:

- ➤ `sys.dm_exec_cached_plans`—You can use this to view a cached query plan for a CLR query.

- ➤ `sys.dm_exec_query_stats`—This contains a row per query statement within the cached plan.

With these DMVs, you can gather aggregate performance statistics for cached query plans. This information can help you determine how any queries in your assemblies are performing.

CLR Integration Design Goals

When integrating SQLCLR in your architecture, you should keep the following design goals in mind:

- ➤ **Performance**—Best practice states that a CLR assembly should not be used to query data. This is what T-SQL is meant to do. CLR assemblies should not spend their time accessing data. Send the data you want worked on to the assembly, instead of having the assembly pull it from SQL Server.

- ➤ **Scalability**—SQL Server and SQLCLR handle memory management differently. SQL Server is more cooperative, and supports a non-preemptive threading model. CLR supports a preemptive threading model, and does not differentiate between physical and virtual memory. These differences present an interesting challenge when building systems that need to scale. Thus, as you design your database architecture, do so in such a way that the scalability and the integrity of the system are not compromised by user code calling unnecessary APIs for threading and memory directly.

- ➤ **Security**—Have a security plan and a set of rules for implementing SQLCLR, and stick to those rules. Ensure that any managed code follows the rules of SQL Server authentication and authorization. Not every piece of managed code needs access to external resources either.

- ➤ **Reliability**—The key with reliability is that any user code should not be allowed to execute any operations that compromise the integrity of the database and Database Engine, including not overwriting internal data structures or memory buffers.

SUMMARY

SQLCLR integration opens up a new world of capabilities for data querying and processing. None of this is truly new, though; it has been around for more than six years. Thus, the purpose of this chapter is to simply provide a look at why you should consider using SQLCLR, what to expect, and some guidance for how to use it.

A great addition to working with SQLCLR is the SQL Server Data Tools, which provide an easy way to work with database objects. You can work with different types of SQLCLR objects, including stored procedures and user-defined functions. Regardless of the type of CLR object you create, the key is to understand why you use SQLCLR over T-SQL. While SQLCLR isn't a replacement for T-SQL, it is a great tool to have in your arsenal, and enables you to do things that are difficult or impossible to do with straight T-SQL.

Managed code has its place within SQL Server. In fact, the SQL Server engine uses CLR for some of its data types, such as the XML data type and the geographic data types. Benefits certainly exist to using SQLCLR, and the more you work with it the more you will find places where you can use it to improve your applications.

While this chapter covered some of the security issues related to CLR integration, Chapter 8 deals with the important topic of securing the database as a whole. Database security consists of authentication and authorization. Authentication consists of proving the identity of the user, while authorization consists of granting or denying access to database objects. After completing the chapter, you will have a solid understanding of the authentication and authorization process.

Securing the Database Instance

WHAT'S IN THIS CHAPTER?

- ➤ Understanding SQL Server authentication types
- ➤ Understanding Windows authentication types
- ➤ Authorizing object-level security
- ➤ Maintaining row-level security

WROX.COM CODE DOWNLOADS FOR THIS CHAPTER

The wrox.com code downloads for this chapter are found at www.wrox.com/go/prosql2014admin on the Download Code tab. The code is in the Chapter 8 download and individually named according to the names throughout the chapter.

Security of a Microsoft SQL Server instance is probably one of the least sexy topics out there today. And, unfortunately, that will probably remain the case for many years to come, if not forever. However, proper security for the database instance is extremely important because without it, there is no way to guarantee that the data stored within the SQL Server instance is the data expected to be there.

Changes that an attacker could make to the data within an instance of SQL Server could be as small as simply changing names or changing the prices for products, to injecting JavaScript or HTML that is served to customers or employees via their web browser, which then executes unexpected code on their machine. These changes could be minor; however, more than likely, they could install some sort of dangerous application on the user's computer such as a Trojan horse or key logger.

So, in reality, anything can happen, and it is best to be prepared for all scenarios. Your corporate databases are key strategic assets, and the data in them must be protected from leakage and tampering. You don't want your company to be the next subject of headlines about leaking customer information to identity thieves.

The key concepts of software security are authentication and authorization. Authentication is the way the software securely identifies who is trying to connect and authorization is the way the software decided what the user can do once connected. Authentication will keep bad guys out, and authorization will keep authenticated users from doing things they shouldn't. SQL Server 2014 has very sophisticated authentication and authorization features that provide many options for securing data. This chapter covers the options and how to configure them.

AUTHENTICATION TYPES

Securing data consists of two essential parts: *authentication* (which is proving you are who you say you are) and *authorization* (which defines the data you have access to, and what you can do to the data). You authenticate yourself to SQL Server by providing something only you have—your fingerprints, a smart card, or a password, for example.

You have two ways to authenticate to the Microsoft SQL Server instance: via SQL Server authentication and via Windows authentication. When you install SQL Server, you have an option to select whether the SQL Server instance should support Windows authentication only, or whether it should support both Windows and SQL Server authentication.

SQL Authentication

SQL Server authentication was the original authentication method supported by SQL Server when it was based on the Sybase codebase. With SQL Server authentication, the application or the user specifies the username and password to be used to authenticate against the SQL Server instance. When specified, the username and password are put into the connection string, which the application then uses when it connects to the SQL Server instance. With SQL Server authentication, the actual username and password are stored in the master database within the database instance.

When you use SQL Server authentication, the account and password are passed to the database instance, which then hashes the password and compares the username and password hash against the list of SQL accounts stored within the master database. If the passed-in username and password hash match an account stored within the master database, authentication succeeds. You can connect, and the rights associated with the SQL account are granted to you. If no match is found, an authentication error is returned.

You can configure SQL Server logins to follow the Windows password security policies to enforce password strength and password expiration. This means that even if SQL Server must use SQL Server authentication, the SQL Server passwords can be protected by the security policies defined by your organization for Windows passwords.

You can enable two domain policy settings: the first is to follow the domain password policies that control password complexity, and the second is to enforce password expiration.

> **NOTE** *Configuring password policies is extremely complex and is outside the scope of this book.*

You can set the password policies via SQL Server Management Studio by editing the login, and checking or unchecking the needed policies. You can also enable or disable the settings by using the `ALTER LOGIN` statement as shown in the following code snippet:

```
ALTER LOGIN chain_test
WITH CHECK_POLICY = ON, CHECK_EXPIRATION=ON
```

The password policy is verified only when the account is created or when the password is changed. This means that a SQL login could be created with a password that doesn't meet the domain policy requirements. Then, after it is created, the check policy setting could be enabled, and it would be assumed that the account meets the domain policy requirements when, in fact, it doesn't.

Windows Authentication

Windows authentication was introduced to the SQL Server database engine in SQL Server 6.0. With Windows authentication, SQL Server relies on Windows to authenticate users. Windows passes the user's identity to SQL Server when the user connects. When you create a login with Windows authentication, you associate a Windows identity with the SQL Server login. Other than the authentication method, a login for Windows authentication is the same as a login for SQL Server authentication. Rights to connect to the SQL Server instance and to databases within the instance can be granted to individual Windows accounts, or to groups that are created and managed within the Windows Active Directory domain.

When you connect to the SQL Server database using Windows authentication, the SQL Server isn't actually the one handling the Windows authentication. When you log in to the Windows operating system, an authentication token is generated by the domain controller, which is then passed to the client computer and stored within the computer's memory. When you attempt to connect to the SQL Server using Windows authentication, this token is then passed from the client computer's operating system to the SQL Server. The SQL Server then uses its operating system to verify with the domain controllers that the token is valid. It verifies that your Security Identifier (SID) can access the SQL Server instance, and determines what level of permissions you should be granted.

The Windows identity used for authentication can be either an individual Windows user or a Windows group. A best practice is to authenticate to SQL Server with a Windows group. That way, the SQL Server administrator only has to configure a small number of groups one time, and then the Windows security administrators can control access by assigning users to the Windows groups configured as logins in SQL Server.

> **NOTE** *The full Windows authentication process is complex and has been documented in a couple of different places. You can dig through the Microsoft TechNet website to find the various articles that make up the documentation, or you can look at Chapter 3 of* Securing SQL Server: Protecting Your Database from Attackers *by Denny Cherry (Amsterdam, The Netherlands: Syngress, 2010), in which the Windows authentication process is spelled out step by step.*

SQL versus Windows Authentication

Because of the differences in SQL Server and Windows authentication, SQL Server authentication is considered to be much less secure, and should be disabled whenever possible. When SQL Server authentication is enabled, those who want to attack the SQL Server instance can use brute force attacks to attempt to break in. This is because the username and password are simply sent to the SQL Server instead of the Windows authentication process that passes in the Windows token. With Windows authentication, the user connects from Windows without the need to provide another password, thus providing a better user experience.

LOGINS AND USERS

A SQL Server login is an identity that is configured in the SQL Server instance. The login is used to authenticate a client to SQL Server. When an administrator creates a login, it is associated with credentials—a SQL Server password or Windows identity. The login can be associated with some SQL Server instance-level privileges, but most data access privileges are associated with SQL Server database users. Users are stored in each database of the instances and get their authenticated identity by being linked to a login. Each login can be associated with one or more database users.

Because the database user is associated with a login stored in the master database of the instances, if a database is moved to a different SQL Server instance, the logins associated with the database users must be created in the new instance to allow users to access the database. This has been an issue with database mirroring and log shipping. When the SQL Server team implemented AlwaysOn Availability Groups in SQL Server 2012, they recognized that keeping logins synchronized for multiple secondary databases would be a significant issue.

SQL Server 2012 introduced a new concept called the *contained user*, which is used within contained databases. Contained users exist only within a single database and are not associated with an instance-level login. This means that instance-level permissions such as cross-database connectivity cannot be assigned to a contained user. Contained users are created with the CREATE USER statement by specifying the password parameter instead of the FROM LOGIN parameter, as shown in the following code snippet:

```
CREATE USER MyContainedUser WITH PASSWORD='MySecurePassword'
GO
```

Within the context of the database in which the contained user is created, rights to objects and permission chains all work in exactly the same process as a traditional or non-contained user.

Contained users can be created based on local or domain Windows accounts, or they can be created as SQL Server users. A *contained Windows user* is simply a Windows account that doesn't have a corresponding login at the server level. Contained SQL users do not have the option of being configured to follow domain policies like traditional SQL logins.

AUTHORIZING SECURABLES

Proper object-level security within the database is key to keeping data within the SQL Server instance safe from intruders. This object-level security extends from instance-level objects (such as

Availability Groups) and the ability to view the instances' server state objects, to securing specific objects within the user databases.

Rights can be granted at both the server level and the database level, or to specific objects. Permissions can also be chained together, which simplifies the permissions both within the database by using permissions chains, as well as across databases by using cross-database chaining.

The following three statements are used when changing permissions in SQL Server:

➤ GRANT is used to assign rights.

➤ DENY is used to prevent access.

➤ REVOKE is used to remove either a GRANT or a DENY.

When granting permissions in SQL Server, you must remember that DENY always overwrites a GRANT. If a user is a member of three different roles, and two of the roles have been granted rights to query from a table, and the third role has been denied rights to query the table, then the user cannot query from the table.

> **NOTE** *Figuring out many of the object rights in this chapter can be difficult to visualize when simply reading through descriptions. Microsoft has a visual diagram that can make this easier. You can download it from* http://social .technet.microsoft.com/wiki/cfs-file.ashx/__key/communityserver-wikis-components-files/00-00-00-00-05/5710.Permissions_5F00_ Poster_5F00_2008_5F00_R2_5F00_Wiki.pdf.

The same applies if higher-level sets of rights are granted. For example, if you have been granted rights to SELECT from a schema and denied the right to query a specific table, you cannot query from the table. If you have been granted rights to query from a table and denied rights to query at the schema level, you cannot query from any table within the schema, no matter what rights have been granted to the table.

You can use a second syntax when granting rights to users: the WITH GRANT syntax. As shown in following code snippet, adding WITH GRANT to the end of the GRANT statement enables the user who has been granted the right to grant the right to other users within the database:

```
GRANT SELECT, INSERT ON dbo.Users TO MyUser WITH GRANT
```

Server Securables

Dozens of instance-wide privileges can be granted at the instance level. These include connecting and managing the various endpoints within the SQL Server instance, managing the logins within the SQL Server instance, various instance-wide settings, the AlwaysOn availability groups, and the user-defined server roles that were introduced in SQL Server 2012.

The biggest difference between instance-wide privileges and database-wide privileges is that instance-wide privileges are granted directly to the login, whereas database-wide privileges are granted to users, and these users are mapped to logins.

> **NOTE** *The terms* logins *and* users *get interchanged often, but within the scope of Microsoft SQL Server, these are two very different things. Logins are used to log in to the database instance, whereas users are mapped to a login from within the SQL Server databases.*

Now, let's take a look at the different endpoint privileges available to the various objects within the scope of the SQL Server instance.

Endpoints

You can manage the following five privileges for each endpoint within the SQL Server instance:

➤ **Alter**—The Alter right enables the login that has the privilege to make configuration changes to the endpoint.

➤ **Connect**—The Connect privilege enables the user that has the privilege to connect to the endpoint. By default, all logins are granted the privilege to connect to the default endpoints.

➤ **Control**—The Control privilege grants the other four privileges.

➤ **Take Ownership**—The Take Ownership privilege enables the login to become the owner of the endpoint.

➤ **View Definition**—The View Definition privilege enables the login to view the configuration of the endpoint without being able to make changes to the endpoint.

Logins

You can manage the following four privileges for each login within the SQL Server instance:

➤ **Alter**—The Alter privilege enables the login that has been given that right to make changes to the second login to which the right was granted. For example, if there were two logins named login1 and login2, login1 can alter login2 with this permission. Altering a login enables the granted login to change the password, default database, default language, and so on, of the grantee login.

➤ **Control**—The Control privilege grants the granted user the other three privileges to the grantee login. For example, if there were two logins named login1 and login2, login1 can control login2 with control permissions.

➤ **Impersonate**—The Impersonate privilege enables the granted user to use the EXECUTE AS syntax, specifying the grantee login the ability to execute code as the grantee login.

➤ **View Definition**—The View Definition privilege enables the granted user to view the configuration of the granter login.

Instance-Wide Settings

Table 8-1 shows privileges that can be granted to a specific login and their meanings.

TABLE 8-1: Instance Privileges and Meanings

PRIVILEGE NAME	PRIVILEGE DEFINITION
Administrator Bulk Options	Grants the user to bulk-insert data into the SQL Server instance using the `BULK INSERT` statement, the `bcp` command-line application, and the `OPENROWSET(BULK)` operation.
Alter Any Availability Group	Grants the user the right to alter or fail over any AlwaysOn Availability Group. Granting this privilege also grants to the Create Availability Group privilege.
Alter Any Connection	Grants the user the right to kill any user connection.
Alter Any Credential	Grants the user the right to alter any credential within the database instance.
Alter Any Database	Grants the user the right to change the database options for any database within the database instance. Granting this privilege also grants the Create Any Database privilege.
Alter Any Endpoint	Grants the user the right to alter any endpoint that has been created on the SQL Server instance. Granting this privilege also grants the Create Any Endpoint privilege.
Alter Any Event Notification	Grants the user the right to alter any event notification that has been created within the SQL Server instance. Granting this privilege also grants the Create Trace Event Notification privilege.
Alter Any Linked Server	Grants the user the right to alter any linked server within the SQL Server instance.
Alter Any Login	Grants the user the right to alter any login within the instance.
Alter Any Server Audit	Grants the user the right to change any server audit specification.
Alter Any Server Role	Grants the user the right to change the user-defined server roles within the SQL Server instance.
Alter Resources	Grants the user the right to change system resources.
Alter Server State	Grants the user the right to change the server state. Granting this privilege also grants the View Server State privilege.
Alter Settings	Grants the user the right to change instance-wide settings.
Alter Trace	Grants the user the right to change other users' profiler and server-side traces.

continues

TABLE 8-1 *(continued)*

PRIVILEGE NAME	PRIVILEGE DEFINITION
Authenticate Server	Grants the user the right to authenticate against the SQL Server instance.
Connect SQL	Grants the user the right to connect to the SQL Server instance.
Control Server	Grants a superset of instance-level rights: Administrator bulk options, Alter Any Availability Group, Alter Any Connection, Alter Any Credential, Alter Any Database, Alter Any Endpoint, Alter Any Event Notification, Alter Any Linked Server, Alter Any Login, Alter Any Server Audit, Alter Any Server Role, Alter Resources, Alter Server State, Alter Settings, Alter Trace, Authenticate Server, Connect SQL, External Access Assembly, Shutdown, Unsafe Assembly, and View Any Definition.
Create Any Database	Enables the user to create a new database, or to restore a database from backup.
Create Availability Group	Enables the user to create a new AlwaysOn Availability Group.
Create DDL Event Notification	Grants the user the right to create a DDL trigger.
Create Endpoint	Grants the user the right to create a SQL Server endpoint.
Create Server Role	Grants the user the right to create a user-defined server role.
Create Trace Event Notification	Grants the user the right to create a trace event notification.
External Access Assembly	Grants the user the right to create an assembly that requires the external access setting.
Shutdown	Grants the user the right to shut down the SQL Server instance by using the `SHUTDOWN T-SQL` statement.
Unsafe Assembly	Grants the user the right to create an assembly that requires the unsafe setting.
View Any Database	Grants the user the right to view the definition of any database within the SQL Server instance.
View Any Definition	Grants the user the right to view the definition of any object within the SQL Server instance. Granting this right also grants the View Any Database privilege.
View Server State	Grants the user the right to view the server state objects. These server state objects include the SQL Server's Dynamic Management Views (DMVs) and functions.

> **WARNING** *The Control Server right can be granted to users who need a higher permission level without needing the full-blown set of administrative rights that come with being a member of the* sysadmin *fixed server role. Heed the warning that a user with this right has elevated permissions to the SQL Server instance, so this right should not be given out often.*

New SQL Server 2014 Settings

SQL Server 2014 added three new instance-level permissions and one new database-level permission, as shown in Table 8-2.

TABLE 8-2: New SQL Server 2014 Permissions

PRIVILEGE NAME	PRIVILEGE DEFINITION
Connect Any Database	This permission allows a login to connect to any database in the instance. Denying this permission prevents a user from connecting to any database.
Impersonate Any Login	This permission allows a login to impersonate any other login defined in the server. This is a dangerous permission, and should be used with caution primarily in test and debugging situations. Denying this permission keeps the user from impersonating other users. This is a useful thing to limit, but test carefully—sometimes impersonation is required for legitimate operations.
Select All User Securables	This permission allows a login to read any data in the whole instance. This might be useful for an auditor who needs to read all the data, but shouldn't be able to change it. This permission is actually more interesting as a DENY permission. If a login is configured with DENY Select All User Securables, it will not be able to read any data in the instance. This means you can set up an administrator with permissions to back up databases, rebuild indexes, and so on, but no ability to read data. Security auditors often make this a requirement, and, until now, this was very difficult to do.
Alter Any Database Event Session	This permission allows a user to administer extended event sessions.

Availability Groups

Availability groups have the following four rights that can be granted to user-defined server roles:

➤ **Alter**—The Alter privilege enables the user who has been assigned the privilege to make changes to the AlwaysOn Availability Group.

➤ **Control**—The Control privilege grants the other three privileges to the user.

➤ **Take Ownership**—The Take Ownership privilege enables the user who has been assigned the privilege to change the ownership of the Availability Group.

➤ **View Definition**—The View Definition privilege enables the user who has been granted the right to view the definition of the Availability Group.

User-Defined Server Roles

SQL Server 2012 introduced user-defined server roles. User-defined server roles are similar to fixed server roles, except that they are created by the SQL Server administrator, and not by Microsoft. The user-defined server roles can be made members of any other server role, either fixed or user-defined. Any server-wide right (shown earlier in this chapter) that can be granted to a login can be granted to a user-defined server role. User-defined server roles make it possible to define an administrator role with only the permissions that particular administrator needs to do his or her job. This makes it easier to follow the "least privilege" security practice.

The following four privileges can be granted to a login for each user-defined server role:

➤ **Alter**—The Alter privilege enables the login to alter the user-defined server role. This includes adding other logins as members of the fixed server roles.

➤ **Control**—The Control privilege grants the other three privileges.

➤ **Take Ownership**—The Take Ownership privilege enables the login to set himself or herself as the owner of the user-defined server role.

➤ **View Definition**—The View Definition privilege enables the login to view the user-defined server role without having the ability to alter the user-defined server role.

Fixed Server Roles

SQL Server has nine fixed server roles that are predefined by Microsoft and cannot be changed. Eight of these fixed server roles have existed since at least SQL Server 7, and the ninth role was added in SQL Server 2005. The newer role is the *bulkadmin* fixed server role. This role gives the members of the role the right to bulk insert data into the database. In other previous versions of SQL Server, bulk loading data into the database required being a member of the most powerful fixed server role, *sysadmin*, which provides the ability to perform any action against any database without restriction. Other fixed server roles grant various rights to the members of the roles and are discussed in the following list:

➤ The *dbcreator* fixed server role grants the user the right to create databases.

➤ The *diskadmin* fixed server role grants the user the rights to manage the physical database files.

➤ The *setupadmin* fixed server role grants the user the rights to add and remove linked servers.

➤ The *processadmin* fixed server role grants the rights to kill other users' processes within the SQL Server instance.

➤ The *securityadmin* fixed server role enables the members of the role to GRANT, DENY, and REVOKE all server-level permissions, as well as any database-level permissions for the databases to which they have rights.

➤ The *serveradmin* fixed server role enables the members to change any server-wide configuration option, as well as use the SHUTDOWN command to shut down the SQL Server instance.

➤ The *public* fixed server role grants no rights; all logins on the instance are members of the *public* role.

➤ The *sysadmin* role, while not considered a fixed server role, grants all rights in the instance. No permission checks are performed on members of the sysadmin role.

Database Securables

Objects of various kinds exist within each SQL Server database, all of which have their own permissions. These permissions grant specific users rights to those objects so that the users can perform the functions needed to complete their tasks. It is a best practice to grant the users who will be using the database the minimum permissions needed to complete their jobs. This is so that the users don't have rights to objects or data within the database that they don't need. An added benefit of this practice is to prevent someone who breaks into the database from gaining access to more secure data.

Database Permissions

Permissions can be granted against the database itself. Some of these rights are specific to the database level, whereas some cascade down to objects within the database (such as tables, views, and stored procedures).

Tables and Views

When dealing with tables and views, ten different rights can be granted to specific users or user-defined database roles. These are listed in Table 8-3.

TABLE 8-3: Rights for Tables and Views

RIGHT	DEFINITION
Alter	Enables the user to change the schema of the object.
Control	Grants the user all other rights on the object.
Delete	Enables the user to delete data from the object.
Insert	Enables the user to insert data into the table.
References	Enables the user to create a foreign key on the table. This right does not apply to views.
Select	Enables the user to select the data from the object.
Take Ownership	Enables the user to change the ownership of the object.
Update	Enables the user to change data within the table.
View Change Tracking	Enables the user to view the change, tracking information for the object in question.
View Definition	Enables the user to view the schema design of the object.

Stored Procedures and Functions

Stored procedures, functions, and most other database objects within SQL Server contain only five permissions that can be granted to users or roles, and are listed in Table 8-4.

TABLE 8-4: Rights for Stored Procedures, Functions, and Most Other Database Objects

PERMISSION	DEFINITION
Alter	Enables the user to change the schema of the database object to which the right was granted.
Control	Grants the user the other rights to the object.
Execute	Enables the user to execute the object.
Take Ownership	Enables the user to change the owner of the object.
View Definition	Enables the user to view the schema of the object without having the ability to change the object.

Permission Chains

Database permissions are chained from higher-level code objects to lower-level objects referenced within the object. As shown in the following code snippet, if a table and stored procedure existed, and a user were granted rights to execute the stored procedure, the permission chain would enable the user to query the table, but only from within the context of the stored procedures. Any queries run from outside the stored procedure do not work unless the user has been granted specific rights to the table.

```
CREATE USER SampleUser WITHOUT LOGIN
GO
CREATE TABLE dbo.Users
(UserId INT IDENTITY (1,1) PRIMARY KEY,
UserName varchar(100),
Password varchar(100))
go
CREATE PROCEDURE dbo.SignIn
     @UserName varchar(100),
     @Password varchar(100)
AS
SELECT UserId
FROM Users
WHERE UserName = @UserName
     and Password = @Password
GO
GRANT EXEC ON dbo.SignIn to SampleUser
GO
```

Permission chains work only within the context of the same execution of the parent object. This is a fancy way of saying that the permission chain does not work with dynamic SQL. When using dynamic SQL, the user must be granted rights to the specific objects called within the dynamic SQL.

Permission chaining works within all native SQL Server objects, including stored procedures, scalar functions, table-valued functions, and views. This chains down to other stored procedures, scalar functions, table-valued functions, views, tables, and service broker objects. Permission chaining is enabled by default and cannot be disabled. Permission chaining is what enables the best practice of only granting the minimum set of permissions needed because it only requires execution rights on the stored procedures that are called and not the base objects.

Cross-Database Permission Chains

Cross-database permission chaining is a feature of SQL Server, introduced in SQL Server 2000 Service Pack 3a. Cross-database permission chaining is an extension of traditional permission chaining, but it allows the permission chaining to apply between databases. Without cross-database permission chaining, accessing objects in a second database using the three-part name of the object would require that the user have the necessary rights on the object. Looking at the script shown in the following code snippet, for the stored procedure to work as written, the user would need to have the SELECT privilege.

```
USE master
GO
CREATE DATABASE Sample1
GO
CREATE DATABASE Sample2
GO
USE Sample1
GO
CREATE TABLE dbo.Users
(UserId INT IDENTITY (1,1) PRIMARY KEY,
UserName varchar(100),
Password varchar(100))
go
USE Sample2
GO
CREATE TABLE dbo.Users
(UserId INT IDENTITY (1,1) PRIMARY KEY,
UserName varchar(100),
Password varchar(100))
go
CREATE PROCEDURE dbo.VerifyUsers
AS
SELECT *
FROM dbo.Users b
WHERE NOT EXISTS (SELECT * FROM Sample1.dbo.Users a WHERE a.UserId = b.UserId)
GO
```

Cross-database chaining is a database-level setting that is disabled by default on all databases. To enable it, the cross-database setting must be enabled on both the database in which the procedure exists and the database in which the table exists. You can see if cross-database chaining is enabled in a couple ways. The easiest way is to query the sys.databases catalog view, specifically looking at the is_db_chaining_on column that returns a 0 when cross-database chaining is disabled and a 1 when cross-database chaining is enabled, as shown in Figure 8-1.

	name	is_db_chaining_on
1	master	1
2	tempdb	1
3	model	0
4	msdb	1
5	SampleDatabase	0
6	ChainedDatabase	1
7	QueueReceiver	0

FIGURE 8-1

You can also view the status of the database chaining by looking at the Properties window of the database. You can do this by connecting to the database instance in the Object Explorer. Follow these steps:

1. Navigate to Databases, and then select the database in question.

2. Right-click the database and select Properties from the context menu that opens.

3. Select the Options page, and scroll down in the Other Options section, as shown in Figure 8-2.

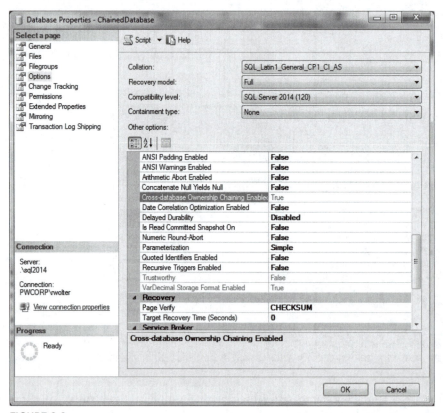

FIGURE 8-2

4. Within the Miscellaneous section, the Cross-Database Ownership Chaining Enabled field is visible, although grayed out. View the setting from the screen shown in Figure 8-2. However, you must use T-SQL to change this setting using the AlTER DATABASE statement.

As stated, enabling cross-database chaining requires using the T-SQL `ALTER DATABASE` statement so that the `DB_CHAINING` option is enabled, as shown in the following code snippet. The `ALTER DATABASE` statement must be used against both databases so that the stored procedure shown in the previous code snippet works as written.

```
ALTER DATABASE Sample1 SET DB_CHAINING ON
GO
ALTER DATABASE Sample2 SET DB_CHAINING ON
GO
```

One additional right must be granted for cross-database chaining to work correctly. The user must be added as a user within the second database. The user does not need any additional rights within the database except to exist as a user within the second database either by creating a user that maps to the same login to which the first database user is mapped, or by enabling the guest user within the second database. Enabling the guest user is not recommended because that would grant other users rights to the database that they do not need.

Although cross-database chaining is a convenient way to allow queries between related databases, it should be used with caution because it may have unintended consequences. Suppose a somewhat nefarious owner of a minor database is in the same instance as the credit card database. As a DBO, he or she can create users in the database linked to the same logins as users in the credit card database. If cross-database chaining is on, the nefarious DBO can access objects he or she probably shouldn't.

ROW-LEVEL SECURITY

Row-level security is something people are always asking about because Oracle has the concept of virtual private databases, which enables the DBA to specify which rows the user can access.

The easiest way to do this is to create a view for each user who needs access, or create a single view for each group of users that needs rights to specific rows within the database table. The user is then granted rights to the view and not to the table, and the user can then view only the rows that match the `WHERE` clause within the view.

Another technique that you can use is to design row-level security into the database schema. For example, if there were a department table and all managers needed to query the table and access only their direct reports' information, you could build this into a view so that a single view could be used for all managers within the system. You can do this via some system functions such as `suser_sname()` or `current_user()`. Listing 8-1 shows the `suser_sname()` function (code file: `Using the suser_sname function.sql`).

LISTING 8-1: Using the suser_sname() Function.sql

```
CREATE TABLE dbo.Employee
(EmployeeId INT IDENTITY(1,1) PRIMARY KEY,
LastName varchar(100),
FirstName varchar(100),
Emailaddress varchar(255),
ManagerId INT,
```

continues

LISTING 8-1 *(continued)*

```
Username varchar(100))
GO
INSERT INTO dbo.Employee
(LastName, FirstName, EmailAddress, ManagerId, UserName)
VALUES
('Smith', 'John', 'jsmith@contonso.com', 0, 'CONTOSO\jsmith'),
    ('Gates', 'Fred', 'fgates@contonso.com', 1, 'CONTOSO\fgates'),
    ('Jones', 'Bob', 'bjones@contonso.com', 1, 'CONTOSO\bjones'),
    ('Erickson', 'Paula', 'perickson@contonso.com', 1, 'CONTOSO\perickson')
GO
CREATE VIEW dbo.EmployeeView
AS
SELECT *
FROM dbo.Employee
WHERE ManagerId = (SELECT EmployeeId FROM Employee WHERE UserName = suser_sname())
GO
```

> **NOTE** *Microsoft has released an excellent whitepaper that discusses row-level security in more detail. You can find more information about the whitepaper on the Public Sector blog hosted on MSDN at* `http://blogs.msdn.com/b/public-sector/archive/2011/08/23/row-level-security-for-sql-server-2008.aspx.` *Microsoft has also created a row- and/or cell-based security feature that has been released on Codeplex* (`http://sqlserver1st.codeplex.com/`). *This was created by the SQL Server engineering team, so it is well maintained and robust.*

SUMMARY

Database security must be implemented correctly because without it, all the information can be accessed by people who shouldn't have access to the data. This can leave the database susceptible to internal and external threats. Security shouldn't be limited to just the database and instance.

You must implement a variety of levels of security both outside and inside the database. This includes properly securing the network, the Windows operating system that hosts the database, the instance, the database permissions, and the application that needs to be secured to ensure that SQL Injection attacks are not successful.

With each release of Microsoft SQL Server, the face of security within the platform changes, and administrators must adapt. The user-defined server roles enable a much more flexible security model.

Chapter 9 covers the In-Memory OLTP feature, which is new for SQL Server 2014. You will learn to use in-memory tables and native compiled stored procedures to optimize your key OLTP table for greatly improved application performance. The chapter covers how to determine which tables are good candidates for In-Memory OLTP, and how to configure and manage the tables chosen.

In-Memory OLTP

WHAT'S IN THIS CHAPTER?

➤ Using and implementing in-memory OLTP

➤ Creating natively compiled stored procedures

➤ Getting to know the Analyze, Report, and Migrate (ARM) tool

WROX.COM CODE DOWNLOADS FOR THIS CHAPTER

The wrox.com code downloads for this chapter are found at `www.wrox.com/go/ prosql2014admin` on the Download Code tab. The code is in the Chapter 9 download and individually named according to the names throughout the chapter.

In-memory online transaction processing (OLTP) represents one of the most significant changes in SQL Server 2014. To fully appreciate in-memory OLTP, you must understand what the technology is, what it is meant to do, and how it is comparable to other in-memory technologies that are competitors of Microsoft. This holistic view of the technology will enable you to determine if and when you should use in-memory OLTP.

In this chapter, you learn how to create in-memory OLTP tables, how to create natively compiled stored procedures, how in-memory OLTP is integrated into the traditional SQL Server stack, and how to leverage the Analyze, Report, and Migrate (ARM) tool.

USING AND IMPLEMENTING IN-MEMORY OLTP

In-memory OLTP is an enterprise-level feature that brings to businesses and users of all sizes performance that was previously only attainable to organizations that could afford to spend several hundreds of thousands of dollars on hardware. It is available in SQL Server 2014 Developer, Evaluation, and Enterprise editions only. To perform the exercises that follow, you must be running one of those editions. In-memory OLTP is also referred to as *memory-optimized* tables.

Memory-optimized tables are stored in a completely different format than regular tables. You add a filegroup with FILESTREAM data to an existing database, or specify one when you create a database. Data is not stored on data pages. It is stored in memory in an optimized format. A checkpoint file is kept on disk.

> **NOTE** *For a review of data records (compressed and uncompressed), pages, extents, allocation bitmaps, Index Allocation Map (IAM) chains, and allocation units, see Chapter 11, "Optimizing SQL Server 2014."*

After you have created your filegroup, you can decide if you would like your table to be durable or non-durable. *Durable data* is saved, persisted to disk, data. Durable data will survive a restart of SQL Server. *Non-durable data* (also known as *schema-only* data) saves only the structure of your table, but does not persist any data upon restart. Non-durable data is stored in memory, and memory is flushed and reset for an application when it is restarted. Your instinct could be to immediately determine that all data should be durable. However, there may be valid scenarios where non-durable data is best for performance, based on the way that an application uses data.

In-memory OLTP is not the end goal to fix all of your SQL Server performance issues. It can offer tremendous performance increases of between 9 and 150 times performance improvement. Many examples can be found at the Microsoft Case Studies website (http://www.microsoft.com/casestudies/). An example of 150 times improvement comes from the Baltika Breweries Case Study (http://www.microsoft.com/casestudies/Microsoft-SQL-Server-2014/Baltika-Breweries/Brewer-Increases-CRM-System-Capacity-by-54-Percent-with-Data-Solution/710000004225).

However, in-memory OLTP will not be right for every workload. Remember to use the proper tool for the proper job. Later in this chapter, you learn about the Analyze, Report, and Migration (ARM) tool, and how to use it to find the proper candidates for in-memory OLTP.

Enabling In-Memory OLTP

The first thing you must do to begin working with in-memory OLTP is to create a database that will store your data. As mentioned, this requires making a database and adding a FILESTREAM data filegroup, or adding one to an existing database. You can use the following code (code file: BradleyBall_Chapter9_Code.sql) to create a new database, or you can also add a FILESTREAM data filegroup to your AdventureWorks database. Notice the keyword CONTAINS MEMORY_OPTIMIZED_DATA. You may also notice that you do not need to enable FILESTREAM on your SQL Server instance to use in-memory OLTP.

```
    Create In Memory OLTP Example DB
    */
    USE [master]
    GO
    CREATE DATABASE [example_InMemOLTP]
     CONTAINMENT = NONE
     ON PRIMARY
```

```
( NAME = N'example_InMemOLTP', FILENAME = N'E:\MSSQL\example_InMemOLTP_xtp.mdf' ,
    SIZE = 3264KB , MAXSIZE = UNLIMITED, FILEGROWTH = 1024KB ),
 FILEGROUP [college_xtp_mod] CONTAINS MEMORY_OPTIMIZED_DATA DEFAULT
( NAME = N'example_InMemOLTP_mod1', FILENAME = N'F:\MSSQL\example_InMemOLTP_mod1'
    , MAXSIZE = UNLIMITED)
 LOG ON
( NAME = N'example_InMemOLTP_log',
    FILENAME = N'E:\MSSQL\example_InMemOLTP_log.ldf' ,
    SIZE = 270016KB , MAXSIZE = 2048GB , FILEGROWTH = 10%)
GO
/*
Alter AdventureWorks to add Filegroup with Memory optimized data
*/
IF NOT EXISTS(SELECT * FROM AdventureWorks.sys.data_spaces WHERE type='FX')
ALTER DATABASE AdventureWorks
ADD FILEGROUP [AdventureWorks_Mod] CONTAINS MEMORY_OPTIMIZED_DATA
GO
IF NOT EXISTS(SELECT * FROM AdventureWorks.sys.data_spaces ds join
    AdventureWorks.sys.database_files df on ds.data_space_id=df.data_space_id
    where ds.type='FX')
ALTER DATABASE AdventureWorks
ADD FILE (name='AdventureWorks_Mod', filename='F:\MSSQL\Adventure_Works_Mod')
    TO FILEGROUP AdventureWorks_Mod
```

Now that you have created a database (or modified an existing one), you are ready to create your first table. Before you begin, let's review some of the limitations of memory-optimized tables:

➤ No schema changes are permitted once the memory-optimized table has been created. No `ALTER TABLE` statements are allowed. All indexes must be created inline. There is no support for `CREATE`, `DROP`, or `ALTER INDEX` statements.

➤ Each table must have at least one index.

➤ Only hash indexes and range indexes can be created on in-memory optimized tables.

➤ Any data type that is not an `in_row_data` type cannot use in-memory OLTP.

➤ There is a maximum of eight indexes per memory-optimized table. There are no unique indexes, except for the Primary Key index.

➤ `IDENTITY` property is available, but you must increment by 1 and start at 1.

➤ No Data Manipulation Language (DML) or Data Definition Language (DDL) triggers, foreign keys, or check constraints are allowed.

➤ There is no support for `LOB` or `ROW_OVER_FLOW` data types. You cannot define a row in a table with more than 8,060 bytes.

➤ You cannot partition or compress a memory-optimized table.

➤ You cannot apply a sort order to hash indexes.

➤ `SAVEPOINT` in explicit transactions, bound transactions, and Distributed Transaction Coordinator (DTC) cannot use memory-optimized tables.

> **NOTE** *For a full list of unsupported syntax and features with this edition of in-memory OLTP, see the MSDN article, "Transact-SQL Constructs Not Supported by In-memory OLTP," at* `http://msdn.microsoft.com/en-us/library/dn246937.aspx.`

In-Memory OLTP Structures

As you continue learning about in-memory OLTP, it is important to get a good understanding of the data structures that make up in-memory OLTP tables. To do this, you should understand the data hierarchy, and how data is stored from its lowest form to its highest. Figure 9-1 shows a list from bottom to top.

FIGURE 9-1

Records

You will start from the bottom and move up through the different storage levels for in-memory OLTP. Rows are the lowest level of storage, and are synonymous with a row in a table. The structure of an in-memory OLTP row is the row header, key, and payload. Figure 9-2 shows a detailed visual representation.

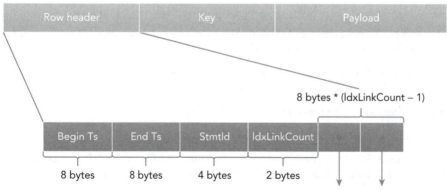

FIGURE 9-2

There are two 8-byte fields that hold timestamps denoted as Begin Ts and End Ts. These are populated from two internal counters (the Transaction-ID counter and the Global Transaction counter) that generate timestamps for any database that supports in-memory OLTP.

Transaction-ID is a unique value that is reset when SQL Server restarts, while the Global Transaction is global and unique. Global Transaction is not reset upon restart of SQL Server, but is initialized during recovery with the highest transaction timestamp found in the recovered records. This value is incremented each time a transaction ends, and the new value is the current timestamp for the current transaction (a new row).

A 4-byte statement ID is the next value in the header. The `StmtId` is unique per transaction. This allows the transaction to script the rows already created by it, if they are accessed again.

The headers also contains a 2-byte value, `idxLinkCount`. This is a reference count indicating how many indexes are referencing this row. After this there is a pointer for each index on the table.

The remaining key columns and data in the row are in the payload. The payload is dependent upon the table definition. All in-memory structures are compiled code, and this leaves the structure for all objects unchangeable after the object is created. In order to add, remove, or alter a column, you must drop and re-create the table. This also means that you must define all of your indexes upon creation.

Indexes

When defining an in-memory OLTP table, you must define at least one index. There are no IAM pages in in-memory OLTP. The index pointers are the only method of linking rows into a table. This is why each table must have a minimum of one index.

In-memory OLTP offers you two new types of indexes to utilize: hash indexes and range indexes.

Hash Indexes

Hash indexes use a hashing function to take values of arbitrary and fixed size (with slight differences in input data) and return a value with very big differences in output data. Each hashed value is stored in a *hash bucket*. Hash buckets are essentially an array of pointers. Those pointers make up a hash index. Figure 9-3 shows one row in a hash index on the `Student` column.

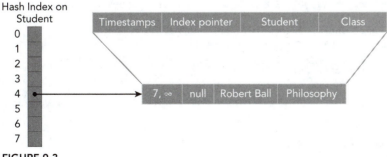

FIGURE 9-3

This example shows eight buckets in the hash array. Hash buckets will always be declared to the nearest power of two. You will learn more about this as you progress through this chapter. The Student record for Robert Ball is stored in hash bucket 4. You can see by the null value in the index pointer that this is the first record in the index. Figure 9-4 shows how you add another row to the table by inserting Robert Noel, and now you have the beginning of an index chain. The Robert Noel row occupies the same bucket as the Robert Ball row. The Robert Noel row has an index pointer that is directed to the previous row.

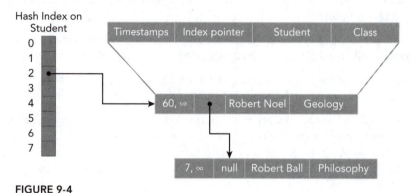

FIGURE 9-4

Typically, you want hash values to occupy their own buckets. Too many hash values in the same bucket can degrade query performance. In the next exercise, you use the following script to create a simple table and a hash index.

```
use AdventureWorks
go
if exists(select name from sys.tables where name='mytable1')
begin
     drop table mytable1
end
go
use AdventureWorks
go
create table mytable1(
              myid int identity(1,1)
              ,mychar1 char(500)  COLLATE Latin1_General_100_bin2 default
                 'a' not null
              ,mychar2 char(3000) default 'b' not null
              constraint pk_mytbl_1 primary key
     nonclustered hash     (myid,mychar1) with (bucket_count = 10)) with
         (memory_optimized = on)

declare @i int
set @i =0
while (@i<16)
begin
     insert into mytable1
     default values
     set @i=@i+1
end
```

You use the `sys.dm_db_xtp_hash_index_stats` DMV to view the number of hash buckets created, and how they are occupying their current spaces. Figure 9-5 shows the details on the DMV results.

```
SELECT OBJECT_NAME(S.object_id) as TableName
 , I.name AS IndexName
 , S.total_bucket_count
 , S.empty_bucket_count
 , S.avg_chain_length
 , S.max_chain_length
FROM sys.dm_db_xtp_hash_index_stats S
JOIN sys.indexes I
on S.index_id = I.index_id
 AND
 S.object_id = I.object_id;
```

	TableName	IndexName	total_bucket_count	empty_bucket_count	avg_chain_length	max_chain_length
1	mytable1	pk_mytbl_1	16	4	1	2

FIGURE 9-5

You can see that, even though you only defined 10 hash buckets, you were allocated 16. This is because SQL Server allocates buckets to the power of 2—8 is a power of 2, 10 is greater than 8, so SQL Server needs to go to the next power of 2, which is 16.

Despite having 16 buckets, you have 4 empty buckets. The average chain length per bucket is 1. This is good. You want your hashed values to have a high level of uniqueness to ensure that a unique row is found on seek operations when a hash bucket and its array of pointers is reviewed.

You have a max chain length of 2, indicating that some hash buckets contain multiple rows. However, 2 is not an unacceptable number, but keep in mind that you must declare the number of required hash buckets during the table definition. There can be no DDL updates. You cannot use ALTER TABLE or ALTER INDEX to change the hash definition. If you were to insert thousands of rows into this table, the hash buckets would be overflowing.

If a seek operation examines a hash bucket and attempts to find a row, this would cause multiple values to be examined, thus slowing down the retrieval process. You want to be as precise as possible when defining the index.

Remember the hash index is still an index. You use it to retrieve data from your table. Declare a hash index on columns that you plan to use as predicates in queries. A query using the `mychar2` column would perform a full table.

You may be asking yourself, "When should I use a hash index?" This is an excellent question. You want to use hash indexes when you know you will be doing a lot of seek operations. You want to have specific queries where you are getting only one row, or a set of very specific rows. For example, say that you wrote a query that read as follows:

```
select * from dbo.mytable1 where myid=1
```

You are looking for a specific row. If this was an orders table, looking up one order at a time would be a valid example. However, if you wanted to find a range of values such as orders that occurred after a different date, then a hash index is not the type of index you should use.

If you need to query a range, then the type of index that you should use is the range index.

Range Indexes

The *range index* is conceptually very similar to indexes that you are used to dealing with in SQL Server. They store, sort, and guide the use of data stored in a range of values. For example, A to Z is an alpha numeric range, and 1 to 100 is a numeric range. When you think of ordering values in a particular manner, that is what a range index does.

Internally, the range index is based on the Bw-tree design that was created by Microsoft Research back in 2011. The general structure of the Bw-tree is very similar to the B-tree you currently have within clustered and nonclustered indexes. However the Bw-tree uses multi-concurrent versions, allowing for latch- and lock-free structures, which offer performance improvements over disk-bound tables.

> **NOTE** *To read more on the Bw-tree, see the white paper, "The Bw-Tree: A B-tree for New Hardware Platforms,"* at `http://research.microsoft.com/pubs/178758/bw-tree-icde2013-final.pdf`. *This white paper introduces the lock-free, latch-free structure that was the basis for the range index that is used in in-memory OLTP.*

Range index pages sizes are not a fixed size. Once they are created, they are unchangeable. The default page size is 8K, but that can vary based on the data that occupies the index. Each index page contains a set of ordered key values.

You still have a root, intermediate, and leaf level pages. However, since the pages cannot update, a new version is created when records are inserted or deleted.

With so many changes to index pages, you may be wondering how your queries will effectively transverse the index chains to perform seek operations. This is where the *page mapping table* is used. The page mapping table tracks the PID, which is the logical page ID, instead of the physical page number. When a new index page is created because of an update operation, the page mapping table is updated, and when queries are no longer using the index page, it is marked for garbage collection. Figure 9-6 shows the structure of a range index.

Notice that the high value from each leaf level page is raised up to the non-leaf level pages. This is a difference between Bw-tree and B-trees. The leaf level pages still contain the key values, but instead of the PID contained in the non-leaf level pages, they store the actual memory address where the data is stored.

Leaf level page changes are tracked using *delta tables*. The delta table adds one row for insert and delete operations. Update operations add a row that contains the previous value, as well as the updated value.

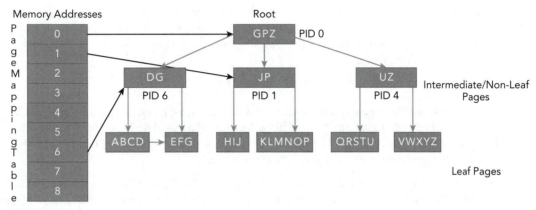

FIGURE 9-6

There is a header within each index page that contains the following values:

➤ PID—This is the pointer to the mapping table.

➤ Page type—This is the type of page allocated within the index.

➤ Right PID—This is the PID for the page to the right of the current page.

➤ Height—This is the the current number of levels from the current page to the leaf.

➤ Page statistics—This is the count of records on the page, plus the count of the delta records.

➤ Max key—This is the the upper limit of the values on the page.

You have now created or modified your existing database, and have learned about the internal structures. You are now ready to create your first table, as shown here (code file: BradleyBall_Chapter9_Code.sql):

```
/*
First Memory Optimized Table
*/
use example_InMemOLTP
go
CREATE TABLE first_InMemOLTP(
    c1 int identity(1,1) NOT NULL PRIMARY KEY NONCLUSTERED
    ,c2 int NOT NULL INDEX first_xtp_nclx_index
        hash with(bucket_count=10000000)
        ,c3 int NOT NULL INDEX first_xtp_nclx_index2
        hash with(bucket_count=10000000)
        ,c4 int NOT NULL INDEX first_xtp_nclx_index3
        hash with(bucket_count=10000000)
    ,c5 int
    ,c6 char(100) COLLATE Latin1_General_100_bin2 NOT NULL INDEX
        first_xtp_nclx_char
    ,c7 char(80)
)WITH(memory_optimized=on, DURABILITY=SCHEMA_AND_DATA)
```

Notice the differences in the table definition. All indexes are defined inline. There is no clustered index. To define a column on a CHAR, VARCHAR, or Unicode data type, you must specify the inline collation to be a *_BIN2 collation compatible type. To find all the collations that are compatible with *_BIN2, use the following query:

```
select * from sys.fn_helpcollations() where name like '%BIN2'
```

You previously learned that you could choose the durable nature of in-memory OLTP tables. The DURABILITY specified is SCHEMA_AND_DATA. This will ensure that the data is persisted to the log using the write-ahead logging mechanism in SQL Server. The data is a checkpointed for out of memory, and is written to the memory-optimized checkpoint file.

You could also specify the DURABILITY as SCHEMA_ONLY. This would disable the write-ahead logging mechanism for this table. The data would never be checkpointed out of memory. When SQL Server restarts, all the data would be lost. When the table is written back into memory during the database restart, only the schema would be re-written to memory.

CPU Considerations

The hardware that you are using to host SQL Server 2014 must support the instruction cmpxchg16b (allowing for atomic operations on octal words) in order to use in-memory OLTP. This is used for parallel algorithms that use compare and swap data larger than the size of a pointer, and is common in lock-free and wait-free algorithms. All modern x64 processors support cmpxchg16b.

The current release of in-memory OLTP is targeted to perform optimally on servers with 2 to 4 sockets, and fewer than 60 cores.

Virtualization Considerations

If you are using virtualization, the host must support cmpxchg. If you are using Hyper-V, cmpxchg is supported, regardless of the underlying hardware.

In typical virtualized environments, you want to ensure that plenty of resources are available to guest machines from the host. It is a best practice to configure a Minimum Server Memory. (The terminology for this will differ based on virtualization vendor.) Another best practice is not to set the memory pre-allocation value too high. This is to prevent other processes from being starved, and not receiving sufficient memory when they require it.

On virtualized systems using in-memory OLTP, this is *not* the case. When a database that uses the in-memory OLTP feature comes online, it will attempt to restore and recover the data from the checkpoint file. In-memory OLTP brings data into memory more aggressively than dynamic memory allocation may allocate to the database. This could lead to the database remaining in the "Recovery Pending" state, even if you have sufficient memory to hold the data.

As a best practice, you should pre-allocate sufficient memory to hold all of your in-memory OLTP data. Allowing the host system to allocate dynamic memory upon demand (and dependant on a Minimum Server Memory setting) could cause issues for your in-memory OLTP data.

Memory Considerations

You should understand your memory requirements before implementing in-memory OLTP. To do this, you must estimate the amount of memory that you will require. If you are migrating a disk-based table, or creating a new memory-optimized table, the process should be the same.

You add up the number of bytes per row, and then you add in an additional 24 bytes per row for the row header and timestamp. There will be index pointers as well. Each index will have an 8-byte address pointer to the next row in the index.

As an example, examine the following code (code file: `BradleyBall_Chapter9_Code.sql`):

```
CREATE TABLE xtp_Estimate(
     c1 int identity(1,1) NOT NULL PRIMARY KEY NONCLUSTERED
     ,c2 int NOT NULL INDEX xtp_nclx_index
         hash with(bucket_count=10000000)
     ,c3 int NOT NULL INDEX xtp_nclx_index2
         hash with(bucket_count=10000000)
     ,c4 int NOT NULL INDEX xtp_nclx_index3
         hash with(bucket_count=10000000)
     ,c5 int NOT NULL INDEX xtp_nclx_index4
     ,c6 char(100)
     ,c7 char(80)
)WITH(memory_optimized=on)
```

You can see four indexes in the code. As you begin to add up the data per row, you can start with the metadata of the 24-byte header and 32 bytes for indexes, for a total of 56 bytes. You have five rows of integer values at 4 bytes each, for a five-column total of 20. This increases the running total to 76. You have two columns of character data, 100 and 80 bytes each. This increases the total amount of storage to 256 bytes per row.

Table 9-1 provides a full breakdown.

TABLE 9-1: Total Number of Bytes per Row

SIZE TYPE	SIZE (BYTES)
Index pointers	8
Number of indexes	4
Total index size	32
Timestamp/Header	24
Data	200
Total bytes per row	256

This value is very important. Now that you have it, you can estimate the amount of space you will need based on the number of rows that you project you will have in your table. Because of the multi-concurrent version store that is maintained for in-memory OLTP, it is important to multiply that time estimate by four to ensure that you have enough space.

If you were to store 10 million rows in your table, you would require 9.54GB of memory, 50 million rows would require 47.68GB, 100 million rows would require 95.37GB, and so on.

Table 9-2 provides a full breakdown.

TABLE 9-2: Complete Size Estimates

ROW SIZE (BYTES)	NUMBER OF ROWS	SIZE (KB)	SIZE (MB)	SIZE (GB)	SIZE (GB) W/ VERSION STORE TIMES 4
256	10,000,000	2,500,000	2,441.41	2.38	9.54
256	50,000,000	12,500,000	12,207.03	11.92	47.68
256	100,000,000	25,000,000	24,414.06	23.84	95.37
256	500,000,000	125,000,000	122,070.31	119.21	476.84
256	1,000,000,000	250,000,000	244,140.63	238.42	953.67

The hash array size is set by `bucket_count=<value>` in the table definition statement. The `bucket_count` value must be a power of 2. If it is not, it will be rounded to the nearest power of 2.

In the previous code example, you used the number 10,000,000. The nearest power 2 is 2^{24}, or 16,777,216. Each hash bucket is 8 bytes in size. So, you multiply 16,777,216 * 8. After dividing by 1,024 once to convert to kilobytes, and then 1,024 again to convert to megabytes, you arrive at 128MB per hash index. This example has three hash indexes, which brings the hash index size to a total of 384MB.

Table 9-3 provides a breakdown of different powers of 2 and the required memory size.

TABLE 9-3 Breakdown of Hash Index Size Requirements by Power of 2

POWER OF 2	NEAREST POWER OF 2	SIZE (BYTES)	SIZE (KB)	SIZE (MB)
2^15	32,768	262144	256	0.25
2^16	65,536	524288	512	0.5
2^17	131,072	1048576	1,024	1
2^18	262,144	2097152	2,048	2
2^19	524,288	4194304	4,096	4
2^20	1,048,576	8388608	8,192	8

POWER OF 2	NEAREST POWER OF 2	SIZE (BYTES)	SIZE (KB)	SIZE (MB)
2^21	2,097,152	16,777,216	16,384	16
2^22	4,194,304	33,554,432	32,768	32
2^23	8,388,608	67,108,864	65,536	64
2^24	16,777,216	134,217,728	131,072	128

The two types of indexes you can have on memory-optimized tables are *range indexes* and hash indexes. In this example, you saw four indexes in the table definition. Three of those indexes were hash indexes, and the other was a range index. A range index may sound fancy and new, but it is the same type of index that you have used throughout SQL Server. A range index takes a range of values, 1 through 1 million, A–Z, or any list that should be ordered.

Calculating the memory for a range index is not as straightforward as the previous examples. Range indexes have a B+-tree structure, which is similar (yet different) from on-disk B-tree structures. The memory allocated to non-leaf nodes is a very small percentage, and can be safely ignored.

To calculate the leaf nodes, you must use the unique key defined for the table—in this example c1 has a 4-byte identity value. You then add that to your column with the range index—c5 in the example table—plus the pointer size per row. If you have multiple rows with the same key (for example, a non-unique non-clustered index), the rows will be linked together. For the previous example, the math would be as follows:

> Range Index Size =(Pointer (8 bytes) + sum(Key Column (4 bytes) + Defined column (4 bytes)) * Unique Rows)
>
> Range Index Size = (8 + 8) * 100,000,000 Bytes = 1.49 GB

To get the total amount of memory required to store 100,000,000 rows in the example table, this would require adding 95.37GB + 1.49GB + 0.384GB together. This would give you a total of 97.24GB.

If you use in-memory table variables in your queries, that memory is utilized outside of what you have previously defined for this example table. This also does not account for memory space usage for the growth of your table.

It is important to know this up front to ensure that you take this into account when you are purchasing hardware and setting your MAX MEMORY setting for SQL Server. By default, in-memory OLTP will use the buffer pool, and use the memory regularly allocated to other SQL Server processes.

Managing Memory with Resource Governor

Thus far, you have learned quite a bit about estimating the amount of memory that in-memory OLTP uses. By default, databases that use in-memory OLTP are bound to the default pool that houses all user resources within SQL Server.

It is possible to bind a database to a resource pool. A regular database will ignore that setting unless a user is bound to the pool. For a full overview of Resource Governor, see Chapter 11 "Optimizing SQL Server 2014."

Once a database is bound to a pool, it allows you to control the memory that is allocated to that database. To bind the database, you must first determine the MIN_MEMORY_PERCENT and the MAX_MEMORY_PERCENT. Using the tables from earlier in this chapter, those numbers should match up with the high estimate that you have for the memory-optimized tables and indexes you plan to build.

After you determine the minimum and maximum percentages, it is important to realize that 100 percent of that value will not be available to in-memory OLTP. Table 9-4 shows how physical memory can affect the percentage of memory available for memory-optimized tables.

TABLE 9-4: Percentage of Memory Available for In-Memory OLTP

TARGET COMMITTED MEMORY	PERCENT AVAILABLE FOR IN-MEMORY TABLES
<=8 GB	70 percent
<=16 GB	75 percent
<=32 GB	80 percent
<=96 GB	85 percent
>96 GB	90 percent

If your table is 60GB in size, and you have only 100GB of memory, you must determine the maximum percentage. You can do this by taking the 60GB and dividing it by 90 percent for the memory target that will be available to you. This gives you (60 / 0.90)=66.7, roughly, after rounding up. This means that you will need your MAX_MEMORY_PERCENT set at 67 percent.

Changing the MAX_MEMORY_PERCENT is an online operation, meaning that no reboot or restart is required. Implementing the Resource Governor bound database for in-memory OLTP will require the database to be taken offline. You should plan on doing this before the database is in production, or during a maintenance window if it is already deployed.

First, you create the resource pool (code file: BradleyBall_Chapter9_Code.sql). Next, you use the sp_xtp_bind_db_resource_pool system stored procedure to bind the database to the pool. Finally, you use the following script to take the database offline and bring it back online:

```
/*
Create a Resource Pool to Manage the In-Memory DB on AdventureWorks
*/
USE master
go
IF NOT EXISTS (SELECT * FROM sys.resource_governor_resource_pools
    WHERE name=N'Pool_AdventureWorks')
BEGIN
    CREATE RESOURCE POOL Pool_AdventureWorks
        WITH ( MAX_MEMORY_PERCENT = 80 );
```

```
        ALTER RESOURCE GOVERNOR RECONFIGURE;
END
GO
/*
Bind AdventureWorks to the Resource Pool
*/
EXEC sp_xtp_bind_db_resource_pool 'AdventureWorks', 'Pool_AdventureWorks'
GO
/*
Take AdventureWorks offline and back online
*/
ALTER DATABASE AdventureWorks SET OFFLINE WITH ROLLBACK IMMEDIATE
GO
ALTER DATABASE AdventureWorks SET ONLINE
GO
```

To track memory usage, you can use Performance Monitor and the SQLServer:ResourcePool Stats counters. Figure 9-7 shows a view of the memory utilization by resource group.

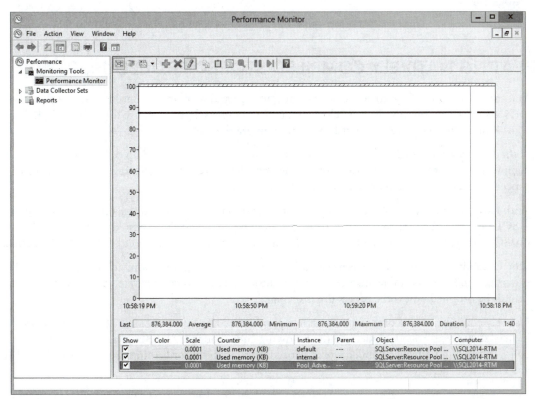

FIGURE 9-7

Figure 9-8 shows a view of memory utilization using Dynamic Management Views (DMVs) and the following script (code file: `BradleyBall_Chapter9_Code.sql`):

```
SELECT pool_id
  , Name
  , min_memory_percent
  , max_memory_percent
  , max_memory_kb/1024 AS max_memory_mb
  , used_memory_kb/1024 AS used_memory_mb
  , target_memory_kb/1024 AS target_memory_mb
FROM sys.dm_resource_governor_resource_pools
```

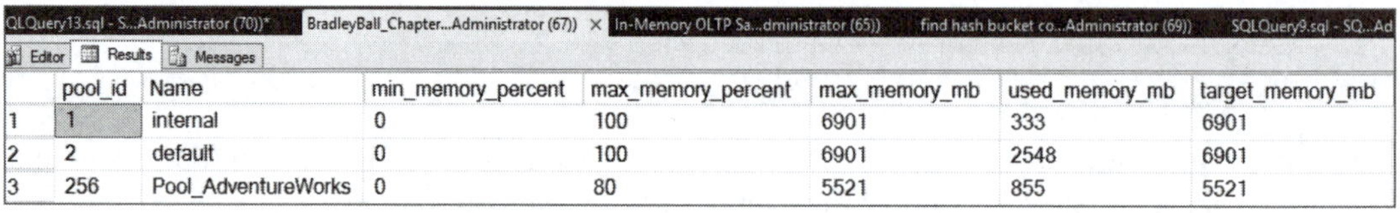

	pool_id	Name	min_memory_percent	max_memory_percent	max_memory_mb	used_memory_mb	target_memory_mb
1	1	internal	0	100	6901	333	6901
2	2	default	0	100	6901	2548	6901
3	256	Pool_AdventureWorks	0	80	5521	855	5521

FIGURE 9-8

CREATING NATIVELY COMPILED STORED PROCEDURES

You can use classic T-SQL to access memory-optimized and regular disk-based tables. SQL Server 2014 also enables you to write natively compiled stored procedures. You use the same T-SQL, but some limitations and a few key words will differentiate the two.

Natively compiled stored procedures are compiled upon creation or load up of SQL Server. The compiled code contains much fewer instructions for CPUs to execute. This results in faster stored procedure execution, and more efficient CPU utilization.

With natively compiled stored procedures, you must declare an ATOMIC transaction. Unlike regular T-SQL, you must declare this explicit transaction, and you cannot have nested transactions. If you do, SQL Server will automatically create a SAVEPOINT before entering the next ATOMIC transaction.

Schema binding is required between the natively compiled stored procedure and the base table. The procedure and the base table must be bound to the schema to which they refer. This means the table cannot be dropped unless the procedure is dropped.

Natively compiled stored procedures do not support EXECUTE AS A CALLER. They can only operate in the EXECUTE AS OWNER mode. Use the following code (code file: `BradleyBall_Chapter9_Code .sql`) to create a natively compiled stored procedure to insert records into the `xtp_Estimate` table you created earlier:

```
if exists(select name from sys.procedures where name='p_ins_new_record')
begin
    DROP PROCEDURE dbo.p_ins_new_record
```

```
end
go
CREATE PROCEDURE dbo.p_ins_new_record (@rowcount int)
WITH NATIVE_COMPILATION
,SCHEMABINDING
,EXECUTE AS OWNER
AS
BEGIN ATOMIC WITH
(TRANSACTION ISOLATION LEVEL=SNAPSHOT, LANGUAGE='us_english')
declare @i int=0
while @i<@rowcount
    begin
        set @i=@i+1
        INSERT INTO dbo.xtp_Estimate(c2, c3, c4, c5, c6, c7)
        VALUES(@i, @i, @i, @i, 'a','b')
    end
END
```

To show the power and performance of natively compiled stored procedures, let's create a disk-based table with a similar structure to the xtp_Estimate table you used earlier (code file: BradleyBall_Chapter9_Code.sql). Then, let's create two additional stored procedures. The first will insert a new row of data into the disk_Estimate table, and the second will use a classic T-SQL stored procedure to insert a row into the xtp_Estimate table. You will load 10,000 rows into each table and see which is the most performant:

```
/*
create disk based structures
*/
use example_InMemOLTP
go
if exists(select name from sys.objects where name='disk_Estimate')
begin
    drop table disk_Estimate
end
go
CREATE TABLE disk_Estimate(
    c1 int identity(1,1) NOT NULL PRIMARY KEY NONCLUSTERED
    ,c2 int NOT NULL INDEX disk_nclx_index
    ,c3 int NOT NULL INDEX disk_nclx_index2
    ,c4 int NOT NULL INDEX disk_nclx_index3
    ,c5 int NOT NULL INDEX disk_nclx_index4
    ,c6 char(100)
    ,c7 char(80)
)

if exists(select name from sys.procedures where name='p_ins_new_disk_record')
begin
    DROP PROCEDURE dbo.p_ins_new_disk_record
end
go
CREATE PROCEDURE dbo.p_ins_new_disk_record (@c2 int, @c3 int, @c4 int, @c5 int,
```

```
            @c6 char(100), @c7 char(80))
AS
BEGIN
INSERT INTO dbo.disk_Estimate(c2, c3, c4, c5, c6, c7)
VALUES(@c2, @c3, @c4, @c5, @c6, @c7)
END
GO
if exists(select name from sys.procedures where name='p_ins_tsql_xtp_record')
begin
     DROP PROCEDURE dbo.p_ins_tsql_xtp_record
end
go
CREATE PROCEDURE dbo.p_ins_tsql_xtp_record (@c2 int, @c3 int, @c4 int, @c5 int,
     @c6 char(100), @c7 char(80))
AS
BEGIN
INSERT INTO dbo.xtp_Estimate(c2, c3, c4, c5, c6, c7)
VALUES(@c2, @c3, @c4, @c5, @c6, @c7)
END
GO
/*
execute the stored procedure
*/
declare @starttime datetime2=sysdatetime()
declare @timems int
declare @i int
--disk based table & classic t-sql stored procedure
set @starttime=sysdatetime()
set @i=0
while @i<10000
begin
     set @i=@i+1
     exec dbo.p_ins_new_disk_record @i, @i, @i, @i, 'a', 'b'
end

set @timems = datediff(ms, @starttime, sysdatetime())
select 'Disk based table and T-SQL stored proc: ' + cast(@timems as varchar(10))
     + ' ms'
--Memory Optimized Table & Classic t-sql stored procedure
set @starttime=sysdatetime()
set @i=0
while @i<10000
begin
     set @i=@i+1
     exec dbo.p_ins_tsql_xtp_record @i, @i, @i, @i, 'a', 'b'
end

set @timems = datediff(ms, @starttime, sysdatetime())
select 'Memory Optimized table and T-SQL stored proc: '
     + cast(@timems as varchar(10)) + ' ms'
--natively compiled
```

```
set @starttime=sysdatetime()
exec dbo.p_ins_new_record 10000

set @timems = datediff(ms, @starttime, sysdatetime())
select 'Natively Compiled stored proc: ' + cast(@timems as varchar(10)) + ' ms'
```

Figure 9-9 shows the results of the run. The disk-based table and classic T-SQL stored procedure completed its run in 3,628 milliseconds (ms). The memory-optimized table and classic T-SQL stored procedure completed in 3,103 ms. The natively compiled stored procedure completed in 79 ms.

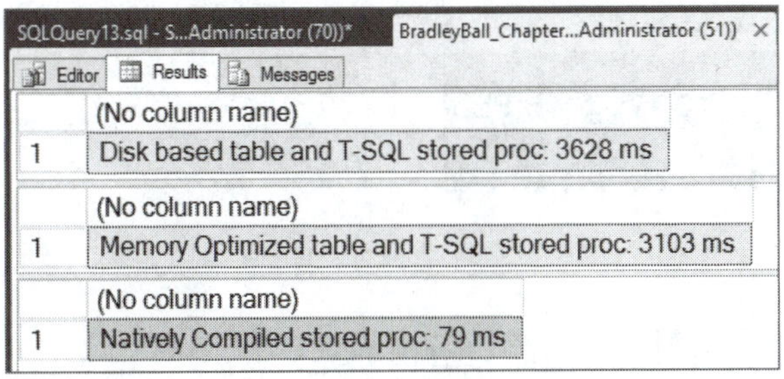

FIGURE 9-9

OVERVIEW OF THE ANALYZE, MIGRATE, AND REPORT (ARM) TOOL

Management Data Warehouse (MDW) got a big upgrade with SQL Server 2014. It was given new functionality with the Transaction Performance data collectors. These collectors look at the physical structure and the utilization of your tables using the Table Usage Analysis data collector. MDW will then make recommendations for candidate tables and procedures to migrate to in-memory OLTP. Stored procedures will be examined for a number of executions and CPU utilization using the Stored Procedure Usage Analysis data collector.

> **NOTE** *To learn more about the other data collectors, see Chapter 12, "Monitoring Your SQL Server."*

Now, let's will walk through the deployment of these data collectors and examine the results.

Connect to your SQL Server 2014 instance using SQL Server Management Studio. Expand the Management node and right-click Data Collection. Select Tasks ➪ Configure Management Data Warehouse, as shown in Figure 9-10.

On the Welcome screen for the Management Data Warehouse Wizard, click Next, as shown in Figure 9-11.

Select a database to hold the MDW schema. If you need to create a MDW database, click the New button, as shown in Figure 9-12.

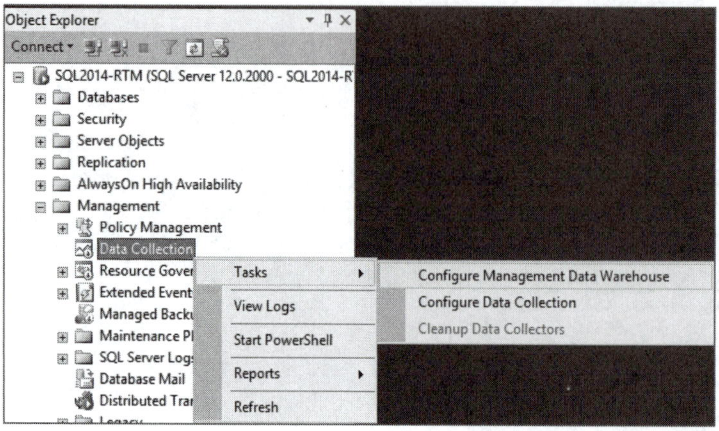

FIGURE 9-10

FIGURE 9-11

As shown in Figure 9-13, name the database to hold the MDW schema. For this example, call the database mdw.

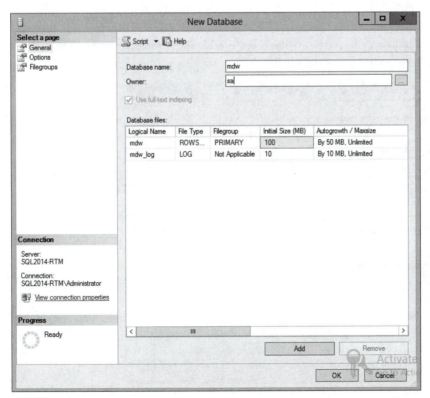

FIGURE 9-12

FIGURE 9-13

After you have named the database, click Next, as shown in Figure 9-14.

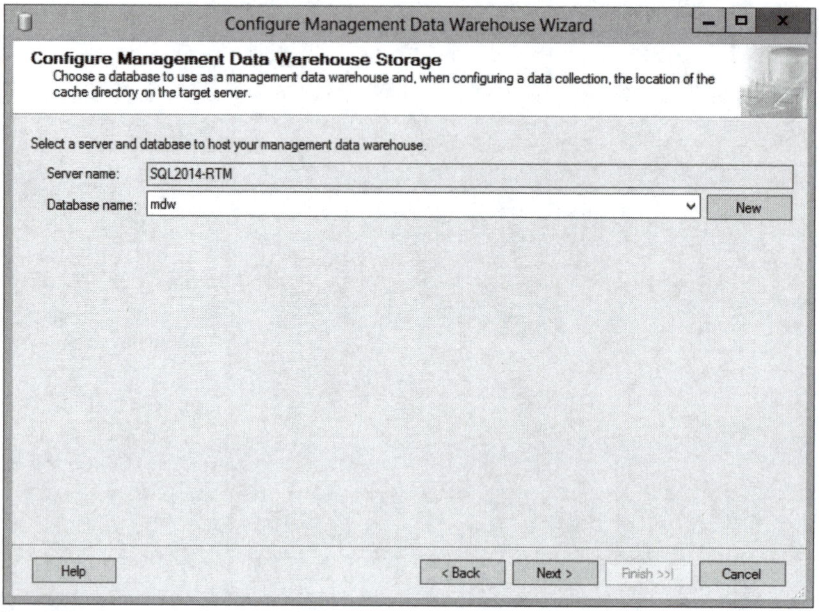

FIGURE 9-14

On the "Map Logins and Users" screen shown in Figure 9-15, select the permissions you will require. For this example, check `mdw_admin`. Click Next.

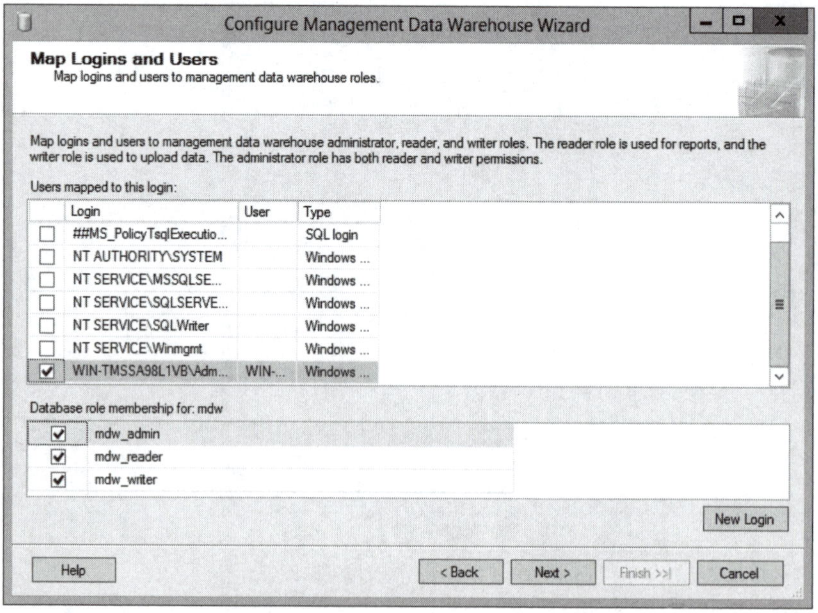

FIGURE 9-15

You should see the "Complete the Wizard" page shown in Figure 9-16. Click Finish.

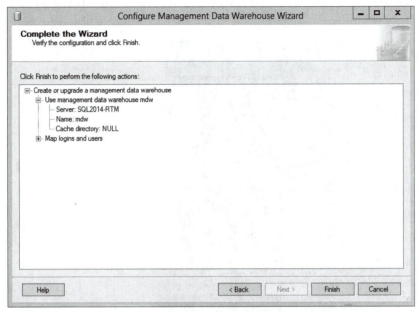

FIGURE 9-16

While you are waiting for the data collectors to deploy, you will see their progress, as shown in Figure 9-17.

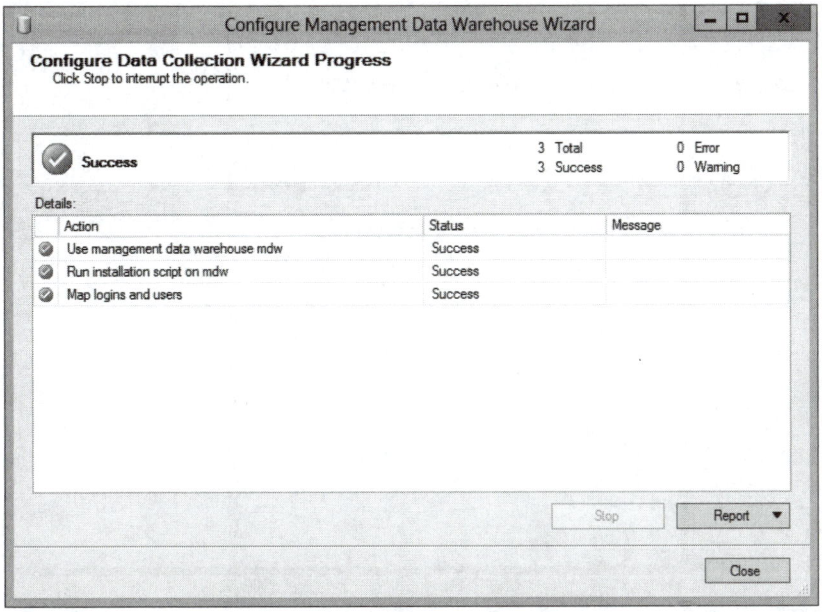

FIGURE 9-17

Now that the database has been deployed with the schema, you must configure data collection. Expand the Management node again, and right-click Data Collection. Select Tasks ⇨ Configure Data Collection, as shown in Figure 9-18.

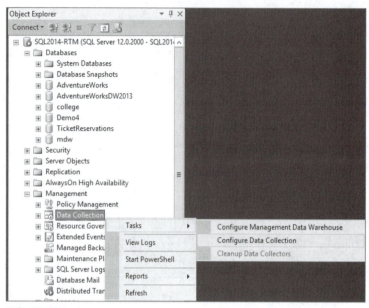

FIGURE 9-18

On the Welcome screen shown in Figure 9-19, click Next.

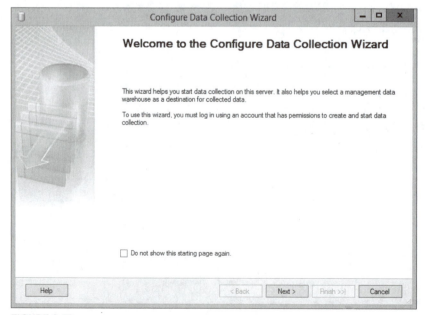

FIGURE 9-19

You must declare the SQL Server instance that will be the repository for the MDW data that the collectors will gather. Figure 9-20 shows the screen where you will do this.

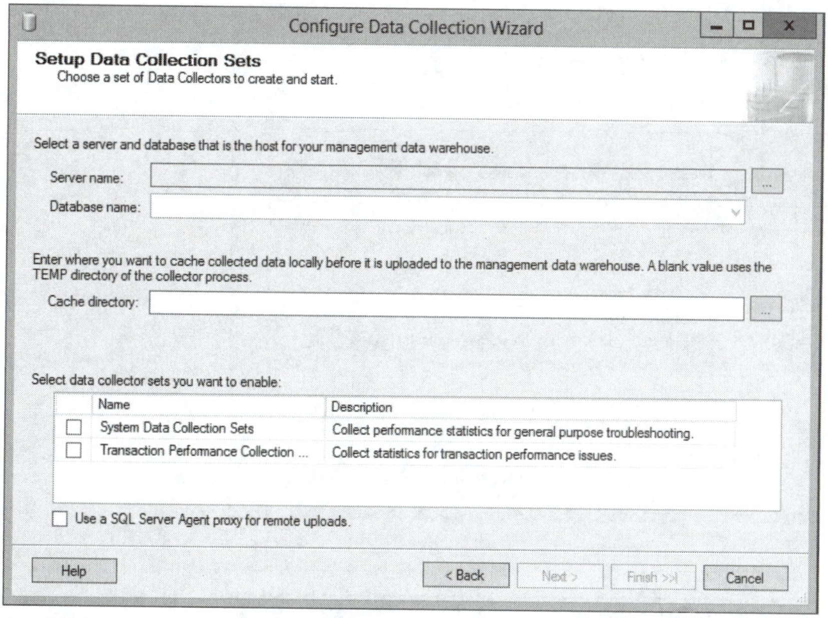

FIGURE 9-20

Click the ellipsis button to connect to your SQL Server instance and select the MDW database you created earlier. Specify a cache directory for the query uploads that will monitor your table usage. Finally, check the Transaction Performance Collection Sets data collector, as shown in Figure 9-21. Click Next.

You should see the "Complete the Wizard" page shown in Figure 9-22. Click Finish.

While you are waiting for the data collectors to deploy, you will see their progress, as shown in Figure 9-23. Once they are deployed, click Close.

The standard collection time is one hour before cached files are uploaded for analysis. Once data is collected, you should begin examining the reports that the data collectors have brought in.

> **NOTE** *Data collectors can be scripted out and deployed to earlier versions of SQL Server 2008 and up, in order to find candidates for in-memory OLTP. You must use some SQL Server 2014–specific language and functions. This will create an error if it is deployed on a version of SQL Server prior to 2014. You must edit these scripts before deploying them.*

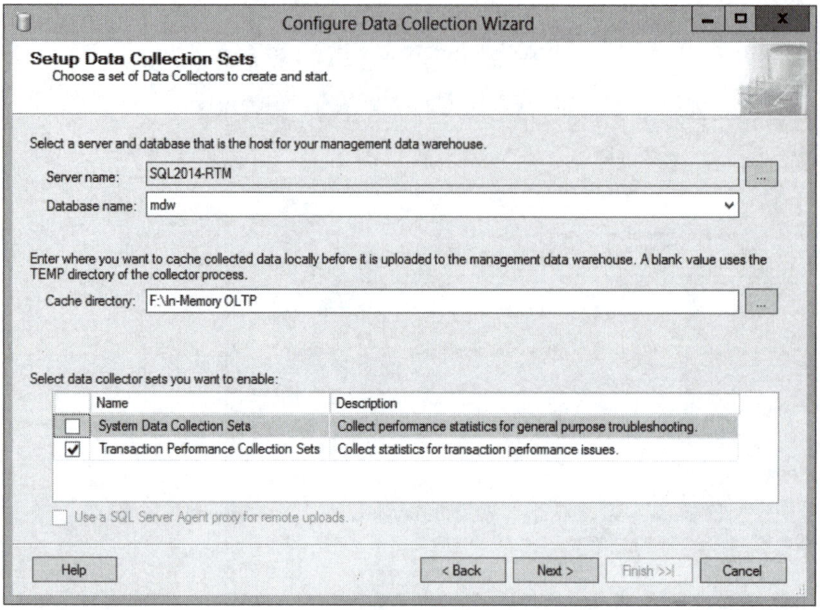

FIGURE 9-21

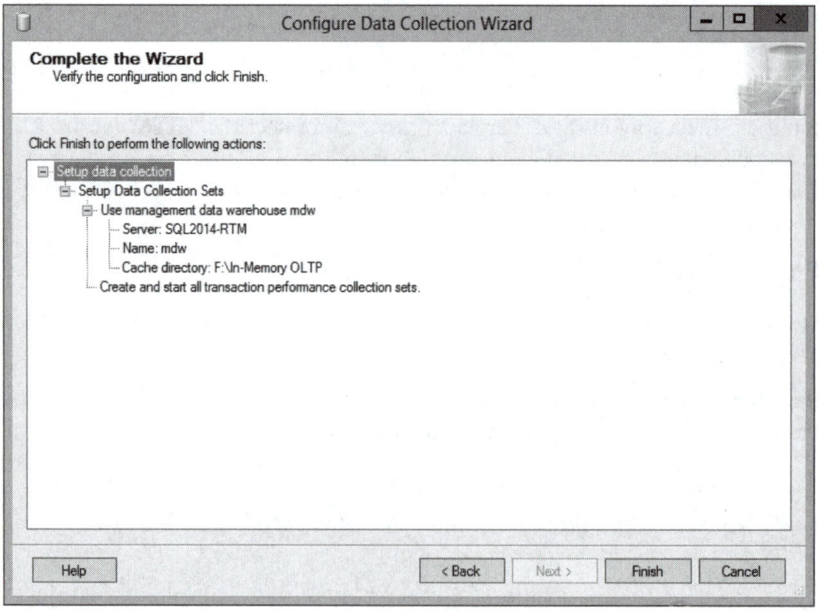

FIGURE 9-22

Expand your database tree and right-click the mdw database you created earlier. Click
Reports ⇨ Management Data Warehouse ⇨ Transaction Performance Analysis Overview, as shown
in Figure 9-24.

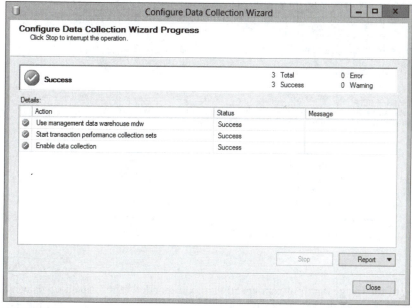

FIGURE 9-23

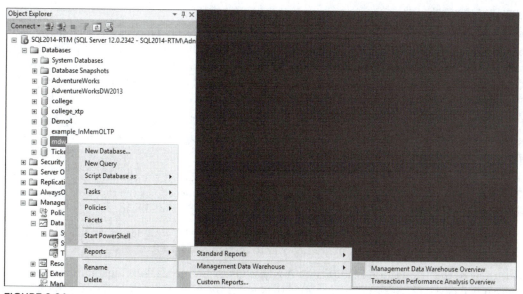

FIGURE 9-24

This launches the Transaction Performance Analysis Overview. From here, you select the reports you want to view on your current system. For this example, start with the Usage Analysis report, as shown in Figure 9-25.

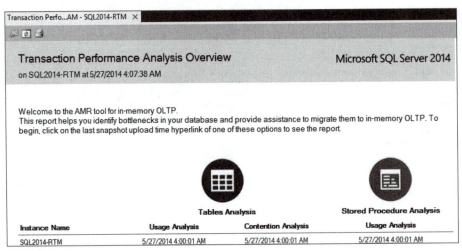

FIGURE 9-25

As shown in Figure 9-26, the Usage Analysis report shows recommended tables based on usage. It collects data per database. By default, only five tables will initially be shown, but you can increase that number by selecting an available number from the left side of the main graph. "All databases" is selected by default. You can click any of the databases on your SQL Server 2014 instance to see how the tables rate.

As you can see, not every table is a candidate for in-memory OLTP. The usage is such that you would expect to get low performance gains. Some tables may be very difficult to migrate based on the number of foreign-key constraints, incompatible data types, or other feature usage. However, clearly others will require minimal migration work, and based on their usage, you could expect to see high performance gains.

If you click the `students` table, you see further details about the table, as shown in Figure 9-27. You get lookup, range scan, latch, and lock statistics. You also see information on query Interop Gain and possibly Native (natively compiled) Gain.

Returning to the Transaction Performance Analysis Overview, next you should explore the Contention Analysis report, as shown in Figure 9-28. This report shows the top table candidates for memory-optimized tables based on the contention of your current workload.

Clicking a table shows the same report as you saw in Figure 9-27, with details on the table statistics, as well as the perspective gain by migrating over to in-memory OLTP.

Returning to the Transaction Performance Analysis Overview, now take a look at the Stored Procedure Based on Usage Analysis report shown in Figure 9-29. This report defaults to the top five stored procedures, which are candidates to be migrated to natively compiled stored procedures. You can increase the number of procedures to 15 on the report at a time. You can also select specific databases to examine only the stored procedures contained within them.

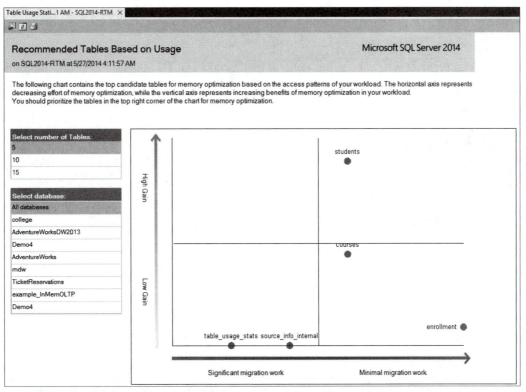

FIGURE 9-26

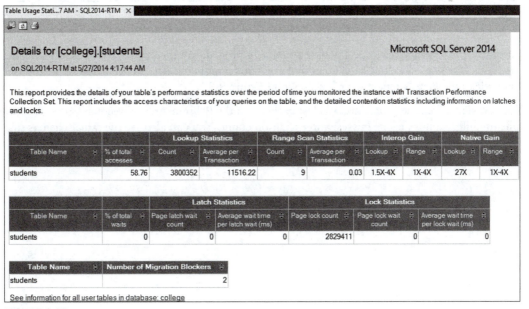

FIGURE 9-27

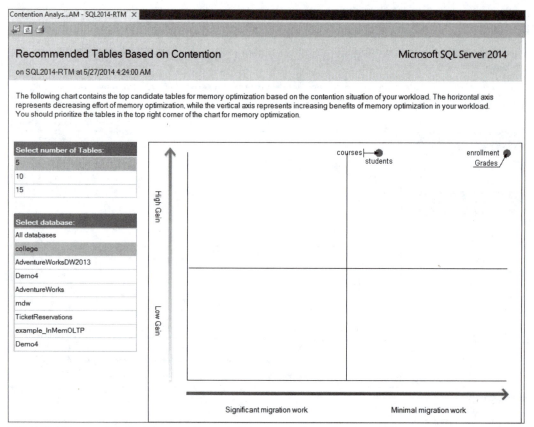

FIGURE 9-28

Currently, the `AdventureWorks` database contains a procedure called `p_calc_revenue_for_each_product`. This procedure has been identified as a good candidate. If you click a stored procedure, you will see the details report for it, as shown in Figure 9-30.

You can view when the procedure was last cached, total CPU time (in milliseconds), total execution time (in milliseconds), cache misses, and execution count. You can also see the table schemas that are referenced by the stored procedure.

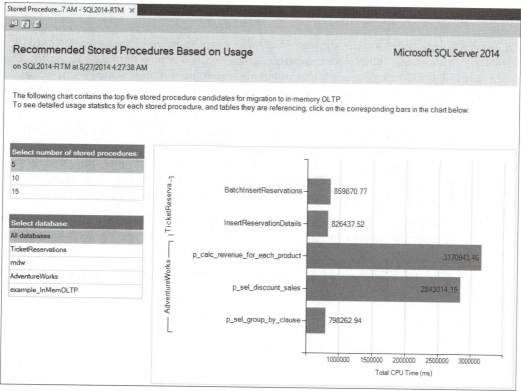

FIGURE 9-29

FIGURE 9-30

SUMMARY

SQL Server 2014 provides some of the biggest changes and advantages in performance that SQL Server has ever received. Unlike most competitors (such as SAP Hannah or Oracle Times 10), you do not have to buy an expensive appliance, or migrate your code and database to a new platform. Furthermore, you can continue to use the advanced features that a SQL Server Enterprise Edition license gives you.

The performance of in-memory OLTP will vary upon implementation, and it is not right for all of the code or objects within a database. If you go to Microsoft Case Studies at `http://www.microsoft.com/casestudies/`, you can search for in-memory OLTP to find real-world scenarios where companies have achieved 9 to 150 times performance improvements by implementing in-memory OLTP. Many of these implementations were able to be done on existing hardware.

Remember to size your utilization, estimate table and index space requirements, and to utilize the ARM to facilitate data collection and analysis. Always test your results in a comparable development (or QA environment) before deploying changes to production.

In Chapter 10, you learn how to configure SQL Server for optimal performance. You will take a close look at the hardware and how it can impact SQL Server.

10

Configuring the Server for Optimal Performance

WHAT'S IN THIS CHAPTER?

- ➤ Defining good performance
- ➤ Understanding what every DBA needs to know about performance
- ➤ Configuring server hardware
- ➤ Understanding the details of CPU configuration
- ➤ Understanding memory configuration and options
- ➤ Understanding I/O design and options

In the IT industry today, many different types of professionals are responsible for databases and for the systems where those databases reside. The *Developer DBA* is primarily responsible for database design, and for generating code (queries, stored procedures, and so on). The *Production DBA* is primarily responsible for database and database system configuration, maintenance, and availability. The *Business Intelligence (BI) DBA* is primarily responsible for the BI stack that is associated with SQL Server and relevant systems. One person may even be responsible for a combination of these tasks, and is then referred to as a *Hybrid DBA*. Additionally, some DBAs have never had formal training, or may have taken over database servers out of necessity because of staff shortages. These are known as *accidental DBAs*. The accidental DBA normally wears many hats, and will need to get things right the first time because of resource constraints. (Refer to Chapter 1 , "SQL Server 2014 Architecture," for a more detailed description of each of these types of database professional.)

Developer DBAs must know how to optimize performance to ensure that anything they design will perform up to its potential. Developer DBAs must ensure that, as inevitable changes are made to the system throughout its life cycle, they are made in a way that enables the application to continue to perform. As the system grows in terms of data, users, and functionality, it needs to grow in ways that keep the system operating optimally.

Similarly, Production DBAs must understand performance so that the system they maintain starts out performing well, and then continues to do so throughout the system's life cycle. Several different elements factor into this, from getting the server set up correctly, to monitoring the system as it starts working, to implementing a full monitoring strategy to keep the system operating optimally.

Following are the three most important pillars that support the capability to deliver high performance around scalability, response time, reliability, and usability:

➤ Setting Power Configuration to High Performance from Balanced

➤ Enabling Instant Database File Initialization in order to minimize IOps during file growth

➤ Understanding Microsoft trace flags (trace flags allow functionality within SQL Server that is turned off by default)

➤ Knowing what your system can deliver in terms of CPU, memory, input/output (I/O)

➤ Finding the bottlenecks and determining ways to resolve them

This chapter discusses all these issues, and addresses the most pressing questions about performance and configuring a server.

WHAT EVERY DBA NEEDS TO KNOW ABOUT PERFORMANCE

This chapter lays out a lot of recommendations that can enable you to improve the performance of your system. However, shaving milliseconds off a transaction time isn't always worth the time and hardware budget you spend to accomplish that goal. Frequently, good planning up front is worth more than clever optimization later. Always keep the following three things in mind regarding performance:

➤ The performance tuning cycle

➤ Defining good performance

➤ Focusing on what is most important

The Performance Tuning Cycle

Too often, performance and optimization are tacked on at the end. *Performance tuning* is an iterative process, and ideally starts at the beginning of the design process. Obtaining favorable performance starts with configuring the server, and continues with designing an efficient schema and specifying tuned SQL statements, which leads to ideal index selection. The monitoring and analysis of performance can then feed back to changes to the server configuration, schema design, or any other point in this process.

There are many third-party tools that can be purchased to assist in monitoring your SQL Server Instances and environment. Microsoft SQL Server comes with Management Data Warehouse (see

Chapter 12 , "Monitoring Your SQL Server," for more details). Utilizing monitoring tools or scripts is a core part of the tuning process.

Figure 10-1 illustrates this design system.

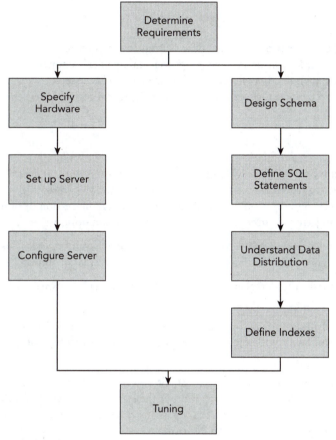

FIGURE 10-1

In the case of a new application, you don't have an existing system to measure. In the best case, you have some metrics from either an existing user base, or management predictions about who the users will be, what they do on a daily basis, and how that would impact the new application.

In the case of an existing system that you are either moving to a new server or to which you are adding functionality, you can measure specific metrics on system resource usage and use those as a starting point. Then you can add information about any new functionality, including the answers to questions such as the following:

➤ Will this increase the user base?

➤ Will it increase the processing load on the server?

➤ Will it change the data volume?

This information enables you to make a good estimate of the new system's impact on resources. Before you implement the new system, while testing is taking place, you have a great opportunity to start evaluating your estimates against the actual resource requirements and the performance you get from your test servers.

Configuration

Out-of-the-box configuration for SQL Server is not the optimum configuration. Before and after installing SQL Server, you must make configuration changes to power management, changes to group policies, configure `tempdb`, and enable beneficial default trace flags. These steps cover advanced configuration options that go beyond those given in Chapter 2, "Installing SQL Server 2014 Best Practices."

Power Configuration

Windows has had power configuration options since Windows 2003. *Power configuration* describes the way the operating system behaves regarding power consumption. Each Windows operating system comes with three default power configuration options. Custom power configuration options can be created and deployed. Following are the three default power configuration options:

Balanced—This setting matches capacity to demand. This will utilize the CPU compute power based on overall application load. It targets good energy efficiency with minimal performance impact.

High Performance—This setting increases the performance of the CPU and server hardware at the expense of energy consumption.

Power Saver—This setting limits performance to save energy and reduce operating costs. Unlike Balanced and High Performance, Power Saver will cap processor frequency at a percentage of the maximum.

Starting with Windows 2008 (Windows Server 2012 R2), the default power configuration setting is now Balanced. This is bad for your SQL Server. In the description of the settings note, you read that Balanced features *minimal performance impact*. Anything that causes performance impact on your SQL server is bad. Thus, the setting you should use is High Performance.

Leaving the power configuration option to Balanced can cause an issue called *core parking*. This is when, instead of being used, certain cores from your CPU are parked, or not being used. This can be a separate issue from poor performance caused by the power configuration being set to Balanced.

You must measure the utilization of your individual CPUs. To measure the effect of improperly setting the power configuration, use the free tool CPU-Z, which can be downloaded at http://www.cpuid.com/softwares/cpu-z.html.

The graphic on the left of Figure 10-2 is taken from a server with the power configuration set to Balanced. As you can see, this reduced the power of a 2.8GHz processor to only using about 0.798GHz, a reduction of nearly 70 percent. The image on the right is from the same server after the power configuration was set to High Performance. You can see the cores of the machine are now operating at peak performance.

> **NOTE** *Starting in Windows Server 2012, default core parking has been disabled. You must still set the power configuration settings for full CPU utilization. However, with Windows Server 2012 onward, as an operating system, you will not have to worry about core parking. For full details on what core parking is and how you can detect it using Resource Monitor, see Microsoft Knowledge Base article 281479 at* http://support.microsoft.com/kb/2814791.

 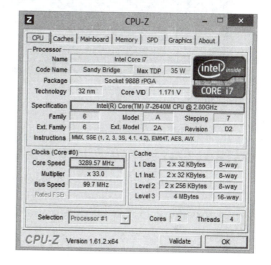

FIGURE 10-2

In order to set this up, you must first go into the BIOS of your server and set the BIOS to allow the operating system to handle power management. If you do not configure this at the BIOS, the operating system will continue to operate in Balanced configuration even if you have High Performance selected. Changing the BIOS requires the server to be rebooted in order to access the BIOS menu. Downtime will be required for this change.

Once you have set up the BIOS, you must next configure the operating system. To do so, simply open PowerShell on your Server. Figure 10-3 shows the commands you will need to type. In order to find what power configuration setting is active, type **powercfg –list**. The option selected with an asterisk(*) is the mode currently active. In order to change it, type **powercfg –setactive** and insert the GUID to the corresponding power configuration mode you would like to select.

```
Select Administrator: Windows PowerShell                    _  □  ×

PS C:\Users\Administrator> powercfg -list

Existing Power Schemes (* Active)
-----------------------------------
Power Scheme GUID: 381b4222-f694-41f0-9685-ff5bb260df2e  (Balanced) *
Power Scheme GUID: 8c5e7fda-e8bf-4a96-9a85-a6e23a8c635c  (High performance)
Power Scheme GUID: a1841308-3541-4fab-bc81-f71556f20b4a  (Power saver)
PS C:\Users\Administrator> powercfg -setactive 8c5e7fda-e8bf-4a96-9a85-a6e23a8c635c
PS C:\Users\Administrator> powercfg -list

Existing Power Schemes (* Active)
-----------------------------------
Power Scheme GUID: 381b4222-f694-41f0-9685-ff5bb260df2e  (Balanced)
Power Scheme GUID: 8c5e7fda-e8bf-4a96-9a85-a6e23a8c635c  (High performance) *
Power Scheme GUID: a1841308-3541-4fab-bc81-f71556f20b4a  (Power saver)
PS C:\Users\Administrator> _
```

FIGURE 10-3

Instant Database File Initialization

When you copy a large file to a file server or from one computer to another, you sometimes get the window where you see a folder passing papers back and forth. Depending on the size of the file, this can go on for several moments before you get status bar showing you the amount of file that has been transferred, and the amount of time until it will complete. Figure 10-4 shows an example of such an operation.

FIGURE 10-4

In the moments before you get a number back for the file that is being copied, the Windows operating system is zeroing out the file. This is a process of zero initializing every bit of data that the file will be written to, before the file is copied. In SQL Server, you can skip the zero initialization of the data files, database backups, and log backups. Table 10-1 shows this can improve performance.

TABLE 10-1: Example Instant Database File Initialization

PERFORMANCE TEST WITHOUT INSTANT DATABASE FILE INITIALIZATION ACTION	RESULTS (MIN/SECONDS)
CREATE DATABASE w/ 20GB Data file	11:57
ALTER DATABASE by 10GB	5:59
BACKUP 30GB DATABASE (Empty)	00:17
RESTORE 30GB DATABASE (Empty Backup)	17:46
RESTORE 30GB DATABASE (12GB Backup)	25:07
BACKUP 30GB DATABASE (12GB of Data)	17:21
PERFORMANCE TEST WITH INSTANT DATABASE FILE INITIALIZATION ACTION	RESULTS (MIN/SECONDS)
CREATE DATABASE w/ 20GB Data file	00:12
ALTER DATABASE by 10GB	00:00
BACKUP 30GB DATABASE (Empty)	00:13
RESTORE 30GB DATABASE (Empty Backup)	00:07
RESTORE 30GB DATABASE (12GB Backup)	6:50
BACKUP 30GB DATABASE (12GB of Data)	13:43

In order to enable this feature, you must have a domain or local service account that is located within the Perform Volume Maintenance Tasks group. In order to do that, open `gpedit.msc` in the Microsoft Management Console. The easiest way to do this to open the Run box and type *gpedit .msc*, as shown in Figure 10-5.

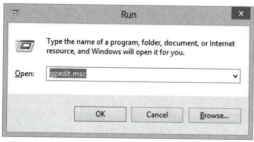

FIGURE 10-5

As shown in Figure 10-6, expand `Windows Settings`, `Security Settings`, `Local Policies`, and, finally, `User Rights Assignment`. Double-click "Perform volume maintenance tasks" and add the SQL Service Account.

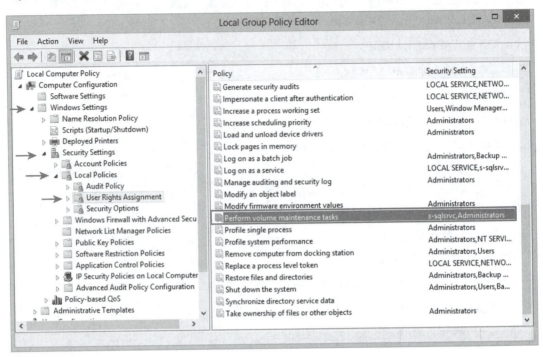

FIGURE 10-6

In order to validate if you currently have Instant Database File Initialization turned on inside your database, you can run the following query and examine the SQL Server Error Log:

```
exec sp_cycle_errorlog
go
DBCC TRACEON(3605)
DBCC TRACEON(3004)
go
USE master
go
CREATE DATABASE IITest
DROP DATABASE IITest
go
```

Figure 10-7 shows an example of a system in which Instant Database File Initialization is *not* turned on. Trace Flag 3605 turns on logging of DBCC commands to the SQL Server Error Log. Trace Flag 3004 turns on the logging of information and changes to physical data files. You will see in Figure 10-7 that the `.mdf` file and the `.ldf` file were zeroed out as the database was created. If

Instant Database File Initialization had been turned on, only the `.ldf` would be zeroed out. The `.mdf` entry would not have occurred.

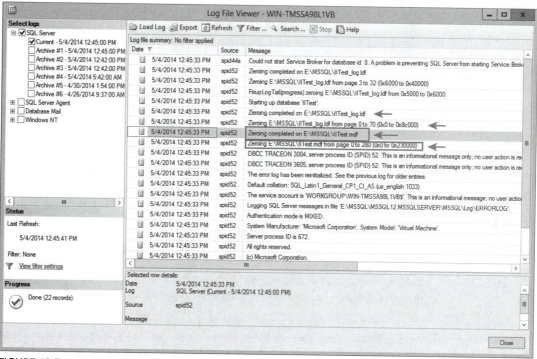

FIGURE 10-7

You can run this on an existing database to see if the setting is currently turned on. If it is not, you will need to restart the SQL Service after adding the account to the group policy before it will take effect.

> **NOTE** *If you have Group Policies pushed down to your servers from an Active Directory Domain server, it will override the settings on the local server. This means if you utilize Active Directory Group Policies, you should speak with your network administrator about adding this policy to the Active Directory policies. Also, Instant Database File Initialization does not work with Transparent Data Encryption or Transaction Logs. There is a possibility that the bits left behind from previously deleted files could be recovered in the* `.mdf` *and* `.ndf` *of files backed up and restored. You would need data forensic tools to get this data and extract it. Always exercise caution with whom you allow to have access to your data files.*

Trace Flags

Microsoft SQL Server has many active builds at any given time. As errors are found and fixed, new behaviors are added to SQL Server. Trace Flags are added to SQL Server using startup parameters such as –T<Trace Flag #> and separated by a semicolon. (To see how to set startup parameters, see Chapter 2.) This will allow specific functionality that is automatically disabled. Some trace flags are very beneficial to performance, and are described in Table 10-2.

TABLE 10-2: Trace Flags that Are Beneficial to Performance

TRACE FLAG	DEFENTION
–T1118	Turns off Single Page Allocations for all databases within SQL Server. Normally used to prevent SGAM contention within tempdb.
–T2371	Allows for increased update of statistics in a database. By default, statistics are updated when 20 percent of the base table plus 500 rows are updated. For small tables, this is okay. But for large tables with millions or billions of rows, this could cause statistics to be out of date very easily. This trace flag lowers the threshold percentage that is required on the base table for statistics to update.
–T4199	Enables all the fixes that were previously made for the query processor during the release of Service Packs or updates in previous versions of SQL Server.
–T3226	This turns off the constant writing of backups to the SQL Server Error log. If you have an instance with tens to hundreds of databases, then you will see a message per database. If those databases are in full recovery mode, and are logging transaction log backups, this can make the error log virtually unreadable.

There are other trace flags that can be enabled. Most have specific uses. Trace flags T1222 and T1204 are commonly used for tracking and tracing deadlocks. Trace flag T610 can be used to streamline bulk loading of clustered and non-clustered indexes. However, the T610 trace flag could have negative consequences in a fully logged OLTP system, and is typically used in data warehouses.

Each trace flag should be tested before it is placed on a production system in order to determine what the overall effect would be.

Defining Good Performance

The fundamental question that every DBA must answer before refining a system is simple: Does the system in question have good performance now? Without either a specific target or some baseline to compare against, you will never know. Planning, sizing, testing, and monitoring can provide you with the information you need to start answering this question. You can break down this process into three steps:

1. Start by identifying your critical targets for CPU, memory, and I/O.

2. Then create a baseline.

3. Finally, after deploying, monitor your critical measurements.

For example, consider how performance requirements can vary in the case of an online store. Here, response time to users is critical to keep them shopping. A database such as this is likely to have clearly defined response times for the most important queries, and there may be a broad requirement that is defined by the management of the business that no query can take longer than 2 or 3 seconds. On a different database server that delivers management reports on warehouse inventory levels, there may be an expectation that these reporting queries take some time to gather the right information, so response times as long as a few minutes may be acceptable. However, there may still be some queries that have much shorter response time requirements. In yet another database, the key performance criterion might be the time it takes to back up the database, or the time to load or unload data.

After the critical targets have been identified, the current system must be measured to create a baseline. SQL Server monitoring methodology is covered more in Chapter 12, of this book.

Focus on What's Most Important

The final essential aspect of performance is to focus on what's important—achieving the performance that users demand. You must know what you need to measure, how to measure it, and what the limitations of that measurement might be.

Consider a typical system. The end users' experience is the net sum of all performance from their client machine through many layers to the database server and back again. Because the focus of this book is the DBA and SQL Server 2014, you can focus on measuring SQL Server 2014 performance, but it's worthwhile to have a basic understanding of the big picture that DBAs fit into, and some of the tools and metrics that may have an impact on your system.

Figure 10-8 shows a schematic diagram of a typical web-based architecture. This schematic is typical of any enterprise customer using the Microsoft Windows Server System Reference Architecture to implement an enterprise solution. This may be the first time that many DBAs have looked at something like this and understood where their puzzle piece (that is, the database) fits into the big picture.

Reviewing a diagram of a possible infrastructure, it is important to understand what a DBA's role *should be*, and what a good team member's role *is*. During troubleshooting, the phrase "that's not my job" should not be used. Understanding the aspects of how the end-user application, network configuration, and security influence or utilize SQL Server is critical to ensuring that SQL Server is being used properly.

When the user calls the help desk and complains of poor performance, finding the culprit involves a lot of possible candidates, so there may be a lot of time spent identifying which piece of the complex system architecture might be guilty. Unfortunately, a large, complex system needs multiple support personnel all focusing on their piece of the puzzle. For example, the firewall and security server are supported by the network team, the web server and application server are supported by the application team, the authentication is handled by the Windows team, and the SQL Server is supported by the database administration team. Understanding who is responsible in large and small shops for independent tasks provides the opportunity to communicate with each team to help facilitate holistic problem resolutions.

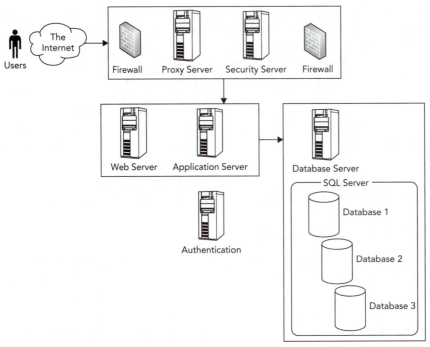

FIGURE 10-8

WHAT THE DEVELOPER DBA NEEDS TO KNOW ABOUT PERFORMANCE

Good performance is built on a solid foundation upon which the rest of your application can be implemented. For a SQL database, this foundation is a well-designed database schema. The performance-tuning rules to follow are less simple than traditional concepts such as "normalize to the nth form." Instead, they require that you have a solid understanding of the use of the system, including the usage pattern, the SQL statements, and the data. The optimal schema for an online transaction processing (OLTP) system may be less preferable for a Decision Support System (DSS), or for a Data Warehousing (DW) system.

Users

You first need to know who is going to use the system: the number of users and their concurrency, peak usage level, and what they are going to do. The users usually fall into different groups based on either job function or feature usage. For an e-commerce–based system, for example, the user groups might be browsers, purchasers, order trackers, customers needing help, and others. For a sales analytics system, the user groups may be primarily analysts reading the data with report tools such as PerformancePoint Server, Power View, or Excel, and perhaps running reporting for the sales team. The e-commerce–based system example is an OLTP database workload optimized for fewer and faster reads, updates, and writes requests, whereas the sales analytics system example is a DSS database workload optimized for large queries to generate reports.

SQL Statements

After determining the different groups of users, you must understand what they do, which SQL statements will be run, and how often each of these is run for a user action. In the e-commerce example, a browser might arrive at the site, which invokes the homepage, for example, requiring 20 or 30 different stored procedures or SQL statements to be executed. When users click something on the homepage, each action taken can require another set of stored procedures to be executed to return the data for the next page. So far, it looks like everything has been read-only, but for ASP .NET pages, there may be the issue of session state, which may be kept in a SQL database. If that's the case, you may already have seen a lot of write activity just to get to this stage.

Data Usage Patterns

The final part of the picture is the data in the database. You need an understanding of the total data volume in each table, including how that data gets there and how it changes over time. For the e-commerce example, the main data elements of the site are the catalog of items available for sale. The catalog could come directly from the suppliers' websites through an Internet portal. After this data is initially loaded, it can be refreshed with updates as suppliers change their product line and as prices vary. The overall volume of data won't change much unless you add or remove items or suppliers.

What will change (hopefully quickly) is the number of registered users, any click-tracking you do based on site personalization, the number of orders placed, the number of line items sold, and the number of orders shipped. Of course, you hope that you can sell a lot of items, which results in a lot of new data growth every day.

A sound knowledge of the data, its distribution, and how it changes helps you find potential hot spots, which could be either frequently retrieved reference data, frequently inserted data, or frequently updated data. All these could result in bottlenecks that might limit performance.

Database Schema

An understanding of all the preceding pieces—users, SQL statements, and data—needs to come together to help implement a well-designed and well-performing application. If the foundation of your database schema is not solid, anything you build on top of that foundation is going to be unstable. Although you may achieve something that's acceptable, you are unlikely to achieve an optimal solution.

How does all this information help you tune the server? Understanding data types can help you understand what advanced features you can utilize. Only in-row-data compresses, however. Therefore, if you use a, large object (LOB) data type like `varbinary(max)`, text, or image, you cannot utilize page and row compression. Likewise, you cannot utilize columnstore indexes or In-Memory OLTP when you require constraints.

Foreign-key constraints are often good candidates for non-clustered indexes. Partitioning keys should be static the majority of the time to prevent data movement throughout partitions. These are simple examples, but each relates to how knowing the data within your database can help you have a better understanding of how to implement SQL Server in an optimized fashion.

You must understand where the hot spots are in the data to enable the physical design to be implemented in the most efficient manner. If you are going through the process of designing a logical data model, you normally would not plan for optimum performance through database design. However, when you are ready to design the physical model, you should take this information into account and modify the design to incorporate your knowledge of data access patterns.

WHAT THE PRODUCTION DBA NEEDS TO KNOW ABOUT PERFORMANCE

The Production DBA's life is considerably different from that of the Developer DBA in that a Production DBA is dealing with a system that someone else may have designed, built, and handed over, either as a new or as an already-running system. The Production DBA may also face challenges with performance on old systems running legacy applications on outdated hardware. In this case, the scenario changes from designing an efficient system to making the system you have been given work as well as possible on that limited hardware.

The starting point for this process must be an understanding of what the hardware can deliver, what hardware resources the system needs, and what the expectations of the users are in terms of user response time. The key elements to understanding the hardware are processor speed, type, and cache size. Additionally you need to know how much memory there is, and what the bus speed is. Finally, it is important to determine the number of I/O disks, how they are configured, and how many network interface cards (NICs) exist.

The next step is determining how each component of the system is required to perform. Are there any performance-related Service-Level Agreements (SLAs) that have been implemented between the business and the DBA team? If any performance guidelines are specified anywhere, are you meeting them, exceeding them, or failing them? In all cases, you should also know the trend. Have you been maintaining the status quo, getting better, or, as is most often the case, slowly getting worse? The Production DBA must understand all this, and then know how to identify bottlenecks and resolve them to get the system performing at the required level again.

Following are the tools that the Production DBA uses to perform these tasks:

➤ **Task Manager**—This gives a quick, high-level view of server performance and use of resources.

➤ **System Performance Monitor (or Resource Monitor in Windows 2012 and Windows 8, sometimes called Perfmon)**—This provides a more detailed view of Windows server performance and per-instance SQL Server–specific counters.

➤ **SQL Server Management Data Warehouse (MDW)**—The MDW is a relational database that collects and stores Perfmon and Data Collector outputs for retrieval when the DBA needs to troubleshoot a system issue. In SQL Server 2014, you also gain the capability to profile data for in-memory OLTP enhancements.

➤ **SQL Server Management Studio (SSMS)**—This enables long-running transactions to be analyzed, and for bottlenecks to be found and resolved. SSMS enables the DBA to run queries against Dynamic Management Views (DMVs) and Extended Events to gather this data.

➤ **Dynamic Management Views (DMVs)**—These are system objects that contain server state information that can be used to diagnose problems and monitor the health of a SQL Server.

➤ **Extended Events**—This is a lightweight monitoring system that collects data about the performance of the SQL Server. This data can be viewed through the Session user interface (UI) that was introduced in SQL Server 2012. New additional Extended Events have been added in SQL Server 2014 to assist in monitoring and troubleshooting technologies.

Chapter 13, "Performance Tuning T-SQL," covers these tools in more detail.

> **NOTE** *MDW gets a big upgrade in SQL 2014 with the Transaction Performance Analysis Overview. This enables you to deploy collectors to SQL 2008 and up, and collect the data on a SQL 2014 instance to determine in-memory OLTP candidate tables and procedures. For more information, see Chapter 9 "In-Memory OLTP."*

Optimizing the Server's Hardware

The rest of this chapter covers optimizing the server. This includes the hardware and operating system configuration to provide SQL Server with the best environment in which to execute. You should consider three key resources any time you discuss optimization or performance:

➤ CPU

➤ Memory

➤ I/O

Starting with the CPU, you don't have a lot of options to play with here other than the number and type of processors. This part of the chapter focuses on understanding the different processor attributes so that you can make the right purchasing decisions.

Memory has more options, and it's a lot easier to add or remove system memory (Random Access Memory, or RAM) than it is to change the number or type of processors in a server. When you initially configure the server, you should have some idea of how much memory you might need, and understand the available configuration options. You can discuss these options with the specific hardware vendor of your choice. Because SQL Server 2014 is (and will remain) available solely as a 64-bit server application, you should install it on 64-bit hardware on top of Windows Server 2012 R2 64-bit, which is discussed in more detail later in this chapter.

In many ways, I/O performance is perhaps the most important part of the server configuration to get right because everything you do lives on the disk. All the code you run in the operating system, SQL Server, and any other applications start off as files on the disk. All the data you touch in SQL Server also lives on the disk: it starts out there, is read into memory, and then has to be written back to disk before it becomes a permanent change. Every change that is made to a SQL Server database is written to the database transaction log file, which also lives on the disk. All these factors make a good I/O configuration an essential part of any SQL Server system.

The following sections cover these key resources in great detail, but before you dig in, it will be helpful to put each of the three server resources back into perspective in terms of their relative performance to each other. As you refer to this book in the future, you can easily pencil in the current start of processor, memory, and I/O performance to see how the relative speeds of different elements have changed.

Within SQL Server, you can't do much to alter how much data is processed by each cycle of the CPU, before SQL Server 2014. Natively compiled stored procedures, discussed in Chapter 9, "In-Memory OLTP," offer a way to compile T-SQL stored procedures to reduce the instruction set required for processing.

Not all T-SQL code will be right for Natively Compiled stored procedures. For example, complex query logic, constraints, and functions will not work with Natively Compiled stored procedures. Natively Compiled stored procedures will also be limited to using In-Memory OLTP data types only. You should still consider obtaining processors with larger caches, and at high speeds. Add more memory, and design your storage subsystem to deliver the fastest performance possible within your requirements for speed, size, and cost.

The conclusion here is the slowest piece of hardware will restrict the remainder of the system. Magnetic physical disks will never be as fast as memory. SQL Server, whether using In-Memory OLTP or traditional T-SQL Tables, is an in-memory application, meaning all work is done on data that is first read into memory. When determining the hardware specifications for SQL Server, ensure that you get enough memory to satisfy your SQL Server. It is rare to hear of a DBA complaining about an instance that had too much memory; too little is a frequent performance problem.

Hardware Management

On most small- to medium-size database servers, a common configuration is to make a BIOS change to enable hyper-threading. (See your server's documentation for details.) In the "Hyper-Threading" section later in this chapter, you can determine whether hyper-threading can provide a performance improvement for your scenario. Once the hyper-threading option has been decided, most of the remaining tasks are related to physically installing RAM, I/O adapters, such as NICs, and disk adapters for Small Computer Systems Interface (SCSI) or Serial Advanced Technology Attachment (SATA). Review the vendors' documentation for any additional configuration options that they recommend.

On nearly all systems, you can find a variety of management software to help you configure, operate, and maintain the hardware. Most hardware vendors have their own version of this kind of software, offering a wide variety of capabilities and options. Examples of these are the iLO from Hewlett Packard (HP), the RSA from IBM, or the DRAC from Dell.

On large enterprise systems such as the HP Superdome 2, NEC Express5800, or SGI Altix UV, configuring the server hardware enters a whole new dimension. On these larger enterprise systems, you can find a *management processor (MP)* within the server. The management processor and its software interface control the hardware—from booting a hardware partition, to configuring a different hardware partition, to changing memory layout, and to managing the power to different hardware components. The management processor handles all these tasks.

The tasks that need to be achieved to manage all the large systems are similar, but the way each hardware vendor implements its interface is unique, from the Java/website approach on SGI to the Telnet-based command-line interface on HP and NEC systems.

> **NOTE** *The Windows Server Catalog (*www.windowsservercatalog.com*) should be your first stop when considering purchasing any new hardware. If the new hardware isn't in the catalog, it's not supported to run Windows Server 2012 and won't be supported when running SQL Server either.*

CPU

SQL Server 2014 operates in a different environment than previous versions of SQL Server. When SQL Server 2000 launched, a huge server used for SQL Server may have had four to eight processors. Now, SQL Server 2014 can run on the largest servers, with up to 64 processors and up to 320 cores. Additionally, SQL Server 2014 can run on machines with up to 4TB of RAM running Windows Server 2012 R2 Standard Edition. The only reason to get Windows Server 2012 R2 Data Center is to get more than two sockets for CPUs. SQL Server 2014 is supported on one processor architecture only: 64-bit (x64).

x64

x64 was originally introduced by AMD and implemented by Intel as EM64T. It is compatible with x86 machine code and can support 64-bit micro-code extensions. The x64 platform can run SQL Server 2014 (using Windows Server 2012 R2), delivering memory beyond 4GB and up to 4TB of natively addressable memory and up to 64 physical CPUs and 320 logical cores.

> **NOTE** *The x64 platform is the only server platform for SQL Server 2014 database workloads. The Itanium 64 (IA64) and x32 (x86-32) series of processors are not supported by SQL Server 2014. Various editions and versions of SQL Server 2008 and 2008 R2 can be found that will be supported on these CPU families.*

Cache

The reason modern processors need onboard cache is because the processor runs at 2 to 3 GHz, and, though main memory is improving, it still cannot keep up with the processor's memory appetite. To try to alleviate this, processor designers added several layers of flash memory to keep recently used data in small, fast caches so that if you need to reuse that data, it will already be available.

The cache on modern processors is typically implemented as multiple layers: L1, L2, and L3. Each subsequent layer is physically farther from the processor core, and is larger (but slower) until you are back at main memory. Some caches are general-purpose and hold copies of any memory such as L2 and L3.

To put the cache performance into perspective, system memory has an average latency of 50 to 100ns, and will range in size from 16 to 1,024GB in total. Solid State Disks (SSDs) have latency and size figures of 30–100 microseconds (µs) and 50–1,024GB respectively. Enterprise-specification hard disk drives will have latency figures in the range of 2–50 milliseconds (ms), and will range in size from 80–2,048GB.

The performance of your SQL Server is extremely dependent on the size of the cache available. Processor manufacturers offer a large variety of models that have a range of L2 and L3 sizes. The high-performance nature of the cache means that it is very costly. This is reflected in the cost of the processors that contain large amounts of cache. You should purchase the fastest processor with the biggest cache memory for your server. In addition, if a compromise must be made, it is always easier and cheaper to upgrade RAM than it is to upgrade a CPU.

> **NOTE** *In 2013, Intel released the first chipset with a massive 128MB of L4 cache. This is currently only available for mobile device CPUs. However, it is rumored that Broadwell (the successor to Haswell) will have L4 cache on the CPU. As of the writing of this book, Broadwell is not yet available. It is currently reported that L4 cache will have a 50 to 60ns latency.*

Hyper-Threading

Hyper-threading (officially dubbed *Hyper-threading Technology*) is Intel proprietary technology that works by duplicating certain sections of the physical processor core to improve parallelization of computations. What this means is that, for each physical core present, two logical cores appear to the operating system. Although the system schedules multiple threads to be executed by the processor, the shared resources may cause certain threads to wait for other ones to complete prior to execution.

There is actually only one question about hyper-threading that you need to ask: Should you run with hyper-threading enabled or disabled? Hyper-threading should be enabled by default and only disabled when it has been proven to cause performance degradation.

One important factor when considering hyper-threading is to understand the maximum theoretical performance benefit that you might get from it. Intel's documentation on hyper-threading reveals that the maximum theoretical performance gain is 30 percent. Understand that hyper-threading can give you only a maximum performance increase of 1.3 times non–hyper-threading performance at best, and, in practice, it may be closer to 1.1 to 1.15 times.

In some cases, hyper-threading (at least theoretically) won't provide any benefit. For example, in any database workload where the code runs a tight loop entirely from cache, hyper-threading won't help because there is only a single execution engine. This scenario could result in degraded performance because the operating system tries to schedule activity on a processor that isn't physically there.

To measure this benchmark, you should perform a comparative test that includes the following steps:

1. First, refer to your specific system's documentation to find out how to turn off hyper-threading and do so.

2. Now, run your benchmark test a number of times and get an average execution time.

3. Then, turn hyper-threading on again.

4. Run the benchmark test the same number of times again, and compare results. What you will be looking for is the average run time of each test to be quicker with hyper-threading turned on. You should then calculate how much quicker it is, and use that information to make a decision on the value of hyper-threading.

Multicore Terminology

Before continuing, it's worth defining some clear terminology here to avoid confusion when discussing multicore systems:

➤ The *socket* is the physical socket into which you plug the processor. Before multicore systems arrived, there used to be a direct one-to-one relationship between sockets and execution units.

➤ A *core* is equivalent to an *execution unit*, or what you would previously have considered to be a processor. With a multicore processor there will be two or more of these per socket.

➤ A *thread* in this context is not the same as the thread you might create in your program, or the operating system threads. It is relevant only in the context of hyper-threading. A hyper-threading thread is not a new execution unit, but rather a new pipeline on the front of an existing execution unit. Refer to the previous section, "Hyper-threading," for more details about how this is implemented.

SQL Server 2014 licensing requires a minimum of four cores licensed per instance. Whether physical or virtual, this means each SQL 2014 Server should have four cores. An important note on hyper-threading is that you only pay for the physical cores on a physical instance of SQL Server. You are not charged extra for hyper-threaded cores presented as logical cores.

NUMA

NUMA stands for "non-uniform memory access." This architecture is often also referred to as ccNUMA, meaning a cache-coherent version of NUMA. The main difference between an old SMP system and a NUMA system is where the memory is connected, and how processors are arranged on the system bus.

Whereas on an SMP system the memory was connected to all the processors symmetrically via a shared bus, on a NUMA system, each group of processors has its own pool of "local" memory. The advantage of this is that each processor doesn't pay a cost of going to a bus past more than its local processors to access memory, provided the data it wants is in the local memory pool. If the data it wants is in the memory pool from another NUMA node, the cost of accessing it is a little higher than on an SMP system. Therefore, one of the objectives with a NUMA system is to try to maximize the amount of data you get from local memory, as opposed to accessing memory on another node.

NUMA systems typically have a two-sockets-per-node configuration and implement multiple nodes up to the system maximum.

Smaller configurations that are any multiple of a 2-socket node can usually be accommodated, allowing for highly configurable servers and highly scalable servers. For example, a company could start with a single 2-socket node and scale up all the way to 16 4-socket nodes for 64 sockets.

Intel Xeon and AMD Opteron use different architecture implementations to access memory. Intel uses a Front Side Bus (FSB) whereby the sockets are connected through the bus to the external controller to the memory; as a result, all sockets are equal distance to the memory. AMD uses an integrated memory controller on each socket to connect to its local memory and the other sockets with their own memory by means of the HyperTransport link. This non-uniform memory arrangement is referred to as NUMA, and the data latency depends on where the data requested by the CPU core is located in memory.

For example, if the data is on a directly connected memory bank, access is fast. If it is on a remote memory bank that is on another socket, it can incur some latency. Although, in the case of the Intel architecture, the FSB delivers equal-distance memory to each CPU core, the inefficiency with this approach is FSB contention, which Intel reduces by implementing larger caches.

MEMORY

Another hardware subsystem to consider is memory—specifically, memory on the server, including some of the issues associated with memory, the options you can use, and how they can impact the performance of the server. Following is a basic introduction to operating system memory. Then, you'll jump straight into the details of how to configure a server for different memory configurations.

Physical Memory

Physical memory is the RAM you install into the server. You are probably already familiar with memory in the form of Dynamic Inline Memory Modules (DIMMs) that go into desktop PCs and servers, which is one example of physical memory, or RAM. This memory is measured in megabytes, gigabytes, or (if you are lucky) terabytes, as the latest editions of Windows Server 2012 R2 Datacenter and Standard Editions can now support systems with 4TB of RAM. Future editions of the operating system will increase this number as customers demand increasingly powerful systems to solve increasingly complex business problems.

Physical Address Space

The *physical address space* is the set of addresses that the processor uses to access anything on its bus. Much of this space is occupied by memory, but some parts of this address space are reserved for things such as mapping hardware buffers, and interface-specific memory areas such as video RAM. On a 32-bit processor, this was limited to a total of 4GB of memory addresses. On 32-bit Intel server processors with Physical Address Extension (PAE), the address bus was 36 bits, which enabled the processor to handle 64GB of memory addresses. You might assume that on a 64-bit processor the address bus would be 64 bits, but because there isn't a need for systems that can address 18 exabytes (EB) of memory yet, or the capability to build a system that large, manufacturers have limited the address bus to 48 bits, which is enough to address 256TB of memory. The architecture enables an extension of this to 52 bits in the future, which would enable systems up to 4 petabytes (PB) of memory.

Virtual Memory Manager

The *Virtual Memory Manager (VMM)* is the part of the operating system that manages all the physical memory and shares it between all the processes that need memory on the system. Its job is to provide each process with memory when it needs it, although the physical memory is actually shared between all the processes running on the system at the same time.

The VMM does this by managing the virtual memory for each process, and, when necessary, it takes back the physical memory behind virtual memory, and puts the data that resided in that memory into the page file so that it is not lost. When the process needs to use that memory again, the VMM retrieves the data from the page file, finds a free page of memory (either from its list of free pages or from another process), writes the data from the page file into memory, and maps the new page back into the processed virtual address space. The resulting delay or interruption is called a *page fault*. To determine whether SQL Server or another process is the cause of excessive paging, monitor the Process: Page Faults/sec counter for the SQL Server process instance. See the section, "Page Faults," later in this chapter for a more in-depth look at these.

On a system with enough RAM to give every process all the memory it needs, the VMM doesn't need to do much other than hand out memory and clean up after a process is done with it. On a system without enough RAM to go around, the job is a little more involved. The VMM must do some work to provide each process with the memory it needs when it needs it. It does this by using the page file to store data in pages that a process isn't using, or that the VMM determines it can remove from the process.

The Page File

The *page file* is a disk file that the computer uses to increase the amount of physical storage for virtual memory. In other words, when the memory in use by all of the existing processes exceeds the amount of available RAM, the Windows operating system takes pages of one or more virtual address spaces and moves them to the page file that resides on physical disk. This frees up RAM for other uses. These "paged out" pages are stored in one or more page files that are located in the root of a disk partition. There can be one such page file on each partition.

On a server running SQL Server, the objective is to try to keep SQL Server running using just the available physical memory. SQL Server itself goes to great lengths to ensure that it doesn't over-allocate memory, and tries to remain within the limits of the physical memory available.

Given this basic objective of SQL Server, in most cases, there is limited need for a page file. However, a frequently asked question is, "Is there a recommended size for the page file?" The answer to this question, of course, is "it depends." It depends on the amount of RAM installed, and what virtual memory will be required above and beyond SQL Server. A general guideline is to configure a page file total of 1.5 to 2 times the amount of RAM installed in the server.

However, in large systems with a large amount of RAM (more than 128GB), this may not be possible because of the lack of system drive space. Following are some good guidelines to keep in mind for these cases:

➤   Configure an 8GB page file on the system drive.

➤   Ensure that the Windows operating system startup parameters are configured to capture a kernel dump in the event of a failure.

> **NOTE** *See the article at* http://support.microsoft.com/kb/307973 *from Microsoft Support to learn more about how to configure this setting.*

➤   Optionally, you might configure multiple page files (on disk volumes other than the system volume) that will be available for the operating system to utilize if a larger page file is desired.

In some cases, SQL Server and the operating system might not cooperate well on sharing the available memory, and you may start to see system warnings about low virtual memory. If this occurs, you should ideally add more RAM to the server, reconfigure SQL to use less memory, or increase the size of the page file. It may be better to reconfigure SQL Server to remain within the available physical memory rather than increase the size of the page file. Reducing paging always results in better performance. If paging occurs, for best performance, the page file should be on fast disks that have minimal disk usage activity, and the disks should be periodically defragmented to ensure that the page file is contiguous on the disks, reducing the disk head movement and increasing performance. The metric in the Windows System Monitor to measure page file usage is Paging file: %Usage, which should be less than 70 percent.

Page Faults

Page faults are generally problematic for SQL Server, but not all page faults are the same. Some are unavoidable, and some have limited impact on performance, whereas others can cause severe performance degradation and are the kind you want to avoid.

SQL Server is designed to work within the available physical memory to avoid the bad kind of page faults. Unfortunately, the System Performance Monitor page fault counter doesn't indicate whether you are experiencing the benign or bad kind of page fault, which means it doesn't tell you whether you are experiencing good or bad performance.

Soft Page Faults

The most common kind of page fault you will experience is the *soft page fault*. These occur when a new page of memory is required. Any time SQL Server wants to use more memory, it asks the VMM for another page of memory. The VMM then issues a soft page fault to bring that memory into SQL Server's virtual address space. This actually happens the first time SQL Server tries to use the page, and not when SQL Server first asks for it. This means that SQL Server is calling `VirtualAlloc` to commit a page of memory. The page fault occurs only when SQL Server tries to write to the page the first time.

Hard Page Faults

Hard page faults are the ones you want to try to avoid. A hard page fault occurs when SQL Server tries to access a page of its memory that has been paged out to the page file. When this happens, the VMM must step in and take some action to get the needed page from the page file on disk, find an empty page of memory, read the page from disk, write it to the new empty page, and then map the new page into SQL Server's address space. All the while, the SQL Server thread has been waiting. Only when the VMM has replaced the missing page of memory can SQL Server continue with what it was doing.

I/O

I/O configuration is actually too big of a subject to cover in one chapter; it requires a book of its own. This section introduces you to some of the available I/O options, and then walks you through several scenarios to provide some insight into how to make the right storage configuration decisions.

I/O encompasses both network I/O and hard disk I/O. In most cases with SQL Server, you are primarily concerned with disk I/O because that's where the data resides. However, you also need to understand the effect that poor network I/O can have as a bottleneck to performance.

Configuring I/O for a server storage system is perhaps the place where you have the most options, and it can have the largest impact on the performance of your SQL Server system. When you turn off your computer, the only thing that exists is the data stored on your hard drive. When you turn the power on, the processor starts running, the operating system is loaded, and SQL Server is started. All this happens by reading data and code from the disk.

This basic concept is true for everything that happens on a computer. Everything starts its life on the disk and must be read from the disk into memory, and, from there, through the various processor caches before it reaches the processor and can be used as either code or data. Any results the processor arrives at must be written back to disk to persist any system event (for example, shutdown, failure, maintenance, and so on).

SQL Server is sensitive to disk performance, more so than many other applications, because of the manner in which it manages large amounts of data in user databases. Many applications have the luxury of loading all their data from disk into memory, and then running for long periods of time without having to access the disk again. SQL Server strives for that model because it is by far the fastest way to get anything done. Unfortunately, when the requested operation requires more data than can fit into memory, SQL Server must do some shuffling around to keep going as fast as it can. It starts to flush the write buffer, and it must start writing that data back to disk, so it can use that memory to generate some new results.

At some point in the life of SQL Server data, every piece of data that SQL Server uses must be read from disk, and changed data must be written back to disk.

Network

Referring back to Figure 10-8, you can see that the network is a key component in any SQL Server system. The network is the link over which SQL Server receives all its requests to do something, and by which it sends all its results back to the client. In most cases, today's high-speed networks provide enough capacity to enable a SQL Server system to use all its other resources (CPU, memory, and disk) to their maximum before the network becomes a bottleneck.

In some systems, the type of work done on the SQL Server is relatively small compared to the number of requests sent to the server, or to the amount of data returned to the client. In either of these cases, the network can be a bottleneck. Network bottlenecks can occur anywhere in the network. They can be on the NIC of the client, where the client is an application server that's serving the database server with hundreds of thousands of requests per second. Bottlenecks can occur on the fabric of the network between the server and the client (application server, web server, or the user's workstation). This network fabric can consist of many pieces of network infrastructure, from the simplest system in which two machines connect over a basic local area network (LAN), to the most complex network interconnected systems in either the Internet or a global corporate wide area network (WAN).

In these larger, more complex interconnected systems, much of the network can be beyond your control, and may introduce bandwidth or latency issues outside of acceptable limits. In these cases, you can do little more than investigate, document, and report your findings.

The parts of networking that you examine here are those over which you may have direct control, and all are on the SQL Server system. You can assume that the remainder of the network fabric is up to the job of supporting the number of requests received, and of passing the results back to the client in a timely manner.

In particular, one thing to be aware of is the speed and duplex settings for the network. It is, unfortunately, easy to cause a duplex mismatch, the result of which is that the network will work at a much slower rate than normal. The standard setting is for the network to be set to full duplex. This means that communications are transmitted in both directions simultaneously. This requires the use of approved cabling. Current networks operate at a rate of 10GB/s.

When examining network wait stats, ASYNC_NETWORK_IO is a common wait. This wait occurs when SQL Server completes a query sent to it by the user application. In order not to overwhelm the client application, SQL Server sends an initial packet, and waits for the application to buffer that packet and send an acknowledgment. The wait stat accumulated during this period of time is ASYNC_NETWORK_IO.

One option to combating this type of wait stat is to first ensure that the packet size can be transmitted over the current network infrastructure, and alter the Network Packet Size to 16383, which is very common packet size, as shown in Figure 10-9.

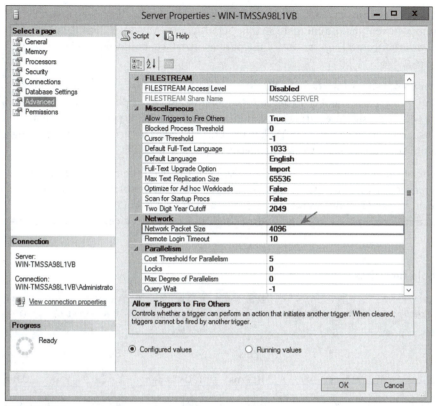

FIGURE 10-9

Magnetic Disks

Magnetic disks are still very prevalent in servers, so they are worth covering. However, they are less superior to SSD/Flash drives and the SSD/Flash drive arrays available from vendors such as Violin Memory. As long as it is properly configured, SSD performance will outperform magnetic hard drives. The fault tolerance of current SSD architectures is improving quickly, but the cost for storage is an area where magnetic drives still win.

The other area of I/O is disk I/O. With earlier versions of SQL Server, disks were quite simple, leaving you with limited options. In most cases, you had only a couple of disks to deal with. Now, enterprise systems have the option to use Storage Area Network (SAN) or Network Attached Storage (NAS) storage, and some may use external disk subsystems using some form of Redundant Array of Independent Disks (RAID), and most likely using an SCSI interface that enables you to build disk subsystems with hundreds if not thousands of disks.

Various interfaces are used in disk storage systems:

➤ **Advanced Technology Attachment (ATA)**—This is also known as Integrated Drive Electronics (IDE), which refers not only to the connector and interface definition, but also to the fact that the drive controller is integrated into the drive. Parallel ATA (PATA) interfaces allow the data to be transferred between the motherboard and the disk using a parallel stream up to a current maximum of 133MB/s. Serial ATA (SATA) has been developed to overcome the architectural limitations of the parallel interface, and can transmit data at speeds up to 3GB/s.

➤ **Small Computer Systems Interface (SCSI)**—This is a set of standards that was developed to connect and transfer data between computers and a myriad of peripheral devices, including disks. This was also using the parallel stream of data transfer with speeds up to a maximum of 640MB/s. Serial Attached SCSI (SAS) has been developed as an evolution of the SCSI standard, and utilizes a serial data stream for speeds of up to 4800MB/s.

Now, consider some of the basic physics involved in disk performance. You must understand the fundamental differences between different types of disks, because they explain differences in performance. This, in turn, helps you make an informed decision about what kinds of disks to use. Table 10-3 demonstrates example values (under ideal conditions) of the typical, fundamental disk latency information.

TABLE 10-3: Example Hard Disk Drive Latency

DISK ROTATIONAL SPEED	ROTATIONAL LATENCY	TRACK-TO-TRACK LATENCY	SEEK TIME	DATA TRANSFER RATE	TRANSFER TIME FOR 8KB	TOTAL LATENCY
5,400 RPM	5.5ms	6.5ms	12ms	90MB/sec	88 μs	12.1ms
7,200 RPM	4.1ms	6.5ms	10.7ms	120MB/sec	66 μs	10.8ms
10,000 RPM	3ms	1.5ms	4.5ms	166MB/sec	48 μs	4.6ms
15,000 RPM	2ms	1.5ms	3.5ms	250MB/sec	32 μs	3.5ms

More Disks

More disks are invariably faster than fewer disks. For example, if you have to build a 4TB volume, it's going to deliver higher performance if it's built from a lot of small disks (ten 400GB disks) versus a few larger disks (two 2TB disks). This is true for various reasons. First, smaller disks are usually faster than larger disks. Second, you stand a better chance at success when you use more spindles to spread read-and-write traffic over multiple disks when you have more disks in the array. This gives you throughput that, in some cases, is the sum of individual disk throughput. For example, if those 400GB disks and 2TB disks all delivered the same throughput, which was, say, 20MB/sec, you would sum that for the two 2TB disks to achieve just 40MB/sec. However, with the ten smaller disks, you would sum that to arrive at 200MB/sec, or five times more.

Faster Disks

Not surprisingly, faster disks are better for performance than slower disks. However, this doesn't just mean rotational speed, which is but one factor of overall disk speed. What you are looking for is some indicator of the disk's capability to handle the I/O characteristics of the workload in which you are specifically interested.

Unfortunately, disk manufacturers rarely, if ever, provide any information other than rotational speed and theoretical disk bus speeds. For example, you often see a 10K or 15K RPM SCSI disk rated as delivering a maximum throughput of 300MB/sec because it's on an SCSI 320 bus. However, if you hook up that disk and start running some tests using a tool such as SQLIO, the chances are good that for small-block-size, non-queued random reads, you will be lucky to get much more than 2–4MB/sec from that disk. Even for the fastest I/O types, large-block sequential I/O, you will rarely get more than 60–70MB/sec. That's a long way from 300MB/sec.

> **NOTE** *You can download the SQLIO Disk Subsystem Benchmark tool from* `www.microsoft.com/download/en/details.aspx?id=20163`. *You can find a very good tutorial to follow when starting out with SQLIO at* `http://sqlserverpedia.com/wiki/SAN_Performance_Tuning_with_SQLIO`.

Cache—Read and Write

Embedded on the controller board of every hard drive is a set of memory that is called the *disk buffer* or *disk cache*. This cache acts as a buffer between the disk and the attached system, and is used to store the data that is being read from or written to the disk. The size of this cache ranges from 8 to 64MB. In the same way, disk controllers (whether they are internal to the server, or external as part of a SAN) also have a cache that is used to store read and written data. The size of controller cache can vary from 512MB to 512GB.

Following are some of the many uses for disk cache:

> ➤ **Read-ahead/read-behind**—When a read operation is sent to the disk, the disk may read unrequested data it deems SQL Server is going to need at a later date.

> ➤ **Write acceleration**—The disk controller may signal to SQL Server that the write operation has succeeded immediately after receiving the data, even though the data has not actually been written to the disk. The data is then stored in the write cache and written later. This does introduce the risk of data loss that could occur if the hard drive loses power before the data is physically written. To combat this very risk, most disk array controllers have a battery backup to ensure that all outstanding write operations complete even if the enclosure loses main power.

> ➤ **Input/Output speed balancing**—The rate of read and write operations sent to the disk may fluctuate during the normal course of operation. To ensure that the requests get serviced in a timely manner, the cache is used to store data waiting to be transferred in and out.

In most configurations, the read and write cache share the same set of memory and the CPU of the disk (or array) controls the nuances of that arrangement. In some cases, certain OLTP database configurations can have their read cache disabled on the storage to free up more memory for the write cache.

Solid State/Flash Drives

Making a comparison between SSDs and magnetic hard drives is difficult. Traditional hard drive benchmarks tend to focus on the performance characteristics that are poor within hard drives (such as rotational latency and seek time). SSDs do not need to spin, and, therefore, they do not have rotational latency. SSDs can have challenges with mixed reads and writes. Their performance may degrade over time.

Flash memory has two types: NAND and NOR. NOR operates like RAM and requires power to store data. NAND is non-volatile, and it doesn't require electricity to maintain data stored in it. For that reason, let's focus on NAND.

NAND SSDs are made up of flash chips, and within those chips, they are either single layer cells (SLCs) or multi-layer cells (MLCs). An SLC can hold only one data bit, yielding a value of either 0 or 1. An MLC can hold more than one, with today's technologies generally yielding two bits per cell. The data density in MLC is higher. This is why MLCs have higher capacity than SLCs.

Reads on MLCs can be slower, because the error correction for cleanup mistakes takes more time to guarantee. MLCs require a full write of a page to a cell versus SLCs, which use the page write more effectively by writing partial data to pages to cells. That being said, most companies are moving away from SLC SSDs and more toward MLCs. A page for SSDs is typically 4KB. Pages are written within blocks. Blocks are typically 128KB to 512KB.

Initial writes on an SSD are less expensive because they only write a single page. However, subsequent writes such as deleting and rewriting data require a page erase and overwriting of the block. As for performance, reads are typically 25 microseconds, the first 4KB page write is 250 microseconds, and erases and rewrites of a 256KB block will take 2 milliseconds.

SSD drives also eventually wear out. There is only a certain amount that can be done before the drives begin to wear out. Typically, it will take 100,000 erase cycles before SLC failure, and 5,000 to 10,000 for MLC to fail. If you were to execute a update and erase cycle on one block per second, it would take more than five years to reach the wear-out rating of 10,000 cycles. However, if you did the same erase and rewrite on the same block for 10,000 cycles, you could wear it out in 3 hours.

One advantage to an SSD is when the writes do begin to fail you can still read from a failed drive; you just cannot write to it.

Storage Considerations

After all that talk about the different pieces of a storage system, it's time to get serious about figuring out how best to configure your storage system. This is a challenging task, because there is no single simple way to configure storage that's going to suit every purpose. SQL Server systems can be required to do dramatically different things, and each implementation could require a radically different storage configuration to suit its peculiar I/O requirements. The following sections offer a set of guidelines, and then provide the details that show how you can figure out what works best for you. You can also use these guidelines during discussions with the teams responsible for the storage.

Use the Vendors' Expertise

The vendors of each piece of hardware should be the people you turn to for expertise regarding how to configure their hardware. They may not necessarily know how to configure it best for SQL

Server, however, so this is where you must convey SQL Server's requirements in a manner the hardware vendor can understand. This is best done by quoting specific figures for reads versus writes, sequential versus random I/O, block sizes, I/Os per second, MB/sec for throughput, and minimum and maximum latency figures. This information can help the vendors provide you with the optimal settings for their pieces of the hardware, be it disks, an array controller, fiber, networking, or some other piece of the storage stack.

Every System Is Different

Each SQL Server system may have different I/O requirements. Understand this, and don't try to use a cookie-cutter approach to I/O configuration (unless you have already done the work to determine that you do have SQL systems with the exact same I/O requirements).

Simple Is Better

It is an age-old engineering concept that simpler solutions are easier to design, easier to build, easier to understand, and hence easier to maintain. In most cases, this holds true for I/O design as well. The simpler solutions invariably work faster, are more robust and reliable, and require less maintenance than more complex designs. Unless you have a compelling, specific reason to use a complex storage design, keep it simple.

Test

Testing is an absolutely essential part of any configuration, optimization, or performance-tuning exercise. Too often, you speak with customers who have been convinced that black is white based on absolutely nothing more than a gut feeling, or some half-truth overheard in a corridor conversation.

Until you have some test results in your hand, you don't truly know what the I/O subsystem is doing. Forget all that speculation, which is nothing more than poorly informed guesswork, and start testing your I/O systems to determine what's actually going on. IOMeter is a commonly used tool for I/O subsystem measurement and characterization to baseline an I/O subsystem. It is both a workload generator and a measurement tool that can emulate a disk or network I/O load. You can find it at www.iometer.org.

> **NOTE** *For a good tutorial to follow when starting out with IOMeter, see* www.techrepublic.com/article/test-storage-system-performance-with-iometer/5735721.

A commonly used disk performance metric is disk latency, which is measured by Windows System Performance Monitor using the Avg Sec/Read, Avg Sec/Write, and Avg Sec/Transfer counters. Target disk latencies are as follows:

- ➤ **Database transaction log**—Less than 5ms, ideally 0ms
- ➤ **OLTP data**—Less than 10ms
- ➤ **Decision Support Systems (OLAP and Reporting) data**—Less than 25ms

After you have set up the system and tested it, you must keep monitoring it to ensure that you are aware of any changes to the workload or I/O subsystem performance as soon as it starts. If you have a policy of monitoring, you can also build a history of system performance that can be invaluable for future performance investigations. Trying to track down the origins of a slow-moving trend can be difficult without a solid history of monitoring data. See Chapter 13, "Performance Tuning T-SQL," for more specifics on what and how to monitor.

RAID

As part of the "how many disks do you need?" question, you must consider the RAID level you require because this can influence the total number of disks required to build a storage system of a certain size and with the I/O characteristics you require. Consider the following:

➤ **Availability**—The first factor when thinking about RAID is the level of availability you need from the storage.

➤ **Cost**—An important part of any system is meeting the cost requirements. There's no point in specifying the latest, greatest high-performance system if it costs 10, 100, or 1,000 times your budget.

➤ **Space**—Another major factor in combination with cost is how much physical space you need to provide.

➤ **Performance**—The performance of the storage is another major factor that should help you determine what level of RAID you should choose.

RAID 0—Striping without Parity or Mirroring

A RAID 0 set contains two or more disks, and the data is striped across all the disks. This RAID level provides no redundancy or fault tolerance because a disk failure destroys the array. During a write operation, the data is broken up into blocks, and the blocks are written onto the disks simultaneously.

This increases bandwidth during read operations because multiple sections of the entire chunk of data are able to be read in parallel. However, RAID 0 does not implement any error checking. This is not recommended for any SQL Server volume.

RAID 1—Mirroring without Striping or Parity (Two Disks)

With RAID 1, one disk is mirrored onto another—meaning two disks are needed to be configured in the RAID set. This is fast because reads can (but not always) occur from both disks, and writes incur minimal performance reduction. It provides redundancy from a disk failure, but increases storage costs because usage capacity is 50 percent of the available disk drives. For storage cost reasons, backups and data loads database operations may not require this level of protection.

RAID 10—Striping with Mirroring (Minimum Four Disks)

RAID 10 (also known as RAID 1+0) is a mirrored set in a striped set with a minimum of four disks. There will always be an even number of disks in the set.

This is normally the fastest arrangement available. RAID 5 (discussed next) is faster during read operations when the same number of disks is used in the set. Reads can occur from multiple disks, and writes incur minimal performance reduction. It also provides redundancy—it can survive more than one disk failure, provided that the disk failures are not in the same mirrored set—but increases storage costs, because usage capacity is 50 percent of the available disk drives.

Database systems that require the most I/O read/write performance and redundancy should be deployed on RAID 10. For storage cost reasons, backups, data loads, and read-only database operations may not require this level of protection. RAID 0+1 is an alternative to RAID 1+0 in that it creates a second striped set to mirror the first striped set, as opposed to RAID 1+0, which creates a striped set from a series of mirrored drives.

RAID 5—Striping with Parity (Minimum Three Disks)

Raid 5 is striping with parity with a minimum of three disks. During writes it must calculate the data parity—for example, for each write operation in a three-disk array, it writes data across two disks and parity across the third disk. The RAID firmware distributes the parity blocks across all the disks in the RAID set to avoid a write hot spot.

There is a performance penalty to calculating the parity and, therefore, RAID 5 is not a good choice for databases that must handle a significant amount of writes. Another downside of RAID 5 is that, in the event of a disk failure, performance can be seriously degraded while rebuilding the array with the new disk. If running with a failed disk, performance can also suffer because parity needs to be calculated per each read to return the data.

During read operations, RAID 5 may perform faster than some other RAID type because multiple disks are able to serve the data in parallel. As a result, RAID 5 is efficient for predominantly read databases such as a DSS. In addition, RAID 5 is more cost-effective than RAID 1 or RAID 10 because the disk space of one single drive is required for parity storage for each RAID 5 set, whereas for RAID 1 or RAID 10, it requires 50 percent of the disk space for redundancy.

RAID 6—Striping with Double Parity (Minimum Four Disks)

A RAID 6 set contains a minimum of four disks, and distributes two copies of the parity across the disks. This provides enhanced fault tolerance because two drive failures could occur without destroying the data on the array. This RAID implementation makes large RAID groups more practical because larger capacity drives extend the time needed to recover from a drive failure.

However, RAID 6 should not be used. It is actually Dual Parity and takes the parity region from RAID 5 and duplicates it so each disk has two parity regions. While this allows it to recover from the possible loss of two drives, it has a performance penalty as well.

RAID-Level Recommendations

You should use fast, robust storage for SQL data files and SQL log files. In general, for most SQL Server implementations, the recommendation for both is to use striping with mirroring (RAID 10).

When unable to use RAID 10, RAID 5 should be the alternative. If the nature of the database implementation is to service an application that has a high number of read operations compared to writes, or the database is configured to be read-only, then RAID 5 with a large number of disks per RAID set is acceptable.

Additionally, if you know your application is going to make extensive use of `tempdb`, use the fastest, most robust storage available. This might seem a little strange because the data in `tempdb` is always transitory, but the requirement for robustness comes from the need to keep the system running, not from a concern about losing data. If the rest of the system uses robust storage but `tempdb` doesn't, a single disk failure can prevent that SQL Server instance from running. The requirement for speed comes from the fact that `tempdb` is highly random I/O utilization data file.

The operating system and SQL binary files can live on a simple mirror, although, in many cases, the time it takes to rebuild the operating system and SQL may be within acceptable downtime, in which case a single disk can suffice.

> **WARNING** *Remember that, even if the time taken to rebuild and patch the operating system, install and patch SQL, and attach the databases is less than the outage window, the cost of staff time to rebuild everything will be much higher than the cost of a second disk with the two disks set up in a RAID 1 array.*

For critical systems, the operating system and SQL binary files should be on a mirrored disk array, but it needs to be only a single mirrored pair. Operating system and SQL binary files don't have high I/O requirements. They are typically read once when the application is loaded, and then not touched until new code paths need to be used, and then a few more 4KB random reads are issued. Therefore, these files don't require high-performance storage.

SUMMARY

Performance tuning can be tricky when a system has been operating sub-optimally for an extended period of time. The performance issues can be multiplied when the underlying system has not been designed in an optimal way from the outset.

Before starting to make decisions about a system's hardware layout, multiple areas of the system need to be discussed: user interaction with the system; data usage patterns; number and type of SQL statements that will be run against the system; schema design; and more.

You must make a number of hardware decisions when configuring a server for optimal performance. The CPU of the server plays a large role in determining if the system will perform acceptably under the expected workload. CPU components such as cache, hyper-threading, multi-core, and system architecture should be investigated, and the available options need to be weighed. You should also consider the memory and the various technologies that are at work within the memory. These technologies include physical and virtual address spaces, the virtual memory manager, and the page file.

The slowest part of a system is I/O. Care should be taken to choose between the myriad of options when designing network and storage subsystems. Some of the questions that you must answer include: How fast should the network be? How much storage space do I need? How many disks? What type of disks? How fast do the disks need to be? SAN or NAS? What RAID should I use? Storage adapter cards? Allocation unit size?

You should now have many tools to choose from when configuring a SQL Server for optimal performance.

In Chapter 12, you learn about monitoring your SQL Server.

11

Optimizing SQL Server 2014

WHAT'S IN THIS CHAPTER?

➤ Understanding the benefits of optimizing application performance

➤ Using partitioning and compression to improve performance

➤ Tuning I/O, CPU, and memory to increase the speed of query results

WROX.COM CODE DOWNLOADS FOR THIS CHAPTER

The wrox.com code downloads for this chapter are found at www.wrox.com/go/prosql2014admin on the Download Code tab. The code is in the Chapter 11 download and individually named according to the names throughout the chapter.

Configuration is only one part of maintaining SQL Server. In every release of SQL Server, features have been added, largely to the Enterprise edition. SQL Server has additional features that, when utilized, can allow for better scale and optimization of specific areas. Partitioning, compression, buffer pool extensions, proper configuration of data files, log files, and even query parameters can all have an important effect on SQL Server's capability to function properly and efficiently.

APPLICATION OPTIMIZATION

You can squeeze more performance out of your SQL Server in many ways, and it is a good idea to ensure that the application is running optimally. Therefore, the first order of business for scaling SQL Server 2014 on the Windows Server platform is optimizing the application. If the application is not well written, getting a bigger hammer only postpones your scalability issues, rather than resolving them. In this chapter, you will read about tuning with regard to CPU workloads and parallelism, but performance tuning a specific application is beyond the scope of this chapter.

The goal of performance tuning SQL Server 2014 is to minimize the response time for each SQL statement and increase system throughput. This can maximize the scalability of the entire database server by reducing network-traffic latency, as well as optimizing disk I/O throughput and CPU processing time.

Defining a Workload

A prerequisite to tuning any database environment is a thorough understanding of basic database principles. Two critical principles are the logical and physical structure of the data, and the inherent differences in the application of the database. For example, different demands are made by an online transaction processing (OLTP) environment than are made by a decision support (DSS) environment. A DSS environment often needs a heavily optimized I/O subsystem to keep up with the massive amounts of data retrieval (or reads) it performs. An OLTP transactional environment needs an I/O subsystem optimized for more of a balance between read-and-write operations.

In most cases, it is not possible to test SQL Server to scale with the actual demands on the application while in production. As a preferred practice, you must set up a test environment that best matches the production system, and then use a load generator such as Quest Benchmark Factory, Idera SQLscaler, or the built-in Distributed Replay Adapter (SQL Developer and Enterprise Edition only) to simulate the database workload of the targeted production data-tier environment. This technique enables offline measuring and tuning of the database system before you deploy it into the production environment.

Further, the use of this technique in a test environment enables you to compartmentalize specific pieces of the overall solution to be tested individually. As an example, using the load-generator approach enables you to reduce unknowns or variables from a performance-tuning equation by addressing each component on an individual basis (hardware, database, and application).

THE SILENT KILLER: I/O PROBLEMS

Improper configuration of data and log files can be just as costly as a set of physical disks that have poor IOPS. For the past several years, I/O has always been viewed as a culprit. In the last five years, it is more likely that you will have undersized memory or CPU infrastructure. I/O can still be a costly problem if there is a problem with the disk subsystem or configuration.

SQL Server I/O Process Model

Windows Server 2012 works with the SQL Server 2014 operating system to satisfy disk I/O requests. Windows Server I/O Manager handles all I/O operations and fulfills all I/O (read or write) requests by means of *scatter-gather* or asynchronous methods. Scatter-gather refers to the process of gathering data from, or scattering data into, the disk or the buffer.

The SQL Server storage engine manages when disk I/O operations are performed, how they are performed, and the number of operations that are performed. However, the Windows operating system (I/O Manager Subsystem) performs the underlying I/O operations, and provides the interface to the physical media.

The job of the database storage engine is to manage or mitigate as much of the cost of these I/O operations as possible. For example, the database storage engine allocates much of its virtual memory space to a data buffer cache. This cache is managed via cost-based analysis to ensure that memory is optimized to efficiently use its memory space for data content—that is, data frequently updated or requested is maintained in memory. This benefits the user's request by performing a logical I/O and avoiding expensive physical I/O requests.

In-memory OLTP represents a major advance for SQL Server in the effort to optimize servers, as well as the code they run, and alleviate I/O contention.

Keep in mind that, when using in-memory OLTP, you must reserve memory outside of the buffer pool for in-memory structures. The amount of memory should be roughly four times the size of the in-memory structures or their estimated size, if they are non-durable.

> **NOTE** *For more information on in-memory OLTP, see Chapter 9, "In-Memory OLTP."*

Database File Placement

SQL Server stores its database on the operating system files—that is, physical disks or Logical Unit Numbers (LUNs) surfaced from a disk array. The database is made up of three file types: a primary data file (.mdf), one or more secondary data files (.ndf), and transaction log files (.ldf).

> **NOTE** *In SQL Server 2014, as in some previous versions, the use of* .mdf, .ndf, *and* .ldf *file extensions is optional.*

Database file location is critical to the I/O performance of the Database Management System (DBMS). Using a fast and dedicated I/O subsystem for database files enables it to perform most efficiently. As described in Chapter 10 "Configuring the Server for Optimal Performance," available disk space does not equate to better performance. Rather, the more, faster physical drives there are (or SSDs), the better your database I/O subsystem can perform. You can store data according to usage across data files and filegroups that span many physical disks. A *filegroup* is a collection of data files used in managing database data-file placement.

> **NOTE** *To maximize the performance gain, make sure you place the individual data files and the log files all on separate physical LUNs. You can place reference-archived data or data that is rarely updated in a read-only filegroup. This read-only filegroup can then be placed on slower disk drives (LUNs) because it is not used very often. This frees up disk space and resources so that the rest of the database may perform better.*

tempdb Considerations

Because database file location is so important to I/O performance, you should consider functional changes to the `tempdb` database when you create your primary data-file placement strategy. The reason for this is that `tempdb` performance has a rather large impact on system performance because it is the most dynamic database on the system, and needs to be the quickest.

Like all other databases, `tempdb` typically consists of primary data and log files. `tempdb` is used to store user objects and internal objects. It also has two version stores. A *version store* is a collection of data pages that hold data rows required to support particular features that use row versioning. These two version stores are as follows:

➤ Row versions generated by data modification transactions in `tempdb` that use snapshot or read-committed row versioning isolation levels

➤ Row versions in `tempdb` generated by data-modification transactions for features such as online index operations, Multiple Active Result Sets (MARS), and AFTER triggers

Beginning with SQL Server 2005 and continuing in SQL Server 2014, `tempdb` has added support for the following large set of features that create user and internal objects or version stores:

➤ Table Variables, Temp Tables, Global Temp Tables

➤ Query

➤ Triggers

➤ Snapshot isolation and read-committed snapshots

➤ MARS

➤ Online index creation

➤ Temporary tables, table variables, and table-valued functions

➤ Database Console Command (DBCC) check

➤ Large Object (LOB) parameters

➤ Cursors

➤ Service Broker and Event Notifications

➤ XML and LOB variables

➤ Query notifications

➤ Database Mail

➤ Index creation

➤ User-defined functions

As a result, placing the `tempdb` database on a dedicated and extremely fast I/O subsystem can ensure good performance. A great deal of work has been performed on `tempdb` internals to improve scalability.

> **NOTE** *Consider reading Books Online under "Capacity Planning for tempdb" for additional information and functionality details regarding* tempdb *usage. You can find this at* http://msdn.microsoft.com/en-us/library/ms345368.aspx.

When you restart SQL Server, tempdb is the only database that returns to the original default size of 8MB, or to the predefined size set by the administrator. It can then grow from there based on use. During the autogrow operation, threads can lock database resources during the database-growth operation, affecting server concurrency. To avoid timeouts, you should set the autogrow operation to a growth rate that is appropriate for your environment. In general, you should set the growth rate to a number that will be large enough to allow normal query activity to continue without other growth iterations. This should be in a minimum of 1GB increments. If you have instant database file initialization turned on, the typical blocking that occurs for data file growths should not occur.

If you notice your tempdb files growing in between restarts, make the default file size equivalent to the highest level of growth. Be sure to make every file the same size.

You should do at least some type of capacity planning for tempdb to ensure that it's properly sized and can handle the needs of your enterprise system. At a minimum, perform the following:

1. Take into consideration the size of your existing tempdb.

2. Monitor tempdb while running the processes known to affect tempdb the most. The following query outputs the five executing tasks that make the most use of tempdb:

   ```
   SELECT top 5 * FROM sys.dm_db_session_space_usage
   ORDER BY (user_objects_alloc_page_count + internal_objects_alloc_page_count) DESC
   ```

3. Rebuild the index of your largest table online while monitoring tempdb. Don't be surprised if this number turns out to be two times the table size because this process now takes place in tempdb.

Following is a recommended query that must be run at regular intervals to monitor tempdb size. It is recommended that this is run every week, at a minimum. This query identifies and expresses tempdb space used (in kilobytes) by internal objects, free space, version store, and user objects.

```
select sum(user_object_reserved_page_count)*8 as user_objects_kb,
    sum(internal_object_reserved_page_count)*8 as internal_objects_kb,
    sum(version_store_reserved_page_count)*8  as version_store_kb,
    sum(unallocated_extent_page_count)*8 as freespace_kb
from sys.dm_db_file_space_usage
where database_id = 2
```

The output on your system depends on your database setup and usage. The output of this query might appear as follows:

user_objects_kb	internal_objects_kb	version_store_kb	freespace_kb
256	640	0	6208

> **NOTE** *If any of these internal SQL Server objects or data stores run out of space,* `tempdb` *will run out of space, and SQL Server will stop. For more information, please read the BOL article on* `tempdb` *disk space at* `http://msdn` `.microsoft.com/en-us/library/ms176029.aspx`*.*

Taking into consideration the preceding results, you must perform the following actions when configuring `tempdb`:

➤ Pre-allocate space for `tempdb` files based on the results of your testing, but to prevent SQL Server from stopping, leave autogrow enabled in case `tempdb` runs out of space.

➤ Per SQL Server instance, as a rule of thumb, create one `tempdb` data file per CPU or processor core, all equal in size up to eight data files. While there are reasons to go past eight files, this should not be done unless there is some sort of contention within the `tempdb` that you need to troubleshoot.

➤ Ensure that `tempdb` is in simple recovery mode, which enables space recovery.

➤ Place `tempdb` on a fast and dedicated I/O subsystem.

➤ Use instant database file initialization. See Chapter 10 for more information on setting up instant database file initialization.

In general, you should create alerts that monitor not just your `tempdb` data files and logs, but also all of the files for all of the databases on your system. You can do this by using SQL Server Agent or Microsoft System Center Operations Manager with SQL Knowledge Pack to ensure that you track for error 1101 or 1105 (`tempdb` is full). This is crucial, because the server stops processing if it receives those errors. Right-click `SQL Server Agent` in SQL Server Management Studio and fill in the dialog box, as shown in Figure 11-1. Moreover, you can monitor the following counters using Windows System Performance Monitor:

➤ **SQLServer:Databases—Log File(s) Size(KB)**—Returns the cumulative size of all the log files in the database.

➤ **SQLServer:Databases—Data File(s) Size(KB)**—Returns the cumulative size of all the data files in the database.

➤ **SQLServer:Databases—Log File(s) Used(KB)**—Returns the cumulative used size of all log files in the database. A large active portion of the log in a database can be a warning sign that a long transaction is preventing log cleanup.

Another great tool is the `sys.dm_db_task_space_usage` Dynamic Management View (DMV), which provides insight into `tempdb`'s space consumption on a per-task basis. Keep in mind that once the task is complete, the counters reset to zero. In addition, you should monitor the per-disk Avg. Sec/Read and Avg. Sec/Write as follows:

➤ Less than 10 milliseconds (ms) = Very good

➤ Between 10–20 ms = Borderline

➤ Between 20–50 ms = Slow, needs attention

➤ Greater than 50 ms = Serious I/O bottleneck

> **NOTE** *If you have large* tempdb *usage requirements, read the Q917047 article, "Microsoft SQL Server I/O subsystem requirements for tempdb database" at* http://support.microsoft.com/kb/917047 *or look in SQL Server 2012 Books Online for "Optimizing tempdb Performance."*

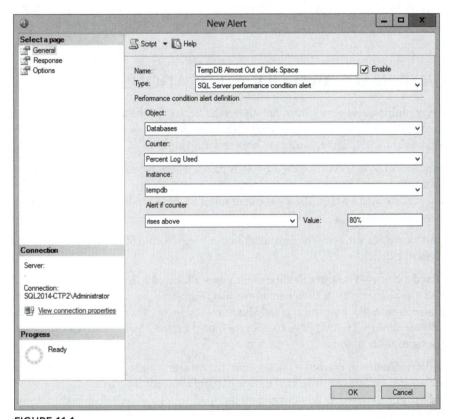

FIGURE 11-1

One of the most common questions about tempdb is, "How many files should I use?" As with most questions in the SQL Server world, the answer is, "It depends."

Use one file per CPU core up to eight files. Microsoft has performed extensive testing that shows diminishing returns (with very few exceptions) when you use more than eight files per filegroup. Table 11-1 provides a good reference.

TABLE 11-1: Determining the Number of Data Files

NUMBER OF CPU PROCESSOR CORES	NUMBER OF TEMPDB DATA FILES
1	1
2	2
4	4
8	8
16	8
32	8

SQL SERVER INTERNALS AND FILE ALLOCATIONS

The reason for having multiple `tempdbs` within any user SQL Server database is because of the way that data is allocated within SQL Server. At the 10,000-foot level, you may see tables, rows, and columns. However, deep within SQL Server, you may see the following:

➤ **Pages**—Data within SQL Server is stored on 8KB pages. There are many different types of pages within SQL Server. There are data pages, index pages, text tree pages, and multiple types of internal metadata pages. Each page contains a 96-byte header, and the remainder of the data is written to the page.

➤ **Extents**—An extent is a grouping of eight contiguous pages within SQL Server. Following are the two types of extents:

  ➤ **Mixed extents**—These are the first eight pages allocated when a table or index is created one at a time from anywhere in the filegroup. This means that when you create a large `temp` table, you will typically have at least eight CALLs to the Shared Global Allocation Map (SGAM) page to allocate mixed extents. Mixed extents can also belong to other objects.

  ➤ **Dedicated/uniform extents**—These occur after the first eight pages are allocated. All subsequent extents are dedicated to one particular object, and an extent represents eight pages allocated to an object, even if not all pages are needed at that moment. These extents are allocated from Global Allocation Map (GAM) pages.

Allocation bitmaps track the way that space and data is allocated in pages, tables, and for metadata objects using extents. Following are the three most pertinent allocation bitmaps when dealing with with databases and `tempdb`:

➤ **Page Free Space (PFS)**—This tracks the allocated pages and the page status. PFS pages track one page per byte allocating an extent per page. The PFS page is always page 1, and occurs every 8,088 pages (or roughly every 64MB).

➤ **Global Allocation Map (GAM)**—This tracks dedicated extents with 1 bit per extent. It is page 2 in a database, and occurs for every 64,000 extents (or roughly 4GB per GAM interval). A GAM page is allocated every 511,230 pages.

➤ **Shared Global Allocation Map (SGAM)**—This tracks mixed extents with 1 bit per extent. It is page 3 in a database, and occurs for every 64,000 extents (or roughly 4GB per GAM interval). An SGAM page is allocated every 511,230 pages.

➤ **Index Allocation Map (IAM)**—This page tracks all other pages that are allocated to one particular object. IAM pages are created for IN_ROW_DATA, ROW_OVERFLOW_DATA, and LOB data. Each table, heap, or index can have multiple IAM pages. Each partition of an object will also have up to three IAM pages. However, IAM pages are not shared between objects.

The term *GAM contention* in tempdb refers to these allocation pages exactly. The creation and destruction of many unique temporary objects can lead to the need for multiple files. Multiple files will allow the load on the allocation bitmaps to be spread among different allocation bitmaps on different files.

Unlike user databases, tempdb can only have one filegroup, the primary filegroup. User databases can create user-defined filegroups, and specify the location for the object to be created. This allows a specific way to alleviate contention for user databases that is not available for tempdb.

Following are the two processes based on algorithms used to allocate space within all SQL Server data files:

➤ *Proportional fill* determines how much data is written to each of the files in a multi-file filegroup based on the proportion of free space within each file. This allows the files to become full at roughly the same time, if they are sized equivalently.

➤ *Round Robin* is the pattern in which a new filegroup is selected in a multi-file filegroup once that file has met its proportional fill limit before a growth operation is required.

Why does this matter? When you create a new table the following operations must occur:

1. You issue a create table statement.

2. An entry is made into an SGAM page creating a reservation for an IAM page, in order to dedicate that IAM page to an object (the table in this instance).

3. The IAM page makes an entry into a PFS page in order to track how full it is.

4. You issue an insert statement to create a data page.

5. An entry is created in the SGAM to allocate one page.

6. An entry is created within the IAM page to track the page.

7. An entry is created within the PFS page to track the page.

8. A data page is created.

Steps 4 through 8 are performed repeatedly up until the first eight pages are created. After eight pages, a GAM page steps in for the SGAM page and eight pages are reserved at a time in dedicated extents.

In the case of `tempdb` (where you will create and drop tables over and over again), this can cause a bottleneck to occur on the PFS, SGAM, or GAM pages. Each data file added to a database contains its own PFS, SGAM, and GAM pages. Because you evenly allocate data across multiple files, this helps keep contention from occurring on allocation bitmaps.

It is important to remember that the files maintain an even size in order to keep an even distribution of data to each file in a multi-file filegroup. If one of the files is sized larger than the others, it will grow in an un-proportional manner in contrast to the other files. For `tempdb` (which is allocating pages every time a temporary object is created, and deallocating them when they are destroyed), this is particularly costly. A hot spot that focuses disproportionate file allocations on one file will occur.

TABLE AND INDEX PARTITIONING

Simply stated, *partitioning* is the breaking up of a large object (such as a table) into smaller, manageable pieces. A *row* is the unit on which partitioning is based.

Partitioning has been around for a while. This technology was introduced as a distributed portioned view (DPV) during the SQL 7.0 launch. This feature provided the capability for the optimizer to eliminate partitions (or tables) joined by a union of all statements on a view. These partitions could also be distributed across servers using linked servers. This is still the same concept as Sharding which runs queries against a DPV on multiple linked servers. This could be slower than running the same query against tables on the same server because of the network overhead. As systems have become increasingly faster and more powerful, the preferred method has become to use the SQL Server capability to partition database tables and their indexes over filegroups within a single database. One important note is that partitioning requires an Enterprise Edition of SQL Server, whereas DPVs can be used outside of Enterprise Edition.

One of the key features in utilizing partitioning for performance is the ability to perform the `alter table…. switch` command.

When you use the `switch` T-SQL command, you reassign the data from one table to another at the allocation bitmap level. Instead of logging inserts on one table and deletes on another table, acquiring multiple locks, latches, and creating a transaction log record for every insert, update, or delete of user and metadata, you change only the 8KB allocation bitmaps that reference where the data is located.

Keep in mind that you can only switch data into empty partitions. The table you switch data into must have the exact same schema as the table you are switching out of.

Why Consider Partitioning?

You might have large tables for a variety of reasons. When these tables (or databases) reach a certain size, it becomes difficult to perform activities such as database maintenance, backup, or restore operations that consume a lot of time. Environmental issues such as poor concurrency caused by a large number of users on a sizable table result in lock escalations, which translates into further challenges.

When you use partitioning, data size matters. You should not partition a table that is less than 25GB. You may not see performance benefits if the table is too small, and may even create additional overhead. When configuring partitioning you should plan out your partitioning strategy for the data you want to keep on hand, as well as a potential archiving strategy.

If you are still unsure whether to implement partitioning, run your workload through the Database Tuning Advisor (DTA), which makes recommendations for partitioning and generates the code for you. Chapter 15 "Replication," covers the DTA, which you can find under the "Performance Tools" section of the Microsoft SQL Server 2014 program menu.

> **NOTE** *Various chapters in this book cover partitioning to ensure that you learn details in their appropriate contexts.*

Following is a high-level process for partitioning:

1. Create a partition function to define a data-placement strategy.
2. Create filegroups to support the partition function.
3. Create a partition scheme to define the physical data distribution strategy (map the function data to filegroups).
4. Create a table or index on the partition function.
5. Examine query plans to see partitions accessed as verification that only a subset of data was returned.

After implementation, partitioning can positively affect your environment and most of your processes. Make sure you understand this technology to ensure that every process benefits from it. The following list presents a few processes that may be affected by partitioning your environment:

➤ Database backup and restore strategy (support for partial database availability)

➤ Index maintenance strategy (rebuild), including index views

➤ Data management strategy (large insert or table truncates)

➤ End-user database workload

➤ Concurrency:

> ➤ **Parallel partition query processing**—In SQL Server 2005, if the query accessed only one table partition, all available processor threads could access and operate on it in parallel. If more than one table partition were accessed by the query, only one processor thread was allowed per partition, even when more processors were available. For example, if you have an eight-processor server and the query accessed two table partitions, six processors would not be used by that query. In SQL Server 2012,

parallel partition processing was implemented whereby all available processors are used in parallel to satisfy the query for a partition table. You can enable or disable the parallel feature based on the usage requirements of your database workload.

➤ **Table partition lock**—Partitioning has the capability to lock at the partition level before escalating to table level locks. This is not on by default, but should be enabled on every partitioned table. You turn this on by issuing the following command.

```
ALTER TABLE TableName SET (LOCK_ESCALATION=AUTO)
```

➤ **SQL Server 2014**—This new version provides the capability to have incremental statistics per partition, and the capability to rebuild statistics per partition.

➤ Enhanced distribution or isolated database workloads using filegroups

Creating a Partition Function

A *partition function* is your primary data-partitioning strategy. When creating a partition function, the first order of business is to determine your partitioning strategy. Identifying and prioritizing challenges is the best way to decide on a partitioning strategy. Whether it's to move old data within a table to a slower, inexpensive I/O subsystem, enhance database workload concurrency, or simply maintain a large table, identifying and prioritizing is essential. After you select your strategy, you must create a partitioning function that matches that strategy.

Remember to evaluate a table for partitioning because the partition function is based on the distribution of data (selectivity of a column and the range or breadth of that column). The range supports the number of partitions by which the table can be partitioned. There is a product limit of 15,000 partitions per table.

Each file that is added to a database adds to the overall startup of that database. When SQL Server starts up, it must crack open the file header for each file and read it into memory. For example, 1,000 files on a database can slow recovery time by as much as 5 minutes. Use file ranges judiciously; less than 100 files should not affect restart time much, but remember to test before placing a partition strategy into production.

A range should also match up with the desired file strategy—for example, spreading out (or partitioning) a huge customer table by order date. It is very rare to have a partition strategy that is not based on date. When you do select your partition range, you want to ensure that you partition on a key value that will always be used in the `where` statement of your queries. If you do not utilize that value as a query predicate, then you will have performance issues because partition elimination does not occur, and you scan the entire table looking for values.

> **NOTE** *You cannot implement user-defined data types, alias data types, timestamps, images, XML,* `varchar(max)`, `nvarchar(max)`, *or* `varbinary(max)` *as partitioning columns.*

For example, consider a partition of a trouble-ticketing system for a telephone company. When a trouble ticket is generated based on an outage, it is submitted to the database. At this point, many activities are initiated. Technicians are dispatched, parts are replaced or reordered, and service can be rerouted within the network. Service-level agreements (SLAs) are monitored and escalations are initiated. All these activities take place because of the trouble ticket. In this system, the activities table and ticketing table have hot spots, as shown in Figure 11-2.

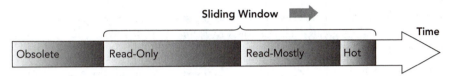

FIGURE 11-2

In Figure 11-2, the information marked as Hot is the new or recent data, which is only relevant or of interest during the outage. The information marked as Read-Only and Read-Mostly is usually used for minor analysis during postmortem processes, and then for application reporting. Eventually, the data becomes obsolete and should be moved to a warehouse. Unfortunately, because of internal regulatory requirements, this database must be online for seven years.

Partitioning this environment can provide sizable benefits. Under a *sliding-window* scenario (explained in the "Creating a Partition Scheme" section later in this chapter), every month (or quarter), a new partition would be introduced to the environment as a retainer for the current (Hot) data for the tickets and activities tables. As part of this process, a partition with data from these tables that is older than seven years would also be retired.

As described earlier, there is a one-to-many relationship between tickets and activities. Although obvious size differences exist between these tables, you must put them through identical processes. This enables you to run processes that affect resources shared by and limited to these objects. To mitigate the impact of doing daily activities such as backups and index maintenance on all this data, these tables will be partitioned based on date ranges. You can create a right partition function based on the `ticketdate` column, as outlined in Listing 11-1 (code file: `c11_BradleyBall_sqlscripts .sql`). (If you execute the following statement, remove the line breaks.)

LISTING 11-1: CreatePartitionFunction

```
CREATE PARTITION FUNCTION
PFL_Years (datetime)
AS RANGE RIGHT
FOR VALUES (
'20050101 00:00:00.000', '20070101 00:00:00.000',
'20090101 00:00:00.000', '20110101 00:00:00.000',
'20120101 00:00:00.000')
```

> **NOTE** *SQL Server rounds time to 0.003 seconds, meaning that a time of 0.997 would be rounded up to 1.0 second.*

➤ The leftmost partition is the first partition and includes all values less than `'20050101 00:00:00.000'`.

➤ The boundary value `'20050101 00:00:00.000'` is the start of the second partition, and this partition includes all values greater than or equal to `'20050101 00:00:00.000'` but less than `'20070101 00:00:00.000'`.

➤ The boundary value `'20070101 00:00:00.000'` is the start of the third partition, and this partition includes all values greater than or equal to `'20070101 00:00:00.000'` but less than `'20090101 00:00:00.000'`.

➤ The boundary value `'20090101 00:00:00.000'` is the start of the fourth partition and this partition includes all values greater than or equal to `'20090101 00:00:00.000'` but less than `'20110101 00:00:00.000'`.

➤ The boundary value `'20110101 00:00:00.000'` is the start of the fifth partition and includes all values greater than or equal to `'20110101 00:00:00.000'` but less than `'20120101 00:00:00.000'`.

➤ Finally, the boundary value `'20120101 00:00:00.000'` is the start of the sixth partition, and this partition consists of all values greater than `'20120101 00:00:00.000'`.

The range partition function specifies the boundaries of the range. The `left` or `right` keyword specifies to which side of each boundary value interval (left or right) the `boundary_value` belongs, when interval values are sorted by the Database Engine in ascending order from left to right. If this keyword is not specified, `left` is the default. There can be no holes in the partition domain; all values must be obtainable. In this code sample, all transactions must fall within a date specified by the sample value range.

Creating Filegroups

You should create filegroups to support the strategy set by the partition function. As a best practice, user objects should be created and mapped to a filegroup outside of the primary filegroup, leaving the primary filegroup for system objects. This ensures database availability if an outage occurs that affects the availability of any filegroup outside of the primary filegroup.

> **NOTE** *To continue with this example exercise, you must create filegroups CY04, CY06, CY08, CY10, CY11, and CY12 in the database before creating the partition scheme.*

Creating a Partition Scheme

A *partition scheme* is what maps database objects such as a table to a physical entity such as a file-group, and then to a file. You definitely have backup, restore, and data-archival considerations when making this decision. (These are discussed in Chapter 17, "Backup and Recovery.") Listing 11-2 (code file: c11_BradleyBall_sqlscripts.sql) maps the partition functions or dates to individual filegroups. The partition scheme depends on the PFL_Years partition function to be available from the earlier example.

LISTING 11-2: CreatePartitionScheme1

```
CREATE PARTITION SCHEME CYScheme
AS
PARTITION PFL_Years
TO ([CY04], [CY06], [CY08], [CY10], [CY11], [CY12])
```

This supports the placement of filegroups on individual physical disk subsystems. Such an option also supports the capability to move old data to an older, inexpensive I/O subsystem and to reassign the new, faster I/O subsystem to support Hot data (CY12). When the older data has been moved to the inexpensive I/O subsystem, filegroups can be marked as read-only. When this data has been backed up, it no longer needs to be part of the backup process. SQL Server automatically ignores these filegroups as part of index maintenance.

The other option for a partition-function scheme enables the mapping of the partition scheme to map the partition function to a single filegroup. Listing 11-3 maps the partition function to the default filegroup (code file: c11_BradleyBall_sqlscripts.sql).

> **WARNING** *This code will fail if you have not created the* PFL_Years *partition function.*

LISTING 11-3: CreatePartitionScheme2

```
CREATE PARTITION SCHEME CYScheme2
AS
PARTITION PFL_Years
TO ([Default], [Default], [Default], [Default], [Default], [Default])
```

Partitioning enables you to delete or insert gigabytes of data on a 500+GB partitioned table with a simple metadata switch and will only affect around 125 allocation bitmaps, reducing the transaction from 500GB to less than 1MB, provided that the delete or insert is based on the partitioned column. The process used to accomplish this is called *sliding window*. On a non-partitioned table, this process would take hours because of lock escalation and index resynchronization.

This process could be repeated in reverse to insert a new partition with data into this source partitioned table as the repository for the Hot data. Again, the only impact to the source partitioned table is a brief pause while a schema-lock is placed during the partition swaps, which can take a few seconds. This switch process can be performed only on partitions within the same filegroup. Implementation details and best practices are covered later in this chapter and in upcoming chapters.

Partitioned table parallelism is also affected by the Max Degree of Parallelism (MAXDOP) setting. A thread can be leveraged across each partition. Had the query been limited to a single partition, multiple threads would be spawned up to the MAXDOP setting. You learn more about MAXDOP later in this chapter.

DATA COMPRESSION

SQL Server data compression is largely unchanged in SQL Server 2014. The investments made in the technology in previous versions are still very robust and worth using. When compression is enabled, it saves space not only in your production system, but in any development, test/QA, and COOP/DR environment as well.

When used in production, compression leads to better I/O utilization because fewer reads and read-ahead reads are required. Data is compressed on disk and *in memory,* so the space savings are not just limited to disk. This allows for a more efficient use of buffer pool resources.

> **WARNING** *Data compression is only available in SQL Server 2014 Enterprise and Developer Editions. Monitor enterprise features that are enabled on a database by querying* `sys.dm_db_persisted_sku_features`.

You can use data compression on the following database objects:

- ➤ Tables (but not system tables)
- ➤ Clustered indexes
- ➤ Non-clustered indexes
- ➤ Index views
- ➤ Partitioned tables and indexes where each partition can have a different compression setting

Row Compression

Row compression is the most basic level of compression in SQL Server. It affects data at the row level and changes the internal structure completely. To understand this fully, look at Figure 11-3 to see an uncompressed data record compared to the structure of a compressed data record.

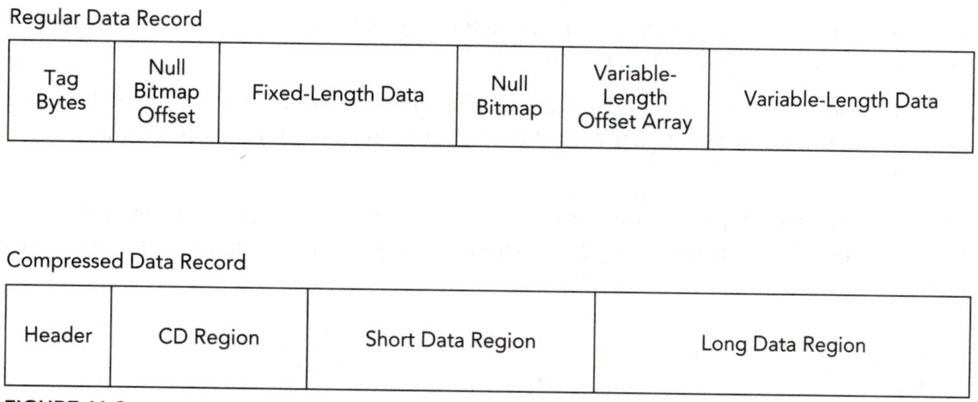

Regular Data Record

Tag Bytes	Null Bitmap Offset	Fixed-Length Data	Null Bitmap	Variable-Length Offset Array	Variable-Length Data

Compressed Data Record

Header	CD Region	Short Data Region	Long Data Region

FIGURE 11-3

The uncompressed data record has *tag bytes* signifying what type of information and also what state the data is in (for example, versioned or ghosted records, containing or not containing variable-length data). After the tag bytes is the *null bitmap offset*. This was introduced in SQL 2005 and points forward to the NULL bitmap as an optimization that allows skipping NULL fields between one another. Next is the *fixed-length data*. Fixed-length data is anything that contains a constant amount of reserved space. For example, if you have a CHAR(50) field and you insert the word 'Test' in it, you have used 4 bytes and have 46 bytes of space left over. SQL Server still stores all 50 bytes no matter what.

After the fixed-length data region is the *NULL bitmap* that contains two bytes per row. It represents the length of each non-NULL row, and identifies which rows contain NULL values. Next is the *variable-length offset array,* which contains forward pointers to each of the *variable-length data fields*. The variable-length offset array and variable-length data fields are read in a loop with the offset pointing to the data, and then looping back to read the next offset.

The difference between fixed-length data and variable-length data is simple. In the previous example, if you create a VARCHAR(50) and insert the word 'Test', you have only used 4 bytes of space, and SQL Server does not store the additional 46 characters of empty/blank spaces.

Looking at Figure 11-3, you can also see a *compressed data record*. Immediately, you can see that the physical structure is different. The reason for this is that row compression pulls all the empty leftover space out of fixed-length data records.

First, you see the *header* of the compressed record, which contains metadata about the compressed record very similarly to tag bytes. However, there is no variable-length data in the compressed record, so you do not require those types of identifiers.

Next, you see the *column descriptors* (CD) region. The CD region contains one bit per row instead of bytes that identify if the record resides in the *short data region, long data region,* or is contained off row in an uncompressed state. LOB data pages and ROW_OVER_FLOW data pages are the only pages that can store uncompressed data off row.

The short data region contains any rows that are equal to or less than 8 bytes. The long data region contains any rows that are greater than 8 bytes, but small enough to fit on a regular IN_ROW_DATA page.

You can turn row compression on or off very easily. You can apply compression when you first create a heap or an index. You can also apply compression when you are rebuilding a heap or an index. Run the following code to see the results:

```
/*
CREATE OUR DEMO DATABASE
AND TABLE
*/
USE MASTER
GO
IF EXISTS(SELECT NAME FROM SYS.DATABASES WHERE NAME='COMPRDEMOS')
BEGIN
        DROP DATABASE COMPRDEMOS
END
GO
CREATE DATABASE COMPRDEMOS
GO
USE COMPRDEMOS
GO
CREATE TABLE UNCOMPRESSED
        (
                MYID INT IDENTITY(1,1)
                ,MYCHAR CHAR(500) DEFAULT 'A'
        )
GO
/*
INSERT 5000 UNCOMPRESSED ROWS
INTO OUR TABLE
*/
INSERT INTO UNCOMPRESSED
DEFAULT VALUES
GO 5000
/*
EXAMINE THE SPACE USED BY TABLE
UNCOMPRESSED BEFORE APPLYING
ROW COMPRESSION AND AFTER
*/

SP_SPACEUSED 'UNCOMPRESSED'
GO
ALTER TABLE UNCOMPRESSED
REBUILD WITH(DATA_COMPRESSION=ROW)
GO
SP_SPACEUSED 'UNCOMPRESSED'
```

As you can see from the code, you create a 5,000-row table with 3,144KB of data. After applying compression, you have only 72KB of space used by the table.

Page Compression

Page compression includes row compression and then implements two other compression operations:

➤ **Prefix compression**—For each page and each column, a prefix value is identified that can be used to reduce the storage requirements. This value is stored in the Compression Information (CI) structure for each page. Then, repeated prefix values are replaced by a reference to the prefix stored in the CI.

➤ **Dictionary compression**—This involves searches for repeated values anywhere in the page, which are replaced by a reference to the CI.

When page compression is enabled for a new table, new inserted rows are row-compressed until the page is full, and then page compression is applied. Afterward, if there is space in the page for additional new inserted rows, they are inserted and page-compressed; if not, the new inserted rows go onto another page. Using page compression, nonleaf pages of the indexes are compressed using row compression only. To create a new compressed table with page compression, use the following commands:

```
USE AdventureWorks
GO
CREATE TABLE [Person].[AddressType_Compressed_Page](
  [AddressTypeID] [int] IDENTITY(1,1) NOT NULL,
  [Name] [dbo].[Name] NOT NULL,
  [rowguid] [uniqueidentifier] ROWGUIDCOL  NOT NULL,
  [ModifiedDate] [datetime] NOT NULL,
)
WITH (DATA_COMPRESSION=PAGE)
GO
```

To change the compression setting of a table, use the ALTER TABLE command, as shown here:

```
USE AdventureWorks
GO
ALTER TABLE Person.AddressType_Compressed_Page REBUILD
WITH (DATA_COMPRESSION=PAGE)
GO
```

Moreover, on a partitioned table or index, compression can be applied or altered on individual partitions. The following code shows an example of applying compression to a partitioned table and index:

```
USE AdventureWorks
GO

CREATE PARTITION FUNCTION [TableCompression](Int)
AS RANGE RIGHT
FOR VALUES (1, 10001, 12001, 16001);
GO

CREATE PARTITION SCHEME KeyRangePS
AS
PARTITION [TableCompression]
```

```
TO ([Default], [Default], [Default], [Default], [Default])
GO

CREATE TABLE PartitionTable
(KeyID int,
Description varchar(30))
ON KeyRangePS (KeyID)
WITH
(
DATA_COMPRESSION = ROW ON PARTITIONS (1),
DATA_COMPRESSION = PAGE ON PARTITIONS (2 TO 4)
)
GO

CREATE INDEX IX_PartTabKeyID
 ON PartitionTable (KeyID)
WITH (DATA_COMPRESSION = ROW ON PARTITIONS(1),
DATA_COMPRESSION = PAGE ON PARTITIONS (2 TO 4 ) )
GO
```

Table partition operations on a compression partition table have the following behaviors:

➤   **Splitting a partition**—Both partitions inherit the original partition setting.

➤   **Merging partitions**—The resultant partition inherits the compression setting of the destination partition.

➤   **Switching partitions**—The compression setting of the partition and the table to switch must match.

➤   **Dropping a partitioned clustered index**—The table retains the compression setting.

In addition, you can manage data compression from SQL Server Management Studio in Object Explorer by choosing the table or index to data compress. For example, to compress a table, follow these steps:

1.   Choose the table and then right-click. From the pop-up menu, choose Storage ➪ Manage Compression.

2.   On the Data Compression Wizard that opens, click Next, and in the Select Compression Type dialog box of the Data Compression Wizard, select the Compression Type drop-down to change the compression (None, Row, or Page). Figure 11-4 shows the Select Compression Type dialog box.

3.   After making a Compression Type change, click the Calculate button to see the estimated space savings. Then, click Next to complete the wizard.

Estimating Space Savings

Prior to enabling data compression, you can evaluate the estimated compression cost savings. For example, if a row is more than 4KB and the whole value precision is always used for the data type, there may not be much compression savings. The sp_estimate_data_compression_savings stored procedure creates a sample data set in tempdb and evaluates the compression space savings, returning the estimated table and sample savings. It can evaluate tables, clustered indexes, nonclustered indexes, index views, and table and index partitions for either page or row compression. Moreover, this stored procedure can estimate the size of a compressed table, index, or partition in the uncompressed state. This stored procedure performs the same cost-saving calculation that was performed by the Data Compression Wizard shown in Figure 11-4 when you clicked the Calculate button.

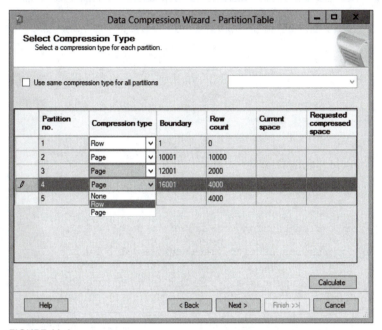

FIGURE 11-4

Following is the syntax of the `sp_estimate_data_compression_savings` stored procedure:

```
sp_estimate_data_compression_savings
[ @schema_name = ] 'schema_name'
, [ @object_name = ] 'object_name'
, [@index_id = ] index_id
, [@partition_number = ] partition_number
, [@data_compression = ] 'data_compression'
[;]
```

In this code:

➤ `@schema_name` is the name of the schema that contains the object.

➤ `@object_name` is the name of the table or index view that the index is on.

➤ `@index_id` is the ID number of the index. Specify NULL for all indexes in a table or view.

➤ `@partition_number` is the partition number of the object; it can be NULL or 1 for nonpartitioned objects.

➤ `@data_compression` is the type of compression to evaluate; it can be NONE, ROW, or PAGE.

Figure 11-5 shows an example of estimating the space savings for the `PartionTable` table in the sample `c11_BradleyBall_sqlscripts.sql` database provided on this book's companion website using page compression.

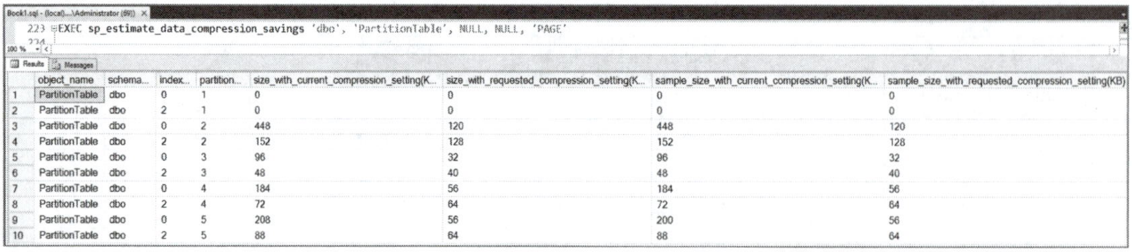

```
223 EXEC sp_estimate_data_compression_savings 'dbo', 'PartitionTable', NULL, NULL, 'PAGE'
```

	object_name	schema...	index...	partition...	size_with_current_compression_setting(K...	size_with_requested_compression_setting(K...	sample_size_with_current_compression_setting(K...	sample_size_with_requested_compression_setting(KB)
1	PartitionTable	dbo	0	1	0	0	0	0
2	PartitionTable	dbo	2	1	0	0	0	0
3	PartitionTable	dbo	0	2	448	120	448	120
4	PartitionTable	dbo	2	2	152	128	152	128
5	PartitionTable	dbo	0	3	96	32	96	32
6	PartitionTable	dbo	2	3	48	40	48	40
7	PartitionTable	dbo	0	4	184	56	184	56
8	PartitionTable	dbo	2	4	72	64	72	64
9	PartitionTable	dbo	0	5	208	56	200	56
10	PartitionTable	dbo	2	5	88	64	88	64

FIGURE 11-5

As shown in the result information in Figure 11-5:

- `index_id` identifies the object. In this case, 1 = clustered index (includes table); 2 and 3 are nonclustered indexes.
- `size_with_current_compression_setting` is the current size of the object.
- `size_with_requested_compression_setting` is the compressed size of the object.

In this example, the clustered index, including the table, is 9,952KB but when page-compressed, it is 4,784KB, saving a space of 5,168KB.

> **WARNING** *Be careful when using* `sp_estimate_data_compression_savings`*. The way the stored procedure works is that it takes 5 percent of the base table's data, moves it into* `tempdb`*, applies compression, and extrapolates the results to the table. This is fine for tables that are a couple of megabytes in size. However, you should not perform this action on your terabyte-size table with 2 billion rows unless you first test this in a development environment.*

Monitoring Data Compression

For monitoring data compression at the SQL Server 2014 instance level, two counters are available in the `SQL Server:Access Method` object that is found in Windows Performance Monitor:

- Page compression attempts/sec counts the number of page compression attempts per second.
- Pages compressed/sec counts the number of pages compressed per second.

However, this will give you very limited information because Performance Monitor is limited by the nature of its function as an application. The `sys.dm_db_index_operational_stats` Dynamic Management Function (DMF) includes the `page_compression_attempt_count` and `page_compression_success_count` columns, which are used to obtain page compression statistics for individual partitions. It is important to take note of these metrics because failures of attempted compression operations waste system resources. If the ratio of attempts to successes gets too high, there may be performance impacts that could be avoided by removing compression. In addition, the `sys.dm_db_index_physical_stats` DNF includes the `compressed_page_count` column, which displays the number of pages compressed per object and per partition.

To identify compressed objects in the database, you can view the `data_compression` column (0=None, 1=Row, 2=Page) of the `sys.partitions` catalog view. From SQL Server 2014 Management Studio in Object Explorer, choose the table and right-click. Then, from the pop-up menu, choose Storage ⇨ Manage Compression for the Data Compression Wizard.

> **NOTE** *For detailed information on data compression, refer to "Data Compression" in SQL Server 2014 Books Online, which you can find at* `http://msdn.microsoft.com/en-us/library/cc280449(v=SQL.120).aspx`.

The best way to monitor compression is to use extended events to track which pages and which reasons for failed compression attempts have occurred. Use the `SQLSERVER` package and the `Page_Compression_Attempt_Failed` and `Page_Compression_Tracing` events.

Data Compression Considerations

When deciding whether to use data compression, keep the following items in mind:

➤ Data compression is available with SQL Server 2014 Enterprise and Developer Editions only.

➤ Enabling and disabling table or clustered index compression can rebuild all nonclustered indexes.

➤ Data compression cannot be used with sparse columns.

➤ LOBs that are out-of-row are not compressed.

➤ Nonleaf pages in indexes are compressed using only row compression.

➤ Nonclustered indexes do not inherit the compression setting of the table.

➤ When you drop a clustered index, the table retains those compression settings.

➤ Unless specified, creating a clustered index inherits the compression setting of the table.

When deciding what to compress, do the following:

➤ Look for the largest tables in your database.

➤ Look at the type of allocation units used for each table. Remember, `IN_ROW_Data` compresses, LOB and `ROW_OVERFLOW` pages do not.

➤ Look at the usage patterns of your tables using `sys.dm_db_index_operational_stats`. Look for high `SEEK` and `SCAN` utilization. High update utilization indicates that you may want to skip compressing the object if you are CPU-bound.

➤ Test and monitor the execution plans of queries and their performance before and after to validate that compression has helped your performance.

> **WARNING** *When applying compression, transaction log records may reduce in size based on the compression level of the data. Every logged insert, update, or delete will store the previous copy of data and the new copy of data, regardless of compression setting. Compressed data can take up less space than non-compressed data. Page compression attempts are logged outside of user processes, and will not cause overhead on user transactions.*

UNDERSTANDING SQL SERVER AND CPUS

SQL Server 2014 (and previous versions since SQL 2005) has a special algorithm for scheduling user processes using the SQLOS. The SQLOS manages one scheduler per one logical core for user processes. There are two types of schedulers within SQL Server:

➤ *Hidden schedulers* are used by internal SQL Server processes. There is currently a 1:1 ratio of Hidden schedulers plus four additional schedulers used to monitor internal processes for AlwaysOn, the Dedicated Administrator Connection, and In-Memory OLTP.

➤ *Visible schedulers* are available for user queries and user processes. The SQLOS is the internal operating system built in SQL Server. It provisions CPU utilization, thread scheduling, task execution, and memory distribution.

You may find it odd that SQL Server has its own operating system within it. The reason for this SQLOS is that Windows is not a good operating system for database applications. Windows utilizes *preemptive scheduling*, and the SQLOS uses *cooperative* (or *non-preemptive*) *scheduling*. To understand the two different scheduling types, let's take a look at a short example to illustrate the differences between them.

Say you and another adult are in a room with 15 children. The other adult gives those children cake, candy, soda, and sugar. The other adult then whispers something to them, and they all get very, very excited. Then the other adult points to you and says, "Go tell that adult over there." You would be initially overwhelmed! You have 15 screaming children jumping up and down, yelling over one another, and your job is to listen to them. You would grab one and say, "I can listen to you for a second," then grab another and say, "I can listen to you for a second," then another, and another, and another. You would listen as fast as you could for only a small amount of time, not letting any of them finish as you frantically go to the next child.

This is analogous to preemptive scheduling. In the case of the operating system, let's say you have Internet Explorer (IE) with 10 tabs open and running—an instance of SQL Server 2014, a virtual machine (VM) with SQL Server 2014, Excel, Word, Notepad, Outlook, Lync, Remote desktop, Skype, and PowerPoint. Your CPU is running around saying, "I can listen to you for a second, now you, now you, now you...." This doesn't work for your queries. You don't want an operating system cutting them off before they are finished.

Now, let's say that those 15 children are now nice, neat, mannerly, and standing in a single-file line. They now wait one at a time patiently to speak with you. If the first child needs to think (in other words, fetch some detail from his little hard drive), then he steps out of line, off to the side, and allows the next little one (think worker thread) to take his place. While he is in the corner waiting, he is generating Wait Statistics in the Waiting Queue. His state is switched to SUSPENDED. Once he buffers his thought back into memory, he then goes to the back of the line (the runnable queue), and his state will switch to RUNNABLE. When all the children in the line have spoken with you, and it is finally his turn again, his state switches to RUNNING, and his task is finally completed.

In this example, you are the scheduler. You listen to the story, which is analogous to a query task. Keep in mind there is one scheduler per logical core on your server, and they allow processes to scale.

NUMA and Hot Add CPUs

For years, the standard hardware configuration has been Non-Uniform Memory Access (NUMA). Fortunately, SQL Server has been NUMA-aware since SQL Server 2005. For a reminder of how NUMA sections out processors and memory, check out Figure 11-6.

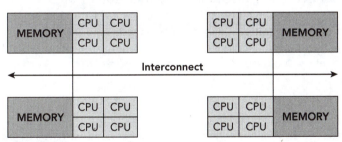

FIGURE 11-6

With Windows 2012 and SQL Server 2014, SQL Server supports *hot-add* CPU, whereby CPUs can be dynamically added while the server is online. Following are the system requirements to support hot-add CPU:

➤ Hardware support for hot-add CPU.

➤ Supported by the 64-bit edition of Windows Server 2012.

➤ Supported by SQL Server 2014 Enterprise Edition.

➤ SQL Server 2014 must not be configured for soft NUMA.

> **NOTE** *For more information about soft NUMA, search for the following topics online: "Understanding Non-Uniform Memory Access" and "How to Configure SQL Server to Use Soft-NUMA."*

Once you have met these requirements, execute the `RECONFIGURE` command to have SQL Server 2014 recognize the new dynamically added CPU.

Cache Coherency

For reasons of data integrity, only one processor can update any piece of data at a time. Other processors that have copies in their caches can have their local copy "invalidated" and thus must be reloaded. This mechanism is referred to as *cache coherency*, which requires that all the caches are in agreement regarding the location of all copies of the data, and which processor currently has permission to perform the update.

SQL Server Work Scheduling Using Affinity Mask

You can use the affinity mask configuration setting to assign a subset of the available processors to the SQL Server process. SQL Server worker threads are scheduled by the scheduler.

If the quanta of time that the scheduler has expires, the thread voluntarily yields, at which time the scheduler selects another worker thread to begin execution. If it cannot proceed without access to a resource such as disk I/O, it sleeps until the resource is available. When access to that resource is available, the process is placed on the run queue before being put back on the processor. When the Windows kernel transfers control of the processor from an executing process to another that is ready to run, this is referred to as a *context switch*.

Context Switching

Context switching is expensive because of the associated housekeeping required to move from one running thread to another. *Housekeeping* refers to the maintenance of keeping the context or the set of processor register values and other data that describes the process state. The Windows kernel loads the context of the new process, which then starts to execute. When the process taken off the processor next runs, it resumes from the point at which it was taken off the processor. This is possible because the saved context includes the instruction pointer. In addition to this *user mode* time, context switching can take place in the Windows operating system (OS) for *privileged mode* time.

The total processor time is equal to the privileged mode time plus the user mode time.

Privileged Mode

Privileged mode is a processing mode designed for operating system components and hardware-manipulating drivers. It enables direct access to hardware and all memory. Privileged time includes time-servicing interrupts and deferred process calls (DPCs).

SQL Server Lightweight Pooling

Context switching can often become problematic. In most environments, context switching should be less than 1,000 per second per processor. The SQL Server lightweight pooling option provides relief for this by enabling tasks to use NT "fibers," rather than threads, as workers.

A *fiber* is an executable unit that is lighter than a thread, and operates in the context of user mode. When lightweight pooling is selected, each scheduler uses a single thread to control the scheduling of work requests by multiple fibers. A fiber can be viewed as a "lightweight thread," which, under certain circumstances, takes less overhead than standard worker threads to context switch. The number of fibers is controlled by the Max Worker Threads configuration setting.

> **WARNING** *99.99 percent of the time, you should not alter the Max Worker Thread Configuration. Only if your Wait Stats point to CPU waits, and there are no other waits, and perfmon counters back up those findings, should you consider changing this setting.*

Affinity Mask

The affinity mask configuration option restricts a SQL Server instance to running on a subset of the processors. If SQL Server 2014 runs on a dedicated server, allowing SQL Server to use all processors can ensure best performance. In a server consolidation or multiple-instance environment, for more predictable performance, SQL Server may be configured to bind CPUs to specific instances, reducing the chance for cross-instance contention (see Figure 11-7).

Incoming connections are assigned to the CPU node. SQL Server assigns the batch request to a task or tasks, and the tasks are managed across schedulers. At any given time, only one task can be scheduled for execution by a scheduler on a processor. A *task* is a unit of work scheduled by the SQL Server. This architecture guarantees an even distribution of the hundreds (or, in many cases, thousands) of connections that can result from a large deployment.

Max Degree of Parallelism (MAXDOP)

By default, the MAXDOP value is set to 0, which enables SQL Server to consider all processors when creating an execution plan. In most systems, a MAXDOP setting equivalent to the number of cores in one NUMA node is recommended. This limits the overhead introduced by parallelization.

The general recommendation to set MAXDOP to 1 is normally to mask poorly written code that cannot handle parallel operations. The authors have seen advice in SQL Server forums where people complain of CXPacket wait statistics. Occasionally, the authors will see advice to set MAXDOP to 1. This is generally terrible, absolutely terrible, advice. CXPacket wait statistics occur when packets (information) are exchanged between CPUs during parallel operations. If you have a perfectly tuned SQL Server, then CXPacket wait statistics are merely indicative of the behavior of your workload.

However, there are some systems (based on application-workload profiles) with such a huge number of transactions per second where parallel query operations could have negative consequences for the application. In those cases, it is recommended that you set this value to 1. This prevents the query optimizer from choosing parallel query plans. Using multiple processors to run a single query is not always desirable in an OLTP environment.

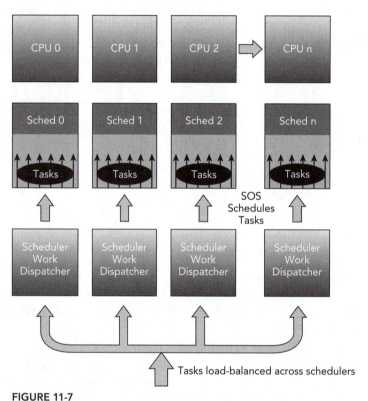

FIGURE 11-7

> **NOTE** *Any change to the MAXDOP setting from 0 should be tested before you put it into production. Test in a development or QA environment, run a workload captured from a production server, and ensure query performance does not suffer as a result.*

Another setting to examine is Cost Threshold for Parallelism.

Cost Threshold for Parallelism

Cost Threshold for Parallelism was added In SQL Server 7.0. The value of that cost was 5. It is still 5 in SQL Server 2014. The Cost Threshold for Parallelism is exactly what it sounds like.

When SQL Server looks at the overall cost of a serial query plan, depending on the level of optimization, the SQL Server optimizer can also generate a parallel plan to compare which is the "cheaper" and thus easiest to execute. If the serial query plan is greater than the Cost Threshold for Parallelism, then a parallel plan will be generated for comparison.

In the SQL 7.0 days, the value of 5 was originally the value on the desktop computer of one of the members of the SQL Server Optimizer Team. In the last 17 years, computers have grown by leaps and bounds to be much more powerful than their predecessors. The query plan that would benefit from parallel execution back in 1997 may operate more efficiently as a serial plan in 2014 hardware. One word of caution, though, before applying this to a live production system, always remember to test, test, and re-test! Never change a server-level setting, on an active server, without being certain that you will not negatively affect performance.

The way you would test this setting on an active system would be first to identify the cost of parallel plans on your system. Use the following query to find parallel plans on your server and what their cost would be. This query should be run in a maintenance window. Scanning your plan cache for XML shredding during a heavy workload could have negative performance impact.

```
SET TRANSACTION ISOLATION LEVEL READ UNCOMMITTED;

WITH XMLNAMESPACES
    (DEFAULT 'http://schemas.microsoft.com/sqlserver/2004/07/showplan')
SELECT
        query_plan AS CompleteQueryPlan
        ,i.value('(@StatementText)[1]', 'VARCHAR(4000)') AS StatementText
        ,i.value('(@StatementOptmLevel)[1]', 'VARCHAR(25)') AS OptimizationLevel
        ,i.value('(@StatementSubTreeCost)[1]', 'VARCHAR(128)') AS QueryCost
        ,i.query('.') AS ExecutionPlan
        ,decp.usecounts as TimesExecuted
FROM sys.dm_exec_cached_plans AS decp
CROSS APPLY sys.dm_exec_query_plan(plan_handle) AS deqp
CROSS APPLY query_plan.nodes('/ShowPlanXML/BatchSequence/Batch/Statements/
    StmtSimple') AS qpn(i)
WHERE  i.query('.').exist('//RelOp[@PhysicalOp="Parallelism"]') = 1
```

Figure 11-8 shows the results of this query. You see that two stored procedures each have a cost of over 5, but under 15.

The next step would be to test each of those stored procedures specifying the query hint of MAXDOP 1, to force a serial execution plan. Compare the run times to see which query is more efficient (see Figure 11-8).

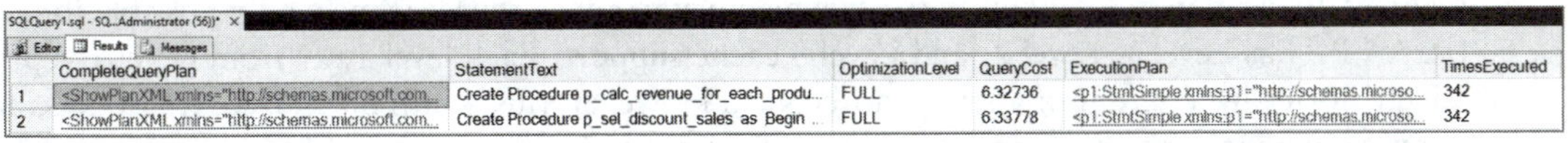

	CompleteQueryPlan	StatementText	OptimizationLevel	QueryCost	ExecutionPlan	TimesExecuted
1	<ShowPlanXML xmlns="http://schemas.microsoft.com...	Create Procedure p_calc_revenue_for_each_produ...	FULL	6.32736	<p1:StmtSimple xmlns:p1="http://schemas.microso...	342
2	<ShowPlanXML xmlns="http://schemas.microsoft.com...	Create Procedure p_sel_discount_sales as Begin ...	FULL	6.33778	<p1:StmtSimple xmlns:p1="http://schemas.microso...	342

FIGURE 11-8

In most cases you, can safely change this value to between 15 and 20 on new systems. Figure 11-9 shows the Cost Threshold for Parallelism.

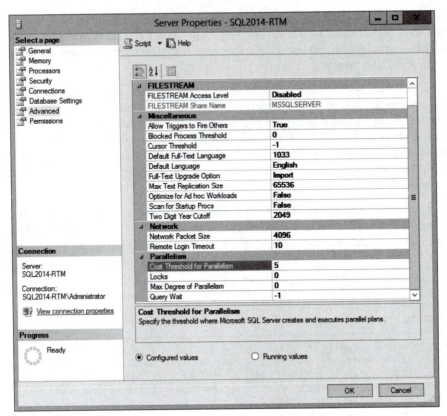

FIGURE 11-9

MEMORY CONSIDERATIONS AND ENHANCEMENTS

There are a few memory considerations and enhancements in SQL Server 2014 that you should keep in mind.

Buffer Pool Extensions

SQL Server 2014 offers the capability to scale memory in a way that was once only possible for CPUs. A CPU has Level 1, Level 2, and Level 3 cache support. Each level away from Level 1 is progressively slower by a matter of a few nanoseconds. However, this is still much faster than making the jump to memory, which is a jump in hundreds of nanoseconds.

Before SQL Server 2014, after system memory was exhausted, you would begin to page files to physical disk, which resulted in being slower orders of magnitude (nanoseconds to milliseconds). With Buffer Pool Extensions (BPEs), you now have the capability to extend the buffer pool. The main system memory will be considered the L1 (Level 1) buffer pool, and the BPE will be considered the L2 (Level 2) buffer pool.

Using the following script, you can create a BPE and place it on a physical disk. The second query can be used to query what is being stored in your buffer pool by database, and whether it is stored in the regular buffer pool or in a BPE.

```
ALTER SERVER CONFIGURATION
SET BUFFER POOL EXTENSION ON
     (FILENAME = 'F:\Example.BPE', SIZE = 20 GB);



SELECT
     DB_NAME(database_id) AS [Database Name]
     , case is_in_bpool_extension
          when 1 then 'BPool Extension'
          when 0 then 'Reg Buffer Pool'
          end as is_in_pbool_extension
     ,COUNT(*) * 8/1024.0 AS [Cached Size (MB)]
FROM
     sys.dm_os_buffer_descriptors
WHERE
     database_id > 4 -- system databases
     AND database_id <> 32767 -- ResourceDB
GROUP BY DB_NAME(database_id), is_in_bpool_extension
ORDER BY [Cached Size (MB)] DESC OPTION (RECOMPILE);
```

The multilevel caching hierarchy created by the BPE occurs when clean, non-dirty pages, are written to the L2 BPE cache. Dirty pages (that is, data pages that have been modified by an insert, update, or delete) will remain written to the L1 buffer pool. Figure 11-10 shows an example of how data flows throughout SQL Server with a BPE.

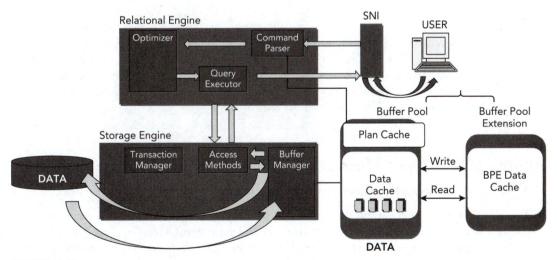

FIGURE 11-10

Additional DMVs, columns, and Extended Events were added to SQL Server 2014 to assist you in understanding how BPEs work, and how your system is using them. Table 11-2 shows a list of pertinent DMVs and Extended Events.

TABLE 11-2: DMVs and Extended Events for Tracking and Monitoring BPEs

OBJECT NAME	TYPE	DESCRIPTION
`sys.dm_os_buffer_pool_exten-sion_configuration`	DMV	A query that returns the configuration information about the BPE in SQL Server. Returns the physical file path, file_id, state, state description, and current size in kilobytes.
`sys.dm_os_buffer_descriptors`	DMV	This DMV is modified in SQL Server 2014 to include a column `is_in_pbool_extension`. Use this column to determine if the buffers in the data cache are stored in physical memory or on a BPE.
`sqlserver.buffer_pool_exten-sion_pages_written`	Extended Event	This event fires when a page or contiguous set of pages are evicted from the buffer pool and written to the BPE.
`sqlserver.buffer_pool_exten-sion_pages_read`	Extended Event	This event fires when a page is read from the BPE.
`sqlserver.buffer_pool_exten-sion_pages_evicted`	Extended Event	This event fires when a page is evicted from the BPE.
`sqlserver.buffer_pool_evic-tion_thresholds_recalculated`	Extended Event	This event fires when the eviction threshold is recalculated.

> **WARNING** *SQL Server does not know the difference between an SSD and a regular magnetic hard drive. Be sure that you define your BPE on an SSD. If you create one on a magnetic hard drive, you will see no performance improvement, and may see performance degradation similar to beyond what the cost of paging out to your physical hard drive was previously.*

Tuning SQL Server Memory

A number of performance counters are available from the System Performance Monitor.

The SQL Server Cache Hit Ratio signifies the balance between servicing user requests from data in the data cache and having to request data from the I/O subsystem. Accessing data in RAM (or data cache) is exponentially faster than accessing the same information from the I/O subsystem; thus, the wanted state is to load all active data in RAM. Unfortunately, RAM is a limited resource. A wanted cache hit ratio average should be well over 90 percent. This does not mean that the SQL Server environment would not benefit from additional memory. A lower number signifies that the system memory or data cache allocation is below the wanted size.

Another reliable indicator of instance memory pressure is the SQL Server:Buffer Manager:Page-life-expectancy (PLE) counter. This counter indicates the amount of time that a buffer page remains in memory (in seconds). The ideal number for PLE varies with the size of the RAM installed in your particular server, and how much of that memory is used by the plan cache, Windows operating system, and so on. The rule of thumb nowadays is to calculate the ideal PLE number for a specific server using the following formula: `MaxSQLServerMemory(GB) x 75`. So, for a system that has 128GB of RAM and has a `MaxServerMemory` SQL setting of 120GB, the "minimum PLE before there is an issue" value is 9000. This can give you a more realistic value to monitor PLE against than the previous yardstick of 300.

Be careful not to under-allocate total system memory, because it forces the operating system to start moving page faults to a physical disk. A *page fault* is a phenomenon that occurs when the operating system goes to a physical disk to resolve memory references. The operating system may incur some paging, but when excessive paging takes places, it uses disk I/O and CPU resources, which can introduce latency in the overall server, resulting in slower database performance. You can identify a lack of adequate system memory by monitoring the Memory: Pages/sec performance counter. It should be as close to zero as possible, because a higher value indicates that more hard-paging is taking place, as can happen when backups are taking place.

SQL Server 2014 has several features that should help with this issue. With Windows Server 2012, SQL Server 2014 has support for hot-add memory, a manager framework, and other enhancements.

As mentioned earlier in this chapter, the SQLOS is a thin layer that sits between SQL Server and Windows to manage the interaction between these environments. It enables SQL Server to scale on any hardware. Figure 11-11 highlights the SQLOS components that perform thread scheduling and synchronization, perform SQL Server memory management, provide exception handling, and host the Common Language Runtime (CLR).

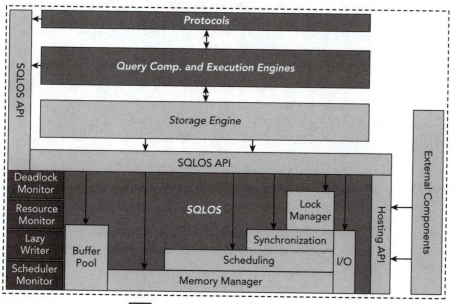

FIGURE 11-11

The goal of this environment is to empower the SQL Server platform to exploit all of today's hardware innovation across the X64 platform. SQLOS was built to bring together the concepts of data locality, support for dynamic configuration, and hardware workload exploitation. This architecture also enables SQL Server 2014 to better support both Cache Coherent Non-Uniform Memory Access (CC-NUMA).

The architecture uses the concept of a *memory node*, which is one hierarchy between memory and CPUs. There is a memory node for each set of CPUs to localize memory and its content to these CPUs.

A *CPU node* is also a hierarchical structure designed to provide logical grouping for CPUs. The purpose is to localize and load-balance related workloads to a CPU node.

The relationship between a CPU node and a memory node is explicit. There can be many CPU nodes to a memory node, but there can never be more than one memory node to a CPU node. Each level of this hierarchy provides localized services to the components that it manages, resulting in the capability to process and manage workloads in such a way as to exploit the scalability of whatever hardware architecture SQL Server runs on. SQLOS also enables services such as dynamic affinity, load-balancing workloads, dynamic memory capabilities, Dedicated Admin Connection (DAC), and support for partitioned resource management capabilities.

SQL Server 2014 leverages the common caching framework (also part of SQLOS) to achieve fine-grain control over managing the increasing number of cache mechanisms (Cache Store, User Store, and Object Store). This framework improves the behavior of these mechanisms by providing a common policy that can be applied to internal caches to manage them in a wide range of operating conditions.

Previous versions of SQL Server introduced a memory-tracking enhancement called the *Memory Broker*, which enables the tracking of OS-wide memory events. Memory Broker manages and tracks the dynamic consumption of internal SQL Server memory. Based on internal consumption and pressures, it automatically calculates the optimal memory configuration for components such as buffer pool, optimizer, query execution, and caches. It propagates the memory configuration information back to these components for implementation. SQL Server 2014 also supports dynamic management of conventional, locked, and large-page memory, as well as the hot-add memory feature mentioned earlier.

Hot-add memory provides the capability to introduce additional memory in an operational server without taking it offline. In addition to OEM vendor support, Windows Server 2012 and SQL Server 2014 Enterprise Edition are required to support this feature.

Data Locality

Data locality is the concept of having all relevant data available to the processor on its local NUMA node while it's processing a request. All memory within a system is available to any processor on any NUMA node. This introduces the concepts of *near memory* and *far memory*. Near memory is the preferred method because it is accessed by a processor on the same NUMA node. As shown in Figure 11-12, accessing far memory is expensive because the request must leave the NUMA node and traverse the system interconnect crossbar to get the NUMA node that holds the required information in its memory.

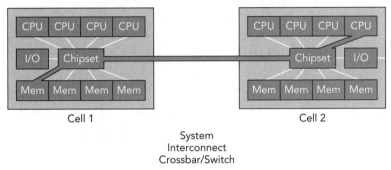

FIGURE 11-12

The cost of accessing objects in far memory versus near memory is often threefold or more. Data locality is managed by the system itself, and the way to mitigate issues with it is to install additional memory per NUMA node.

Max Server Memory

When "Maximum server memory" is kept at the default dynamic setting, SQL Server acquires and frees memory in response to internal and external pressure. SQL Server uses all available memory if left unchecked, so the "Maximum server memory" setting is strongly recommended. The Windows operating system needs some memory to function, so you should configure a value of 8GB to 16GB less than the total system memory. Table 11-3 shows some configuration guidelines.

TABLE 11-3: Configuration Guidelines for Maximum Server Memory

TOTAL SYSTEM MEMORY (GB)	OS RESERVED MEMORY (GB)	MAX SQL SERVER MEMORY (GB)
16	4	12
32	4	28
64	4	60
128	8	120
256	8	248

See Figure 11-13 for an example of setting Maximum Server memory on SQL Server 2014.

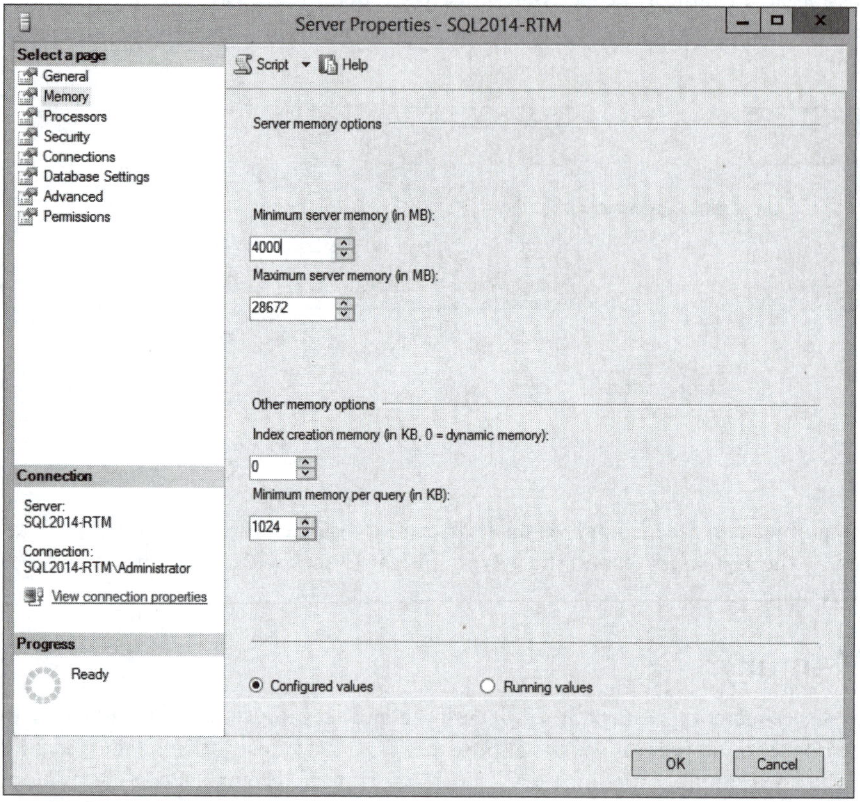

FIGURE 11-13

RESOURCE GOVERNOR

Resource Governor is a SQL Server technology that limits the amount of resources that can be allocated to each database workload from the total resources available to SQL Server 2014. When enabled, Resource Governor classifies each incoming session and determines to which workload group the session belongs. Each workload group is then associated to a resource pool that limits those groups of workloads. Moreover, Resource Governor protects against runaway queries on the SQL Server and unpredictable workload execution, and sets workload priority. For Resource Governor to limit resources, it must differentiate workloads as follows:

➤ Classify incoming connections to route them to a specific workload group

➤ Monitor resource usage for each workload group

➤ Pool resources to set limits on CPU, memory, and I/O to each specific resource pool

➤ Identify workloads and group them together to a specific pool of resources

➤ Set workload priority within a workload group

The constraints on Resource Governor are as follows:

➤ It applies only to the SQL Server Relational Engine and not to Analysis Services, Report Services, or Integration Services. Resource Governor is also an Enterprise feature, which requires an Enterprise Edition license.

➤ It cannot monitor resources between SQL Server instances. However, you can use Windows Resource Manager (part of Windows) to monitor resources across Windows processes, including SQL Server.

➤ It can limit CPU bandwidth, memory, and I/O.

➤ A typical OLTP workload consists of small and fast database operations that individually take a fraction of CPU time and may be too miniscule to enable Resource Governor to apply bandwidth limits.

The Basic Elements of Resource Governor

The main elements of Resource Governor include resource pools, workload groups, and classification support, explained in the following sections.

Resource Pools

The *resource pools* are the physical resources of the SQL Server. During SQL Server installation, two pools are created: *internal* and *default*. The resources that can be managed are min and max CPU, and min and max memory. By default, the Resource Governor is disabled. To enable it, use the ALTER RESOURCE GOVERNOR RECONFIGURE command. You can disable it again with the ALTER RESOURCE GOVERNOR DISABLE command.

The internal pool is used for SQL Server's own internal functions. It contains only the internal workload group; it cannot be altered, and it is not restricted.

The default pool is the predefined user resource pool. It contains the default workload group, and can contain user-defined workload groups. It can be altered, but cannot be created or dropped.

You can create user-defined pools using the CREATE RESOURCE POOL DDL statement, or by using SQL Server Management Studio. Moreover, you can modify a pool by using the ALTER RESOURCE POOL command, and delete it by using the DROP RESOURCE POOL command. You can define any number of resource pools, up to a maximum of 20. This includes the internal and default pools.

The following syntax creates a resource pool for Resource Governor:

```
CREATE RESOURCE POOL pool_name
[ WITH
        ( [ MIN_CPU_PERCENT = value ]
    [ [ , ] MAX_CPU_PERCENT = value ]
```

```
    [ [ , ] CAP_CPU_PERCENT = value ]
    [ [ , ] AFFINITY {SCHEDULER = AUTO | (Scheduler_range_spec) | NUMANODE =
        (NUMA_node_range_spec)}]      [ [ , ] MIN_MEMORY_PERCENT = value ]
    [ [ , ] MAX_MEMORY_PERCENT = value ]
    [ [ , ] MIN_IOPS_PER_VOLUME = value ]
    [ [ , ] MAX_IOPS_PER_VOLUME = value ])
]   [;]
```

> **NOTE** *Note that* `MIN_IOPS_PER_VOLUME` *and* `MAX_IOPS_PER_VOLUMNE` *are new options available in SQL Server 2014. See the Books Online topic for more information at* `http://msdn.microsoft.com/en-us/library/bb934024(v=SQL.120).aspx`.

Workload Groups

A *workload group* is a container for similar sessions according to the defined classification rules, and applies the policy to each session of the group. It also contains two predefined workload groups: *internal* and *default*. The internal workload group relates to the internal resource pool and cannot be changed. The default workload group is associated with the default resource pool, and is the group used when no session classification user-defined function exists, when a classification failure occurs, or when a classification user-defined function returns NULL.

You can create the user-defined workload group by using the CREATE WORKLOAD GROUP command, modify it by using the ALTER WORKLOAD GROUP command, and drop it by using the DROP WORKLOAD GROUP command.

The following syntax creates a workload group for Resource Governor:

```
CREATE WORKLOAD GROUP group_name
[ WITH
    ( [ IMPORTANCE = { LOW | MEDIUM | HIGH } ]
          [ [ , ] REQUEST_MAX_MEMORY_GRANT_PERCENT = value ]
          [ [ , ] REQUEST_MAX_CPU_TIME_SEC = value ]
          [ [ , ] REQUEST_MEMORY_GRANT_TIMEOUT_SEC = value ]
          [ [ , ] MAX_DOP = value ]
          [ [ , ] GROUP_MAX_REQUESTS = value ] )
]
[ USING { pool_name | "default" } ] [ ; ]
```

You can apply several configuration settings to a workload group:

➤ Maximum memory allocation per request

➤ Maximum CPU time per request

➤ Maximum IOPS per request/per second

➤ Minimum IOPS per request/per second

➤ Resource timeout per request

➤ Relative importance setting per request

➤ Workgroup limit per number of requests

➤ Maximum degree of parallelism

➤ Specific resource pool

Classification

Resource Governor supports classifying incoming connections into existing workload groups. It supports system-wide provided rules and user-defined rules using connection-specific attributes. In the absence of a user-defined classification function, it can use the default workload group. After the user-defined classification function is registered with Resource Governor, the function is executed for every new connection, and the connection is routed to one of the existing workload groups to be limited by the resource pool. Only one user-defined classification function can be designated as a classifier; and after registering it, it takes effect after an ALTER RESOURCE GOVERNOR RECONFIGURE command is executed.

Resource Governor uses connection-specific functions such as HOST_NAME(), APP_NAME(), SUSER_NAME(), SUSER_SNAME(), IS_SRVROLEMEMBER(), and IS_MEMBER() to identify each connection.

Figure 11-14 shows the components of Resource Governor and their relationships.

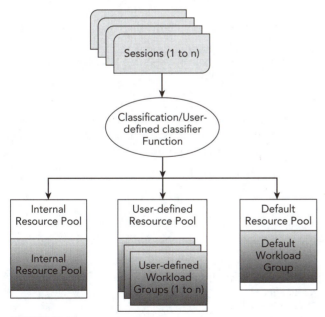

FIGURE 11-14

Listing 11-6 (code file: c11_BradleyBall_sqlscripts.sql) shows a Resource Governor Implementation example that creates three resource pools to support the resource requirements for three different workload groups.

1.   First, create three resource pools: adhoc, reports, and admin requests.

LISTING 11-6: ResourcePools

```
USE Master;
BEGIN TRAN;
CREATE RESOURCE POOL poolAdhoc with
( MIN_CPU_PERCENT = 10, MAX_CPU_PERCENT = 30,
MIN_MEMORY_PERCENT= 15, MAX_MEMORY_PERCENT= 25,
MIN_IOPS_PER_VOLUME=0, MAX_IOPS_PER_VOLUME=2147483647);

CREATE RESOURCE POOL poolReports with
( MIN_CPU_PERCENT = 20, MAX_CPU_PERCENT = 35,
MIN_MEMORY_PERCENT= 15,  MAX_MEMORY_PERCENT= 45,
MIN_IOPS_PER_VOLUME=0, MAX_IOPS_PER_VOLUME=2147483647);

(MIN_IOPS_PER_VOLUME=0, MAX_IOPS_PER_VOLUME=2147483647);
 ALTER RESOURCE POOL Customer2Pool WITH (MIN_IOPS_PER_VOLUME=0,
     MAX_IOPS_PER_VOLUME=2147483647);

CREATE RESOURCE POOL poolAdmin with
( MIN_CPU_PERCENT = 15, MAX_CPU_PERCENT = 25,
MIN_MEMORY_PERCENT= 15,  MAX_MEMORY_PERCENT= 30);
```

2.   Next, create three workload groups and associate them with the three resource pools:

```
CREATE WORKLOAD GROUP groupAdhoc using poolAdhoc;
CREATE WORKLOAD GROUP groupReports with (MAX_DOP = 8) using poolReports;
CREATE WORKLOAD GROUP groupAdmin using poolAdmin;
GO
```

3.   Create a user-defined classification function that identifies each new session and routes it to one of the three workload groups. Any request that cannot be identified by the user-defined classification function is directed to the default workload group:

```
CREATE FUNCTION rgclassifier_v1() RETURNS SYSNAME
WITH SCHEMABINDING
AS
BEGIN
    DECLARE @grp_name AS SYSNAME
      IF (SUSER_NAME() = 'sa')
         SET @grp_name = 'groupAdmin'
      IF (APP_NAME() LIKE '%MANAGEMENT STUDIO%')
         OR (APP_NAME() LIKE '%QUERY ANALYZER%')
         SET @grp_name = 'groupAdhoc'
      IF (APP_NAME() LIKE '%REPORT SERVER%')
         SET @grp_name = 'groupReports'
    RETURN @grp_name
END;
GO
```

4.   Next, the user-defined classification function must be registered to Resource Governor. All these operations are contained inside an explicit transaction. That's a preventive measure so

that if a user error occurs, it can be rolled back. In addition, only one user-defined classification function can be registered to the Resource Governor at any one time.

```
ALTER RESOURCE GOVERNOR WITH (CLASSIFIER_FUNCTION= dbo.rgclassifier_v1);
COMMIT TRAN;
```

5. Finally, to have these new changes take effect or to enable Resource Governor, run the following command:

```
ALTER RESOURCE GOVERNOR RECONFIGURE;
```

Using Resource Governor from SQL Server 2014 Management Studio

From inside SQL Server 2014 Management Studio in Object Explorer, Resource Governor is in the Management node. By default, Resource Governor is disabled. To enable it, right-click Resource Governor and then click Enable. Moreover, from Object Explorer inside the Management node, right-click Resource Governor, and then click Properties to add, delete, or modify properties of the resource pools and workload groups, or to add or remove a user-defined classification function and enable Resource Governor.

From the Resource Governor Properties dialog box, you can see that two resource pools, Internal and Default, with two corresponding workload groups, are visible. These are created by SQL Server 2014 during installation. No classification function is available until one is created. If Resource Governor is enabled, it uses the default system-defined rules and the default pool, as configured in Figure 11-15.

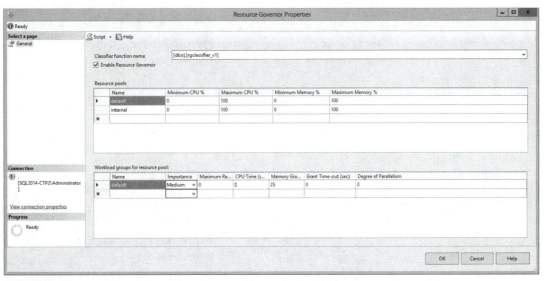

FIGURE 11-15

After running the script in Listing 11-6 to create the three user-defined resource pools, workload groups, and the user-defined classification function, and after enabling the Resource Governor, the properties should match what is shown in Figure 11-16.

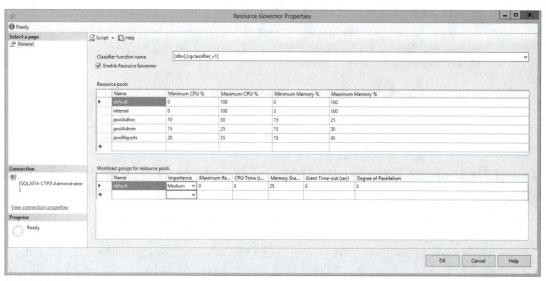

FIGURE 11-16

Monitoring Resource Governor

SQL Server 2014 includes two performance objects to collect workload group and pool statistics for each SQL Server instance:

➤ SQLServer—Resource Pool Stats for resource-specific statistics—For more information, see the article at `http://msdn.microsoft.com/en-us/library/cc645958(v=SQL.120).aspx`.

➤ SQLServer—Workload Group Stats for workload-specific statistics—For more information, see the article at `http://msdn.microsoft.com/en-us/library/cc627354(v=SQL.120).aspx`.

Moreover, Resource Governor DMVs return information specific to resource statistics, as indicated in Table 11-4.

TABLE 11-4: Resource Governor DMVs

RESOURCE GOVERNOR DYNAMIC MANAGEMENT VIEWS	DESCRIPTION
`sys.dm_resource_governor_configuration`	For current in-memory configuration state
`sys.dm_resource_governor_resource_pools`	For resource pool state, configuration, and statistics
`sys.dm_resource_governor_workload_groups`	For workload group `statisticvs` and in-memory configuration

> **NOTE** *For more detailed information on Resource Governor, refer to SQL Server 2014 Books Online under "Resource Governor" at* `http://msdn.micro-soft.com/en-us/library/bb933866(v=SQL.120).aspx.`

SUMMARY

You have many important points to consider when setting up and configuring SQL Server 2014. You should place database files (data and log files) on separate LUNs, which are made up of fast disks. You should place `tempdb` on its own set of disks, which should be the fastest possible. You can use partitioning to increase performance, which also offers manageability advantages. You can use compression to increase I/O performance, but you must take care not to overtax the CPU. You can tweak CPU and memory from within SQL Server, but you must be careful not to use settings that are detrimental. Remember: test, test, test!

If you apply these lessons correctly, SQL Server 2014 is more than capable of tuning itself automatically to predictably provide the availability and performance to support the requirements of your enterprise.

In Chapter 12, you learn about monitoring your SQL Server.

12

Monitoring Your SQL Server

WROX.COM CODE DOWNLOADS FOR THIS CHAPTER

The wrox.com code downloads for this chapter are found at `www.wrox.com/go/ prosql2014admin` on the Download Code tab. The code is in the Chapter 12 download and individually named according to the names throughout the chapter.

Implementing good monitoring enables you to move from reactively dealing with events to proactively diagnosing problems and fixing them before your users are even aware there is a problem. This chapter teaches you how to proactively monitor your SQL Server system so that you can prevent or react to events before the server gets to the point where users begin calling.

Here's a quick example. Say you recently took over an existing system after the DBA moved to a different team. This system's applications ran well, but there was something that needed fixing every other day—transaction logs filling up, `tempdb` out of space, too many locks, and filegroups filling up—nothing major, just a slow, steady trickle of problems that needed fixing. This is the DBA's death of 1,000 cuts. Your time is sucked away doing these essential maintenance tasks until you get to the point where you don't have time to do anything else.

After a few weeks of this, you manage to put some new monitoring in place and make several proactive changes to resolve issues before anything breaks. These changes aren't rocket science; they are simple things such as moving data to a new filegroup, turning on autogrow for several files and extending them to allow a known amount of growth, and rebuilding badly fragmented indexes that were reserving unneeded space. All this takes considerably less time than dealing with the steady stream of failures, and provides a greatly improved experience for the users of this system.

So, what does it take to monitor this system? Nothing dramatic—just a few simple steps, mostly some T-SQL monitoring of tables, database and filegroup free space, index usage, and fragmentation. You do a few things to monitor resource usage and help find the key pain points. After you understand the pain points, you can take a few steps to get ahead of the curve on fixing things.

Now that you've seen the value in monitoring SQL Server, you can learn how to do this for yourself.

THE GOAL OF MONITORING

The goal when monitoring databases is to see what's going on inside SQL Server—namely, how effectively SQL Server uses the server resources (CPU, memory, and I/O). You want this information so that you can see how well the system performs. The data must be captured over time to enable you to build a profile of what the system normally looks like: How much of what resource do you use for each part of the system's working cycle? From the data collected over time, you can start to build a baseline of "normal" activity. That baseline enables you to identify abnormal activities that might lead to issues if left unchecked.

Abnormal activity could be an increase in a specific table's growth rate, a change in replication throughput, or a query or job taking longer than usual or using more of a scarce server resource than you expected. Identifying these anomalies before they become an issue that causes your users to call and complain makes for a much easier life. Using this data, you can identify what might be about to break, or where changes need to be made to rectify the root cause before the problem becomes entrenched.

Sometimes this monitoring is related to performance issues such as slow-running queries or deadlocks, but in many cases, the data points to something that you can change to avoid problems in the future.

This philosophy is about the equivalent of "an apple a day keeps the doctor away"—preventative medicine for your SQL Server.

Determining Your Monitoring Objectives

Before you start monitoring, you must first clearly identify your reasons for monitoring. These reasons may include the following:

- ➤ Establishing a baseline
- ➤ Identifying new trends before they become problems
- ➤ Monitoring database growth
- ➤ Identifying daily, weekly, and monthly maintenance tasks
- ➤ Identifying performance changes over time
- ➤ Auditing user activity
- ➤ Diagnosing a specific performance problem

Establishing a Baseline

Monitoring is extremely important to help ensure the smooth running of your SQL Server systems. However, just monitoring by itself (and determining the value of a key performance metric at any point in time) is not of great value unless you have a sound baseline to compare the metric against. Are 50 transactions per second good, mediocre, or bad? If the server runs at 75 percent CPU, is that normal? Is it normal for this time of day, on this day of the week, during this month of the year? With a baseline of the system's performance, you immediately have something to compare the current metrics against.

If your baseline shows that you normally get 30 transactions per second, then 50 transactions per second might be good; the system can process more transactions. However, it may also be an indication that something else is going on, which has caused an increase in the transactions. What your baseline looks like depends on your system, of course. In some cases, it might be a set of Performance Monitor logs with key server resource and SQL counters captured during several periods of significant system activity, or stress tests. In another case, it might be the results of an analysis of a SQL Profiler trace, or an Extended Events log captured during a period of high activity. The analysis might be as simple as a list of the stored procedure calls made by a particular application, with the call frequency.

To determine whether your SQL Server system performs optimally, take performance measurements at a regular interval over time, even when no problem occurs, to establish a server performance baseline. How many samples and how long each needs to be are determined by the nature of the workload on your servers. If your servers have a cyclical workload, the samples should aim to query at multiple points in several cycles to allow a good estimation of minimum, maximum, and average rates. If the workload is uniform, fewer samples over shorter periods can provide a good indication of minimum, maximum, and average rates. At a minimum, use baseline performance to determine the following:

➤ Peak and off-peak hours of operation

➤ Query or batch response time

Another consideration is how often the baseline should be recaptured. In a system that is rapidly growing, you may need to recapture a baseline frequently. When current performance has changed by 15 to 25 percent compared to the old baseline, it is a good point to consider recapturing the baseline.

Comparing Current Metrics to the Baseline

A key part of comparing current metrics to those in the baseline is determining an acceptable limit from the baseline outside of which the current metric is not acceptable, and thus flags an issue that needs investigating.

What is acceptable here depends on the application and the specific metric. For example, a metric looking at free space in a database filegroup for a system with massive data growth and an aggressive archiving strategy might set a limit of 20 percent free space before triggering some kind of alert. On a different system with little database growth, that same metric might be set to just 5 percent.

You must make your own judgment of what is an acceptable limit for deviation from the baseline based on your knowledge of how your system is growing and changing.

CHOOSING THE APPROPRIATE MONITORING TOOLS

After you define your monitoring goals, you should select the appropriate tools for monitoring. The following list describes the basic monitoring tools:

➤ **Performance Monitor**—Performance Monitor is a useful tool that tracks resource use on Microsoft operating systems. It can monitor resource usage for the server, and provide information specific to SQL Server either locally or for a remote server. You can use it to capture a baseline of server resource usage, or it can monitor over longer periods of time to help identify trends. It can also be useful for ad hoc monitoring to help identify any resource bottlenecks responsible for performance issues. You can configure it to generate alerts when predetermined thresholds are exceeded.

➤ **Extended Events**—Extended Events (XEvents) provide a highly scalable and configurable architecture to enable you to collect information to troubleshoot issues with SQL Server. It is a lightweight system with a graphical user interface (GUI) that enables new sessions to be easily created.

XEvents provides the `system_health` session. This is a default health session that runs with minimal overhead, and continuously collects system data that may help you troubleshoot your performance problem without having to create your own custom XEvents session.

While exploring the `Extended Events` node in SQL Server Management Studio, you may notice an additional default session, the `AlwaysOn_health` session. This is an undocumented session created to provide health monitoring for Availability Groups.

➤ **SQL Profiler**—This tool is a graphical application that enables you to capture a trace of events that occurred in SQL Server. All SQL Server events can be captured by this tool into the trace. The trace can be stored in a file, or written to a SQL Server table.

SQL Profiler also enables the captured events to be replayed. This makes it a valuable tool for workload analysis, testing, and performance tuning. It can monitor a SQL Server instance locally or remotely. You can also use the features of SQL Profiler within a custom application, by using the Profiler system-stored procedures.

SQL Profiler was deprecated in SQL Server 2012, so you should plan on moving away from using this tool, and instead use XEvents for trace capture activities, and Distributed Replay (discussed later in this chapter) for replaying events.

➤ **SQL Trace**—SQL Trace is the T-SQL stored procedure way to invoke a SQL Server trace without needing to start up the SQL Profiler application. It requires a little more work to set up, but it's a lightweight way to capture a trace. And because it's scriptable, it enables the automation of trace capture, making it easy to repeatedly capture the same events.

With the deprecation of SQL Server Profiler, you should start moving all your trace-based monitoring to XEvents.

➤ **Default trace**—Introduced with SQL Server 2005, the default trace is a lightweight trace that runs in a continuous loop and captures a small set of key database and server events. This is useful in diagnosing events that may have occurred when no other monitoring was in place.

➤ **Activity Monitor in SQL Server Management Studio**—This tool graphically displays the following information:

  ➤ Processes running on an instance of SQL Server

  ➤ Resource waits

  ➤ Data File I/O activity

  ➤ Recent expensive queries

➤ **Dynamic Management Views and Dynamic Management Functions**—Dynamic Management Views (DMVs) and Dynamic Management Functions (DMFs) return server state information that you can use to monitor the health of a server instance, diagnose problems, and tune performance. These are some of the best tools added to SQL Server for ad hoc monitoring. These views provide a snapshot of the exact state of SQL Server at the point they are queried. This is extremely valuable, but you may need to do a lot of work to interpret the meaning of some of the data returned, because they often provide just a running total of some internal counter. You must add quite a bit of additional code to provide useful trend information. Numerous examples in the "Monitoring with Dynamic Management Views and Functions" section later in this chapter show how to do this.

➤ **System-stored procedures**—Some system-stored procedures provide useful information for SQL Server monitoring, such as `sp_who`, `sp_who2`, `sp_lock`, and several others. These stored procedures are best for ad hoc monitoring, not trend analysis.

➤ **Standard reports**—The standard reports that ship with SQL Server are a great way to get a look into what's happening inside SQL Server without needing to dive into DMVs, XEvents, and the default trace.

➤ **System Center Advisor**—An extension of the SQL Server Best Practice Analyzer, this is a cloud-based utility to analyze your SQL Servers and provide feedback on their configuration and operation against the set of accepted best practices for configuring and operating SQL Server.

Now that you have a general idea of what these tools can do, let's take a more detailed look at them.

PERFORMANCE MONITOR

Performance Monitor (also known as Perfmon, or System Monitor) is the user interface (UI) that most readers will become familiar with as they work with performance monitoring. Performance Monitor is a Windows tool that's found in the `Administrative Tools` folder on any Windows PC, or server. It has the capability to graphically show performance counter data as a graph (the default setting) or as a histogram, or in a textual report format.

Performance Monitor is an important tool because it not only informs you about how SQL Server performs, but it is also the tool that indicates how Windows performs. Performance Monitor provides a huge set of counters, but don't be daunted. This section covers a few of them, but there is likely no one who understands all of them.

This section is not an introduction to using Performance Monitor. (Although, later in this section, you learn about two valuable tools—Logman and Relog—that make using Performance Monitor a lot easier in a production environment.) This section instead focuses on how you can use the capabilities of this tool to diagnose performance problems in your system. For general information about using Performance Monitor, look at the Windows 8 or Windows Server 2012 documentation.

As mentioned earlier, you need to monitor three server resources:

➤ CPU

➤ Memory

➤ I/O (primarily disk I/O)

To gather a baseline of normal behavior, you should monitor these key counters over a "typical" interesting business usage period. Depending on your business usage cycles, this could be a particular day, or couple of days when the system experiences peaks of usage. You would not gather data over a weekend or holiday. You want to get an accurate picture of what's happening during typical business usage, and not when the system is idle. You should also take into account any specific knowledge of your business, and monitor for peaks of activity such as end of week, end of month, or other special activities. Once you have a good baseline, you should capture performance data continuously, and store it in a repository for post-mortem analysis of an unexpected performance problem. This data is also valuable as a capacity planning aid.

DETERMINING SAMPLE TIME

The question of what sample period to use often comes up. (A "sample period" is displayed as the "Sample Every" value on the General tab of a Performance Monitor chart's property page.)

A general rule of thumb is that the shorter the overall monitoring period, the shorter the sample period. If you are capturing data for 5–10 minutes you might use a 1-second sample interval. If you are capturing data for multiple days, then 15 seconds, 30 seconds, or even 1–5 minutes might be better sample periods.

The real decision points center on managing the overall capture file size, and ensuring that the data you capture has fine enough resolution to let you discern interesting events. If you are looking for something that happens over a short period of time, you need an even shorter sample time to be able to see it. So, for an event that you think might last 10–15 seconds, you should aim for a sample rate that gives you at least 3–5 samples during that period. For the 15-second event, you might choose a 3-second sample period, which would give you 5 samples during the 15-second event.

One last point to consider is that if you're interested in maintenance activity performance (such as for backups, index maintenance, data archival, and so on), that actually is a case where you might want to monitor at night and on weekends, and during normal business downtime, because that's when the maintenance activities are typically scheduled to run.

CPU Resource Counters

Several counters show the state of the available CPU resources. Bottlenecks caused by CPU resource shortages are frequently caused by problems such as more users than expected, one or more users running expensive queries, or routine operational activities such as index rebuilding.

The first step to finding the cause of the bottleneck is to identify that the bottleneck is a CPU resource issue. The following counters can help you do this:

➤ **Object: Processor - Counter: % Processor Time**—This counter determines the percentage of time each processor is busy. There is a _Total instance of the counter that (for multiprocessor systems) measures the total processor utilization across all processors in the system. On multiprocessor machines, the _Total instance might not show a processor bottleneck when one exists. This can happen when queries execute that run on either a single thread or fewer threads than there are processors. This is often the case on online transaction processing (OLTP) systems, or where MAXDOP has been set to less than the number of processors available.

In this case, a query can be bottlenecked on the CPU because it's using 100 percent of the single CPU it's scheduled to run on, or in the case of a parallel query, because it's using 100 percent of multiple CPUs. But, in both cases, other idle CPUs are available that this query is not using.

If the _Total instance of this counter is regularly at more than 80 percent, that's a good indication that the server is reaching the limits of the current hardware. Your options here are to buy more or faster processors, or optimize the queries to use less CPU. See Chapter 11, "Optimizing SQL Server 2014," for a detailed discussion on hardware.

➤ **Object: System - Counter: Processor Queue Length**—The processor queue length is a measure of how many threads sit in a ready state waiting on a processor to become available to run them. Interpreting and using this counter is an advanced operating system performance-tuning option needed only when investigating complex multithreaded code problems. For SQL Server systems, processor utilization can identify CPU bottlenecks much more easily than trying to interpret this counter.

➤ **Object: Processor - Counter: % Privileged Time**—This counter indicates the percentage of the sample interval when the processor was executing in kernel mode. On a SQL Server system, kernel mode time is time spent executing system services such as the memory manager, or more likely, the I/O manager. In most cases, privileged time equates to time spent reading and writing from disk or the network.

It is useful to monitor this counter when you find an indication of high CPU usage. If this counter indicates that more than 15 percent to 20 percent of processor time is spent executing privileged code, you may have a problem, possibly with one of the I/O drivers, or possibly with a filter driver installed by antivirus software scanning the SQL data or log files.

➤ **Object: Process - Counter: % Processor Time - Instance: sqlservr**—This counter measures the percentage of the sample interval during which the SQL Server process uses the available processors. When the Processor % Processor Time counter is high, or you suspect a CPU bottleneck, look at this counter to confirm that it is SQL Server using the CPU, and not some other process.

➤ **Object: Process - Counter: % Privileged Time - Instance: sqlservr**—This counter measures the percentage of the sample that the SQL Server process runs in kernel mode. This will be the kernel mode portion of the total %ProcessorTime shown in the previous counter. As with the previous counter, this counter is useful when investigating high CPU usage on the server to confirm that it is SQL Server using the processor resource, and not some other process.

➤ **Object: Process - Counter: % User Time - Instance: sqlservr**—This counter measures the percentage of the sample that the SQL Server process runs in User mode. This is the User mode portion of the total %ProcessorTime shown in the previous counter. Combined with %Privileged, the time should add up to %ProcessorTime.

> **NOTE** *After determining that you have a processor bottleneck, the next step is to track down its root cause. This might lead you to a single query, a set of queries, a set of users, an application, or an operational task causing the bottleneck. To further isolate the root cause, you need to dig deeper into what runs inside SQL Server. See the "Performance Monitoring Tools" section later in this chapter to help you do this. After you identify a processor bottleneck, consult the relevant chapter for details on how to resolve it. See Chapter 10 for information on "Configuring the Server for Optimal Performance," Chapter 11 for "Optimizing SQL Server 2014," Chapter 13 for "Performance Tuning T-SQL," and Chapter 14 for information on "Indexing Your Database."*

Disk Activity

SQL Server relies on the Windows operating system to perform I/O operations. The disk system handles the storage and movement of data on your system, giving it a powerful influence on your system's overall responsiveness. Disk I/O is frequently the cause of bottlenecks in a system. You must observe many factors in determining the performance of the disk system, including the level of usage, the rate of throughput, the amount of disk space available, and whether a queue is developing for the disk systems.

Unless your database fits into physical memory, SQL Server constantly brings database pages into and out of the buffer pool. This generates substantial I/O traffic. Similarly, log records must be flushed to the disk before a transaction can be declared committed. SQL Server 2005 started to make considerably more use of tempdb, and this hasn't changed with SQL Server 2014, so beginning with SQL Server 2005, tempdb I/O activity can also cause a performance bottleneck.

Many of the disk I/O factors are interrelated. For example, if disk utilization is high, disk throughput might peak, latency for each I/O might start to increase, and eventually a queue might begin to form. These conditions can result in increased response time, causing performance to slow.

Several other factors can impact I/O performance, such as fragmentation or low disk space. Make sure you monitor for free disk space, and take action when it falls below a given threshold. In general, the level of free space to raise an alert is when free disk space falls below 15 percent to 20 percent. Above this level of free space, many disk systems start to slow down because they need to spend more time searching for increasingly fragmented free space.

You should look at several key metrics when monitoring I/O performance:

➤ **Throughput, IOPS**—How many I/Os per second (IOPS) can the storage subsystem deliver?

➤ **Throughput, MB/sec**—How many MB/sec can the I/O subsystem deliver?

➤ **Latency**—How long does each I/O request take?

➤ **Queue depth**—How many I/O requests are waiting in the queue?

For each of these metrics, you should also distinguish between read-and-write activity.

Physical versus Logical Disk Counters

There is often confusion around the difference between physical and logical disk counters. This section explains the similarities and differences, provides specific examples of different disk configurations, and explains how to interpret the results shown on the different disk configurations.

One way to think about the difference between the logical and the physical disk counters is that the *logical disk counters* monitor I/O where the I/O request leaves the application layer (or as the requests enter kernel mode), whereas the *physical disk counters* monitor I/O as it leaves the bottom of the kernel storage driver stack. Figure 12-1 shows the I/O software stack and illustrates where the logical disk and physical disk counters monitor I/O.

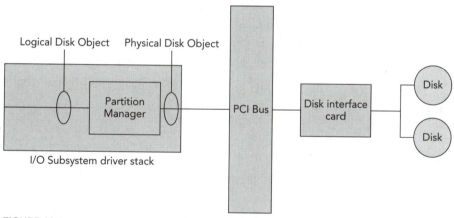

FIGURE 12-1

In some scenarios, the logical and physical counters provide the same results; in others, they provide different results.

The different I/O subsystem configurations that affect the values displayed by the logical and physical disk counters are discussed in the following sections.

Single Disk, Single Partition

Figure 12-2 shows a single disk with a single partition. In this case, there will be a single set of logical disk counters and a single set of physical disk counters. This configuration works well in a small SQL Server configuration with a few disks, where the SQL data and log files are already spread over multiple single disk, single partition disks.

Physical Disk 0

FIGURE 12-2

Single Disk, Multiple Partitions

Figure 12-3 shows a single disk split into multiple partitions. In this case, you have multiple instances of the logical disk counters, one per partition, and just a single set of physical disk counters. This kind of configuration doesn't provide any performance advantages, but it does allow more accurate monitoring of I/O to the different partitions. If you place different sets of data onto different partitions, you can see how much I/O goes to each set by monitoring the logical disk counters.

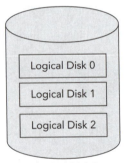

Physical Disk 0

FIGURE 12-3

One danger with this configuration is that you may be misled into thinking you actually have different physical disks, and so you think you are isolating data I/O from log I/O from tempdb I/O because they are on different "drives," when in fact, all the I/O is going to the same physical disk.

An example of this might be to put SQL log files on one partition, tempdb data files on another partition, a filegroup for data on another partition, a filegroup for indexes on another partition, and backups on another partition.

Multiple Disks, Single Volume—Software RAID

Figure 12-4 shows multiple disks configured in a software RAID array and mounted as a single volume. In this configuration, there is a single set of logical disk counters and multiple sets of physical disk counters.

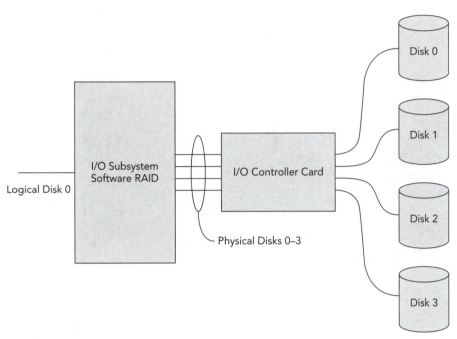

FIGURE 12-4

This configuration works well in a small SQL Server configuration where the hardware budget won't stretch to a RAID array controller, but multiple disks are available and you want to create a RAID volume spanning them. For more information on RAID, refer to Chapter 10, "Configuring the Server for Optimal Performance."

Multiple Disks, Single Volume—Hardware RAID

Figure 12-5 shows a hardware RAID array. In this configuration, multiple disks are managed by the hardware RAID controller. The operating system sees only a single physical disk presented to it by the array controller card. The disk counters appear to be the same as the single disk, single partition configuration—that is, a single set of physical disk counters and a corresponding single set of logical disk counters.

Monitoring I/O Throughput—IOPS

The Object: Physical Disk - Counter: Disk Writes/Sec and Object: Physical Disk - Counter: Disk Reads/Sec counters provide information about how many I/O operations are performed per second over the sample interval. This information is useful to determine whether the I/O subsystem is approaching capacity. It can be used in isolation to compare against the theoretical ideal for the I/O subsystem based upon the number and type of disks in the I/O subsystem. It is also useful when compared against the I/O subsystem baseline to determine how close you are to maximum capacity.

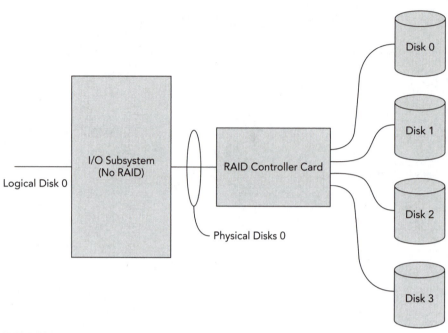

FIGURE 12-5

Monitoring I/O Throughput—MB/Sec

The Object: Physical Disk - Counter: Disk Write Bytes/Sec and Object: Physical Disk - Counter: Disk Read Bytes/Sec counters provide information about how many MB/sec are read and written to and from the disk over the sample interval. This is an average over the sample period, so with long sample periods, it may average out to big peaks and troughs in throughput. Over a short sample period, this may fluctuate dramatically, because it sees the results of one or two larger I/Os flooding the I/O subsystem. This information is useful in determining whether the I/O subsystem is approaching its capacity.

As with the other disk I/O counters, Disk Read Bytes/Sec and Disk Write Bytes/Sec can be used in isolation to compare against the theoretical throughput for the number and type of disks in the I/O subsystem, but it is more useful when it can be compared against a baseline of the maximum throughput available from the I/O subsystem.

Monitoring I/O Latency

The Object: Physical Disk - Counter: Avg. Disk Sec/Write and Object: Physical Disk - Counter: Avg. Disk Sec/Read counters provide information on how long each read-and-write operation is taking. These two counters show average latency. It is an average taken over every I/O issued during the sample period.

This information is extremely useful and can be used independently to determine how well the I/O subsystem deals with the current I/O load. Ideally, these counters should be below 5–10 milliseconds (ms).

On larger data warehouse or decision-support systems, it is acceptable for the values of these counters to be in the range of 10–20 ms. Sustained values over 50ms are an indication that the I/O subsystem is heavily stressed, and that a more detailed investigation of I/O should be undertaken.

These counters show performance degradations before queuing starts. These counters should also be used with the following disk queue length counters to help diagnose I/O subsystem bottlenecks.

Monitoring I/O Queue Depth

The Object: Physical Disk - Counter: Avg. Disk Write Queue Length and Object: Physical Disk - Counter: Avg. Disk Read Queue Length counters provide information on the read-and-write queue depth. These two counters show the average queue depth over the sample period. Disk queue lengths greater than 2 for a single physical disk indicate that there may be an I/O subsystem bottleneck.

Correctly interpreting these counters is more challenging when the I/O subsystem is a RAID array, or when the disk controller has built-in caching and intelligence. In these cases, the controller will have its own queue, which is designed to absorb and buffer, and effectively hide from this counter, any queuing going on at the disk level. For these reasons, monitoring these counters is less useful than monitoring the latency counters. If these counters do show queue lengths consistently greater than 2, it's a good indication of a potential I/O subsystem bottleneck.

Monitoring Individual Instances versus Total

In multidisk systems with several disks, monitoring all the preceding counters for all available disks provides a mass of fluctuating counters to monitor. In some cases, monitoring the _Total instance (which combines the values for all instances) can be a useful way to detect I/O problems. The scenario in which this doesn't work is when I/O to different disks has different characteristics. In this case, the _Total instance shows a reasonably good average number, although some disks may sit idle and others melt from all the I/O requests they service.

Monitoring Transfers versus Read and Write

One thing you may have noticed in the list of counters is that the transfer counters are missing. This is because the transfer counters average out the read-and-write activity. For a system that is heavy on one kind of I/O at the expense of the other (reads versus writes), the transfer counters do not show an accurate picture of what happens.

In addition, read I/O and write I/O usually have different characteristics, and different performance than the underlying storage. Monitoring a combination of two potentially disparate values doesn't provide a meaningful metric.

Monitoring %Disk Counters

Another set of disk counters missing from this list are all the %Disk counters. Although these counters can provide interesting information, enough problems with the results can occur (that is, the total percentage can often exceed 100) and these counters won't provide a useful detailed metric.

If you can afford to monitor all the counters detailed in the preceding sections, you can have a much more complete view of what's going on with your system.

If you want a few simple metrics that provide a good approximate indication of overall I/O subsystem activity, the %Disk Time, %Disk Read Time, and %Disk Write time counters can provide that.

Isolating Disk Activity Created by SQL Server

All the counters you should monitor to find disk bottlenecks have been discussed. However, you may have multiple applications running on your servers, and one of those other applications could cause a lot of disk I/O. To confirm that the disk bottleneck is being caused by SQL Server, you should isolate the disk activities created by SQL Server. Monitor the following counters to determine whether the disk activity is caused by SQL server:

➤ SQL Server: Buffer Manager: Page reads/sec

➤ SQL Server: Buffer Manager: Page writes/sec

Sometimes your application is too big for the hardware you have, and a problem that appears to be related to disk I/O may be resolved by adding more RAM. Make sure you do a proper analysis before making a decision. That's where trend analysis is helpful because you can see how the performance problem evolved.

Is Disk Performance the Bottleneck?

With the help of the disk counters, you can determine whether you have disk bottlenecks in your system. Several conditions must exist for you to make that determination, including a sustained rate of disk activity well above your baseline, persistent disk queue length longer than two per disk, and the absence of a significant amount of paging. Without this combination of factors, it is unlikely that you have a disk bottleneck in your system.

Sometimes your disk hardware may be faulty, and that could cause a lot of interrupts to the CPU. Another possibility could be that a processor bottleneck is caused by a disk subsystem, which can have a system-wide performance impact. Make sure you consider this when you analyze the performance data.

> **NOTE** *If, after monitoring your system, you come to the conclusion that you have a disk bottleneck, you need to resolve the problem. See Chapter 10 for more details on configuring SQL Server for optimal performance, Chapter 11 for optimizing SQL Server, and Chapter 13, "Performance Tuning T-SQL" for SQL query tuning.*

Memory Usage

Memory is perhaps the most critical resource affecting SQL Server performance. Without enough memory, SQL Server is forced to keep reading and writing data to disk to complete a query. Disk access is anywhere from 1,000 to 100,000 times slower than memory access, depending on exactly how fast your memory is.

Because of this, ensuring SQL Server has enough memory is one of the most important steps you can take to keep SQL Server running as fast as possible. Monitoring memory usage, how much is available, and how well SQL Server uses the available memory is therefore a vitally important step.

In an ideal environment, SQL Server runs on a dedicated machine, and shares memory only with the operating system and other essential applications. However, in many environments, budget or other constraints mean that SQL shares a server with other applications. In this case, you must monitor how much memory each application uses, and verify that everyone plays well together.

Low memory conditions can slow the operation of the applications and services on your system. Monitor an instance of SQL Server periodically to confirm that the memory usage is within typical ranges. When your server is low on memory, *paging*—the process of moving virtual memory back and forth between physical memory and the disk—can be prolonged, resulting in more work for your disks. The paging activity might need to compete with other transactions performed, intensifying disk bottleneck.

Because SQL Server is one of the best-behaved server applications available, when the operating system triggers the low memory notification event, SQL releases memory for other applications to use. It actually starves itself of memory if another memory-greedy application runs on the machine.

The good news is that SQL releases only a small amount of memory at a time, so it may take hours, and even days, before SQL starts to suffer. Unfortunately, if the other application desperately needs more memory, it can take hours before SQL frees up enough memory for the other application to run without excessive paging. Because issues such as those mentioned can cause significant problems, monitor the counters described in the following sections to identify memory bottlenecks.

Monitoring Available Memory

The Object: Memory - Counter: Available Mbytes counter reports how many megabytes of memory are currently available for programs to use. It is the best single indication that there may be a memory bottleneck on the server.

Determining the appropriate value for this counter depends on the size of the system you monitor. If this counter routinely shows values less than 128MB, you may have a serious memory shortage.

On a server with 4GB or more of physical memory (RAM), the operating system can send a low memory notification when available memory reaches 128MB. At this point, SQL releases some of its memory for other processes to use.

Ideally, aim to have at least 256MB to 500MB of Available MBytes. On larger systems with more than 16GB of RAM, this number should be increased to 500MB–1GB. If you have more than 64GB of RAM on your server, increase this to 1–2GB.

Monitoring SQL Server Process Memory Usage

Having used the Memory – Counter: Available Mbytes counter to determine that a potential memory shortage exists, the next step is to determine which processes use the available memory. Because your focus is on SQL Server, you hope that it is SQL Server that uses the memory. However, you should always confirm that this is the case.

The usual place to look for memory usage by a process is in the `Process` object under the instance for the process. For SQL Server, these counters are detailed in the following list:

➤ **Object: Process – Instance: sqlserver - Counter: Virtual Bytes**—This counter indicates the size of the virtual address space allocated by the process. Virtual address space (VAS) is used by a lot of processes that aren't related to memory performance. This counter is of value when looking for the root cause of SQL Server out-of-memory errors.

➤ **Object: Process – Instance: sqlservr – Counter: Working Set**—This counter indicates the size of the working set for the SQL Server process. The working set is the total set of pages currently resident in memory, as opposed to being paged to disk. It can provide an indication of memory pressure when this is significantly lower than the Private Bytes for the process.

➤ **Object: Process – Instance: sqlservr – Counter: Private Bytes**—The Private Bytes counter tells you how much memory this process has allocated that cannot be shared with other processes—that is, it's private to this process. To understand the difference between this counter and virtual bytes, you just need to know that certain files loaded into a process's memory space—the EXEs, any DLLs, and memory-mapped files—will automatically be shared by the operating system. Therefore, Private Bytes indicates the amount of memory used by the process for its stacks, heaps, and any other virtually allocated memory in use. You could compare this to the total memory used by the system. When this value is a significant portion of the total system memory, it is a good indication that SQL Server memory usage is the root of the overall server memory shortage.

Other SQL Server Memory Counters

The following is a list of some additional SQL Server memory counters. When looking at memory issues, these counters can provide more detailed information than the counters already described:

➤ **Buffer Cache Hit Ratio**—This counter indicates how many page requests were found in the buffer pool. It tends to be a little coarse in that 98 percent and above is good, but 97.9 percent might indicate a memory issue.

➤ **Free Pages**—This counter indicates how many free pages SQL Server has for new page requests. Acceptable values for this counter depend on how much memory you have available, and the memory usage profile for your applications. Having a good baseline is useful, because the values for this counter can be compared to the baseline to determine whether there is a current memory issue, or whether the value is part of the expected behavior of the system.

This counter should be read with the Page Life Expectancy counter.

➤ **Page Life Expectancy**—This counter provides an indication of the time (in seconds) that a page is expected to remain in the buffer pool before being flushed to disk. The current Best Practices from Microsoft state that values above 300 are generally considered okay. Values approaching 300 are a cause for concern. Values below 300 are a good indication of a memory shortage. These Best Practices are now getting a bit dated, however. They were written when a large system might have 4 dual or quad-core processors, and 16GB of RAM. Today's commodity hardware comes with a 2P system with 10, 12, 16+ cores, and the capability to have 256GB or more of memory. Therefore, those Best Practice numbers are less relevant. Because of this, you should interpret this counter in conjunction with other counters to understand if there really is memory pressure.

Read this counter with the Free Pages counter. You should expect to see Free Pages drop dramatically as the page life expectancy drops below 300. When considered together, Free Pages and Page Life Expectancy provide an indication of memory pressure that may result in a bottleneck.

Scripting Memory Counters with Logman

Listing 12-1 shows a Logman script (code file: `logman_create_memory.cmd`) that can create a counter log of the memory counters discussed in this section. (See the "Logman" section later in this chapter for more information.)

LISTING 12-1: logman_create_memory.cmd

```
Logman create counter "Memory Counters" -si 05 -v nnnnnn -o
"c:\perflogs\Memory Counters" -c "\Memory\Available MBytes"
"\Process(sqlservr)\Virtual Bytes" "\Process(sqlservr)\Working Set"
"\Process(sqlservr)\Private Bytes" "\SQLServer:Buffer Manager\Database
pages" "\SQLServer:Buffer Manager\Target pages" "\SQLServer:Buffer
Manager\Total pages" "\SQLServer:Memory Manager\Target Server Memory (KB)"
"\SQLServer:Memory Manager\Total Server Memory (KB)"
```

Resolving Memory Bottlenecks

The easy solution to memory bottlenecks is to add more memory. But, as previously stated, tuning your application always comes first. Try to find queries that are memory-intensive, for example, queries with large worktables—such as hashes for joins and sorts—to see if you can tune them. You can learn more about tuning T-SQL queries in Chapter 13, "Performance Tuning T-SQL."

In addition, refer to Chapter 10 to ensure that you have configured your server properly.

Performance Monitoring Tools

A few tools are well hidden in the command-line utilities that have shipped with Windows operating systems for some time. Two of these that are extremely valuable when using Performance Monitor are Logman and Relog.

Logman

Logman is a command-line way to script performance monitoring counter logs. You can create, alter, start, and stop counter logs using Logman.

You have already seen an example earlier in this chapter of using Logman to create a counter log. Listing 12-2 shows a short command-line script file (code file: `logman_start_memory.cmd`) to start and stop a counter collection.

> **LISTING 12-2:** logman_start_memory.cmd
>
> ```
> REM start counter collection
> logman start "Memory Counters"
> timeout /t 5
> REM add a timeout for some short period
> REM to allow the collection to start
> REM do something interesting here
> REM stop the counter collection
> logman stop "Memory Counters"
> timeout /t 5
> REM make sure to wait 5 to ensure its stopped
> ```

Complete documentation for Logman used to be available through the Windows help system, but was removed with Windows 8. The documentation is now only available online. Either execute the command `logman /?`, search on Bing for "Logman," or see `http://technet.microsoft.com/en-us/library/cc753820.aspx`.

Logman Script for I/O Counters

Listing 12-3 shows a script (code file: `logman_create_io.cmd`) that can create a new counter log called `IO Counters` and collect samples for every counter previously detailed (for all instances) with a 5-second sample interval, and write the log to `c:\perflogs\IO Counters`, appending a six-digit incrementing sequence number to each log.

> **LISTING 12-3:** logman_create_io.cmd
>
> ```
> Logman create counter "IO Counters" -si 05 -v nnnnnn -o "c:\perflogs\IO
> Counters" -c "\PhysicalDisk(*)\Avg. Disk Bytes/Read" " \PhysicalDisk(*)\Avg.
> Disk Bytes/Write" "\PhysicalDisk(*)\Avg. Disk Read Queue Length"
> "\PhysicalDisk(*)\Avg. Disk sec/Read" "\PhysicalDisk(*)\Avg. Disk sec/Write"
> "\PhysicalDisk(*)\Avg. Disk Write Queue Length" "\PhysicalDisk(*)\Disk Read
> Bytes/sec" "\PhysicalDisk(*)\Disk Reads/sec" "\PhysicalDisk(*)\Disk Write
> Bytes/sec" "\PhysicalDisk(*)\Disk Writes/sec"
> ```

After running this script, run the following command to confirm that the settings are as expected:

```
logman query "IO Counters"
```

Relog

Relog is a command-line utility that enables you to read a log file and write selected parts of it to a new log file.

You can use it to change the file format from `blg` to `csv`. You can use it to resample data and turn a large file with a short sample period into a smaller file with a longer sample period. You can also use it to extract a short period of data for a subset of counters from a much larger file.

Complete documentation for Relog used to be available through the Windows help system, but was removed with Windows 8. The documentation is now only available online. Either execute the command `relog /?`, search on Bing for "relog," or see `http://technet.microsoft.com/en-us/library/cc771669.aspx`.

MONITORING EVENTS

Events are fired at the time of some significant occurrence within SQL Server. Using events enables you to react to the behavior at the time it occurs, and not have to wait until some later time. SQL Server generates many different events, and has several tools available to monitor some of these events.

The following list describes the different features you can use to monitor events that happened in the Database Engine:

➤ **Extended Events**—XEvents were new with SQL Server 2008 and extend the event notification mechanism. They are built on the Event Tracing for Windows (ETW) framework. Extended events are a different set of events from those used by Event Notifications and can be used to diagnose issues such as low memory conditions, high CPU use, and deadlocks. The logs created when using SQL Server XEvents can also be correlated with other ETW logs using `tracerpt.exe`.

> **NOTE** *See the topic on "Extended Events" in SQL Server Books Online for more references to information on using ETW and* `tracerpt.exe`. *For more details, see the section, "SQL Server Extended Events," later in this chapter.*

➤ `system_health` **Session**—The `system_health` session is included by default with SQL Server. It starts automatically when SQL starts, and runs with no noticeable performance impact. It collects a minimal set of system information that can help resolve performance issues.

➤ **Default Trace**—Initially added in SQL Server 2005, this is perhaps one of the best-kept secrets in SQL Server. It's virtually impossible to find any documentation on this feature. The default trace is basically a flight data recorder for SQL Server. It records the last 5MB of key events. The events it records were selected to be lightweight, yet valuable when troubleshooting a critical SQL event.

➤ **SQL Trace**—This records specified events and stores them in a file (or files) that you can use later to analyze the data. You must specify which Database Engine events you want to trace when you define the trace. Following are two ways to access the trace data:

➤ Using SQL Server Profiler (a GUI)

➤ Through T-SQL system-stored procedures

➤ **SQL Server Profiler**—This exploits all the event-capturing functionality of SQL Trace and adds the capability to trace information to or from a table, save the trace definitions as templates, extract query plans and deadlock events as separate XML files, and replay trace results for diagnosis and optimization. Another option (and perhaps least understood) is using a database table to store the trace. Storing the trace file in a database table enables the use of T-SQL queries to perform complex analysis of the events in the trace.

➤ **Event notifications**—These send information to a Service Broker service about many of the events generated by SQL Server. Unlike traces, event notifications can be used to perform an action inside SQL Server in response to events. Because event notifications execute asynchronously, these actions do not consume any resources defined by the immediate transaction. This means, for example, that if you want to be notified when a table is altered in a database, then the ALTER TABLE statement would not consume more resources or be delayed because you have defined event notification.

Following are a few reasons why you should monitor events that occur inside your SQL Server:

➤ **Find the worst-performing queries or stored procedures**—You can do this using either XEvents or through SQL Profiler/SQL Trace. To use SQL Profiler, you can find a trace template on this book's website at www.wrox.com that you can import into your SQL Server Profiler to capture this scenario. This includes the Showplan Statistics Profile, Showplan XML, and Showplan XML Statistics Profile under Performance event groups. These events are included because, after you determine the worst-performing queries, you need to see what query plan was generated by them. Just looking at the duration of the T-SQL batch or stored procedure does not get you anywhere. Consider filtering the trace data by setting some value in the Duration column to retrieve only those events that are longer than a specific duration so that you minimize your data set for analysis.

➤ **Audit user activities**—You can either use the SQL Audit capabilities in XEvents to create a SQL Audit, or create a trace with Audit Login events. If you choose the latter, select the EventClass (the default), EventSubClass, LoginSID, and LoginName data columns; this way you can audit user activities in SQL Server. You can add more events from the Security Audit event group or data columns based on your need. You may someday need this type of information for legal purposes in addition to your technical purposes.

➤ **Identify the cause of a deadlock**—You can do this using XEvents. Much of the information needed is available in the system_health session that runs by default on every instance of SQL Server. You look into how to do that in more detail later in this chapter.

➤ **Collect a representative set of events for stress testing**—For some benchmarking, you want to reply to the trace generated. SQL Server provides the standard template TSQL_Replay to capture a trace that can be replayed later. If you want to use a trace to replay later, ensure that you use this standard template because to replay the trace, SQL Server needs some specific events captured, and this template does just that. Later in this chapter, you see how to replay the trace.

➤ **Create a workload to use for the Database Engine Tuning Adviser**—SQL Server Profiler provides a predefined Tuning template that gathers the appropriate Transact-SQL events in the trace output, so it can be used as a workload for the Database Engine Tuning Advisor.

➤ **Take a performance baseline**—Earlier you learned that you should take a baseline and update it at regular intervals to compare with previous baselines to determine how your application performs. For example, suppose you have a batch process that loads some data once a day and validates it, does some transformation, and so on, and puts it into your warehouse after deleting the existing set of data. After some time, there is an increase in data volume, and suddenly your process starts slowing down. You would guess that an increase in data volume is slowing down the process, but is that the only reason? In fact, there could be more than one reason. The query plan generated may be different—because the stats may be incorrect, because your data volume increased, and so on. If you have a statistic profile for the query plan taken during the regular baseline, with other data (such as performance logs) you can quickly identify the root cause.

The following sections provide details on each of the event monitoring tools.

The Default Trace

The default trace was introduced in SQL Server 2005. This trace is always on and captures a minimal set of lightweight events. If, after learning more about the default trace, you decide you actually do not want it running, you can turn it off using the T-SQL code shown in Listing 12-4 (code file: `default_trace_off.sql`).

LISTING 12-4: default_trace_off.sql

```
-- Turn ON advanced options
exec sp_configure 'show advanced options', '1'
reconfigure with override
go
-- Turn OFF default trace
exec sp_configure 'default trace enabled', '0'
reconfigure with override
go
-- Turn OFF advanced options
exec sp_configure 'show advanced options', '0'
reconfigure with override
go
```

> **NOTE** *If you do turn the default trace off, and then you realize how valuable it is and want to turn it back on again, you can do that by using the same code you used to turn it on, just set the* sp_configure *value for* 'default trace enabled' *to* 1 *and not* 0.

The default trace logs 30 events to five trace files that work as a First-In, First-Out (FIFO) buffer, with the oldest file being deleted to make room for new events in the next `trc` file.

The default trace files live in the SQL Server Logs folder. Among the SQL Server Error log files, you can find five trace files. These are just regular SQL Server trace files, so you can open them in SQL Profiler.

The key thing is to have some idea of what events are recorded in the default trace, and remember to look at it when something happens to SQL Server. The events captured in the default trace fall into six categories:

➤ **Database**—These events are for examining data and log file growth events, as well as database mirroring state changes.

➤ **Errors and warnings**—These events capture information about the error log and query execution–based warnings around missing column stats, join predicates, sorts, and hashes.

➤ **Full-Text**—These events show information about full text crawling, when a crawl starts, stops, or is aborted.

➤ **Objects**—These events capture information about `User` object activity, specifically `Create`, `Delete`, and `Alter` on any `User` object. If you need to know when a particular object was created, altered, or deleted, this could be the place to look.

➤ **Security Audit**—This captures events for the major security events occurring in SQL Server. There is quite a comprehensive list of sub events (not listed here). If you're looking for security-based information, then this should be the first place you look.

➤ **Server**—This category contains just one event, Server Memory Change. This event indicates when SQL Server memory usage increases or decreases by 1MB, or 5 percent of max server memory, whichever is larger.

You can see these categories by opening one of the default trace files in SQL Server Profiler and examining the trace file properties. By default, you don't have permission to open the trace files while they live in the `Logs` folder, so either copy the file to another location, or alter the permissions on the file that you want to open in Profiler.

When you open the trace file properties, you see that, for each category, all event columns are selected for all the events in the default trace.

system_health Session

The `system_health` session is a default XEvents session that is created for you by SQL Server. It is very lightweight and has minimal impact on performance. With previous technologies like SQL Server Profiler and the default trace, customers have worried about the performance impact of running these monitoring tools. XEvents and the `system_health` session mitigate those concerns.

The `system_health` session contains a wealth of information that can help diagnose issues with SQL Server. Following is a list of some of the information collected by this session.

➤ SQL text and Session ID for sessions that:

  ➤ Have a severity ≥ 20

  ➤ Encounter a memory-related error

  ➤ Have waited on latches for ≥ 15 seconds

  ➤ Have waited on locks for ≥ 30 seconds

➤ Deadlocks

➤ Nonyielding scheduler problems

SQL Trace

As mentioned earlier, you have two ways to define the SQL Trace: using T-SQL system-stored procedures and SQL Server Profiler. This section first explains the SQL Trace architecture. Then you study an example to create the server-side trace using the T-SQL system-stored procedure.

Before you start, you need to know some basic trace terminology:

➤ **Event**—This is the occurrence of an action within an instance of the Microsoft SQL Server Database Engine or the SQL Server Database Engine (such as the `Audit:Logout` event, which happens when a user logs out of SQL Server).

➤ **Data column**—This is an attribute of an event, such as the `SPID` column for the `Audit:Logout` event, which indicates the SQL SPID of the user who logged off. Another example is the `ApplicationName` column, which gives you an application name for the event.

> **NOTE** *In SQL Server, trace column values greater than 1GB return an error, and are truncated in the trace output.*

➤ **Filter**—This is criteria that limit the events collected in a trace. For example, if you are interested only in the events generated by the SQL Server Management Studio – Query application, you can set the filter on the `ApplicationName` column to SQL Server Management Studio – Query, and you see only events generated by this application in your trace.

➤ **Template**—In SQL Server Profiler, this is a file that defines the event classes and data columns to be collected in a trace. Many default templates are provided with SQL Server, and these files are located in the directory `\Program Files\Microsoft SQL Server\110\Tools\Profiler\Templates\Microsoft SQL Server\110`.

> **NOTE** *For even more terminology related to trace, refer to the Books Online section "SQL Trace Terminology."*

SQL Trace Architecture

You should understand how SQL Trace works before looking at an example. Figure 12-6 shows the basic form of the architecture. Events are the main unit of activity for tracing. When you define the trace, you specify which events you want to trace. For example, if you want to trace the SP: Starting event, SQL Server traces only this event (with some other default events that SQL Server always captures). The event source can be any source that produces the trace event, such as a T-SQL statement, deadlocks, other events, and more.

After an event occurs, if the event class has been included in a trace definition, the event information is gathered by the trace. If filters have been defined for the event class (for example, if you are interested only in the events for `LoginName= 'foo'`) in the trace definition, the filters are applied and the trace event information is passed to a queue. From the queue, the trace information is written to a file, or it can be used by Server Management Objects (SMO) in applications, such as SQL Server Profiler.

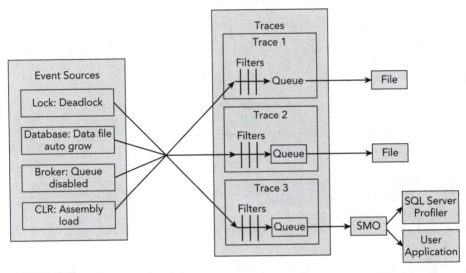

FIGURE 12-6

SQL Server Profiler

SQL Server Profiler is a rich interface used to create and manage traces and analyze and replay trace results. SQL Server Profiler shows how SQL Server resolves queries internally. This enables you to see exactly what T-SQL statements or multidimensional expressions are submitted to the server, and how the server accesses the database or cube to return result sets.

> **NOTE** *In SQL Server 2012, SQL Server Profiler was marked as being deprecated. Because of this, you should move any monitoring capabilities using this tool to the newer tools based on extended events.*

You can read the trace file created using a T-SQL stored procedure with SQL Profiler. To use SQL Profiler to read the trace file, just go to the File menu and open the trace file you are interested in.

> **NOTE** *In SQL Server 2008, the server reported both the duration of an event and CPU time used by the event (in milliseconds). In SQL Server 2005, the server reported the duration of an event in microseconds (one millionth of a second) and the amount of CPU time used by the event in milliseconds (one thousandth of a second). In SQL Server 2000, the server reported both duration and CPU time in milliseconds. In SQL Server 2005, the SQL Server Profiler GUI displayed the* Duration *column in milliseconds by default, but when a trace was saved to either a file or a database table, the* Duration *column value was written in microseconds. If you want to display the duration column in microseconds in SQL Profiler, go to Tools ⇨ Options and select the option Show Values in Duration Column in Microseconds (SQL Server 2005 only).*

Being able to capture and examine the XML plan for a particular query is very valuable when trying to troubleshoot issues. SQL Server Profiler makes this possible using the XML Showplan option. Additionally, being able to correlate a Profiler trace with a Performance Monitor chart can help to diagnose performance problems by enabling you to correlate which queries are executing in a Profiler trace against performance counters captured in Performance Monitor. With this capability you can see exactly what was executing when a particular behavior was observed in the Performance Monitor graph.

> **NOTE** *When the Showplan XML event class is included in a trace, the amount of overhead significantly impedes performance. Showplan XML stores a query plan that is created when the query is optimized. To minimize the overhead incurred, limit the use of this event class to traces that monitor specific problems for brief periods of time, and be sure to use the data column filter based on specifics you are going to trace.*

Replaying a Trace

Replay is the capability to take a saved trace and replay it later. This functionality enables you to reproduce the activity captured in a trace. When you create or edit a trace, you can save the trace to replay it later. Be sure to choose the predefined template called TSQL_Replay when you create the trace using SQL Profiler. SQL Server needs specific events and data columns to be captured to replay the trace later. If you miss those events and data columns, SQL Server does not replay the trace.

Trace replay supports debugging by using the Toggle Breakpoint and the Run to Cursor options on the SQL Server Profiler Replay menu. These options especially improve the analysis of long scripts because they can break the replay of the trace into short segments so they can be analyzed incrementally.

The following types of events are ignored when you replay the trace:

➤ **Traces that contain transactional replication and other transaction log activity**—These events are skipped. Other types of replication do not mark the transaction log, so they are not affected.

➤ **Traces that contain operations involving globally unique identifiers (GUIDs)**—These events are skipped.

➤ **Traces that contain operations on** `text`, `ntext`, **and** `image` **columns involving the** `bcp` **utility, the** `BULK INSERT`, `READTEXT`, `WRITETEXT`, **and** `UPDATETEXT` **statements, and full-text operations**—These events are skipped.

➤ **Traces that contain session binding** (`sp_getbindtoken` **and** `sp_bindsession` **system-stored procedures)**—These events are skipped.

➤ **Traces collected by Microsoft SQL Server version 7.0 or earlier**—SQL Server Profiler does not support replaying these traces.

In addition, some requirements must be met to replay the trace on the target server:

➤ All logins and users contained in the trace must be created already on the target and in the same database as the source.

➤ All logins and users in the target must have the same permissions they had in the source.

➤ All login passwords must be the same as those of the user who executes the replay. You can use the Transfer Login task in SQL Server Integrated Services (SSIS) to transfer the logins to the target server on which you want to replay the trace.

➤ The database IDs on the target ideally should be the same as those on the source. However, if they are not the same, matching can be performed based on the database name if it is present in the trace, so ensure that you have the `DatabaseName` data column selected in the trace.

➤ The default database on the target server for a login should be the same as on the source when the trace was taken.

➤ Replaying events associated with missing or incorrect logins results in replay errors, but the replay operation continues.

Distributed Replay

Distributed Replay, a tool for replaying traces from multiple machines, was introduced in SQL Server 2012. Although SQL Profiler can replay a trace, it can only do so from a single machine. Distributed Replay can also replay traces, but can do so from a pool of machines. Because of this, Distributed Replay provides a more scalable solution than SQL Profiler, and is better at simulating mission-critical workloads.

Profiler versus Distributed Relay

Now that you have two tools for replaying traces, the question becomes when to use which tool. As a general rule, you should use SQL Profiler for all trace replays, and always for replaying traces against Analysis Services. You only need to resort to Distributed Replay *if* the concurrency in the captured trace is so high that a single server cannot sufficiently simulate the load you want to put onto the target server.

A Distributed Replay system known as a *Distributed Replay Utility* consists of a number of different servers, the Admin tool, the controller, a number of clients, and the target SQL Server.

Because Distributed Replay can replay a trace from multiple servers, you must do a little additional work on the trace file before it can be used in a distributed replay. Specifically, you must preprocess the trace file and spilt it into multiple streams of commands that are replayed from the different client servers in the Distributed Replay Utility.

Performance Considerations When Using Trace

SQL Server tracing incurs no overhead unless it captures an event, and most events need few resources. Profiler can become expensive as you add events, and increase the amount of event data captured for each event. Normally, you see a maximum of 10 percent to 20 percent overhead. If you see more than this, or even if this level of overhead is impacting the production system, you can reduce the number of events, reduce the amount of data, or use an alternate approach. Most of the performance hit results from a longer code path; the actual resources that the trace needs to capture event data aren't particularly CPU-intensive. In addition, to minimize the performance hit, you can define all your traces as server-side traces, avoiding the overhead of producing row sets to send to the Profiler client.

Event Notifications

Event Notifications are special database objects that send messages to the Service Broker service (see Chapter 6, "Service Broker in SQL Server 2014," for details on the Service Broker) with information regarding server or database events. Event Notifications can be programmed against some of the same events captured by SQL Trace, but not all. Event Notifications can also be programmed against many DDL events. Unlike creating traces, Event Notifications can be used to perform an action inside an instance of SQL Server in response to events. Later in this chapter, you see an example that shows how to create an event notification for specific events, and take actions if needed.

To subscribe to an event, you must create the Service Broker queue that receives the details regarding the event. In addition, a queue requires the Service Broker service to receive the message. Then you must create an event notification. You can create a stored procedure and activate it when the event message is in the queue to take a certain action. This example assumes you know how the Service Broker works, so be sure to read Chapter 6, "Service Broker in SQL Server 2014," if you don't already know about the Server Broker.

You can also be notified for grouped events. For example, if you want to be notified when a table is created, altered, or dropped, you don't need to create three separate event notifications. You can use the group event called `DDL_TABLE_EVENTS` and just create one event notification to achieve the same thing. Another example is related to monitoring all the locking events using the event group `TRC_LOCKS`. When you create an event notification with this group, you can be notified about the following events: `LOCK_DEADLOCK`, `LOCK_DEADLOCK_CHAIN`, `LOCK_ESCALATION`, and `DEADLOCK_GRAPH`.

> **NOTE** *Refer to the Books Online topic, "DDL Event Groups for Use with Event Notifications," for all the event groups.*

Event Notifications can be used to do the following:

➤ Log and review changes or activity occurring on the database or server.

➤ Perform an action in response to an event in an asynchronous, rather than synchronous, manner.

Event notifications can offer a programming alternative to DDL triggers and SQL Trace.

> **NOTE** *Event notifications are created at the server or database level.*

You can create an event notification in a database whereby you will be notified when a new table is created. To do so, perform the following steps:

1. Open the script `CreateDatabase.sql` shown in Listing 12-5 (code file: `CreateDatabase.sql`). This script creates a database called `StoreEvent` for the example.

LISTING 12-5: CreateDatabase.sql

```
IF NOT EXISTS(SELECT 1 FROM sys.databases WHERE name = 'StoreEvent')
CREATE DATABASE StoreEvent
GO

USE StoreEvent
GO

IF OBJECT_ID('EventTable') IS NULL
CREATE TABLE EventTable
(
 RID int IDENTITY (1,1) NOT NULL
,EventDetails xml NULL
,EventDateTime datetime NULL
)
```

2. Next, open the `CreateQueue.sql` script, shown in Listing 12-6 (code file: `CreateQueue.sql`).

LISTING 12-6: CreateQueue.sql

```sql
USE StoreEvent
GO

--CREATE QUEUE to receive the event details.
IF OBJECT_ID('dbo.NotifyQueue') IS NULL
CREATE QUEUE dbo.NotifyQueue
WITH STATUS = ON
    ,RETENTION = OFF
GO

--create the service so that when event happens
--server can send the message to this service.
--we are using the pre-defined contract here.
IF NOT EXISTS(SELECT * FROM sys.services WHERE name =
'EventNotificationService')
CREATE SERVICE EventNotificationService
ON QUEUE NotifyQueue
([http://schemas.microsoft.com/SQL/Notifications/PostEventNotification])

IF NOT EXISTS(SELECT * FROM sys.routes WHERE name = 'NotifyRoute')

CREATE ROUTE NotifyRoute
WITH SERVICE_NAME = 'EventNotificationService',
ADDRESS = 'LOCAL';
GO
```

3. This script creates a queue in the StoreEvent database to store the event data when a table is created in the StoreEvent database. It creates a Service Broker service EventNotificationService such that SQL Server can send the message when a subscribed event happens. The route NotifyRoute helps route the message to a local SQL server instance. Run this script.

4. You must now create the event notification. Open the script CreateEventNotification.sql, shown in Listing 12-7 (code file: CreateEventNotification.sql).

LISTING 12-7: CreateEventNotification.sql

```sql
USE StoreEvent
GO
CREATE EVENT NOTIFICATION CreateTableNotification
ON DATABASE
FOR CREATE_TABLE
TO SERVICE 'EventNotificationService', 'current database' ;
```

This script creates an event notification called CreateTableNotification that notifies you when a table is created in the StoreEvent database.

Messages are sent from one service to another, as discussed in Chapter 6. In this case, you have created the target end of the service, which is EventNotificationServer; the initiator end of the service is SQL Server itself.

5. When a table is created in the `StoreEvent` database, you get the message in the queue `NotifyQueue`, so create a table and run the following script to see what's in the queue:

```
SELECT CAST(message_body AS xml)
FROM NotifyQueue
```

6. Following is what the final XML message in the queue looks like:

```
<EVENT_INSTANCE>
  <EventType>CREATE_TABLE</EventType>
  <PostTime>2014-01-18T21:53:14.463</PostTime>
  <SPID>55</SPID>
  <ServerName>STEVENS_LAPTOP</ServerName>
  <LoginName>MicrosoftAccount\steven_wort@hotmail.com</LoginName>
  <UserName>dbo</UserName>
  <DatabaseName>StoreEvent</DatabaseName>
  <SchemaName>dbo</SchemaName>
  <ObjectName>TestTable1</ObjectName>
  <ObjectType>TABLE</ObjectType>
  <TSQLCommand>
    <SetOptions ANSI_NULLS="ON" ANSI_NULL_DEFAULT="ON" ANSI_PADDING="ON"
         QUOTED_IDENTIFIER="ON" ENCRYPTED="FALSE" />
      <CommandText>create table test (
a   int null,
b   varchar(5) null,
c   datetime null
)</CommandText>
    </TSQLCommand>
  </EVENT_INSTANCE>
```

You can take some action with this event if you create a stored procedure and have it activated when a message arrives in the queue. You create the server-wide event in the same way. For a full list of the events for which you can be notified, you can query the `sys.event_notification_event_types` view. Refer to the script `Metadata_EventNotification.sql` to get the catalog view list that stores the metadata about event notifications.

SQL Server Extended Events

SQL Server Extended Events (XEvents) was a completely new feature for SQL Server 2008. XEvents has been enhanced in SQL Server 2014 with increased event coverage and a new GUI interface in SQL Server Management Studio. Extended events provide a deep insight into SQL Server internals and are designed to enable faster diagnosis of issues with SQL Server. They provide the capability to act either synchronously or asynchronously to SQL events, and are designed to be extremely light-weight and highly scalable. The `system_health` session is a lighter weight and more powerful version of the `default_trace`. Extended events are also lighter weight and more flexible and scalable than SQL Server Trace and SQL Profiler.

Extended events are designed to replace some of the older monitoring technologies such as SQL Server Profiler. All the events and columns available in SQL Server Profiler are available through the XEvents feature.

XEvent Objects

This section introduces the objects in XEvents. Figure 12-7 shows the object hierarchy for XEvent objects.

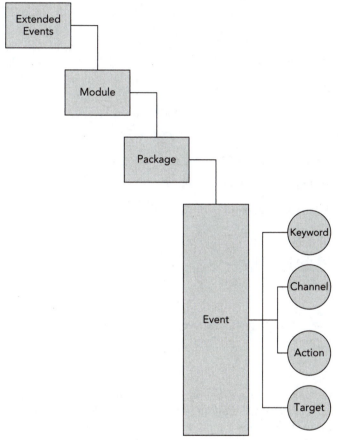

FIGURE 12-7

Module

The `Module` object is equivalent to the binary that contains the events. `Module` is equivalent to `SQLServr.exe`, or `MyDll.dll` if you were to write your own code and load it into SQL Server. The only place you see the module is as an attribute of the package in the `sys.dm_xe_packages` DMV.

Package

A *package* is a container object within the module. You can see the packages that come with SQL Server in the `sys.dm_xe_packages` DMV. The following code lists the contents of this DMV, the results of which are shown in Table 12-1.

```
select name, description
from sys.dm_xe_packages
```

TABLE 12-1: sys.dm_xe_packages

NAME	DESCRIPTION
package0	Default package (contains all standard types, maps, compare operators, actions, and targets)
sqlos	Extended events for SQL operating system
sqlserver	Extended events for Microsoft SQL Server
SecAudit	Security Audit events
Ucs	Extended events for Unified Communications Stack
Sqlclr	Extended events for SQL CLR
Filestream	Extended events for SQL Server FILESTREAM and FileTable
sqlserver	Extended events for Microsoft SQL Server
XtpRuntime	Extended events for the XTP Runtime
XtpCompile	Extended events for the XTP Compile
XtpEngine	Extended events for the XTP Engine
qds	Extended events for Query Store

As with modules, you won't be creating any packages unless you write your own code and create your own new events.

Event

Events are the first "real" objects in the hierarchy. An *event* represents an occurrence of a significant activity within SQL Server. To get a better understanding of events, take a look at some of the events available. You can find these in the sys.dm_xe_objects DMV and they have a type of 'event'. The following code outputs a list of event types:

```
select name
from sys.dm_xe_objects
where object_type ='event'
order by name
```

This returns a list of 777 different events. This is quite an increase from the 254 event types that were originally available in SQL Server 2008, and a small increase from the 618 available in SQL Server 2012. Following are a select few:

```
checkpoint_begin
checkpoint_end
lock_acquired
lock_deadlock
lock_released
locks_lock_waits
sp_statement_completed
sp_statement_starting
```

```
sql_statement_completed
sql_statement_starting
wait_info
wait_info_external
```

All events have two additional attributes: `Keyword` and `Channel`. The `Keyword` for an event is a way to group events based on who fires the event, so keywords are `memory`, `broker`, `server`, and so on. The `Channel` for an event reflects who might be interested in the event. Following are four channels in SQL Server 2014:

➤ `debug`

➤ `analytical`

➤ `operational`

➤ `administration`

To see the `Channel` and `Keyword` for the events, you must join several of the XEvent DMVs, as shown in the following code:

```
select p.name as package_name
, k.event
, k.keyword
, c.channel
, k.description
from (
select c.object_package_guid as event_package
, c.object_name as event
, v.map_value as keyword
, o.description
from sys.dm_xe_object_columns as c inner join sys.dm_xe_map_values as v
  on c.type_name = v.name
  and c.column_value = v.map_key
  and c.type_package_guid = v.object_package_guid
inner join sys.dm_xe_objects as o
  on o.name = c.object_name
  and o.package_guid = c.object_package_guid
where c.name = 'keyword'
) as k inner join (
select c.object_package_guid as event_package
, c.object_name as event
, v.map_value as channel
, o.description
from sys.dm_xe_object_columns as c inner join sys.dm_xe_map_values as v
  on c.type_name = v.name
  and c.column_value = v.map_key
  and c.type_package_guid = v.object_package_guid
inner join sys.dm_xe_objects as o
  on o.name = c.object_name
  and o.package_guid = c.object_package_guid
where c.name = 'channel'
) as c
on
k.event_package = c.event_package and k.event = c.event
inner join sys.dm_xe_packages as p on p.guid = k.event_package
order by keyword
, channel
, event
```

Table 12-2 shows a few of the events, including their keywords and channels.

TABLE 12-2: Select Extended Events

PACKAGE NAME	EVENT	KEYWORD	CHANNEL	DESCRIPTION
sqlserver	broker_acti-vation_task_aborted	broker	Admin	Broker activation task aborted
sqlserver	broker_acti-vation_task_started	broker	Analytic	Broker activation task started
sqlserver	change_tracking_cleanup	change_tracking	Debug	Change Tracking Cleanup
sqlserver	app_domain_ring_buffer_recorded	clr	Debug	AppDomain ring buffer recorded
sqlserver	cursor_manager_cursor_end	cursor	Analytic	Cursor manager cursor end
sqlserver	checkpoint_begin	database	Analytic	Checkpoint has begun
sqlserver	database_started	database	Operational	Database started
sqlserver	deadlock_moni-tor_state_tran-sition	deadlock_monitor	Debug	Deadlock Monitor state transition
sqlserver	error_reported	errors	Admin	Error has been reported
sqlserver	trace_print	errors	Debug	Trace message published
sqlserver	assert_fired	exception	Debug	Assert fired
sqlos	dump_exception_routine_executed	exception	Debug	Dump exception routine executed
sqlserver	sql_statement_starting	execution	Analytic	SQL statement starting
sqlserver	databases_log_file_size_changed	io	Analytic	Database log file size changed
sqlserver	file_read	io	Analytic	File read
sqlserver	flush_file_buf-fers	io	Debug	FlushFileBuffers called

Action

Actions are what you want to happen when an event fires. They are invoked synchronously on the thread that fired the event. The available actions are stored in the `sys.dm_xe_objects` DMV with an `object_type = 'action'`. The action enables you to do things such as correlate a `plan_handle` and T-SQL stack with a specific event. This kind of flexibility creates an incredibly powerful framework that exceeds anything that SQL Trace and SQL Profiler could do.

The following query returns all the actions available:

```
select name
from sys.dm_xe_objects
where object_type = 'action'
order by name
```

This query returns 50 actions, some of which are listed here:

```
attach_activity_id
attach_activity_id_xfer
callstack
collect_cpu_cycle_time
collect_system_time
create_dump_all_thread
create_dump_single_thread
database_context
database_id
debug_break
plan_handle
session_id
sos_context
sql_text
transaction_id
tsql_stack
```

Predicate

A *predicate* is a filter that is applied to the event right before the event is published. As a boolean expression, it can be either local or global and can store state.

Predicates are stored in the `sys.dm_xe_objects` DMV and you can see them by using the following T-SQL:

```
select name, description
from sys.dm_xe_objects
where object_type = 'pred_compare'
order by name
-- 77 rows

select name, description
from sys.dm_xe_objects
where object_type = 'pred_source'
order by name
-- 44rows
```

Table 12-3 shows a few of the `pred_compare` objects.

TABLE 12-3: Selected pred_compare Objects

NAME	DESCRIPTION
divides_by_uint64	Whether a uint64 divides another with no remainder
equal_ansi_string	Equality operator between two ANSI string values
greater_than_equal_float64	Greater-than or equal operator between two 64-bit double values
greater_than_i_sql_ansi_ string	Greater than operator between two SQL ANSI string values
less_than_ansi_string	Less-than operator between two ANSI string values
less_than_equal_i_unicode_ string_ptr	Less-than or equal operator between two Unicode string pointer values
less_than_int64	Less-than operator between two 64-bit signed int values
not_equal_ptr	Inequality operator between two generic pointer values

Table 12-4 lists some of the pred_source objects.

TABLE 12-4: Selected pred_source Objects

NAME	DESCRIPTION
Counter	Counts the number of times evaluated.
cpu_id	Gets the current CPU ID.
current_thread_id	Gets the current Windows thread ID.
database_id	Gets the current database ID.
node_affinity	Gets the current NUMA node affinity.
partitioned_counter	Per-CPU partitioned counter. The value is aggregated and approximate.
scheduler_address	Gets the current scheduler address.
scheduler_id	Gets the current scheduler ID.
session_id	Gets the current session ID.
system_thread_id	Gets the current system thread ID.
task_address	Gets the current task address.

NAME	DESCRIPTION
task_elapsed_quantum	Gets the time elapsed since quantum started.
task_execution_time	Gets the current task execution time.
transaction_id	Gets the current transaction ID.
worker_address	Gets the current worker address.

Target

A *target* is a way to define what you want to happen to the events you monitor. Table 12-5 shows the 17 targets defined for SQL Server 2014. Like the other XEvent objects, you can find them in the sys.dm_xe_objects DMV with object_ type = 'target'. The two new targets for SQL Server 2014 are asynchronous_security_audit_mds_log_target and compressed_history.

TABLE 12-5: Targets

NAME	DESCRIPTION
asynchronous_router	Route events to asynchronous listeners.
asynchronous_security_ audit_event_log _target	Asynchronous security audit NT event log target.
asynchronous_security_ audit_file _target	Asynchronous security audit file target.
asynchronous_security_ audit_mds_log_target	Asynchronous security audit MDS log target.
asynchronous_security_ audit_security _log_target	Asynchronous security audit NT security log target.
compressed_history	Use the history target to preserve event stream in highly compressed form.
etw_classic_sync_target	Event Tracing for Windows (ETW) synchronous target.
Event_counter	Counts the number of occurrences of each event in the event session.
Event_file	Saves the event data to an Expression Encoder Log (XEL) file, which can be archived and used for later analysis and review. You can merge multiple XEL files to view the combined data from separate event sessions.
Event_stream	Asynchronous live stream target.

continues

TABLE 12-5 *(continued)*

NAME	DESCRIPTION
`histogram`	Aggregates event data based on a specific event data field or action associated with the event. The histogram enables you to analyze distribution of the event data over the period of the event session.
`pair_matching`	Pairing target.
`ring_buffer`	Asynchronous ring buffer target.
`router`	Routes events to listeners.
`synchronous_security_ audit_event_log _target`	Synchronous security audit NT event log target.
`synchronous_security_ audit_file _target`	Synchronous security audit file target.
`synchronous_security_ audit_security _log_target`	Synchronous security audit NT security log target.

The following T-SQL code returns the list of targets from `sys.dm_xe_objects`:

```
select name, description
from sys.dm_xe_objects
where object_type = 'target'
order by name
```

Event Session

The *event session* is where all the objects detailed earlier are brought together to actually do something. You create the event session to define which of those objects you want to use to perform your event capture.

You create event sessions using the DDL `CREATE EVENT SESSION` syntax. This one statement enables you to define all the objects you need to create a new event session. The only thing you cannot do is start the session. For transaction consistency, you must create the session first. When it has been created, you can start it using the `ALTER EVENT SESSION` syntax, as shown here:

```
ALTER EVENT SESSION <session name>  STATE = START
```

Listing 12-8 (code file: `XE_long_running_queries.sql`) shows an example of code to create a new event session that gathers `sql_text`, and the `tsql_stack` for any SQL statement that has a duration > 30ms. It then writes the output to the XML file specified in the target specification, and flushes results from memory to the file every second.

LISTING 12-8: XE_long_running_queries.sql

```
-- Create a new event session
CREATE EVENT SESSION [long_running_queries] ON SERVER
ADD EVENT sqlserver.sql_statement_completed(
    SET collect_statement=(1)
    ACTION(sqlserver.sql_text
        ,sqlserver.tsql_stack)
    WHERE (([duration]>(30)))
ADD TARGET package0.event_file(SET
        filename=N'C:\ch12_samples\XEvents\long_running_queries.xel')
WITH (MAX_MEMORY=4096 KB
    ,EVENT_RETENTION_MODE=ALLOW_SINGLE_EVENT_LOSS
    ,MAX_DISPATCH_LATENCY=5 SECONDS
    ,MAX_EVENT_SIZE=0 KB
    ,MEMORY_PARTITION_MODE=NONE
    ,TRACK_CAUSALITY=OFF
    ,STARTUP_STATE=OFF)
GO
with (max_dispatch_latency = 1 seconds)
```

ALTER SESSION is probably most frequently used to start and stop sessions, but you can also use it to add or remove events from an existing session. The following code snippet shows how to start the session you created in Listing 12-8.

```
-- Which event session do we want to alter
alter event session long_running_queries on server
-- Now make any changes
-- change the state to start
state = start
```

The code shown in Listing 12-9 (code file: XE_alter_long_running_queries.sql) shows how to use ALTER SESSION to add an additional event to the existing event session.

LISTING 12-9: XE_alter_long_running_queries.sql

```
-- Which event session do we want to alter
alter event session long_running_queries on server
-- Now make any changes
-- add another event, this time the long_io_detected event
add event sqlserver.long_io_detected
(
-- for this event get the sql_text, and tsql_stack
    action(sqlserver.sql_text, sqlserver.tsql_stack)
        -- No predicate, we want all of these to see if there is any correlation
)
```

To see which sessions are currently active, use the following queries:

```
select * from sys.dm_xe_sessions

select * from sys.dm_xe_session_events
```

Catalog Views

Following are several of the catalog views that expose information about XEvents:

➤   `server_event_sessions`

➤   `server_event_session_targets`

➤   `server_event_session_fields`

➤   `server_event_session_events`

➤   `server_event_session_actions`

DMVs

You have already seen some of the XEvents DMVs in action. For completeness, here is the full list:

➤   `sys.dm_xe_map_values`—Returns a mapping of internal numeric keys to human-readable text.

➤   `sys.dm_xe_object_columns`—Returns the schema information for all the objects.

➤   `sys.dm_xe_objects`—Returns a row for each object exposed by an event package. Objects can be one of the following:

➤   **Events**—Indicate points of interest in an execution path. All events contain information about a point of interest.

➤   **Actions**—Run synchronously when events fire. An action can append runtime data to an event.

➤   **Targets**—Consume events, either synchronously on the thread that fires the event or asynchronously on a system-provided thread.

➤   **Predicate sources**—Retrieve values from event sources for use in comparison operations. Predicate comparisons compare specific data types and return a boolean value.

➤   **Types**—Encapsulate the length and characteristics of the byte collection, which is required to interpret the data.

➤   `sys.dm_xe_packages`—Lists all the packages registered with the XEvents engine.

➤   `sys.dm_xe_session_event_actions`—Returns information about event session actions. Actions are executed when events are fired. This management view aggregates statistics about the number of times an action has run, and the total run time of the action.

➤   `sys.dm_xe_session_events`—Returns information about session events. Events are discrete execution points. Predicates can be applied to events to stop them from firing if the event does not contain the required information.

➤   `sys.dm_xe_session_object_columns`—Shows the configuration values for objects that are bound to a session.

➤ `sys.dm_xe_session_targets`—Returns information about session targets.

➤ `sys.dm_xe_sessions`—Returns information about an active XEvents session. This session is a collection of events, actions, and targets.

Working with Extended Event Sessions

You can create, modify, display, and analyze sessions and session data in several ways.

You can manipulate extended events using DDL in T-SQL as you saw in some of the previous examples. Additional T-SQL examples on creating XEvents sessions are shown later in this section.

Two GUIs that you can use with XEvents are the New Session Wizard and the New Session UI.

New Session Wizard

The New Session Wizard guides you through the creation of a new session with the following steps:

1. In SQL Server Management Studio, open the `Management` node, then the `Extended Events` node, and then the `Session` node. Right-click Sessions, and choose New Session Wizard. This launches the New Session Wizard and displays the Introduction page, as shown in Figure 12-8.

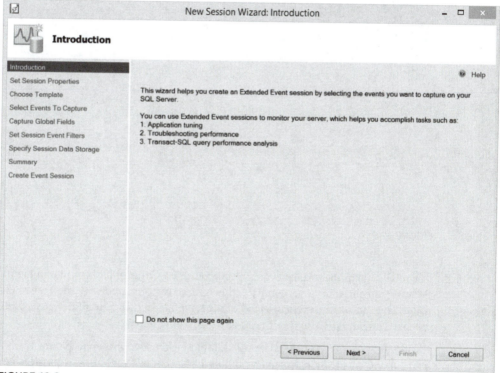

FIGURE 12-8

2. Click Next to move on to the Set Session Properties page shown in Figure 12-9. Here you provide a session name, and select if you want the session to start up each time the server starts. For this example, enter the name **chapter_12_test**.

3. Click Next to move on to the Choose Template page shown in Figure 12-10. Here you choose a predefined template for the events in the template, or you can select to not use a template and manually select events. In this example, select "Use this event session template," which populates the list of event session templates. For this example, select the "Query Wait Statistics" template, and click Next.

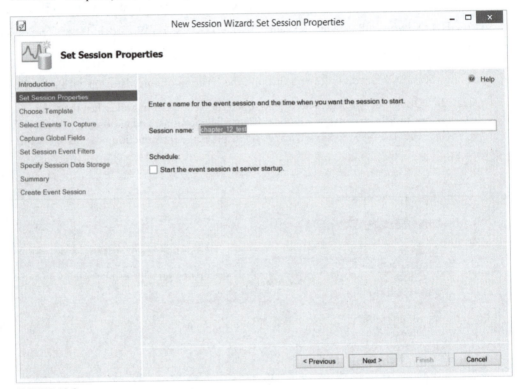

FIGURE 12-9

4. The next page in the wizard is the Select Events To Capture page shown in Figure 12-11. Because you chose to use a template, this is already populated with the events from the template. You can see the event selected in the template in the "Selected events" box. Because you used a template, you don't need to do anything here.

5. Click Next to move on to the Capture Global Fields page shown in Figure 12-12. Again, because you selected a template, a number of global fields are already preselected. The preselected fields are those with a check box next to them. In Figure 12-12, you can see `client_app_name` and `database_id` are checked. Scrolling down shows the other fields that are selected from the template.

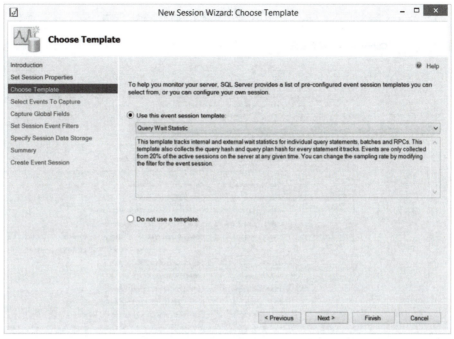

FIGURE 12-10

FIGURE 12-11

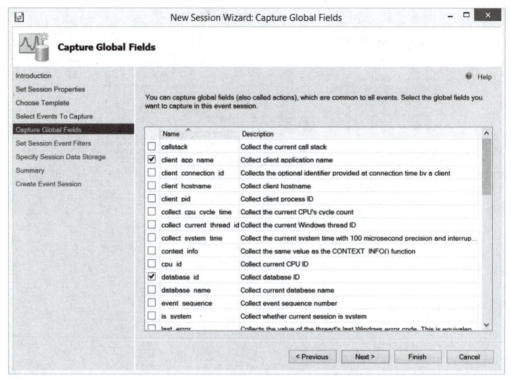

FIGURE 12-12

6. Click Next to move on to the Set Session Event Filters page shown in Figure 12-13. Here you can select any filters (also known as *predicates*) that would restrict the amount of data to be captured. For this example, you do not apply any filters.

7. Click Next to move on to the Specify Session Data Storage page shown in Figure 12-14. Here you can specify where you want the data to be collected. The two options are to "Save data to a file for later analysis," or to put it into a ring buffer. For this example, select "Save data to a file for later analysis (event_file target)," and leave the default values for the filename, maximum file size, enable file rollover, and maximum number of files.

8. Click Next to move on to the Summary page shown in Figure 12-15. This page provides a summary of the selections made throughout the wizard. Note that in Figure 12-15, all the nodes have been expanded so that you can see all the options chosen through the wizard. This provides one last opportunity to confirm the values selected before the wizard applies these settings and creates the new event session.

9. Click Finish and the wizard creates the new event session. If it creates the event session successfully, you see the Create Event Session Success page shown in Figure 12-16. You then have the option to start the event session immediately and watch live data as it is captured. Select both options ("Start the event session immediately after session creation" and "Watch live data on screen as it is captured").

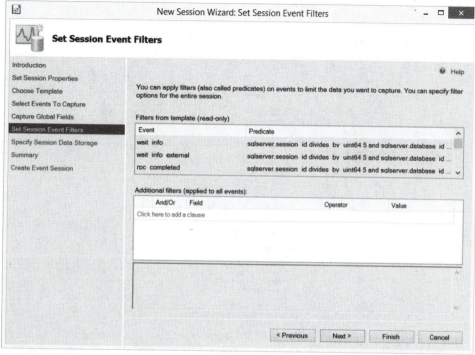

FIGURE 12-13

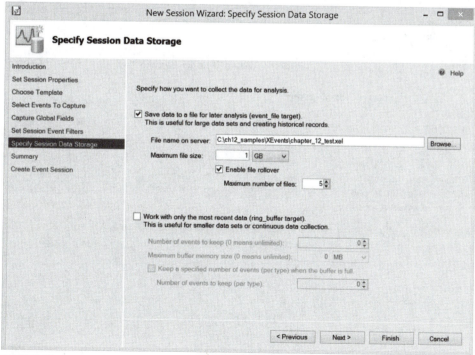

FIGURE 12-14

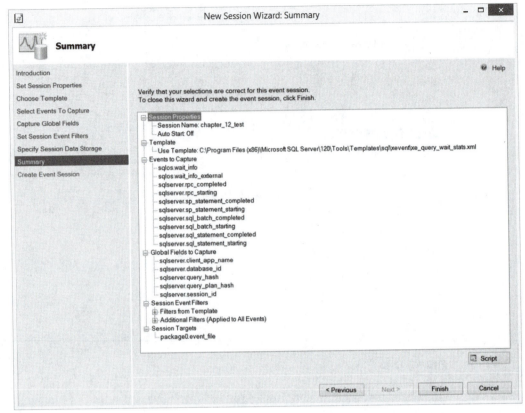

FIGURE 12-15

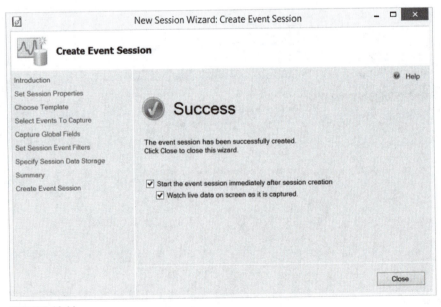

FIGURE 12-16

10. Click Close to close the wizard, start the event session, and watch live data being captured. The wizard closes, and SQL Server Management Studio displays a new tab showing the Live Data for the new session.

New Session UI

You launch the New Session UI from SQL Server Management Studio. To start using this interface, perform the following steps:

1. Open the Management node, then the Extended Events node, and then the Session node. Right-click Sessions and choose New Session. This opens the New Session UI on the General page. Enter a session name of **chapter_12_test2**, and select the Connection Tracking template, as shown in Figure 12-17. Select "Start the event session at server startup."

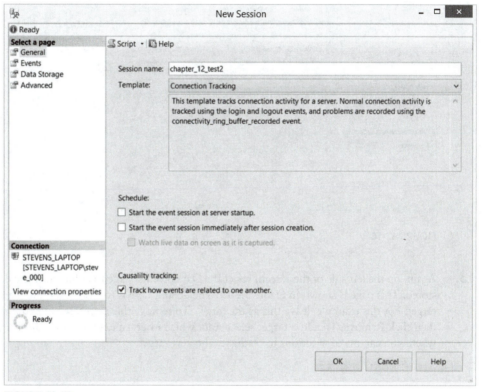

FIGURE 12-17

2. On the left side of the screen, select the Events page to see which events have been preselected with this template (see Figure 12-18). Because you selected a template, there is no need to change anything here.

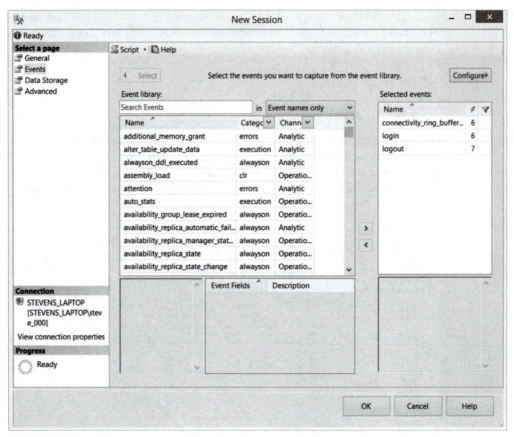

FIGURE 12-18

3.   Again, on the left side of the screen, select the Data Storage page to define how the data will be stored. This page is shown in Figure 12-19. The default here is to store data into a `ring_buffer` target. For this example, leave this as the target. To remove this target, select `ring_buffer` and then click Remove. To add a target select Add, which inserts a new row into the Targets table, where you can make selections to configure the new target.

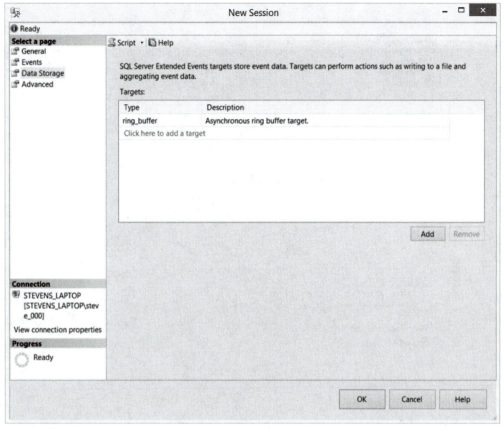

FIGURE 12-19

4. On the left side of the screen, select the Advanced page to specify advanced settings for the New Session. The Advanced page is shown in Figure 12-20. These settings are acceptable for this example.

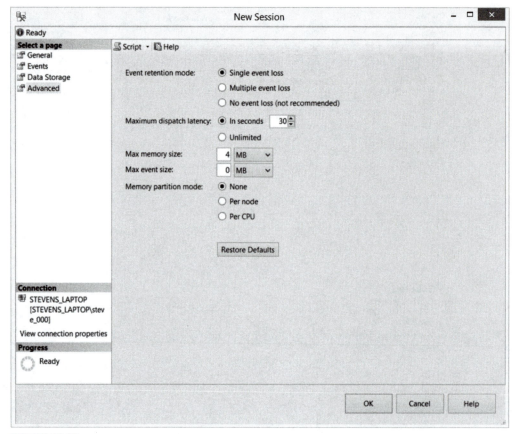

FIGURE 12-20

5. At this point, you have examined all the options for creating the new session. To create the new session, click OK. The UI disappears, and if you look in SQL Server Management Studio under Management ⇨ Extended Events ⇨ Sessions, you see that a new session called `chapter_12_test2` has been created. Because of the options you selected, it is not currently running.

6. To start the new session, right-click it and select Start Session. To view live data for the session, right-click it and select Watch Live Data.

Editing a Session

To edit a session, select it in SQL Server Management Studio by right-clicking its node, and select Properties. This brings up the same set of pages seen in the New Session UI, but this time preloaded with the session information and with some options disabled. Select Properties on the `chapter_12_test2` session to display the dialog box shown in Figure 12-21.

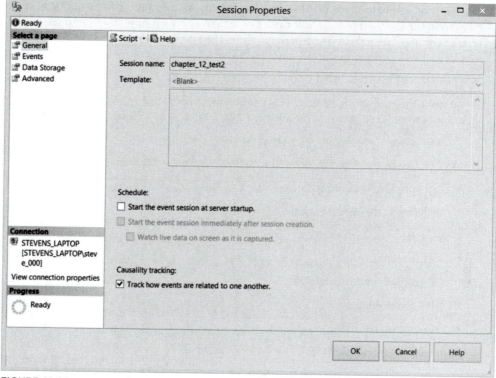

FIGURE 12-21

Using this dialog box, you can edit many of the session properties (additional options throughout the session UI have not been discussed here). Most of these options are self-explanatory, but you should explore these in conjunction with the available documentation in Books Online.

MONITORING WITH DYNAMIC MANAGEMENT VIEWS AND FUNCTIONS

Dynamic Management Views (DMVs) and Dynamic Management Functions (DMFs) are a godsend to the DBA. They provide plenty of information about server and database state. DMVs and DMFs are designed to give you a window into what's going on inside SQL Server. They return server state information that you can use to monitor the health of a server instance, diagnose problems, and tune performance. Following are two types of DMVs and DMFs:

➤ Server-scoped

➤ Database-scoped

All DMVs and DMFs exist in the sys schema and follow the naming convention dm_*. To view the information from a server-scoped DMV, you have to grant the SERVER VIEW STATE permission to the user. For database-scoped DMVs and DMFs, you must grant the VIEW DATABASE STATE permission to the user. After you grant the VIEW STATE permission, that user can see all the views; to restrict the user, deny the SELECT permission on the DMVs or DMFs that you do not want the user to access. The following example grants the VIEW SERVER STATE permission to the user J_Smith:

```
GRANT VIEW SERVER STATE TO [NorthAmerica\J_Smith]
```

If you want the user [NorthAmerica\J_Smith] to be restricted from viewing information in the view sys.dm_os_wait_stats, you must use DENY SELECT as follows:

```
DENY SELECT ON sys.dm_os_wait_stats TO [NorthAmerica\J_Smith]
```

DMVs and DMFs are generally divided into the following categories:

➤ Always On Availability Group

➤ Change Data Capture-related

➤ Change Tracking-related

➤ CLR-related

➤ Database mirroring-related

➤ Database-related

➤ Execution-related

➤ Filestream and FileTable

➤ Full-Text-Search and Semantic Search

➤ Index-related

➤ I/O-related

➤ Object-related

➤ Query notifications–related

➤ Replication–related

➤ Resource Governor

➤ Security-related

➤ Service Broker–related

➤ SQL Server OS–related

➤ Transaction-related

Rather than describe all the views here, this section looks at examples for the common tasks a DBA would perform to monitor a SQL Server. For details about all the DMVs and DMFs, see the Books Online topic "Dynamic Management Views and Functions."

Following are some of the scenarios in which you can use DMVs and DMFs. You can also open a sample DMV to get all the scripts. Following are just a few examples, but in the sample DMV solution, you can find many examples for monitoring your SQL Server.

What's Going on Inside SQL Server?

The following sections illustrate querying the DMVs to determine what is currently going on inside SQL Server.

Currently Running Queries

Listing 12-10 (code file: `current running queries.sql`) shows the SQL text for currently running queries. It helps you find which queries are currently running and displays the SQL text for each currently running query. This is useful when you try to determine what is currently running in terms of T-SQL code, and not just SPIDs/`session_ids`.

LISTING 12-10: current running queries.sql

```
select r.session_id
    ,r.status
    ,substring(qt.text,r.statement_start_offset/2,
    (case when r.statement_end_offset = -1
    then len(convert(nvarchar(max), qt.text)) * 2
    else r.statement_end_offset end - r.statement_start_offset)/2)
    as query_text
    ,qt.dbid
    ,qt.objectid
    ,r.cpu_time
    ,r.total_elapsed_time
    ,r.reads
    ,r.writes
    ,r.logical_reads
    ,r.scheduler_id
from sys.dm_exec_requests as r
cross apply sys.dm_exec_sql_text(sql_handle) as qt
inner join sys.dm_exec_sessions as es on r.session_id = es.session_id
where es.is_user_process = 1
order by r.cpu_time desc
```

Who Is Using Which Resources?

Listing 12-11 (code file: `Resource Usage.sql`) samples the system tables (which are now deprecated). It samples `sysprocesses` over a 10-second interval and reports on the delta between the first and second sample. It reports on the CPU, Physical I/O, and memory resource usage. Although `sysprocesses` is deprecated, it has all the information nicely formatted in one place, whereas the corresponding DMVs require joins to multiple DMVs. Because `sysprocesses` is so easy to use, you are better off using it for as long as it is available.

LISTING 12-11: Resource Usage.sql

```
-- Who is using all the resources?
select spid, kpid, cpu, physical_io, memusage, sql_handle, 1 as sample,
getdate() as sampleTime, hostname, program_name, nt_username
```

continues

LISTING 12-11 *(continued)*

```
into #Resources
from master..sysprocesses

waitfor delay '00:00:10'

Insert #Resources
select spid, kpid, cpu, physical_io, memusage, sql_handle, 2 as sample,
getdate() as sampleTime, hostname, program_name, nt_username
from master..sysprocesses

-- Find the deltas
select r1.spid
, r1.kpid
, r2.cpu - r1.cpu as d_cpu_total
, r2.physical_io - r1.physical_io as d_physical_io_total
, r2.memusage - r1.memusage as d_memusage_total
, r1.hostname, r1.program_name, r1.nt_username
, r1.sql_handle
, r2.sql_handle
from #resources as r1 inner join #resources as r2 on r1.spid = r2.spid
    and r1.kpid = r2.kpid
where r1.sample = 1
and r2.sample = 2
and (r2.cpu - r1.cpu) > 0
order by (r2.cpu - r1.cpu) desc

select r1.spid
, r1.kpid
, r2.cpu - r1.cpu as d_cpu_total
, r2.physical_io - r1.physical_io as d_physical_io_total
, r2.memusage - r1.memusage as d_memusage_total
, r1.hostname, r1.program_name, r1.nt_username
into #Usage
from #resources as r1 inner join #resources as r2 on r1.spid = r2.spid
    and r1.kpid = r2.kpid
where r1.sample = 1
and r2.sample = 2
and (r2.cpu - r1.cpu) > 0
order by (r2.cpu - r1.cpu) desc

select spid, hostname, program_name, nt_username
, sum(d_cpu_total) as sum_cpu
, sum(d_physical_io_total) as sum_io
from #Usage
group by spid, hostname, program_name, nt_username
order by 6 desc

drop table #resources
drop table #Usage
```

Who Is Waiting?

Listing 12-12 (code file: who is waiting.sql), which shows the tasks that are currently waiting, uses the same sampling principle as the preceding query.

LISTING 12-12: who is waiting.sql

```
select
* , 1 as sample
, getdate() as sample_time
into #waiting_tasks
from sys.dm_os_waiting_tasks

waitfor delay '00:00:10'

insert #waiting_tasks
select
* , 2
, getdate()
from sys.dm_os_waiting_tasks

-- figure out the deltas
select w1.session_id
, w1.exec_context_id
,w2.wait_duration_ms - w1.wait_duration_ms as d_wait_duration
, w1.wait_type
, w2.wait_type
, datediff(ms, w1.sample_time, w2.sample_time) as interval_ms
from #waiting_tasks as w1 inner join #waiting_tasks as w2 on w1.session_id =
w2.session_id
and w1.exec_context_id = w2.exec_context_id
where w1.sample = 1
and w2.sample = 2
order by 3 desc

-- select * from #waiting_tasks

drop table #waiting_tasks
```

Wait Stats

Listing 12-13 (code file: wait stats.sql) samples the wait stats to see what has changed over the sample period.

LISTING 12-13: wait stats.sql

```
select *, 1 as sample, getdate() as sample_time
into #wait_stats
from sys.dm_os_wait_stats
```

continues

LISTING 12-13 *(continued)*

```
waitfor delay '00:00:30'
insert #wait_stats
select *, 2, getdate()
from sys.dm_os_wait_stats

-- figure out the deltas

select w2.wait_type
,w2.waiting_tasks_count - w1.waiting_tasks_count as d_wtc
, w2.wait_time_ms - w1.wait_time_ms as d_wtm
, cast((w2.wait_time_ms - w1.wait_time_ms) as float) /
cast((w2.waiting_tasks_count - w1.waiting_tasks_count) as float) as avg_wtm
, datediff(ms, w1.sample_time, w2.sample_time) as interval
from #wait_stats as w1 inner join #wait_stats as w2 on w1.wait_type =
w2.wait_type
where w1.sample = 1
and w2.sample = 2
and w2.wait_time_ms - w1.wait_time_ms > 0
and w2.waiting_tasks_count - w1.waiting_tasks_count > 0
order by 3 desc

drop table #wait_stats
```

Viewing the Locking Information

Listing 12-14 (code file: `locking.sql`) can help you get the locking information in a particular database.

LISTING 12-14: locking.sql

```
SELECT l.resource_type, l.resource_associated_entity_id
,OBJECT_NAME(sp.OBJECT_ID) AS ObjectName
,l.request_status, l.request_mode,request_session_id
,l.resource_description
FROM sys.dm_tran_locks l
LEFT JOIN sys.partitions sp
 ON sp.hobt_id = l.resource_associated_entity_id
WHERE l.resource_database_id = DB_ID()
```

Viewing Blocking Information

Listing 12-15 (code file: `blocking.sql`) returns blocking information on your server.

LISTING 12-15: blocking.sql

```
SELECT
t1.resource_type
,t1.resource_database_id
,t1.resource_associated_entity_id
```

```
,OBJECT_NAME(sp.OBJECT_ID) AS ObjectName
,t1.request_mode
,t1.request_session_id
,t2.blocking_session_id
FROM sys.dm_tran_locks as t1
JOIN sys.dm_os_waiting_tasks as t2
  ON t1.lock_owner_address = t2.resource_address
LEFT JOIN sys.partitions sp
  ON sp.hobt_id = t1.resource_associated_entity_id
```

Index Usage in a Database

Listing 12-16 (code file: `index usage stats.sql`) can give you index usage for the database in which you run the query. It creates a table and stores the results in that table so that you can analyze it later. This query can be helpful in determining which indexes are truly useful in your application. Ensure that you run these queries for several days (rather than looking at data for just one day) because this can give you a better idea of the overall picture. Keep in mind that DMVs are volatile, and whenever SQL Server is restarted, these views are initialized again.

LISTING 12-16: index usage stats.sql

```
-------------------------------------------------------------------
IF OBJECT_ID('dbo.IndexUsageStats') IS NULL
CREATE TABLE dbo.IndexUsageStats
(
 IndexName sysname NULL
,ObjectName sysname NOT NULL
,user_seeks bigint NOT NULL
,user_scans bigint NOT NULL
,user_lookups bigint NOT NULL
,user_updates bigint NOT NULL
,last_user_seek datetime NULL
,last_user_scan datetime NULL
,last_user_lookup datetime NULL
,last_user_update datetime NULL
,StatusDate datetime NOT NULL
,DatabaseName sysname NOT NULL
)

GO
----Below query will give you index USED per table in a database.
INSERT INTO dbo.IndexUsageStats
(
 IndexName
,ObjectName
,user_seeks
,user_scans
,user_lookups
,user_updates
,last_user_seek
,last_user_scan
```

continues

LISTING 12-16 *(continued)*

```
,last_user_lookup
,last_user_update
,StatusDate
,DatabaseName
)
SELECT
 si.name AS IndexName
,so.name AS ObjectName
,diu.user_seeks
,diu.user_scans
,diu.user_lookups
,diu.user_updates
,diu.last_user_seek
,diu.last_user_scan
,diu.last_user_lookup
,diu.last_user_update
,GETDATE() AS StatusDate
,sd.name AS DatabaseName
FROM sys.dm_db_index_usage_stats  diu
JOIN sys.indexes si
  ON diu.object_id = si.object_id
 AND diu.index_id = si.index_id
JOIN sys.all_objects so
  ON so.object_id = si.object_id
JOIN sys.databases sd
  ON sd.database_id = diu.database_id
WHERE is_ms_shipped <> 1
  AND diu.database_id = DB_ID()
```

Indexes Not Used in a Database

Listing 12-17 (code file: `indexes not being used.sql`) can give you information about which indexes are not being used. If certain indexes are not used, you should consider dropping them because they take unnecessary time to create or maintain. The results stored in the table, `NotUsedIndexes`, to indicate which indexes are not used. Ensure that you run this query for several days (rather than looking at data for just one day) because this can give you a better idea of the overall picture. Keep in mind that DMVs are volatile, and whenever SQL Server is restarted, these views are initialized again.

LISTING 12-17: indexes not being used.sql

```
-----------------------------------------------------------------------
--This will store the indexes which are not used.
IF OBJECT_ID('dbo.NotUsedIndexes') IS NULL
CREATE TABLE dbo.NotUsedIndexes
(
 IndexName sysname NULL
```

```
,ObjectName sysname NOT NULL
,StatusDate datetime NOT NULL
,DatabaseName sysname NOT NULL
)

----Below query will give you indexes which are NOT used per table in a database.
INSERT dbo.NotUsedIndexes
(
 IndexName
,ObjectName
,StatusDate
,DatabaseName
)
SELECT
 si.name AS IndexName
,so.name AS ObjectName
,GETDATE() AS  StatusDate
,DB_NAME()
FROM sys.indexes si
JOIN sys.all_objects so
  ON so.object_id = si.object_id
WHERE si.index_id NOT IN (SELECT index_id
                              FROM sys.dm_db_index_usage_stats diu
                              WHERE si.object_id = diu.object_id
                                AND si.index_id = diu.index_id
                          )
      AND so.is_ms_shipped <> 1
```

View Queries Waiting for Memory Grants

Listing 12-18 (code file: `waiting for memory grants.sql`) indicates the queries waiting for memory grants. SQL Server analyzes a query and determines how much memory it needs based on the estimated plan. If memory is not available at that time, the query is suspended until the memory required is available. If a query is waiting for a memory grant, an entry shows up in the `sys.dm_exec_query_memory_grants` DMV.

LISTING 12-18: waiting for memory grants.sql

```
SELECT
  es.session_id AS SPID
 ,es.login_name
 ,es.host_name
 ,es.program_name, es.status AS Session_Status
 ,mg.requested_memory_kb
 ,DATEDIFF(mi, mg.request_time
 , GETDATE()) AS [WaitingSince-InMins]
FROM sys.dm_exec_query_memory_grants mg
JOIN sys.dm_exec_sessions es
  ON es.session_id = mg.session_id
WHERE mg.grant_time IS NULL
ORDER BY mg.request_time
```

Connected User Information

Listing 12-19 (code file: `connected users.sql`) can tell you which users are connected, and how many sessions each of them has open.

LISTING 12-19: connected users.sql

```sql
SELECT login_name
, count(session_id) as session_count
FROM sys.dm_exec_sessions
GROUP BY login_name
```

Filegroup Free Space

Listing 12-20 (code file: `filegroup free space.sql`) indicates how much free space remains in each filegroup. This is valuable when your database uses multiple filegroups. Note that this query uses catalog views rather than DMVs.

LISTING 12-20: filegroup free space.sql

```sql
-- Find the total size of each Filegroup
select data_space_id, (sum(size)*8)/1000 as total_size_MB
into #filegroups
from sys.database_files
group by data_space_id
order by data_space_id

-- Find how much we have allocated in each FG
select ds.name, au.data_space_id
, (sum(au.total_pages) * 8)/1000 as Allocated_MB
, (sum(au.used_pages) * 8)/1000 as used_MB
, (sum(au.data_pages) * 8)/1000 as Data_MB
, ((sum(au.total_pages) - sum(au.used_pages) ) * 8 )/1000 as Free_MB
into #Allocations
from sys.allocation_units as au inner join sys.data_spaces as ds
    on au.data_space_id = ds.data_space_id
group by ds.name, au.data_space_id
order by au.data_space_id
-- Bring it all together
select f.data_space_id
, a.name
, f.total_size_MB
, a.allocated_MB
, f.total_size_MB - a.allocated_MB as free_in_fg_MB
, a.used_MB
, a.data_MB
, a.Free_MB
from #filegroups as f inner join #allocations as a
on f.data_space_id = a.data_space_id
order by f.data_space_id

drop table #allocations

drop table #filegroups
```

Query Plan and Query Text for Currently Running Queries

Use the query shown in Listing 12-21 (code file: `query plan for running queries.sql`) to find out the query plan in XML and the query text for the currently running batch for a particular session. Ensure that you use a grid to output the result in SQL Server Management Studio. When you get the result, you can click the link for the XML plan, which opens an XML editor inside Management Studio. If you want to look at the graphical query plan from this XML plan, click the link to the XML plan, and it opens in a new window in SQL Server Management Studio.

LISTING 12-21: query plan for running queries.sql

```
SELECT
  er.session_id
 ,es.login_name
 ,er.request_id
 ,er.start_time
 ,QueryPlan_XML = (SELECT query_plan FROM
sys.dm_exec_query_plan(er.plan_handle))
 ,SQLText = (SELECT Text FROM sys.dm_exec_sql_text(er.sql_handle))
FROM sys.dm_exec_requests er
JOIN sys.dm_exec_sessions es
  ON er.session_id = es.session_id
WHERE es.is_user_process = 1
ORDER BY er.start_time ASC
```

Memory Usage

Listing 12-22 (code file: `memory usage.sql`) indicates the memory used (in KB) by each internal SQL Server component.

LISTING 12-22: memory usage.sql

```
SELECT
  name
 ,type
 ,pages_kb AS MemoryUsedInKB
FROM sys.dm_os_memory_clerks
```

Buffer Pool Memory Usage

Listing 12-23 (code file: `buffer pool memory usage.sql`) lists out all the objects within the buffer pool, along with the amount of space used by each. This is a great way to see who uses the buffer pool.

LISTING 12-23: buffer pool memory usage.sql

```
SELECT count(*)AS cached_pages_count
    ,name ,index_id
FROM sys.dm_os_buffer_descriptors AS bd
```

continues

LISTING 12-23 *(continued)*

```
        INNER JOIN
        (
            SELECT object_name(object_id) AS name
                ,index_id ,allocation_unit_id
            FROM sys.allocation_units AS au
                INNER JOIN sys.partitions AS p
                    ON au.container_id = p.hobt_id
                        AND (au.type = 1 OR au.type = 3)
            UNION ALL
            SELECT object_name(object_id) AS name
                ,index_id, allocation_unit_id
            FROM sys.allocation_units AS au
                INNER JOIN sys.partitions AS p
                    ON au.container_id = p.partition_id
                        AND au.type = 2
        ) AS obj
            ON bd.allocation_unit_id = obj.allocation_unit_id
    WHERE database_id = db_id()
    GROUP BY name, index_id
    ORDER BY cached_pages_count DESC;
```

MONITORING LOGS

Another aspect of monitoring that is frequently overlooked is monitoring the various log files available. SQL Server writes its own error log, and you also have the Windows Event Logs; you may find events logged in the Application, Security, or System Event logs.

Traditionally, the SQL Server and Windows Event Logs have been viewed through separate applications: Windows Logs through the Windows Event Viewer, and SQL Logs through a text editor. The SQL Server Management Studio Log File viewer enables you to combine both sets of logs into a combined view. Root-level nodes for SQL Server, SQL Server Agent, Database Mail, and Windows NT enable you to do this.

Monitoring the SQL Server Error Log

The SQL Server Error Log is the location where SQL Server writes all its error information, and also a lot of additional informational messages about how it is working and what it is doing.

The error log is a text file written to the `C:\Program Files\Microsoft SQL Server\MSSQL12 .MSSQLSERVER\MSSQL\Log` folder. A new log file is opened each time the SQL Server process starts. SQL Server keeps seven log files: the current one is called simply `errorlog`, and the oldest one is called `errorlog.6`.

The error log contains a lot of useful information. Any time a significant issue occurs, the first place to search for additional information should be the SQL Server Error Log. Additionally, you can use both Event Notifications and Extended Events if additional data is required to help troubleshoot a particular issue.

Monitoring the Windows Event Logs

Three Windows Event Logs may hold entries of relevance to a SQL Server event:

➤ Application Event Log

➤ Security Event Log

➤ System Event Log

These event logs contain additional event information about the server environment, other processes/applications operating on the server, and also additional information about the SQL Server process that may not be logged in to the SQL Server Error Log. These logs should be another place that you go to look for additional information about any issues that arise with SQL Server.

SQL SERVER STANDARD REPORTS

One of the best-kept secrets in SQL Server is the standard reports that started shipping with the SQL Server 2005 Performance dashboard reports. Since then, each edition of SQL Server has added to the standard reporting capabilities. Today, they provide a comprehensive set of reports that provide a great deal of detailed information on what's going on inside SQL Server.

The standard reports are accessible through SQL Server Management Studio. Starting with the Server Node, right-click the server node, then Reports, and then Standard Reports to see the list of reports for the SQL Server Instance. Figure 12-22 shows the list of standard reports in which the server node is shown.

As you navigate through the various nodes in the Object Explorer, different reports are available at different key nodes. In some cases, no standard reports exist, and you just see a custom report node that's empty. In other cases, such as when you select a specific database, a long list of standard reports is available. Figure 12-23 shows the standard reports for a database.

Unfortunately, these are not documented anywhere, so you have to find your own way around the various nodes in the Object Explorer by clicking nodes and looking in the Reports menu to find any standard reports. Figure 12-24 shows one more location where you can find standard reports, which is under Security ⇨ Logins.

SYSTEM CENTER ADVISOR

System Center Advisor (SCA) is the natural evolution of SQL Server Best Practice Analyzer (BPA). One of the challenges with SQL BPA is that the set of rules are encoded into each version for BPA that's released, and knowledge about best practices can change more quickly than new versions can be released. SQL BPA is also a tool that must be manually executed on each server.

SCA is the result of a lot of effort by folks who work with SQL Server and the SQL teams within Product Support Services (PSS) to deliver a more effective tool for validating SQL Server configurations.

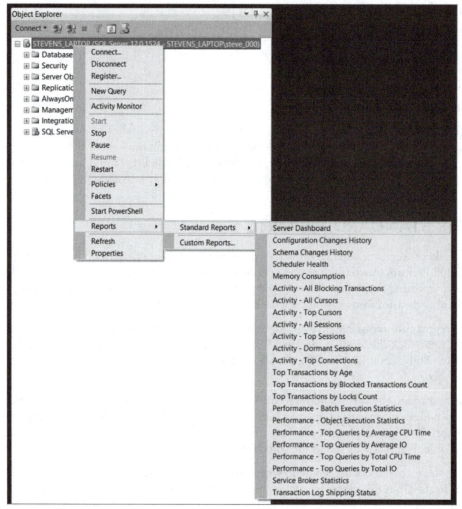

FIGURE 12-22

SCA is a cloud-based configuration monitoring tool that can continuously monitor a large number of servers and provide online analysis of the results. One of the benefits of being cloud-based is that new best practices can be incorporated into the validation checks quickly, and with no activity on your (the end user's) part. The SCA team can introduce a new rule with minimal effort, and every server being monitored by SCA can immediately gain the benefit of being checked against the new rule.

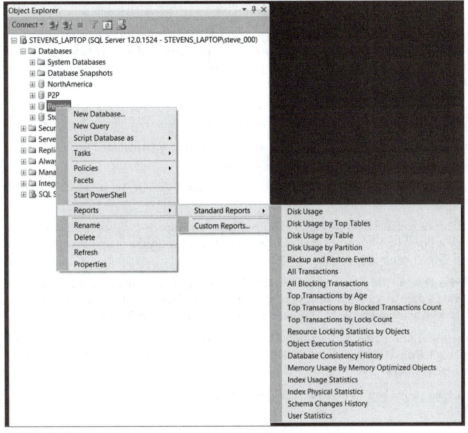

FIGURE 12-23

FIGURE 12-24

SUMMARY

Monitoring SQL Server regularly and gathering performance data is key to helping identify performance problems. Increasingly, today's DBAs must cover more systems than ever before, and must spread their net widely. The tools and techniques introduced in this chapter help DBAs move from a hands-on approach to an event-driven approach.

Performance Monitor enables the DBA to monitor resource usage for a server, and helps troubleshoot performance issues with server and SQL resource usage.

The SQL Trace architecture with SQL Profiler, SQL Trace, and now Distributed Replay provide tools for capturing, analyzing, and replaying SQL Server events.

Event Notifications provides a framework to execute actions outside SQL Server asynchronously in response to events occurring inside the server.

XEvents provides a scalable framework for capturing data when specific events occur within SQL Server. This is a powerful framework that enables complex data collection to assist with troubleshooting SQL Server issues.

The SQL Server Dynamic Management Views (DMVs) and Dynamic Management Functions (DMFs) provide a deep insight into what's going on inside SQL Server, and the samples provided help illustrate how to use some of the DMVs and DMFs to troubleshoot specific issues.

System Center Advisor provides a cloud-based service for best practices, as well as for patch and update checking to help you keep your SQL Servers current with the very latest knowledge around SQL Server Best Practices.

In Chapter 13, you learn how to performance-tune T-SQL.

13

Performance Tuning T-SQL

WHAT'S IN THIS CHAPTER ?

➤ Understanding query processing

➤ Reading query plans

➤ Using query operators

➤ Performance tuning in a production environment

WROX.COM CODE DOWNLOADS FOR THIS CHAPTER

The wrox.com code downloads for this chapter are found at www.wrox.com/go/ prosql2014admin on the Download Code tab. The code is in the Chapter 13 download and individually named according to the names throughout the chapter.

Performance tuning on a SQL Server is the process of looking at T-SQL statements and identifying queries that don't return results in a timely manner. Performance tuning T-SQL involves some knowledge of the internal workings of SQL Server, as well as the syntax of the query being written. You must understand how individual statements are analyzed, and how SQL Server's compilation engine uses various resources (for example, indexes, statistics, query plans, data tables, and compilation steps) to help a user create T-SQL statements that are more efficient and process faster. The process of tuning T-SQL statements includes measuring actual performance, reviewing the query plans, and then modifying architecture and T-SQL statements to optimize the query performance. Sometimes a very simple change to a query plan can result in a substantially better-performing query. But understanding how to identify those changes can be tedious and frustrating unless you first understand how the SQL compilation engine handles individual parts of query statements.

To optimize a query, you must understand the impact of each T-SQL statement on the optimizing engine. You also need to know how to use the monitoring tools that SQL Server provides to measure query performance. Lastly, you must understand what choices you have for improving slow-performing queries.

In this chapter, you learn how a query is processed, how to identify performance problems using SQL Server tools, and how to read query plans to identify performance issues.

> **NOTE** *One of the primary performance upgrades in SQL Server 2014 is the capability to store online transaction processing (OLTP) tables in memory and use natively compiled stored procedures. This chapter does not focus on those features, because they are covered elsewhere in this book. The performance tuning techniques in this chapter focus on regular disk-based tables, indexes, and stored procedures.*

OVERVIEW OF QUERY PROCESSING

This chapter is not meant to be a complete explanation of the internal workings of the compilation engine in SQL Server, but instead an overview of some of the important query processing steps that you should understand when performance tuning queries.

SQL Server performs two main steps to produce the desired result when a query is executed. As you would guess, the first step is query compilation, which generates the query plan, or the physical steps that will be executed to return the information requested. The second step is the execution of that query plan, which returns results to the calling program. The focus of this chapter is on the first step that generates the query plans. Performance tuning the execution step involves tuning the disks and storage systems to provide the highest I/O speeds, which won't be covered here because those tasks are very unique to each installation.

The compilation phase in SQL Server goes through three steps: parsing, algebrization, and optimization. The SQL Server team spent considerable effort during SQL 2012 development to re-architect and rewrite several parts of SQL Server compilation process. This effort paved the way for additional improvements in SQL Server 2014—a better Cardinality Estimator for cost-based optimization (discussed in this chapter), and natively compiled stored procedure optimizations for in-memory tables.

Let's investigate basic compilation and recompilation of queries, starting with a look at how the compilation engine impacts performance, and then identify improvements in SQL Server 2014.

Let's first review the basic query processing steps. Figure 13-1 shows a high-level overview of how a SQL statement flows through the compilation engine, is executed, and returns results.

When a T-SQL query (statement, batch, stored procedure, trigger, or other group of T-SQL statements) is executed, the compilation process tries to find a query plan in the plan cache that matches the statements in the submitted query. The Plan Guide Match feature in the engine determines whether an existing query plan for a particular statement or batch exists. If it exists, it uses the query plan for that statement or batch for execution. Keep in mind that not all query plans that are created are put into the cache. For example, if a stored procedure was created with the WITH RECOMPILE option included, that plan is not cached, and the stored procedure gets a new query plan each time it's executed. Additionally, estimated query plans generated by development tools are not stored. If a matching query plan is found, the execution engine uses that plan to process the query.

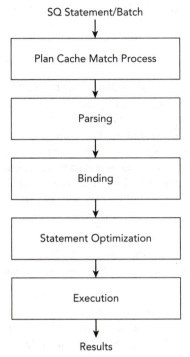

SQ Statement/Batch

Plan Cache Match Process

Parsing

Binding

Statement Optimization

Execution

Results

FIGURE 13-1

A number of things can impact whether a matching query plan is found and executed. For example, changed statistics, additional indexes, or some SET options can cause a query plan to be marked as "incorrect" and recompiled. Excessive or unnecessary recompilations can impact overall system performance.

If a plan is not found, or an existing plan is found but determined to be incorrect, the query must be compiled or recompiled. The query statement is passed to the parsing engine, which validates the syntax and creates a *parse tree*. This parse tree (or *logical tree*) represents the high-level logical steps that are necessary to execute the entire T-SQL statement or batch.

The binding process uses that parse tree to validate that all of the objects exist, and then matches the names to the corresponding ObjectIDs that are in the system catalog. This *algebrized tree* is then sent to the Query Optimizer.

It is the Query Optimizer that determines the performance criteria for any executed T-SQL statements. This optimizer creates query plans that determine how the actual statements will be executed, and in what order. The query optimization process maps the logical query operators defined in the binding process to the physical processing operations that will be performed by the execution engine. At a high level, the optimizing engine determines the physical steps and execution order for the steps that will return the result set.

The Query Optimizer creates candidate execution plans that will satisfy the end result, creates a cost for each plan based on available information, and selects the most cost-effective plan for execution. The Query Optimizer will attempt to find the most cost-effective query, but depending on the number of possibilities it finds, may choose the "good enough" option. Let's take a closer look at how query plans are generated and selected for execution.

Generating Execution Plans

The Query Optimizer engine generates a series of query plans for a T-SQL statement or batch. The basic purpose of this engine is to analyze all of the different solutions for a query, and determine the option with the least cost. Even a simple query may have many ways of resolving, so determining the "lowest" cost for a query is important. Remember that cost is measured by the time it takes to return results to the user, as well as the amount of system resources required. In theory, a cost-based optimizer should generate and analyze all of the possible execution plans, but some complex queries may have millions of plans to consider. Therefore, the Query Optimizer will spend a "reasonable" amount of time to find a "reasonable" plan, which may not be the "best" plan. One way of tuning the performance of your system is to create queries that result in simpler query plans so that the "best" plan is found in that "reasonable" amount of time.

Once an optimized query plan is generated, that plan is sent to the execution engine to retrieve the actual data and return it to the calling program. The query plan is stored in cache to be used again.

You have several ways to generate query plans that can be analyzed for performance improvements. Graphical or text-based query plans can be reviewed in SQL Server Management Studio, they can be gathered by Extended Events, and some query performance metrics can be monitored by reading system Dynamic Management Views (DMVs) and system Dynamic Management Functions (DMFs). You learn about reviewing and reading query plans later in this chapter.

Statistics

Before looking at specific optimization steps, it is important to understand SQL Server statistics and how they impact query performance. These statistics tell the optimizer engine how to pick the different join operations based on the content of the tables. Making sure that your system has updated statistics is critical to building valid query plans.

SQL Server collects statistical information about the distribution of values in one or more columns of a table or indexed view. The uniqueness of data found in a particular column is known as *cardinality*. *High cardinality* refers to a column with values that are unique, whereas *low cardinality* refers to a column that has many values that are the same. The two types of statistics are single-column or multicolumn. Each statistical object includes a histogram that displays the distribution of values in the first column of the list of columns contained in that statistical object.

The Query Optimizer uses these statistics to estimate the cardinality and, thus, the selectivity of expressions. When those are calculated, the sizes of intermediate and final query results are estimated. Good statistics enable the optimizer to accurately assess the cost of different query plans and choose a high-quality plan. All information about a single statistics object is stored in several columns of a single row in the sys.indexes table, and in a statistics binary large object (statblob) kept in an *internal-only* table.

If your execution plan has a large difference between the estimated row count and the actual row count, the first things you should check are the statistics on the join columns and the column in the WHERE clause for that table. Be careful with the inner side of loop joins; the row count should match the estimated rows multiplied by the estimated executions.

As noted earlier, it is important when performance tuning queries to make sure that the statistics are current. One way to verify this is to check the UpdateDate, Rows, and Rows Sampled columns returned by sys.dm_db_stats_properties Dynamic Management View (DMV). You must keep up-to-date statistics to maintain quality query plans for optimal system performance. Up-to-date statistics are a reflection of the data, not the age of the statistics. With no data changes, statistics can be valid indefinitely.

You can use the following views (and command) to get details about statistics:

➤ To see how many statistics exist in your table, you can query the sys.stats view.

➤ To view which columns are part of the statistics, you can query the sys.stats_columns view.

➤ To view the histogram and density information, you can query the sys.dm_db_stats_properties view.

SQL 2014 Query Optimization Improvements—The New Cardinality Estimator

In SQL 2014, a new Cardinality Estimator was introduced, and it has a direct impact on query performance and the development of query plans. Cardinality estimates determine the potential number of rows that will be returned in the actual query. This estimate has a direct impact on how tables are joined, and the types of joins used in the physical processing.

> **NOTE** *In most cases, the new Cardinality Estimator will not have a negative impact on current queries, but Microsoft has produced a white paper to address the primary changes to the Estimator and how it will impact queries. Refer to the document at the bottom of the page at* http://msdn.microsoft.com/en-us/library/dn673537.aspx *for more information.*

This chapter focuses on some possible situations where this will improve query performance, and how to turn this new estimator on and off to maintain consistency with earlier query plans.

Using the New Cardinality Estimator

The new Cardinality Estimator has been rewritten with optimized functionality for data warehouse and OLTP workloads. Any new databases created in SQL Server 2014 will have this estimator enabled by default (assuming the model database is set to compatibility level 120).

If you have upgraded to SQL 2014, and your Database Compatibility Level is set to 110, you will be using the SQL Server 2012 Cardinality Estimator.

The SQL Server team has written articles that they believe that most user queries will not be negatively impacted, and, in fact, most should improve with the new estimator. However, it is always a good practice to validate your queries with an engine change and benchmark the new performance metrics.

One good recommendation is to run your queries with the Database Compatibility Level set to your previous compatibility level (the one prior to your SQL Server 2014 upgrade/installation) by using the following command:

```
ALTER DATABASE database_name
SET COMPATIBILITY_LEVEL = 110 | 100)
```

The following compatibility levels can be set for SQL 2014. For SQL 2012, use compatibility level 110. For SQL 2008/2008R2, use compatibility level 100. SQL 2014 does not support earlier compatibility levels. If your previous SQL installation was a version prior to SQL 2008, then you can upgrade that database to SQL 2008, and test against that version with compatibility level 100.

Next, measure the performance of your queries, reset the Database Compatibility Level to 120, and re-test the queries. You should identify any queries with degraded performance, and use a trace flag 2312 to modify the Cardinality Estimator for just those queries.

The trace flag 2312 enables you to run a query with a previous version of the Cardinality Estimator. The QUERYTRACEON query hint enables you to override the new Cardinality Estimator and use the SQL 2012 Cost Estimator to evaluate a specific query. For example, OPTION (QUERYTRACEON 2312) at the end of a query statement would optimize that particular query using the SQL Server 2012 Cost Estimator.

Following are some of the areas that have been impacted by the new Cardinality Estimator:

➤   Recently added ascending keys.

➤   The assumption that filtered predicates on the same table have the same correlation.

➤   The assumption that filtered predicates on different tables are independent.

IDENTIFYING SQL QUERY PERFORMANCE TUNING ISSUES

When you are performance tuning on a SQL Server, you discover that how fast a query performs is a function of the amount of CPU required to process the query, and the time it takes to read the disks and return a valid set of rows and columns. A server can have other performance issues (slow CPU, slow disks), but this chapter focuses on identifying performance issues with SQL queries, and how to troubleshoot those issues.

Monitoring Query Performance

You can identify and monitor stored procedure and T-SQL performance issues on a SQL Server in several ways. Chapter 12 "Monitoring your SQL Server" discusses many of these monitoring methods. One of the common ways is to run one of the built-in system reports that monitor queries. Figure 13-2 shows the Standard reports available for any database.

These reports can help an administrator identify any long-running or resource-hogging queries or stored procedures. This is a good place to start when looking for possible system performance issues. Another good set of reports are the Standard Performance reports available from the Instance level on the Object Explorer, as shown in Figure 13-3.

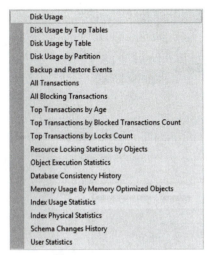

FIGURE 13-2

Ideally, as an administrator, you are looking for queries that consume a large amount of system resources (memory, CPU, or I/O). Even if a query performed fine in testing before being deployed, it can be recompiled without warning, and the query plan can become non-optimal. Also, queries that run with low amounts of data may be recompiled and run non-optimally over time. Monitoring real-time production queries is the best way to identify possible problems before they become issues.

One tip is to remember that a relatively fast query that runs many times per second or per minute can actually be a poor-performing query, even though an individual execution may look very fast (that is, less than a few hundred milliseconds). When looking for poor performers, it is worth evaluating the total amount of system resources and time used when the query numbers are aggregated by each query.

What to Do When You Find a Slow-Performing Query

A "slow-performing" query is a relative term—what runs slow in one system may be considered fast in another system. Individual query execution time itself may not a good measure of whether a query is running slow. For example, a query that runs in 300 milliseconds (ms) might be considered by many to be fast, unless that query is executed hundreds of times per second, resulting in heavy CPU usage. So, the first thing to do is to decide if the query is a poor performer by reviewing individual and aggregated performance metrics captured when running the queries.

When you find a stored procedure or T-SQL statement that is consuming more resources than expected, the next step is to take a closer look at the query performance itself, and understand the individual query plan that is being used.

Entire books are dedicated to reading and understanding query plans and the internal workings of the SQL compiler. This discussion focuses on some troubleshooting tips, and some basic performance tuning steps.

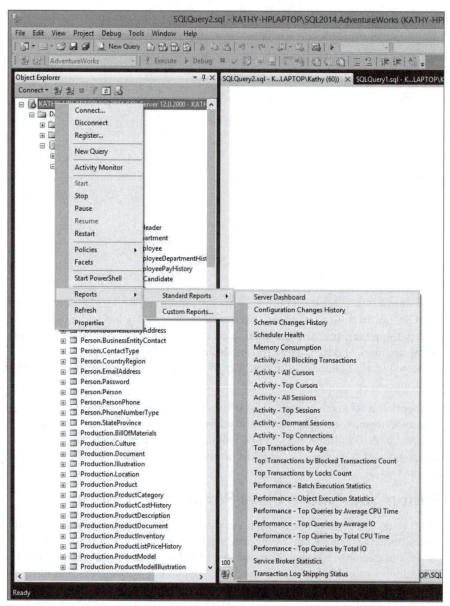

FIGURE 13-3

Generating the Query Plans

The first step in troubleshooting a problem T-SQL query is generating the query plan. When a query is processed, the logical steps required are translated into a series of physical steps that will provide the required results. There can be many query plans built, and the SQL engine will try to evaluate the most cost-effective query plan and implement it. However, accurate query plan costing depends on several things—appropriate indexes, updated and valid statistics, and a level of complexity that allows the engine to analyze a reasonable number of plans.

The SQL Server query plan comes in different flavors: textual, graphical, and XML format. Reading the graphical display is usually a fast way to identify problems in the query because many visual cues are illustrated in the graphical query plan. A *Showplan* event in the query engine describes any of these query plan flavors, and different types of Showplans have different information. SQL Server can produce a graphical plan with visual cues to performance issues, or a text plan (in text or XML format) that will give more details about the execution of the query.

Table 13-1 summarizes the various Showplan formats. For the demonstrations in this chapter, you will be using the graphical query plans. After becoming better skilled in reading query plans, advanced users may choose to use the text or XML formats to read the query plans.

TABLE 13-1: Showplan Formats

PLAN CONTENTS	TEXT FORMAT	GRAPHICAL FORMAT	XML FORMAT
Operators	`SET SHOWPLAN_TEXT ON`	N/A	N/A
Operators and estimated costs	`SET SHOWPLAN_ALL ON`	Displays the estimated execution plan in SQL Server Management Studio	`SET SHOWPLAN_XML ON`
Operators plus estimated cardinalities and costs, plus runtime information	`SET STATISTICS PROFILE ON`	Displays the actual execution plan in SQL Server Management Studio	`SET STATISTICS XML ON`

Query plans come in two forms: estimated and actual. You can generate an *estimated query plan* before running a query that will show the steps the query engine is likely to use. This plan is not necessarily the final query plan, but is usually a good evaluation of the execution of the query. To do this, highlight the statement in SQL Server Management Studio and click the Estimated Query Plan button in the toolbar, as shown in Figure 13-4.

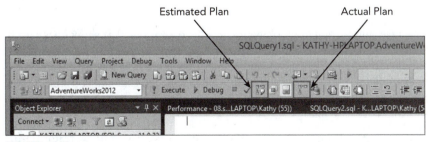

FIGURE 13-4

The estimated query plan is a good indicator of actual performance, but it is not a true query plan. Many things can influence the final query plan, including parameters, parallelism, and outdated statistics. The *actual query plan* will show you the steps that were executed when the query was run. Figure 13-4 also highlights the Actual Query Plan button on the toolbar. Both query plans are also available from the Query menu, as illustrated in Figure 13-5.

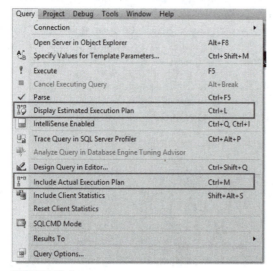

FIGURE 13-5

Reading the Query Plan

In a graphical query plan, logical and physical operations are represented by icons, each identifying the type of operation that is executed.

> **NOTE** *To learn more about each of the physical operations represented in a graphical query plan, see the Microsoft Books Online page at* `http://msdn` `.microsoft.com/en-us/library/ms191158(v=sql.120).aspx`.

When you are performance tuning, you are looking for specific operations that show unexpected high reads or writes that would consume system resources. In many types of queries, large volumes of reads are a normal operation—but depending on the query type, unnecessary reads can slow down the query. For example, if a table must be sorted prior to reading, that can consume a large volume of reads when the addition of an index might eliminate the table sort and return a much lower volume of reads to process the query.

Consider a system that has high CPU utilization. Let's say that the database administrator (DBA) has identified a query that is consuming a large amount of CPU cycles during processing. In this example, two tables are joined together, but are missing indexes to make the join work efficiently. To ensure that the performance is measured accurately in this example, caches are cleared prior to execution, which forces both a recompile of the stored procedure and clearing of the data cache. Statistics for both time and I/O are turned on to help identify possible problems. Figure 13-6 shows the statements used to test this query without indexes.

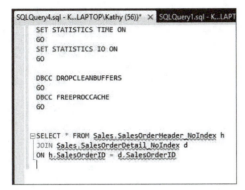

FIGURE 13-6

The example query was set up with a copy of two tables from the AdventureWorks database. The first query is made up of two tables that have no indexes or primary keys. When this simple table join executes, a query plan is generated to produce the joined results.

Figure 13-7 shows the query plan for the sample query from above. A hash join (explained later in this chapter) is used to match rows from one table to the rows in the other table. The graphical query plan identifies that the majority of the cost for this query is in the processing steps, not the steps that read the actual data tables. Looking at the query plan in Figure 13-7, the two Table Scan operations consume 32 percent of the cost, while all of the remaining processing steps (Hash Join, Parallel Operations) consume the remaining 68 percent of the query cost. If the bottleneck on the system was CPU, and the goal was to reduce CPU, using a more efficient query that reduces the cost of the processing steps would improve the results.

The query plan generator recognizes that an index on at least one of these tables would speed up processing, and the generator makes a recommendation. By adding the proper indexes (including the recommended index), the same query should run with less CPU cost, as shown in Figure 13-8. The query plan generator also recognized a potential challenge with an implicit data conversion for the final SELECT statement, but that can be addressed after indexing.

Now the same query runs against the table with the valid indexes. The new query plan shows that 82 percent of the query cost is in the read operations instead of the processing steps. The processing steps in this query have been reduced to 18 percent of the cost. The same number of rows have been read (both are table scans), but the amount of processing time has been greatly reduced, improving the CPU performance. Since you assumed that the sample system had a CPU bottleneck, making this improvement can improve overall system performance, even though the overall execution time has not been largely impacted.

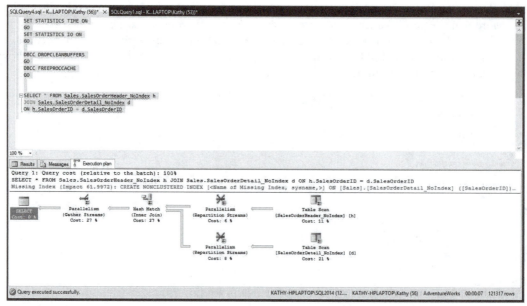

FIGURE 13-7

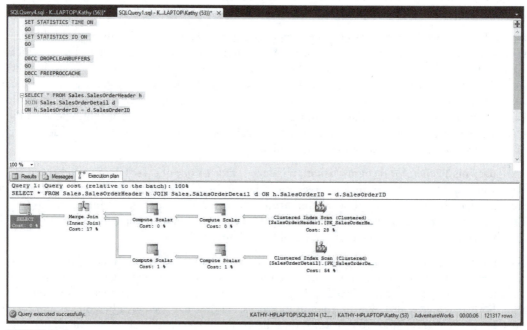

FIGURE 13-8

A review of the I/O and time statistics for each of these queries also shows the improvement in CPU performance. The first non-indexed query returns these results:

```
(121317 row(s) affected)
Table 'SalesOrderHeader_NoIndex'. Scan count 9, logical reads 780, physical reads
0, read-ahead reads 780, lob logical reads 0, lob physical reads 0, lob read-ahead
reads 0.
Table 'SalesOrderDetail_NoIndex'. Scan count 9, logical reads 1494, physical reads
0, read-ahead reads 1494, lob logical reads 0, lob physical reads 0, lob read-ahead
reads 0.
Table 'Workfile'. Scan count 0, logical reads 0, physical reads 0, read-ahead
reads 0, lob logical reads 0, lob physical reads 0, lob read-ahead reads 0.
Table 'Worktable'. Scan count 0, logical reads 0, physical reads 0, read-ahead
reads 0, lob logical reads 0, lob physical reads 0, lob read-ahead reads 0.

(1 row(s) affected)

 SQL Server Execution Times:
   CPU time = 2375 ms,  elapsed time = 6762 ms.
SQL Server parse and compile time:
   CPU time = 0 ms, elapsed time = 0 ms.

 SQL Server Execution Times:
   CPU time = 0 ms,  elapsed time = 0 ms.
```

The second query with proper indexing returns these results:

```
(121317 row(s) affected)
Table 'SalesOrderDetail'. Scan count 1, logical reads 1246, physical reads 3, read-
ahead reads 1277, lob logical reads 0, lob physical reads 0, lob read-ahead
reads 0. Table 'SalesOrderHeader'. Scan count 1, logical reads 689, physical reads
2, read-ahead reads 685, lob logical reads 0, lob physical reads 0, lob read-ahead
reads 0.

(1 row(s) affected)

 SQL Server Execution Times:
   CPU time = 1469 ms,  elapsed time = 6638 ms.
SQL Server parse and compile time:
   CPU time = 0 ms, elapsed time = 0 ms.
```

Although the overall execution time (6,762 ms versus 6,638 ms) is not a huge reduction in time, the CPU processing time has been reduced significantly (2,375 ms versus 1,469 ms), which will reduce the CPU bottleneck in the example.

When performance tuning a poor-performing query, the query plan and Statistics I/O and Statistics Time reports can provide good indications of where performance improvements can be made, and they can help validate and measure those improvements.

DATA ACCESS OPERATORS IN QUERY PLANS

The graphical query plan returns the different types of access operators that SQL Server uses to read the data. This section explores ways that these operators are different from each other, and how the access methods may affect performance of the query.

This section is not intended to be an all-encompassing explanation of all of the query plan options, but it will highlight the most common operators and give you an overview of how query performance tuning uses these operators to improve performance.

To follow along with the examples in the next sections, restore a copy of your AdventureWorks database as AW_2 so that you can drop and re-create indexes and compare results.

Table Scan

A *table scan* involves a sequential scan of all data pages belonging to the table. Run the following script in the AW_2 database:

```
SELECT * INTO dbo.New_SalesOrderHeader
FROM Sales.SalesOrderHeader
```

After you run this script to make a copy of the SalesOrderHeader table, run the following script. Remember to click the Graphical Query Plan button on top of the query window to display the query plan. If you prefer, you can always get the actual textual plan using SET STATISTICS PROFILE ON.

```
SELECT SalesOrderID, OrderDate, CustomerID
FROM dbo.New_SalesOrderHeader
```

Because this is a heap table, this statement causes a table scan. Figure 13-9 shows the graphical plan.

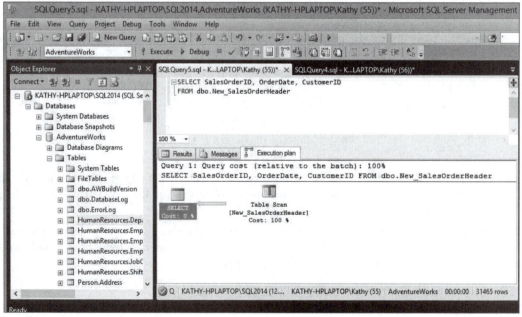

FIGURE 13-9

Now, look at the STATISTICS IO output for the example query shown in Listing 13-1 (code file: IndexAccess1.sql). This is a session-level setting. STATISTICS IO provides you with I/O-related statistics for the query statement that caused a table scan to be run.

```
DBCC DROPCLEANBUFFERS
GO
SET STATISTICS IO ON
GO
SET STATISTICS PROFIL ON
GO
SELECT SalesOrderID, OrderDate, CustomerID
FROM dbo.New_SalesOrderHeader
GO
SET STATISTICS IO OFF
GO
SET STATISTICS PROFILE OFF
GO
```

The statistics I/O information is as follows:

```
(31465 row(s) affected)
Table 'New_SalesOrderHeader'. Scan count 1, logical reads 780, physical reads 0,
read-ahead reads 780, lob logical reads 0, lob physical reads 0, lob read-ahead
reads 0.
```

The Scan count tells you how many times the table was accessed for this query. If you have multiple tables in your query, you see statistics showing I/O information for each table. In this case, the New_SalesOrderHeader table was accessed once.

The logical reads counter indicates how many pages were read from the data cache. In this case, 780 reads were done from cache. The logical reads number may be a little different on your machine. As mentioned earlier, because of the whole table scan, the number of logical reads equals the number of pages allocated to this table.

You can also run the following query to verify the number of pages allocated to the table:

```
select in_row_reserved_page_count
from sys.dm_db_partition_stats
  WHERE OBJECT_ID = OBJECT_ID('New_SalesOrderHeader')
```

The physical reads counter indicates the number of pages read from the disk. It shows 0 for the preceding code. This doesn't mean that there were no physical reads from disk, though.

The read-ahead reads counter indicates the number of pages from the physical disk that are placed into the internal data cache when SQL Server guesses that you will need them later in the query. In this case, this counter shows 780, which is the total number of physical reads that occurred. Both the physical reads and read-ahead reads counters indicate the amount of physical disk activity. These numbers may, too, be different on your machine.

The `lob logical reads`, `lob physical reads`, and `lob read-ahead reads` are the same as the other reads, but these counters indicate reads for the large objects—for example, if you read a column with the data types `varchar(max)`, `nvarchar(max)`, `xml`, or `varbinary(max)`. When T-SQL statements retrieve `lob` columns, some `lob` retrieval operations might require traversing the `lob` tree multiple times. This may cause SET STATISTICS IO to report higher-than-expected logical reads.

Clustered Index Scan

For this exercise, you add a clustered index to the table to see the impact on the query. A clustered index maintains the entire table's data at its leaf level, sorted by the *clustered index key*.

> **NOTE** *A clustered index is not a copy of the table's data; it is the data.*

Now, run the script shown in Listing 13-2 (code file: `IndexAccess2.sql`) and query to see the effect of adding a clustered index.

LISTING 13-2: IndexAccess2.sql

```
CREATE CLUSTERED INDEX IXCU_SalesOrderID ON New_SalesOrderHeader(SalesOrderID)
GO
DBCC DROPCLEANBUFFERS
GO
SET STATISTICS IO ON
GO
SELECT SalesOrderID, RevisionNumber, OrderDate, DueDate
FROM New_SalesOrderHeader
GO
SET STATISTICS IO OFF
GO
```

The results of STATISTICS IO are shown here, and the query plan is shown in Figure 13-10:

```
(31465 row(s) affected)
Table 'New_SalesOrderHeader'. Scan count 1, logical reads 799, physical reads 0,
read-ahead reads 788, lob logical reads 0, lob physical reads 0, lob read-ahead
reads 0.
```

As shown in the Statistics IO output, the number of page reads was 799 (logical reads), which is just a little more than the heap table scan because actual row sizes are slightly larger in a clustered index. The clustered index row also includes the unique key values, and pointers to the previous-next rows. In this case, the scan did not use the pointers in the rows, but just read all of the pages unordered. You can see this if you use the graphical interface, and show the details of the table scan by hovering your mouse over the Clustered Index Scan icon, as shown in Figure 13-11.

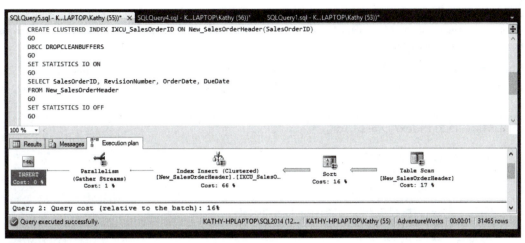

FIGURE 13-10

FIGURE 13-11

From the detail scan information, you can see that the index was not ordered (ORDERED = FALSE), which indicates that the access method did not rely on the linked list to read the pages, and that the leaf-level pages maintain the logical order of the data, which makes this operation similar to the table scan operation.

An ordered clustered index scan is also a full scan of the clustered index, but the data is returned in order by the clustering key. Pages will be read using the link list that points from each row to the next row in the sort order.

This time, run the query shown in Listing 13-3 (code file: `IndexAccess3.sql`). This query can access the same table, but is ordered by the `SalesOrderID` column, which is the clustered index key.

LISTING 13-3: IndexAccess3.sql

```
DBCC DROPCLEANBUFFERS
GO
SET STATISTICS IO ON
GO
SELECT SalesOrderID,RevisionNumber, OrderDate, DueDate
FROM New_SalesOrderHeader
ORDER BY SalesOrderID
GO
SET STATISTICS IO OFF
GO
```

The `STATISTICS IO` information is as follows:

```
(31465 row(s) affected)
Table 'New_SalesOrderHeader'. Scan count 1, logical reads 799, physical reads 0,
read-ahead reads 788, lob logical reads 0, lob physical reads 0, lob read-ahead
reads 0.
```

The query plan is shown in Figure 13-12.

As you can see, the query plan is the same in Figure 13-12 as the one in Figure 13-11, but here you have `Ordered = True`. The `STATISTICS IO` information is also the same as the unordered clustered index scan. Unlike the unordered clustered index scan, the performance of the ordered clustered index scan may depend on the amount of fragmentation in the file. In spinning-disk–based technologies, pages that are not physically located next to each other slow down the sequential reads.

Nonclustered Index Scans

A *nonclustered index scan* can occur when a nonclustered index can return all of the required fields without reading the actual data pages. Every nonclustered index includes the clustered key fields (or `rowid` for a heap table), the nonclustered index fields (for sorting), and any `INCLUDE` fields added that do not affect the sorting. If a nonclustered index can be used to satisfy a query, it is called a *covering index*. A covering index generally performs faster than a clustered index scan because the individual rows are smaller since they do not contain all of the fields in the actual table. An index may be covering even if it does not include extra fields, as long as the fields required in the query can be returned from an index.

A great example of this is `COUNT(*)` queries. For a count query, the Query Optimizer will almost always choose an index to scan rather than the data table so that the amount of data read (that is, the number of pages) is fewer, and it returns the total number of rows by counting the rows in the index instead of the rows in a table.

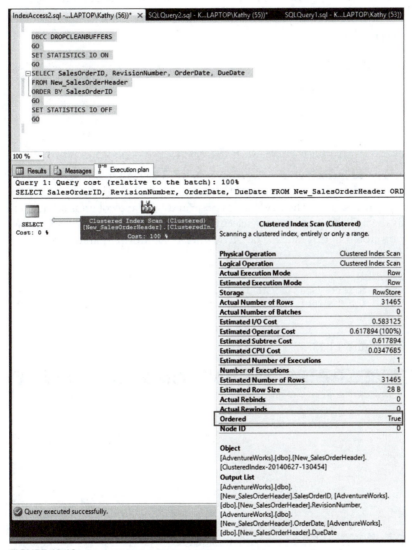

FIGURE 13-12

The following query creates a nonclustered index on the New_SalesOrderHeader table that can be used in queries. Execute the code in Listing 13-4 (code file: IndexAccess4.sql) in your database, and review the STATISTICS IO output and query plan.

LISTING 13-4: IndexAccess4.sql

```
CREATE NONCLUSTERED INDEX IXNC_SalesOrderID ON New_SalesOrderHeader(OrderDate)
INCLUDE(RevisionNumber, DueDate)
GO
DBCC DROPCLEANBUFFERS
GO
SET STATISTICS IO ON
GO
SELECT SalesOrderID, RevisionNumber, OrderDate, DueDate
FROM New_SalesOrderHeader
GO
SET STATISTICS IO OFF
GO
```

This script creates a nonclustered index on the OrderDate column. The clustered index key of the table will be included in each index row, and the INCLUDE clause will instruct the index to store the columns RevisionNumber and DueDate. The RevisionNumber and DueDate columns are included because your query needs them. The optimizer will select this index to resolve the query because all of the required fields are stored in this index. The STATISTICS IO information for the query is shown here:

```
(31465 row(s) affected)
Table 'New_SalesOrderHeader'. Scan count 1, logical reads 108, physical reads 1,
read-ahead reads 106, lob logical reads 0, lob physical reads 0, lob read-ahead
reads 0.
```

The query plan is shown in Figure 13-13.

FIGURE 13-13

As you can see from the STATISTICS IO result, only 108 logical reads were done to fulfill this query. The results returned by the clustered index query and the covering nonclustered index query are identical (number of columns and number of rows), but there were 799 logical reads in the clustered index and only 108 logical reads in the nonclustered scan because the nonclustered index has covered the query and served the data from its leaf level.

As with a clustered index scan, a nonclustered index scan can be ordered or unordered. To determine if your query is ordered, you can hover your mouse over the NonClustered Index Scan icon in the graphical query plan, and validate the ORDERED clause.

Connecting Access Operators

When reading a query plan, one of the visual cues provided to help troubleshoot performance problems are the pipes that connect the data access operators. The size of the pipe is displayed as an indicator of the number of rows being processed in between steps. Figure 13-14 shows an aggregation query on tables in AdventureWorks that returns seven rows of data.

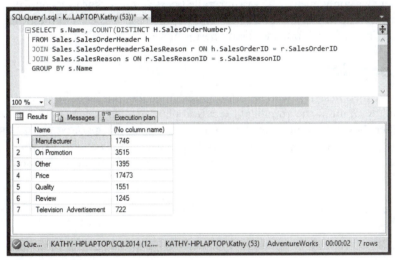

FIGURE 13-14

The query plan for this statement shows that during the query process, a large number of rows are read in order to produce the final seven rows. Figure 13-15 shows a portion of this query.

This portion of the query plan gives you an easy view indicating where a large number of rows are processed with a smaller number of rows in the actual operation. Holding your cursor over each of the pipes that join the operators shows the estimated and actual number of rows sent through that pipe to the operator. One tip when troubleshooting is to look for a difference between the actual number of rows processed and the estimated row count. If there is a large difference, this is a good indicator that your statistics are out of date.

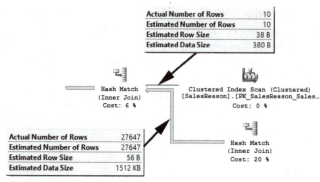

FIGURE 13-15

JOIN OPERATORS

Before SQL Server 7.0, there was only one join algorithm, called *nested loops*. Since version 7.0, SQL Server also supports *hash* and *merge join* operators. This section describes each of these and explains the conditions under which each provides better performance.

Nested Loop or Loop Join

The nested loop join (also called *nested iteration* or *loop join*) uses one join input as the outer input table (shown as the top input in the graphical execution plan, as seen in Figure 13-16) and the other input as the inner (bottom) input table. The outer loop consumes the outer input table row by row. The inner loop, executed once for each outer row, searches for matching rows in the inner input table. Listing 13-5 (code file: Join.sql) is an example that produces a nested loop join.

LISTING 13-5: Join.sql

```
--Nested Loop Join

DBCC DROPCLEANBUFFERS
GO
SET STATISTICS IO ON
GO
  SELECT C.CustomerID, c.TerritoryID
  FROM Sales.SalesOrderHeader oh
  JOIN Sales.Customer c
    ON c.CustomerID = oh.CustomerID
  WHERE c.CustomerID IN (11000,11002)
  GROUP BY C.CustomerID, c.TerritoryID
GO
SET STATISTICS IO OFF
GO
```

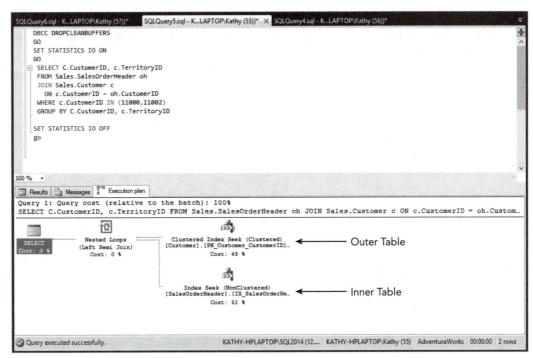

FIGURE 13-16

In this example, a row is read from the Customer table, and then all matching rows are found in the SalesOrderHeader table. Because only two Customer records are required based on the WHERE clause, this means the SalesOrderHeader table will only be read twice. Because there is a nonclustered index on the SalesOrderHeader table that will return the required fields, that index is used in a SEEK operation (read the index tree to find a specific row). This query is very efficient because the outer table has very few rows returned, and the inner table has a matching index to speed up finding the matching rows.

A nested loop join is particularly effective if the outer input is small and the inner input is sorted and large. In many small transactions (such as those affecting only a small set of rows), indexed nested loop joins are superior to both merge joins and hash joins (described in detail shortly). In large queries, however, nested loop joins are often not the optimal choice. The presence of a nested loop join operator in the execution plan doesn't indicate whether it's an efficient plan, but when performance tuning, you must validate that it is a correct join type for the most efficient way to return rows. You should also verify that the nested loop join has a valid index to perform a seek in the inner query and that it is not performing a table scan or index scan.

Hash Join

The hash join has two inputs like every other join: the *build input* (outer table) and the *probe input* (inner table). The Query Optimizer assigns these roles so that the smaller of the two inputs is the build input. A variant of the hash join (*hash aggregate physical operator*) can do duplicate removal and grouping, such as SUM (OrderQty) or GROUP BY TerritoryID. These modifications use only one input for both the build and probe roles.

Listing 13-6 (code file: Join2.sql) shows an example of a hash join, and the graphical execution plan is shown in Figure 13-17.

LISTING 13-6: Join2.sql

```
--Hash Match

DBCC DROPCLEANBUFFERS
GO
SET STATISTICS IO ON
GO

  SELECT p.Name As ProductName, ps.Name As ProductSubcategoryName
  FROM Production.Product p
  JOIN Production.ProductSubcategory ps
    ON p.ProductSubcategoryID = ps.ProductSubcategoryID
  ORDER BY p.Name,  ps.Name

SET STATISTICS IO OFF
GO
```

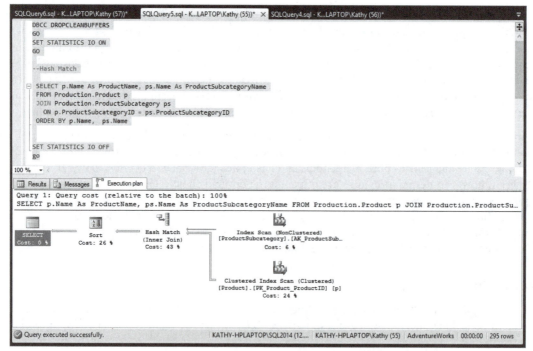

FIGURE 13-17

The hash join first scans or computes hash values for the entire build input, and then builds a hash table. In Figure 13-17, the build input is the `Production.ProductSubCategory` table.

This build phase is followed by the probe phase. The entire probe input (it is the `Production.Product` table in Figure 13-17) is scanned or computed one row at a time. For each probe row (from the `Production.Product` table), the hash key's value is computed, the corresponding hash bucket (the one created from the `Production.ProductSubCategory` table) is scanned, and the matches are produced. This strategy is called an *in-memory hash join*.

Normally, a hash table is produced in memory. In the case of very large tables, your system may not have enough memory to hold a complete hash table. If the build input does not fit in memory, a hash join has extra steps to store the hash table on disk. This can cause slower performance on a large hash join, because the table must be processed in several passes to accommodate the lack of memory. When this happens, the hash table is partitioned into smaller groups that will fit into memory, and processed as individual steps. The hash partition function assures that rows that need to join together will be processed in the same partition. A *recursive hash join* will be created if the hash tables are so large that they must be partitioned in many steps and into many levels in each step.

> **NOTE** *SQL Server always starts with an in-memory hash join and changes to other strategies if necessary.*

Recursive hash joins (or *hash bailouts*) cause reduced performance in your server. If you see many Hash Warning events in an Extended Events trace file (the Hash Warning event is under the Errors and Warnings event class), update statistics on the columns that are being joined. You should capture this event if you see that you have many hash joins in your query. This ensures that hash bailouts are not causing performance problems on your server. When appropriate indexes on join columns are missing, the optimizer normally chooses the hash join, which is a good indicator that there may be a performance improvement by adding an index to the table to support the join.

Merge Join

The merge join relies on sorted input to match records from two tables, and is an efficient algorithm if both inputs are available sorted the same way.

In the query shown in Listing 13-7 (code file: `Join3.sql`), both tables have a clustered index on the `SalesOrderID` column, so the optimizer chooses a merge join, as shown in Figure 13-18. Sometimes the optimizer chooses the merge join even if one of the inputs is not presorted by an index, by adding a sort to the plan. The optimizer would do that if the input were small enough to justify the cost of the sort, as opposed to building a hash join or nested lookup join. If the optimizer chooses to sort before the merge, it is worth checking to ensure that adding a covering index to the table would allow the query to process faster, eliminating the need for the sort. The covering index is performing the sort of the required data ahead of time, and persisting the results so that when the query executes, the data is available.

LISTING 13-7: Join3.sql

```
--Merge Join

DBCC DROPCLEANBUFFERS
GO
SET STATISTICS IO ON
GO

SELECT oh.SalesOrderID, oh.OrderDate,od.ProductID
  FROM Sales.SalesOrderDetail od
  JOIN Sales.SalesOrderHeader oh
    ON oh.SalesOrderID = od.SalesOrderID

SET STATISTICS IO OFF
GO
```

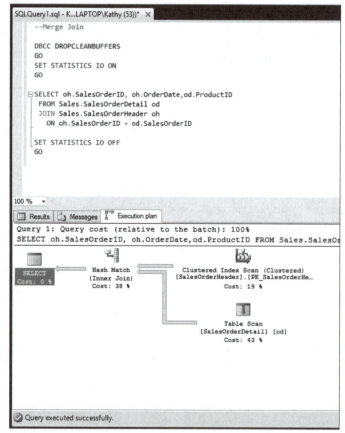

FIGURE 13-18

In this query, the sorted rows in each table are scanned one by one, and when a match on each side is detected, the joined rows are returned. Two types of merge joins can occur.

Merge joins are very effective when the query matches up two large tables that have the same leading values in the clustered index key, or have covering indexes that are sorted the same. On a unique key, the merge join will run faster (one-to-many merge). In a non-unique index, a temporary table will be used to match up the many-to-many records that are returned in the join. Either way, it is important when performance tuning to determine if adding an index can eliminate a costly join operation to speed up the results.

DATA MODIFICATION QUERY PLAN

When you execute data modifications, the generated plan has two stages. The first stage is read-only, which determines which rows must be inserted, updated, or deleted.

During this first stage, the execution plan generates a data stream that describes the changes. For INSERT statements, you have column values, so the data stream contains the column values. DELETE statements have key column(s), and UPDATE statements have data streams, the changed columns' values, and the table key. If you have foreign keys, the plan includes performing constraint validation. It also maintains indexes. And if any triggers exist, it fires these triggers as well.

The two maintenance strategies for INSERT, UPDATE, and DELETE statements are per-row and per-index. Consider the following DELETE query, which has a per-row query plan:

```
DELETE FROM New_SalesOrderHeader
WHERE OrderDate = '2007-07-01 00:00:00.000'
```

The query plan is shown in Figure 13-19.

With a per-row plan, SQL Server 2014 maintains the indexes and the base table together for each row affected by the query. The updates to all nonclustered indexes are performed with each row update on the base table. The base table could be a heap or a clustered index. If you look at the clustered index delete information box in Figure 13-19, in the Object information highlighted in the illustration, you can see that both the clustered index and the nonclustered index are listed, which indicates that the indexes are maintained with a per-row operation.

> **NOTE** *Because of the short code path and update to all indexes and tables together, the per-row update strategy is more efficient in terms of CPU cycles.*

Now, consider another query plan with the following query:

```
DELETE FROM Sales.SalesOrderHeader
WHERE OrderDate < '2006-07-01 00:00:00.000'
```

The change in this query is to the WHERE clause (changed to <) to impact a larger group of rows, and this query uses the Sales.SalesOrderHeader table to produce the plan for this example. Inspection of this table shows that it has six indexes on it. The query plan is shown in Figure 13-20.

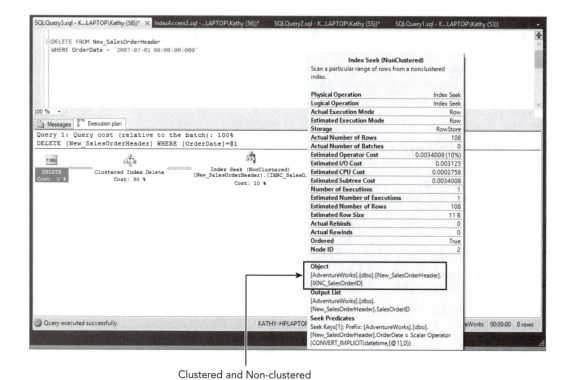

FIGURE 13-19

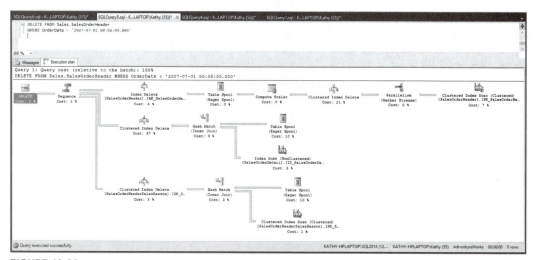

FIGURE 13-20

This query plan performs per-index maintenance. The plan first deletes qualifying rows from the clustered index, and, at the same time, it builds the temporary spool table containing the clustering key values for the other nonclustered indexes that must be maintained. SQL Server 2014 reads the spool data as many times as the number of nonclustered indexes on the table. The `sort` operator between the index `delete` operator and the `spool` operator indicates that SQL Server 2014 sorts the data according to the key column of the index it is about to delete so that the index pages can be accessed optimally. The `sequence` operator enforces the execution order of each branch. SQL Server 2014 updates the indexes one after another from the top of the plan to the bottom.

As shown in the query plan, per-index maintenance is more complicated. But because it maintains individual indexes after sorting the key (`Sort` operator), it never visits the same page again, saving in I/O. Therefore, when you update many rows, the optimizer usually chooses the per-index plan.

Query Processing on Partitioned Tables and Indexes

Before delving further into this topic, you may want to refer to the section "Partitioned Tables and Indexes" in Chapter 14 for a better understanding of partitioned tables. The following discussion assumes that you have a basic knowledge of partitioned tables and indexes.

In addition to system administration benefits, partitioning tables and indexes can benefit query performance. Partitioning tables changes the way parallelism is applied, and can help limit the size of scans on larger tables.

> **NOTE** *Partitioned tables and indexes are supported only in SQL Server Enterprise and Developer editions.*

Partition-Aware Operations

Several of the operations in query plans can be impacted by partitioned tables and indexes. Partitioning tables allows the query processor to add a partition index ID to the clustered index key in order to break the table down into smaller groups. A table that is partitioned will always have a `PartitionID` as a hidden field leading the clustered index key. If the WHERE clause of a query contains the partition key, it is translated to the `PartitionID`, and only those rows with the valid partition key are read. Also, if the partition key is not a part of the query and multiple partitions are read, parallelism operators help improve performance by using more processes to read the data.

Operations that are partition-aware will have additional attributes in the detail description for the operation. Figure 13-21 shows the detail from a query plan operator that supports partitioned operations and the number of actual partitions processed.

In this example, a partition scheme and function were built to separate this table into 42 monthly partitions. When the Query Optimizer starts processing this query, it inserts a hidden `PartitionID` column that represent the partition number in a partitioned table as a leading column in the SEEK or SCAN operation. The Query Optimizer looks at this clustered index key with `PartitionID` as the leading column of the composite key.

In this example the composite key would be `PartitionID, LastModifiedDate`. It then needs to analyze which partitions would be read to satisfy the query requirements. The `PartitionID` acts as a first-level seek value to limit the rows that are processed in the query. Once specific partitions have been identified, the normal SEEK operation will take over and find the matching records to return to the query. In this example, the partition-aware `Table Scan` operator will read data from only 13 of the 42 partitions in order to cover all of the dates requested by the query.

The following operators are partition-aware, and will use partition attributes when building the query plan:

- ➤ `Table Scan`
- ➤ `Index Scan`
- ➤ `Index Seek`
- ➤ `Insert`
- ➤ `Update`
- ➤ `Delete`
- ➤ `Merge`

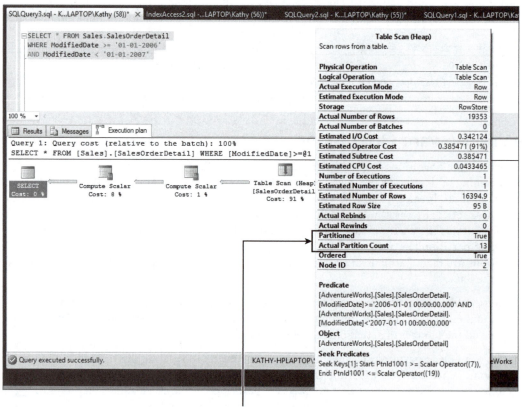

Additional Partitioning
Attributes

FIGURE 13-21

Parallel Query Execution Strategy for Partitioned Objects

SQL Server also uses parallelism to improve query performance when you access the partitioned table. If the number of threads is less than the number of partitions, the query processor assigns each thread to a different partition, initially leaving one or more partitions without an assigned thread. When a thread finishes executing on a partition, the query processor assigns it to the next partition until each partition has been assigned a single thread. This is the only case in which the query processor reallocates threads to other partitions.

If the number of threads is equal to the number of partitions, the query processor assigns one thread to each partition. When a thread finishes, it is *not* reallocated to another partition.

If the number of partitions is less than the number of available threads, the query processor will assign more than one thread to each partition. It may assign an uneven number of threads to partitions if there is an uneven match between available threads and partitions.

Remember the following key points to achieve better query performance on partitioned tables when you access large amounts of data:

➤ Take advantage of the fact that multicore processors are on a commodity server because SQL Server can also use it for parallel query-processing capabilities.

➤ Use due diligence when planning table partitioning. Ensure that the impact on queries has been tested to minimize poor performance.

➤ Keep in mind that the best partitioning for data maintenance may not be the best partitioning for queries.

➤ Remember to validate nonclustered partitioned index performance to ensure whether the indexes can be partitioned aligned.

➤ Ensure that you have a clustered index on partitioned tables so that the query processor can take advantage of index scanning optimizations.

➤ If you aggregate a large amount of data from a partitioned table, ensure that you have enough `tempdb` space on your server.

> **NOTE** *See the article "Capacity Planning for tempdb" in Microsoft Books Online for more information on how to monitor* `tempdb` *space usage.*

ANALYZING QUERY PERFORMANCE IN A PRODUCTION ENVIRONMENT

Previously in this chapter, you learned how to review query plans using the graphical query plan in SQL Server Management Studio. There will be times when monitoring system performance that you will have to do more detailed analysis than you can get with SQL Server Management Studio. Tracking queries in a production environment is critical to troubleshooting production problems.

Instead of gathering plans using sample or test queries in the SQL Server Management Studio, it will be important to gather information and query plans and performance metrics from queries being executed by users in the production environment. The Extended Events monitor allows for the capture of query plans and other query processing performance metrics from real-time queries as they run in production.

> **WARNING** *Use great caution when gathering query plans using Extended Events. This can be a very resource-intensive activity that can negatively impact system performance if done improperly. For more information, refer to* `http://connect.microsoft.com/SQLServer/feedback/details/732870/` `sqlserver-query-post-execution-showplan-performance-impact`.

Chapter 12 "Monitoring Your SQL Server" describes how to monitor system events using the Extended Events monitoring tool. Here you learn about using some of these techniques to capture errors, warnings, and query plans.

To capture query plans for production queries, launch an Extended Events session and monitor the following events:

➤ `query_post_compilation_showplan`

➤ `query_post_execution_showplan`

➤ `query_pre_execution_showplan`

These events return an XML description of the Showplan that you can use to determine the query processing steps. You can also monitor other events to get further detail on the processing steps and performance problems.

Ensure that you set appropriate filters for your monitoring criteria when you are gathering the profiling data because the log file size can grow quickly, and the XML Showplans can generate a lot of disk activity as they are written to the log files.

If used appropriately, the Extended Events monitoring can provide a lot of detailed information on slow-running queries from a production environment. You can then use that information to tune your T-SQL statements to execute more efficiently in your production environment.

System Dynamic Management Views (DMVs)

One of the performance tuning activities you may need to do is to investigate heavy CPU utilization and slow performance caused by query recompilation. Recompilation can be caused by several things, including parameterization, out-of-date statistics, and a large volume of data changes.

Some system DMVs can be used to investigate query plan recompilation issues. The most important one is `sys.dm_exec_cached_plans`. This view presents one row for every cached plan, and can be used in conjunction with the `sys.dm_exec_sql_text` view to retrieve the SQL text of the query contained in the plan cache. Following is an example of this:

```
SELECT st.text, cp.plan_handle, cp.usecounts, cp.size_in_bytes,
  cp.cacheobjtype, cp.objtype
FROM sys.dm_exec_cached_plans cp
  CROSS APPLY sys.dm_exec_sql_text(cp.plan_handle) st
ORDER BY cp.usecounts DESC
```

The information to gather here is located in the following columns:

➤ text—SQL text of the query that generated the query plan.

➤ usecounts—Number of times a query plan has been reused. This number should be high and, if large amounts of low numbers are found, the system is dealing with a large number of recompilations.

➤ size_in_bytes—Number of bytes consumed by the plan.

➤ cacheobjtype—Type of the cache object (that is, if it's a compiled plan or something similar).

Another system DMV to investigate is sys.dm_exec_query_stats. You can use this view to return performance statistics for all queries, aggregated across all executions of those queries. The following query returns the top 50 CPU-consuming queries for a specific database (for example, AdventureWorks):

```
-- Top 50 CPU Consuming queries
USE AdventureWorks
GO
SELECT TOP 50
  DB_NAME(DB_ID()) AS [Database Name],
  qs.total_worker_time / execution_count AS avg_worker_time,
  SUBSTRING(st.TEXT, (qs.statement_start_offset / 2) + 1,
    ((CASE qs.statement_end_offset
      WHEN -1 THEN DATALENGTH(st.TEXT)
      ELSE qs.statement_end_offset
    END - qs.statement_start_offset) / 2) + 1)
AS statement_text, *
FROM
  sys.dm_exec_query_stats AS qs
  CROSS APPLY sys.dm_exec_sql_text(qs.sql_handle) AS st
ORDER BY avg_worker_time DESC;
```

Using system DMVs to monitor recompilations will help keep your system performing optimally, and can prevent problems in your production environment.

PUTTING IT ALL TOGETHER

Performance tuning is the process of evaluating system performance and specific query performance using tools, query plans, and DMVs/DMFs. You will be evaluating all of this data to determine if individual queries are being processed efficiently. The graphical and textual query plans give detailed information on processing operators, data flows, and processing steps. From these detailed plans, you will be able to determine if additional indexes, T-SQL changes, updated statistics, additional hardware, or other modifications are necessary.

A key success factor in performance tuning your environment is baselining performance metrics, and measuring changes in performance after system or code changes are implemented. Using Extended Events to measure system performance can give you a good indication of problems before they become a crisis. Reading the query plans from either testing or your production system can help isolate poorly performing queries.

The most successful database administrators have a lot of knowledge about the performance metrics of their systems—from CPU utilization to I/O and memory utilization. Keeping track of these metrics and identifying unexpected changes to them will help avoid that dreaded system overload when a query suddenly changes performance.

SUMMARY

In this chapter, you learned how to read query plans, how queries are processed in SQL Server, and how to identify potential performance improvements. You learned the steps a query goes through when it is compiled and executed: it is parsed into logical operators, optimized into physical operators, and then sent to the execution engine for actual processing. Cost optimization and the impact of the new SQL Server 2014 Cardinality Estimator were discussed. You also learned about the impact of statistics on the Cardinality Estimator, and the value of having updated statistics for accurate query plans.

You learned the impact of various query plan operators on performance, including several data access operators (`Table Scan`, `Index Scan`), and several join operators (`Hash Join`, `Nested Loops Join`, and `Merge Join`). This chapter also covered partitioning and its impact on query performance.

Identifying and isolating problem queries should be a standard part of system administration for a SQL Server environment, and Microsoft and other third-party vendors provide many tool sets for monitoring the environment and measuring performance. You learned that the Extended Events monitoring tool can provide a lot of detail that can be used to troubleshoot performance problems, and that the key is understanding expected behavior versus unexpected behavior. You also learned that system DMVs are useful for monitoring query recompile activity.

Now that you understand the basics of SQL performance tuning, you can move to Chapter 14, in which you learn more about creating indexes that will help your query performance.

14

Indexing Your Database

WHAT'S IN THIS CHAPTER?

➤ Getting to know the index-related features available in SQL Server 2014 and previous versions

➤ Understanding how partitioned tables and indexes enable your databases to be more manageable and scalable

➤ Implementing partitioned tables and indexes

➤ Maintaining and tuning indexes

One of the most important functions of Production DBAs is to ensure that query times are consistent with Service-Level Agreements (SLAs) or within user expectations. One of the most effective techniques to improve query performance is to create indexes.

Query performance is generally measured by the amount of time the query takes to run, and the amount of work and resources it consumes. Long-running and expensive queries consume resources over an extended period of time, and may slow down or cause applications, reports, and other database operations to time out.

For this reason, understanding what indexing features are available in SQL Server 2014 and how to implement them is essential to any Production DBA.

This chapter offers an overview of the indexing-related features available in SQL Server 2014, including the newest features for columnstore indexes (clustered and updatable), which can greatly enhance the features introduced in SQL Server 2012.

> **NOTE** *This chapter does not cover index features included for in-memory table optimizations, including the new HASH index type. See Chapter 9, "In-Memory OLTP," for a discussion about in-memory index improvements, including the HASH indexes.*

WHAT'S NEW FOR INDEXES IN SQL SERVER 2014

The *columnstore index* is a type of index first introduced in SQL Server 2012. It is a column-based, nonclustered index geared toward increasing query performance for workloads that involve large amounts of data, typically found in data warehouse fact tables.

SQL Server 2014 introduces two new features for columnstore indexes: the capability to have a clustered columnstore index, and the capability to update an existing clustered columnstore index.

In SQL Server 2012, when the columnstore index was introduced, you could only create nonclustered columnstore indexes, and this index was not updatable once it was created. With SQL Server 2014, you can create a clustered columnstore index (which is the table), and that table/columnstore index is then updatable.

SQL Server 2014 also introduces some major enhancements to online indexing. With SQL Server 2014, single partitions can now be rebuilt, which was not allowed in previous versions of SQL Server. This is a very important improvement for companies that have very large tables and must break up their maintenance operations over a series of days.

Another new feature in SQL Server 2014 is the capability to show columnstore index information in a `SHOWPLAN` query plan. The `EstimatedExecutionMode` and `ActualExecutionMode` properties of the `SHOWPLAN` have two possible values: `Batch` or `Row`. The `Storage` property also has two possible values: `RowStore` and `ColumnStore`.

Although the core index functionality hasn't changed, there have been a number of enhancements in the past few releases of SQL Server. Table 14-1 highlights many of the index-related features introduced in previous versions of SQL Server that are now part of SQL Server 2014.

TABLE 14-1: Evolution of Index Functionality

FEATURE	INTRODUCED IN	DESCRIPTION (AS OF INITIAL RELEASE)
Columnstore indexes	SQL Server 2012	A columnstore index is a column-based, nonclustered index geared toward increasing query performance for workloads that involve large amounts of data, typically found in data warehouse fact tables. There can only be a single columnstore index on a table, and this index is not updatable. Columnstore indexes are more efficient for certain types of queries, especially read-intensive queries like data warehouse queries. Columnstore indexes have some limitations. Only a single columnstore index can be created on a table. A columnstore index can be partitioned, but only as a partitioned-aligned index (partitioning aligns with the table). Some data types were not included, including `binary`, `varbinary`, `text`, `image`, `varchar(max)`, `nvarchar(max)`, and others.

FEATURE	INTRODUCED IN	DESCRIPTION (AS OF INITIAL RELEASE)
Selective XML indexes	SQL Server 2012	This feature was introduced to allow developers to design an XML index that follows a specific path, rather than index the entire XML document.
Online index operations	SQL Server 2012	This feature included online index operations for large object (LOB) data types, including `image`, `text`, `ntext`, `varchar(max)`, `nvarvchar(max)`, and XML.
Support for up to 15,000 partitions	SQL Server 2008	In SQL Server 2008 Service Pack 2 and SQL Server 2008 R2 Service Pack 1 (SP1), the limit of 999 table partitions increased to 15,000.
Filtered indexes and statistics	SQL Server 2008	You can use a predicate to create filtered indexes and statistics on a subset of rows in the table. Prior to SQL Server 2008, indexes and statistics were created on all the rows in the table. As of the release of SQL Server 2008, you can include a WHERE predicate in the index or statistics you create to limit the number of rows to be included in the indexes or stats. Filtered indexes and statistics are especially suitable for queries that select from well-defined subsets of data; columns with heterogeneous categories of values; and columns with distinct ranges of values.
Compressed storage of tables and indexes	SQL Server 2008	Support was added for on-disk storage compression in both row and page format for tables, indexes, and indexed views. Compression of partitioned tables and indexes can be configured independently for each partition.
Spatial indexes	SQL Server 2008	Support was added for spatial data and spatial indexes. *Spatial data* in this context represents geometric objects or physical location. SQL Server supports two spatial data types: geography and geometry. A *spatial column* is a table column that contains data of a spatial data type, such as geometry or geography. A *spatial index* is a type of extended index that enables you to index a spatial column. SQL Server uses the NET CLR (Common Language Runtime) to implement this data type. Refer to the topic "Working with Spatial Indexes (Database Engine)" in Books Online (BOL) for details.
Partitioned tables and indexes	SQL Server 2005	As of the release of SQL Server 2005, you can create tables on multiple partitions and indexes on each partition. This enables you to manage operations on large data sets (such as loading and unloading a new set of data) more efficiently by indexing just the new partition, rather than having to re-index the whole table.

continues

TABLE 14-1: *(continued)*

FEATURE	INTRODUCED IN	DESCRIPTION (AS OF INITIAL RELEASE)
Online index operations	SQL Server 2005	Online index operations were added as an availability feature in SQL Server 2005. They enable users to continue to query against a table while indexes are built or rebuilt. The main scenario for using this new feature is when you need to make index changes during normal operating hours. The new syntax for using online index operations was the addition of the `ONLINE = ON` option with the `CREATE INDEX`, `ALTER INDEX`, `DROP INDEX`, and `ALTER TABLE` operations.
Parallel index operations	SQL Server 2005	Parallel index operations are another useful feature from SQL Server 2005. They are available only in Enterprise Edition and only apply to systems running on multiprocessor machines. The key scenario for using this feature is when you need to restrict the amount of CPU resources that index operations consume. This might be either for multiple index operations to coexist, or, more likely, when you must allow other tasks to complete while performing index operations. They enable a DBA to specify the `MAXDOP` for an index operation. This is useful on large systems, enabling you to limit the maximum number of processors used in index operations. It's effectively a `MAXDOP` specifically for index operations, and it works with the server-configured `MAXDOP` setting. The new syntax for parallel index operations is the `MAXDOP = n` option, which can be specified on `CREATE INDEX`, `ALTER INDEX`, `DROP INDEX` (for clustered indexes only), `ALTER TABLE ADD` (constraint), `ALTER TABLE DROP` (clustered index), and `CONSTRAINT` operations.
Asynchronous statistics update	SQL Server 2005	This is a performance `SET` option: `AUTO UPDATE STATISTICS_ ASYNC`. When this option is set, outdated statistics are placed on a queue and are automatically updated by a worker thread later. The query that generated the autoupdate request continues before the stats are updated. Asynchronous statistics updates cannot occur if any data definition language (DDL) statements such as `CREATE`, `ALTER`, or `DROP` occur in the same transaction.
Full-text indexes	SQL Server 2005	Beginning with SQL Server 2005, Full-Text Search supports the creation of indexes on XML columns. It was also upgraded to use MSSearch 3.0, which includes additional performance improvements for full-text index population. It also means that there is now one instance of MSSearch for each SQL Server instance.

FEATURE	INTRODUCED IN	DESCRIPTION (AS OF INITIAL RELEASE)
Nonkey columns in non-clustered indexes	SQL Server 2005	As of the release of SQL Server 2005 and SQL Server 2008, nonkey columns can be added to a nonclustered index. This has several advantages. It enables queries to retrieve data faster because the query can now retrieve everything it needs from the index pages without having to do a bookmark lookup into the table to read the data row. The nonkey columns are not counted in the limits for the nonclustered index number of columns (16 columns) or key length (900 bytes). The new syntax for this option is `INCLUDE (column Name, ... )`, which is used with the `CREATE INDEX` statement.
Index lock granularity changes	SQL Server 2005	In SQL Server 2005, the `CREATE INDEX` and `ALTER INDEX` T-SQL statements were enhanced by the addition of new options to control the locking that occurs during the index oper-ation. `ALLOW_ROW_LOCKS` and `ALLOW_PAGE_LOCKS` specify the granularity of the lock to be taken during the index operation.
Indexes on XML columns	SQL Server 2005	This type of index on the XML data in a column enables the Database Engine to find elements within the XML data without having to shred the XML each time.
Dropping and rebuild-ing large indexes	SQL Server 2005	The Database Engine was modified in SQL Server 2005 to treat indexes occupying more than 128 extents in a new, more scal-able way. If a drop or rebuild is required on an index larger than 128 extents, the process is broken down into logical and physi-cal stages. In the logical phase, the pages are simply marked as deallocated. After the transaction commits, the physical phase of deallocating the pages occurs. The deallocation takes place in batches, occurring in the background, thereby avoiding taking locks for a long period of time.
Indexed view enhance-ments	SQL Server 2005	Indexed views were enhanced in several ways. They can now contain scalar aggregates and (with restrictions) some user-defined functions (UDFs). In addition, the Query Optimizer can now match more queries to indexed views if the query uses scalar expressions, scalar aggregates, UDFs, interval expressions, and equivalency conditions.
Version Store	SQL Server 2005	Version Store provides the basis for the row-versioning frame-work used by Online Indexing, Multiple Active Result Sets (MARS), triggers, and the new row-versioning–based isolation levels.

continues

TABLE 14-1: *(continued)*

FEATURE	INTRODUCED IN	DESCRIPTION (AS OF INITIAL RELEASE)
Database Tuning Advisor (DTA)	SQL Server 2005	The Database Tuning Advisor (DTA) replaced SQL Server 2000's Index Tuning Wizard (ITW). DTA offers the new features that include time-bound tuning, the capability to tune across multiple databases, the capability to tune a broader class of events and triggers, a tuning log, what-if analysis, more control over tuning options, XML file support, partitioning support, offloading tuning load to lower-spec hardware, and execution by database owners.

> **NOTE** *This chapter uses the sample databases* AdventureWorks *and* AdventureWorksDW, *which are available for download at* http://msftdbprodsamples.codeplex.com/.

ABOUT INDEXES AND PARTITIONED TABLES

This section offers an overview of the process that goes into creating indexes and using indexes with partitioned tables to manage and scale large tables.

Understanding Indexes

Good index design starts with a good understanding of the benefits indexes provide. In books, a table of contents helps readers locate a section, chapter, or page of interest. SQL Server indexes serve the same function as a table of contents in a book. Indexes enable SQL Server to locate and retrieve as fast as possible the data requested in a query.

Consider a 500-page book with dozens of sections and chapters and no table of contents. To locate a section of a book, readers would need to flip and read through every page until they located the section of interest. Imagine if you have to do this for multiple sections of the book. It would be a time-consuming task.

This analogy also applies to SQL Server database tables. Without proper indexes, SQL Server must scan through all the data pages that contain the data in a table. For tables with large amounts of data, this becomes time-consuming and resource-intensive. This is the reason why indexes are so important.

Indexes can be classified in several ways, depending on the way they store data, their internal structure, their purpose, and the way they are defined. The following sections briefly describe these various types of indexes.

Row-Based (Rowstore) Indexes

A *row-based (or rowstore) index* is a traditional index in which data is stored as rows in data pages. These indexes include clustered indexes and nonclustered indexes.

Clustered Indexes

Clustered indexes store and sort the table's leaf-level data based on the key column(s). The actual storage pages are linked together so that you can sequentially read the tables in the clustered key order with minimal I/O. There can only be one clustered index per table, because data can be sorted in only one order, and the clustered index represents the actual table data.

Having the actual data clustered can help performance in sequential reads. A single page of data will contain (hopefully) several to many rows of actual data that are all sorted together.

The clustered key fields are carried in all non-clustered indexes for a reference back to the leaf-level row. This can impact the size of non-clustered indexes if a large clustered index key is selected.

A clustered index is created by default when a table definition includes a primary key constraint. A good clustered index has some of the same properties of a good primary key—the fields don't change, and they are always increasing. This type of clustered index key can help reduce page splitting when new records are added.

Nonclustered Indexes

Nonclustered indexes contain index key values and row locators that point to the actual data row. If there is no clustered index, the row locator is a RowID pointer to the actual data row. When a clustered index is present, the row locator is the clustered index key values for the row.

Nonclustered indexes can be optimized to satisfy more queries, improve query response times, and reduce index size. Following are the two most important of these optimized nonclustered indexes.

Covering Indexes

Covering indexes are indexes that can satisfy (cover) all of the field requirements for a specific query. A non-clustered index can contain nonkey columns in the leaf level to help cover a query by using the INCLUDE phrase in the CREATE INDEX statement. These types of indexes improve query performance and reduce I/O operations because the columns necessary to satisfy a query are included in the index itself either as key or nonkey columns, eliminating the need to read the actual data rows.

The INCLUDE phrase also makes non-clustered indexes more flexible, because fields included in the key can have data types not normally allowed in a key, and they are not counted when calculating the index size or number of key columns.

Filtered Indexes

Filtered indexes use a WHERE clause to indicate which rows are to be indexed. Because you index only a portion of rows in a table, you can create a smaller set of data that will be stored in the index. Filtered indexes are always non-clustered indexes, because they select a subset of the total records set, which is represented in a clustered index on the table. And a filtered index will be selected in a query plan if the WHERE clause of the query can be satisfied with rows from the WHERE clause in the filtered index.

Why would you need a nonclustered index that references a subset of data in a table? A well-designed filtered index can speed up table reads for selected groups of rows because there are fewer index pages to read. For example, if you have a large table, a full table index will also be large. If that table has a smaller, well-defined group of rows that are accessed heavily, a filtered index that selects only those heavily accessed rows will help those types of queries run faster because there will be fewer index pages to read (shallow index depth, and fewer rows in the index). In addition, statistics on a filtered index will be more reliable because they will analyze a smaller set of data, and be more likely to represent the distribution of values in the smaller set of rows. Having better statistics and a smaller data set will almost always result in a more efficient query plan and faster performance.

In addition, there are some administrative benefits to a smaller index size. The index can be rebuilt quicker, statistics will be built faster and more accurately, and it will take up less space.

Column-Based Indexes

Column-based indexes are indexes that are created on single columns. The two main types of column-based indexes are columnstore indexes (first delivered in SQL Server 2012), and XML indexes, which provide indexes to values in an XML Column.

Columstore Indexes

Columstore indexes were first introduced in SQL Server 2012. With these column-based indexes, an index of row values is created for each column, then all of the indexes are joined together to represent the base data storage for the table. These indexes are based on the Vertipaq engine implementation, which is capable of high compression ratios, and handles large data sets. In SQL Server 2012, these indexes were not updatable—to add values to the index, you had to rebuild it.

A non-clustered columnstore index has the following limitations:

➤ Can index a subset of the columns on the table (clustered or heap).

➤ Can only be updated by rebuilding the index.

➤ Can be combined with other indexes on the table.

➤ Needs extra space to store a copy of the columns in the index separate from the row values.

In SQL Server 2014, a clustered columnstore index is updatable with some limitations:

➤ The clustered columnstore index cannot have any non-clustered indexes, it is the only index on the table.

➤ A table stored as a clustered columnstore index cannot be used in replication.

➤ A table stored as a clustered columnstore index cannot have change data capture is a SQL Server feature.

➤ A table stored as a clustered columnstore index cannot have any FILESTREAM columns associated with it.

➤ Clustered columnstore indexed tables are only available in Enterprise, Developer, or Evaluation editions of SQL Server 2014.

➤ A primary key cannot be created on a columnstore clustered index, and no referential integrity constraints can be created.

SQL Server also offers an additional compression option for columnstore indexes (COLUMSTORE_ ARCHIVE) that provides an additional level of compression. This feature is applicable to both clustered and nonclustered columnstore indexes. This further compresses the index or partitioned index to a smaller size. This is very useful when the data must be stored in the smallest amount of space, and you can afford the extra CPU overhead for decompression.

A clustered columnstore index contains all of the fields in the table but a unique key is not required. There is no concept of a "key" column because all columns are indexed in the columnstore without a key to the row. Once a clustered columnstore index is created, standard T-SQL statements for loading data can be used to load the table, including bulk loading. No other indexes can be created on the data. Data that is modified or deleted is marked for deletion, and space is reclaimed when the index is rebuilt.

If the table is a rowstore-style table (that is, traditional storage), a nonclustered columnstore index can be created using a subset of the columns in the table. A rowstore table can have both nonclustered columnstore indexes and other indexes, but the columnstore indexes are not updatable and can have changes applied only by rebuilding the index. Nonclustered columnstore indexes also cannot be used as primary or foreign key indexes, cannot be defined as "unique," cannot include SPARSE or FILESTREAM columns, and do not store statistics.

Columnstore indexes were designed for use in data warehouse applications as opposed to OLTP applications, where tables are traditionally not updated (often), will require referential integrity, and are often partitioned. It is possible for some queries to have worse performance with columnstore indexes. A good performance tip is to re-create the columnstore indexes on partitions that have been recently updated, rather than the entire table, to improve availability and limit issues and problems.

Tables can be converted between columnstore and rowstore storage formats by dropping and re-creating the indexes. A columnstore table will be converted to a heap table by dropping the columnstore index. A rowstore clustered index can then be created if required. A rowstore table can be converted to a columnstore table by dropping all of the indexes, then adding the clustered columnstore index.

Memory Optimized Indexes

In SQL 2014, new indexes have been created to support *memory-optimized tables*. A *hash index* is in-memory, used to access data in the memory-optimized (Hekaton) tables. The amount of memory required is related to the bucket-count used by the hash index.

A memory-optimized non-clustered index sorts data that will be accessed from a memory-optimized table. These indexes can only be created with CREATE TABLE and CREATE INDEX statements, and are created for range-ordered scans (reading large volumes of data in sorted order). These indexes are created when the in-memory table is loaded into memory, and are not persisted in the physical table.

Other Index Types

There are a few other types of indexes in SQL Server that support very specific development topics. This section reviews the basics of some of these types, but for more detailed information on any of these index topics, review information in Microsoft Books Online Indexing sections.

XML Indexes

XML indexes are a special type of index that indexes values stored in an XML column. These indexes shred an XML column and store the details for faster retrieval in a SQL query. XML columns can be very large, and shredding the XML data into readable data elements at run time can slow down large XML queries. By using XML indexes, this shredding is persisted ahead of time, and is faster to read at run time.

There are two types of XML index—a Primary and Secondary index. The first index created on an XML column must be a *Primary index*. A Primary index indexes all tags, values, and paths within the XML column. For each XML object, the index creates a row of data for each shredded element of the blob. The number of rows created will be approximately the same as the number of nodes within the XML object. Each row created will store the tag name, node value, node type, document order information, the path, and the primary key (or RowID) for the base table.

A *Secondary index* can be created on the XML columns that will provide additional indexing for PATH, VALUE, and PROPERTY values in the primary index.

Full-Text Index

Full-text indexes are created to support the Full-Text Search feature in SQL Server. This allows users and applications to query character-based data in SQL Server tables. A Full-Text index must be created on a table before it can be included in a Full-Text search.

Columns that are defined as char, varchar, nchar, nvarchar, text, ntext, image, xml, or varbinary(max), and FILESTREAM can be indexed for a Full-Text search. A Full-Text search can perform a linguistic search on words and phrases stored in these columns. Each full-text index indexes one or more columns within a table, and each column can be defined to use a different language in the search.

Full-Text searching is an optional feature of SQL Server that must be turned on before using. The Full-Text searches perform linguistic searches of words and phrases based on rules for the languages defined in the columns to do basic matching. Full-text indexes help speed up these searches.

Spatial Indexes

A *spatial index* indexes columns of spatial data, which contains values of type GEOMETRY or GEOGRAPHY. These indexes support operations that act on spatial data, such as the built-in geography methods (STContains(), STDistaince(), STEquals(), STIntersects, and so on). In order for the query to be selected by the optimizer, the methods must be used in the JOIN or WHERE clause of a query.

How Indexes Are Used by SQL Server

A good understanding of how indexes are used by SQL Server is also important in a good index design. In SQL Server, the Query Optimizer component determines the most cost-effective option to execute a query. The Query Optimizer evaluates a number of query execution plans, and selects the execution plan with the lowest cost. Chapter 13, "Performance Tuning T-SQL," explains how indexes are used in query execution and performance tuning.

Creating Indexes

At this point you should be familiar with the different types of indexes and how they are used in execution plans. This understanding is crucial for you to design and fine-tune indexes to improve query performance.

Indexes are created manually by using T-SQL commands, or by using a graphical user interface (GUI) such as SQL Server Management Studio. Introduced in SQL Server 2005, the Database Engine Tuning Advisor (DTA) tool suggests and generates missing indexes for you. This tool is discussed later in this chapter.

An index key can be made up of one or more fields in the table. As mentioned, indexes can be created as clustered or non-clustered indexes. The leaf level of the clustered index contains the actual data pages containing all of the columns for each row of data, but the leaf-level data on a non-clustered index contains only the fields specified in the index and any INCLUDE columns defined. The CREATE INDEX statement by default will create a non-clustered index.

Indexes can be defined as unique, or can contain duplicates. Defining a unique index means that no two rows can contain the same set of values as described in the index key. Multiple fields can be used to define uniqueness, and individual values can be NULL, but multiple rows with the same NULL values in a key will be considered duplicate. A Primary Key constraint will create a unique index that does not allow NULL values. A Unique constraint will also create a unique non-clustered index. Each table can have up to 999 nonclustered indexes, including indexes created by constraints.

Indexes can be enabled or disabled. When an index is enabled, users have access to it. Disabling an index makes it unavailable to users, so if a clustered index is disabled, the underlying table becomes unavailable to the users. Disabled indexes are unavailable to the users until the indexes are rebuilt.

To create an index using T-SQL commands, perform the following steps:

1. Open SQL Server Management Studio and connect to the SQL Server instance.

2. Make sure you have a copy of the AdventureWorks database installed from http://msftdbprodsamples.codeplex.com/. This database comes in several versions, so if your version does not match the example, correct the syntax below to work with your AdventureWorks installation.

3. Open a new query window and follow one of the sample syntaxes provided in the following list:

   First make a copy of one of the tables. In this example, you will make a copy of the HumanResources.Employee table using the following script that will eliminate fields not needed for these examples:

```
SELECT BusinessEntityID, NationalIDNumber,

    LoginID, OrganizationLevel,
     JobTitle, BirthDate, MaritalStatus,

    Gender, HireDate, SalariedFlag,

    VacationHours, SickLeaveHours,
```

```
        CurrentFlag, rowguid, ModifiedDate
INTO HumanResources.EmployeeNew
FROM HumanResources.Employee
```

➤ To create a clustered index on the table you just created, use the CREATE CLUSTERED INDEX T-SQL command, as shown here:

```
CREATE CLUSTERED INDEX cix_BusinessEntityID
ON HumanResources.EmployeeNew(BusinessEntityID)
```

➤ To create a nonclustered index, use the CREATE NONCLUSTERED INDEX T-SQL command. NONCLUSTERED is the default index type and can be omitted,

```
CREATE NONCLUSTERED INDEX idx_BirthDate
ON HumanResources.EmployeeNew (BirthDate)
```

or:

```
CREATE INDEX idx_BirthDate
ON HumanResources.EmployeeNew (BirthDate)
```

➤ To create a covering index, use the CREATE NONCLUSTERED INDEX T-SQL command along with the INCLUDE keyword, as shown here:

```
CREATE NONCLUSTERED INDEX cidx_HireDate
ON HumanResources.EmployeeNew (HireDate)
INCLUDE (MaritalStatus, Gender, JobTitle)
```

➤ To create a filtered index, use the CREATE NONCLUSTERED INDEX T-SQL command, along with the WHERE keyword, as shown here:

```
CREATE NONCLUSTERED INDEX idx_GenderFemale
ON HumanResources.EmployeeNew (Gender)
WHERE Gender = 'Female'
```

➤ To create a clustered columnstore index, first you should drop all of the other indexes on the table. Then use the CREATE COLUMNSTORE INDEX T-SQL command as follows:

```
CREATE CLUSTERED COLUMNSTORE INDEX idx_EmployeeNew ON HumanResources.
EmployeeNew;
```

➤ Convert that clustered columnstore index back to a Rowstore table by dropping the clustered index:

```
DROP INDEX idx_EmployeeNew on HumanResources.EmployeeNew;
```

➤ To create a nonclustered columnstore index, use the CREATE COLUMNSTORE INDEX T-SQL command, as shown here:

```
CREATE NONCLUSTERED COLUMNSTORE INDEX idx_EmployeeNew
ON HumanResources.Employee (FirstName, LastName, MaritalStatus, Gender);
```

Using Partitioned Tables and Indexes

In Chapter 11, you learned about partitioning tables to help optimize your system. Partitioned tables are a way to spread a single table over multiple units, and having the option of placing each unit on a separate filegroup. When used appropriately, partitions and indexes help manage large volumes of data and return information to the queries faster.

Partitions are created to help divide tables into smaller units and give the SQL Query Engine better techniques for optimizing the queries, including parallelism and partition elimination. Chapter 11 and Chapter 13 both discuss how the query engine uses partitions to help optimizations. Indexing along with partitioning helps the engine further by adding a level of data access to help identify and locate the rows required to satisfy a query.

Each partition has not only the key fields for the clustered index, but also the partition key in each row. Rows within a partition are physically located together based on the partition key. Indexes built on partitioned tables can be partitioned with the same partition function/scheme as the partitioned table, or they can have their own partition function and scheme, or they can be non-partitioned. When a non-clustered index is partitioned with the same partition key as the underlying base table (the clustered index key), this is referred to as a *partition-aligned index*. Partition-aligned indexes must be in place for the "sliding window" partition application. By aligning partitions to the underlying clustered index, individual partitions along with their indexes can be swapped in and out, and can be maintained individually.

However, you may find out that adding other non-partition-aligned indexes can help performance. If the partition key is not in many of the queries, some query performance may actually suffer. In this case, creating non-clustered non-partitioned aligned indexes should restore query performance. If you need to add non-partitioned-aligned indexes, and you also need to have partition swapping scenarios, then you will need to drop the non-partition-aligned indexes prior to partition swapping, and then rebuild those indexes after the swapping is done.

The partition key is not required to be a part of the index key, except when the index is unique.

INDEX MAINTENANCE

A very important task of the Production DBA is to monitor existing index health, and identify where new indexes are needed. Every time data is inserted, updated, or deleted in SQL Server tables, indexes are accordingly updated. As indexes are updated, data on leaf-level pages is moved around to support the sort order of the index, which can cause index fragmentation.

In a rowstore index, rows that are deleted or modified can reuse empty space, but page splits can lead to fragmentation. With columnstore indexes, it is important to regularly rebuild indexes to reclaim space from deletes and updates, as well as update any nonclustered columnstore indexes.

Over time, the distribution of data in data pages can become unbalanced. Some data pages become loosely filled, whereas others are filled to the maximum. Too many loosely filled data pages create performance issues because more data pages must be read to retrieve the requested data.

On the other hand, pages filled close to their maximum may create page splits when new data is inserted or updated. When page splits occur, about half of the data is moved to a newly created data page. This constant reorganization consumes resources and creates data page fragmentation.

The goal is to store as much data into the smallest number of data pages with room for growth to prevent excessive page splits. You can achieve this delicate balance by fine-tuning the index fill factor.

> **NOTE** *For more information on fine-tuning the index fill factor, refer to Books Online at* `http://msdn.microsoft.com/en-us/library/ ms177459(v=SQL.110).aspx.`

Monitoring Index Fragmentation

You can monitor index fragmentation (including columnstore indexes) through the provided Data Management Views (DMVs) available in SQL Server 2014. One of the most useful DMVs is sys .dm_db_index_physical_stats, which provides average fragmentation information for each index.

For example, you can query the sys.dm_db_index_physical_stats DMV as follows:

```
SELECT index_id,avg_fragmentation_in_percent
FROM sys.dm_db_index_physical_stats
(
DB_ID('AdventureWorks'),
OBJECT_ID('AdventureWorks'),
NULL, NULL, 'DETAILED'
) ORDER BY avg_fragmentation_in_percent desc
```

Figure 14-1 shows the results of this query.

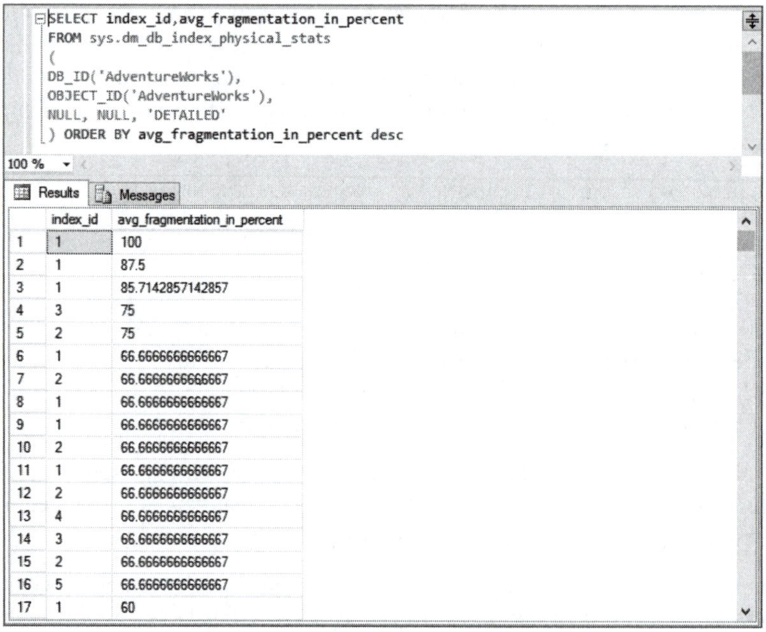

FIGURE 14-1

From execution results of this DMV, you can observe indexes with high fragmentation. Indexes with high defragmentation percentages must be defragmented to avoid performance issues. Heavily fragmented indexes are stored and accessed inefficiently by SQL Server depending on the type of fragmentation, (internal or external). *External fragmentation* means that data pages are not stored in logical order. *Internal fragmentation* means that pages store much less data than they can hold. Both types of fragmentation cause query execution to take longer. Further DMV queries can identify the specific indexes that need defragmenting.

A new feature in SQL 2014 enables you to clean up and defragment individual partitions within a partitioned index, which helps DBAs with minimal impact, and limits downtime for maintenance activities.

Cleaning Up Indexes

Index cleanup should always be part of all database maintenance operations. You must perform these index cleanup tasks on a regular basis, depending on how fragmented indexes become because of changes to the data. If your indexes become highly fragmented, you can defragment them by reorganizing or rebuilding the indexes.

➤ The reorganization of an index does the following:

   ➤ Reorders and compacts leaf-level pages

   ➤ Performs index reordering online, with no long-term locks

   ➤ Is good for indexes with low fragmentation percentages

➤ The rebuilding of an index does the following:

   ➤ Re-creates a new index, then drops the original index

   ➤ Reclaims disk space

   ➤ Reorders and compacts rows in contiguous pages

   ➤ Provides an online index rebuild option in Enterprise Edition

   ➤ Is better for highly fragmented indexes

Table 14-2 shows the general syntax that would be used for index operations on a table called `DimCustomer`.

TABLE 14-2: Index/Operations Syntax for DimCustomer Table

OPERATION	SYNTAX
Create index	`CREATE INDEX IX_DimCustomer_CustomerAlternateKey ON DimCustomer (CustomerAlternateKey)`
Reorganize index	`ALTER INDEX IX_DimCustomer_CustomerAlternateKey ON DimCustomer REORGANIZE`
Reorganize index on a single partition	`ALTER INDEX IX_DimCustomer_CustomerAlternateKey ON DimCustomer REORGANIZE PARTITION = 1`
Reorganize index on all partitions	`ALTER INDEX IX_DimCustomer_CustomerAlternateKey ON DimCustomer REORGANIZE PARTITION = ALL`
Rebuild index	`ALTER INDEX IX_DimCustomer_CustomerAlternateKey ON DimCustomer REBUILD`
Rebuild index on a single partition	`ALTER INDEX IX_DimCustomer_CustomerAlternateKey ON DimCustomer REBUILD PARTITION = 1`
Rebuild index on all partitions	`ALTER INDEX IX_DimCustomer_CustomerAlternateKey ON DimCustomer REBUILD PARTITION = ALL`
Drop index	`DROP INDEX IX_DimCustomer_CustomerAlternateKey ON DimCustomer`

Indexes may become heavily fragmented over time. Deciding whether to reorganize or rebuild indexes depends in part on their level of fragmentation, and your maintenance window. Generally accepted fragmentation thresholds to perform an index rebuild range between 20 percent and 30 percent. If your index fragmentation level is below this threshold, performing a reorganize index operation may be good enough.

But, why not just rebuild indexes every time? You can, if your maintenance window enables you to do so. Keep in mind that index rebuild operations take longer to complete, time during which locks are placed and all inserts, updates, and deletions have to wait. If you are running SQL Server 2005 or higher Enterprise Edition, you can take advantage of online index rebuild operations. Unlike standard rebuild operations, online index operations allow for inserts, updates, and deletions during the time the index is being rebuilt. And with SQL Server 2014 Single Partition Index Rebuild/Reorganize, you are able to spread out your cleanup for a table over the span of multiple days, thus limiting your maintenance activities even more.

IMPROVING QUERY PERFORMANCE WITH INDEXES

SQL Server 2014 includes several DMVs that enable you to fine-tune queries. DMVs are useful to surface execution statistics for a particular query (such as the number of times it has been executed, number of reads and writes performed, amount of CPU time consumed, index query usage statistics, and so on).

For example, you can use the execution statistics obtained through DMVs to fine-tune a query by refactoring the T-SQL code to take advantage of parallelism and existing indexes. You can also use DMVs to identify missing indexes, indexes not utilized, and, as mentioned earlier, identify indexes that require defragmentation.

For example, explore the existing indexes in the `FactInternetSales` table from the `AdventureWorksDW` database. As shown in Figure 14-2, the `FactInternetSales` table has been indexed fairly well.

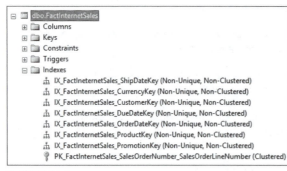

FIGURE 14-2

To illustrate the query-tuning process, follow these steps to generate execution statistics that can surface through DMVs:

1. Drop the existing `ProductKey` and `OrderDateKey` indexes from the `FactInternetSales` table as follows:

```
USE [AdventureWorksDW]
GO
-- Drop ProductKey index
IF  EXISTS (SELECT * FROM sys.indexes
WHERE object_id = OBJECT_ID(N'[dbo].[FactInternetSales]') AND
name = N'IX_FactInternetSales_ProductKey')
DROP INDEX [IX_FactInternetSales_ProductKey] ON [dbo].[FactInternetSales]
GO
-- Drop OrderDateKeyIndex
IF  EXISTS (SELECT * FROM sys.indexes WHERE object_id =
    OBJECT_ID(N'[dbo].[FactInternetSales]')
AND name = N'IX_FactInternetSales_OrderDateKey')
DROP INDEX [IX_FactInternetSales_OrderDateKey] ON [dbo].[FactInternetSales]
  GO
```

2. Execute the following script three times:

```
/*** Internet_ResellerProductSales ***/
SELECT
 D.[ProductKey],
 D.EnglishProductName,
 Color,
 Size,
 Style,
ProductAlternateKey,
 sum(FI.[OrderQuantity]) InternetOrderQuantity,
 sum(FR.[OrderQuantity]) ResellerOrderQuantity,
 sum(FI.[SalesAmount]) InternetSalesAmount,
 sum(FR.[SalesAmount]) ResellerSalesAmount
FROM [FactInternetSales] FI
 INNER JOIN DimProduct D
  ON FI.ProductKey = D.ProductKey
 INNER JOIN FactResellerSales FR
  ON FR.ProductKey = D.ProductKey
GROUP BY
 D.[ProductKey],
 D.EnglishProductName,
 Color,
 Size,
 Style,
 ProductAlternateKey
```

Figure 14-3 shows the T-SQL script executed, along with results. Your execution results may vary depending on the resources available to your machine.

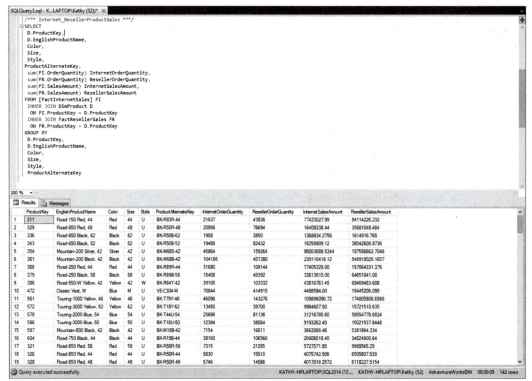

FIGURE 14-3

3.   Run the following script to analyze the execution statistics of the previous query:

```
SELECT TOP 10
  SUBSTRING(qt.TEXT, (qs.statement_start_offset/2)+1,
  ((CASE qs.statement_end_offset WHEN -1 THEN DATALENGTH(qt.TEXT)
  ELSE qs.statement_end_offset
  END - qs.statement_start_offset)/2)+1) QueryText,
  qs.last_execution_time,
  qs.execution_count ,
  qs.last_logical_reads,
  qs.last_logical_writes,
  qs.last_worker_time,
  qs.total_logical_reads,
  qs.total_logical_writes,
  qs.total_worker_time,
  qs.last_elapsed_time/1000000 last_elapsed_time_in_S,
  qs.total_elapsed_time/1000000 total_elapsed_time_in_S,
  qp.query_plan
FROM
  sys.dm_exec_query_stats qs
  CROSS APPLY sys.dm_exec_sql_text(qs.sql_handle) qt
  CROSS APPLY sys.dm_exec_query_plan(qs.plan_handle) qp
ORDER BY
```

```
        qs.last_execution_time DESC,
        qs.total_logical_reads DESC
```

Figure 14-4 shows the execution statistics reported mainly by the `sys.dm_exec_query_stats` DMV.

FIGURE 14-4

From this DMV you can observe that there was a large number of reads and a long period of time during which the processor was busy executing the query. Keep these baseline numbers in mind. At the end of this example, you can reduce these numbers.

4. Query the `sys.dm_db_missing_index_details` DMV to check if missing indexes are reported:

```
SELECT * FROM sys.dm_db_missing_index_details
```

Figure 14-5 shows the results of the `sys.dm_db_missing_index_details` DMV. The sys `.dm_db_missing_index_details` DMV is a great way to quickly identify if you need indexes.

The Database Engine Tuning Advisor (DTA) is another way to identify missing indexes, and has a wizard to help walk you through the process of identifying missing indexes. The DTA can be executed from the Tools menu of SQL Server Management Studio.

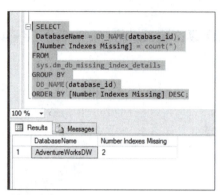

```
SELECT
    DatabaseName = DB_NAME(database_id),
    [Number Indexes Missing] = count(*)
FROM
    sys.dm_db_missing_index_details
GROUP BY
    DB_NAME(database_id)
ORDER BY [Number Indexes Missing] DESC;
```

100 %

Results   Messages

	DatabaseName	Number Indexes Missing
1	AdventureWorksDW	2

FIGURE 14-5

> **NOTE** *You could also try to identify which indexes are needed by analyzing the query text captured by the* `sys.dm_exec_sql_text` *(refer to Figure 14-5).*

5. Continuing with your query-tuning endeavor, create the `ProductKey` and `OrderDateKey` indexes on the `FactInternetSales` table as follows:

```
USE [AdventureWorksDW]
GO
IF  EXISTS
  (SELECT * FROM sys.indexes
   WHERE object_id = OBJECT_ID(N'FactInternetSales')
   AND name = N'IX_FactInternetSales_OrderDateKey')
   DROP INDEX IX_FactInternetSales_OrderDateKey ON
   FactInternetSales
GO
IF NOT EXISTS
  (SELECT * FROM sys.indexes
   WHERE object_id = OBJECT_ID(N'[dbo].[FactInternetSales]') AND
   name = N'IX_FactInternetSales_ProductKey')

   CREATE NONCLUSTERED INDEX IX_FactInternetSales_ProductKey ON
   FactInternetSales
  (ProductKey ASC)
   WITH
   (PAD_INDEX = OFF,
    STATISTICS_NORECOMPUTE = OFF,
    SORT_IN_TEMPDB =  OFF,
    DROP_EXISTING = OFF,
    ONLINE = OFF,
    ALLOW_ROW_LOCKS = ON,
```

```
      ALLOW_PAGE_LOCKS = ON
   ) ON [PRIMARY]
GO
```

6. Execute the `Internet_ResellerProductSales` query defined in step 2 three more times. Figure 14-6 shows that the number of reads for this query improved substantially, which will improve the overall execution time for the query.

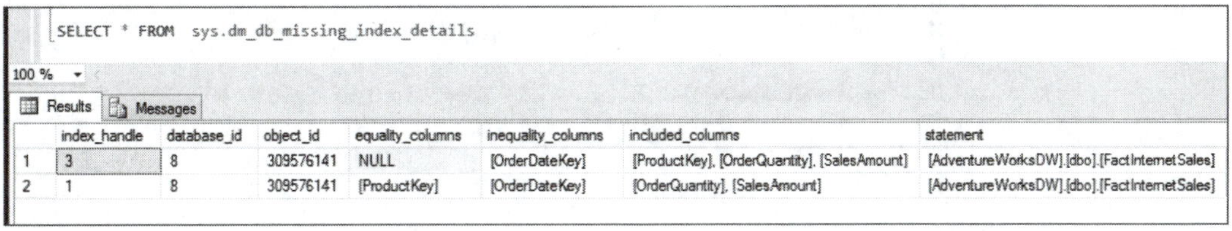

	index_handle	database_id	object_id	equality_columns	inequality_columns	included_columns	statement
1	3	8	309576141	NULL	[OrderDateKey]	[ProductKey], [OrderQuantity], [SalesAmount]	[AdventureWorksDW].[dbo].[FactInternetSales]
2	1	8	309576141	[ProductKey]	[OrderDateKey]	[OrderQuantity], [SalesAmount]	[AdventureWorksDW].[dbo].[FactInternetSales]

`SELECT * FROM sys.dm_db_missing_index_details`

FIGURE 14-6

DATABASE TUNING ADVISOR

One of the more useful tools available for DBAs since SQL Server 2005 is the Microsoft Database Engine Tuning Advisor (DTA). As you learned earlier in this chapter, the DTA enables you to analyze a database for missing indexes and other performance-tuning recommendations such as partitions and indexed views. The DTA accepts the following types of workloads:

➤ SQL script files (`*.sql`)

➤ Trace files (`*.trc`)

➤ XML files (`*.xml`)

➤ Trace table

➤ Plan cache

Figure 14-7 shows the DTA's workload selection screen, including the Plan Cache option. One of the great benefits of the DTA to DBAs and SQL Server developers is the capability to rapidly generate database performance improvement recommendations without knowing the underlying database schema, data structure, usage patterns, or even the inner workings of the SQL Server Query Optimizer.

In addition, starting in SQL Server 2012, the plan cache can also be used as part of a DTA workload. This new workload option eliminates the need to manually generate a workload for analysis (such as trace files).

The Cost of Too Many Indexes

The saying, "Too much of a good thing is not always good" holds true when discussing indexes. Too many indexes create additional overhead associated with the extra amount of data pages that the Query Optimizer must go through. Also, too many indexes require too much space, and add to the time it takes to accomplish index maintenance.

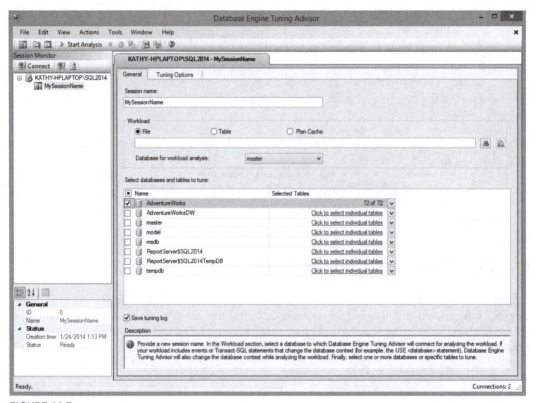

FIGURE 14-7

Still, the DTA typically recommends a large number of indexes, especially when analyzing a workload with many queries. The reason behind this is because queries are analyzed on an individual basis. It is a good practice to incrementally apply indexes as needed, always keeping a baseline to compare if the new index improves query performance.

SQL Server 2014 provides several DMVs to obtain index usage information, including the following:

➤ `sys.dm_db_missing_index_details`—Returns detailed information about a missing index.

➤ `sys.dm_db_missing_index_columns`—Returns information about the table columns that are missing an index.

➤ `sys.dm_db_missing_index_groups`—Returns information about a specific group of missing indexes.

➤ `sys.dm_db_missing_index_group_stats`—Returns summary information about missing index groups.

➤ `sys.dm_db_index_usage_stats`—Returns counts of different types of index operations and the time each type of operation was last performed.

➤ `sys.dm_db_index_operational_stats`—Returns current low-level I/O, locking, latching, and access method activity for each partition of a table or index in the database.

➤ `sys.dm_db_index_physical_stats`—Returns size and fragmentation information for the data and indexes of the specified table or view.

For example, to obtain a list of indexes that have been used and those that have not been used by user queries, query the `sys.dm_db_index_usage_stats` DMV. From the list of indexes that have been used, you can obtain important statistics that help you fine-tune your indexes. Some of this information includes index access patterns such index scans, index seeks, and index bookmark lookups. Remember that rebuilding an index will change the results of the query, so be sure to run the query often.

To obtain a list of indexes that have been used by user queries, execute the following script:

```
SELECT
 SO.name Object_Name,
 SCHEMA_NAME(SO.schema_id) Schema_name,
 SI.name Index_name,
 SI.Type_Desc,
 US.user_seeks,
 US.user_scans,
 US.user_lookups,
 US.user_updates
FROM sys.objects AS SO
 JOIN sys.indexes AS SI
  ON SO.object_id = SI.object_id
 INNER JOIN sys.dm_db_index_usage_stats AS US
  ON SI.object_id = SI.object_id
  AND SI.index_id = SI.index_id
WHERE
 database_id=DB_ID('AdventureWorks')
 AND SO.type = 'u'
 AND SI.type IN (1, 2)
 AND (US.user_seeks > 0 OR US.user_scans > 0 OR US.user_lookups > 0 );
```

To obtain a list of indexes that have not been used by user queries, execute the following script:

```
SELECT
 SO.Name TableName,
 SI.name IndexName,
 SI.Type_Desc IndexType,
 US.user_updates
FROM sys.objects AS SO
 INNER JOIN sys.indexes AS SI
  ON SO.object_id = SI.object_id
 LEFT OUTER JOIN sys.dm_db_index_usage_stats AS US
  ON SI.object_id = US.object_id
  AND SI.index_id = US.index_id
WHERE
 database_id=DB_ID('AdventureWorks')
 AND SO.type = 'u'
 AND SI.type IN (1, 2)
 AND (US.index_id IS NULL)
 OR  (US.user_seeks = 0 AND US.user_scans = 0 AND US.user_lookups = 0 );
```

Indexes that are not used by user queries should be dropped, unless they have been added to support mission-critical work that occurs at specific points in time (such as monthly or quarterly data extracts and reports). Unused indexes add overhead to insert, delete, and update operations, as well as to index maintenance operations.

Index usage statistics are only available as long as the index (or heap) metadata is in the metadata cache. The usage statistics are initialized to empty when the cache object is removed. For example, when the SQL Server service restarts, the database is detached or shut down, or when the AUTO_CLOSE property is turned on.

SUMMARY

In this chapter, you learned about the types of indexes available in SQL Server, including rowstore indexes, columnstore indexes, and some other index types (XML, spatial, and full-text indexes).

Rowstore indexes are combinations of columns that are stored in sorted order that provide a pointer to the leaf-level data for the table. A "covering" index is an index that contains all of the columns required to satisfy the needs of a query.

Columnstore indexes are column-based, nonclustered indexes that store data based on discrete values found in a column. This type of index has greater advantages over regular row-based indexes. These advantages include smaller-sized indexes and faster retrieval of data. In SQL Server 2014, these indexes became updatable, and have a new compression option (COLUMNSTORE_ARCHIVE).

An important part of indexing your database includes optimizing access by creating partitions and indexes, along with advanced indexing techniques such as filtered indexes and covering indexes. Reorganizing and rebuilding indexes is an important maintenance operation to reduce and eliminate index fragmentation.

You can put the finishing touches on your database by tuning a query with indexes, which you can accomplish by utilizing the data from Data Management Views (DMVs). It is also important to remember the benefits of finding indexes that are not used by user queries and removing them.

In Chapter 15, you learn how replication is used to distribute data across locations.

15

Replication

WHAT'S IN THIS CHAPTER?

➤ Understanding the different types of replication

➤ Getting to know replication models

➤ Setting up snapshot replication

➤ Setting up the distributor

➤ Understanding how snapshot differs from transactional and merge replication

➤ Understanding peer-to-peer replication

➤ Monitoring replication

WROX.COM CODE DOWNLOADS FOR THIS CHAPTER

The wrox.com code downloads for this chapter are found at www.wrox.com/go/prosql2014admin on the Download Code tab. The code is in the Chapter 15 download and individually named according to the names throughout the chapter.

Today's enterprise needs to distribute its data across many departments and geographically dispersed offices. SQL Server replication provides ways to distribute data and database objects among its SQL Server databases, databases from other vendors (such as Oracle), as well as mobile devices such as smartphones, tablets, and point-of-sale terminals. Along with log shipping, database mirroring, and clustering, replication provides functionalities that satisfy customers' needs for load balancing, high availability, and scaling.

This chapter introduces you to the concept of replication, explaining how to implement basic snapshot replication, and noting things you should pay attention to when setting up transactional and merge replication.

REPLICATION OVERVIEW

SQL Server replication closely resembles the magazine publishing process, so that analogy is used here to explain its overall architecture. Consider a popular magazine. The starting point is the large pool of journalists writing *articles*. From all of the available articles, the editor picks which ones to include in the current month's magazine. The selected set of articles is then published in a *publication*. After a monthly publication is printed, it is shipped out via various distribution channels to *subscribers* all over the world.

SQL Server replication uses similar terminology. The pool from which a publication is formed can be considered a *database*. Each piece selected for publication is an *article*; it can be a table, a stored procedure, or another database object. Like a magazine publisher, replication also needs a *distributor* to deliver publications, keep track of delivery status, and track a history of synchronization to maintain data consistency.

Depending on the kind of replication model you choose, articles from a publication can either be stored as files in a folder to which both publisher and subscriber(s) have access, or as records in tables in a distribution database synchronously or asynchronously. Regardless of how publications are delivered, replication always needs a distributor database to keep track of delivery status. Depending on the capacity of the publication server, the distributor database can be located on the publisher, the subscriber, or on another server that might be dedicated purely to serving as the distribution database.

Conceptually, however, differences exist between SQL Server replication and a magazine publishing company, with the biggest being the contributor-like role the subscriber can sometimes take on. For example, in some replication models, a subscriber or subscribers can update articles and have them propagated back to the publisher or other subscribers. In the peer-to-peer replication model, each participant of replication acts both as publisher and subscriber so that changes made in different databases replicate back and forth between multiple servers.

Replication Components

Now that you have an idea of how replication works in comparison to magazine publishing, it is time to examine what these terms and functions mean in direct relation to the SQL Server. SQL Server replication is comprised of several key components that are grouped into the following areas:

- ➤ Replication roles
- ➤ Replication data
- ➤ Replication agents
- ➤ Replication internal components (maintenance jobs)

Replication Roles

Following are three key roles in replication:

- ➤ **Publisher**—The publisher is the server (or database instance) that is the source (or master) for the articles being published.

- ➤ **Distributor**—The distributor is the intermediary in the act of publishing and subscribing, and, in some types of replication, is the medium whereby the data gets from the publisher to the subscriber. The distributor stores the data to be replicated from the publisher, and also stores the location of snapshots. The distributor is a database that can live on the publishing server, its own dedicated server, or on the subscriber.

➤ **Subscriber**—The subscriber is the server (or database instance) that is the destination for the articles being published. In some replication models, the subscriber can also be a publisher. The subscriber can republish articles when they must be sent on to another subscriber in the Updating Subscriber model. The subscriber can also republish articles in a peer-to-peer model (explained in the "Replication Types" section later in this chapter).

> **NOTE** *Subscriptions can be set up as either push or pull subscriptions. The difference is where the agent executes. For a push subscription, the agent executes on the publisher, and so when it executes, it pushes changes down to the subscriber. For a pull subscription, the agent runs on the subscriber, and pulls changes down from the publisher.*

Replication Data

Following are three key components to replication data:

➤ **Article**—An article is the smallest set of data that can be configured for replication. It can consist of a table, a view, or a stored procedure, and can have additional restrictions on the rows and columns included in each article.

➤ **Publication**—A publication is a grouping of articles published together. Using a publication enables the replication of logically grouped articles to be managed together, rather than having to manage each article individually.

➤ **Subscription**—A subscription is a request to receive data from one or more publications. It can add additional constraints to the publication regarding how and when the data is distributed.

Replication Agents

Replication agents are executable programs that perform much of the work of replication. They are commonly executed through SQL Server Agent jobs, but can also be run manually. The following SQL Server Agent jobs are created by replication:

➤ **Snapshot agent**—The Snapshot agent is executed by a SQL Agent job that takes and applies a snapshot for the three types of replication: transactional, merge, or snapshot replication. These types are explained in greater detail in the "Replication Types" section later in this chapter. For transactional and merge replication, the snapshot is only needed when replication is being set up, or when an article is added or changed significantly. For snapshot replication, the Snapshot agent is run on every synchronization.

➤ **Log Reader agent**—The Log Reader agent is executed by a SQL Agent job that reads the transaction log on the publisher, and records the transactions for each article being published into the distribution database.

➤ **Distribution agent**—The Distribution agent is executed by a SQL Agent job that reads the transactions written to the distribution database, and applies them to the subscribing databases for transactional replication.

➤ **Merge agent**—The Merge agent is executed by a SQL Agent job that moves changes at the publisher to the subscriber, moves changes from the subscriber to the publisher, and initiates the conflict-resolution process if necessary. It is used during merge replication.

➤ **Queue Reader agent**—The Queue Reader agent is used to read messages stored in a SQL Server queue, or a Microsoft Message Queue. It then applies those messages to the publisher. The Queue Reader agent is used in either snapshot or transactional replication publications, which allow queued updating (see the "Replication Types" section later in this chapter for details on snapshot and transactional replication).

Replication Maintenance Jobs

Replication uses the following additional SQL Agent jobs to perform maintenance:

➤ **Agent History Cleanup**—This job removes replication agent history that is stored in the distribution database. This job is scheduled to run every ten minutes.

➤ **Distribution Cleanup**—This job removes transactions from the distribution database after they are no longer needed. This job is scheduled to run every ten minutes.

➤ **Expired Subscription Cleanup**—This job determines when a snapshot has expired, and removes it. This job is scheduled to run once a day at 1 A.M.

➤ **Reinitialize Failed Subscriptions**—This job looks for subscriptions that have failed, and marks them for reinitialization. This job is not enabled by default, so you can either run it manually when required, or you can create a custom schedule to suit your needs.

➤ **Replication Agent Monitor**—This job monitors the execution of the SQL Agents, and writes to the Windows event log when a job step fails. This job is scheduled to run every ten minutes.

➤ **Replication Agents Checkup**—This job monitors the execution of the replication agents on a distributor. It checks for replication agents that are running, but have not logged any history within the specified heartbeat interval.

Replication Types

SQL Server 2014 provides the following three types of replication:

➤ Snapshot replication

➤ Transactional replication

➤ Merge replication

Peer-to-peer replication and Oracle Publishing replication are variations of these three types of replication, and are also discussed in this section.

Snapshot Replication

As its name implies, snapshot replication takes a snapshot of a publication and makes it available to subscribers. When the snapshot is applied on the subscribing database, the articles at the subscriber (such as tables, views, and stored procedures) are dropped and re-created. Snapshot replication is a one-shot deal; there is no continuous stream of data from the publisher to the subscriber. The data at the publisher at the time the snapshot is taken is applied to the subscriber.

Snapshot replication is best suited for fairly static data, at times when it is acceptable to have copies of data that are out of date between replication intervals, or when article size is small. For example, suppose you have to look up tables that maintain ZIP codes. Those tables can be good snapshot replication candidates in most cases because they are typically static.

> **WARNING** *During the period when a snapshot refresh is being applied, the article is unavailable for use.*

Transactional Replication

Transactional replication replicates changes to an article as they occur. To set up transactional replication, a snapshot of the publication is taken and applied to the subscriber once to create the same set of data. After the snapshot is taken, the Log Reader agent reads all the transactions that occur against the articles being published, and records them in the distribution database. The transactions are then applied to each subscriber according to the subscription's configuration.

Transactional replication enables faster data synchronization with less latency. Depending on how it is set up, this data synchronization can occur in nearly real time, so it is useful for cases in which you want incremental changes to happen quickly on the subscriber.

Merge Replication

Merge replication is usually used whenever there is a slow or intermittent network connection between the publisher and subscriber. It enables sites to work fairly autonomously, and to synchronize the changes to the data when they are next online. It needs a snapshot to initialize the replication, after which subsequent changes are tracked with triggers.

One side effect of merge replication is the possibility of conflicts when offline changes are synchronized in. Merge replication automatically resolves these issues in the Merge agent using the conflict-resolver model chosen when the publication was created. If you don't want to use automatic conflict resolution, you can configure the publication for interactive conflict resolution. When the publication is configured for interactive conflict resolution, each conflict must be resolved manually. You can do this using the Interactive Resolver user interface.

Other "Types" of Replication

The following two options are often considered additional types of replication, but they are not actually separate replication types. Instead, these are just variations of the ones listed previously.

➤ **Peer-to-peer replication**—Peer-to-peer replication is a subtype of transactional replication. In peer-to-peer replication, each publisher owns a subset of the total set of rows in an article. Each peer publishes its own rows, to which each of its peers subscribes, and it subscribes to the other rows from each of its peers. You learn more details about peer-to-peer transactional replication later in this chapter.

➤ **Oracle Publishing**—SQL Server 2000 enabled the capability to subscribe to data published from an Oracle database. Using Oracle Publishing, you can subscribe using either snapshot or transactional replication, but not merge replication.

> **NOTE** *This chapter does not cover programming replication using Replication Management Objects (RMOs). RMO is a managed code-programming model for SQL Server replication. All of the steps and processes discussed in this chapter can be programmed using RMO. For more information on RMO, see the sample applications and code samples from Books Online.*

REPLICATION MODELS

You can set up replication in quite a few different ways. This section covers some of the most common replication topologies. These are the basic building blocks, and from these, considerably more complex topologies can be constructed.

Single Publisher, One or More Subscribers

A Single Publisher model is perhaps the simplest topology to use with a single publishing database that has one or more subscription databases. You might use this topology where you need to keep a hot standby system, or distribute data from a central office to multiple field offices. Figure 15-1 shows the basic structure of this topology with the distributor on the publishing server.

Figure 15-2 shows a more advanced option with a separate server for the distribution database. Use this option when you need more performance at the distributor than you can get from a single server acting as the publisher and distributor.

Figure 15-3 shows the next variant of the Single Publisher model, with multiple subscription databases.

Multiple Publishers, Single Subscriber

A Point of Service (POS) application is a good example of a Multiple Publisher model. A POS application has multiple publishers, but only one subscriber. In a POS, it is often necessary to send data from the many POS terminals in a store to a central system either in the store, or at the head office where the individual transactions can be consolidated. The replication topology to use for this is a Multiple Publisher, Single Subscriber model. Figure 15-4 shows this topology.

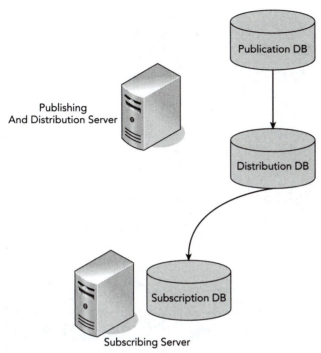

Publishing
And Distribution Server

Publication DB

Distribution DB

Subscription DB

Subscribing Server

FIGURE 15-1

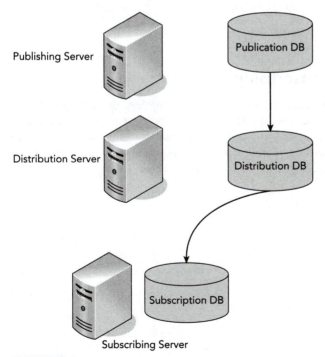

Publishing Server

Distribution Server

Publication DB

Distribution DB

Subscription DB

Subscribing Server

FIGURE 15-2

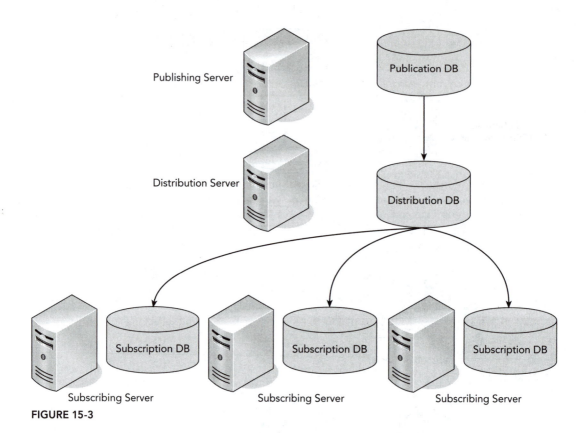

FIGURE 15-3

Multiple Publishers Also Subscribing

A Customer Resource Management (CRM) application is a good example of the Multiple Publishers also Subscribing model. In the CRM application, it might be necessary to have an address book containing all contacts that is updated locally, yet is synchronized across all sites. One way to do this is to have each branch office publish the updates made at that office, and also subscribe to the updates made by all other branch offices. Figure 15-5 shows how to achieve this.

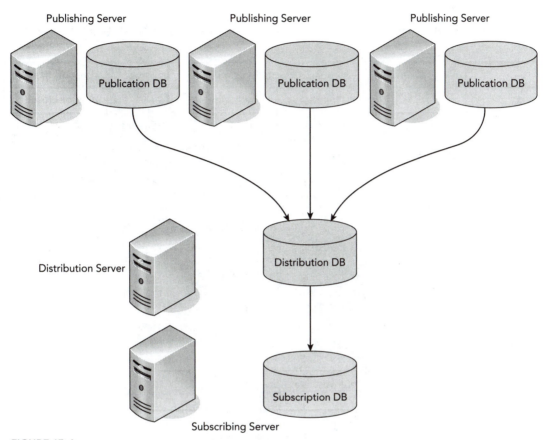

FIGURE 15-4

Updating Subscriber

The CRM application can also be implemented when using an Updating Subscriber model. In this topology, the master copy of the contacts is held at a central location. This would be published to all branch offices. Any changes at the branch offices are then updated back to the publisher using the Updating Subscriber feature built into replication. Figure 15-6 shows the Updating Subscriber topology.

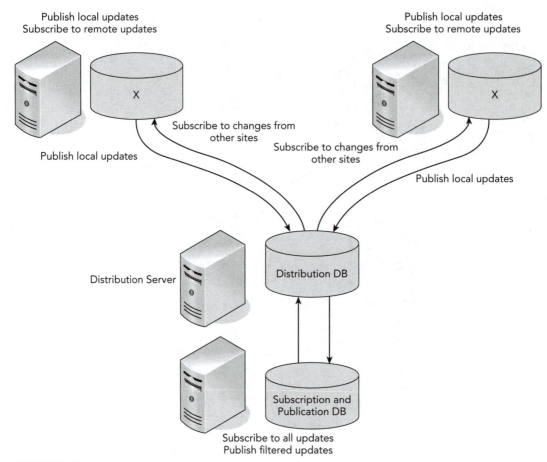

Publish local updates
Subscribe to remote updates

Publish local updates
Subscribe to remote updates

X

X

Subscribe to changes from
other sites

Subscribe to changes from
other sites

Publish local updates

Publish local updates

Distribution Server

Distribution DB

Subscription and
Publication DB

Subscribe to all updates
Publish filtered updates

FIGURE 15-5

Peer-to-Peer

Finally, a peer-to-peer topology is also exemplified by implementing the CRM application. The peer-to-peer model doesn't have the concept of a master copy of the data. Instead, each instance owns its own set of rows, and receives any updates made at the other instances. Figure 15-7 shows a peer-to-peer topology.

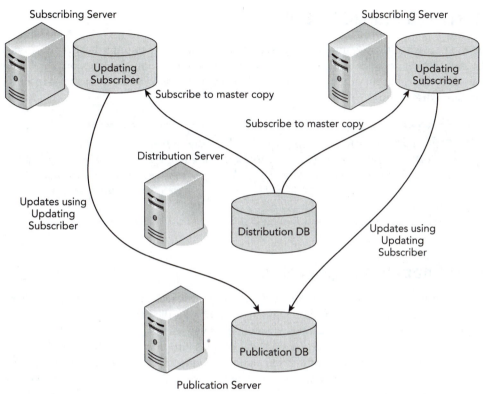

FIGURE 15-6

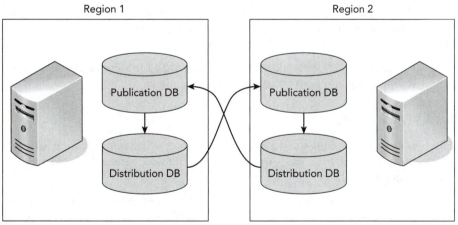

FIGURE 15-7

IMPLEMENTING REPLICATION

Now that you've learned the terminology, types, and models, it is time to implement replication. To start with, this section provides an exercise to set up snapshot replication. Transactional and merge replication are similar, but they each have a few differences that are reviewed after the snapshot replication setup discussion.

> **NOTE** *It's always worth reminding yourself that, after a fresh install of SQL Server, all the external protocols are disabled. To talk to a remote SQL Server, you must run the SQL Server Configuration Manager, enable one of the external protocols (either Named Pipes or TCP-IP), and then remember to restart the SQL Service.*

Setting Up Snapshot Replication

To keep things simple, you only create two new databases in this replication example: a new database called Publisher that is the publisher, and a new database called Subscriber that is the subscriber. For the purposes of this example, you create a sales schema, and, in that schema, you create a single table, Cars. You then insert a small set of rows into that table. The scenario is based on a car company that sells fuel-efficient hybrid cars in the United States, China, and Sweden. You set up snapshot replication between database servers in the United States and China to refresh data. Furthermore, you can set up transactional replication between database servers in the United States and Sweden. The data can also be used to set up merge replication.

Replication can be implemented through both GUI wizard pages and scripting. If you are new to replication, you should first go through the GUI and property pages using SQL Server Management Studio. As you work through the GUI, you are able to generate SQL scripts at the end of processes, which you can save to a file and edit for other deployments.

You must implement a distributor before you can create publications and subscribe to publications, so first create the distributor that you need for all types of replications.

Setting Up Distribution

As mentioned earlier, a distributor consists of a distribution database (where replication history, status, and other important information are stored) and a shared folder (where data and articles can be stored, retrieved, and refreshed).

The distributor database can live on either the Publisher (the default location), or a separate server. For low volumes of transactions, using the Publisher works well. For a higher volume of transactions, using a separate server will give better performance.

To begin setting up distribution, you must find out the domain name and account that will be used during the process to run various replication agents, such as the Snapshot agent, Log Reader agent, and Queue Reader agent. For the purpose of this example, you can just choose to impersonate the SQL Server Agent account, but when you put things into production, a dedicated domain account is recommended for security reasons.

Following is a step-by-step process of how to set up distribution:

1. Using SQL Server Management Studio, connect to the distributor server. Expand the server in Object Explorer.

2. Right-click Replication and select Configure Distribution.

> **WARNING** *If you use a fresh default install of SQL Server 2014, by default, the Agent XPs are disabled. This prevents you from starting the SQL Agent service. If SQL Agent is not running, you see an error when you try to complete step 2. To prevent this error, enable the Agent XPs using the following script, and then start the SQL Agent service, either from SSMS or SQL Server Configuration Manager:*
>
> ```
> sp_configure 'show advanced options', 1;
> GO
> RECONFIGURE;
> GO
> sp_configure 'Agent XPs', 1;
> GO
> RECONFIGURE
> GO
> ```
>
> *After executing this script, the SQL Server Agent node in SSMS will no longer have the "Agent XPs disabled" tag appended.*

3. At the Welcome screen, click Next. You see the Distributor screen, where you pick which server to use as the distributor. This example uses the current machine. For a more complex topology, you can choose a separate server.

4. Click Next. The SQL Server Agent Start page appears. This enables you to configure the SQL Server Agent to start automatically or manually. Select the option to start the agent automatically.

5. Click Next. The Snapshot Folder screen appears. Here you can enter the snapshot folder. If you want to use a pull subscription, the path you enter here should be a network path. This example sets up a local replication topology, so a network path is not necessary.

6. After you pick the snapshot folder, move to the Distribution Database screen shown in Figure 15-8, where you configure the name of the distribution database (distribution, in this example), and the folder locations for the database and log files. Click Next to continue.

7. Next you see the Publishers screen, shown in Figure 15-9, where you set the list of servers that can use this distribution database.

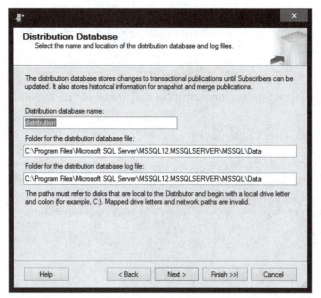

FIGURE 15-8

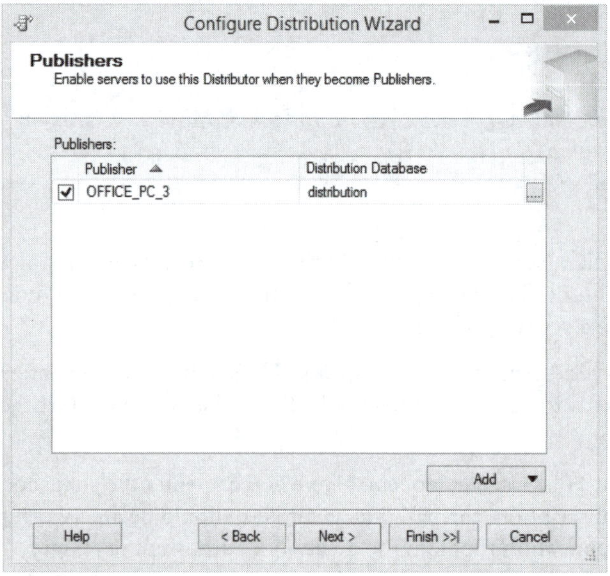

FIGURE 15-9

8. Next, define what the wizard should do from the Wizard Actions screen, shown in Figure 15-10. Choose to either configure the distribution database or create scripts. If you want to create scripts, select both options.

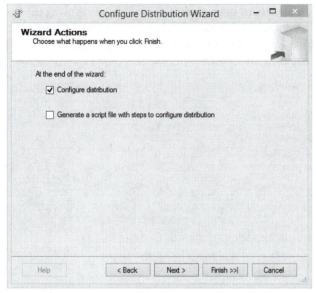

FIGURE 15-10

9. The next page of the wizard displays a list of actions the SQL Server can perform. Confirm that the list of actions is what you expect and click Finish. If it's not correct, go back and fix the incorrect settings. You then see a screen indicating the progress the wizard has made at executing the actions you selected.

10. Figure 15-11 shows the wizard actions completed successfully. If any errors are reported, investigate and resolve each one before attempting to rerun the wizard.

FIGURE 15-11

After executing the wizard you can browse to the new distribution database using the Server Explorer in Management Studio. The new distribution database appears under `System Databases`, as shown in Figure 15-12. Additionally, you can expand the SQL Server Agent in Object Explorer and open the `Jobs` folder, where you see that a number of new jobs were created for the replication, as shown in Figure 15-13.

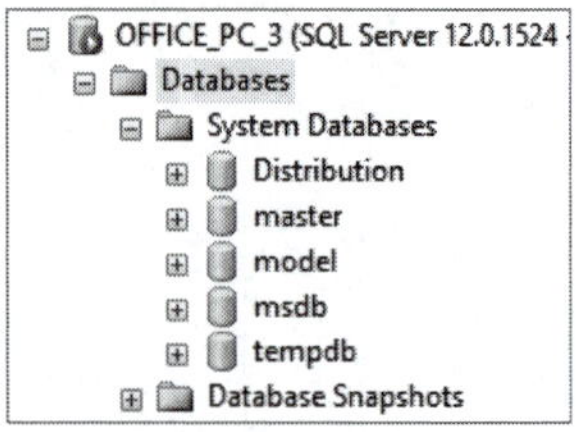

FIGURE 15-12

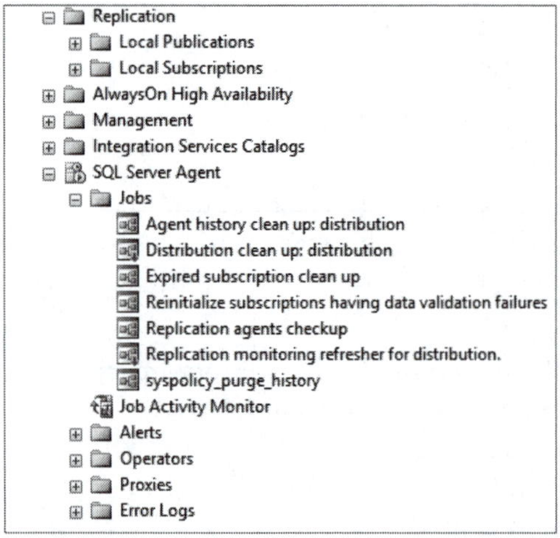

FIGURE 15-13

Implementing Snapshot Replication

Now that you've set up the distributor, you can use that for the replication exercise later in this chapter. Before you set up snapshot replication, though, you must create the databases to use as the publisher and subscriber.

In this example, you create these databases on a single server. You can find a script to create these databases in the code samples, `01 Create Databases.sql`, or you can create them manually using Management Studio. To create them manually, follow these steps:

1. Right-click the `Databases` node and select the New Database option.

2. Make sure the publication database is called `Publisher`, and the subscription database is called `Subscriber`. You can leave all other settings at default for now.

3. After creating the publisher, you also need to create some tables and load some data. To do this, download and run the script in the samples called `02 Create and load sales.sql`.

After you complete these initial steps, you can move on to the steps involved in setting up Snapshot Publication, which is covered in the next section.

Setting Up Snapshot Publication

The best way to set up Snapshot Publication is to use Management Studio and elect to have everything scripted at the end of the process. Follow these steps:

1. Within Management Studio, while connected to the server where the publication database resides, expand the `Replication` folder. Right-click `Local Publications` and select New Publication.

2. You see the Publication Wizard welcome screen; click Next. On the Publication Database screen, pick a database for publication. Select `Publisher` as your database to create a publication, and click Next.

3. Figure 15-14 shows the Publication Type screen where you select the type of replication. In this case, select Snapshot Publication and click Next to continue.

FIGURE 15-14

4. Next is the Articles screen where you select the tables in this article. By default, nothing is selected, so you must expand the `Tables` node and pick the tables you want to publish. Once you expand, select the `Cars` table you created earlier for publication and its children, as shown in Figure 15-15. You can see that the `Cars` table under the Sales schema is selected. In other scenarios, if necessary, you can pick and choose columns of the table for publication by unchecking the box next to the column name.

   You can also set properties of articles that you choose to publish. These properties affect how the article is published and some behaviors when it is synchronized with the subscriber.

Don't change the default properties here; however, they can be useful in other situations. Click Next to continue.

FIGURE 15-15

5. On the Filter Table Rows page, the wizard gives you an option to filter out rows. Click the Add button to display the Add Filter page.

6. As mentioned earlier, because you want to replicate data to the Chinese market, you need to filter the cars by country. To do this, add a WHERE clause to the "filter statement" to match the following SQL text, as shown in Figure 15-16.

```
SELECT <published_columns>
FROM [Sales].[Cars]
WHERE [Country] = 'China'
```

After you click OK, the filter is applied. This returns you to the previous screen, which now has a filter defined, as shown in Figure 15-17. Click Next to continue.

7. Figure 15-18 shows the Snapshot Agent screen, where you define how the snapshot should be created, and when it should be scheduled to run. In this case, don't schedule it or create one immediately. Instead, in the example, you will invoke it manually by running a SQL Server Agent job yourself. Click Next to continue.

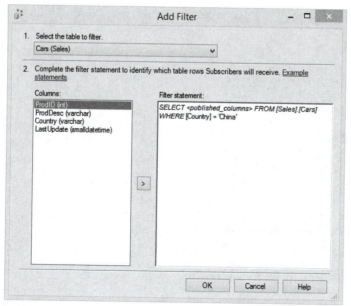

FIGURE 15-16

FIGURE 15-17

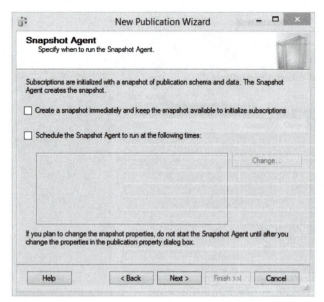

FIGURE 15-18

8. The next screen is the Snapshot Agent Security screen, where you can specify the accounts used to run the Snapshot Agent job and to connect to the publisher. As mentioned earlier, different replication models call for different agents to be run. Click the Security Settings button to configure the accounts needed for your replication model.

It is convenient to have a dedicated domain account with a secure password that doesn't need to be changed often for this purpose. However, if you don't have that access, you can choose to impersonate the SQL Server Agent account, as mentioned previously. Even though you will do so for this exercise, it is a best practice to always use a dedicated account.

If you chose to use a dedicated Windows account, then the account must be a member of the db_owner database role in the distribution database, and have write permissions on the snapshot share.

Enter the account details on the Snapshot Agent Security screen, as shown in Figure 15-19. After the account is set, click OK. On the Agent Security page, click Next.

9. Figure 15-20 shows the Wizard Actions screen, where you can specify whether you want the wizard to create the publication, or script the creation. For now, leave these settings on the default, and just create the publication.

10. The next screen is the wizard action confirmation screen. Here you can assign a name to this publication. Enter the name **Pub_Cars_China** in the Publication Name text box. Review the actions specified here, and if anything is incorrect go back and fix it. When everything is correct, click Finish.

11. The next screen (see Figure 15-21) confirms your actions, which, in this case, are to Create the Publication and then add the articles (of which you have just one). The status should indicate

success, showing that you have now successfully created a new publication. If any errors are reported, investigate and resolve them before attempting to execute the actions again.

FIGURE 15-19

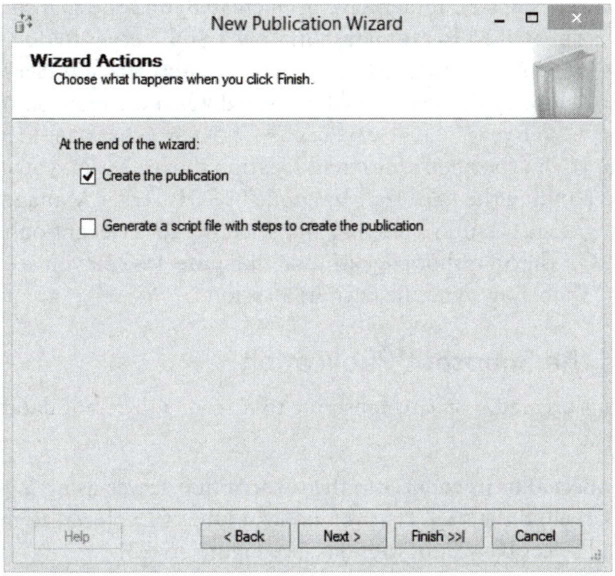

FIGURE 15-20

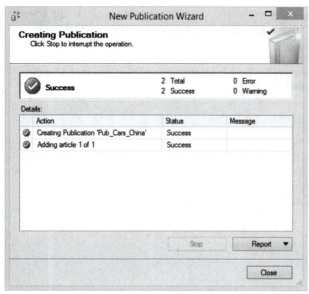

FIGURE 15-21

The rest of the process is quite similar to the distributor creation documented earlier. After you click Finish, the Snapshot Publication is created. Again, you can use Object Explorer to see the publication and SQL Server jobs created during this process.

At this point, no files or folders in the snapshot folder have been created, and the snapshot has not been created because no one is subscribed to the snapshot. To get SQL Server to do anything further, you must subscribe to the new publication. When there is a subscriber, SQL Server creates all the necessary files. You can find these in the shared folder defined when the distributor was set up earlier. The default location is `C:\Program Files\Microsoft SQL Server\MSSQL12` `.MSSQLSERVER\MSSQL\ReplData`. If you specified a different location during setup, you can always retrieve the current location by expanding the `Replication` node in SQL Server Management Studio Object Explorer, expanding `Local Publications`, and selecting the relevant publication. Right-click and select Properties. On the Snapshot page (shown in Figure 15-22), you see a section titled "Location of snapshot files" that shows you the current location.

Setting Up a Subscription to the Snapshot Publication

Now that a Snapshot Publication is created, you can subscribe to it from a different database, or a different server. Follow these steps:

1. If you are not already connected to it, connect to the subscription server using SQL Server Management Studio, and expand the `Replication` node in Object Explorer. Right-click `Local Subscription` and select New Subscriptions (see Figure 15-23).

2. You see the welcome screen of the New Subscription Wizard. Click Next to choose the publication you want to subscribe to.

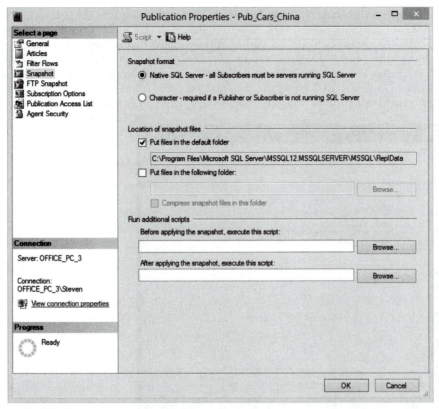

FIGURE 15-22

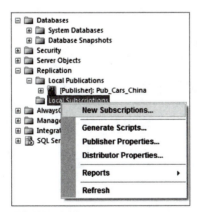

FIGURE 15-23

This example has the publisher and subscriber on the same server, so the page should already be populated with the available publications. In a real scenario in which the publisher and subscribers are on different servers, you must find the publishing server. Do this by selecting "<Find SQL Server Publisher...>" from the drop-down list (see Figure 15-24). You see the typical Connect to Server window that is common in SQL Server Management Studio. To connect to the server where you set up the Snapshot Publication earlier, select the publishing server, and click Connect. You then see the Publication screen, as shown in Figure 15-25. Expand the database (Publisher) and select the publication you just created by the name you gave it: Pub_Cars_China. Click Next to continue.

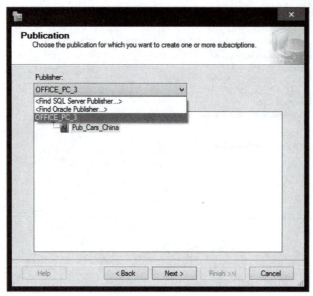

FIGURE 15-24

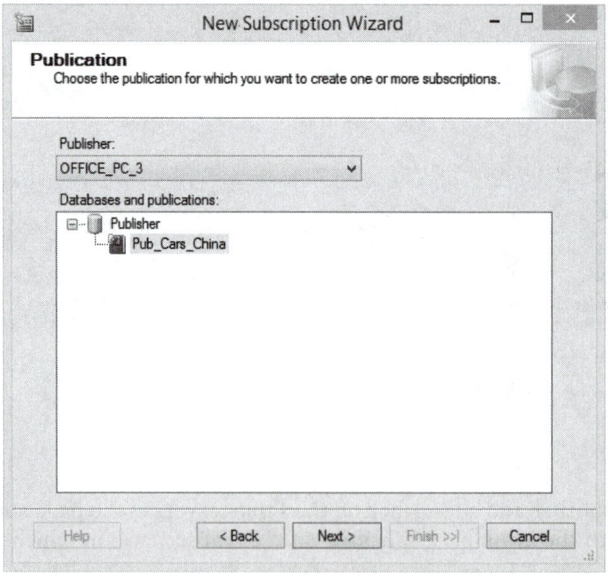

FIGURE 15-25

3.   The next screen is the Distribution Agent Location screen, shown in Figure 15-26. Here, select the location for the distribution agents to execute. This can be either at the distributor for a *push subscription* or at the subscriber for a *pull subscription*. Make your subscription a push subscription by selecting the first option, "Run all agents at the Distributor," and click Next.

FIGURE 15-26

4.   The next screen is the Subscribers screen (shown in Figure 15-27), where you can set the subscriber properties. Select the server where the subscriber will be; in this case, it is the current server. Then select the subscription database. If you want to add additional subscribers, you can do so on this page as well by using the Add Subscriber button. Select Next to move to the next screen.

5.   Figure 15-28 shows the Distribution Agent Security screen, where you see the familiar screen used for setting agent security settings. Click the ellipsis (...) to set up the security options. If you want to specify a different domain account for Distribution Agent Security, fill out the account information here. For this example, select the options shown in Figure 15-29.

FIGURE 15-27

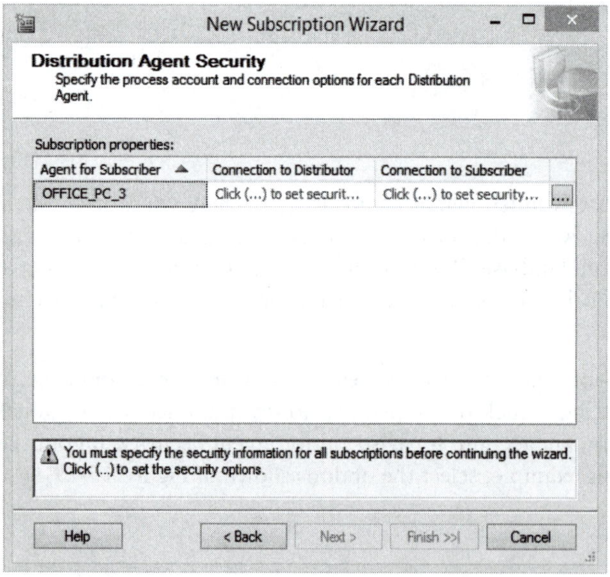

FIGURE 15-28

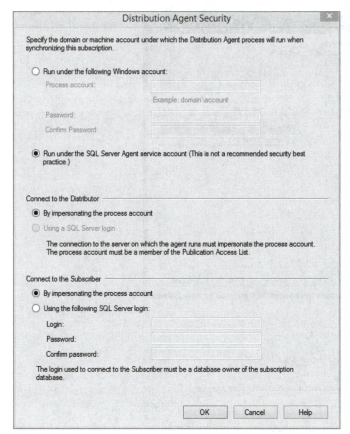

FIGURE 15-29

6. Specify the synchronization schedule. Because this is just your first test example, make it simple and set it to run on demand. Click the drop-down and select "Run on demand only," as shown in Figure 15-30. Click Next to continue.

7. Figure 15-31 shows the Initialize Subscriptions screen where you specify when the snapshot is initialized. Check the box to select initialization; and in the drop-down, choose to initialize immediately.

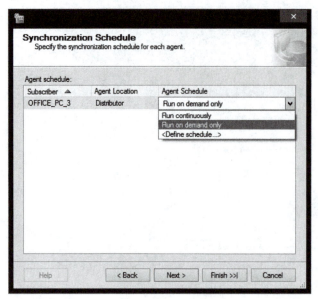

FIGURE 15-30

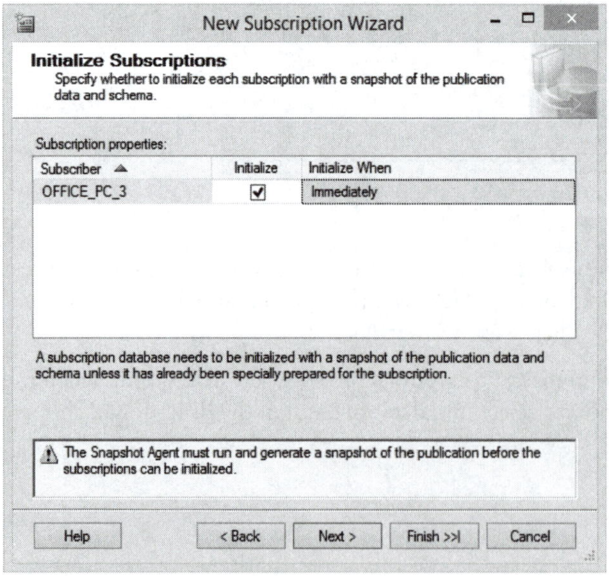

FIGURE 15-31

8. Next is the Wizard Actions screen shown earlier (refer to Figure 15-20), where you can choose to create the subscription and script the creation. Make your selection and click Next to continue.

9. From the confirmation screen that appears, confirm that the actions are as you expect. If not, go back and fix anything before executing the wizard actions you selected. When you are satisfied, click Finish.

10. The next screen shows the actions and their status. You should see three actions, with the last of these indicating a warning. Clicking the message for this action should reveal a message indicating that the snapshot is not available. Although you marked the subscription to initialize immediately, it must wait until you manually run the Snapshot agent to create a snapshot that is available to be applied. You can see this in Figure 15-32. If this step shows any errors, investigate and resolve them before attempting to rerun the wizard.

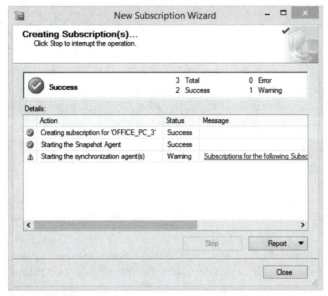

FIGURE 15-32

Verifying Snapshot Replication

So far, the setup is simple, but how do you know it actually works? Following are some tests you can conduct to make sure it does indeed work properly:

1. Connect to the publication server and verify the records there using the following SQL code (code file: `03 verify publisher.sql`):

```
use publisher;
 select * from Sales.Cars;

ProdID     ProdDesc          Country      LastUpdate
1       ProEfficient Sedan     US        2014-05-18 09:18:00
2       ProEfficient Van       US        2014-05-18 09:18:00
3       JieNeng Crossover      China      2014-05-18 09:18:00
4       Jieneng Utility        China      2014-05-18 09:18:00
```

```
5       EuroEfficient Wagon    Sweden    2014-05-18 09:18:00
6       EuroEfficient Pickup   Sweden    2014-05-18 09:18:00
 (6 row(s) affected)
```

2. Now, connect to the subscription server using the following SQL code (code file: `04 verify subscriber.sql`). You've already initialized the subscription, so you see only cars for the Chinese market.

```
use subscriber;
 select * from Sales.Cars;

 ProdID      ProdDesc                              Country LastUpdate
 ----------- ------------------------------------- ------- -----------------------


 3              JieNeng Crossover                  China   2014-05-07 12:43:00
 4              Jieneng Utility                    China   2014-05-07 12:43:00
 (2 row(s) affected)
```

3. Now, suppose you made some changes to cars for the Chinese market and upgraded `JieNeng Crossover` to `JieNeng Crossover LE` at the publication server. To make these changes, use the following code (code file: `05 Update Publication.sql`).

```
  use publisher;

update Sales.Cars set proddesc = 'JieNeng Crossover LE' where prodid = 3;
```

4. You've updated records at the publisher, so you must take a new snapshot by running the SQL Server Agent jobs. You can do this using either of the following methods:

   ➤ In Object Explorer, expand the SQL Server Agent `Jobs` folder, You should see a job with a name similar to the format `<Your Server Name>-Publisher-Pub_Cars_China-1`. Right-click the job, and select Start Job from the context menu.

   ➤ In Object Explorer right-click the `Replication` node, and select Launch Replication Monitor. Using Replication Monitor is covered in the "Monitoring Replication" section later in this chapter. In the example, this should open up, and because you're connected to the current server, it already knows about the local publications. So, under the `My Publications` node, you see the local server, in this case called `OFFICE-PC`. Open that node and you see the publication you set up on the `Publisher` database called `[Publisher]: Pub_Cars_China`. Right-click and select Generate Snapshot. This creates the new snapshot, but has not yet applied it to the subscriber.

5. Because you implemented a push subscription, go to the distributor and run the job to refresh this snapshot. Again, you can do this by either running the specified job, or through the Replication Monitor.

   ➤ To run the specified job, open Object Explorer on the subscriber and expand the SQL Server Agent `Jobs` folder. Locate the job with a name of `OFFICE-PC-Publisher-Pub_Cars_Chine-OFFICE-PC-1`, right-click the job, and select Start Job from the context menu.

   ➤ In the Replication Monitor, select the node for your publication. In the right pane, select the Agent tab. Right-click the line for the Snapshot Agent job, and select Start Agent.

6. Now, ensure that the data is indeed refreshed by running the same SQL code from step 2 (code file: `04 verify subscriber.sql`):

```
use subscriber;

select * from Sales.Cars;
```

```
ProdID      ProdDesc                                Country LastUpdate
----------- --------------------------------------- ------- -----------------------
3           JieNeng Crossover LE                    China   2014-05-24 12:43:00
4           Jieneng Utility                         China   2014-05-24 12:43:00
 (2 rows affected)
```

Implementing Transactional and Merge Replication

Procedurally, setting up transactional and merge replication is similar to the snapshot replication discussed earlier; refer back to that section for step-by-step instructions. This section notes the additions, exceptions, and a few other noteworthy highlights.

Transactional Replication

The typical transactional replication is not too different from snapshot replication, but with one major component added: the Log Reader agent. This agent tracks all changes made to the article so that it can be propagated to the subscriber. As a result, the load on the distribution database is higher than with snapshot replication, which means you must keep a closer eye on it, especially the log file of the distribution database.

One variation of transactional replication you may encounter is having updatable subscriptions. If you implement a transactional publication with an updatable subscription, changes at the subscriber are applied back to the publisher. To enable this, SQL Server adds one additional column in tables included in the publication to track changes. This column is called `MSrepl_tran_version` and is a unique identifier column. Therefore, code such as the following fails because it does not have a column list:

```
insert into Sales.Cars values (9,'English Car','UK', getdate());
```

As a result, the application of that code must be updated. To fix that, the column list that corresponds to the values in parentheses must be provided right after the table name, as shown here:

```
insert into Sales.Cars (prodid, proddesc, country, lastupdate)
values (9,'English Car','UK', getdate());
```

For transactional replication with updatable subscription, a linked server is used among SQL Server publishing and subscribing databases. The linked server uses the MS Distributed Transaction Coordinator (MS DTC) to coordinate transactions; therefore, MS DTC on the publisher must be enabled to accept remote connections.

Merge Replication

For merge replication, all articles must have a unique identifier column with a unique index and the `ROWGUIDCOL` property. If they don't have it, SQL Server adds one for you. Just like the transactional replication with an updatable subscription, an `INSERT` statement without the column list will fail.

Additional agents are used for transactional and merge replication, such as the Log Reader agent and Queue Reader agent. The agents require a domain account to run under. The domain account can be their own or shared with other agents. How you choose to implement that depends on your company's security policy.

PEER-TO-PEER REPLICATION

In peer-to-peer replication, every participant is both a publisher and a subscriber. It is suitable for cases in which user applications need to read or modify data at any of the databases participating in the setup. It provides an interesting alternative for load-balancing and high-availability scenarios. This feature is available only in the Enterprise Edition of SQL Server. Oracle calls this kind of replication *multimaster*, whereas DB2 calls it *update anywhere*.

Consider the following when evaluating and setting up peer-to-peer replication:

➤ It is designed for a small number of participating databases. A good rule-of-thumb number is less than ten. If you use more than that, you are likely to encounter performance issues.

➤ Peer-to-peer replication handles conflict resolution, but in a different way from merge replication. Starting with SQL Server 2008, peer-to-peer replication causes a critical error to occur when it detects a conflict. This critical error causes the Distribution agent to fail. Because of this, you should design your application so that you do not have conflicts.

➤ Peer-to-peer does not support data filtering. That would defeat its purpose, because everyone is an equal partner here for high availability and load balancing.

➤ Applications can scale out read operations across multiple databases, and databases are always online. Participating nodes can be added or removed for maintenance.

➤ As mentioned previously, peer-to-peer replication is available only in the Enterprise Edition. However, for your testing purposes, it is available in the Developer Edition of SQL Server 2014.

Setting Up Peer-to-Peer Replication

From an implementation standpoint, the process to set up peer-to-peer replication is similar to setting up snapshot, transactional, or merge replication. However, some differences exist, as you will see in the following sections as you walk through an example to set up peer-to-peer replication.

1. To start out, begin with one database, back it up, and restore it on all other participating databases. This way, you start from a clean and consistent slate.

2. All nodes in the topology need a distributor, so set one up here. Although you can use a single distribution database for all publications, this is not recommended for a production system. The examples here use a local distribution database, one on each publishing server.

3. After the distributor is set, create a publication just like a regular transactional replication publication, except that there is now a new replication type to choose from: peer-to-peer

publication. Choose this new option as the Publication Type on the Publication Type page (previously shown in Figure 15-14).

4. After selecting the replication type of peer-to-peer publication, complete the New Publication Wizard, which is similar to the steps used to create the Snapshot Publication previously.

5. After the new peer-to-peer publication is created, you must create additional peer-to-peer publications to act as peers in the topology. This example has two separate publications, one with a peer-to-peer publication called NorthAmerica_P2P, and the other with a peer-to-peer publication called Europe-P2P. You can use the same sample code from the previous snapshot replication example to create a single table to be replicated in each of these systems.

6. Proceed with the rest of the setup by right-clicking the publication and selecting Configure Peer-to-Peer Topology. The resulting dialog box is shown in Figure 15-33. This option is only available for a peer-to-peer publication. Click Next to continue.

FIGURE 15-33

Configuring Peer-to-Peer Replication

After setting up peer-to-peer replication, a welcome screen appears. From here, you can begin configuring the peer-to-peer topology. Follow these steps:

1. Select which peer-to-peer publication will configure the topology. For this example, choose to configure the topology from the local publication, which is NorthAmerica_P2P.

2. After choosing NorthAmerica_P2P, click Next, and you see the Configure Topology page, which presents you with a designer surface that looks like the screen shown in Figure 15-34. To add nodes to the topology, right-click the designer surface, and select Add a New Peer Node.

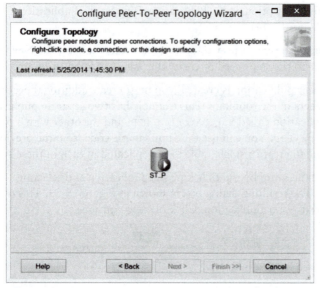

FIGURE 15-34

3. You now see the standard SQL Server Management Studio server connection dialog box, where you can specify which server the peer is on. In this example everything is on the same server, so specify "." as a reference to the local server.

4. Next, you see the Add a New Peer Node dialog box, as shown in Figure 15-35. Select the `Europe` database, as shown in the figure.

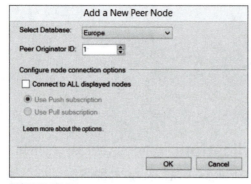

FIGURE 15-35

5. Click OK, and the node is added to the topology designer, as shown in Figure 15-36. It is difficult to know which node is which just by looking at the display surface. Fortunately, extensive tips are available when you hover your mouse over each node.

FIGURE 15-36

6. The next step is to connect the nodes in the topology. To connect the two nodes, right-click either node on the designer and select either "Connect to ALL displayed nodes," or "Add a new peer connection." For this example, select "Connect to ALL displayed nodes" because you have only two nodes displayed. This adds a two-way arrow between the two nodes.

   Because this particular example has only two nodes, you could have done this previously by selecting "Connect to ALL displayed nodes" (refer to Figure 15-35), but you can perform this step earlier (and should) when you have only two nodes.

7. Click next and the wizard moves onto the Log Reader Agent Security page. Set the security information by clicking the ellipsis (…) button, and choose the "Run under the SQL Server Agent service account" option. Click Next and the Distribution Agent Security page appears.

8. On the Distribution Agent Security page, you must provide security information for the distribution agents on all nodes in the topology. For this example, select the same options for both servers: "Run under the SQL Server Agent service account," and choose "By impersonating the process account" for how you connect to the distributor and subscriber, as shown in Figure 15-37. Click Next to move onto the next page.

9. The next page in the wizard is the New Peer Initialization page, where you can specify how the new peer should be initialized. In this case, the databases were created manually, and the same data was loaded into each database, so you can select the first option. Click Next to move onto the next page.

10. The Complete the Wizard page displays. Here, you see all the choices you made in the wizard. If these all appear to be correct, click Finish to start applying the actions selected in the wizard.

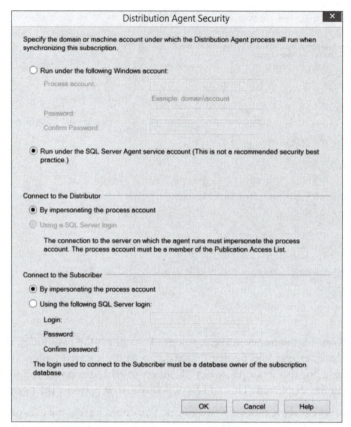

FIGURE 15-37

11.   The final page in the wizard shows the actions as they are executed, and reports any warnings or errors with the process. If any actions report something other than success, you need to investigate each and resolve the reported issue before attempting to rerun the topology wizard.

You have just completed the build out of a peer-to-peer topology. You can alter the topology at any time by re-running the Configure Topology Wizard and adding additional nodes, removing existing nodes, and changing connections.

SCRIPTING REPLICATION

For many, the preferred interface for managing replication is the graphical interface provided in SQL Server Management Studio in the various replication wizards. However, DBAs want to create a script that can be checked into a source code control system such as Visual Source Safe or Visual Studio Team Foundation Server.

For script replication, you have two options. You can use either the various replication wizards (which provide a scripting option), or you can use SQL Server Management Studio and script individual objects.

You can save the scripts into your source code control system, where you can version-control them and use them to deploy a replication configuration to development, test, QA, preproduction, and production systems.

MONITORING REPLICATION

You can use three tools for monitoring replication: Replication Monitor, Performance Monitor, and the replication-related Dynamic Management Views (DMVs). This section discusses these three tools in detail.

Replication Monitor

Replication Monitor is built into SQL Server Management Studio. It shows the status of replication, and can be used to make configuration changes. It can also show the current latency and the number of outstanding commands. It does not show the transaction or command rates; nor does it show any history of what happened at any time before the current snapshot of data was read.

You can invoke the Replication Monitor from Management Studio:

1. First, navigate to either the context menu of the top-level `replication` node, or the context menu of any server listed under `Local Publications` or `Local Subscriptions`.

2. From here, choose the Launch Replication Monitor option. Figure 15-38 shows the Replication Monitor after it has been started when running on a server with a local replication configuration. If you start Replication Monitor from a computer without a local replication configuration, you must specify the servers with the replication topology to see any information.

Following are a few of the key options in the Replication Monitor that you can choose from once invoked:

➤ You can see the SQL Server 2014 Distributor view by selecting the root node Replication Monitor. Doing this displays the options in the right pane to Add Publisher or to Switch to Distributor View. Selecting this second option changes the display to present nodes based on their distributor. This example uses a local distributor, so this doesn't change the display. In a more complex configuration with multiple replication streams using multiple distributors, this would change the ownership of publications and subscriptions to live under their parent distributor. To switch back, select the root node again, and select Switch to Publisher Group View.

➤ To look at subscription status (as shown in Figure 15-39), double-click any entry of the All Subscriptions tab to bring up a window where you can easily view reports and the status of publication to distribution, distribution to subscription, and undistributed commands. This is a user-friendly tool that provides a good overview of all your replication status information.

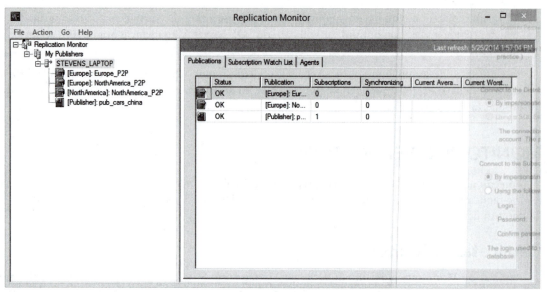

FIGURE 15-38

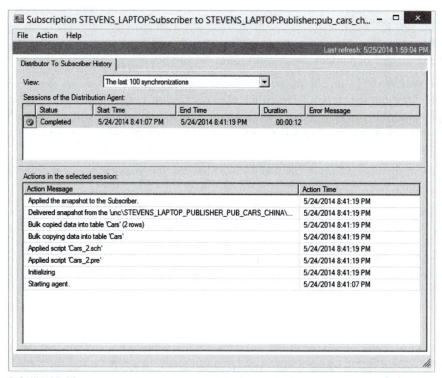

FIGURE 15-39

➤ Tracer tokens are a way to measure the current performance of replication. The Tracer Tokens tab is shown in Figure 15-40. Think of a tracer token as a dummy record that the Replication Monitor uses to gauge the performance of your replication model. It can give you a good idea of latency between your publisher, distributor, and subscriber.

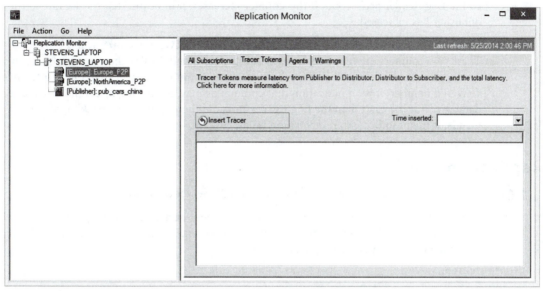

FIGURE 15-40

Performance Monitor

You can monitor several replication-related Performance Monitor objects and counters in SQL Server.

➤ **SQLServer: Replication Agent**—Has a single counter called Running that shows the number of replication agents running on the server

➤ **SQL Server: Replication Log Reader**—Shows the statistics for the Log Reader, with counters for Commands per second, Transactions per second, and Latency

➤ **SQL Server: Replication Dist**—Shows the statistics for the distributor with the same counters as for the Log Reader

➤ **SQL Server: Replication Merge**—Shows the statistics for the Merge agent, with counters for Conflicts per second, Downloaded changes per second, and Updates per second

➤ **SQL Server: Replication Snapshot**—Shows the statistics for the Snapshot agent, with counters for Delivered commands per second and Delivered transactions per second

When considering which performance counters to use, your replication type is the key factor to consider. For snapshot replication, look at the Replication Snapshot counters. For merge replication, look at the Replication Merge counters. For transactional replication, look at the Replication Log Reader and Replication Dist counters.

Here is some more information on the counters you should monitor for transactional replication:

➤ **Object: SQL Server:Replication Log Reader - Counter: LogReader: Delivered Cmds/Sec and Tx/Sec**—These two counters are repeated for each publication; they display the commands or transactions read per second, and indicate how many commands or transactions are read by the Log Reader per second. If this counter increases, it indicates that the Tx rate at the publisher has increased.

➤ **Object: SQL Server: Replication Dist. - Counter: Dist:Delivered Cmds/Sec and Tx/Sec**— These two counters are repeated for each subscription, and display the commands or transactions per second delivered to the subscriber. If this number is lower than the Log Reader delivered number, it is an indication that commands may be backing up on the distribution database. If it is higher than the Log Reader rate and there is already a backlog of commands, it might indicate that replication is catching up.

Replication DMVs

Following are four replication-related DMVs in every SQL Server database:

➤ `sys.dm_repl_articles`—Contains information about each article being published. It returns data from the database being published, and returns one row for each object being published in each article. The syntax is as follows:

```
select
* from sys.dm_repl_articles
```

➤ `sys.dm_repl_schemas`—Contains information about each table and column being published. It returns data from the database being published, and returns one row for each column in each object being published. The syntax is as follows:

```
select
* from sys.dm_repl_schemas
```

➤ `sys.dm_repl_tranhash`—Contains information about the hashing of transactions. The syntax is as follows:

```
select
* from sys.dm_repl_tranhash
```

➤ `sys.dm_repl_traninfo`—Contains information about each transaction in a transactional replication. The syntax is as follows:

```
select
* from sys.dm_repl_traninfo
```

These DMVs show information about what is being published from a specific database. They cannot help you monitor what's going on with replication. For that, you must either run the `sp_replcounters` system stored procedure (discussed in the next section), or go digging into the distribution database. It's much easier to just execute the `sp_replcounters` stored procedure than dig into the inner workings of replication in the MSDB or distribution databases. However, it may not have all the information you want to monitor. If you do need more information, you must search the distribution database. This is currently undocumented territory, but a good place to start is the source code for the replication stored procedures. Use these to begin determining where the data you want is located, and take it from there.

sp_replcounters

The sp_replcounters replication system stored procedure returns information about the transaction rate, latency, and first and last log sequence number (LSN) for each publication on a server. Run it on the publishing server. Calling this stored procedure on a server that is acting as the distributor or subscribing to publications from another server does not return any data.

Table 15-1 is an example of the output of this stored procedure. The results have been split over two lines for clarity.

TABLE 15-1: Example Output from sp_replcounters

DATABASE	REPLICATED TRANSACTIONS	REPLICATION RATE TRANS/SEC	REPLICATION LATENCY (SEC)
Publisher	178	129.0323	0.016
REPLBEGINLSN	**REPLNEXTLSN**		
0x0002FACC003458780001	0x0002FACC003459A1003D		

SUMMARY

Replication is an important technology within SQL Server for moving data between servers. The various types of replication include snapshot, transactional, and merge—and the different topologies that can be used with replication include Single Publishers, Multiple Publishers, Updating Subscribers, and peer-to-peer. You can monitor replication using Replication Monitor, Performance Monitor, and relevant performance counters. Additionally, some of the replication DMVs and system-stored procedures help to identify the root cause of issues when they occur.

Along with AlwaysOn, log shipping, database mirroring, and clustering, SQL Server 2014 provides many features to satisfy customers' needs for load balancing, high availability, disaster recovery, and scaling.

In Chapter 16, you will learn about clustering SQL Server 2014.

16

Clustering SQL Server 2014

WHAT'S IN THIS CHAPTER?

➤ Getting to know clustering and mastering its intricacies

➤ Researching hardware and software configurations to identify what works best for your organization

➤ Configuring hardware

➤ Configuring and clustering the operating system

➤ Configuring SQL Server 2014 on the cluster

➤ Testing the installation

➤ Administering and troubleshooting the production SQL Server 2014 cluster

With this chapter's tried-and-true information, you can successfully install, configure, and administer a clustered instance of SQL Server 2014. In this chapter, you learn how a Windows Failover Cluster Instance (FCI) works, and whether it's the right solution for your organization. The newly adopted name is AlwaysOn Failover Cluster Instance as of SQL Server 2012, which is synonymous with Windows Server Failover Cluster. You learn how to choose between upgrading a previous version of a Windows Failover Cluster and building a new cluster; how to plan for clustering, including hardware and the operating system; and how to install SQL Server 2014 on a Windows Failover Cluster. Finally, you learn how to maintain and troubleshoot an operational instance of SQL Server on a cluster.

Although you can deploy a geographically dispersed cluster in Windows 2012 R2, this chapter primarily focuses on co-located clustering, as well as the most commonly deployed Windows Failover Cluster configuration.

> **NOTE** *If you don't have a Storage Area Network (SAN) or the hardware to create these examples on physical hardware, consider using a Hyper-V virtual machine (VM) solution with Windows Server 2012 file server configured as a Server Message Block (SMB) file share for the shared disks. For more information, see "Install SQL Server with SMB Fileshare as a Storage Option" at* `http://msdn.microsoft.com/en-us/library/hh759341.aspx`.

CLUSTERING AND YOUR ORGANIZATION

Many DBAs seem to have difficulty understanding exactly what clustering is. What follows is a good working definition.

Microsoft Windows Failover Clustering Instance (FCI) is a high-availability option designed to increase the uptime of SQL Server instances. A typical *cluster* includes two or more physical servers, called *nodes*; identical configuration is recommended. One is identified as the *active node*, on which a SQL Server instance is running the production workload, and the other is a *passive node*, on which SQL Server is installed, but not running. If the SQL Server instance on the active node fails, its passive node becomes the active node, and begins to run the SQL Server production workload with some minimal failover downtime. Additionally, you can deploy a Windows Failover Cluster to have both nodes active, which means running different SQL Server instances where any SQL Server instances can failover to the other node. The common component between the nodes is the shared storage. Remember that a SQL Server cluster only maintains one set of data, so it does not provide protection against database corruption.

This definition is straightforward, but it has a lot of unclear implications, which is where many clustering misunderstandings arise. One of the best ways to more fully understand what clustering can and cannot do is to drill down into the details.

What Clustering Can Do

Clustering is designed to improve the availability of the physical server hardware, operating system, and SQL Server instances, but excludes the shared storage. Should any of these aspects fail, the SQL Server instance fails over. The other node in a cluster automatically takes over the failed SQL Server instance to reduce downtime to a minimum. Behind the scenes, the passive node takes control over the shared storage. The passive node starts its local copy of the SQL Server services and connects to the shared storage that houses all the user and system databases.

Additionally, the use of Windows FCI can help reduce downtime when you perform maintenance on cluster nodes. For example, if you must update hardware on a physical server or install a new service pack on the operating system, you can do so one node at a time. To do so, follow these steps:

1. Upgrade the passive node that is not running a SQL Server instance.

2. Manually fail over from the active node to the now upgraded node, which becomes the active node.

3. Upgrade the currently passive node.

4. After it is upgraded, if you choose, you can fail back to the original node. This cluster feature helps to reduce the overall downtime caused by upgrades.

When running an upgrade, you must ensure that you do not manually failover to a node that has not been upgraded; that would cause instability because the binary would not have been updated.

> **NOTE** *A Windows Failover Cluster should be migrated to a Windows 2012 R2 Failover Cluster. Create a Windows 2012 R2 Failover Cluster and migrate the databases.*

What Clustering Cannot Do

Clustering is just one part of many important and required pieces in a puzzle to ensure high availability. Other aspects of high availability (such as ensuring redundancy in all hardware components) are just as important. Without hardware redundancy, the most sophisticated cluster solution in the world can fail. If all the pieces of that puzzle are not in place, spending a lot of money on clustering may not be a good investment. The section, "Getting Prepared for Clustering," later in this chapter discusses this in further detail.

Some DBAs believe that clustering can reduce downtime to zero. This is not the case. Clustering can mitigate downtime, but it can't eliminate it. For example, the failover itself causes an outage lasting from seconds to a few minutes while the SQL Server services are stopped on one node, then started on the other node, and database recovery is performed.

Nor is clustering designed to intrinsically protect data because the shared storage is a single point of failover in clustering. This is a great surprise to many DBAs. Data must be protected using other options, such as backups, log shipping, AlwaysOn Availability Groups, or disk mirroring. In actuality, the same database drives are shared (albeit without being seen at the same time) by all servers in the cluster, so corruption in one would carry over to the others.

Clustering is not a solution for load balancing either. *Load balancing* is when many servers act as one, spreading your load across several servers simultaneously. Some DBAs may think that clustering provides load balancing between the cluster nodes. This is not the case; clustering helps improve only uptime of SQL Server instances. If you need load balancing, you must look for a different solution. A possibility might be Peer-to-Peer Transactional Replication, discussed in Chapter 15, "Replication."

Clustering purchases require Standard or Datacenter versions of the Windows Server 2012 R2 operating system and SQL Server Standard, Enterprise, or Business Intelligence (BI) editions. Clustering is usually deployed within the confines of a data center, but can be used over geographic distances (known as *geoclusters*). To implement a geocluster, work with your storage vendor to enable the storage across the geographic distances to synchronize the disk arrays. SQL Server 2014 also supports another option: multi-site clustering across subnets. The same subnet restriction was eliminated with the release of SQL Server 2012.

> **NOTE** *Clustering requires experienced DBAs to be highly trained in hardware and software, and DBAs with high-availability experience command higher salaries.*

Although SQL Server is cluster-aware, not all client applications that use SQL Server are cluster-aware. For example, even if the failover of a SQL Server instance is relatively seamless, a client application may not have the reconnect logic. Applications without reconnect logic require that users exit and then restart the client application after the SQL Server instance has failed over, and users may lose any data displayed on their current screen.

Choosing SQL Server 2014 Clustering for the Right Reasons

When it comes right down to it, the reason for a clustered SQL Server is to improve the availability of the whole SQL Server instance, which includes all user/system databases, logins, and SQL Jobs. But this justification makes sense only if the following are true:

➤ You have experienced DBA staff to install, configure, and administer a clustered SQL Server.

➤ The cost (and pain) resulting from downtime is more than the cost of purchasing the cluster hardware and software, as well as maintaining it over time.

➤ You have in place the capability to protect your storage with redundancy. Remember that clusters don't protect data.

➤ For a geographically dispersed cluster across remote data centers, you have a certified third-party hardware and software solution.

➤ You have in place all the necessary peripherals required to support a highly available server environment (for example, backup power and so on).

If all these things are true, your organization is a good candidate for installing a clustered SQL Server, and you should proceed. But if your organization doesn't meet these criteria, and you are not willing to implement them, you would probably be better off with an alternative, high-availability option, such as one of those discussed next.

Alternatives to Clustering

SQL Server clustering is just one of many options available to help provide high availability within your SQL Server 2014 instances, and high-availability solutions consist of multiple layers of solutions to ensure uptime. This section takes a brief look at alternatives to clustering, starting with the least-expensive and easy-to-implement options, and working along to the more-expensive and more-difficult-to-implement options.

Cold Backup Server

A *cold backup* refers to having a spare physical server available that you can use as your SQL Server 2014 server should your production server fail. Generally speaking, this server does not have SQL

Server 2014 or any database backups installed on it. This means that it can take time to install SQL Server 2014, restoring the databases and redirecting applications to the new server, before you are up and running again. It also means that you may lose some of your data if you cannot recover the last transaction logs from the failed production server, and you have only your most recent database backups to restore from.

If being down a while or possibly losing data is not a major concern, having a cold backup server is the least-expensive way to ensure that your organization stays in business should your production SQL Server 2014 server go down.

Warm Backup Server

The major difference between a cold backup server and a *warm backup* server is that your spare server (the "warm" one) has SQL Server 2014 preinstalled, and may be used as a development server where it has some less-recent production databases installed. This means that you save a lot of installation and configuration time, getting back into production sooner than you would with the use of a cold backup server. You still need to redirect your database applications, refresh the data to the most current, and you may lose some of your data should you not recover the last transaction logs from the failed server.

Log Shipping

In a log-shipping scenario, you have two SQL Servers: the primary (production) server and a secondary. The secondary server also has SQL Server 2014 installed and configured. The major difference between a warm backup server and log shipping is that log shipping adds the capability not only to restore database backups from the production server to the secondary server automatically, but also to ship database transaction logs and automatically restore them. This means there is less manual work than with a warm backup server, and less chance for data loss, because the most data you might lose would be the equivalent of one transaction log. For example, if you create transaction logs every 15 minutes, in the worst case you would lose only 15 minutes of data.

> **NOTE** *Log shipping is covered in detail in Chapter 18, "SQL Server 2014 Log Shipping."*

Replication

Many experts include SQL Server replication as a means to increase high availability, but the authors are not among them. Although replication is great for moving data from one SQL Server to others, it's not a good high-availability option. It is much too complex and limited in its capability to easily replicate entire databases to be worth the effort of spending any time trying to make it work in failover scenarios, unless you already have the replication expertise.

> **NOTE** *Replication is covered in detail in Chapter 15.*

Database Mirroring

Database mirroring in many ways is a good alternative to clustering SQL Server. Like clustering, you can use database mirroring to automatically fail over a failed SQL Server instance to the mirror server, on a database-by-database basis. The biggest difference between clustering and database mirroring is that data is actually protected when you have two different copies of the data stored in mirroring. In clustering, the shared disk can be a single point of failure. In addition, database mirroring can operate over long distances, is less expensive than clustering, requires less knowledge to set up and manage, and the failover can be fully automated in some circumstances, like clustering is. In some cases, database mirroring may be a better choice than clustering for high availability.

> **NOTE** *Database mirroring was added to the deprecated list as of the release of SQL Server 2012. It still exists in SQL Server 2014, but may not be present in the next release of SQL Server. The technology is being replaced with the AlwaysOn Availability Groups.*

AlwaysOn Availability Groups

AlwaysOn Availability Groups is a high-availability and disaster-recovery solution that was new with SQL Server 2012. It enables you to maximize availability for one to many user databases as a group. Deploying this technology involves configuring one or more Availability Groups. Each Availability Group defines a set of user databases that can fail over as a single unit by leveraging a Windows Failover Cluster and the clustered SQL Server name and IP address.

The Availability Group involves a set of nine failover partners, known as *availability replicas.* This support for nine replicas is new to SQL Server 2014, because it was limited to five in SQL Server 2012. Each availability replica possesses a non-shared copy of each of the databases in the Availability Group where the data can be maintained either synchronously or asynchronously. One of these replicas, known as the *primary replica*, maintains the primary copy of each database. The primary replica makes these databases (known as *primary databases*) available to users for read-write access. For each primary database, other availability replicas (known as *secondary replicas*) maintain a failover copy for each database that can also be configured for read-only access. Also note that you can have up to three replicas participating in Synchronous mode, and up to two nodes with automatic failover.

> **NOTE** *See Chapter 25, "AlwaysOn Availability Groups," for more information on this subject.*

Third-Party Clustering Solutions

In addition to Microsoft, some third-party partners also offer high-availability solutions for SQL Server. In general, these options may be more expensive than (and as complex as) Microsoft's FCI option, but some offer additional features and benefits beyond what Microsoft offers.

What to Do?

Although this brief introduction clarifies your options, it may not be enough information for you to make a good decision. If the best solution is not self-evident, you should spend time researching the preceding options before determining what is best for your organization.

CLUSTERING: THE BIG PICTURE

Before you can deploy and manage clustering, you must know how it works, including clustering configuration options.

How Clustering Works

In this section, you learn about terminologies such as active and passive nodes, the shared disk array, the quorum, public and private networks, and the cluster server. Then, you learn how a failover works.

Active Nodes versus Passive Nodes

A Windows Failover Cluster built on Windows Server 2012 can support up to 64 nodes. However, typical clustering deployment is only two nodes. A single SQL Server 2014 instance can run on only a single node at a time, and should a failover occur, the failed instance can fail over to another node. You should consider clusters of three or more physical nodes when you need to cluster many SQL Server instances. Larger clusters are discussed later in this chapter.

In a two-node Windows Failover Cluster with SQL Server, one of the physical nodes is considered the active node, and the second one is the passive node for that single SQL Server instance. It doesn't matter which of the physical servers in the cluster is designated as active or passive, but you should specifically assign one node as the active and the other as the passive. This way, there is no confusion about which physical server is performing which role at the current time.

When referring to an active node, this particular node is currently running a SQL Server instance accessing that instance's databases, which are located on a shared disk array.

When referring to a passive node, this particular node is not currently running the SQL Server. When a node is passive, it is not running the production databases, but it is in a state of readiness. If the active node fails and a failover occurs, the passive node automatically runs production databases and begins serving user requests. In this case, the passive node has become active, and the formerly active node becomes the passive node (or the failed node, if a failure occurs that prevents it from operating).

Shared Disk Array

Standalone SQL Server instances usually store their databases on local disk storage or non-shared disk storage. Clustered SQL Server instances store data on a shared disk array. *Shared* means that all nodes of the Windows Failover Cluster are physically connected to the shared disk array, but only the active node can access that instance's databases. To ensure the integrity of the databases, both nodes of a cluster never access the shared disk at the same time.

Generally speaking, a shared disk array can be an iSCSI, a fiber-channel, SAS connected, a RAID 1, a RAID 5, or a RAID 10 disk array housed in a standalone unit, or a SAN. This shared disk array must have at least two logical disk partitions. One partition is used for storing the clustered instance's SQL Server databases, and the other is used for the quorum drive, if a quorum drive is used. Additionally, you need a third logical partition if you choose to cluster Microsoft Distributed Transaction Coordinator (MSDTC). SQL Server 2014 also adds support for Cluster Share Volumes (CSV) for a supported storage configuration, where a single Virtual Hard Drive (VHD) file can actively be read from and written to by multiple nodes.

Starting with SQL Server 2012 and currently supported in SQL Server 2014, system databases (`master`, `model`, `msdb`, and `tempdb`), and Database Engine user databases can be installed with Server Message Block (SMB) file server as a storage option. This applies to both SQL Server standalone and AlwaysOn Failover Cluster Instance installations (FCI). For more information on using SMB as shared storage, see `http://msdn.microsoft.com/en-us/library/hh759341.aspx`.

The Quorum

When both cluster nodes are up and running and participating in their respective active and passive roles, they communicate with each other over the network. For example, if you change a configuration setting on the active node, this configuration is propagated automatically (and quickly) to the passive node, thereby ensuring synchronization.

As you might imagine, though, you can make a change on the active node and have it fail before the change is sent over the network and made on the passive node. In this scenario, the change is never applied to the passive node. Depending on the nature of the change, this could cause problems, even causing both nodes of the cluster to fail.

To prevent this change from happening, a Windows Failover Cluster employs a quorum. A *disk quorum* is essentially a log file, similar in concept to database logs. Its purpose is to record any change made on the active node. This way, should any recorded change not get to the passive node because the active node has failed and cannot send the change to the passive node over the network, the passive node (when it becomes the active node) can read the quorum log file to find out what the change was. The passive node can then make the change before it becomes the new active node. If the state of this drive is compromised, your cluster may become inoperable.

In effect, each cluster quorum can cast one "vote," where the majority of total votes (based on the number of these cluster quorums that are online) determine whether the cluster continues running on the cluster node. This prevents more than one cluster node from attempting to take ownership of the same SQL Server instance. The voting quorums are cluster nodes or, in some cases, a *disk witness* or *file share witness*. Each voting cluster quorum (with the exception of a file share witness) contains a copy of the cluster configuration. The cluster service works to keep all copies synchronized at all times.

Starting with Windows 2012, Windows Failover Cluster implemented Dynamic Quorum, which is on by default. This capability will adjust the quorum (based on the available voting resources) that modifies the vote of the cluster when nodes are brought down sequentially. For example, in a five-node cluster, four nodes can be down for planned maintenance, while leaving the last node running SQL Server. Then, as nodes are brought back online, the cluster gives its votes back and participates in the quorum calculations. To change the default, select the "Advanced quorum configuration and witness selection" option. To check the current votes of a cluster, run the following `Get-ClusterNode` Windows PowerShell cmdlet:

```
PS C:\> Get-ClusterNode | ft name, dynamicweight, nodeweight, state -AutoSize
```

Following are the four supported Windows Failover Cluster quorum modes:

> ➤ **Node Majority**—Each node that is available and in communication can vote. The cluster functions only with a majority of the votes.

> ➤ **Node and Disk Majority**—Each node plus a designated disk in the cluster storage (the "disk witness") can vote, whenever they are available and in communication. The cluster functions only with a majority of the votes.

> ➤ **Node and File Share Majority**—Each node plus a designated file share created by the administrator (the "file share witness") can vote, whenever they are available and in communication. The cluster functions only with a majority of the votes.

> ➤ **No Majority: Disk Only**—The cluster has a quorum if one node is available and in communication with a specific disk in the cluster storage. Only the nodes that are also in communication with that disk can join the cluster. The disk is the single point of failure, so use highly reliable storage. A *quorum drive* is a logical drive on the shared disk array dedicated to storing the quorum and as a best practice should be around 1GB of fault-tolerant disk storage.

Table 16-1 describes clusters based on the number of nodes and other cluster characteristics, and lists the quorum mode that is recommended in most cases.

TABLE 16-1: Cluster Quorum Recommendations

DESCRIPTION OF CLUSTER	QUORUM RECOMMENDATION
Odd number of nodes	Node Majority
Even number of nodes (but not a geocluster)	Node and Disk Majority
Even number of nodes, geocluster	Node and File Share Majority
Even number of nodes, no shared storage	Node and File Share Majority

You can switch the quorum configuration after the cluster has been deployed based on the number of clustered nodes and user requirements. To do so, select Configure Cluster Quorum Settings.

Public and Private Networks

Each node of a cluster must have at least two network cards to be a fully supported installation. One network card is connected to the public network, and the other network card is connected to a private cluster network.

> ➤ The *public network* is the network to which the client applications connect. This is how they communicate to a clustered SQL Server instance using the clustered IP address and clustered SQL Server name. You should have two teamed network cards for the public network for redundancy and to improve availability.

➤ The *private network* is used solely for communications between the clustered nodes. It is used mainly for the *heartbeat communication*. Two forms of communications are executed:

➤ **LooksAlive**—Verifies that the SQL Server service runs on the online node every 5 seconds by default

➤ **IsAlive**—Verifies that SQL Server accepts connections by executing `sp_server_diagnostics`.

This health-detection logic determines if a node is down, or suffering from lack of resources, and the passive node then takes over the production workload.

The SQL Server Instance

Surprisingly, SQL Server client applications don't need to know how to switch communicating from a failed cluster node to the new active node or anything else about specific cluster nodes (such as the NETBIOS name or IP address of individual cluster nodes). This is because each clustered SQL Server instance is assigned a network name and IP address, which client applications use to connect to the clustered SQL Server. In other words, client applications don't connect to a node's specific name or IP address, but instead to the cluster SQL network name or cluster SQL IP address that stays consistent and fails over. Each clustered SQL Server will belong to a Failover Cluster Resource Group that contains the following resources (which will fail together):

➤ SQL Server Network Name

➤ IP Address

➤ One or more shared disks

➤ SQL Server Database Engine service

➤ SQL Server Agent

➤ SQL Server Analysis Services, if installed in the same group

➤ One file share resource (if the FILESTREAM feature is installed)

How a Failover Works

Assume that a single SQL Server 2014 instance runs on the active node of a cluster, and that a passive node is available to take over when needed. At this time, the active node communicates with both the database and the quorum on the shared disk array. Because only a single node at a time can access the shared disk array, the passive node does not access the database or the quorum.

Because SQL Server 2014 supports a CSV (which is a distributed file-access solution allowing simultaneous access to the shared filesystem, but not to the same files), cluster storage provisioning is simplified. In addition, the active node sends out heartbeat signals over the private network, and the passive node monitors them, so it can take over if a failover occurs. Clients are also interacting with the active node via the clustered SQL Server virtual network name and IP address while running production workloads.

Now, assume that the active node stops working because of a power failure. The passive node (which is monitoring the heartbeats from the active node) notices that the heartbeats stopped.

After a predetermined delay, the passive node assumes that the active node has failed and initiates a failover. As part of the failover process, the passive node (now the active node) takes over control of the shared disk array and reads the quorum, looking for any unsynchronized configuration changes. It also takes over control of the clustered SQL Server virtual network name and IP address. In addition, as the node takes over the databases, it performs a SQL Server startup and recovers the databases.

The time this takes depends on many factors, including the performance of the hardware and the number of transactions that might have to be rolled forward or back during the database recovery process. When the recovery process is complete, the new active node announces itself on the network with the clustered SQL Server virtual network name and IP address, which enables the client applications to reconnect and begin using the SQL Server 2014 instance after this minimal interruption.

A nice feature introduced in SQL Server 2012 was the Flexible Failover Policy. This is still supported in SQL Server 2014. Since, as mentioned previously, the health detection now uses the `sp_server_diagnostics` stored procedure, the administrator can set various levels to initiate a failover. This is set through the properties of the SQL Server service in Failover Cluster Manager. Various levels exist, and can be set to designate the condition to initiate a failover. Following are the levels that can initiate a failover:

- **Level 0**—No failover or restart will be triggered automatically.
- **Level 1**—Failover or restart on server down.
  - SQL Server Service is down.
- **Level 2**—Failover or restart on server unresponsive.
  - SQL Server Service is down.
  - SQL Server instance is non-responsive.
- **Level 3 (default)**—Failover or restart on critical server errors.
  - SQL Server Service is down.
  - SQL Server instance is non-responsive.
  - `sp_server_diagnostics` returns "system error."
- **Level 4**—Failover or restart on moderate server errors.
  - SQL Server Service is down.
  - SQL Server instance is non-responsive.
  - `sp_server_diagnostics` retuens "system error."
  - `sp_server_diagnostics` returns "resource error."
- **Level 5**—Failover or restart on any qualified failure condition.
  - SQL Server Service is down.
  - SQL Server instance is non-responsive.

➤ `sp_server_diagnostics` returns "system error."

➤ `sp_server_diagnostics` returns "resource error."

➤ `sp_server_diagnostics` returns "query_processing error."

> **NOTE** *You can find more information about the Flexible Failover Policy at* `http://msdn.microsoft.com/en-us/library/ff878664.aspx`.

Clustering Options

Up to this point, you've learned about simple two-node, single-instance cluster, or multi-instance running a single SQL Server instance. However, this is only one of many options you have when clustering SQL Server. Two other popular options include active/active clustering and multi-node clustering. Additionally, you can also cluster multiple instances of SQL Server on the same server. The following sections discuss these alternatives in detail.

Multi-Instance Cluster

The examples so far have described what is called a *single-instance cluster*. This is a two-node cluster in which there is only one active instance of SQL Server 2014. Should the active node fail, the passive node takes over the single instance of SQL Server 2014, becoming the active node.

To save hardware costs, some organizations like to configure a *multi-instance cluster*. Like a single-instance cluster, this is also a two-node cluster, but instead of only a single SQL Server instance running, you have two instances, one on each physical node of the cluster.

The advantage of a multi-instance cluster is that you make better use of the available hardware. Both nodes of the cluster are in use instead of just one, as in a single-instance cluster. The disadvantage is that when a failover occurs, both SQL Server instances are running on a single physical server, which can reduce performance of both instances where memory may need to be readjusted to ensure that each has adequate memory. To help overcome this problem, both of the physical servers can be oversized to better meet the needs of both instances should a failover occur.

Chances are good, however, that the perfect balance will not be met and there will be some performance slowdown when failing over to the other node. In addition, if you have an active/active cluster running two SQL Server instances, each instance needs its own logical disk on the shared disk array. Logical disks cannot be shared among SQL Server instances.

In the end, if you want to save hardware costs and don't mind potential application slowdowns, use a multi-instance two-node cluster.

Multi-Node Clusters

If you think you will be adding even more clustered SQL Server 2014 instances in the future, you may want to consider a third option: *multi-node clusters*. For the more conservative, a three-node cluster, or *multi-instance with a passive standby*, is a good option that provides more redundancy, and it won't cause any application slowdown should a failover occur with the passive node. If you don't mind the complexity of large clusters, you can add even more nodes.

The number of physical nodes supported for SQL Server clustering depends on which version of the software you purchase, along with which version of the operating system you intend to use. Also, keep in mind that the quorum model to use depends on whether there is an odd or even number of nodes in the cluster.

Purchasing the Right Software

One of the reasons it is important to research your clustering needs is that they directly affect what software you need, along with licensing costs. Following are your options:

- ➤ **SQL Server 2014 Standard Edition (32-bit or 64-bit)**—Supports up to two-node clustering.
- ➤ **SQL Server 2014 BI Edition (32-bit or 64-bit)**—Supports up to two-node clustering.
- ➤ **SQL Server 2014 Enterprise Edition (32-bit or 64-bit)**—Supports up to the operating system maximum, which, as of this writing, is 64 nodes.

If you need only a two-node cluster, you can save by licensing Windows Server 2012 Standard Edition and SQL Server 2014 Standard Edition. If you want more than a two-node cluster, your licensing costs will escalate quickly because you will need SQL Server 2014 Enterprise Edition, although Windows Server 2012 Standard Edition supports up to 64 nodes.

> **NOTE** *SQL Server 2014 is supported on Windows 2008 SP2 and later operating systems. You should use the latest Windows operating system for best performance and features, which at the time of this writing is Windows Server 2012 R2.*

Number of Nodes to Use

As discussed earlier, in a two-node cluster, a SQL Server instance runs on the active node, while the passive node is currently not running SQL Server, but is ready to do so when a failover occurs. This same principle applies to multi-node clusters.

As an example, say that you have a three-node cluster. In this case, you have two active nodes running their own individual SQL Server instances, and the third physical node acts as a passive node for the other two active nodes. If either of the two active nodes fails, the passive node can take over. You can set up a failover preferred node to predetermine the failover sequence from node to node.

Now, consider an eight-node cluster. In this case, you have seven active nodes and one passive. Should any of the seven active nodes fail, the passive node takes over after a failover. In this case, with a large number of nodes, it is more preferable to have a passive node to avoid multiple node failures that cause the surviving nodes to carry all that additional workload.

In an active/passive configuration, the advantage of many nodes is that less hardware is used for failover needs. For example, in a two-node cluster, 50 percent of your hardware is used for redundancy; but in an eight-node cluster, only 12.5 percent of your cluster hardware is used for redundancy.

Ultimately, deciding how many nodes your cluster has should depend on business restrictions like your budget, your in-house expertise, and your level of aversion (if any) to complexity. Some organizations have many different SQL Server instances that they need to cluster, but choose to use multiple two-node active/passive clusters instead of a single multi-node cluster, working under the impression that it is best to keep things as simple as possible.

Clustering Multiple Instances of SQL Server on the Same Server

As indicated in the types of clustering discussed previously, a single SQL Server instance can run on a single physical server. However, this is not a requirement. SQL Server Enterprise Edition can actually support up to 64 SQL instances on a single clustered configuration. If SMB file shares are used for shared storage, the limit jumps up to 50 instances of SQL Server 2014. The effectiveness of this depends on the business requirements, the capacity of the hardware, SLAs, and the expertise of the IT organization managing it.

The purpose of clustering is to boost availability. Adding many SQL Server instances to a cluster adds complexity, and complexity can increase risk and failover points in the solution. But complexity can also be managed, depending on the IT expertise to support it. Speak to your IT support when considering this option.

UPGRADING SQL SERVER CLUSTERING

If your organization is like many, it probably already has some older versions of SQL Server clusters in production. If so, it is time to decide how to upgrade them to SQL Server 2014. Your available options include the following:

➤ Don't upgrade.

➤ Perform an in-place SQL Server 2014 upgrade.

➤ Rebuild your cluster from scratch, and then install SQL Server 2014 clustering. Or, leave the Windows Failover Cluster intact if it is a Windows 2008 SP2 or later, but install a new SQL Server 2014 on it and migrate the databases.

This section considers each of these three options.

Don't Upgrade

This is an easy decision. Not upgrading is simple and doesn't cost anything. Just because a new version of SQL Server comes out doesn't mean you have to upgrade. If your current SQL Server cluster is running satisfactorily, it may not be worth the costs and upgrade work. A properly configured Windows 2012 R2 cluster is stable running SQL Server 2008 R2 and 2012.

On the other hand, SQL Server 2014 offers scalability, ease of use, new capabilities, reliability, and new functionality, all of which you may want to take advantage of. Before you upgrade, do the research to determine whether the new features of SQL Server 2014 are what you need. Otherwise, you can choose to stay on the current SQL Server version, provided that it is still supported by Microsoft.

Upgrading Your SQL Server 2014 Cluster In-Place

Before talking about how to upgrade a Windows Failover Cluster to SQL Server 2014, first consider what operating system you currently run. If you are on Windows Server 2008 SP2 or later, you can upgrade in-place to SQL Server 2014.

You should deploy Windows 2008 SP2 or later, preferably Windows 2012 R2. Upgrading from a previous Windows version in a Failover Cluster is not supported; a total rebuild is required.

If you run a Windows 2008 SP2 Failover Cluster where SQL Server needs to be upgraded to SQL Server 2014, you can perform a rolling upgrade with minimum downtime by performing the following steps:

1. Identify the cluster node that you want to upgrade first.

2. Failover all the SQL instances from that node. As a result, no SQL instances will run on that node. Therefore, that node becomes passive.

3. Install prerequisites on each passive node, and upgrade the shared SQL Server components.

4. Restart passive nodes as prompted.

5. Run the SQL Server 2014 setup to perform an in-place upgrade. Prior to doing any upgrades, you should follow SQL upgrade validation procedures. Set up a test environment, run the SQL Server 2014 Upgrade Advisor, upgrade the test environment to SQL 2014, replay a production SQL Profiler trace, and test the application's connectivity and performance test. Not following upgrade procedures can result in a failed upgrade that also results in a need to back out, which is more complex in a Windows Cluster than in a standalone SQL Server environment.

6. After more than half of the passive nodes have been upgraded, the upgrade process automatically initiates a failover to the upgraded nodes and maintains a list of possible owners to which the resources can fail while the remaining nodes are upgraded.

> **NOTE** *Not all SQL instances need to be upgraded. Windows Failover Cluster supports a mix of SQL Server 2008 (and R2), 2012, and 2014 on a single Windows Failover Cluster.*

Rebuilding Your Cluster

Rebuilding your cluster from scratch is a good idea if any one of the following conditions exists:

➤ You need to upgrade your current hardware. (It is either old or underpowered.)

➤ The server is using an older Windows operating system.

➤   The current cluster installation is unstable.

➤   You have disdain for upgrading software in-place and prefer a fresh install.

If you do decide to upgrade from scratch, you must also decide whether to install on new hardware or use your old hardware. If you install on new hardware, you have the convenience of building the cluster and testing it at your own pace while the current cluster is still in production. This helps to ensure that you have done an outstanding job and, at the same time, relieves some of the stress that you might experience if you have to reuse your old hardware and then rebuild the cluster during a brief and intense time period.

If you don't have the luxury of acquiring new hardware, you must identify a downtime when your system can be shut down while the rebuild occurs. This could range from a 4-hour period to a 12-hour period, depending on the size of the cluster and complexity. In addition to the time your cluster will be down, there is also the added risk of unexpected problems. For example, you might make an installation mistake halfway through the upgrade and have to start over. Because of the uncertainty involved, you should first estimate how much time you think the upgrade will take under good circumstances, and then double that estimate as the size of your requested downtime window. This way, your users are prepared.

Whether you upgrade using new hardware or old hardware, you must consider two additional issues:

➤   Will you reuse your current clustered SQL Server name and IP address, or select new ones?

➤   How will you move your data from the previous cluster to the new cluster?

The clients that access your current SQL Server cluster do so using the cluster's SQL Server name and IP address. If you want the clients to continue using the same clustered SQL Server name and IP address, you must reuse the old clustered SQL Server name and IP address in the new cluster. This is the most common approach, because it is generally easier to change a single clustered SQL Server name and IP address than to reconfigure dozens (if not hundreds) of clients that access the SQL Servers on the Windows Failover Cluster.

If you upgrade using old hardware, reusing the former clustered SQL Server name and IP address is not an issue because the old cluster is brought down and then the new one is brought up, so there is never a time when the clustered SQL Server name and IP address are on two clusters at the same time (which won't work).

If you upgrade by using new hardware, you must assign a clustered SQL Server virtual network name and IP address for testing, but you won't use the old ones because they are currently in use. In this case, you must use a temporary clustered SQL Server name and IP address for testing. When you are ready for the actual changeover from the old cluster to the new cluster, follow these general steps:

1.   Back up the data.

2.   Remove SQL Server clustering from the old cluster, or turn off the old cluster.

3.   On the new cluster, change the clustered SQL Server virtual network name and IP address from the old cluster.

4.   Restore the data.

How you move the data from the old cluster to the new cluster depends on both the size of the databases and, somewhat, on whether you use old hardware or new hardware.

Regardless of the option you choose, before you proceed, back up all the databases. Remember, identify any objects in the System databases such as SQL jobs, SSIS packages, and logins, and re-create them in the new Windows Failover Cluster. If you use old hardware, all you have to do is back up or detach the user databases. When the cluster rebuild is complete, restore or re-attach the user databases.

If you move to new hardware or change the database file locations, you should first back up or detach user databases. Next, move these to the new cluster or new database location. Then, when the cluster rebuild completes, restore or re-attach the user databases.

> **NOTE** *There isn't space here to include detailed steps for every possible scenario, such as what happens if the drive letter changes, and so on. The key to success is to plan all these steps and, if possible, perform a trial run before you do an actual cutover.*

Back-Out Plan

No matter how you decide to upgrade to SQL Server 2014 clustering, you need to have a back-out plan. Essentially, a *back-out plan* is what you do if your upgrade fails. Typically, a back-out plan consists of reinstalling SQL Server, restoring the system and user databases, and incurring at least a few hours of outage.

However, because each particular circumstance can vary, it is impossible to create one set of steps to follow for all back-out plans. Therefore, as you plan your upgrade, consider how the plan could fail, and come up with options to get you back in business should things not go well. Your job could depend on how good your back-out plan is. Typically speaking, the most risk is associated with an in-place upgrade of SQL Server because there is no rollback plan. For that reason, you should perform a side-by-side upgrade if at all possible, and, of course, ensure that you back up all databases before any upgrade process.

Which Upgrade Option Is Best?

Speaking from experience, the authors always prefer to upgrade by rebuilding clusters from scratch on new hardware. This is the easiest, fastest, least risky, and least stressful way. Unfortunately, you may not have this option for whatever reasons based on your circumstances. In this case, you must work with what you have been given. The key to a successful upgrade is a lot of detailed planning, as much testing as possible, and, of course, having a complete back-out plan.

GETTING PREPARED FOR CLUSTERING

For SQL Server 2014 clustering, the devil is in the details. If you take the time to ensure that every step is done correctly and in the right order, your cluster installation will be smooth and relatively quick and painless. But if you don't like to read instructions, and instead prefer the trial-and-error approach to computer administration, expect to face a lot of frustration and a lot of time installing and reinstalling your SQL Server 2014 cluster.

The best way to ensure a smooth cluster installation is to create a detailed, step-by-step plan for the installation, down to the screen level. Yes, this is boring and tedious, but it forces you to think through every option, and how it can affect your installation and your organization (after it is in production). In addition, such a plan can come in handy the next time you build a cluster, and can be great documentation for your disaster-recovery plan.

Preparing the Infrastructure

Before you begin building a SQL Server 2014 cluster, you must ensure that your network infrastructure is in place. Following is a checklist of everything required before you begin installing a SQL Server 2014 cluster. In many cases, these items are the responsibility of others on your IT staff, but it is your responsibility to ensure that all these are in place before you begin building your SQL Server 2014 cluster.

- ➤ Your network must have at least one Active Directory domain controller, and ideally two for redundancy.

- ➤ Your network must have at least one DNS server, and ideally two for redundancy.

- ➤ Your network must have available switch ports for the public network cards used by the nodes of the cluster. Be sure to set them to match the manually set network card settings used in the nodes of the cluster. SQL Server 2014 supports nodes in different subnets. (This functionality was not supported before the release of SQL Server 2012.)

- ➤ You must secure IP addresses for all the public network cards (which is preferable), or use Dynamic Host Configuration Protocol (DHCP).

- ➤ You must decide how you will configure the private heartbeat network. Choose between using a direct network-card-to-network-card connection using a crossover cable (only possible with a two-node cluster), or use a hub or switch. The hub or switch should be different than the one supporting the public network for redundancy. Although a heartbeat network is no longer required, it is still recommended.

- ➤ You must secure IP addresses for the private network cards. Generally, you should use a private network subnet such as 10.0.0.0–10.255.255.255, 172.16.0.0–172.31.255.255, or 192.168.0.0–192.168.255.255. Remember, this is a private network seen only by the nodes of the cluster.

- ➤ Ensure that you have proper electrical power for the new cluster nodes and shared disk array.

- ➤ Ensure that battery backup power is available to all the nodes in your cluster and your shared disk array.

- ➤ If you don't already have one, create a SQL Server service account to be used by the SQL Server services running on the cluster. This must be a domain account with the password set to never expire.

➤ Determine a name for your Windows Failover Cluster and secure an IP address for it. This name will be used for management of the cluster after it is created.

➤ Determine a name for your SQL Server 2014 cluster and secure an IP address for it. This will be the name that clients will connect to.

These preparations will come back into play during the installation process.

Preparing the Hardware

Hardware typically presents certain issues, often taking the most time to research and configure. Part of the reason for this is that many hardware options are available, some of which work, some of which don't. Unfortunately, there is no complete resource you can use to help you sort through this. Each vendor offers different hardware, and the available hardware is always changing, along with new and updated hardware drivers, making this entire subject a moving target with no easy answers. In spite of all this, here is what you need to know to start selecting the proper hardware for your SQL Server 2014 cluster.

Finding Your Way through the Hardware Jungle

This section describes the basic hardware you need for a SQL Server cluster. To keep things simple, only a two-node active/passive cluster is discussed, although these same recommendations apply to multi-node clusters. Additionally, some Windows Failover Clusters are configured with a quorum drive, so assume a quorum drive configuration. The following are the authors' minimum hardware recommendations. If you check out Microsoft's minimum hardware requirements for a SQL Server 2014 cluster, they will be somewhat less.

> **NOTE** *Each node in your cluster should be identical. This will avoid installation and administrative headaches.*

The minimum specifications for the server nodes should be the following:

➤ Dual CPUs, 2GHz or higher, 2MB L2 Cache (32-bit or 64-bit)

➤ 4GB or more RAM

➤ Local mirrored SCSI drive for the application drive (RAID 10, 5, or 1) (C:), 9GB or larger

➤ SCSI DVD drive

➤ SCSI connection for local SCSI drive and DVD drive

➤ SCSI or fiber connection to shared disk array or SAN or shared ISCSI drives

➤ Redundant power supplies

➤ Private network card

➤ Public network card

➤ Mouse, keyboard, and monitor (can be shared)

The shared disk array should have an SCSI-attached RAID 10, 5, or 1 array with an appropriate high-speed SCSI connection. With Microsoft Windows Failover clustering, SCSI is supported only if you have a two-node cluster. If you want to cluster more than two nodes, you must use iSCSI, SMB 3.0 file shares, fiber-attached disk array, or SAN with RAID 10, 5, or 1, and an appropriate high-speed connection.

If you are new to clustering, contact your hardware vendor for specific hardware recommendations. Keep in mind that you will be running SQL Server 2014 on this cluster, so ensure that whatever hardware you select meets the needs of your predicted production workload.

Preparing the Hardware

As a DBA, you may not be the one who installs the hardware. In any case, here are the general steps most people follow when building cluster hardware:

1. Install and configure the hardware for each node in the cluster as if it will be running as a standalone server. This includes installing the latest approved drivers and firmware.

2. After the hardware is installed, install the operating system and the latest service pack, along with any additional required drivers. Then run Windows Update.

3. Configure the nodes to the public network. To make things easy to identify, name the network used for public connections **public network**.

4. Configure the private heartbeat network. To make things easy to identify, name the private heartbeat network **private network**.

5. Set up and configure the shared disk array, iSCSI targets, or fiber channel SAN.

6. Install and configure the iSCSI or fiber cards in each of the nodes, and install the latest drivers. In this case, you must set up the iSCSI initiators to connect to the drives.

7. One at a time, connect each node to the shared disk array, iSCSI drive, or SAN, following the instructions for your specific hardware. It is critical that you do this one node at a time. In other words, only one node at a time should be physically on and connected to the shared disk array or SAN and configured. After that node is configured, turn it off and turn the next node on and configure it, and so on, one node at a time. If you do not follow this procedure, you risk corrupting the disk configuration on your nodes, requiring you to start the process over.

8. Use Disk Administrator to configure and format the drives on the shared disk array. You need at minimum two logical drives on the shared disk array: one for storing your SQL Server databases, and the other for the quorum drive. The data drive must be big enough to store all the required data and the quorum drive must be at least 500MB (which is the smallest size that an NTFS volume can efficiently operate). When configuring the shared drives using Disk Administrator, each node of the cluster is required to use the same drive letter when referring to the drives on the shared disk array or SAN. For example, you might want to assign your data drive as drive "F:" on all the nodes, and assign the quorum drive letter "Q:" on all the nodes.

9. When all the hardware is put together, ensure that no problems exist before you begin installing clustering services by checking the Windows Event Viewer. Although you may do some diagnostic hardware testing before you install the operating system, you need to wait until after installing the operating system before you can fully test the hardware.

10. Ensure that you can ping the cluster nodes over the public and then the private networks. Likewise, ensure that you can ping the domain controller and DNS server to verify that they are available.

11. Write a file in the shared disks next to one node, which should be visible by the other node.

12. Additionally, verify that the drive letters correspond between nodes and that there is not a mismatch in drive letters from the shared disks between nodes.

After all the hardware has been configured and tested, you are ready to install Windows Failover clustering.

CLUSTERING WINDOWS SERVER 2012 R2

Before you can install SQL Server 2014 on the cluster, you must first install Windows Server 2012 R2 Failover Cluster services. After it is successfully installed and tested, you can cluster SQL Server. This section takes a high-level, step-by-step approach to installing and configuring a Windows Failover Cluster.

Before Installing Windows 2012 R2 Clustering

To install Windows Failover clustering, you must perform a series of important steps. This is especially important if you didn't build the cluster nodes, because you want to ensure everything is working correctly before you begin the actual cluster installation. When they are completed, you can install Windows 2012 R2 Failover clustering. Following are the steps you must perform:

1. Ensure that all the physical nodes are working properly and are configured identically (hardware, software, and drivers).

2. Verify that none of the physical nodes have been configured as a domain controller or for any other critical services such as Exchange. Also, ensure that you have multiple domain controllers in your environment.

3. Verify that all drives are NTFS and are not compressed.

4. Ensure that the public and private networks are properly installed and configured.

5. SQL Server failover cluster installation supports Local Disk only for installing the `tempdb` files. Ensure that the path specified for the `tempdb` data and log files is valid on all the cluster nodes. During failover, if the `tempdb` directories are not available on the failover target node, the SQL Server resource will fail to come online.

6. Verify that you have disabled NetBIOS for all private network cards.

7. Verify that no network shares are on any of the shared drives.

8. If you intend to use SQL Server encryption, install the server certificate with the fully qualified DNS name of the clustered SQL Server on all cluster nodes.

9. Check all the error logs to ensure that no problems exist. If they do, resolve them before proceeding with the cluster installation.

10. Add the SQL Server and clustering service accounts to the Local Administrators group of all the cluster nodes.

11. Verify that no antivirus software has been installed on the cluster nodes. Antivirus software can reduce the availability of a cluster. If you want to check for possible viruses on a Windows Failover Cluster, run scans on the cluster nodes remotely from another computer.

You have many things to check, but each is important. If skipped, any one of these steps could prevent your cluster from installing or working properly.

Installing Windows Server 2012 R2 Failover Clustering

Now that all your physical nodes and shared disk array, iSCSI device, or SAN are ready, you are ready to install a Windows 2012 R2 Failover Cluster. This section describes the process from beginning to end.

To begin, you must enable the clustering feature for each of the Windows 2012 R2 node candidates. In Windows 2008, the decision was made to reduce the Windows surface area by disabling the feature by default. To enable the failover clustering feature, from the Server Manager, open the "Add Roles and Features Wizard." As shown in Figure 16-1, check Failover Clustering, and the wizard completes the installation for you. This doesn't actually cluster your machines, but installs the necessary components on your server to manage the cluster and perform the failover. You must repeat this step on each physical node participating on the Windows Failover Cluster.

Validating the Windows Failover Cluster

Before you create the cluster, you want to validate that the cluster physical nodes run on supported hardware. You can tell if this is true if the nodes pass the cluster validation tests. To do this, open the Failover Cluster Management tool, and click "Validate a Configuration." This opens the "Validate a Cluster Configuration Wizard," which runs a full diagnosis of your cluster prior to the installation.

Additionally, you can also use this wizard after installation of the cluster to ensure that you still meet the cluster hardware requirements, and that all the hardware is in proper working condition.

> **NOTE** *Microsoft supports a Windows Failover Cluster if it passes the cluster validation. Gone are the days of looking over a long compatibility matrix list to determine whether your Windows Failover Cluster was supported on a given hardware platform!*

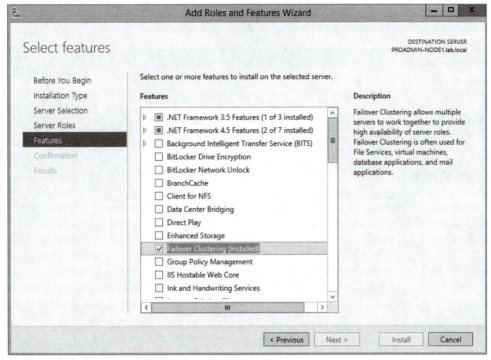

FIGURE 16-1

When you're in the "Validate a Configuration Wizard," you will be asked which physical nodes or potential nodes you want to validate. Enter each of them into the list, and click Next. You are then asked what types of tests you want to run. The tests begin to run, and you get a visual confirmation as the validation tests move from step to step, as shown in Figure 16-2. If you fail a test, do not install the cluster, even though you can override the test and still cluster the nodes. Review the report. You see a component-by-component evaluation of your configuration to determine whether your hardware is suitable.

Viewing the report is as easy as clicking the View Report button. Doing so takes you to an HTML report, a granular report about each of your hardware components, and whether they're cluster-approved.

Installing the Clustered Nodes

Windows 2012 R2 Failover Cluster has been simplified substantially from previous Windows versions. This is mainly because you can now cluster all nodes at once in a wizard that asks you two questions. If you've deployed an older Windows Failover Cluster, you will be amazed when you see how easy the steps are to cluster Windows Server 2012 R2:

1. From within the Failover Cluster Management, click "Create a Cluster." This opens the Create Cluster Wizard. The first screen after the welcome screen asks you which physical

nodes will participate in the cluster. Type in each physical node and click Add, as shown in Figure 16-3. You can add more physical nodes later if need be.

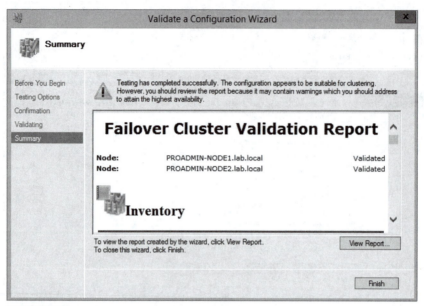

FIGURE 16-2

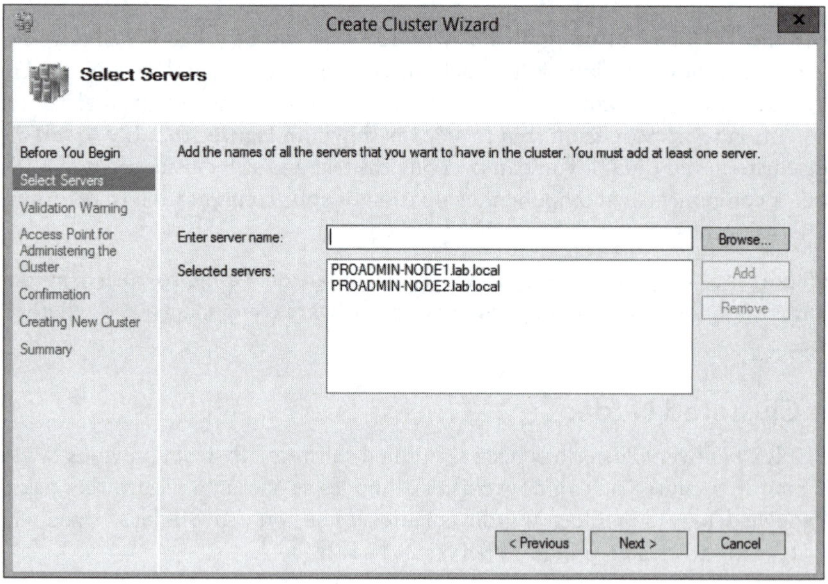

FIGURE 16-3

2. Assign the Windows cluster an IP address, and specify which network you want the cluster to use, as shown in Figure 16-4. In the figure, you can see that PROADMIN-WSFC was the Windows cluster name used for management. Also, the cluster object gets assigned an IP address, which, in this case, is 10.10.10.27.

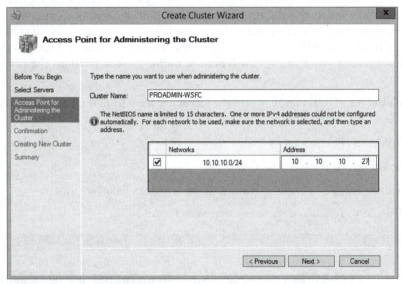

FIGURE 16-4

The wizard then begins to create and configure the cluster (see Figure 16-5), and you will be notified when the build process is done. This is a much shorter process than in previous Windows versions. It took no more than 2 minutes in a test environment.

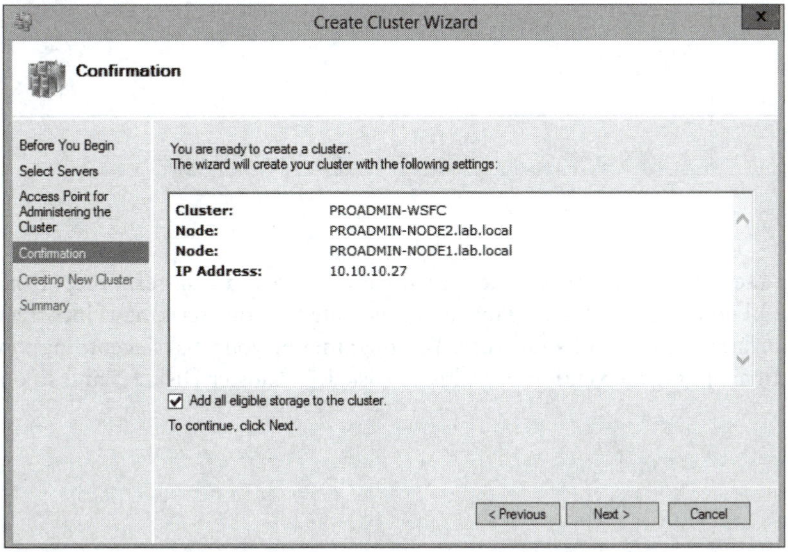

FIGURE 16-5

Preparing Windows Server 2012 R2 for Clustering

Before you can install SQL Server, you must perform one small step, and that is to prepare the cluster for SQL Server. In the previous section, you clustered Windows, but didn't tell Windows which are the shared disks. This is because Microsoft now deploys a minimalist approach to clustering during the installation, doing the absolute minimum it needs to get it clustered, and then enabling you to add the necessary components later. You have the option to add all eligible storage at the end of the Create Cluster Wizard, which is not required for the cluster to be created successfully. If you did not check that option, you will need to follow these steps to get the storage added to the cluster.

To prepare the cluster for SQL Server, perform the following steps from the Failover Cluster Management tool:

1. Under Navigate, click Storage ⇨ Disks.

2. From the Actions pane, click Add Disk.

3. Add any disks that you want to be visible to the Windows Failover Cluster.

4. Click OK, and you should see a screen similar to Figure 16-6.

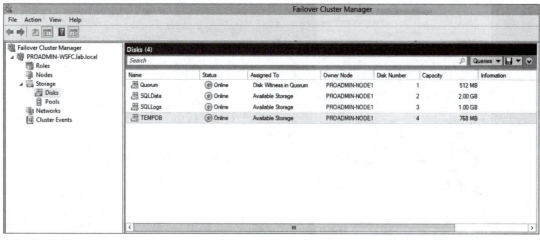

FIGURE 16-6

If you cannot see the shared disks, they are either already added as a disk resource, or the disks are not visible to all nodes in the cluster. This might indicate that the masking is incorrect, or that there's a communication problem of some sort. You might name your disks according to when they will be added with a naming convention of "Cluster Disk 1," "Cluster Disk 2," and so on. At this point, you have added all the available/eligible storage to the cluster before attempting to install SQL Server 2014.

CLUSTERING MICROSOFT DISTRIBUTED TRANSACTION COORDINATOR

To coordinate transactions across SQL Servers in a clustered environment, you must leverage the Microsoft Distributed Transaction Coordinator (MSDTC) to make it highly available.

Windows 2003 supported only one cluster MSDTC resource; as a result, all applications across the cluster needed to use the single MSDTC instance. However, when an MSDTC is highly utilized, it can become a bottleneck. On Windows 2008 and later, for better performance, you can install multiple MSDTC instances on a single Windows Failover Cluster as shown in the following steps. The first MSDTC instance installed becomes the default instance, but can be changed from the Component Services Management Console (`dcomcnfg`):

1. Launch the Component Services Management Console from the `Administration` folder, or by executing `dcomcnfg` from a command prompt.

2. Expand `Computers`, and then right-click `My Computer`.

3. Click Properties, click the MSDTC tab, and select the default coordinator.

If multiple MSDTC instances exist, SQL Server uses the following rules to identify the MSDTC instance to be chosen in priority order:

1. Use the MSDTC instance installed to the local SQL Server group.

2. Use the mapped MSDTC instance. To create a mapping, execute the following at the command prompt:

```
msdtc -tmMappingSet -name <MappingName>
-service <SQLServerServiceName> -clusterResource <MSDTCResourceName>
```

In this code snippet, the following is true:

➤ `<MappingName>` is any chosen name to identify the mapping.

➤ `<SQLServerServiceName>` is the service name from the SQL Server instance, such as `MSSQLServer` or `MSSQL$<InstanceName>`.

➤ `<MSDTCResourceName>` is the MSDTC resource name to map.

3. Use the cluster's default MSDTC instance.

4. Use the local node MSDTC instance.

SQL Server automatically uses its local group MSDTC instance if it exists; otherwise, it uses the default instance. If the local group MSDTC instance fails, you must tell SQL Server to use another MSDTC instance; it does not automatically use the default instance. To create a cluster MSDTC instance, use the Failover Cluster Management tool, and follow these steps:

1. Identify a small shared disk to store the MSDTC log file. It is best to put the log file on its own shared disk or mount point to protect it from any other service that may corrupt the disk.

2. If the MSDTC resource is installed within a SQL Server Resource Group, it can share the IP and clustered SQL Server name of that group.

3. The default MSDTC should be installed on its own Cluster Resource Group to avoid a failover of MSDTC, which, in turn, fails other services contained in that resource group. When installed on its own resource group, it needs its own IP and network name, in addition to a shared disk.

After creating the MSDTC resource(s), you must enable MSDTC network access to allow MSDTC to access network resources, and for applications to access it. To do so, perform these steps:

1. Launch the Component Services Management Console from the `Administration` folder, or by executing `dcomcnfg` from a command prompt.

2. Expand `Computers`. Expand `Distributed Transaction Coordinator` and then expand `<Your instance of MSDTC>`.

3. Right-click the Properties of your MSDTC instance.

4. Under Security Settings, check the Network DTC Access box and the Allow Inbound and Allow Outbound check boxes, and click OK.

CLUSTERING SQL SERVER 2014

The procedure to install a SQL Server instance onto a Windows Failover Cluster is one of the easiest parts of getting your SQL Server cluster up and running. The SQL Server 2014 setup program is used for the install, and does the heavy lifting for you. All you have to do is make a few (but critically important) decisions, and then sit back and watch the installation complete. The setup program even goes to the trouble of verifying that your nodes are all properly configured. And if not, it suggests how to fix any problems before the installation begins. SQL Server 2014 binaries are installed on the local drive of each node, and the system databases are stored on the shared disk array you designate.

The next section shows the step-by-step instructions for installing a SQL Server 2014 instance in a Windows Failover Cluster. The assumption for this example is that you will install this instance in a two-node active/passive cluster. Even if you install in a two-node active/active or a multi-node cluster, the steps in this section are applicable. The only difference is that you must run SQL Server 2014 setup on every node for which you want to install SQL Server, and you must specify a different logical drive on the shared disk array for each SQL Server instance.

Step-by-Step Instructions to Cluster SQL Server

To begin installing your SQL Server on the cluster, you need the installation media (DVD or ISO). You can either install it directly from the media, or copy the install files from the media to the current active node of the cluster, and run the setup program from there. The general process for SQL Server installation is the same as a normal, non-clustered installation. (This is covered in Chapter 2 , "Installing SQL Server 2014 Best Practices.") Therefore, the following steps outline the differences from a normal non-clustered installation:

1. To begin installation, run `Setup.exe`. The prerequisite components (which you learned about in Chapter 2) install first. It is a good idea to run these prerequisites on each of the nodes prior to clustering, because doing so can save time and enable you to debug visually if something goes wrong during the installation.

2. When you get to the SQL Server Installation Center, click New SQL Server Failover Cluster Installation. In this screen you can also add new nodes to the cluster after the installation, as shown in Figure 16-7.

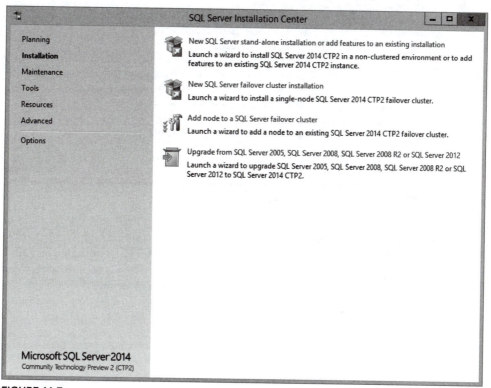

FIGURE 16-7

For the most part, the cluster installation is exactly the same as the standalone SQL Server installation, with the exception of just a few screens. When you get to the Setup Support

Rules page, you notice a number of new rules that are checked (see Figure 16-8). For example, a check is made to determine whether MSDTC is clustered. Although SQL Server can work without MSDTC clustered, some features such as distributed transactions for linked servers or SSIS will not work without it.

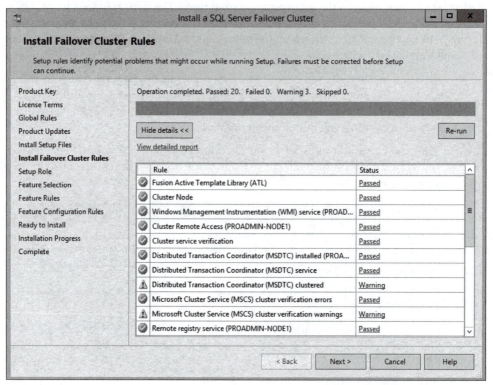

FIGURE 16-8

3. In the Instance Configuration dialog box, specify the clustered SQL Server Network Name for your SQL Server instance, as shown in Figure 16-9. This is the name that all the client applications use to connect in their connection strings. The name of the directory where your program files will be copied is also based on this name by default. Click Next.

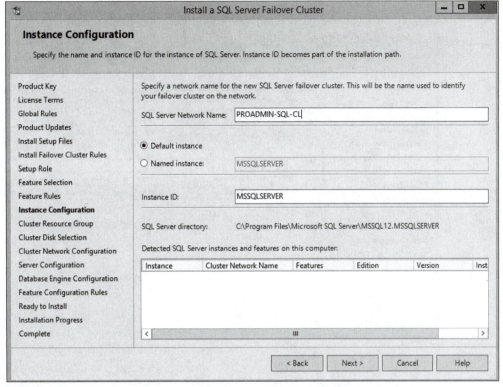

FIGURE 16-9

4. On the Cluster Resource Group page, specify the cluster resource group that will group all your SQL Server resources, such as your network name, IP, and SQL Server services, as shown in Figure 16-10. Click Next.

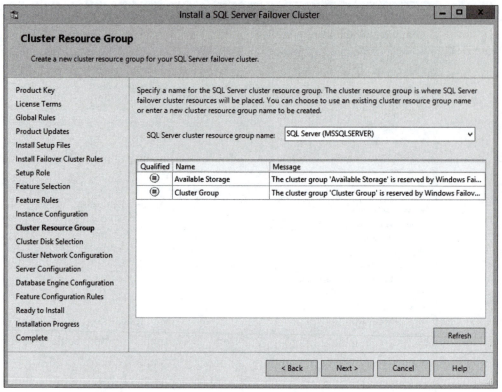

FIGURE 16-10

5. A nice improvement since SQL Server 2008 is that you can have SQL Server use multiple drives in a cluster during the installation. In SQL Server 2005, you had to configure this behavior afterward, and you weren't able to back up to another disk other than the main SQL Server disk until you fixed the dependencies. In SQL Server 2014, simply check which clustered drive resources you want SQL Server to access, as shown in Figure 16-11. Click Next.

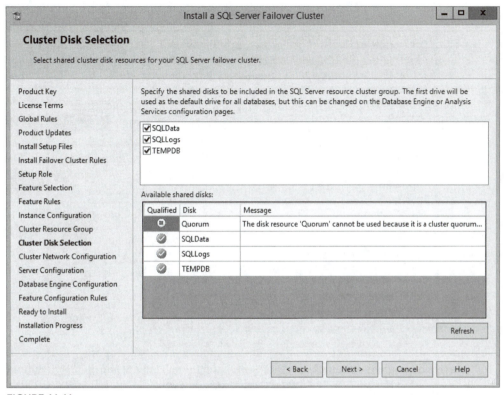

FIGURE 16-11

6. With the drive configuration complete, on the Cluster Network Configuration page, specify the network that SQL Server will use to communicate with client applications, and choose an IP address for each of the networks. This IP address should have been obtained earlier from a network administrator. Notice in Figure 16-12 that Windows 2012 R2 can also use DHCP. Click Next.

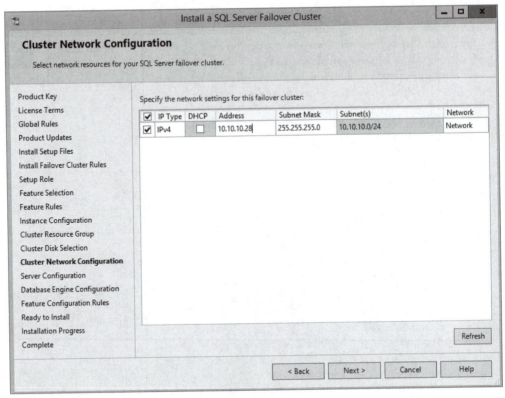

FIGURE 16-12

7. On the Server Configuration page, specify the service accounts and collation configuration, as shown in Figure 16-13.

Continue with the installation to proceed to copy the files to the cluster node and run the setup. Additionally, all the SQL cluster resources will be created and configured. When finished with that cluster node, you can go to the other cluster node and click Add Node to join each additional node to become part of the SQL Server cluster instance. Unlike clustering SQL Server 2005 where the SQL setup program copied the SQL binary to all clustered nodes, starting in SQL Server 2008, the SQL setup program clusters the current node onto where the setup is executing.

To add another node for SQL Server 2008 or later, perform the following steps:

1. Log in to the node that you want to join to the cluster.

2. Run the SQL Setup on the node.

3. Choose "Add Node to a SQL Server Failover Cluster."

4. As the setup proceeds, you will be asked for the name of the SQL cluster to join to. Provide the appropriate name.

5. Then the setup will proceed to join that node. If you want to add more nodes to the cluster, follow the previous steps for each node.

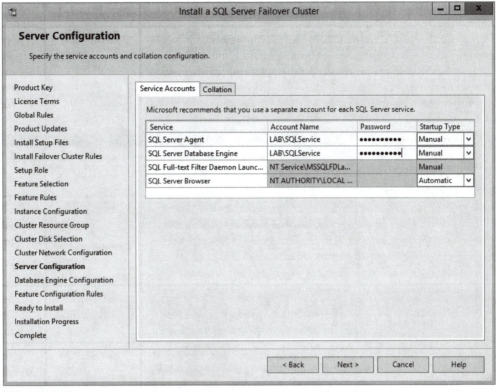

FIGURE 16-13

When the cluster installation completes, from within the Windows Failover Cluster Manager, your two-node cluster installation should look similar to Figure 16-14.

> **NOTE** *Like clustering the SQL Server relational engine that is fully integrated with the Windows Failover Cluster, Analysis Services is fully clustered. Moreover, SSIS can only be clustered as a generic resource, whereas Reporting Services cannot be clustered. (Although the Reporting Services databases can live on a cluster instance, just not the web front-ends.)*

After each SQL Server instance has been clustered, the resource group should contain the following resources:

➤ Network name.

➤ IP address.

➤ One or more shared disks.

➤ SQL Server Database Engine service.

➤   SQL Server Agent service.

➤   SQL Server Analysis Services service (if installed). As a best practice, install it on its own resource group to avoid a failure in one resource affecting the other.

➤   One file share resource, if the `FILESTREAM` feature is installed.

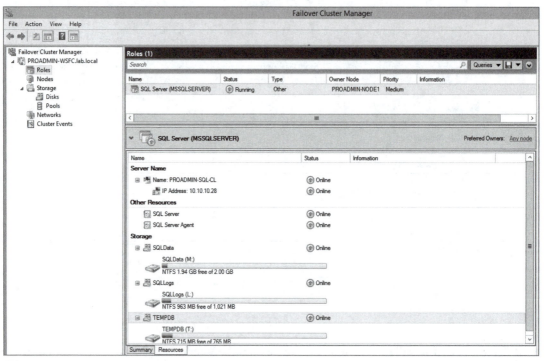

FIGURE 16-14

After the clustered SQL Server installation completes, evaluate the resources' dependencies to identify what other resources in the group must be online before a particular resource can be brought online. For example, SQL Server Agent depends on SQL Server being online, and SQL Server depends on the shared disks and the clustered SQL Server name and IP address. The complete Windows Failover Cluster installation should look like Figure 16-14.

Installing the Service Pack and Cumulative Updates

After you install and cluster SQL Server, your next step is to install any available SQL Server service pack and cumulative updates, which you can download from Windows Update. You can perform a rolling upgrade as described in the "Upgrading Your SQL Server 2014 Cluster In-Place" section. Installing a service pack and/or a cumulative update is fairly straightforward because they are cluster-aware.

Test, Test, and Test Again

After you cluster SQL Server on the nodes, you must thoroughly test the installation, just as you did after first installing Windows 2012 R2 Failover Cluster. For example, check the Windows Event Viewer for any error messages, and validate that you can fail over the SQL Server across nodes and back. However, not only do you want to test the SQL Server cluster, but you also want to test how your client applications "react" to failovers. Because of this, the following testing section is similar to the one you previously read, but has been modified to meet the more complex needs of the additional client application testing you need to perform.

The following is a series of tests you can perform to verify that your SQL Server 2014 cluster and its client applications work properly during failover situations. After you perform each test, verify whether you get the expected results (a successful failover), and be sure you check the Windows log files for any possible problems. If you find a problem during one test, resolve it before proceeding to the next test.

Preparing for the Testing

As with your previous cluster testing, identify a workstation with the Failover Cluster Management tool to interact with your cluster during testing.

To be prepared, you need to test each client application that will be accessing your clustered SQL Server to see what happens should a failover occur. Some client applications deal with clustering failovers by reconnecting, whereas others are not designed with reconnect logic and just fail to reconnect. You must determine beforehand how each client application responds.

To do this, first identify all the client applications; there may be dozens. Each of these must be reconfigured to use the clustered SQL Server name (and IP address) for the new clustered SQL Server instance. In addition, for the client applications to work, you must have the appropriate databases restored or installed on the new cluster. This is necessary if you want a highly available cluster solution.

After you have each of your client applications connected to the SQL Server instance, you are ready for testing. Keep in mind that you are testing multiple things, including the Windows 2012 R2 Cluster, the clustered SQL Server, and the client applications.

Moving Resource Groups between Nodes

The easiest test to perform is to use the Failover Cluster Management tool to manually move the SQL Server resource group from the active node to a passive node, and then back again. To do this, follow these steps:

1. Go to the resource group that contains SQL Server. Right-click to select "Move this service or application to another node," and specify where you'd like to move the resource group. This initiates the resource group move from your active node to the designated passive node.

2. After this happens, check the Failover Cluster Management tool and each of the client applications. Each should continue to operate as if no failover had occurred. The Failover Cluster

Management tool should pass this test easily. The clients are another story; you must check each client application to see if it reconnected. If not, you must determine why not, which is not always easy. Most client applications that stop working after a failover do so because of no reconnect logic. For example, they reconnect if you exit and restart the client application.

3.   When the resource group has been successfully moved from the active node to a passive node, use the same procedure to move the group back to the original node. As before, check the Failover Cluster Management tool, the client applications, and the event logs to see if there were any problems. If you noticed any Windows Failover Cluster or SQL Server problems because of the failover test, you must resolve them before proceeding. If you have a client application problem, you can continue with your testing and try to resolve it later. In most cases, if a client application fails this first test, it will fail all the other tests.

Manually Failing Over Nodes by Turning Them Off

To validate that the failover from node to node is taking place and that each node can take over the SQL Server, you can perform a failover test by manually turning nodes off:

1.   Turn off the active node. When this happens, watch the failover in the Failover Cluster Management tool and the client applications. As before, check for any problems.

2.   Next, turn on the node and wait until it boots back up successfully. Then turn off the now current active node. Again, watch the failover in the Failover Cluster Management tool and the client applications, and check for problems.

3.   Turn the node back on when done.

Manually Failing Over Nodes by Disconnecting the Public Network Connections

You can also manually failover nodes by turning off public network connections:

1.   Unplug the public network connection from the active node. This causes a failover to a passive node, which you can watch in the Failover Cluster Management tool and the client applications. Check for any problems.

2.   Now, plug the public network connection back into the server, and unplug the public network connection from the now-active node. This causes a failover to the current passive node, which you can watch in the Failover Cluster Management tool. Watch the failover in the Failover Cluster Management tool and the client applications, and check for problems.

3.   When the testing is complete, plug the network connection back into the node.

Manually Failing Over Nodes by Breaking the Shared Array Connection

You can perform a third manual failover test by breaking a shared array connection:

1.   From the active node, remove the shared disk array connection. This can cause a failover that you can watch in the Failover Cluster Management tool and client applications. Check for any problems.

2. Next, reconnect the connection from the now-active node, and remove the shared disk array connection. Watch the failover in the Failover Cluster Management tool and the client applications, and check for problems.

3. When done, reconnect the connection.

> **NOTE** *If you run into problems in any of these tests, resolve them before continuing.*

MANAGING AND MONITORING THE CLUSTER

After you have your clustered SQL Server up, running, and tested, you are ready to deploy it into production. This may involve creating new databases, moving databases from older servers to this one, setting up SQL jobs, and so on. In most cases, managing SQL Server on a cluster is the same as managing it as a standalone SQL Server instance.

The key thing to keep in mind is that whenever you access your cluster with any of your SQL Server 2014 administrative tools (such as SQL Server Management Studio), you access it using its SQL cluster network name and IP address. But if you use any of the operating system tools (such as System Monitor), you must use the SQL cluster network or IP address of the node to monitor (which is usually the active node).

In most cases, as a DBA, you probably will administer SQL Server 2014 using SQL Server Management Studio, but sometimes you need to access the individual nodes of the cluster. If you have easy access to the cluster, you can always log on locally; if you prefer remote administration, you can use Remote Desktop (Terminal Services) to access the individual nodes.

When DBAs begin to administer their first Windows Failover Cluster, they get a little confused as to where SQL Server actually runs. Keep in mind that a clustered SQL Server instance consists of an active node that is running a SQL Server and the passive node that is not running SQL Server. At any one time, a SQL Server instance runs on the active node only, so when you need to look at the nodes directly, generally you want to look at the active node. If you don't know which node is currently active, you can find out by using the Failover Cluster Management tool.

When you log in to the active node (or connect to it remotely using Remote Desktop) and then bring up Windows Explorer (a routine task), you can access the SQL Server shared data disks. But if you log on to the passive node, you cannot access the SQL Server shared data disks. This is because drives can be accessed from only a single SQL Server node at a time.

If you access your cluster through Remote Desktop (Terminal Services), be aware of a couple of odd behaviors. For example, if you use Remote Desktop to connect to the cluster using the SQL cluster network name or IP address, you will connect to the active node, just as if you used Remote Desktop to connect to the active node directly (using its network name and IP address). But if a failover should occur and you use Remote Desktop to access the cluster using the SQL cluster network name and IP address, Remote Desktop gets a little confused, especially if you use Windows Explorer. For example, you may discover that your data drives no longer appear to be accessible, even though they actually are. To resolve this problem, you may need to log out of Remote Desktop and reconnect after the failover.

TROUBLESHOOTING CLUSTER PROBLEMS

Troubleshooting cluster-related issues requires a lot of fortitude, persistence, and experience, and a support contract with Microsoft Technical Support. The problem is that clustering is somewhat complex, and requires that you know hardware, shared disk arrays, hardware drivers, operating systems, clustering services, and SQL Server. Any problem you have could be caused by any one of them, and identifying the exact cause of a problem is often difficult.

Another reason cluster troubleshooting is difficult is that the feedback you get (in the form of messages or logs) is not easy to understand, assuming you get any feedback at all. And when you do get feedback, the resources for identifying and remedying problems are minimal.

Because of all this, if you have a Windows Failover Cluster, you should plan to purchase Microsoft Technical Support. This is a good investment, and one that will pay for itself. The authors have used Microsoft Technical Support many times, and, in most cases, it assisted adequately. You don't need to automatically call Support as soon as you have a problem; always try to identify and resolve problems on your own if you can. But, at some point, especially if your cluster is down and you need assistance getting it back up, you must recognize when you can't resolve the problem by yourself and when you need outside help.

The next section includes some general advice to get you started when you need to identify and resolve cluster-related problems.

How to Approach Windows Failover Clustering Troubleshooting

The discussion about how to install clustering in this chapter emphasized the importance of testing each task after it is performed, and only proceeding to the next step if everything works. This methodical approach helps you more easily identify what caused the problem as soon as possible after it happens.

For example, if things work correctly, but you perform a task and the test fails, you can fairly assume that what you just did is directly or indirectly responsible for the problem, making problem identification easier. If you don't perform regular testing and don't notice a problem until after many tasks have been performed, identifying the cause of a problem (or problems) is much more difficult.

Therefore, the best way to troubleshoot problems is to perform incremental testing. This also makes it much easier if you have a detailed installation plan that you can follow, helping to ensure that you perform all the necessary steps (including testing at appropriate places).

Doing It Right the First Time

You can save a lot of troubleshooting problems by preventing them. Here's how:

➤ Be sure that all the hardware for the physical nodes and shared disk array passes the Cluster Validation.

➤ Ensure that you use the latest hardware and software drivers and service packs.

➤ Create a detailed installation plan that you can use as your guide for the installation and for disaster recovery should the need arise.

➤ Learn as much as you can about Windows Failover Cluster before you begin your installation. Many cluster problems are user-created because the people responsible guessed instead of knowing for sure what they needed to do.

➤ Develop a Windows Failover Cluster runbook identifying the state, configuration, and instructions on running each cluster to establish a consistent and stable system.

Gathering Information

To help identify the cause of a problem, you often need a lot of information. Unfortunately, the information you need may not exist, or it may be scattered about in many different locations, or it may be downright misleading. In any event, to troubleshoot problems, you need to find as much information as you can.

To try to combat these issues, use the following guidelines and resources when gathering information to troubleshoot a cluster problem:

➤ **Know what is supposed to happen**—If you expect a specific result, and you are not getting it, be sure that you fully understand what is supposed to happen, and exactly what is happening. In other words, know the difference between the two.

➤ **Know what happened directly before the problem occurred**—This is much easier if you test incrementally, as described earlier.

➤ **Know whether the problem is repeatable**—Not all problems can be easily repeated, but if they can, the repetition can provide useful information.

➤ **Take note of any on-screen error messages**—Be sure to take screen captures of any messages for reference. Some DBAs have the habit of clicking OK after an error message without recording its exact content. Often, the exact content of a message is helpful if you need to search the Internet to learn more about it.

➤ **View logs**—You can view a variety of logs, depending on how far along you are in the cluster setup process. These include the three operating system logs: the cluster log (located at `c:\windows\cluster\cluster.log`), the SQL Server 2014 Setup log files (located at `%ProgramFiles%\Microsoft SQL Server\120\Setup Bootstrap\LOG\Summary.txt`), and the SQL Server 2014 log files. There can be a variety of error messages in the log. Once you identify the error, you can perform a web search to see if anyone else has had this error, and find suggestions on how to resolve the problem.

➤ **Perform an Internet search for the error message**—If the error messages you identify aren't obvious (are they ever?), search on the Internet, including newsgroups.

The more information you can gather about a problem, the better position you are in to resolve the problem.

Resolving Problems

Many cluster problems are because of the complexity of the software involved, and it is sometimes faster to just rebuild the cluster from scratch, including the operating system. This is especially true if you have tried to install Windows Failover Cluster or clustered SQL Server, and the setup process aborted during setup and did not set itself up cleanly.

When you build a new Windows Failover Cluster, rebuilding it to resolve problems is usually an option because time is not an issue. However, suppose you have a clustered SQL Server in production and it fails where neither node works. Because time now becomes an issue, you should bring in Microsoft.

Working with Microsoft

Operating a clustered SQL Server without having a Microsoft Technical Support contract is like operating a car without insurance. You can do it, but if you have any unexpected problems, you will be sorry you went without.

Generally, you have two main reasons to call Microsoft Technical Support for clustering issues. The first situation would be when it's a noncritical issue that you just can't figure out for yourself. In this case, you will be assigned an engineer, and over a period of several days, you work with that engineer to resolve that problem. This may involve running diagnostics to gather information about your cluster so that the Microsoft support engineer can diagnose it.

The second reason to call is because your production cluster is down, and you know of no obvious solutions to get it back up quickly. Generally, in this case, call Microsoft Technical Support as soon as you can to get the problem ticket started. In addition, you should emphasize to the technical call screener (the first person who answers the phone) and the support engineer who is assigned to you that you are facing a production down situation, and that you want to declare a *critical situation* (*critsit*). This tells Microsoft that your problem is top priority, and you will get special attention. When you declare a critsit, the person on the phone will validate that it is a critsit because it causes a chain of events to happen within Microsoft Technical Support. But if your production cluster is down, you need to emphasize the serious nature of your problem. If it is, you can get immediate help with your problem until your Windows Failover Cluster is resolved.

SUMMARY

This chapter represents only the tip of the iceberg when it comes to covering everything the DBA should know about clustering SQL Server 2014 on Windows Server 2012 R2. It is important to understand the basics of installing, configuring, testing, monitoring, troubleshooting, and maintaining a Windows 2012 R2 Failover Cluster running SQL Server 2014.

To successfully install a Windows Failover Cluster, you start by identifying the hardware and verifying that it meets the cluster prerequisites. Follow the step-by-step instructions in this chapter to configure the hardware to be clustered. All of these steps must be configured as described; any variation will likely prevent the cluster from installing successfully.

You should run the Cluster Validation to verify that the cluster configuration can be clustered. If any errors are identified, address them before proceeding. Then, you can proceed with creating the cluster.

Determine the need for one or more MSDTC services and install them. Using the SQL Server 2014 setup, install the SQL Server instance on the cluster. You can have more than one SQL Server instance on a node, or have many nodes each running SQL Server instances supported by a passive node, or even without a passive node. Run the SQL Server 2014 setup to install additional SQL Server cluster instances.

Clustering can be combined to offer high availability and disaster recovery by deploying a *geographically dispersed cluster* where a cluster is established with nodes that live across two data centers, which may even be on different subnets. You can learn more about different Windows Failover Cluster deployed configurations by reading clustering articles, the SQL Server 2014 Books Online, and any additional information from Microsoft's website or elsewhere on the Internet.

In Chapter 17, you learn about backup and recovery with SQL Server 2014.

17

Backup and Recovery

WHAT'S IN THIS CHAPTER?

- ➤ Understanding different types of failures and why they occur
- ➤ Planning for disasters
- ➤ Understanding how backup works
- ➤ Choosing the right backup configuration for your environment
- ➤ Recovering databases when a problem occurs

WROX.COM CODE DOWNLOADS FOR THIS CHAPTER

The wrox.com code downloads for this chapter are found at www.wrox.com/go/prosql2014admin on the Download Code tab. The code is in the Chapter 17 download and individually named according to the names throughout the chapter.

Data is a critical asset. Over the course of many years, organizations amass information about their customers, inventory, purchases, financials, and products. Over the course of many years, organizations amass information to improve the daily customer experience, as well as to leverage this information to support strategic decisions. Downtime is unacceptable, and can be costly for the organization. For example, without their databases, a stock brokerage house cannot take stock orders and an airline cannot sell tickets. Every hour the database is down can add up to millions of dollars of business opportunities lost. To keep their business activities going, organizations deploy high-availability solutions (such as failover clustering, database mirroring, replication, and log shipping) so that when a database server fails, they can continue to run their business on a standby database server. All these topics are covered in other chapters in this book.

In addition, the underlying storage for the database may be protected by the use of fault-tolerant or highly available storage technologies such as Redundant Array of Independent Disks (RAID). Even with these fault-tolerant technologies, businesses still need to have database backups to allow recovery from a data-corrupting event, from data loss, or as part of a disaster-recovery plan to cover the complete failure of the primary data center.

Although a high-availability solution tries to keep the business data online, a database backup plan is crucial to protect the business data asset. If a data-error problem exists and the database is unrecoverable, the DBA can use the database backup to recover the database to a consistent state. Moreover, a good database backup strategy can reduce the amount of data loss for certain kinds of errors encountered during the course of the daily database activities.

This chapter first presents an overview of the backup and restore processes. Then it walks through planning and developing a backup plan, managing backups, and performing restores. It also explores data archiving and disaster-recovery planning.

BACKUP AND RESTORE ENHANCEMENTS

SQL Server 2014 contains the following enhancements for SQL Server Backup and Restore:

➤ SQL Server Backup to URL

➤ SQL Server Managed Backup to Windows Azure

➤ Encryption for backups

SQL Server Backup to URL

SQL Server Backup to URL was introduced in SQL Server 2012 SP1 CU2 and was supported only by Transact-SQL (T-SQL), Windows PowerShell, and Server Management Objects (SMO). In SQL Server 2014, you can use SQL Server Management Studio to back up to or restore from the Windows Azure Blob storage service. The new option is available both for the Backup task and maintenance plans.

SQL Server Managed Backup to Windows Azure

Built on SQL Server Backup to URL, SQL Server Managed Backup to Windows Azure is a service that SQL Server provides to manage and schedule database and log backups. In this release, only backup to Windows Azure storage is supported. SQL Server Managed Backup to Windows Azure can be configured both at the database and at the instance level, allowing for both granular control at the database level and automating at the instance level. SQL Server Managed Backup to Windows Azure can be configured on SQL Server instances running on-premises, as well as SQL Server instances running on Windows Azure virtual machines. It is recommended for SQL Server instances running on Windows Azure virtual machines.

Encryption for Backups

You can now choose to encrypt the backup file during a backup operation. SQL Server 2014 supports several encryption algorithms, including AES 128, AES 192, AES 256, and Triple DES. You must use either a certificate or an asymmetric key to perform encryption during backup.

OVERVIEW OF BACKUP AND RESTORE

Before you can effectively formulate a backup-and-restore plan, you must understand how backup and recovery work on a mechanical level. SQL Server has several different backup and restore processes that you can use, depending on the needs of your organization. This section examines how backup and restore work, and helps you choose the best plan for your needs.

How Backup Works

Database backup is a procedure that safeguards your organization's investment to reduce the amount of data loss. A database backup is the process of making a point-in-time copy of the data and transaction log into an image on either disks or tapes. SQL Server implements versatile backup processes that can be used separately or together to produce the optimal backup strategy required by an organization. Moreover, SQL Server can perform the database backup while it is online and available to users.

The following types of backups are available:

➤ **Full backup**—This is a copy of all data in the database, including the transaction log. Using this backup type, you can restore the database to the point in time when the backup was taken. It is the most basic of the backups, and is often required prior to any of the other backup types. When you restore from a full database backup, all the database files are restored without any other dependencies, the database is available, and it is transactionally consistent.

➤ **Partial backup**—This is a way to back up only those parts of the database that change. This reduces the size of the backup and the time it takes to back up and restore. It is a copy of the primary filegroup and read/write filegroups. To take advantage of this type of backup, you must group the tables that change into a set of filegroups, and group the tables that are static or history into a different set of filegroups. The filegroups containing historical data will be marked read/write or read-only. A partial backup normally includes the primary filegroup and read-write filegroups, but read-only filegroups can optionally be included. A partial backup can speed up the backup process for databases with large read-only areas. For example, a large database may have archival data that does not change, so there is no need to back it up every time, which reduces the amount of data to back up.

➤ **File/filegroup backup**—This is a copy of selected files or filegroups of a database. This method is typically used for large databases for which it is not feasible to do a full database backup. A transaction-log backup is needed with this backup type if the backup includes read/write files or filegroups. The challenge is maintaining the files, filegroups, and transaction-log backups, because larger databases have many files and filegroups. It also requires more steps to restore the database.

> **NOTE** *During a file or filegroup backup, a table and all its indexes must be backed up in the same backup. SQL Server checks for this and sends an error when this rule is violated. To take advantage of file/filegroup backups, you may need to plan the location of your indexes with the backup plan in mind.*

➤ **Differential backup**—This is a copy of all the data that has changed since the last full backup. The SQL Server 2014 backup process identifies each changed extent and backs it up. Differentials are cumulative. If you do a full backup on Sunday night, the differential taken on Monday night includes all the changes since Sunday night. If you take another differential on Tuesday night, it includes all the changes since Sunday night. When restoring, you would restore the last full database backup and the most recent differential backup. Then you would restore any transaction-log backups since the last differential. This can mean quicker recovery. Whether differentials are good for you depends on what percentage of rows change between full database backups. As the percentage of rows changed approaches the number of rows in the database, the differential backup gets closer to the size of an entire database backup. When this occurs, it is often better to get another full database backup and start a new differential. Another benefit to using differential backups is realized when a group of rows is repeatedly changed. Remember that a transaction-log backup includes each change that is made. The differential backup includes only the last change for a row. Imagine a database that keeps track of 100 stock values. The stock value is updated every minute. Each row is updated 1,440 times per day. Consider a full database backup on Sunday night and transaction-log backups during the week. At the end of the day Friday, restoring from all the transaction logs would mean that you have to replay each change to each row. In this case, each row would be updated 7,200 times (1,440 times/day times 5 days). When you include 100 stocks, the restore would have to replay 720,000 transactions. If you had done a differential backup at the end of each day, you would have to replace only the 100 rows. The differential keeps the most recent version only. In some situations, it can be a great solution.

➤ **Partial differential backup**—This works the same as a differential backup, but is matched to data from a partial backup. It is a copy of all extents modified since the last partial backup. To restore from a partial differential backup requires the parent partial backup.

➤ **File differential backup**—This is a copy of the file or filegroup of all extents modified since the last file or filegroup backup. A transaction-log backup is required after this backup for read/write files or filegroups. Moreover, after the restore, you must restore the transaction log as well. Using the file backup and file differential backup methods increases the complexity of the restore procedures. Furthermore, it may take longer to restore the complete database.

➤ **Copy-only backup**—This can be made for the database or transaction log. The copy-only backup does not interfere with the normal backup and restore procedures. A normal full database backup resets the differential backups made afterward, whereas a copy-only backup does not affect the next differential backup. It still contains the changes since the last full backup. A copy-only backup of the transaction log does not truncate the log or affect the next normal transaction-log backup. Copy-only backups are useful when you want to make a copy of the database for testing or development purposes without affecting the restore process.

The transaction log in SQL Server is a main component for a relational database system that maintains the ACID (atomicity, consistency, isolation, and durability) properties for transactions. SQL Server implements the Write Ahead Logging (WAL) protocol, which means that the transaction-log records are written to stable media prior to the data being written to disk, and before SQL Server sends an acknowledgment that the data has been permanently committed. *Stable media* is usually a directly attached disk drive, but it can be any device that guarantees that, on power loss, no data will be lost.

Even on direct attached systems, this can be a challenge. Just as disk drives implement write caches, RAID controllers (even at the simplest level) also implement caches, which either must be write-disabled or battery-backed. Any external storage system such as a Storage Area Network (SAN) system must also be checked to confirm that the cache is battery-backed, and will guarantee the consistency of any written log records during a power failure.

There is a new trend for using solid-state storage devices, which can take many forms. If you leverage these devices, you must ensure that they either deliver guarantees around writes if a power failure occurs, or that they are used in places where write cache performance is not an issue (such as if used for `tempdb`, where all data is deleted in the event of a system restart). An increasingly common trend on high-performance systems that need the highest levels of transaction-log write performance is to place the transaction log on solid-state storage. Although this is great from a performance perspective, you must also guarantee that the log records can survive a power outage.

The SQL Server Database Engine expects the transaction log to be consistent on restart. If it is not, it will identify the database as corrupted because the data consistency of the database cannot be determined.

In addition, when a data modification occurs, SQL Server generates a new *log sequence number (LSN)* used on restart to identify the consistency of the data while performing database recovery. The LSN is used when restoring the transaction log. SQL Server uses it to determine the sequences of each transaction log restored. For example, if a transaction-log backup from a backup log chain is not available, that is known as a *broken log chain*, which prevents a transaction-log recovery past that point. Backing up the transaction log to point-in-time recovery is a critical part of a backup strategy.

Copying Databases

Sometimes you don't need a backup of the database, but might want a copy of the data instead. This section covers several ways that you can copy a database.

Detach/Attach

Detach/Attach is a great way to move a database to a new server. However, you can also use it to create a copy. The Detach/Attach feature detaches the database or shuts down SQL Server. After the files are detached, you can copy the database files to a new location.

> **NOTE** `sp_attach_db` *is now a deprecated feature. Although it still works in SQL Server 2014, you should plan to replace any scripts that use* `sp_attach_db` *with the new* CREATE DATABASE FOR ATTACH *syntax. Note also that* `sp_detach_db` *is not deprecated, so although there is a corresponding* ALTER DATABASE SET OFFLINE *syntax, you can still use* `sp_detach_db`.

To back up the database files using this method, you can detach the database using either the sp_detach_db system stored procedure, or the ALTER DATABASE SET OFFLINE syntax as shown in the following two code samples.

Here is the sp_detach_db example (code file: ch17_code.sql):

```
EXEC master.dbo.sp_detach_db @dbname = N'ch17_samples'
```

Here is the ALTER DATABASE example:

```
ALTER DATABASE ch17_samples SET OFFLINE
```

To restore, you can either create a new database using the CREATE DATABASE syntax, or, if you already have a database and want to update it with a new copy from the other server, simply replace the files and use the ALTER DATABASE SET ONLINE syntax.

Here is the CREATE DATABASE example (code file: ch17_code.sql):

```
CREATE DATABASE [ch17_samples] ON
( FILENAME = N'C:\Program Files\Microsoft SQL Server\MSSQL12.MSSQLSERVER\
    MSSQL\DATA\ch17_samples.mdf' ),
( FILENAME = N'C:\Program Files\Microsoft SQL Server\MSSQL12.MSSQLSERVER\
    MSSQL\DATA\ch17_samples_log.ldf' )
 FOR ATTACH;
```

> **NOTE** *You should change the drive letter "C" (as well as the rest of the file location) to reflect the directory where your data files are stored. The example uses the default location for data files.*

Here is the ALTER DATABASE SET ONLINE example:

```
ALTER DATABASE ch17_samples SET ONLINE;
```

> **NOTE** *If you attach an encrypted database, the database owner must open the master key of the database by using the following command:*
>
> ```
> OPEN MASTER KEY DECRYPTION BY PASSWORD = '<password>'
> ```
>
> *Microsoft recommends you enable automatic decryption of the master key by using the following command:*
>
> ```
> ALTER MASTER KEY ADD ENCRYPTION BY SERVICE MASTER KEY
> ```

BCP

The second backup option is performed through the Bulk Copy Program (BCP). You can run it via a simple batch script and export all the data from a database. This doesn't capture everything in the database, but it can be a useful way to get a copy of specific data within the database.

If you need to export more than 2 billion rows from a table, you *must* use BCP from SQL Server 2008 onward. A bug in older versions of BCP (SQL Server 2005 and older) prevented it from exporting or importing more than 2 billion rows, and it also failed to report any errors.

Following are two example BCP command lines that show how to export (OUT) and import (IN) a table called People from the Seattle_SQL server to the London_SQL server:

```
BCP address OUT address.dat -SSeattle_SQL -T -c -dPeople

BCP address IN address.dat -SLondon_SQL -T -c -dPeople
```

Scripting Wizard

SQL Server Management Studio provides a scripting wizard that enables you to generate scripts for selected objects within the database. This is a great way to keep a record of the scripts needed to regenerate a database and can be a good way to get a version check on any recent changes to the database.

Use this with a source-code control system to determine the delta between previously generated scripts and scripts currently generated to find changes to objects in the database.

Import/Export Wizard

SQL Server Management Studio provides Import/Export capabilities that you can access from the Tasks item on the database context menu (see Figure 17-1).

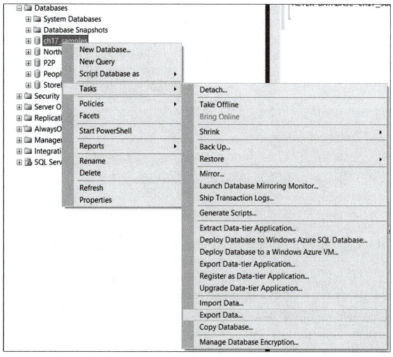

FIGURE 17-1

As you can see, you can drive this from either end. The following example walks you through an export driven from the source database.

> **NOTE** *You can find the sample tables for this exercise in the code file* `ch17_sam-ple_tables.sql`, *available for download on this book's accompanying website at* `www.wrox.com`.

1. Select Export Data to start the Import and Export Wizard. The wizard welcome screen appears as shown in Figure 17-2.

FIGURE 17-2

2. Click Next in the welcome screen and you are taken to the "Choose a Data Source" page, shown in Figure 17-3. Enter the server name and authentication method for this server, and then you can select the database from which you want to export data. In this example, you have chosen the `ch17_samples` database, as shown in Figure 17-3.

3. In the next page in the wizard, the "Choose a Destination" page shown in Figure 17-4, choose a server, authentication method, and then database name. The wizard defaults to using the default database for the login used to authenticate against this server. Click Next.

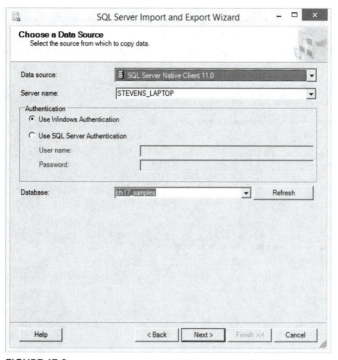

FIGURE 17-3

FIGURE 17-4

4. On the next page shown in Figure 17-5, choose "Copy data from one or more tables or view" to use a table copy, or "Write a query to specify the data to transfer" to write a query to select data. In this example, choose the first option to copy data from one or more tables or views. Click Next.

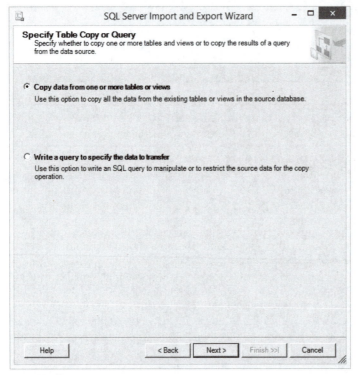

FIGURE 17-5

5. On the "Select Source Tables and Views" screen shown in Figure 17-6, the wizard presents you with a list of all the tables and views that are available. In the example database, you can see only a small number of tables in Figure 17-6. Select the tables and views to be exported and click Next.

6. On the "Save and Run Package" screen shown in Figure 17-7, you now have the option to run the package immediately, or to save the SQL Server Integrated Services (SSIS) package. If you choose to save the package, you can specify whether you want to save it to SQL Server or the filesystem. You can also define a package protection level to secure the package contents. Click Next.

7. On the "Complete the Wizard" screen shown in Figure 17-8, you see the selections you have made.

8. Click Finish to execute the selections you made during the wizard. In this case, the wizard executes one SSIS package to export the selected tables from the source server, creates the new tables in the destination server, and imports the data to the newly created tables. The wizard then reports on the status of the package execution. Figure 17-9 shows that everything completed successfully.

FIGURE 17-6

FIGURE 17-7

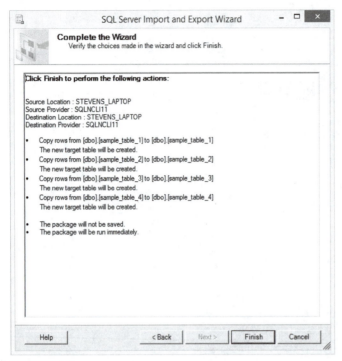

FIGURE 17-8

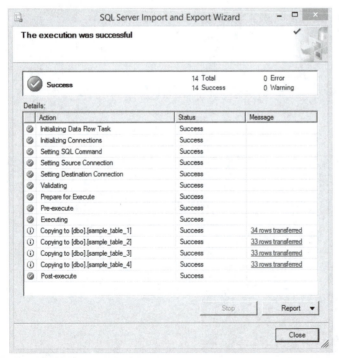

FIGURE 17-9

One thing to note is that if you get errors here and you go back to make changes and rerun the package, you may encounter additional errors because the wizard doesn't attempt any cleanup if it fails partway through.

Some common errors you might encounter are when tables are created, but the data import fails, possibly because of the transaction log being full. In this case, you can resolve the issue by either deleting any tables manually, or viewing the created tables in the destination database and rerunning the package again. Other common errors can come from data truncation, data type differences, and identity insert errors.

> **NOTE** *When you run the package, the SQL Agent service does not need to be running.*

Extract Data Tier Application (DAC)

If your database uses the set of features that are compatible with Data Tier Applications (DACs), you have the added option to create a DAC using this wizard in SQL Server Management Studio. The DAC contains just the database schema, without data, but this can be useful for transferring the schema from development to test to QA and onto production. See the DAC documentation in Books Online for complete details on using DACs.

Copy Database Wizard

SQL Server Management Studio provides a Copy Database Wizard. This can either utilize Attach/Detach or SMO to make a copy of a database and move it to another server. Using Attach/Detach requires the database to be taken offline. Using the SMO method enables the copy to be made while the database remains online. You can find the Copy Database Wizard on the database context menu under the Tasks menu item, as shown in Figure 17-10.

Follow these steps to learn how to use this wizard:

1. Open the Copy Database Wizard and you will see the welcome page shown in Figure 17-11. Click Next.

2. Select your source server, as shown in Figure 17-12. Click Next.

3. On the "Select a Destination Server" page shown in Figure 17-13, select the destination server. The wizard defaults to using the default database for the login used to authenticate against this server. Click Next.

4. On the "Select the Transfer Method" page shown in Figure 17-14, choose how you would like the wizard to make the transfer. You can choose between Attach/Detach or using SMO. For this example, use the SMO method. Click Next.

5. On the "Select Databases" page shown in Figure 17-15, select which databases to copy. You can choose to either copy or move the selected databases. This choice is on a per-database basis, so you can move some databases and copy others if that's what you want to do. Figure 17-15 shows the ch17_samples database being selected to be copied. Click Next.

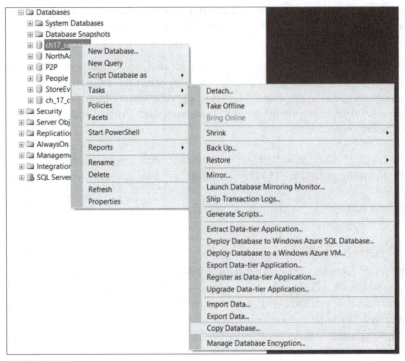

FIGURE 17-10

FIGURE 17-11

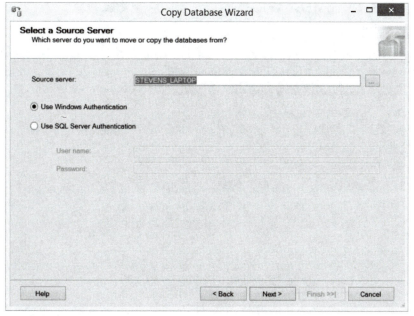

FIGURE 17-12

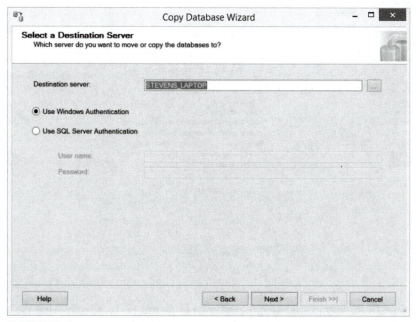

FIGURE 17-13

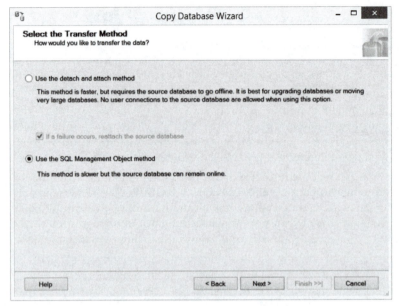

FIGURE 17-14

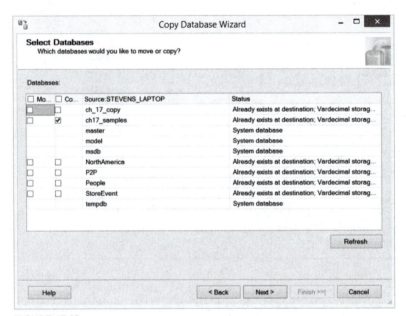

FIGURE 17-15

6. On the "Configure Destination Database" page shown in Figure 17-16, specify what the new database will be called, and which files will be created. By default, these options are pre-populated with the information from the source database. Other options are available on this page that determine what action to take if the destination database exists. Click Next.

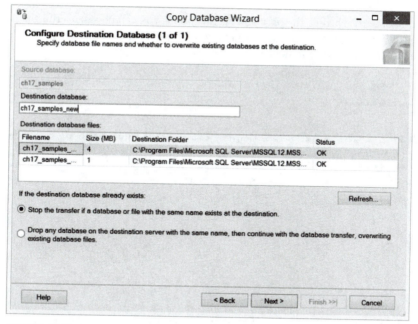

FIGURE 17-16

7. Configure the SSIS package that will perform the database copy, as shown in Figure 17-17. Click Next.

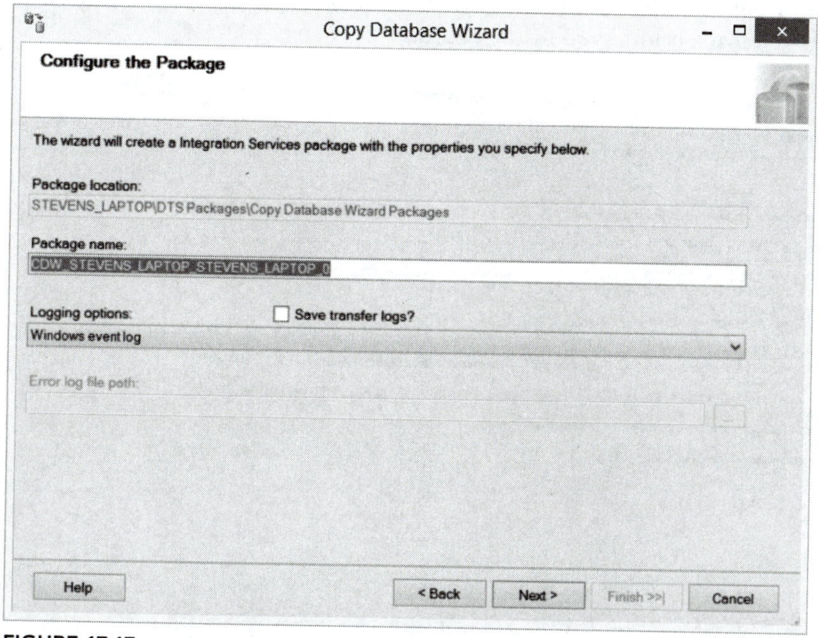

FIGURE 17-17

8. You are ready to schedule the package. At this point, you can choose to run the package immediately or schedule it for execution later. The screen shown in Figure 17-18 shows the choice to run the package immediately. Click Next.

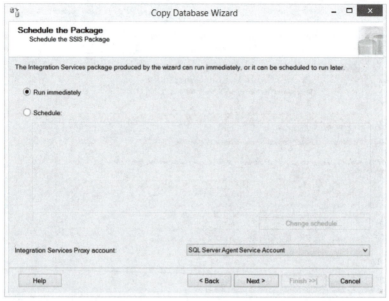

FIGURE 17-18

9. On the "Complete the Wizard" page shown in Figure 17-19, be sure to confirm all the choices you made before running the package.

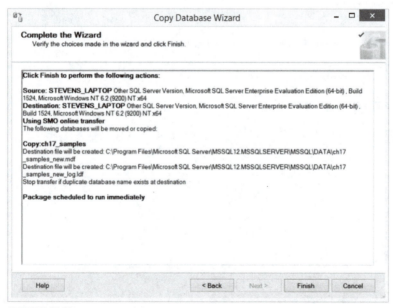

FIGURE 17-19

9. Click Finish to run the package and copy the selected databases and objects from the source to the destination server. While the package is executing, the wizard reports the status of each step. Upon completion, the wizard displays the results of executing the package.

> **NOTE** *Ensure that you have SQL Agent running on the destination server. This is where the package is scheduled to execute, through a SQL Agent job, even if the package is specified to execute immediately. This behavior is different from the SQL Server Import and Export Wizard, which does not need SQL Agent to immediately run the packages it creates.*

Backup Compression

The Backup Compression feature enables you to store the backup files in compressed form. This can lead to both shorter backup times and smaller files containing the backup. The trade-off you make is increased CPU usage to do the compression in exchange for less I/O because of the smaller files.

Generally, the result of backup compression is greatly reduced backup times. Whether you can benefit from using compression is relative to the availability or scarcity of CPU and I/O resources, as well as the degree of compression obtained. You can determine the state of your system by looking at the following performance counters in Performance Monitor:

➤ Windows performance monitor counters for your disks.

➤ SQL Server performance counters:

   ➤ SQLServer:Backup Device/Device Throughput Bytes/sec

   ➤ SQLServer:Databases/Backup/Restore Throughput/sec

> **NOTE** *For more information on monitoring performance counters, see Chapter 12, "Monitoring Your SQL Server" and Chapter 13, "Performance Tuning T-SQL."*

Beginning with SQL Server 7, backup media used a media format called Microsoft Tape Format (MTF). This is the same format that Windows operating system backups used, enabling SQL Server backups to coexist on the same media with Windows backups. This was especially convenient for users with a single tape drive.

Beginning with SQL 2008, however, compressed backups use a different media format, which is incompatible with Windows backups. This leads to some restrictions regarding the use of backup compression:

➤ Compressed and uncompressed backups cannot coexist in the same media set.

➤ Prior versions of SQL Server cannot read compressed backups.

➤ NT backups and compressed backups cannot coexist in the same media set.

If you violate one of these restrictions, SQL Server returns an error.

A new server-level configuration option, backup compression default, enables your default backups to be either compressed or uncompressed. You can set this option via `sp_configure` and from SQL Server Management Studio. Backup compression is turned off by default. You can override the default using the `with compression` or `with no_compression` option in the `backup` T-SQL command, or using the Backup dialog boxes in SQL Server Management Studio or the Database Maintenance Plan Wizard.

How much compression you achieve depends on several factors:

➤ Databases that are compressed do not see additional compression in backups.

➤ Encrypted data does not compress as well as unencrypted data.

➤ Character data types compress better than other data types.

➤ Greater levels of compression are achieved when a page has multiple rows in which a column contains the same value.

Comparing Recovery Models

Understanding the recovery models is essential to developing an effective backup strategy. The recovery model determines how the transaction log is managed by SQL Server. The model you choose depends on the backup/restore plan you have for a database.

In the *full recovery model*, the transaction log records all data modifications, makes available all database recovery options, and implements the highest data protection while using the most transaction-log space. You can use this recovery model with all database backup operations. It is capable of point-in-time recovery, and it enables backing up the transaction log. Most Online Transaction Processing (OLTP) production systems and mission-critical applications that require minimal data loss should use the full recovery model.

> **NOTE** *The first transaction-log backup cannot be completed until after a full database backup has been done.*

The *bulk-logged recovery model* performs minimal logging for certain database operations, including bulk import operations, such as the following:

➤ `BCP`

➤ `BULK INSERT`

➤ `SELECT INTO`

➤ `CREATE INDEX`

➤ `ALTER INDEX REBUILD`

➤ `DBCC DBREINDEX`

Instead of logging every modification for these database operations, the bulk-logged recovery model logs the extent allocations and flags the changed extents. As a result, these operations execute faster (because they are minimally logged), but it presents possible data-loss risks for recovery. A transaction-log backup copies everything in the transaction log, checks the extents flagged as changed, and copies them from the data files into the log backup. In addition, after a bulk-logged operation, point-in-time recovery using transaction-log backup is disallowed.

Consider the same scenario presented earlier. The database uses the bulk-logged recovery model. The full database backup occurred at 1:00 P.M. A transaction log backup occurs at 1:30 P.M. Then a bulk-logged database operation is performed. Next, the physical drives containing the data files fail at 2:00 P.M. You cannot recover up to 2:00 P.M. because the transaction-log backup would need to access the data files to retrieve the data modifications performed during the bulk-logged operations. You cannot perform a tail-log backup. As a result, data will be lost and you can only recover up to 1:30 P.M.

When you do bulk operations in this mode, you are at risk of losing data until you complete a log backup after the bulk operations. You can minimize the data loss in this scenario with some bulk-logged database operations by implementing shorter transactions that perform transaction-log backups during and immediately after the bulk-logged operations. Oftentimes, this recovery model is used when the DBA performs bulk-logged operations and then switches back to full after the bulk-logged operation completes, to improve the performance for bulk operations. In addition, this model is commonly used in an Online Analytical Processing (OLAP) or a reporting database for which nightly bulk data loads occur. A backup is taken, and afterward no data is modified during the day, so if the data is lost because of a failure it can be restored from backup.

The *simple recovery model* implements minimal logging, just like the bulk-logged recovery model, except that it keeps the transaction-log records only until the next checkpoint process occurs, writing the dirty changes to the data files. Then the checkpoint process truncates the transaction log. Transaction-log backups are not allowed; therefore, point-in-time recovery is not available.

Typically, this recovery model is used for development or test servers, where data loss is acceptable and data can be reloaded. Moreover, this model may be used by an OLAP and reporting database for which only a nightly data load may occur and then a full or differential backup is performed. With this model, if the database were to fail during the data load, you would have to start from the beginning, unless a full or differential backup was taken during the process. In addition, if a DBA switches from one of the other recovery models to this one, the transaction-log continuity is broken because it truncates the transaction log and during the time that the database is in this recovery mode, the database is more exposed to potential data loss.

> **NOTE** *Transactional replication, log shipping, or data mirroring is not allowed in the simple recovery model, because there is no persistent storage of transactions in the transaction log.*

Choosing a Model

Choosing the best recovery model depends on the amount of acceptable data loss, the database's read-and-write daily activities, and how critical that database is to the daily business of your organization. Following are recommendations for choosing between the full, bulk-logged, and simple recovery models.

Full Recovery Model

Choose the full recovery model for a mission-critical database to keep data loss to a minimum because it is fully logged. And, in case of damaged data files, you can back up the tail transaction log and used it to restore the database to a given point in time. Therefore, OLTP production systems usually use the full recovery model, except when the database is modified nightly, as is sometimes the case with OLAP or reporting databases.

Bulk-Logged Recovery Model

You can use the bulk-logged recovery model to increase the performance of bulk operations because it does minimal logging. For example, you could do a nightly bulk operation and then switch back to full recovery. The bulk-logged model will fully log, as is the case with the full recovery model, except for the bulk operations. Therefore, you could use bulk-logged recovery as a permanent recovery model, except that it poses a risk of data loss. As long as no bulk-data operations occur, the DBA can back up the transaction log. But oftentimes, unknown to the DBA, the tail transaction-log backup recovery may no longer be available if a bulk operation has been performed.

To guard against someone doing bulk operations without a database backup, and to reduce that data risk, you should switch to bulk-logged only when a bulk operation needs to be performed. Bulk-logged can be a permanent recovery model in an OLAP or reporting database where there is no daily modification activity, because there is limited data-loss risk if the databases are backed up right after any nightly data load. There is no chance of data loss throughout the day, because nothing would have changed. In addition, some data loss may be acceptable, because you can reload the OLAP and reporting databases from the OLTP data source whenever needed.

Simple Recovery Model

The simple recovery model does not save the transaction log; instead, the checkpoint process truncates it. Therefore, no one must maintain the transaction log. This recovery model is commonly used for development, read-only, and test systems for which transaction-log backups are not required. If there is data loss, you can reload a new copy of the data from the OLTP data source. If the DBA switches to this recovery model from one of the others, the transaction-log continuity is broken because there is no way to back up the transaction log. In this recovery model, there is no point-in-time recovery because the DBA cannot back up the transaction log. Therefore, any restore would be from the previous full, and any differential, backups.

Switching Recovery Models

SQL Server provides complete flexibility to switch among the recovery models. However, be aware of the limitations when switching among them, because switching can result in data loss during recovery. The following list outlines the limitations of switching recovery models:

➤ **Switching from full to bulk-logged**—Because bulk-logged database operations may be performed, a transaction-log backup is recommended at a minimum so that the DBA can recover to this last transaction log if the tail transaction log is not available. To change to this recovery model, use this command:

```
ALTER DATABASE ch17_samples SET RECOVERY BULK_LOGGED
```

➤ **Switching from full to simple**—Because the transaction-log continuity is broken by this recovery model, a transaction-log backup is recommended, at minimum, before the switch. After the recovery model switch, transaction-log backups and point-in-time recovery are disallowed. To change to this recovery model, use the following command:

```
ALTER DATABASE ch17_samples SET RECOVERY SIMPLE
```

➤ **Switching from bulk-logged to full**—Because bulk-logged database operations may have been performed, and to minimize potential data loss if the tail transaction log is not accessible, a transaction-log backup is recommended after the switch. To change to this recovery model, use the following command:

```
ALTER DATABASE ch17_samples SET RECOVERY FULL
```

➤ **Switching from bulk-logged to simple**—In this recovery model there is a greater chance of data loss in case of a database failure, so, at a minimum, a transaction-log backup is highly recommended before the switch. To change to this recovery model, use the following command:

```
ALTER DATABASE ch17_samples SET RECOVERY SIMPLE
```

➤ **Switching from simple to full**—To enable the full recovery model to start to apply transaction-log backups, a full, differential, file, or filegroup backup is required after the switch. To change to this recovery model, use the following command:

```
ALTER DATABASE ch17_samples SET RECOVERY FULL
```

➤ **Switching from simple to bulk-logged**—To enable the bulk-logged recovery model to start to apply transaction-log backups, a full, differential, file, or filegroup backup is required after the switch. To change to this recovery model, use the following command:

```
ALTER DATABASE ch17_samples SET RECOVERY BULK_LOGGED
```

The recovery model is configured for each database. You can also switch the recovery model from SQL Server Management Studio by opening the Database Properties and choosing Options, as shown in Figure 17-20.

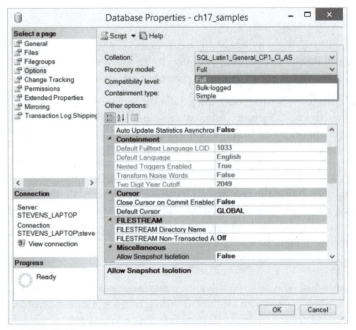

FIGURE 17-20

Backing Up History Tables

SQL Server maintains the backup history for the server in the `msdb` database in a group of tables from which it can identify the backup available for a database. SQL Server presents the restores available for the database in the Restore dialog box. The tables are as follows:

➤   `Backupfile`—A row for each data or log file backed up

➤   `Backupfilegroup`—A row for each filegroup in a backup set

➤   `Backupmediafamily`—A row for each media family

➤   `Backupmediaset`—A row for each backup media set

➤   `Backupset`—A row for each backup set

> **NOTE** *A media set is an ordered collection of all tapes or disks from all devices that took part in the backup. A media family is a collection of all backup media on a single device that took part in the backup. A media backup is a tape or disk device used for backup.*

The following three backup information statements return information from the history backup tables:

➤ RESTORE FILELISTONLY—Returns a list of database and log files in a backup set from the backupfile table:

    RESTORE FILELISTONLY FROM ch17_samples_Backup

➤ RESTORE HEADERONLY—Returns all the backup header information for all the backup sets in a device from the backupset table:

    RESTORE HEADERONLY FROM ch17_samples_Backup

➤ RESTORE LABELONLY—Returns information about the backup media of a backup device from the backupmediaset table:

    RESTORE LABELONLY FROM ch17_samples_Backup

> **NOTE** RESTORE HEADERONLY, RESTORE FILELISTONLY, RESTORE VERIFYONLY, *and* RESTORE LABLELONLY *do not actually restore anything, and, therefore, are completely safe to run. They only provide information. It may be a bit confusing though; just remember to look for the contextual use of* RESTORE.

Permissions Required for Backup and Restore

SQL Server provides granular permission for both the backing up and restoring of a database. A Windows or SQL Server authenticated user or group can be given permission to perform the backup and restore operations. To have permission to back up a database, a user must have (at minimum) the following permissions:

➤ **Server role**—none

➤ **DB role**—db_backupoperator

To restore a database, a user must have at minimum the following permissions:

➤ **Server role**—dbcreater

➤ **DB role**—db_owner

Backing Up System Databases

SQL Server system databases are critical to the operation of each SQL Server instance. These databases are not often modified, but they contain important information that must be backed up. After creating a new SQL Server instance, develop a backup plan to perform a full backup of all the system databases, except for tempdb. SQL Server re-creates tempdb every time it is restarted because it does not contain any data to recover. Backing up these system databases takes only minutes, so there is no excuse for not having a proper backup. You could often schedule these backups nightly and do extra backups to your local hard drive before and after any changes you make. That keeps you safe until the current night's normal backup.

master

The `master` database contains the login information—metadata about each database for the SQL instance. Moreover, it contains SQL Server configuration information. For example, the database is altered every time you do the following:

- ➤ Add, remove, or modify a database-level setting
- ➤ Add or delete a user database
- ➤ Add or remove a file or filegroup in a user database
- ➤ Add, remove, or modify a login's security
- ➤ Modify a SQL Server server-wide configuration
- ➤ Add or remove a logical backup device
- ➤ Configure distributed queries or remote procedure calls (RPC)
- ➤ Add, modify, or remove a linked server or remote login

Although these modifications occur infrequently, when they do, consider doing a full database backup. If a backup is not performed, you stand to lose the modifications if a previous backup of the `master` is restored. Moreover, as a precautionary measure, before and after adding any service pack or hotfix, perform a new backup of the `master` database.

msdb

The `msdb` database contains SQL jobs, backup jobs, schedules, operators, and backup and restore histories. It can also contain SSIS packages and other items. If you create a new job or add a new SSIS package and `msdb` were to fail, the previous backup would not contain these new jobs, and would need to be re-created.

tempdb

`tempdb` cannot be backed up. Because it is re-created every time SQL Server is restarted, no data in it needs to be recovered.

model

Typically, the `model` database changes even less frequently than the other system databases. `model` is the template database used when a new database is created. If you want a certain database object to be present in every new database (such as a stored procedure or table), place it in `model`. In these cases, it should be backed up; otherwise, any `model` modifications will be lost and need to be re-created. In addition, keep scripts of any changes you make to the `model`, just to add another layer of safety.

Full-Text Backup

Full-text search performs fast querying of unstructured data using keywords based on the words in a particular language. It is primarily used to search char, nchar, varchar, and nvarchar fields. Prior to querying, the full-text index must be created by a population or crawl process, during which full-text search performs a breakdown of the keywords and stores them in the full-text index. Each full-text index is then stored in a full-text catalog. Then a catalog is stored in a filegroup.

With SQL Server 2014, a full backup includes the full-text indexes. In SQL 2005, full-text indexes were part of a catalog that existed in a filegroup with a physical path, and was simply treated as a database file. SQL Server 2014 treats the entire catalog as a virtual object—simply a collection of full-text indexes. Full-text indexes are now stored and treated like other indexes for the purpose of backups. To back up all the full-text indexes, you must discover the files that contain any full-text index, and then back up the file or filegroup.

The end result is that backups for full-text indexes are completely incorporated into the standard backup architecture. You can place full-text indexes on separate filegroups and the Primary filegroup, or allow them to live in the same filegroup as the base table. This improvement makes administration easier than in prior releases.

Verifying the Backup Images

With any backup solution, a critical operation is verifying the backup images that they will restore. Often, a DBA may be meticulously doing backups, but along the way the database becomes corrupted, and every backup from that point on is not usable. Plan on doing periodic restores to verify recoverability. In addition, perform database consistency checks to validate the database structures. Use the RESTORE VERIFYONLY T-SQL command to perform validation checks on the backup image. It does not restore the backup, but it performs validation checks, including the following:

➤ Confirms the backup set is complete and readable.

➤ Checks some header fields of database pages.

➤ If the backup were created WITH CHECKSUMS, it will validate it.

➤ Checks destination devices for sufficient space.

However, the RESTORE VERIFYONLY command does not completely guarantee that the backup is restorable. That is why you need a policy to randomly restore a backup to a test server. RESTORE VERIFYONLY simply provides another level of validation. Here's the syntax:

```
RESTORE VERIFYONLY FROM <backup_device_name>
```

Following is an example resulting message:

```
The backup set on file 1 is valid.
```

> **NOTE** RESTORE VERIFYONLY *does not work on database snapshots. If you plan to revert (restore) from a database snapshot, use* DBCC CHECKDB *to ensure that the database is healthy.*

For higher reliability, to guard against a malfunctioning backup device that may render the entire backup unrecoverable, use mirroring of backup sets for redundancy. They can be either disk or tape and have the following restrictions:

➤ Backup devices must be identical.

➤ To create a new (or extend an existing) backup, the mirror backup set must be intact. If one is not present, the media backup set cannot be used.

➤ To restore from a media backup set, only one of the mirror devices must be present.

➤ If one mirror of the media backup set is damaged, no additional mirroring can be performed on that media backup set.

For example, use the following command to use a backup device mirroring on the `ch17_samples` database (code file: `ch17_code.sql`):

```
BACKUP DATABASE ch17_samples
TO DISK = 'x:\ch17_samples\backup\ch17_samples.bak'
MIRROR TO DISK = 'y:\ch17_samples\backup_mirror\ch17_samples.bak'
WITH FORMAT, MEDIANAME='ch17_sample_mirror'
```

How Restore Works

Restore brings back the database in case of a failure, and is a major function of a transactional relational database system. When a DBA restores a database, three restore phases must happen:

➤ Copy phase

➤ Redo phase

➤ Undo phase

RESTORE VERSUS RECOVERY

The terms *restore* and *recovery* are often confused and misused. Restore is what occurs when you use the RESTORE T-SQL command to get a database back.

Recovery is a process that brings a database into a consistent state. This means that committed transactions are applied to disk (redo phase) and transactions that are begun but not yet committed are rolled off (undo phase). The result is a database that contains only committed transactions—a consistent state.

Each time the server starts, an automatic recovery process runs. At startup, you do not know how SQL Server last stopped. It could have been a clean shutdown, or a power outage could have brought the server down. In the case of a power outage, there may have been transactions that were begun but not yet completed. Recovery does the work necessary to ensure that committed transactions are included, and that uncommitted transactions are removed.

The last step in a restore process that you begin is also recovery. The RESTORE command enables you to specify when recovery runs. If recovery has not yet run, you can restore a differential backup or continue to restore transaction logs. After recovery has run, no more log restores can occur, and the database is brought online.

In the *copy phase*, the database image is created and initialized on disk, and then the full backup is copied. That can be followed by any differential and transaction-log backups. You do these via the RESTORE T-SQL command.

After the full backup has been applied and any differential and transaction logs have been restored, the DBA allows recovery to run. During the recovery process, SQL Server performs both a redo phase and an undo phase. During the *redo phase*, all committed transaction records that were in the transaction log but not in the data files are written to the data files. The WAL protocol guarantees that the transaction records that were committed have been written to the transaction-log stable media. Then, during the redo, SQL Server evaluates the transaction-log records and applies the data modifications to the data files in the database.

The duration of the redo phase depends on how many data modifications SQL Server performed, which depends on what SQL Server was doing at the time of the failure and the recovery interval setting. For example, if SQL Server just finished updating 10 million rows from a table and committed the transaction but was unexpectedly shut down right after, during recovery it would have to redo those data modifications to the data. The SQL Server recovery interval setting influences recovery time according to how many dirty pages are kept in memory before the checkpoint process must write them to stable media. By default, the recovery interval is set to 0, which means that SQL Server keeps less than a minute of work that is not yet written to the data files. With that setting, during recovery, there is minimal redo work before the database becomes available for users. The higher the recovery interval value, the longer the recovery may take.

After the redo phase is the *undo phase*, where any transactions that did not complete are rolled back. Depending on the amount of work and the length of the transactions at the time before shutdown, this phase can take some time. For example, if the DBA was in the middle of deleting 10 million rows, SQL Server is required to roll back all those rows during recovery. SQL Server does make the database available to users while in the undo phase, but users should expect some performance impact while in the undo phase.

PREPARING FOR RECOVERY

To mitigate the risk and extent of data loss, one of the DBA's most important tasks is database backup and planning for recovery. You need to develop a backup plan that minimizes data loss, and can be implemented within the maintenance window of time allowed. Choose the best SQL Server backup capabilities to achieve the preferred backup plan—one that meets the continuity and data loss requirements for the business. You must also set up the backup procedure and monitor it every day to ensure that it works successfully. That includes validating that the database backup restores properly.

An organization may be current with its backups and assume that it has the necessary backups to restore the database, only to find that the database was corrupted and some of the recent database backups will not restore. Cases like these can go undiscovered for months until someone needs to restore a database and finds out that it is not recoverable. To reduce this risk, run the database-consistency checks against each database, and design a process to test the recoverability of the database backup. In addition, send database backups offsite to protect them in case of a local disaster, but keep local copies of recent backups in case you need to perform a quick restore.

Another critical task is disaster-recovery planning. If the organization data center were to be completely destroyed, you should quickly deploy a new data center with minimum data loss and minimum business disruption. Disaster-recovery planning is not complete until a team periodically simulates a data center failure, and proceeds through the test drill to deploy a new data center.

Recoverability Requirements

Any backup planning should start with the end goal in mind: the recoverability requirements. Following are a few things you might consider:

➤ Perhaps only part of the database must be online. You can consider a piecemeal restore to reduce your restore time, especially on larger databases for which a restore can take a long time. Determine what parts of the database must be available, and arrange the data into filegroups so that you can recover the most critical filegroups first. Archived data or reporting data is less critical and can be recovered last.

➤ The organization may allocate newer, redundant hardware and RAID storage with a high-availability solution to mitigate downtime. A company might also consider faster and more backup devices to quickly restore the database.

➤ Determine how easy or difficult it would be to re-create lost data for each database. For some databases, you can easily re-create data by extracting data from another system or from flat-file data loads. Typically, decision-support databases use extract, transfer, and load (ETL) tools to extract data. For example, if some unrecoverable data loss occurred, you can execute the ETL tool to reload the data.

➤ What is the acceptable downtime in a media failure, such as a failed disk drive? As disk technology continues to become less expensive, most organizations deploy databases on a fault-tolerant disk array that reduces the exposure of one of the disk drives failing, causing the database to become unavailable. For example, on a RAID 5 set, loss of a single drive can cause a noticeable performance slowdown. If a second drive in the same RAID 5 were to fail, the data would be lost. To mitigate this risk, have spare drives in the disk array system and get a Service-Level Agreement (SLA) from the hardware provider to deliver and install the drives. Another common scenario is a department inside the organization deploying a database in a less-than-ideal hardware environment. With time, the database becomes mission-critical to that department, but it lives under the DBA's radar with no accountability. The DBA should attempt to identify all database sources within the organization and develop a recovery plan.

➤ Determine which databases have any external dependencies on other databases, requiring both databases to be restored for users to perform their daily activities. Determine whether there is any linked server(s), external application(s), or mainframe connectivity on which a database has dependencies.

➤ Identify the available hardware that can be allocated for redeployment and where it is located.

➤ Identify the staff required for backup, restore, and disaster recovery. They need to understand the disaster-recovery procedures, and where they fit in these procedures. Record when all staff members are available, their contact numbers, the chain of communication, and the responsibility of each member. Determine the chain of command and find out whether backup members have the expertise to carry out the duties for backup, restore, and disaster recovery if the lead is unavailable. Find out the expertise of the staff and what additional training they might need to support the environment. Identify any training classes that may be beneficial.

➤ Finally, document any information about stored SQL jobs, linked servers, and logins that may be needed when the database is restored onto another database server.

Data Usage Patterns

Part of your recovery plan should include analyzing how your data is used in a typical scenario. For each database, determine how often the data is modified. You'll require different backup strategies for a database that may have a data load once a day than for others that may be read-only or that change every minute. Separate the tables that are modified from read-only tables. You can place each type on different filegroups, and develop a backup plan around it.

Identify the usage pattern of the databases during the day to determine the backup strategy to use. For example, during high activity, a DBA may schedule more frequent differential or transaction-log backups, whereas full backups may be performed during off-peak hours.

Determine the disk space used by the transaction log during peak times and the log's performance. For example, during peak times, the transaction log may fill the available disk drive allocated to it. Moreover, during peak times, the number of disks allocated for the transaction log may not be adequate to sustain the database's performance. The database recovery model setting affects both disk space and performance.

For a database in the full recovery model, consider switching to bulk-logged mode during bulk operations to improve performance, because that will incur minimal transaction logging. Prior to the start of the bulk operations, you should (at minimum) perform a transactional or differential backup to guard against the risk of a data-drive failure when the tail transaction log may not be accessible.

Also, consider how the database is to be used. If the database is mission-critical, apply redundancy around the hardware. Start with a highly redundant storage system, using RAID 10, and then add on additional hardware capabilities as you can afford them, up to and including a completely duplicate hot standby system using a failover cluster. Identify what level of data loss the company can afford, and plan to back up the transaction log to meet the time requirement. Also use the full recovery model so that you can get recovery to the point of failure.

Maintenance Time Window

Sometimes, the backup strategy is dictated by the maintenance time window available to perform database defragmentation, backups, statistics updates, and other maintenance activities. To keep enhancing the customer experience, organizations demand more timely information and give customers greater access to information, and customers are, therefore, more dependent on having this information. This presents a challenge to create the best customer experience, mitigate the risk of data loss, and enable quick restores if the database system fails.

The task of the DBA is to find the best backup strategy to meet the organization's business require-ments. Usually, the maintenance time window is limited. SQL Server implements various backup options that you can use in combination to meet these requirements. Following are some of the challenges you face when designing a backup strategy:

➤ Available backup time may be limited in a mission-critical, highly available database. Organizations often have SLAs and must finish their maintenance by a certain time when users are back on the system. If the backup takes longer, it may delay other database activities, which might not finish by the time users log in to the system. This could result in opportunity loss for the company.

➤ There may be a large number of databases to back up during the maintenance time window. You can try to optimize your time for all available backup media by performing concurrent backups within the capacity of the database server.

➤ A growing database puts pressure on the maintenance window. Additional backup devices, higher-performance database servers, and faster I/O may be needed to relieve the pressure. Sometimes the maintenance time window can be increased, but oftentimes it cannot. You may need to consider a SAN copy solution to speed the backup process.

➤ Other database activities are likely performed on all the databases in the database server (for example, database-consistency checking, defragmentation, update statistics, and perhaps data loads). As the database grows, these other activities may take longer to perform, too.

➤ Software updates, security patches, service packs, and database structure updates may need to fit within this maintenance time window.

➤ Full-text catalogs may need to be processed.

➤ As more organizations see the benefit of decision-support systems such as SQL Server Analysis Services, the Analysis Services database may need to be processed during this time.

To meet these requirements, a small database can use a full database backup every night. However, as the database becomes larger, that may not be possible. A good next step is to perform a full database backup on the weekend and perform full differential backups nightly. As the database becomes larger, consider moving read-only and read/write data to different filegroups, and then use full partial backups during the weekend and partial differential backups at night. As the database continues to grow, consider a nightly backup of individual files.

Other High-Availability Solutions

When your database has been deployed in a high-availability solution, such as AlwaysOn, failover clustering, log shipping, or database mirroring, it may require additional backup considerations:

➤ If you use the AlwaysOn technology introduced in SQL Server 2012, you can modify your backup plans. For example, one reason to create a secondary replica might be to offload the I/O load from backups from the primary replica to the secondary. In this model, you would not take backups from the primary replica, or other secondary replicas, but have a dedicated secondary replica specifically for taking backups from. You can specify a replica to be the preferred location to run backups using the BACKUP_PRIORITY configuration setting for the Availability Group.

> **NOTE** *For more information on the new AlwaysOn technologies, see Chapter 25, "AlwaysOn Availability Groups."*

➤ In log shipping, the transaction log is backed up by the log-shipping process. No other transaction-log backup should be permitted, because that will break the log chain and prevent any additional transaction-log restores on the standby server. If that occurred, you would need to reconfigure log shipping.

➤ In database mirroring, if the mirror server is down, the principal server transaction log queues all modifications to be sent to the mirror in the transaction log. The transaction log cannot be truncated past the point where it has not sent data modifications to the mirror server.

➤ A failover cluster is a single SQL Instance, so it has no special considerations. However, if the failover cluster is integrated with log shipping or data mirroring, the transaction-log limitations already mentioned apply.

➤ Any use of replication requires you to make a detailed backup recovery plan that includes the synchronization of the source database, the distribution database, and the subscribers. Replication can introduce a new level of complexity to the backup/recovery plan. Although you can recover a replicated database from a backup, additional criteria must be met to make this successful. You should consider whether using backups is a reasonable solution for recovering the subscriber databases. In the case of small databases, it may be easier and more reliable to simply regenerate and apply a new snapshot from the publisher.

> **NOTE** *In transaction replication, if the subscriber is down, the transaction log cannot be truncated past the point at which it has not replicated those data modifications to the subscriber server.*

DEVELOPING AND EXECUTING A BACKUP PLAN

SQL Server provides three methods for planning and executing backups. You can use the graphical interface of SQL Server Management Studio, Database Maintenance Plans, or the T-SQL backup commands. This section covers all of these methods.

Using SQL Server Management Studio

SQL Server Management Studio exposes backup management capabilities for a DBA to either develop a scheduled maintenance plan, or directly perform a backup. Before you start, decide the destination for the backup image. It can be a backup location such as a directory path with a file-name, or a separate backup device.

If you use a backup device, you must first create a logical device that defines where SQL Server will copy the backup image. From SQL Server Management Studio, select Server Objects ➪ Backup Devices ➪ New Backup Device. You see the dialog box shown in Figure 17-21, in which you have two destination options:

➤ **Tape**—Requires that a local tape drive be present on the database server

➤ **File**—Requires a valid disk destination

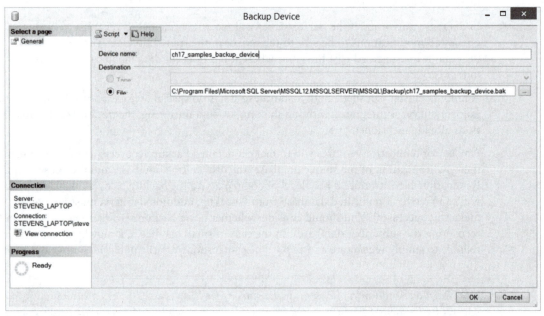

FIGURE 17-21

You do not need to use backup devices when backing up to disk because the location is hard-coded. Instead, create unique backup filenames that include the database name, the backup type, and some date/time information to make the name unique. This is much more flexible than using a backup device. To perform a database backup from SQL Server Management Studio, follow these steps:

1. Select the database you want to back up, right-click, and choose Tasks ➪ Backup. The General page of the Back Up Database dialog box appears, as shown in Figure 17-22.

2. In the Source area of this dialog box, configure the following:

    ➤ **Database**—Choose the database to back up.

    ➤ **Recovery model**—This value is grayed out because it cannot be changed. This is in the full recovery model. If it were the simple recovery model, the transaction log could not be backed up because the transaction log is truncated by the checkpoint process and files, and filegroup backups would not be available, except for read-only files or filegroups.

➤ **Backup type**—Choose among Full, Differential, or Transaction Log.

➤ **Copy-only backup**—Enables you to do a backup that does not affect the transaction chain or truncate the log.

➤ **Backup component**—Choose from the following options.

➤ **Database**—Backs up the database.

➤ **Files and filegroups**—Backs up files or filegroups. This option presents a dialog box from which you can choose one or more files or filegroups.

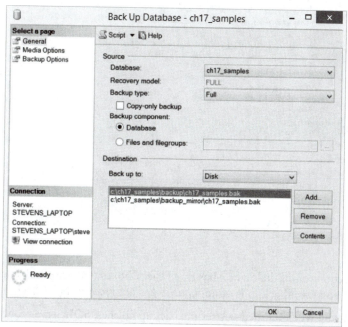

FIGURE 17-22

3. In the Destination area of the dialog box, you can select the destination type from Disk, or, new to SQL Server 2014, the option of URL. In Figure 17-22, you can see two disk files listed. These are the ones created in the examples earlier in this chapter. You can add additional file locations, or remove these.

4. From the left side of the screen, select the Media Options page. This is shown in Figure 17-23.

5. In the "Overwrite media" section, you can choose to back up to the existing media set, in which case you must configure these options:

➤ **Append to the existing backup set**—Preserves the existing backups by appending to that media set. This is the default.

➤ **Overwrite all existing backup sets**—Erases all the existing backups and replaces them with the current backup. This overwrites all existing backup sets unless the "Check media set name and backup set expiration" box is checked.

Alternatively, you can choose to back up to a new media set and erase all existing backup sets, which erases all backups in the media, and begins a media set, according to your specifications.

FIGURE 17-23

6. The Reliability section of this dialog box has three check boxes that are all good recommended practices because a backup is of no value if it is not recoverable. Check these boxes:

➤ **Verify backup when finished**—After the backup finishes, SQL Server confirms that all volumes are readable.

➤ **Perform checksum before writing to media**—SQL Server does a checksum prior to writing to media, which can be used during recovery to verify that the backup was not tampered with. There is a performance penalty with this operation.

➤ **Continue on error**—Backup should continue to run after encountering an error such as a page checksum error or torn page.

7. The "Transaction log" section of this dialog box contains options that only apply during transaction-log backups. If you are performing a transaction-log backup, select whichever of these is appropriate to the log backup you are trying to accomplish:

➤ **Truncate the transaction log**—During normal transaction-log backups, it is common practice to manage the size of the transaction log and to truncate it after it has been backed up to a backup media.

➤ **Back up the tail of the log, and leave the database in the restoring state**—This option is useful when the data files of the database are not accessible. (For example, the physical drives have failed, but the transaction log in separate physical drives is still accessible.) As a result, during database recovery, apply this as the last transaction-log backup to recover right to the point of failure.

8. The "Tape drive" section of the dialog box contains check boxes to let you specify how to handle the tape. The two options include:

➤ Unload the tape after backup

➤ Rewind the tape before unloading

9. From the list on the left side of the page, select the Backup Options page. You arrive at the page shown in Figure 17-24.

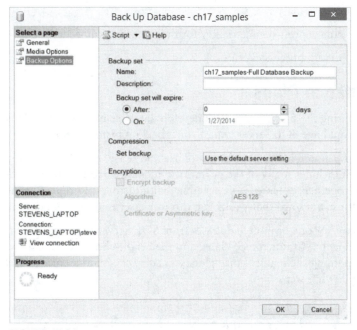

FIGURE 17-24

In the "Backup set" area of this dialog box, configure the following:

➤ **Name**—Give the backup set a name for easier identification. This name distinguishes the backup from others in the backup device.

➤ **Description**—Provide an optional description for this media set.

➤ **Backup set will expire**—Configure these options based on your business's retention policy; this guards against SQL Server's backup process overwriting the backup set.

➤ **After**—This determines the number of days, from 0 to 99,999, after which the set can be overwritten. Zero is the default, which means the set never expires. You can change the server-wide default by choosing SQL Server

Properties ⇨ Database Settings. Change the default backup media retention (in days).

➤ **On**—Specify a date on which the backup set will expire.

10. In the Compression section of this dialog box, specify one of three compression options for the backup:

➤ Use the default server setting

➤ Compress backup

➤ Do not compress backup

11. In the Encryption section, you can choose the encryption options for the backup. This option will be disabled if you have not met the following prerequisites:

➤ Create a database master key.

➤ Create a certificate or asymmetric key for the use of backup encryption.

12. Click OK and the backup process executes.

Database Maintenance Plans

Another approach to executing the backup plan is to develop database maintenance plans for each database, schedule them, and have SQL Server e-mail you a backup history report.

The purpose of the database maintenance plan is ease of use and reuse. A database maintenance plan is beneficial because it includes many of the normal maintenance actions you must do for a database, but grouped all together, executed on a schedule, with history and reporting. You can create a plan manually, or use a wizard that walks you through a series of dialog boxes.

To create maintenance plans for one or more databases from SQL Server Management Studio, choose the folder Management ⇨ Maintenance Plans, and then right-click and choose New Maintenance Plan. After naming the maintenance plan, you go to the maintenance plan design screen and perform the following steps:

> **NOTE** *You may need to display the Maintenance Plan Tasks toolbox, because this no longer shows up by default. To do this, press Ctrl+Alt+X, or use the View ⇨ Toolbox menu option.*

1. Choose the Back Up Database Task, and drag it to the Designer.

2. Right-click the Back Up Database Task, and choose Edit to open the Backup Database Task dialog box, as shown in Figure 17-25.

3. In the Connection field, choose "Local server connection," or, if this maintenance plan is to back up databases on another server, choose "New connection" and provide the connection information.

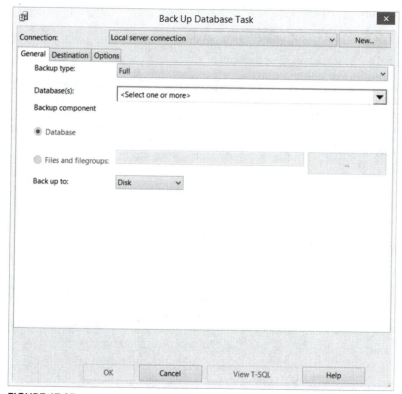

FIGURE 17-25

4. In the Database(s) field, choose `ch17_samples`. You can choose more than one database if they have identical backup requirements.

5. In the "Backup component" field, choose either Database or "Files and filegroups." If you choose "Files and filegroups," you must specify which files or filegroups to back up.

6. In the "Back up to" field, choose either Disk, Tape, or URL.

7. Select the Destination tab, as shown in Figure 17-26. On the Destination tab, you can choose a list of hard-coded files to which you can back up your databases, or have the maintenance plan create an automatically named backup file for each database.

   a. If you choose "Back up databases across one or more files," follow these steps:

      1. Click the Add button to configure the backup location. For disk, provide the full path to the filename or the disk backup device. For tape, provide the tape location or the tape backup device. You can use more than one file or backup device. If more than one is chosen, all the databases will be backed up across them, up to the 64 backup devices that SQL Server supports.

      2. In the "If backup files exist" field, select whether to append to the existing backup file or to overwrite. The default is Append.

b. If you choose "Create a backup file for every database," follow these steps:

1. Select the root directory for the backups.

2. Choose a backup file extension.

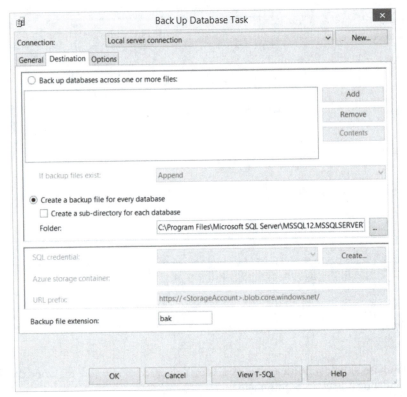

FIGURE 17-26

8. If you selected URL as the destination on the General tab, the SQL Credentials, Azure Storage Container, and URL Prefix options are now enabled. These fields are where you specify SQL credentials for the Azure Storage container. Select the Options tab, as shown in Figure 17-27.

9. On the Options tab, in the "Set backup compression" field, specify whether the backup should be compressed.

10. You can optionally choose an expiration date for the backup set. This prevents accidental overwrites.

11. The Copy-only Backup option lets you create a copy-only backup. A Copy-only backup is independent of the sequence of conventional backups, and so can be used as a complete copy of the database without needed to have all backups and logs in a backup chain. For this example, do not select this option.

12. Click the "Verify backup integrity" check box as a recommended practice.

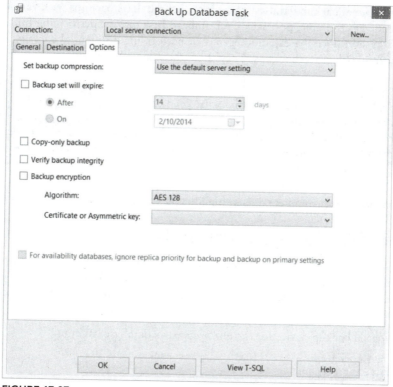

FIGURE 17-27

13. If you enable "Backup encryption," you can select the backup Algorithm, or specify the "Certificate or Asymmetric key."

14. Click OK. This will close the Back Up Database Task properties dialog box, and take you back to the Maintenance Plan Designer.

15. Click the "Reporting and Logging" button on the Maintenance Plan [Design] Menu tab, and choose how to receive the backup history report. If you choose e-mail, Database Mail must be configured. Moreover, a SQL Server Agent Operator must be configured to e-mail the report. Then click OK.

16. Click the Schedule button, and set up the schedule for this maintenance plan.

> **NOTE** *When you allow a maintenance plan to create a backup file for each database, it creates a file formatted as* `ch17_samples_bac kup_2014_01_24_090243_2394128` *for the* `ch17_samples` *database. This includes the backup type, date, and time of the backup, which is good because it means all the backup filenames indicate when the backup was taken, and what type of backup is contained within the file. The downside of using this option is that you get a single backup file, and do not realize the performance benefits of a multi-file backup.*

You can include additional backup database tasks for other database backups with various backup requirements. For example, one Back Up Database Task may be performing full database backups on several databases; another may be performing differential backups; whereas a third may be performing filegroup backups. They share the same schedule.

> **NOTE** *Earlier in this chapter, you organized your databases into categories based on the backup/restore needs. You could create maintenance plans that satisfy the needs of each category. Then, when a new database is created on that server, you simply categorize it, adding it to the appropriate maintenance plan.*

When the maintenance plan is complete, it is automatically scheduled as a SQL job in SQL Agent.

Using Transact-SQL Backup Commands

All the backup commands using SQL Server Management Studio and all functionality are available directly using T-SQL. For a full list of BACKUP syntax, refer to Books Online at http://msdn .microsoft.com/en-us/library/ms186865(v=sql.120).aspx. Following are some examples of the syntax:

> ➤ Create a logical backup device for the ch17_samples database backup:

```
EXEC sp_addumpdevice 'disk', 'ch17_samples_Backup',
'C:\BACKUP\ch17_samples.bak';
```

> **NOTE** *Your drive letters may be different, so you may have to change the file-name reference. If you use a file share, you should use the UNC name instead of a shared drive letter, as shown here:*
>
> ```
> \\myserver\myshare\Backup\ch17_samples.bak.
> ```

> ➤ Create a full ch17_samples database backup:

```
BACKUP DATABASE ch17_samples TO ch17_samples_Backup;
```

> ➤ Create a full differential backup:

```
BACKUP DATABASE ch17_samples TO ch17_samples_Backup WITH DIFFERENTIAL;
```

> ➤ Create a tail transaction-log backup. This type of backup is used only after a database failure when the transaction logs are still available.

```
BACKUP LOG ch17_samples TO tailLogBackup WITH NORECOVERY;
```

> **NOTE** *The previous tail log backup assumes you have created a new backup device called* `tailLogBackup`.

➤ Create a backup filename for the `ch17_samples` database backup:

```
DECLARE @devname varchar(256)
SELECT @devname = 'C:\BACKUP\ch17_samples_Full_'+ REPLACE
(REPLACE(CONVERT(Varchar(40), GETDATE(), 120),'-','_'),':','_') + '.bak';
```

➤ Create a full `ch17_samples` database backup:

```
BACKUP DATABASE ch17_samples TO DISK = @devname;
```

➤ Create a backup filename for the `ch17_samples` differential backup:

```
DECLARE @devname varchar(256)
SELECT @devname = 'C:\BACKUP\ch17_samples_Differential_' + REPLACE
(REPLACE(CONVERT(Varchar(40), GETDATE(), 120),'-','_'),':','_') + '.bak';
```

➤ Create a full differential backup:

```
BACKUP DATABASE ch17_samples TO DISK = @devname     WITH DIFFERENTIAL;
```

➤ Create a backup filename for the `ch17_samples` database backup:

```
DECLARE @devname varchar(256)
SELECT @devname = 'C:\BACKUP\ch17_samples_Log_' + REPLACE
(REPLACE(CONVERT(Varchar(40), GETDATE(), 120),'-','_'),':','_') + '.bak';
```

➤ Create a normal transaction-log backup:

```
BACKUP LOG ch17_samples TO DISK = @devname;
```

When using disk files, place each backup in its own backup file, and name the file appropriately. The name should include the unique database name (which might include some server part, if you have databases named the same in several servers), backup type, and date information. The preceding examples use `yyyy_mm_dd hh_mm_ss` as the date part. It is not unusual to create a stored procedure or user-defined function (UDF) that accepts parameters and returns the name of the backup file.

> **NOTE** *Do not use mapped drive letters in your backup filenames. If backing up to files on file shares, use the UNC name. Mapped drive letters may vary depending on who is logged in to the physical server. You can create permanent mapped drive letters, but UNC names are preferred.*

MANAGING BACKUPS

Managing your backups is another important DBA task. The better your maintenance procedure, the faster and more accurately the backups will be identified and quickly restored. Meticulously running backups does little good if the backups cannot be identified or, worse, were lost or overwritten. The following tips should help your backup management program:

➤ Descriptively label all the backups to prevent overwriting or misplacing a backup. You can use a naming scheme similar to the one previously mentioned by using something like the following: `<Server_Name>_<database_name>_<year>><month>_<day>.bck`.

➤ Set up a retention policy to prevent a tape or disk backup from being overwritten. These may be dictated by corporate policy, government regulations, cost, space, or logistics.

➤ Tapes can go bad, so set up a reuse policy. Define how many times a tape can be reused before throwing it away. This adds a tape cost, but a worn tape can stop a successful restore.

➤ Set up a storage location where the backups can easily be organized, found, and accessed. For example, if you're not available and someone else needs to perform the restore, that person must be able to get to the location and correctly identify the backups. You should also keep a copy of the backups stored offsite in a location where they will be protected from a local disaster. This offsite location should allow 24-hour access in case you need a backup. Moreover, keep a copy of the more recent backups locally in case they are quickly needed for a restore.

➤ The backup storage location should be secured such that unauthorized individuals do not have access to sensitive data. Furthermore, for the most sensitive data, use SQL Server column-level encryption.

➤ You must back up and maintain any encryption keys used with databases that are encrypted. These keys must be backed up again when the accounts (commonly the service account or machine account) change. These certificates *must* be maintained or the database will not be restorable, or the data will not be accessible.

➤ Set up a logistical procedure to promptly move a copy of each backup to the offsite location to prevent it from being destroyed in a disaster.

BACKUP AND RESTORE PERFORMANCE

SQL Server supports 64 backup devices, and uses multiple backup devices in parallel to back up and restore for faster throughput. The backup devices should be on a different controller from the database for better throughput. For disk devices, consider the RAID level used for fault tolerance and performance. Using RAID 5 on drives used to store backups is a bad idea because the additional overhead of calculating parity can reduce I/O throughput, and, therefore, slow down backups. RAID 10 is the preferred choice for write performance, especially if your RAID controller has the intelligence to split writes across both sides of the mirror. This can dramatically increase write throughput. Work with your storage vendor to get recommendations for your storage hardware.

In many cases, disk-based backups are written to large slow disks because of the cost savings from using cheaper, large-capacity disks. This immediately has a performance impact on the capability of the backup process to write to these disks. This is just something that you have to live with for backups, because very few companies are willing to spend large amounts of money on a high-performance disk subsystem to store backups.

A combination of full, differential, and transaction-log backups can improve performance by reducing the amount of data that must be read from the database and written to the backup device. If you take a full backup of a 5TB database every day, that's a lot of data to be backing up so often. If only a small percentage of the database changes every day, taking a full backup once a week (on the weekend, or other slack period, perhaps) with daily differential backups can dramatically reduce the amount of data being read and written during the week.

Network bandwidth can become an issue when backing up to a network device or other server. Ideally, backups should use a dedicated network with enough bandwidth to satisfy all the backup and restore throughput needs.

PERFORMING RECOVERY

Recovery is the action of restoring a database, and bringing it back to a consistent state. This section explains the various methods of recovery, through both SQL Server Management Studio and T-SQL. You also learn how to restore the system databases.

Restore Process

It is a DBA's task to ensure that backups are consistently taken and validated to restore. Each backup sequence is labeled and stored to enable quick identification to restore a database. These restore procedures include the following:

- ➤ Full database restore
- ➤ Transaction-log restore
- ➤ Partial database restore
- ➤ File/filegroup restore
- ➤ Database snapshot restore
- ➤ History tables restore

> **NOTE** *Versions prior to SQL Server 2005 required file initialization by filling the files with zeros to overwrite any existing data inside the file for the following SQL Server operations: creating a database; adding files, logs, or data to an existing database; increasing the size of an existing file; and restoring a database or filegroup. As a result, for a large database, file initialization would take significant time. Beginning with SQL Server 2005, however, data files can use instant file initialization, provided that the SQL Server service account is assigned to the Windows* SE_MANAGE_VOLUME_NAME *permission, which you can do by assigning the account to the Perform Volume Maintenance Tasks security policy. Instant file initialization reduces the time required to create a database or perform other tasks by initializing the new file areas with zeros. Instant file initialization works only on data files, and not on transaction-log files.*

Full Database Restore

A *full restore* contains the complete backup image of all the data in all the files, and enough of the transaction log to enable a consistent restore of committed transactions and uncommitted transactions. A full restore can be the base restore for differential and transaction-log restores to bring the database to a certain point in time. During the full restore, choose whether you want to overwrite the current database, whether the database should be left in operation mode, or whether to allow additional restores (such as differential backups or transaction logs). You must also choose with move if the database files are to be moved to a different directory location or filename. Then, perform the full database restore, followed by all differential and transaction-log backups. The advantage of this process is that it recovers the database in fewer steps. However, it is slow; you need a maintenance window to perform it.

A full differential restore image contains all extents that have been modified since the last full backup. Typically, it is smaller and faster than a full backup image, provided there is not a high turnover of modification activity. A differential restore is commonly used to augment the full restore. During the restore, the full backup is restored, the database is left in NORECOVERY mode, and the differential restore is performed.

Transaction-Log Restore

As mentioned previously, a mission-critical database reduces data-loss exposure by performing periodic transaction-log backups. The *transaction-log restore* requires a full database backup, a file backup, or a filegroup backup as its base. Then you apply the differential restores, and next apply all transaction-log backups in sequence (with the oldest first) to bring the database to a point in time—either by completing all the transaction-log restores, or by stopping at a specific point. For example, you can restore the database to a point before a certain error by using one of the following transaction-log restore options:

➤ With Stopat—Stop the transaction restore at the specified time.

➤ With Stopatmark—Stop the transaction-log restore at the marked transaction.

➤ With Stopbeforemark—Stop the transaction-log restore before the marked transaction.

You can insert a transaction-log mark in the transaction log by using the WITH MARK option with the BEGIN TRANSACTION command. During each mark, a row is inserted into the logmarkhistory table in msdb after the commit completes.

Normally, restoring to a point in time requires that you specify the exact time for the restore point. Perhaps a batch process went awry and you want to restore the database to the point immediately prior to the beginning of the batch process. What time did the batch process begin? That is hard to determine unless you have some sort of log-reading utility. This is where *logmarks* are helpful. For the first transaction in the batch process, add a logmark with a unique name for the batch. That way, if you need to restore to the beginning of the batch, you can restore to the logmark—easy.

An example of a transaction-log restore sequence might be as follows:

1. Restore the full database with NORECOVERY.

2. Restore any differential backups with NORECOVERY.

3. Restore each transaction log with NORECOVERY. You can use the STOP clause to restore the database to a point in time.

4. If you have the tail transaction log, restore it. Then set the database to RECOVERY.

> **NOTE** *After the database is recovered, no additional restores can be performed without starting over.*

Partial Database Restore

A partial backup contains the primary filegroup, all the read/write filegroups, and any read-only filegroups specified. A filegroup is read-only if it was changed to read-only prior to its last backup. A *partial restore* of a read-only database contains only the primary filegroup. This kind of backup is typically used when a database has read-only filegroups and, more importantly, large read-only filegroups that can be backed up to save disk space.

A partial differential backup image contains changes in the primary filegroup, and any changes to read/write filegroups. Restoring a partial differential requires a partial backup image.

File/Filegroup Restore

This is also called a *piecemeal restore*. You first restore the primary filegroup using the PARTIAL keyword. Then, you can restore the remaining filegroups. Each filegroup (when consistent) can be brought online while the other filegroups are being restored. This allows the DBA to make parts of the database available more quickly, without having to wait on the entire database restore.

The following is an example of restoring a database in piecemeal by filegroup, starting with the primary filegroup:

```
RESTORE DATABASE ch17_samples FILEGROUP='PRIMARY' FROM ch17_samples_
Backup WITH PARTIAL, NORECOVERY;
```

The FILEGROUP 'ch17_samples_fg_rw' (which is read/write) is recovered next:

```
RESTORE DATABASE ch17_samples FILEGROUP='ch17_samples_fg_rw' FROM
ch17_samples_Backup WITH NORECOVERY;
```

The FILEGROUP 'ch17_samples_fg_ro' (which is read-only) is restored last, and does not require transaction logs, because it is read-only:

```
RESTORE DATABASE ch17_samples FILEGROUP='ch17_samples_fg_ro' FROM
ch17_samples_Backup WITH RECOVERY;
```

> **NOTE** *File and filegroup backups require that the recovery model is either full or bulk-logged to enable transaction-log backups, unless the database is read-only.*

The previous code example is appropriate when you place many backups in a single device. If you put each backup in its own file, you must use the filenames in the RESTORE commands.

Database Snapshot Restore

SQL Server supports database snapshots whereby a read-only, point-in-time copy of the database can be taken. The snapshot file, when taken, contains no data because it uses the "copy on first write" technology. As the database is modified, the first time a value is modified, the old value is placed in the snapshot file.

This type of restore is not intended for restoring media failures. It is generally used when you want to make a series of changes to the database and then revert back to the original version prior to the changes. If the changes are minimal, this can occur quickly. A common use for this is during testing. Make changes during the test, then revert to the original version. A restore from snapshot returns the database to the point in time when the snapshot was taken.

Snapshots have limitations, as well. Blobs, read-only or compressed filegroups, offline files, and multiple snapshots prevent you from reverting using a snapshot. Reverting a database by restoring a snapshot backup also breaks any backup chain that may have existed before the restore. This means that after a snapshot restore, you must take a full backup (or file backup) before attempting to take any log backups.

To create a database snapshot, use the following syntax:

```
CREATE DATABASE ch17_samples_dbss9AM ON ( NAME = ch17_samples_Data
, FILENAME ='C:\Program Files\Microsoft SQL Server
\MSSQL12.MSSQLSERVER\MSSQL\Data\ch17_samples_data')
AS Snapshot of ch17_samples
```

To restore from a snapshot, use this syntax:

```
USE MASTER
RESTORE DATABASE ch17_samples
FROM DATABASE_SNAPSHOT='ch17_samples_dbss9AM'
```

Beginning with SQL 2005, a much-improved page-level reporting structure has been available. Page errors are now logged in the suspect_pages table in msdb. Along with the capability to log page errors, the DBA now has the capability to restore suspect pages. SQL Server can restore pages while the database remains online and available, even the filegroup and file that contains the suspect pages. Other versions of SQL Server allow only offline restore of suspect pages.

Only data pages can be restored, which excludes allocation pages, full-text indexes, the transaction log, and the database and file boot pages. Page restore also does not work with the simple recovery model.

The restoration process for page restore is just like that of a file restore, except you provide the page numbers you want to restore. The syntax is as follows:

```
RESTORE DATABASE <dbname>
PAGE = '<file:page>,…'
FROM <backup file or device>
WITH NORECOVERY
```

You restore any differential backup and then log backups with NORECOVERY. Then you create a normal log backup and restore it:

```
BACKUP LOG <dbname> TO <filename>
RESTORE LOG <dbname> FROM <filename> WITH RECOVERY
```

You can identify suspect pages from the suspect_pages table in msdb, the SQL error log, SQL event traces, some Database Console Command (DBCC) commands, and the Windows Management Instrumentation (WMI) provider for server events. Page restores can be a great thing. The DBA has the capability to restore pages quickly without having to restore the whole database. This is especially useful when you have hardware failures like controller or disk drive intermittent failures.

History Tables Restore

The msdb database maintains restore-metadata tables, which are restored as part of the msdb database restore. The following list details the metadata tables, and what each contains:

➤ dbo.restorefile—Contains one row for each restored file, including files restored indirectly by filegroup name

➤ dbo.restorefilegroup—Contains one row for each restored filegroup

➤ dbo.restorehistory—Contains one row for each restore operation

SQL Server Management Studio Restore

To restore a database from SQL Server Management Studio, perform the following steps:

1. Choose the Database folder, right-click the database of your choice, and choose Tasks ⇨ Restore ⇨ Database. The Restore Database dialog box shown in Figure 17-28 exposes the restore capability. The default page is the General page.

2. In the Source area of this dialog box, choose between the following options:

➤ **Database**—The name of the database to restore. This information is retrieved from the backup history tables in msdb.

➤ **Device**—Choose either the backup device or the backup filename to restore from. This may be used when restoring a database onto another SQL Server 2014 instance and there is no restore data in the backup tables in msdb.

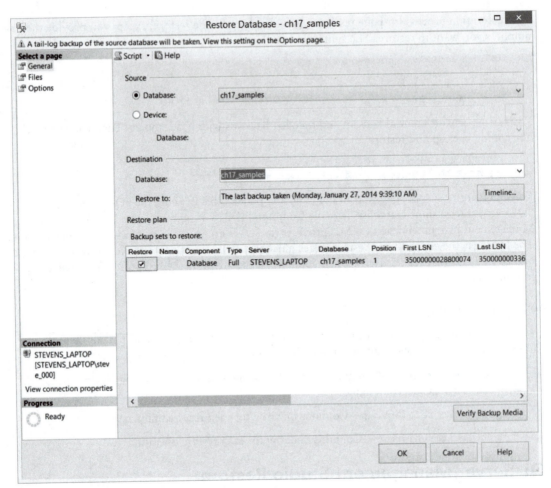

FIGURE 17-28

3. In the Destination area of the Restore Database dialog box, select from the following options:

   ➤ **Database**—Choose the name of an existing database or type the database name.

   ➤ **Restore to**—This defaults to the last Backup taken for the database, but using the Timeline... button, you can view and select a different point in time to recover to. A point in time is commonly used when a database is being restored because of a user or application data modification error and you have identified the time when the error occurred. Therefore, you want to stop the restoration before the error. This option is not possible for the simple recovery model because the transaction log is truncated.

4. Next, select the backup sets to restore from the list at the bottom of the dialog box. When you select the restore source, it populates this field with the backup sets available for the database. It also provides an option to choose which backup sets to restore.

5. Select the Files page, and you will see the options shown in Figure 17-29.

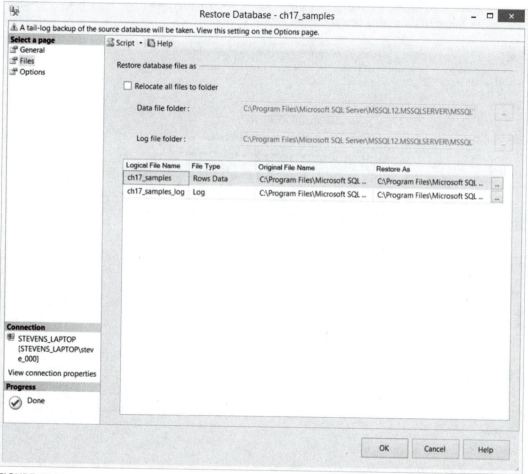

FIGURE 17-29

➤ **Restore database files as**—Here you can choose to restore the database in another directory and with a different filename. For example, if a new database copy has been created in the same directory, you need to change the filename of the restored database. This is equivalent to the MOVE option in the Restore Database command. If the filenames are not changed, SQL Server generates the following error:

```
Restore failed for Server 'STEVENS_LAPTOP'.
(Microsoft.SqlServer.SmoExtended) System.Data.SqlClient.SqlError:
Exclusive access could not be obtained because the database is in
use.(Microsoft.SqlServer.Smo)
```

6. From the Restore Database dialog box, select the Options page from the left side, and you'll be taken to the dialog box shown in Figure 17-30.

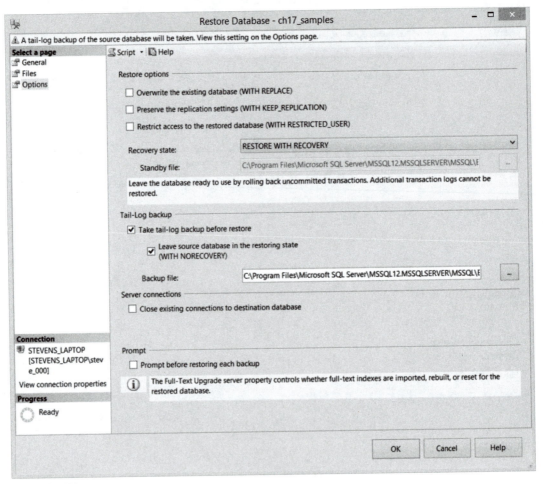

FIGURE 17-30

7. Choose from the following options in the "Restore options" section of this dialog box:

➤ **Overwrite the existing database**—Use this check box when the database you want to restore already exists in the SQL Server instance. Checking this box overwrites the existing database. This is equivalent to the REPLACE option in the Restore Database command.

➤ **Preserve the replication settings**—Use this check box when you restore a publisher database. It is equivalent to the `PRESERVE_REPLICATION` option in the `Restore Database` command.

➤ **Restrict access to the restored database**—Use this check box when you need to perform additional database operations or validation before allowing users to access the database. This option limits database access to members of `db_owner`, `dbcreator`, or `sysadmin`, and is equivalent to the `RESTRICTED_USER` option in the `Restore Database` command.

8. In the "Recovery state" section of this dialog box, select one of these options:

➤ **RESTORE WITH RECOVERY**—The default setting recovers the database, which means that no more backup images can be restored and the database becomes available to users. If additional backup images need to be restored (such as a full database restore followed by several transaction logs), the recovery should be performed after the last step, because after recovery, no additional backup images can be restored without starting the restore over. This is equivalent to the `WITH RECOVERY` option in the `Restore Database` command.

➤ **RESTORE WITH NORECOVERY**—After a backup image is restored, the database is not recovered to enable additional backup images to be applied (such as a database differential or a transaction-log backup). Moreover, the database is not user-accessible while in `NORECOVERY`. This state is used on the mirror server in data mirroring and is one of the states available on the secondary server in log shipping. This is equivalent to the `WITH NORECOVERY` option in the `Restore Database` command.

➤ **RESTORE WITH STANDBY**—After a backup image has been restored, the database is left in a state in which it allows additional backup images to be restored while allowing read-only user access. In this state, for the database to maintain data consistency, the undo and uncommitted transactions are saved in the standby file to allow preceding backup images to commit them. Perhaps you plan to apply additional backup images and want to validate the data before each restore. Oftentimes, this option is used on the secondary server in log shipping to allow users access for reporting. This is equivalent to the `WITH STANDBY` option in the `Restore Database` command.

9. In the Tail-Log Backup section of the Options page, you can select the option to take a tail log backup before the restore. If you select this option, you can also choose to leave the source database in a restoring state after the tail log backup is taken, in preparation for the restore. There is also a Backup File selection, so you can specify where the tail log backup will be written.

10. In the Server Connections section of the Options page, you can select to close existing connections to the destination database before the restore operation starts.

11. In the Prompt section of the Options page, you can select the "Prompt before restoring each backup" check box if you want to swap tapes that contain the backup set.

T-SQL Restore Command

All the restore commands using SQL Server 2014 Management Studio and all functionality are available directly from T-SQL. For example, to conduct a simple restore of a full database backup, use this syntax:

```
RESTORE DATABASE [ch17_samples] FROM  DISK ='
C:\Program
Files\Microsoft SQL Server\MSSQL12.MSSQLSERVER\MSSQL\Backup\ch17_samples.bak'
```

The following is a more complex example of a database restore using a full database, differential, and then transaction-log restore, including the STOPAT option. This option enables the DBA to stop the restore at a point in time before a data modification that caused an error. As a good practice, the STOPAT option has been placed in all the transaction-log backups. If the stop date is in the previous transaction-log backup, it stops there. Otherwise, if the stop date has been passed over, the restore process must be started again.

```
--Restore the full database backup
RESTORE DATABASE ch17_samples FROM ch17_samples_Full_Backup
    WITH NORECOVERY;
--Restore the differential database backup
RESTORE DATABASE ch17_samples FROM ch17_samples_Diff_Backup
    WITH NORECOVERY;
-- Restore the transaction logs with a STOPAT to restore to a point in time.
RESTORE LOG ch17_samples
    FROM ch17_samples_Log1
    WITH NORECOVERY, STOPAT = 'Feb 1, 12:00 AM';
RESTORE LOG ch17_samples
    FROM ch17_samples_Log2
    WITH RECOVERY, STOPAT = 'Feb 1, 2012 12:00 AM';
```

> **NOTE** *Databases that use transparent encryption automatically have their backups encrypted with the same key. When you restore these backups, the server encryption key must also be available. No key—no access to the data. The encryption keys must be saved for as long as the backups.*

Restoring System Databases

The cause of the master database failure determines the procedure to follow to recover it. For a failure that necessitates the installation of a new SQL Server instance, if you have a copy of the most recent master full database backup, follow these steps:

1. Install the new SQL Server instance.

2. Start the SQL Server instance.

3. Install service packs and hotfixes.

4. Stop the SQL Server Agent. If you don't, it may take the only single-user connection. In addition, shut down any other services that may be accessing the SQL Server instance because that may take the only connection.

5. Start the SQL Server instance in single-user mode. You have several ways to set SQL Server to single-user mode: by using SQL Server Configuration Manager, executing the SQL Server binary from the command line, or, from Windows Services, locating the SQL Server service. In all cases, add the –m startup parameter to set SQL Server to single-user mode, and then restart. The recommended approach is to go to SQL Server Configuration Manager, under SQL Server Services, and locate the SQL Server instance. Stop that SQL service. Then, on the Startup Parameters tab of the Service Properties dialog box, add the –m startup parameter to the service, and restart the SQL service, as shown in Figure 17-31.

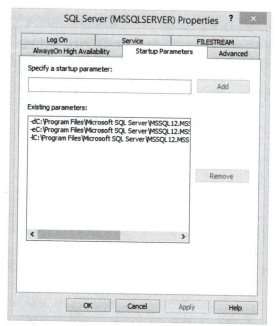

FIGURE 17-31

6. Use SQLCMD or an administration tool to log on to the SQL Server instance with a system administrator account. Restore the master database by executing the following command:

```
RESTORE DATABASE [MASTER] FROM  DISK =
N'C:\Program
Files\Microsoft SQL Server\MSSQL12.MSSQLSERVER\MSSQL\Backup\master.bak'
```

7. If SQL Server does not start because the master database is corrupted and a current master backup is not available, the master database must be rebuilt. Execute the SQL Server setup .exe to repair the system databases.

8. After the rebuild and SQL Server starts, if a current copy of the `master` database backup is available, set the SQL Server instance in single-user mode and restore it, according to the previous instructions. If a current `master` database backup is not available, any modifications to the `master` database (for example, login security, endpoints, or linked server) will be lost and need to be redeployed.

9. Additionally, `setup.exe` creates new `msdb` and `model` databases during the system database rebuild. If current copies of the `model` and `msdb` databases are available, restore them. If not, all modifications performed to the `model` and `msdb` databases must be redeployed. The syntax to rebuild the `master` database is as follows:

```
start /wait setup.exe /qn INSTANCENAME=<InstanceName> REINSTALL=SQL_Engine
```

10. Finally, attach the user databases.

If only the `model` or `msdb` databases are damaged, you can restore them from a current backup. If a backup is not available, you must execute setup.exe, which re-creates all the system databases. Typically, `model` and `msdb` reside in the same disk system with `master`, and if a disk-array failure occurred, most likely all three would be lost. To mitigate disk failure, consider using a RAID array where `master`, `model`, and `msdb` reside. `tempdb` does not need to be restored because it is automatically re-created by SQL Server at startup. `tempdb` is a critical database, and is a single point of failure for the SQL Server instance; as such, it should be deployed on a fault-tolerant disk array.

ARCHIVING DATA

Archiving a large amount of data from large tables can be challenging. For example, selecting millions of rows from a billion-row table, copying them, and then deleting them is a long-running delete process that may escalate to a table lock and reduce concurrency, which is not acceptable, unless no one will be using the table. A commonly used procedure is to periodically delete a small number of rows to improve table concurrency because the smaller number of rows may take page locks and use an index for faster access, completing faster.

An efficient procedure to archive large amounts of data is to use a sliding time window table partitioning scheme. You have two approaches to this solution: using SQL Server table partitioning or using a partitioned view.

SQL Server Table Partitioning

SQL Server supports table partitioning, whereby a table can be carved into as many as 15,000 pieces, with each residing on its own filegroup. Each filegroup can be independently backed up. Different filegroups can also be located on different storage. For example, current data can be held on fast disks, possibly even on solid-state disks. Older/archive data can then be moved to larger, slower disks and more easily deleted when the data is no longer needed. The deletion of a partition can be achieved extremely quickly, and with virtually no impact to queries against the current data.

Look at the following partitioning example in which each partition contains one month's data. With table partitioning, a new empty partition is created when the next monthly data becomes available.

Then the oldest partition can be switched out into a table and moved to an archive table monthly. The basic steps to create a table partition are as follows:

1. Create a partition function that describes how you want the data partitioned.

2. Create a partition schema that maps the pieces to the filegroups.

3. Create one or more tables using the partition scheme.

Following is an example of creating a partition table using a monthly sliding window:

```
--Create partition function
CREATE PARTITION FUNCTION [OrderDateRangePFN](datetime)
AS RANGE RIGHT
FOR VALUES (N'2014-01-01 00:00:00'
, N'2014-02-01 00:00:00'
, N'2014-03-01 00:00:00'
,N'2014-04-01 00:00:00');
--Create partition scheme
CREATE PARTITION SCHEME [OrderDatePScheme]
AS PARTITION [OrderDateRangePFN]
TO ([filegroup1], [filegroup2], [filegroup3], [filegroup4], [filegroup5]);
--Create partitioned table SalesOrderHeader
CREATE TABLE [dbo].[SalesOrderHeader](
    [SalesOrderID] [int] NULL,
    [RevisionNumber] [tinyint] NOT NULL,
    [OrderDate] [datetime] NOT NULL,
    [DueDate] [datetime] NOT NULL,
    [ShipDate] [datetime] NULL,
    [Status] [tinyint] NOT NULL
) ON [OrderDatePScheme]([OrderDate]);
```

This example places each partition on a different filegroup. Splitting and merging partitions requires data movement. You can achieve high-speed splits and merges without table locking or reducing concurrency if you place the partitions on the same filegroup. When partitions are on the same filegroup, switching out a partition or merging is only a schema change and occurs quickly. Several other smaller restrictions for high-speed partitioning exist, but the filegroup restriction is more important.

Partitioned View

This technique has been available since earlier versions of SQL Server. It uses a partition view to group independent, identical tables together (for example, a new table for each month). Following is the procedure:

1. Create individual, identical tables with a check constraint to limit the data that can reside in each.

2. Create a view to unite all these tables.

3. Load the data through the partition view. SQL Server evaluates the table constraint to insert the data in the correct table.

4.   Before the next date period, create a new table with the date period constraint and include it as part of the view definition. Then load the current data through the view.

5.   To archive, remove the oldest table from the view definition and then archive it. Each table can be placed in its own filegroup and backed up individually.

This technique does not have the 15,000-partition limitation, but it requires more management because each table is independent and managed.

SUMMARY

Backup and recovery are the last defenses to recover an organization's data asset when everything else fails. The backup and restore functionality must guarantee that many years of customer information, buying patterns, financial data, and inventory can be recovered.

SQL Server 2014 is a scalable and highly available relational database management system (RDBMS) solution that supports some of the largest databases with the highest number of concurrent users running mission-critical applications. These key backup and restore functionalities ensure that it can support a larger database with less management.

If you followed along throughout this chapter, you should now both understand the details needed to create a robust plan for backing up your company's data, and possess one or more documents that constitute your recovery plan.

In Chapter 18, you learn about log shipping with SQL Server 2014.

18

SQL Server 2014 Log Shipping

WHAT'S IN THIS CHAPTER?

- ➤ Understanding log shipping
- ➤ Taking a look at practical usage scenarios
- ➤ Getting to know log-shipping architecture
- ➤ Understanding log-shipping deployment
- ➤ Role changing within log shipping
- ➤ Monitoring and troubleshooting

Log shipping is a low-cost, efficient, and simple SQL Server technique that became available many releases ago, and has been vital to organizations for their business continuity. In log shipping, the database transaction log from one SQL Server is backed up and restored onto a secondary SQL Server, where it is often deployed for high-availability, reporting, and disaster-recovery scenarios. Beginning with SQL Server 2005, log shipping has delivered business continuity, and continues to be one of the high-availability solutions to maintain a warm standby and, with a secondary server, used for failover.

This chapter covers log-shipping architecture and deployment scenarios, and discusses how to configure log shipping and the various scenarios for switching roles between the primary and secondary servers. You also learn how to troubleshoot your log-shipping setup, and how to integrate log shipping with other high-availability solutions.

LOG-SHIPPING DEPLOYMENT SCENARIOS

Log shipping takes advantage of the transaction-log backup and restore functionalities of SQL Server. The two log-shipping SQL Server partners can be located next to each other for high availability, or across a distance for disaster recovery. The only distance restriction for the two

SQL Servers is that they share connectivity that enables the secondary SQL Server to copy the transaction log and restore it. Log shipping can be deployed in three different scenarios:

➤ **Warm standby server**—A backup database copy is maintained in the same physical location to protect from a primary server failure.

➤ **Disaster-recovery solution**—Two servers are geographically separated in case the local area where the primary server resides suffers from a disaster.

➤ **Reporting solution**—The secondary server is used to satisfy the reporting needs.

Log Shipping to Create a Warm Standby Server

A *warm standby server* involves creating a full backup and periodic transaction-log backups at the primary server, and then applying those backups (in sequence) to the standby server. The standby server is left in a read-only state between restores. When the standby server needs to be made available for use, any outstanding transaction-log backups (including the backup of the active transaction log from the primary server) are applied to the standby server, and the database is recovered. A common log-shipping scenario is to create a warm standby server whereby the log-shipping secondary server is located close to the primary server. If the primary server goes down for planned or unplanned downtime, the secondary server takes over and maintains business continuity. Then, the DBA may choose to failback to the primary server when the primary server becomes available.

It is simple to configure a warm standby server with log shipping because it uses the dependable transaction-log backup, operating system copy file, and transaction-log restore. In most warm standby scenarios, you should configure the log-shipping jobs to execute at a shorter interval to maintain the secondary server closely in sync with the primary server, to reduce the amount of time to switch roles, and to reduce data loss. Additionally, to further limit data loss, if the active portion of the primary server's transaction log is available, the secondary server would be restored to the point in time of the failed primary server.

However, in some situations, the active portion of the transaction log may not be available when the storage where the transaction log resided is not accessible, or some transaction-log files that were in transit may not have made it to the secondary server, causing some data loss. In a typical role-switch scenario, you would recover all in-transit transaction logs and the active portion of the transaction log before recovering the secondary server. Users would also need to be redirected because, unlike Windows failover clustering or other SQL high-availability solutions, log shipping has no automatic user redirect.

Sometimes, when performing a failback, log shipping is used in place of Windows failover clustering because it is a less expensive solution. For example, clustering requires a shared disk system that an organization may not own. Log shipping does not have such hardware requirements, so an organization may already own hardware that is not failover-cluster–compatible that can be used for log shipping. Moreover, in log shipping, the primary and secondary databases exist on separate servers. This is a shared-nothing environment. Windows failover clustering uses a shared disk system with a single copy of your database on that disk, which could become corrupted.

> **NOTE** *Unlike clustering, log-shipping failover is always a manual process. This means that you must initiate and monitor the status of the failover process, and update the client application's connection strings to the new primary. When you use Windows Clustering for SQL Server, the monitoring and failover is done automatically. When you determine that you must failover to the secondary log-shipping server, the execution of the steps can be manual or automated. If you choose automation, you must create scripts that do work on your behalf. Examples of these scripts are covered later in this chapter.*

Another difference between log shipping and clustering is that clustering protects the whole SQL Server instance. In failover clustering, all databases on the instance are included in the solution. Log shipping is by user database. If you need high availability for all the databases on a server, you can achieve it using either clustering or log shipping. But if you choose log shipping, you must set it up for each database on the server. If you want some, but not all, of the databases on a server to be highly available, log shipping is a good choice.

Log Shipping as a Disaster-Recovery Solution

Even if an organization already has a local high-availability solution, regardless of whether it is based around Windows failover clustering or log shipping, an alternative, site-to-site solution is a vital tool to employ. If you deploy log shipping to a secondary server at a remote location, you can protect your organization from a power grid failure or local disaster.

If the transaction-log files in the backup folder or the active transaction log are not accessible (such as in a disaster where the primary server cannot be restarted because of a power grid failure), you can stitch the primary server's active transaction log and transaction-log files together by using a third-party transaction-log analyzer to identify transactions that did not make it across, and apply them manually. However, your availability or recovery plan should not depend on these log analyzers. The transaction-log files backed up by the backup job should be archived to provide point-in-time recovery of the primary server if, for example, a user error modifies some data that needs to be recovered.

Moreover, archiving the transaction logs along with a full database backup offers another disaster-recovery option when needed. To control when the transaction-log files are deleted so that the operating system backup program can back up these files on its own schedule, set the Delete Files Older Than option to a time period greater than that of the operating system backup program schedule. You can find this option in the Transaction Log Backup Settings. For example, if the operating system backup is scheduled to run every night, set the Delete Files Older Than option to at least keep the files there until the operating system backup completes.

The challenges with this scenario are that the network bandwidth must have the capacity to support log shipping large log files to the remote location. Moreover, in the event of a disaster, there is a potential that some of the files may be in transit and may not make it to the secondary server. Even if the bandwidth supports log shipping comfortably, during a disaster, the bandwidth may be constrained by other activity that can slow down the file transfers. That means the possibility of data loss.

The databases are kept in sync using the transaction logs. The amount of data that might be at risk during a disaster is the data included in the transaction log. For mission-critical applications for which you want to minimize any data loss, you may need to choose another solution. For example, database mirroring or Availability Groups can send transactions to be synchronized as soon as the transaction commits, without waiting for a transaction-log backup. If you use log shipping, you may need to accept a greater amount of data loss because of a missing log file, or an inaccessible backup log folder.

Log Shipping as a Report Database Solution

Out of the three deployment solutions for which you can use log shipping, using it as a report database solution is the least effective. However, it does have its advantages. Log shipping is a low-cost solution, it leverages inexpensive hardware, and it is a simple solution to implement and manage. Therefore, in certain scenarios, it may be feasible to use the secondary server's database for production reporting, provided that the database recovery mode is STANDBY. However, several inherent disadvantages exist to using this server for reporting.

The restore process needs exclusive access to the database while restoring. If users run reports, the restore process fails to restore, and the job waits for the next restore interval to try again. Log shipping alerts may trigger, sending an alert that the secondary server has fallen behind. Moreover, at the time of role-switching, there may be transaction logs that have not been applied because reporting prevented it, which increases the role-switching time because these transaction logs were applied.

However, you can configure log shipping to disconnect users who are in the database to restore the transaction logs, but longer-running reports may be kept from completing in that case. As an example, if you have the restore run every 10 minutes, but you have a report that takes 30 minutes to complete, the report would never run to completion because log shipping would kill the connection every 10 minutes. To improve the chances that the report will run to completion, the restore job interval would have to be longer, which makes the secondary server fall further behind. Additionally, the data for the reports will not be current, and the secondary server's database schema cannot be optimized for reporting because it is read-only. For example, if particular indices are beneficial to the report database, the indices must be created in the primary server's database, which may suffer from having the additional indices.

For these reasons, using log shipping for reporting has several challenges and does not make a good reporting solution for some environments. For occasional reporting, provided the organization can live with these challenges, it is possible to use log shipping for reporting. However, a better report solution may be Availability Groups, which allows reporting from replica databases. (See Chapter 25 for more on Availability Groups.) Or, you can use transactional replication, which provides concurrency, granularity, and near real-time synchronization, with the added flexibility to allow modification of the database schema. (See Chapter 15 for more on transactional replication.)

> **NOTE** *The fact that log shipping must have exclusive access to the database can be a big disadvantage. If you apply logs every hour, any currently running report must be killed before the log can be applied. This kind of partial access inconveniences users and might cause them to bypass the use of log shipping for reporting purposes many times. However, if you can live with this issue, log shipping is a viable solution.*

LOG-SHIPPING ARCHITECTURE

Figure 18-1 shows the basic log-shipping architecture. The architecture requires three servers:

➤ Primary server

➤ Secondary server (also known as the standby server)

➤ Monitor server (optional)

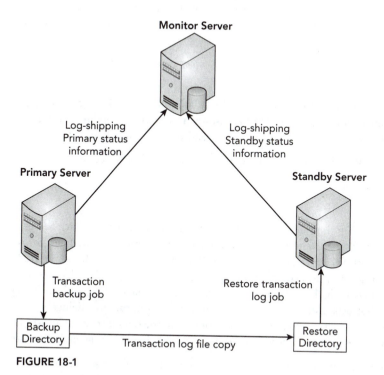

FIGURE 18-1

Primary Server

The primary server is the production server to which users connect and do work. It holds the SQL Server 2014 instance that must be protected in case of hardware failure, software error, natural disaster, or user-induced errors (for example, accidentally deleting data). You can consider configuring the secondary server to restore the log at a delay interval to react to these user-induced errors. In log shipping, the primary server is configured to execute a SQL Agent job to back up the transaction log to a file. For log shipping to function, the server must use the database recovery models of either Bulk-logged or Full. (You can find these in the Database Properties using SQL Server 2014 Management Studio.)

Secondary Server

The secondary server is the backup SQL Server 2014 instance that maintains a copy of the primary server database. The secondary server uses the SQL Agent to copy the transaction-log file from the backup folder (where it was placed by the primary server), and to restore the transaction-log backup. The secondary server is configured with two SQL Agent jobs: one to copy the transaction-log file from the shared backup folder, and the other to restore the transaction log. This server should have similar performance specifications to those of the primary server to maintain a consistent user experience during failover. Log shipping can also support multiple secondary servers at a time. For example, you can set one up for warm-standby, another for reporting, and another may even have a transaction log with a time delay.

You can configure the secondary database using either the STANDBY or NORECOVERY recovery options:

➤ STANDBY—This provides users read-only access to the log-shipped database between transaction-log restores. This means you can offload read-only access to a secondary server. However, for a transaction-log restore to succeed, no read-only access is allowed.

➤ NORECOVERY—The database will not be available for users for read-only access.

Monitor Server

Having a monitor server as part of log shipping is optional, but recommended. The monitor server should be a different physical server to prevent it from becoming a single point of failure from the primary or secondary server. Any SQL Server version including SQL Server Express can be configured as a monitor server. When the monitor server participates in log shipping, it manages the jobs that produce monitoring information, such as the last time the transaction log was backed up on the primary server, the last transaction log that was restored on the secondary server, and the time deltas between the processes. The monitor server can also send alerts to page or e-mail the operator when log-shipping thresholds are crossed. A single monitor server can monitor multiple log-shipping environments.

Having a separate physical monitor server is recommended. Deploying a monitor server on the primary or secondary server has the risk that if that server were to fail, you would lose monitoring server capabilities as well. Without the monitor server, log shipping will continue to operate and monitoring can be performed using Dynamic Management Views (DMVs).

LOG-SHIPPING PROCESS

SQL Agent is used on the participating servers to execute the processes that implement log shipping. Following are the three main processes:

➤ **Back up the transaction log on the primary server**—A SQL Agent job on the primary server backs up the transaction log at a user-configurable time interval to a file in a backup folder. By default, the filename is time-stamped to provide uniqueness—for example, `database-name_yyyymmddhhmmss.trn`. By default, the backup job is named `LSBackup_databasename`, and it executes an operating system command to back up the transaction log:

```
"C:\Program Files\Microsoft SQL Server\120\Tools\Binn\sqllogship.exe"
-Backup 0E5D9AA6-D054-45C9-9C6B-33301DD934E2 -server SQLServer1
```

➤ **Copy the transaction log to the secondary server**—A SQL Agent job on the secondary server uses UNC or a shared drive to access the backup folder on the primary server to copy the transaction-log file to a local folder on the secondary server. By default, the copy job is named `LSCopy_servername_databasename`, and it executes an operating system command to copy the transaction-log file:

```
"C:\Program Files\Microsoft SQL Server\120\Tools\Binn\sqllogship.exe"
-Copy F2305BFA-B9E3-4B1C-885D-3069D0D11998 -server SQLServer1\SQLServer2
```

➤ **Restore the transaction log on the secondary server**—A SQL Agent job on the secondary server restores the transaction log on the secondary server. To restore the transaction log, the database must be in either STANDBY or NORECOVERY mode. The default restore job name is `LSRestore_servername_databasename`, and it executes an operating system command to copy the transaction-log file:

```
"C:\Program Files\Microsoft SQL Server\120\Tools\Binn\sqllogship.exe"
-Restore F2305BFA-B9E3-4B1C-885D-3069D0D11998 -server SQLServer1\SQLServer2
```

> **NOTE** *You can find most of the log-shipping objects in* `msdb`*. For more information, see Microsoft SQL Server 2014 Books Online.*

SYSTEM REQUIREMENTS

The servers that participate in log shipping must meet the minimum SQL Server 2014 hardware requirements. (See Microsoft SQL Server 2014 Books Online for specifics.) Additionally, certain hardware infrastructure requirements are necessary to deploy log shipping. The following sections outline what the system infrastructure requirements are and discuss what you can do to ensure that you follow them accurately.

Network

The log-shipping SQL Servers are required to be networked such that the primary server has access to the backup folder, and the secondary server has access to copy the transaction-log files from the backup folder and into its local folder. In addition, the monitor server must connect to both the primary and secondary servers. To improve copying the transaction-log file in an active log-shipping environment, place the participating servers on their own network segment, and use an additional network card dedicated to log shipping. Log shipping can function with any feasible network speed, but on a slow network, the transaction-log file transfer can take longer, and the secondary server can likely be further behind the primary server.

Identical Capacity Servers

The primary and secondary servers are recommended to have identical performance capacity so that in a failover, the secondary server can take over and provide the same level of performance and user experience. Additionally, some organizations have service-level agreements (SLAs) to meet. The SLA may require that you provide the same performance during failover as you would normally, requiring your secondary server to have the same capacity as the primary. Some businesses allow the secondary server to be of smaller capacity. You should understand the specific requirements of your business and configure the secondary server appropriately.

Storage

Unlike a Windows failover cluster that requires a shared-disk infrastructure, log shipping has no such requirements. On the contrary, to mitigate the risk of storage failure becoming a single point of failure, the primary and secondary servers should not share the same disk system. In a disaster-recovery scenario configuration, the primary and secondary servers would be located at a distance from each other and would be unlikely to share the same disk system. Plan the disk space requirements for the backup share that holds the transaction-log backups to avoid running out of disk space.

Moreover, when identifying the performance specification for the disk systems, consider the log-shipping I/O activities. You can use the SQLIO Disk Subsystem Benchmark Tool to determine the I/O capacity of a given disk system. To download the tool, go to `http://www.microsoft.com/en-us/download/details.aspx?id=20163`.

When deploying log shipping with SQL Server 2014 Management Studio, the SQL Server service and the SQL Agent account (or its proxy running the backup job) must have read-and-write permission to the backup folder. If possible, this folder should reside on a fault-tolerant disk system so that if a drive is lost, all the transaction-log files are not lost.

Software

The following SQL Server editions are supported for log shipping:

➤ SQL Server 2014 Enterprise Edition

➤ SQL Server 2014 Standard Edition

➤ SQL Server 2014 Business Intelligence Edition

➤ Monitor server can be any edition including SQL Express

The log-shipping servers are required to have identical case-sensitivity settings, and the log-shipping databases must use either the full or bulk-logged recovery model.

DEPLOYING LOG SHIPPING

Before you can begin the log-shipping deployment process, you must do some initial configuration. Then you have a choice regarding how you want to deploy: using the SQL Server 2014 Management Studio, or using T-SQL scripts. Typically, a DBA uses SQL Server 2014 Management Studio to configure log shipping, and then generates SQL scripts for future redeployment. Both procedures are covered here.

Initial Configuration

Prior to deploying log shipping, some specific directories are needed for log shipping to copy the transaction-log files, and some SQL configuration is needed to prepare the log-shipping process to execute. To configure your shared directories for log shipping, perform the following steps:

1. First create a backup folder that the primary server can access. Share it, and ensure that it is accessible by the secondary server. For example, you could use the folder `c:\primaryBackupLog`, which is also shared as a UNC path: `\\primaryserver\primaryBackupLog`. Use the UNC when you are accessing the share from a remote server. When the share is local, you can access either by UNC or by the directory letter. The primary server's SQL Agent account must have read-and-write permission to the folder, and the secondary server's SQL Agent account or the proxy account executing the job should have read permission to this folder. Additionally, the SQL Agent account must have permission to execute the log-shipping extended stored procedure.

2. Next, create a destination folder on the secondary server, such as `c:\secondaryBackupDest`. The secondary server's SQL Agent account, or the proxy account executing the job, must have read-and-write permission to this folder. Additionally, the account must have permission to execute the log-shipping extended stored procedures.

> **NOTE** *Log shipping uses extended stored procedures. SQL Agent on the primary and secondary servers must have the extended stored procedures enabled (it is disabled by default), as shown here:*
>
> ```
> EXECUTE sp_configure "Agent XPs", 1;
> GO
> Reconfigure;
> GO
> ```

3. Set the recovery model for the log-shipped database to either `Full` or `Bulk_logged`. You have two ways to do this, depending on how you want to deploy: with Management Studio or with a T-SQL command.

To use Management Studio, open the Database Properties window and select Options. From the "Recovery model" drop-down, choose the recovery model, as shown in Figure 18-2.

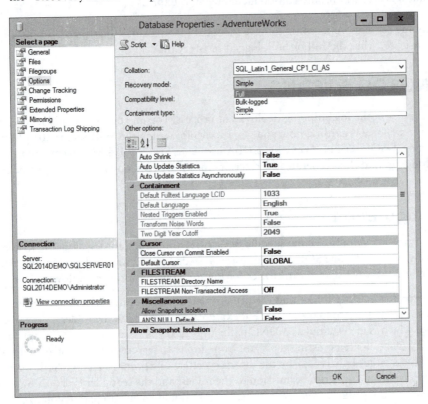

FIGURE 18-2

To use T-SQL, open a SQL query window and use the ALTER DATABASE command to change the recovery model. For example, to change the AdventureWorks database to Full, use this T-SQL:

```
USE master;
GO
ALTER DATABASE AdventureWorks
SET RECOVERY FULL;
GO
```

Deploying with Management Studio

To deploy log shipping with SQL Server Management Studio, perform the following steps:

1. Start by opening the database to be configured and select the database properties. Then select Transaction Log Shipping. Click the check box that reads "Enable this as a primary database in a log shipping configuration," as shown in Figure 18-3.

2. Next, click the Backup Settings button. The Transaction Log Backup Settings dialog box appears, as shown in Figure 18-4.

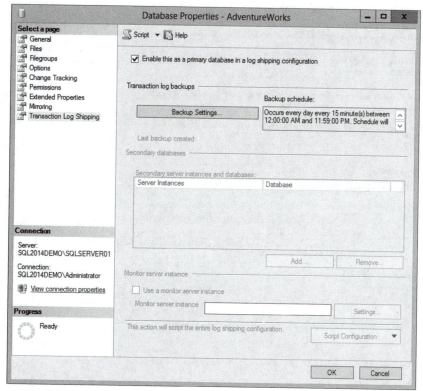

FIGURE 18-3

3. Here, you need to provide the network path to the backup folder and the local path if the folder is local to the primary server. If the folder is local to the primary server, log shipping uses the local path. Remember that the SQL Server service and the SQL Agent account or its proxy running the backup job must have read-and-write permission to this folder. If possible, this folder should reside on a fault-tolerant disk system so that if a drive is lost, all the transaction-log files are not lost.

    Typically, you can delete transaction log backup files that have been applied and are older than the value in the "Delete files older than" field to control the folder size containing older transaction log backup files. However, for an additional level of protection, if the business requires point-in-time recovery, leave the files there until the operating system backup program backs them up to another storage device, provided that a full database backup is also available to apply these transaction logs. The default setting is 72 hours.

4. In the "Alert if no backup occurs within" field, choose a value based on the business requirements. The amount of data your organization can stand to lose determines the transaction backup interval setting, or how critical the data is. The alert time also depends on the transaction backup interval setting. For example, if the business requires a highly available secondary server, where the transaction log is backed up every couple of minutes, this setting should be configured to send an alert if the job fails to run within that interval. The default setting is 1 hour.

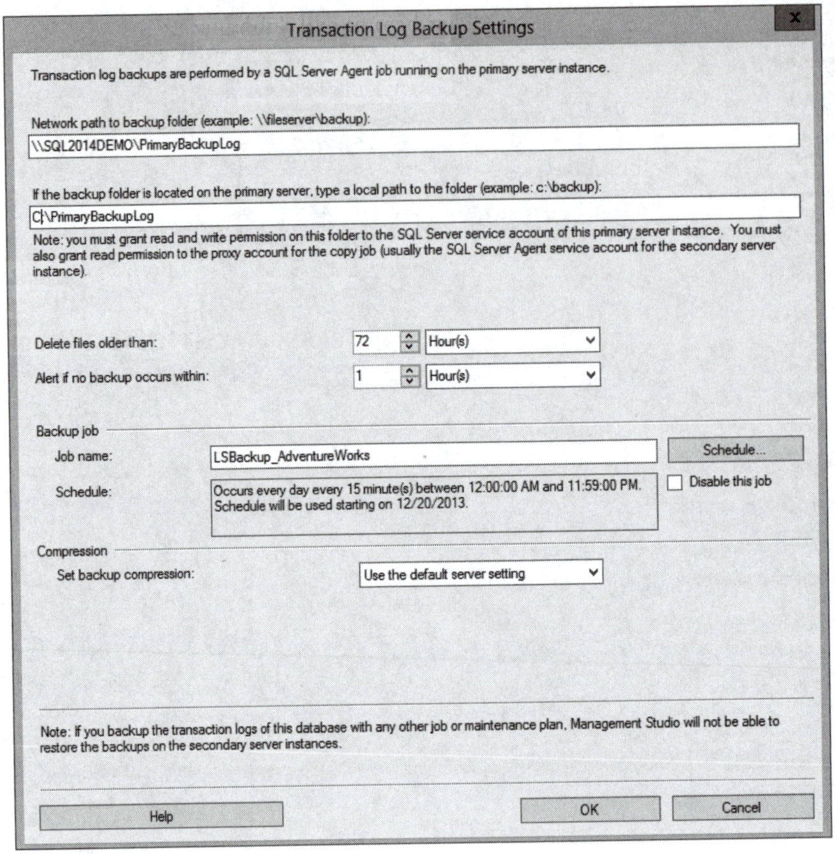

FIGURE 18-4

5. Click the Schedule button to display the Job Schedule Properties page, and set up a schedule for the transaction-log backup job. The important setting is the "Occurs every" field, which defaults to 15 minutes. This setting can be configured to once every minute for higher availability. However, the time interval should be appropriately set to allow the previous transaction-log backup job to complete. This value is the degree to which the primary and secondary servers are in sync. When you're done here, click OK on the Job Schedule Properties page. Then click OK in the Transaction Log Backup Settings dialog box to return to the Database Properties page for Transaction Log Shipping.

6. Click Add to display the Secondary Database Settings dialog box to set up a secondary (standby) server, as shown in Figure 18-5.

   Click Connect and choose the Secondary Server instance. Then choose an existing database or a new database name. On the Initialize Secondary Database tab shown in Figure 18-6, you have three options from which to choose.

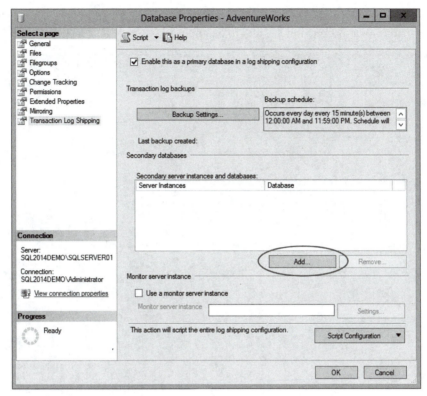

FIGURE 18-5

These options answer the question, "Do you want the Management Studio to restore a backup into the secondary database?"

➤ **Yes, generate a full backup of the primary database and restore it into the secondary database (and create the secondary database if it does not exist)**—This Restore Options setting enables you to set the database folder locations for the data and the log files. If this is not set, the default database locations are used.

➤ **Yes, restore an existing backup of the primary database into the secondary database (and create the secondary database if it does not exist)**—This Restore Options setting enables you to set database folder locations for the data and the log files. You also specify the network location of the backup file you want to restore.

➤ **No, the secondary database is initialized**—This option means that the database has already been created. The transaction logs preceding the database restore must be available to enable log shipping to work. For example, the log sequence number (LSN) of the primary server and the secondary server databases must match. Also, the secondary database must be in either NORECOVERY or STANDBY mode to allow additional transaction-log files to be applied.

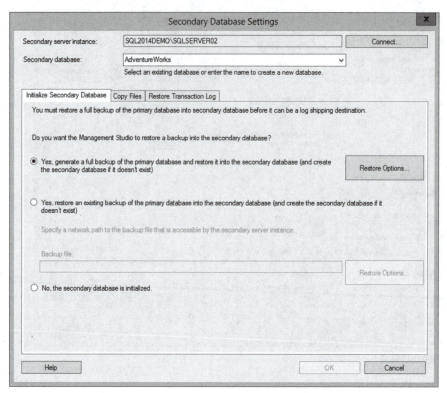

FIGURE 18-6

7. Next, restore the secondary database from the primary backup. The new database file path and name created will be the same as the primary database. You cannot alter the filename, but you can change the path and specify path names in the dialog box by clicking the Restore Options button. For the examples in this section, the primary and secondary databases are on the same Windows server, but different SQL Server 2014 instances. The secondary database AdventureWorks was created with the same filenames as those for the primary database AdventureWorks, but placed in a different directory.

8. On the Copy Files tab shown in Figure 18-7, in the "Destination folder for copied files" text box, type the destination folder (for example, c:\secondaryBackupDest). The "Delete copied files after" option controls the folder size after the transaction log is restored on the secondary server's database. Any files older than the specified time are deleted. The default is 72 hours.

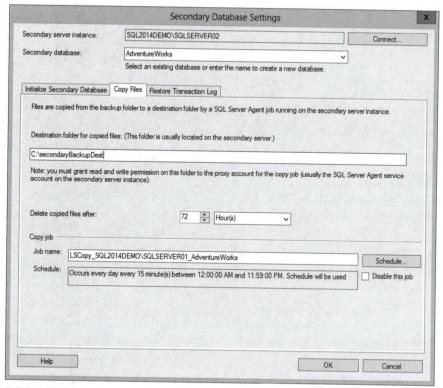

FIGURE 18-7

9. Click the Schedule button to set up a schedule for the transaction-log-file copy job. The important setting is the "Occurs every" field, which defaults to 15 minutes. You can reduce this time to have the secondary closer in data sync with the primary. Click OK when you finish to return to the Secondary Database Settings page.

10. Click the Restore Transaction Log tab, as shown in Figure 18-8.

   You have two options for the "Database state when restoring backups" field:

   ➤ **No Recovery mode**—The secondary database is left in NORECOVERY mode, which enables the server to restore additional transactional-log backups, but doesn't enable user access.

   ➤ **Standby mode**—The secondary database enables read-only operations to be performed in the database (such as reporting). However, as mentioned previously, the restore process needs exclusive access to the secondary database. If users are accessing the database, the restore process cannot complete.

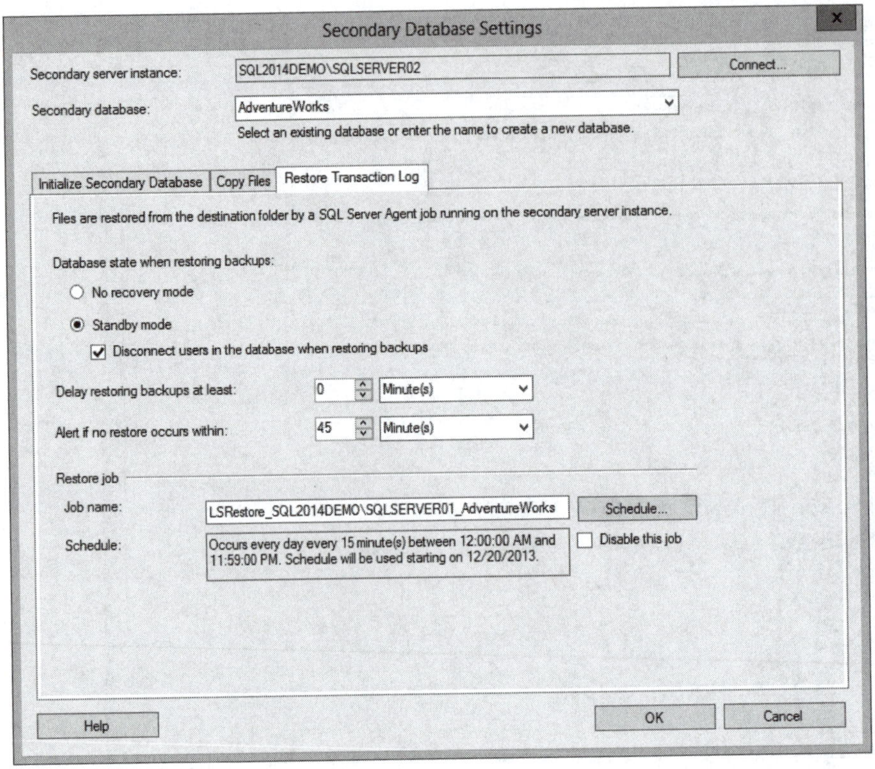

FIGURE 18-8

For the "Delay restoring backups at least" setting, the default is 0 minutes. Typically, you would change this setting if your organization wants to keep the secondary database around in case of a primary database's data corruption or unintended data deletions. This delay may prevent the secondary database from restoring the corrupted transaction-log file.

The "Alert if no restore occurs within" setting defaults to 45 minutes, and should be set to the tolerance level of the business.

> **NOTE** *An alert can be a symptom of a serious error on the secondary database that prevents it from accepting additional transaction-log restores. When this occurs, look in the history of the restore job. The default name is* LSRestore_ *ServerName_PrimaryDatabaseName and is found under SQL Agent jobs on the secondary server. Additionally, look in the Windows Event Viewer for any additional information. You can also copy and paste the restore job command into a SQL command window, which may provide additional error information to help diagnose the problem.*

11. Click OK on the Secondary Database Settings page when you finish. To add another secondary server instance, click Add and follow the same steps to add another secondary server.

12. To add a monitor server, from the Transaction Log Shipping page of the primary database properties, click Use a Monitor Server Instance. Then click Settings. A separate monitor instance from either the primary or secondary server is recommended so that a failure of the primary or secondary server won't bring down the monitor server.

13. On the Log Shipping Monitor Settings page shown in Figure 18-9, click Connect, and then choose a "Monitor server instance" for this log-shipping environment.

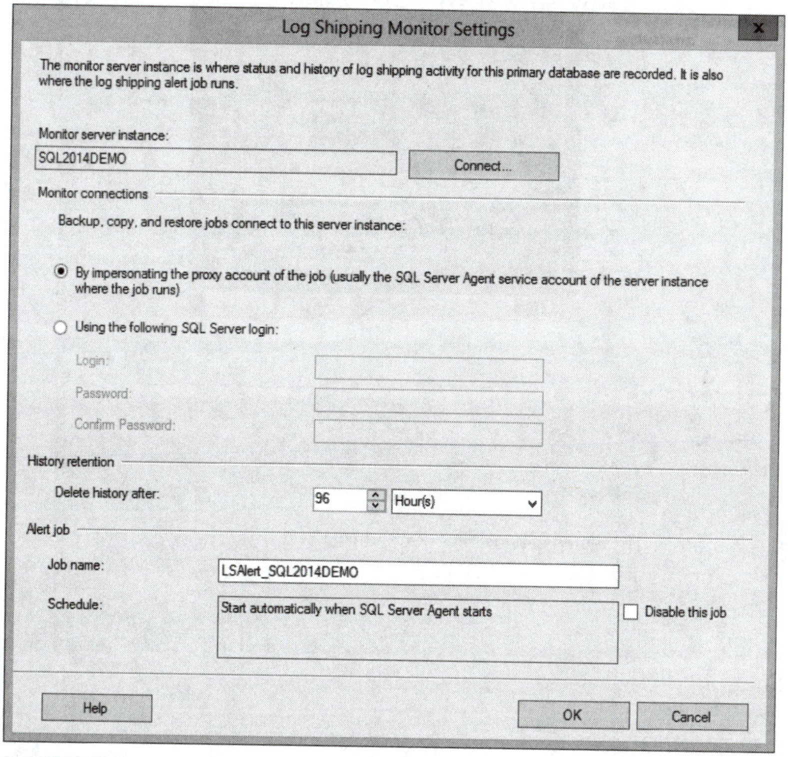

FIGURE 18-9

14. The account must have system administrator permissions on the secondary server. In the "By impersonating the proxy account of the job" or "Using the following SQL Server login" field, choose how the backup, copy, and restore jobs connect to this server instance to update msdb job history information. For integrated security, the jobs should connect by impersonating the proxy account of the SQL Server Agent running the jobs, or by SQL Server login.

The "Delete history after" field controls the amount of history data held in msdb. The default is 96 hours. How long you hold history depends on your business-retention requirements and your available disk space. The default value is fine for most deployments unless you plan to perform data analysis over time; then you should change the default.

15. When you finish, the complete log-shipping setup should look like Figure 18-10. Click OK on the Log Shipping Monitor Settings page. Then click OK on the Database Properties to finish setting up the log-shipping configuration.

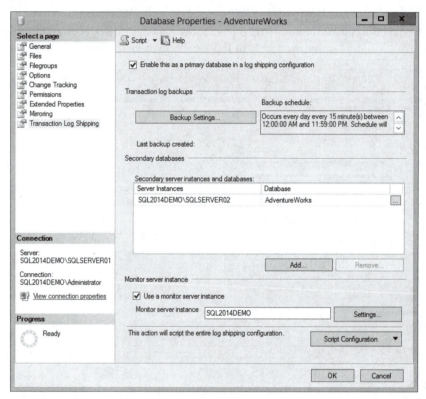

FIGURE 18-10

> **NOTE** *You can find this complete log-shipping script for the preceding exercise in the* `Chapter18_CreateLogShip.sql` *file for download on this book's website at* `www.wrox.com`*.*

Deploying with T-SQL Commands

Another deployment option is to use the actual T-SQL commands to configure log shipping. Even if you choose to use the SQL Server Management Studio to configure log shipping, saving the generated command script enables you to quickly reconfigure the server to expedite a disaster-recovery scenario while avoiding any user-induced errors. The following T-SQL commands are equivalent to the steps you took in SQL Server Management Studio.

On the primary server, execute the following stored procedures:

➤ `master.dbo.sp_add_log_shipping_primary_database`—Configures the primary database for a log-shipping configuration. This configures the log-shipping backup job.

➤ `msdb.dbo.sp_add_schedule`—Creates a schedule for the log-shipping configuration.

➤ `msdb.dbo.sp_attach_schedule`—Links the log-shipping job to the schedule.

➤ `msdb.dbo.sp_update_job`—Enables the transaction-log backup job.

➤ `master.dbo.sp_add_log_shipping_alert_job`—Creates the alert job and adds the job ID in the `log_shipping_monitor_alert` table. This stored procedure enables the alert notifications.

On the secondary server, execute the following stored procedures:

➤ `master.dbo.sp_add_log_shipping_secondary_primary`—Sets up the primary information, adds local and remote monitor links, and creates copy and restore jobs on the secondary server for the specified primary database.

➤ `msdb.dbo.sp_add_schedule`—Sets the schedule for the copy job.

➤ `msdb.dbo.sp_attach_schedule`—Links the copy job to the schedule.

➤ `msdb.dbo.sp_add_schedule`—Sets the schedule for the restore job.

➤ `msdb.dbo.sp_attach_schedule`—Links the restore job to the schedule.

➤ `master.dbo.sp_add_log_shipping_secondary_database`—Sets up secondary databases for log shipping.

➤ `msdb.dbo.sp_update_job`—Enables the copy job.

➤ `msdb.dbo.sp_update_job`—Enables the transaction-log restore.

Back on the primary server, execute this stored procedure:

➤ `master.dbo.sp_add_log_shipping_primary_secondary`—Adds an entry for a secondary database on the primary server.

MONITORING AND TROUBLESHOOTING

Log shipping has monitoring capabilities to identify the progress of the backup, copy, and restore jobs. Additionally, monitoring helps to determine whether the backup, copy, or restore jobs are out of sync with the secondary server. A few indicators that something has gone wrong include a job that has not made any progress or a job that has failed, both of which are discussed later in this section.

You have two approaches to monitoring the progress of the log-shipping operation: using the Transaction Log Shipping Status report (performed through Management Studio) or executing the `master.dbo.sp_help_log_shipping_monitor` stored procedure. Either method can help you determine whether the secondary server is out of sync with the primary server, and the time delta between the two.

Using SQL Management Studio, you can visually see the operation. But using the stored procedure enables setup of a recurring batch SQL Agent job command to monitor the log-shipping operation to send alerts. With both of these methods, you can also determine which jobs are not making any progress, and the last transaction-log backup, copy, and restore filename processed on the secondary server.

To inform you of any errors found, log shipping also performs alert jobs that periodically check if a preset threshold has been exceeded by executing the `sys.sp_check_log_shipping_monitor_alert` stored procedure. If the threshold has been exceeded, the stored procedure raises an alert that is returned to the log-shipping monitoring status. You can choose to modify the log-shipping alert jobs to capture the alert and notify you using SQL Agent.

In log shipping, if a monitor server is deployed, these alerts reside on the monitor server that reports on the transaction-log backup, copy file, and restore transaction log. If not, the primary server manages the alert job for the transaction-log backup, and the secondary server manages the alert job for the copy file and restore transaction log. If the monitoring server is present, the primary and secondary servers will not deploy alert jobs.

The following is an example error that results if the transaction-log backup process has exceeded the preset threshold of 30 minutes:

```
Executed as user: NT AUTHORITY\SYSTEM. The log shipping primary database
SQLServer1.AdventureWorks has backup threshold of 30 minutes and has not
performed a backup log operation for 60 minutes. Check agent log and log shipping
monitor information. [SQLSTATE 42000](Error 14420). This step failed.
```

The next example shows an error that results if the restore transaction-log process has exceeded the preset threshold of 30 minutes:

```
Executed as user: NT AUTHORITY\SYSTEM. The log shipping secondary database
SQLServer2.AdventureWorks has restore threshold of 30 minutes and is out of
sync. No restore was performed for 60 minutes. Restored latency is 15 minutes.
Check agent log and log shipping monitor information. [SQLSTATE 42000]
(Error 14421).
The step failed.
```

As an alternative, you can set up an alert for when errors 14420 or 14221 are raised; SQL Agent sends an alert to the operator.

Monitoring with SQL 2014 Management Studio

The Transaction Log Shipping Status report displays monitoring information from SQL Management Studio. This report executes the `sp_help_log_shipping_monitor` stored procedure. When executed on the primary server, it reports on the transaction-log backup details. When executed on the secondary server, it reports on the copy and transaction-log restore details. When the monitor server is configured, the report executed from the monitor server produces a consolidated report of the transaction-log backup, copy, and transaction-log restore details in one report. To access the Transaction Log Shipping Status report, follow these steps:

1. Connect to the primary, secondary, or monitor server using SQL Server 2014 Management Studio. The monitor server is the most useful option because it has the consolidated log-shipping detail data.

2. If the Object Explorer is not visible, select View ➪ Object Explorer.

3. Right-click the server node in the Object Explorer and select Reports ➪ Standard Reports ➪ Transaction Log Shipping Status.

Figure 18-11 shows an example of a Transaction Log Shipping Status report executed from the monitor server, showing the details for all log-shipping activities with alerts.

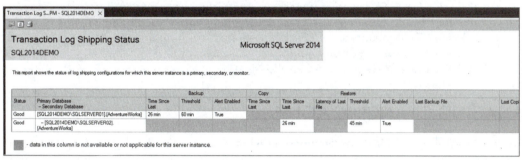

FIGURE 18-11

Monitoring with Stored Procedures

Executing the `sp_help_log_shipping_monitor` stored procedure in the `master` database from a SQL query window produces log-shipping status details, similar to the Transaction Log Shipping Status report. If you execute it from the primary server, it returns detailed information on the transaction-log backup job. If you execute it from the secondary server, it returns information on the copy and transaction-log restore jobs. If it is executed from the monitor server, it returns a consolidated detail result of the transaction-log backup, copy, and transaction-log restore, because the monitor server is visible to all log-shipping processes.

For additional log-shipping operational and troubleshooting detail information, you can query the log-shipping tables using the log-shipping stored procedures found in the `msdb` database. For more information, see SQL Server 2014 Books Online.

Troubleshooting Approach

As mentioned previously, log shipping consists of three basic operations: backing up the transaction log, copying the file, and restoring the transaction log. Troubleshooting this process is simply a matter of identifying which operation is not functioning. You can use both of the log-shipping monitoring capabilities to identify the problem.

For example, say the restore transaction-log file shows that no new files have been restored in the last 60 minutes. You need to look at the log-shipping job history on the secondary server first under the SQL Agent and the Windows Event Viewer to determine the actual error message. For example, if the copy file job is failing, it may be because the network is down. If the restore transaction-log job is failing, it may be because the server is unavailable, or because users are using the database if the database is in standby mode.

> **WARNING** *Be aware that changing the database recovery model to* `Simple` *will break log shipping because the transaction log is truncated instead of backed up. If this occurs, you must reconfigure log shipping. If you saved the log-shipping configuration scripts, the reconfiguration should be fairly simple. Additionally, there should not be any other transaction-log backup operation outside of log shipping, because that will also break log shipping since the log chain will not match on the secondary server. Finally, note that large transaction-log files will take longer to copy and restore, thus increasing latency.*

MANAGING CHANGING ROLES

For business continuity, a high-availability solution must allow smooth role-switching between the current primary and secondary servers. To accomplish this goal, log shipping requires that certain dependencies are available on the secondary server because the scope of log shipping is at the database level. Any object outside of the log-shipped database will not be maintained by log shipping. For example, SQL Server logins are contained in the `master` database, and SQL jobs are contained in `msdb`. Therefore, these dependencies and others need to be systematically maintained by other procedures to enable users to connect to the secondary server after it becomes the new primary server. Furthermore, you need to develop an approach to redirect the client applications to the new primary server. For examples, see the section, "Redirecting Clients to Connect to the Secondary Server" later in this chapter.

Synchronizing Dependencies

Log shipping applies changes that occur inside the log-shipping database, but it does not maintain any outside dependencies. Moreover, log shipping cannot be used to ship system databases. Newly added logins, new database users, jobs, and other dependencies that live in other databases are not synchronized by log shipping.

SQL Server 2014 resolves the login dependency by using the Contained Database property in the database property where user authentication can then be stored directly in the database, and authentication can be made directly to the database removing the login dependency. For new deployments, you should consider using the Contained Database property and removing the login dependency.

In a failover scenario, without using Contained Databases, when users attempt to log in to the secondary server's database, they will not have a login there. Moreover, any jobs configured on the primary server will not be present either; and if the primary server uses linked servers to access a remote SQL Server, then the database operations would fail because they would not find the linked server. Therefore, you must identify the outside dependencies that the log-shipping database uses, and develop a plan to make these resources available during the failover. The following sections describe common log-shipping dependencies and their solutions.

Login and Database Users

When developing a process to synchronize SQL Server logins with the secondary server and database, you should begin by setting it up as a recurring SQL job that runs at certain scheduled intervals. In a planned failover, you should run these SQL jobs before failover to update the secondary server with the most current access information. Following are the steps:

1. Develop an Integration Services (SSIS) package to transfer logins. Open SQL Server Data Tools 2014, and start a new Integration Services project.

2. In the Solution Explorer, name the SSIS project `Transfer Logins`, and rename the SSIS Package to `Transfer Logins`.

3. Click the Toolbox, and drag the Transfer Logins Task into the package.

4. Right-click the Transfer Logins Task, and choose Edit.

5. Click Logins. You see the dialog box shown in Figure 18-12.

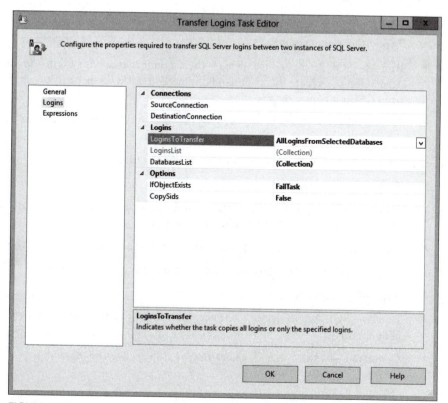

FIGURE 18-12

6. For `SourceConnection`, enter a new connection to the primary server.

7. For `DestinationConnection`, enter a new connection for the secondary server.

8. For `LoginsToTransfer`, choose `AllLoginsFromSelectedDatabases`.

9. For `DatabasesList`, choose the log-shipping database.

10. In the Options section, in the `IfObjectExists` entry, choose what to do if the login exists, such as `FailTask`, `Override`, or `Skip`. If the secondary server is hosting other databases, you may encounter duplicate logins.

11. Save the package, and choose Build ⇨ Build SSIS Transfer Logins to compile the package.

12. From Microsoft SQL Server 2014 Management Studio, connect to the Integration Services of the primary server.

13. Under Stored Packages, choose MSDB. Right-click, and choose Import Package.

This next job resolves the logins on the secondary server after the secondary database has been recovered. The SQL Server Agent service account or a proxy account must have the system administrator role to run this job. Following are the steps to synchronize logins between primary and secondary servers:

1. Create a new SQL Agent job on the primary server and rename it Sync Secondary Server Access Information.

2. Create a step named `BCP Syslogins` with these characteristics:

   ➤ **Type**—Operating system.

   ➤ **Run As**—SQL Agent Service. (This is the account that needs system administrator permission to execute this command and needs read/write permission on the folder from which it copies the file.)

   ➤ **Command**—`BCP Master.sys.syslogins out c:\login1\syslogins.dat /N /S <Server_Name> -T`

3. Create a step named `Copy Syslogins` with these characteristics:

   ➤ **Type**—Operating system.

   ➤ **Run As**—SQL Agent Service. (This account needs read access to the source folder and read/write access to the destination folder.)

   ➤ **Command**—`COPY c:\login1\syslogins.dat \\SecondaryServer\login2`

4. Create a step named `Transfer Logins Task` with these characteristics:

   ➤ **Type**—Operating system.

   ➤ **Run As**—SQL Agent Service. (The account needs sysadmin permission to execute this command.)

   ➤ **Command**—`DTEXEC /sq` *Transfer Logins* `/Ser <Server_Name>`

5. Create a step named `Resolve Logins` with these characteristics:

   ➤ **Type**—Transact-SQL script (T-SQL)

   ➤ **Command**—`EXEC sp_resolve_logins @dest_db = '<Database_Name>',`
   `@dest_path = 'c:\login2\', @filename = 'syslogins.dat'`

> **NOTE** *When using the method of synchronizing logins as described in this section, you should run this SQL job on a regular schedule to avoid inconsistent logins, in case of a primary server failure.*

SQL Agent Jobs

You can use the Integration Services Transfer Jobs Task to synchronize jobs from the primary server to the secondary server:

1. Create a package using SQL Server 2014 Data Tools, and choose the Transfer Jobs Task.

2. Provide the connection information and the jobs to transfer.

3. Compile and import the package into SQL Server 2014 or as an SSIS filesystem.

4. Finally, schedule and execute it as a SQL Agent job to periodically synchronize changes with the secondary server. The frequency depends on how often SQL jobs are changed that then need to be synchronized.

Other Database Dependencies

Make a list of all dependencies on which the log-shipping database relies. These can be distributed queries/linked servers, encrypted data, certificates, user-defined error messages, event notifications and WMI events, extended stored procedures, server configuration, full-text engine, permissions on objects, replication settings, Service Broker applications, startup procedures, triggers, CLR procedures, and Database Mail. Develop a plan to synchronize these to the secondary server.

Switching Roles from the Primary to Secondary Servers

If the primary server were to fail, the secondary server needs to assume the role of the primary server. This is called *role switching*. Two potential types of role switches exist: planned failover and unplanned failover. A *planned failover* is most likely when the DBA needs to perform some type of maintenance, usually scheduled at a time of low business activity or during a maintenance window—for example, switching roles to apply a service pack on the primary server. An *unplanned failover* is when the DBA switches roles for business continuity because the primary server becomes unavailable.

Planned Failover

For a planned failover, identify a time when the primary server has little or no activity. During a time like this, it is likely that the secondary server will not have restored all the transaction logs from the primary server, and transaction logs will be in the process of being copied across by the SQL Agent job that the restore SQL Agent job has not completed. Additionally, the active transaction log may contain records that have not been backed up.

Before you start your planned failover, you must completely synchronize the secondary server, and the active transaction log must be restored on the secondary server. Following are the steps to do that:

1. Stop and disable the primary server transaction-log backup job.

2. Execute the log-shipping copy and restore jobs to reinstate the remainder of the transaction logs. Use the log-shipping monitoring tool or report to verify that the entire set of transaction-log backups has been copied and restored on the secondary server. A manual option is to copy all transaction-log backups that have not been copied from the primary server backup folder to the secondary server folder. Then restore each transaction log in sequence to the secondary server.

3. Stop and disable the secondary server's copy and restore jobs.

4. Execute the Sync Secondary Server Access Information job to synchronize database dependencies and then disable it.

5. Back up the active transaction log from the primary to the secondary server with NORECOVERY:

   ```
   USE MASTER;
   BACKUP LOG <Database_Name> TO DISK =
   'C:\primaryBackupLog\<Database_Name>.trn'
   WITH NORECOVERY;
   ```

   This accomplishes two goals:

   ➤ It backs up the active transaction log from the primary server so that it can be restored to the secondary server to synchronize the secondary database.

   ➤ It changes the old primary server database to NORECOVERY mode to enable transaction logs from the new primary server to be applied without initializing the database by a restore, because the log chain would not have been broken.

6. Copy the backup log files to the secondary server. On the secondary server, restore the tail of the transaction log and then recover the database:

   ```
   RESTORE LOG <Database_Name>
   FROM DISK ='c:\secondaryBackupDest\Database_name.trn'WITH RECOVERY;
   ```

7. If the active transaction log is not accessible, the database can be recovered without it:

   ```
   RESTORE DATABASE <Database_Name>  WITH RECOVERY;
   ```

8. On the new primary server, execute the Resolve Logins job to synchronize the logins. The secondary server's database becomes the primary server's database and starts to accept data modifications.

9. Redirect all applications to the new primary server.

10. Configure log shipping from the new primary server to the secondary server. The secondary server (the former primary server) is already in NORECOVERY mode. During log-shipping configuration, in the Secondary Database Settings dialog box, choose "No, the secondary database is initialized."

11. When you finish configuring log shipping, the new primary server executes the transaction-log backup job, and the secondary server copies and restores the transaction-log files. Set up and enable all SQL jobs that were synchronizing from the old primary server (for example, to synchronize the logins and database users to the old primary server).

Unplanned Failover

If the primary server becomes unavailable in an unplanned situation, some data loss is probable. This could be because the active transaction log cannot be backed up, or some of the transaction-log backup may not be reachable. Therefore, in an unplanned failover, you must verify that the last copy and restore transaction logs have been restored by using the log-shipping monitoring and reporting functions. If the active transaction-log backup is accessible, it should be restored to bring the secondary server in synchronization with the primary server up to the point of failure. Then restore the secondary database with RECOVERY.

After assessing the damage and fixing the old primary server, you will most likely need to reconfigure log-shipping configuration because the active transaction log may not have been accessible, or the log chain may have been broken. When you configure log shipping, in the Secondary Database Settings dialog box, choose either to restore from a previous database backup, or to generate a new database backup to restore. You can choose to switch roles to promote the original primary server, which is discussed next.

Switching Between Primary and Secondary Servers

In a planned failover, after performing the steps to switch the primary and secondary server in a server change whereby the log-shipping jobs have been deployed to both primary and secondary servers; you can switch between primary and secondary servers by following these steps:

1. Stop and disable the primary server's transaction-log backup job.

2. Verify that all the transaction-log backups have been copied and restored, either manually or by executing the SQL jobs.

3. Execute the Sync Logins job.

4. Stop and disable the transaction-log copy and restore jobs on the secondary server.

5. Back up the active transaction log on the primary server with NORECOVERY.

6. Restore the active transaction-log backup on the secondary server.

7. Restore the secondary server's database with RECOVERY.

8. Execute the Resolve Logins job.

9. Enable the transaction-log backup on the new primary server to log-ship to the secondary server.

10.   Enable the secondary server transaction-log copy and restore jobs.

11.   Enable synchronization of the logins and database users.

12.   Enable any other SQL jobs.

Redirecting Clients to Connect to the Secondary Server

After switching roles, the client connections must be redirected to the secondary server with minimal disruptions to users. Log shipping does not provide any client-redirect capability, so you need to choose another approach. The approach you choose may depend on the infrastructure and who controls it, as well as the number of clients that need to be redirected, the required availability of the application (such as an SLA), and the application activity. At minimum, users will experience a brief interruption as the client applications are redirected. The following sections discuss a few common approaches to redirecting client connections to the secondary server.

Application Coding

You can develop the application as failover-aware with the capability to connect to the secondary server either with automatic retry or by manually changing the server name. The application logic would connect to the primary server first, but if it is unavailable, and after the retry logic has run unsuccessfully, the application can attempt to connect to the secondary server if it has been promoted to a primary server.

After the secondary database has been recovered, however, it may not necessarily be ready to serve user requests. For example, you may need to run several tasks or jobs first, such as running the Resolve Logins task. To overcome this circumstance, the database may need to be put into single-user mode to prevent other users from connecting while you perform tasks or jobs. Therefore, the application logic must handle this situation in which the primary server is no longer available and the secondary server is not yet accessible.

Network Load Balancing

Use a network load-balancing solution, either Windows Network Load Balancing (NLB) or a hardware solution. With this solution, the application connects using the load-balancing network name or IP address, and the load-balancing solution directs the application to the database server. Therefore, in a failover scenario, the application continues to connect to the network load balancer's network name or IP address, while the load balancer is updated manually or by script with the new primary server network name and IP address. Then clients are redirected. NLB is included with certain versions of Microsoft Windows. Configuration is straightforward and can act as the cross-reference to direct applications to the current primary server.

Domain Name Service (DNS)

DNS provides name-to-IP address resolution and can be used to redirect clients to the new primary server. If you have access to the DNS server, you can modify the IP address to redirect client applications after a failover, either by script or by using the Windows DNS management tool. DNS acts as a cross-reference for the client applications because they continue to connect to the same name, but the DNS modification redirects the database request to the new primary server.

SQL Client Aliasing

SQL aliasing is another method you can use to redirect clients to the new primary server. To configure aliasing, go to the SQL Server Configuration Manager, under the SQL Native Client Configuration. This method may be less favorable if many client applications connect directly to the database server because the alias would have to be created at each client computer, which may not be feasible. It is more feasible if the client applications connect to a web or application server that then connects to the database server. Then the SQL client alias can be applied on the web or application server, and all the clients would be redirected to the new primary server.

DATABASE BACKUP PLAN

Regardless of the high-availability solution, a database backup plan is strongly recommended to protect data from corruption or user error. A secondary database is not enough, because a corruption in the primary database can cause corruption on the secondary database as well. You can take two routes when choosing a backup plan: a full database backup and a differential database backup.

A *full database backup* copies all the data and the transaction log to a backup device, which is usually a tape or disk drive. It is used in case of an unrecoverable failure so that the database can be restored to that point in time at which it was last backed up. A full database restore is also required as a starting point for differential or transaction-log restores. The backup should be stored offsite so that the database is not lost in the event of a disaster.

A *differential database backup* copies all modified extents in the database since the last full database backup. An *extent* is a unit of space allocation that consists of eight database pages that SQL Server uses to allocate space for database objects. Differential database backups are smaller than the full database backup, except in certain scenarios where the database is active and every extent is modified since the last full backup. To restore from a differential database backup, a full database backup is required prior to the differential backup.

Full or differential database backup operations will not break log shipping, provided no transaction-log operations are performed that change it. However, the inverse is possible in that log shipping can impact some backup and recovery plans in the following ways:

➤ Another transaction-log backup cannot be performed in addition to log shipping because that breaks the log chain for the log-shipping process. SQL Server will not prevent an operator from creating additional transaction-log backup jobs on a log-shipping database.

➤ A transaction-log backup that truncates the transaction log will break the log chain, and log shipping will stop functioning.

➤ If you change the database to the `simple` recovery model, the transaction log will be truncated by SQL Server and log shipping will stop functioning.

INTEGRATING LOG SHIPPING WITH OTHER HIGH-AVAILABILITY SOLUTIONS

Log shipping can be deployed along with other Microsoft high-availability solutions because log shipping provides disaster recovery while the other solution provides high availability, except for Availability Groups, which provide both high availability and disaster recovery within the solution. You can integrate log shipping with three main solutions:

➤ **Data mirroring**—Maintains a remote site if the data-mirroring pair becomes unavailable.

➤ **Windows failover clustering**—Maintains a remote disaster-recovery site if the local Windows failover cluster becomes unavailable.

➤ **Replication**—Maintains a highly available replication publisher.

SQL Server 2014 Data Mirroring

A scenario in which log shipping can be best integrated with a SQL Server 2014 data-mirroring solution would be if an organization deployed local data mirroring and then log shipping from the principal server to a remote disaster-recovery location. However, during a data-mirroring role switch, log shipping does not automatically switch roles. Therefore, manual steps must be taken to enable the former data mirror, which would now be the principal, to start to log ship its transaction log to the secondary server by deploying log shipping from the new principal server.

Windows Failover Clustering

The best scenario in which log shipping can be deployed to ship a database from inside a Windows failover SQL cluster to a remote disaster-recovery location is in a local disaster. During disaster recovery, when the Windows failover cluster is not available, log shipping can offer business conti-nuity at the remote location. Unless an organization deploys a geographically dispersed cluster, the cluster nodes are located near each other, and can both be down during a disaster.

When deploying log shipping in a cluster environment, the backup folder and BCP folder should be set up as a cluster resource and should be in the same cluster group with the SQL Server that contains the log-shipping database. That way, in a cluster-failover scenario, the backup folder will failover while the log-shipping SQL Server remains accessible to the other Windows failover cluster node. Any configuration and data files in that Windows failover cluster that the other cluster node needs to access should also be set up as a cluster resource included in the log-shipping SQL Server cluster group. For example, if you choose to execute the SSIS Transfer Logins Task package from a file instead of storing it in the SQL Server, you should include that folder as a cluster resource to make it available to all cluster nodes.

To set up a folder as a cluster resource, follow these steps:

1. First create the folder.

2. Then, using the cluster administrator, create a new resource and choose Shared Folder. Be sure to place it in the same group with the SQL Server that contains the log-shipping database.

3. Now, inside the Windows failover cluster, you can set SQL Server to depend on the folder. For example, if the folder is not yet online, SQL Server waits for that resource.

> **NOTE** *The decision to make something a dependency is based on whether the resource must be available before SQL Server starts. For example, if the backup folder for the transaction-log files is not available, then SQL Server doesn't need to wait to come online because a database that is up and serving users is more important than the transaction-log backup.*

SQL Server 2014 Replication

A replication topology where the SQL Server 2014 publisher is the data consolidator can quickly become a single point of failure. All the subscribers connect to the distributor who then connects to the publisher to receive data updates, and if the publisher fails, replication stops until the publisher can be brought online again. Log shipping can be used as a high-availability solution to protect the publisher from becoming a single point of failure. Log shipping is supported by transactional and merge replication.

In this configuration, log shipping is protecting the publisher. The primary server, which is also the replication's publisher, log ships its transaction log to a secondary server.

Then, in a role switch, follow the steps in the previous sections, "Switching Between Primary and Secondary Servers" and "Redirecting Clients to Connect to the Secondary Server."

Additionally, you should take the following into consideration when using transactional replication with log shipping:

➤ For replication to continue to work after the role switch, the primary and secondary server configurations must be identical after the switch.

➤ For transactional replication, to prevent the subscribers from having data that has to be shipped to the secondary server, the primary server should be configured to use the `sync with backup` parameter in the transaction-log backup command of log shipping, whereby a transaction is not replicated to the subscribers until a transaction-log backup has been performed. This does introduce a latency penalty whereby the subscribers are not quite in real time because replication needs to wait for log shipping. You can reduce this latency by decreasing the interval to perform the transaction-log backup. Without `sync with backup`, there is a possibility that the subscriber's data may not match with the publisher during a log-shipping role switch, and data loss may occur.

➤ In merge replication, after the role switch, the merge publisher may synchronize any changes lost during the role switch by merge replicating with each subscriber. A more common high-availability solution to prevent a single point of failure for the publisher is to configure a Windows failover cluster so that, in case of a failure, replication fails over to the other cluster node.

REMOVING LOG SHIPPING

Before deleting the log-shipping database, you must remove log shipping from it. When you remove log shipping, all schedules, jobs, history, and error information are deleted. Recall that you have two ways to remove log shipping: with SQL Server 2014 Management Studio and with T-SQL. You may want to script the log-shipping configuration before deleting to quickly redeploy log shipping in the future.

Removing Log Shipping with Management Studio

To use SQL Server 2014 Management Studio to remove log shipping, follow these steps:

1. Connect to the primary server with SQL Server 2014 Management Studio.

2. Choose the primary server's database properties.

3. Under Select a Page, choose Transaction Log Shipping.

4. Clear the "Enable this as a primary database in a log shipping configuration" check box, and click OK.

5. If necessary, choose to remove a secondary server from the primary server's database properties. Under Secondary Databases, choose the secondary server instance, and click Remove.

6. To remove a monitor server instance, uncheck the "Use a monitor server instance" check box.

Removing Log Shipping with T-SQL Commands

To remove log shipping with T-SQL, issue this command on the primary server:

```
Use Master;
sp_delete_log_shipping_primary_secondary  @primary_database, @secondary_server,
@secondary_database;
```

This command deletes secondary information on the primary server from the `msdb.dbo.log_shipping_primary_secondaries` table.

On the secondary server, issue this command:

```
Use Master;
sp_delete_log_shipping_secondary_database @secondary_database;
```

This command deletes the secondary information on the secondary server and its jobs by executing the `sys.sp_delete_log_shipping_secondary_database_internal` stored procedure.

Back on the primary server, issue this command:

```
Use Master;
sp_delete_log_shipping_primary_database @database;
```

This command deletes the log-shipping information from the primary server and its jobs, removes monitor info and the monitor, and deletes the `msdb.dbo.log_shipping_primary_databases` table.

Then, if desirable, you can delete the secondary database.

LOG-SHIPPING PERFORMANCE

A well-performing log-shipping solution is critical to provide faster failover to support the warm standby requirements (such as SLAs). To do this, the following key areas must be tuned and optimized to handle the additional capacity of log shipping:

➤ Networking is required for copying the transaction-log files from the primary to the secondary server.

➤ I/O on both the file share on the primary server (where the transaction-log files are getting backed up) and on the secondary server (that is, receiving the transaction-log files) and then applying them needs to have the read/write throughput. Consider placing the log-shipping backup directory on a separate disk drive from the database files. Additionally, backup compression improves I/O performance. As part of ongoing administration, monitor the I/O performance counters for any bottlenecks (for example, the average second/read and average second/write should preferably be less than 10 ms).

➤ To keep the secondary server more closely in sync with the primary server, maintain shorter database transactions, when possible. A database transaction is log-shipped only after it has been committed on the primary database.

➤ Perform database administration activities (such as index defragmentation) during a period of lower activity. Depending on the level of fragmentation, the transaction-log file will be larger and take longer to back up, copy, and restore, thus increasing latency.

➤ To maintain performance after failover, both the primary and secondary servers should be of identical hardware and server configurations.

> **NOTE** *Both SQL Server 2012 Standard Edition and Enterprise Edition support backup compression. Log shipping uses the default settings for backup compression on the server. Whether a log is compressed depends on the Backup Compression setting.*

This enables it to stay in sync with the primary server. Also, in a role switch, the secondary server can provide the same performance experience that users expect. Similarly, separate the file copy directory from the database; and as part of ongoing administration, monitor I/O performance counters. Furthermore, monitor network bandwidth to ensure that there is capacity to move the transaction-log file in a timely manner.

UPGRADING TO SQL SERVER 2014 LOG SHIPPING

You must follow certain procedures to upgrade an existing log-shipping deployment from an earlier SQL Server version to SQL Server 2014 to prevent disruption to the log-shipping configuration between the primary and secondary server. You have three common approaches to upgrading log shipping: minimum downtime approach, with downtime approach, and deploy log-shipping approach. These are discussed in the following sections.

Minimum Downtime Approach

The minimum downtime approach requires that the secondary server be upgraded in-place using the setup program to SQL Server 2014 first. This does not break log shipping because SQL Server 2008/2008R2/2012 transaction logs can be applied to SQL Server 2014. Afterward, a planned failover takes place where the role-switch procedures are followed, and users are redirected to the secondary server, which is the new primary. After the role switch and users are redirected, perform the following steps:

1. Stop and disable the log-shipping jobs. The newly upgraded SQL Server 2014 primary server cannot log-ship to the old primary server running SQL Server 2008/2008R2/2012.

2. Complete an in-place upgrade on the old primary server using the SQL Server 2014 setup program and leave it as the secondary server.

3. Configure SQL Server 2014 log shipping from the new primary server to the secondary server using the same log-shipping shared folders used by SQL Server 2008/2008R2/2012. Additionally, in the Secondary Database Settings, on the Initialize Secondary Database page, choose "No, the secondary database is initialized." SQL Server 2014 log shipping then starts shipping the transaction log. If you prefer, switch the roles back to the original primary server.

With Downtime Approach

With the downtime approach, the primary and secondary servers are not available during the upgrade because both are upgraded in-place using the setup program. Use this method if you have allocated downtime to upgrade the SQL Server 2008/2008R2/2012 servers. This is the simpler approach because it does not involve going through the failover process.

1. Verify that the secondary server is in sync with the primary server by applying all the transaction-log backups and the active transaction log from the primary server.

2. Stop and disable the log-shipping jobs. Then do an in-place upgrade on the secondary server, followed by an upgrade to the primary server.

3. Reconfigure SQL Server 2014 log shipping using the same shared folders. Additionally, in the Secondary Database Settings, on the Initialize Secondary Database page, choose "No, the

secondary database is initialized." SQL Server 2014 log shipping starts shipping the transaction log without having to take a database backup and restore on the secondary server.

Deploy Log-Shipping Approach

The deploy log-shipping approach is more feasible when the log-shipping databases are small and can quickly be backed up, copied, and restored on the secondary server that has already been upgraded to SQL Server 2014. It is similar to the downtime approach, but instead of verifying and waiting for synchronization of the secondary database, after the upgrade and during the SQL Server 2014 log-shipping configuration, on the Initialize Secondary Database page, choose "Yes, generate a full backup of the primary database." The log-shipping process performs a database backup on the primary server, and restores the backup onto the secondary server to start the log shipping.

SUMMARY

Log shipping is a simple, inexpensive, dependable SQL Server high-availability solution with a long track record. As a disaster-recovery solution, it has been deployed to maintain a secondary server over a distance for business continuity to protect from a local disaster, power grid failure, and network outages. Log shipping can ship the log anywhere in the world. Its only limitation is the network bandwidth capacity to transfer the transaction-log file in a timely manner. It can be combined with a reporting solution when an organization requires point-in-time reporting, rather than real time. Moreover, it has been deployed as an alternative to Windows failover clustering to provide a local, high-availability solution, where it is less expensive to implement because it does not require a shared disk system.

The main challenge in deploying log shipping is that it does not provide any automatic client redirect. Therefore, an operator must have an approach for it. In addition, the role switch requires some user intervention to ensure that all the transaction logs have been restored to the secondary server. Switching the roles back also requires some manual intervention. Another challenge is that log shipping is at the user database level that does not copy new logins, SQL jobs, Integration Services, and linked servers from the primary server. However, using Integration Services' Tasks and SQL Agent jobs, it can be accomplished.

Regardless of the risks and challenges, many organizations have successfully used log shipping by scripting all the processes (such as role switching, login synchronization, and client redirects), and can quickly failover with minimal manual downtime.

Furthermore, because log shipping involves two or more physically separate servers that do not have any shared components (like a Windows failover cluster does), you can achieve patch-management independence whereby one server is patched, the roles are switched, and then the other server is patched.

Database Mirroring is a reliable, high-availability solution in SQL Server 2014 Standard and Enterprise Editions that can be configured for automatic failover and supports synchronous and asynchronous data transfer (see Chapter 19 for more details). These days, it is more commonly deployed with Standard Edition because Availability Groups is available with Enterprise Edition, which offers enhanced capabilities beyond data mirroring.

Availability Groups is the high-availability technology that may eventually replace log shipping. However, log shipping is a time-tested, high-availability solution that many large, strategic customers with mission-critical applications depend on every day to provide local high availability and disaster recovery.

19

Database Mirroring

WROX.COM CODE DOWNLOADS FOR THIS CHAPTER

The wrox.com code downloads for this chapter are found at www.wrox.com/go/prosql2014admin on the Download Code tab. The code is in the Chapter 19 download and individually named according to the names throughout the chapter.

Database mirroring is a reliable, high-availability solution in SQL Server 2014 Standard and Enterprise Editions. These days, it is more commonly deployed with Standard Edition because Availability Groups is available with Enterprise Edition, which offers enhanced capabilities. (Chapter 26 provides more details on Availability Groups.)

> **NOTE** *As of SQL Server 2014, Database Mirroring has been deprecated. It will be continued to be supported, but will be removed in a future product release. For a full list of deprecated Database Engine features in SQL Server 2014, go to* http://msdn.microsoft.com/en-us/library/ms143729%28v=sql.120%29 .aspx.

Maximizing database availability is a top priority for most database administrators (DBAs). It is difficult to explain the pain a DBA goes through when a database goes down. You cannot get it right back online, and at the same time, you're answering pointed questions from your manager. Database mirroring can come to the rescue in certain scenarios, which this chapter explains.

Database mirroring can help you get the database back online with automatic or manual failover to your mirror database, adding another high-availability alternative to the SQL Server 2014 arsenal. This chapter explains database mirroring concepts, shows you how to administer the mirrored database, and provides an example demonstrating how to implement database mirroring. The database snapshot is also discussed, which you can use with database mirroring to read the mirrored databases.

OVERVIEW OF DATABASE MIRRORING

Database mirroring is a high-availability solution at the database level, implemented on a per-database basis. To maximize database availability, you must minimize planned as well as unplanned downtime. Planned downtime is common, such as changes you must apply to your production system, hardware upgrades, software upgrades (security patches and service packs), database configuration changes, or database storage upgrades. These all require your database or server to be unavailable for short periods of time—if everything goes as planned. Unplanned downtime can be caused by hardware failures such as storage failure, by power outages, by human error, or by natural disasters, all of which can cause the production server or data center to be unavailable.

Figure 19-1 illustrates a number of mirroring concepts, which are discussed in detail throughout this chapter.

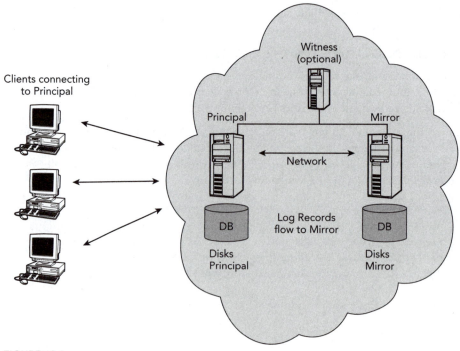

FIGURE 19-1

Database mirroring involves two copies of a single database, residing on separate instances of SQL Server, usually on different computers. You can have separate instances of SQL Server 2014 on the same computer, but that would most likely not fit your high-availability requirements other than for testing purposes.

At any given time, only one copy of the database is available to clients. This copy of the database is the *principal database*. The SQL Server that hosts this principal database is the *principal server*. Database mirroring works by transferring and applying the stream of database log records to the copy of the database. The copy of the database is the *mirror database*. The SQL Server that hosts this mirror database is the *mirror server*.

The principal and mirror servers are each considered a *partner* in a database mirroring *session*. Database mirroring applies every database modification (DML, DDL, and so on) made to the principal database to the mirror database, including physical and logical database changes such as database files and indexes. As you would guess, a given server may assume the role of principal for one database, and the role of mirror for another database. For automatic failover, a third server called the *witness* is required. The witness server is discussed in the later section, "High-Safety Operating Mode with Automatic Failover."

Database mirroring helps minimize both planned and unplanned downtime in the following ways:

➤ It provides ways to perform automatic or manual failover for mirrored databases.

➤ It keeps the mirrored database up to date with the principal database, either synchronously or asynchronously. You can set these operating modes for database mirroring, which are discussed in the next section, "Operating Modes of Database Mirroring."

➤ It enables the mirrored database to be in a remote data center, to provide a foundation for disaster recovery.

> **NOTE** *You cannot mirror the* `master`, `msdb`, `tempdb`, *or* `model` *databases. You can mirror multiple databases from a SQL Server instance, though. You cannot re-mirror the mirror database. Mirroring does not support a principal database having more than one mirrored partner.*

OPERATING MODES OF DATABASE MIRRORING

To keep the mirror database up to date, database mirroring transfers and applies the stream of database log records on the mirror database. For this reason, you need to understand in which *operating mode* database mirroring is configured.

A database mirroring session has three possible operating modes. The exact mode of the operation is based on the transaction safety setting and whether the witness server is part of the mirroring session. Table 19-1 outlines the three operating modes of database mirroring.

TABLE 19-1: Operating Modes of Database Mirroring

OPERATING MODE	TRANSACTION SAFETY	TRANSFER MECHANISM	QUORUM REQUIRED	WITNESS SERVER	FAILOVER TYPE
High Performance	OFF	Asynchronous	No	N/A	Forced failover only (with possible data loss). This is a manual step.
High Safety **without** automatic failover	FULL	Synchronous	Yes	No	Manual or forced.
High Safety **with** automatic failover	FULL	Synchronous	Yes	Yes	Automatic or manual.

When you set up database mirroring, you have two options: SAFETY FULL or SAFETY OFF. When weighing these options, you must decide whether you want the principal database and mirror database to be in sync at all times (SAFETY FULL) or whether you can live with some data loss in case of principal failure (SAFETY OFF). These options are part of the ALTER DATABASE statement when you set up database mirroring.

If you choose SAFETY FULL, you are setting up database mirroring in *high-safety mode* (also known as *synchronous mirroring mode*). As the principal server hardens log records of the principal database to disk (that is, flushes the log buffer to disk), it also sends log buffers to the mirror. The principal then waits for a response from the mirror server. The mirror responds to a commit when it has hardened those same log records to the mirror's transaction log. The commit is then reported to the client. Synchronous transfer guarantees that all transactions in the mirror database's transaction log will be synchronized with the principal database's transaction log so that the transactions are considered safely transferred. Figure 19-2 shows the sequence of events when SAFETY is set to FULL.

Keep in mind that with SAFETY FULL it is guaranteed that you won't lose data, and that both the principal and mirror will be in sync as long as the transaction is committed successfully. There is some performance impact here because the transaction is not committed until it is hardened to the transaction log on the mirror server. There will be a slight, noticeable increase in perceived user response time, and a reduction in transaction throughput because the principal server must wait for an acknowledgment from the mirror that the transaction is hardened to the mirror transaction log.

How long that delay might be depends on many factors, such as server capacity, database workload, network latency, application architecture, disk throughput, and more. An application with a lot of small transactions has more impact on response time than one with long transactions because transactions wait for acknowledgment from the mirror, and the wait time adds proportionately more to the response time of short transactions.

If you choose the SAFETY OFF option, you are setting up database mirroring in high-performance mode, or asynchronous mirroring mode. In this mode, the log-transfer process is the same as in synchronous mode, but the principal does not wait for acknowledgment from the mirror that the log buffer is hardened to the disk on a commit. As soon as step 3 in Figure 19-2 occurs, the transaction is committed on the principal. The database is synchronized after the mirror server catches up to the principal server. Because the mirror server is busy keeping up with the principal server, if the principal suddenly fails, you may lose data. However, it will only be that which hasn't been sent to the mirror. In this operating mode, there is minimal impact on response time or transaction throughput because it does not wait for the mirror to commit.

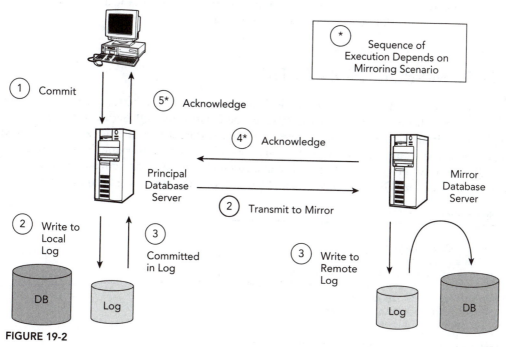

FIGURE 19-2

Note the following three important terms in database mirroring:

➤ **Send queue**—While sending the log records from the principal to the mirror, if the log records can't be sent at the rate at which they are generated, a queue called the *send queue* builds up at the principal in the database transaction log. The send queue does not use extra storage or memory. It exists entirely in the transaction log of the principal. It refers to the part of the log that has not yet been sent to the mirror.

➤ **Redo queue**—While applying log records on the mirror, if the log records can't be applied at the rate at which they are received, a queue called the *redo queue* builds up at the mirror in the database transaction log. Like the send queue, the redo queue does not use extra storage or memory. It exists entirely in the transaction log of the mirror. It refers to the part of the hardened log that remains to be applied to the mirror database to roll it forward. Mostly, a single thread is used for redo, but SQL Server Enterprise Edition implements *parallel redo*— that is, a thread for every four processing units (equivalent to four cores).

➤ **Log stream compression**—When transferring data across the partners, data mirroring uses *log stream compression*, which reduces network utilization and can achieve at least a 12.5 percent compression ratio. In the data mirror scenario, the principal compresses the data before sending it to the mirror, and the mirror uncompresses the data before applying it. This slightly increases the CPU utilization on both the principal and the mirror to compress and uncompress the data, while reducing network utilization. It is especially useful for database workloads that incur a great deal of data modification throughout the day, reducing the amount of network resources that data mirroring uses.

DATABASE MIRRORING IN ACTION

Now that you understand transaction safety, let's look at an example to better understand the operating modes and other mirroring concepts. You must designate three SQL Server instances for this example: one principal server, one mirror server, and one witness server. In this example, as shown in Figure 19-3, you set up high-safety mode with automatic failover. This example assumes that all three SQL Server instances are on the network and run under the same domain account, which is `Administrator` on the SQL Server instance and has access to the other SQL Server instances.

Principal Server

```
1.   Create Certificate on the Principal
2.   Create Endpoint on Principal
7.   Create Login and Grant Connect on Principal
10.  Back Up the AdventureWorks database on Principal
12.  Insert and modify data on Principal
13.  Back Up Transaction Log on Principal
15.  Set Up Principal Server
```

Mirror Server

```
3.   Create Certificate on the Mirror
4.   Create Endpoint on Mirror
8.   Create Login and Grant Connect on Mirror
11.  Restore the AdventureWorks database on Mirror
14.  Set Up Mirror Server
16.  Restore Transaction Log on Mirror
```

Witness Server

```
5.   Create Certificate on the Witness
6.   Create Endpoint on Witness
9.   Create Login and Grant Connect on Witness
17.  Set Up Witness Server
```

FIGURE 19-3

Preparing the Endpoints

For database-mirroring partners to connect, they must trust each other. This trust is established by means of Transmission Control Protocol (TCP) endpoints. Therefore, on each partner, you must create the endpoint using the T-SQL statement CREATE ENDPOINT and grant the connect permission on these endpoints using the GRANT CONNECT ON ENDPOINT statement. The endpoint concept is exactly the same as discussed in Chapter 8, "Securing the Database Instance," so the rules are the same. The only difference is that instead of creating an endpoint for Service Broker, here you are creating an endpoint for database mirroring. The security rules are the same; you can use either Windows authentication or certificates for authentication. This example uses certificates so that you can learn how to use them for transport authentication. Windows authentication is easy to establish, but that is a separate exercise.

> **NOTE** *You can find all the example scripts for this chapter on this book's web-site at* www.wrox.com, *but you need to make a few modifications before running the scripts.*

1. First, for data mirroring to work, the TCP/IP protocol must be enabled. Use the SQL Server Configuration Manager to verify that the TCP/IP protocol is enabled.

2. Second, in the principal, mirror, and witness, create a new folder at a location of your choosing to store the data mirror example.

> **NOTE** <your folder> *refers to the created folder in the scripts in this chapter. You must change this to match your folder name.*

3. Next, create the certificates on each partner server. Connect to the principal server, and execute the CreateCertOnPrincipal.sql script shown in Listing 19-1 (code file: CreateCertOnPrincipal.sql).

LISTING 19-1: CreateCertOnPrincipal.sql

```
USE MASTER
GO
IF NOT EXISTS(SELECT 1 FROM sys.symmetric_keys where name =
'##MS_DatabaseMasterKey##')
CREATE MASTER KEY ENCRYPTION BY PASSWORD = '23%&weq^yzYu3000!'
GO

IF NOT EXISTS (SELECT 1 FROM sys.databases where
[is_master_key_encrypted_by_server] = 1)
ALTER MASTER KEY ADD ENCRYPTION BY SERVICE MASTER KEY
GO
```

continues

LISTING 19-1 *(continued)*

```
IF NOT EXISTS (SELECT 1 FROM sys.certificates WHERE name = 'PrincipalServerCert')
CREATE  CERTIFICATE PrincipalServerCert
WITH SUBJECT = 'Principal Server Certificate'
GO
```

Either Windows authentication or certificates can be used for authentication. This example uses certificates and, for simplicity in the example, you will use certificates created by SQL Server.

```
BACKUP CERTIFICATE PrincipalServerCert TO FILE = '<your folder>
\PrincipalServerCert.cer'
```

The `BACKUP CERTIFICATE` statement backs up the public key certificate for this private key.

4. Now create the endpoint on the principal server. Connect to the principal server, and execute the `CreateEndPointOnPrincipal.sql` script (code file: `CreateEndPointOnPrincipal.sql`):

```
--Check If Mirroring endpoint exists
IF NOT EXISTS(SELECT * FROM sys.endpoints WHERE type = 4)
CREATE ENDPOINT DBMirrorEndPoint
STATE = STARTED AS TCP (LISTENER_PORT = port_num)
FOR DATABASE_MIRRORING ( AUTHENTICATION = CERTIFICATE PrincipalServerCert,
                         ENCRYPTION = REQUIRED
                        ,ROLE = ALL
            .)
```

This code creates the endpoint `DBMirrorEndPoint`, and you have specified the `PrincipalServerCert` certificate to use for authentication. You also specified `ROLE=ALL`, which indicates that this server can act as either the principal, mirror, or witness server. If you want this server to act only as the witness, you can specify `WITNESS` as a parameter. You can also specify the `PARTNER` option, which indicates that the server can act as either the principal or the mirror, but not the witness.

5. Now create the certificates on both the mirror and the witness servers. Connect to the mirror server and execute the `CreateCertOnMirror.sql` script (code file: `CreateCertOnMirror.sql`):

```
USE MASTER
 GO
 IF NOT EXISTS(SELECT 1 FROM sys.symmetric_keys where name =
 '##MS_DatabaseMasterKey##')
 CREATE MASTER KEY ENCRYPTION BY PASSWORD = '23%&weq^yzYu3000!'
GO

 IF NOT EXISTS (select 1 from sys.databases where
 [is_master_key_encrypted_by_server] = 1)
 ALTER MASTER KEY ADD ENCRYPTION BY SERVICE MASTER KEY
 GO
```

```
IF NOT EXISTS (SELECT 1 FROM sys.certificates WHERE name = 'MirrorServerCert')
CREATE   CERTIFICATE MirrorServerCert
WITH SUBJECT = 'Mirror Server Certificate'
GO


BACKUP CERTIFICATE MirrorServerCert TO FILE = '<your folder>\MirrorServerCert
.cer'
```

6. Next, while connected to the mirror server, execute the `CreateEndPointOnMirror.sql` script (code file: `CreateEndPointOnMirror.sql`):

```
--Check If Mirroring endpoint exists
IF NOT EXISTS(SELECT * FROM sys.endpoints WHERE type = 4)
CREATE ENDPOINT DBMirrorEndPoint
STATE=STARTED AS TCP (LISTENER_PORT = port_num)
FOR DATABASE_MIRRORING ( AUTHENTICATION = CERTIFICATE MirrorServerCert,
                         ENCRYPTION = REQUIRED
                        ,ROLE = ALL
                        )
```

7. Connect to the witness server, and execute the `CreateCertOnWitness.sql` script (code file: `CreateCertOnWitness.sql`):

```
USE MASTER
GO
IF NOT EXISTS(SELECT 1 FROM sys.symmetric_keys where name =
'##MS_DatabaseMasterKey##')
CREATE MASTER KEY ENCRYPTION BY PASSWORD = '23%&weq^yzYu3000!'GO

IF NOT EXISTS (select 1 from sys.databases where
[is_master_key_encrypted_by_server] = 1)
ALTER MASTER KEY ADD ENCRYPTION BY SERVICE MASTER KEY
GO


IF NOT EXISTS (SELECT 1 FROM sys.certificates WHERE name = 'WitnessServerCert')
CREATE   CERTIFICATE WitnessServerCert
WITH SUBJECT = 'Witness Server Certificate'
GO


BACKUP CERTIFICATE WitnessServerCert
TO FILE = '<your folder>\WitnessServerCert.cer'
```

8. Finally, while connected to the witness server, execute the `CreateEndPointOnWitness.sql` script (code file: `CreateEndPointOnWitness.sql`):

```
--Check If Mirroring endpoint exists
IF NOT EXISTS(SELECT * FROM sys.endpoints WHERE type = 4)
CREATE ENDPOINT DBMirrorEndPoint
STATE=STARTED AS TCP (LISTENER_PORT = port_num)
FOR DATABASE_MIRRORING
( AUTHENTICATION = CERTIFICATE WitnessServerCert, ENCRYPTION
= REQUIRED
                        ,ROLE = ALL
                        )
```

Because all the partners can talk to each other, each partner needs permission to connect to the others. To do that, you must create logins on each server and associate the logins with certificates from the other two servers. You must grant connect permission to that user on the endpoint:

1. First, copy the certificates created in the previous scripts with the BACKUP CERTIFICATE command to the other two servers. For example, copy the certificate PrincipalServerCert .cer on the principal from the new folder you created earlier to the similar folders on both the witness and mirror servers.

2. Connect to the principal server and execute the Principal_CreateLoginAndGrant.sql script (code file: Principal_CreateLoginAndGrant.sql):

```
USE MASTER
GO


--For Mirror server to connect
IF NOT EXISTS(SELECT 1 FROM sys.syslogins WHERE name = 'MirrorServerUser')
CREATE LOGIN MirrorServerUser WITH PASSWORD = '32sdgsgy^%$!'
IF NOT EXISTS(SELECT 1 FROM sys.sysusers WHERE name = 'MirrorServerUser')
CREATE USER MirrorServerUser;

IF NOT EXISTS(SELECT 1 FROM sys.certificates WHERE name = 'MirrorDBCertPub')
CREATE CERTIFICATE MirrorDBCertPub  AUTHORIZATION MirrorServerUser
FROM FILE = '<your folder>\MirrorServerCert.cer'

GRANT CONNECT ON ENDPOINT::DBMirrorEndPoint TO MirrorServerUser
GO

--For Witness server to connect
IF NOT EXISTS(SELECT 1 FROM sys.syslogins WHERE name = 'WitnessServerUser')
CREATE LOGIN WitnessServerUser WITH PASSWORD = '32sdgsgy^%$!'
IF NOT EXISTS(SELECT 1 FROM sys.sysusers WHERE name = 'WitnessServerUser')
CREATE USER WitnessServerUser;

IF NOT EXISTS(SELECT 1 FROM sys.certificates WHERE name = 'WitnessDBCertPub')
CREATE CERTIFICATE WitnessDBCertPub  AUTHORIZATION WitnessServerUser
FROM FILE = '<your folder>\WitnessServerCert.cer'

GRANT CONNECT ON ENDPOINT::DBMirrorEndPoint TO WitnessServerUser
GO
```

This script creates two users on the principal server: MirrorServerUser and WitnessServerUser. These users are mapped to the certificates from the mirror and the witness. After that, you granted connect permission on the endpoint, so now the mirror and the witness server have permission to connect to the endpoint on the principal server. Perform the same steps on the mirror server and witness server.

3. Next, connect to the mirror server, and execute the Mirror_CreateLoginAndGrant .sql script. Finally, connect to the witness server, and execute the Witness_ CreateLoginAndGrant.sql script.

Now you have configured the endpoints on each server, using certificates. If you want to use the Windows authentication, the steps to configure the endpoints are a bit easier than using certificates.

Simply do the following on each server (this example is for the principal) (code files: `Mirror_CreateLoginAndGrant.sql`, `Witness_CreateLoginAndGrant.sql`):

```
IF NOT EXISTS(SELECT * FROM sys.endpoints WHERE type = 4)
CREATE ENDPOINT DBMirrorEndPoint
STATE = STARTED AS TCP (LISTENER_PORT = 5022)
FOR DATABASE_MIRRORING ( AUTHENTICATION = WINDOWS, ROLE = ALL)

GRANT CONNECT ON ENDPOINT::DBMirrorEndPoint TO
[MyDomain\MirrorServerServiceAccount]
GO

GRANT CONNECT ON ENDPOINT::DBMirrorEndPoint TO
[MyDomain\WitnessServerServiceAccount]
GO
```

Of course, you must change the logins appropriately. In Windows authentication mode, each server uses the service account under which it is running to connect to the other partners, so you must grant connect permission on the endpoint to the service account of SQL Server 2014.

Additionally, you can use SQL Server 2014 Management Studio to configure data mirroring with Windows authentication. Right-click the database you want to mirror, and choose Tasks ➪ Mirror. A wizard starts, as shown in Figure 19-4. Click the Configure Security button, which takes you through the steps to configure database mirroring. The wizard tries to use 5022 as the default TCP port for database mirroring, but you can change it if you want.

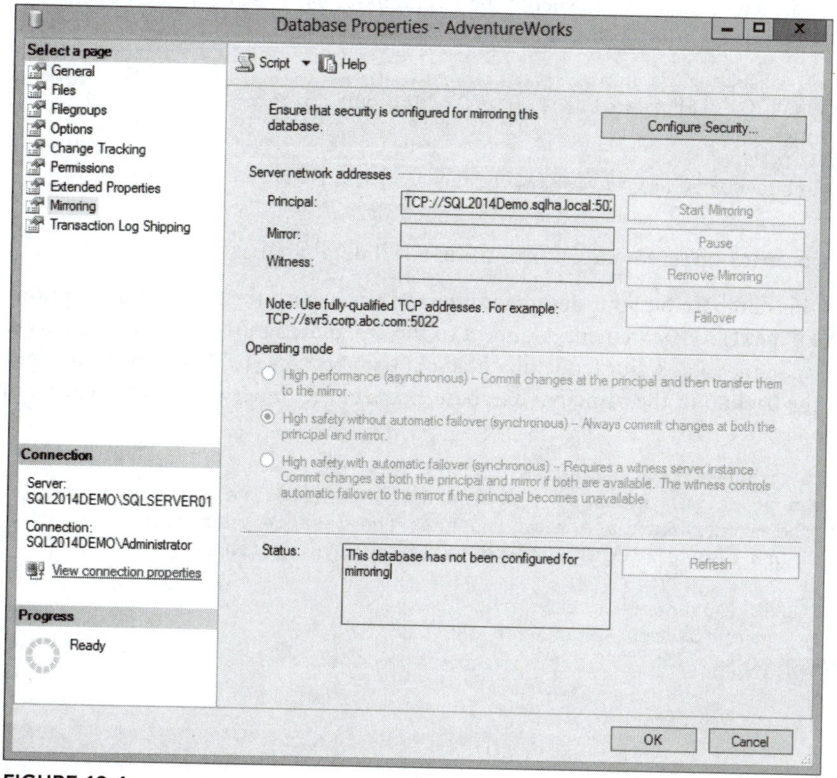

FIGURE 19-4

> **NOTE** *You need only one mirroring endpoint per server; it doesn't matter how many databases you mirror. Be sure to use a port that is not used by other endpoints. You can specify any available port number between 1024 and 32767.*
>
> *Do not reconfigure an in-use database mirroring endpoint (using* ALTER ENDPOINT*). The server instances use each other's endpoints to learn the state of the other systems. If the endpoint is reconfigured, it might restart, which can appear to be an error to the other server instances. This is particularly important in high-safety mode with automatic failover, where reconfiguring the endpoint on a partner can cause a failover to occur.*

Preparing the Database for Mirroring

Before you can set up the data mirroring, you need a database to work with:

1. Use the `AdventureWorks` database for this example, which must be in the recovery model of FULL:

   ```
   -- As a reminder you will need to set the database Recovery model to FULL
   -- recovery in order to establish mirroring.
   ALTER DATABASE AdventureWorks SET RECOVERY FULL
   ```

2. Connect to the principal server and execute the `BackupDatabase.sql` script (code file: `BackupDatabase.sql`):

   ```
   --Take a full database backup.
   BACKUP DATABASE [AdventureWorks] TO DISK = N'<your folder>
   \AdventureWorks.bak'
   WITH FORMAT, INIT,
   NAME = N'AdventureWorks-Full Database Backup',STATS = 10
   GO
   ```

   Using this script, back up `AdventureWorks` using a full database backup.

3. Next, restore this database on your designated mirror server with the NORECOVERY option for the RESTORE DATABASE statement. Connect to the designated mirror server, and execute the `RestoreDatabase.sql` script (code file: `RestoreDatabase.sql`). The following script assumes that the backup of the principal database exists in the folder you created earlier on the mirror server.

   ```
   --If the path of the mirror database differs from the
   --path of the principal database (for instance, their drive letters differ),
   --creating the mirror database requires that the restore operation
   --include a MOVE clause. See BOL for details on MOVE option.

   RESTORE DATABASE [AdventureWorks]
   FROM DISK = '<your folder>\AdventureWorks.bak'
   WITH   NORECOVERY
   ```

```
,MOVE N'AdventureWorks_Data' TO N'<your folder>\AdventureWorks_Data.mdf'
,MOVE N'AdventureWorks_Log' TO N'<your folder>\AdventureWorks_Log.LDF'
```

This code restores the AdventureWorks database in NORECOVERY mode on your mirror server. The NORECOVERY option is required. Now that you have a database ready to be mirrored, you should understand what it takes to do initial synchronization between the principal and mirror servers.

> **NOTE** *To establish the mirroring session, the database name must be the same on both the principal and the mirror. Before you back up the principal database, make sure that the database is in* FULL *recovery mode.*

Initial Synchronization Between Principal and Mirror

You have just backed up and restored the AdventureWorks database for mirroring. Of course, mirroring a database the size of AdventureWorks does not simulate a real-life scenario. In real life, you might mirror a production database with hundreds of thousands of megabytes. Therefore, depending on the database's size and the distance between the servers, it may take a long time to copy and restore the database on the mirror.

During this time, the principal database may have produced many transaction logs. Before you set up mirroring, you must copy and restore all these transaction logs with the NORECOVERY option on the mirror server. If you don't want to bother copying and restoring these transaction logs on the mirror, you can suspend the transaction log backups (if you have a SQL job to do backup transaction logs, you can disable that job) until the database on the mirror is restored, and the database mirroring session is established. (You learn about that soon in the "Establishing the Mirroring" section.) After the database mirroring session is established, you can resume the transaction log backup on the principal server again. It is important to understand that, in this approach, because you have stopped the transaction log backups, the transaction log file will grow, so make sure you have enough disk space for transaction log-file growth.

For the database mirroring session to be established, both databases (principal and mirror) must be in sync, so at some point you must stop the transaction log backup on your principal. Decide when you want to do it: before backing up the full database and restoring on the mirror server, or after backing up the full database. In the first case, you must plan for transaction-file growth. In the second case, you must copy and restore all the transactions logs on the mirror before you establish the mirroring session.

If you are mirroring a large database, it is going to take a longer time to back up and then restore it on the mirror server. To minimize the performance impact on the principal server, try to plan mirroring setup during low-activity periods on your system. On a highly active system, you may want to increase the time between each transaction log backup so that you have a smaller number of logs to copy and restore on the mirror; although this increases the database's data loss exposure in case of a principal failure. If you have minimal database activities, you can stop taking transaction log backups on the principal, back up the database on the principal, restore on the mirror, establish the mirroring session, and then restart the transaction log backup job on the principal.

Establishing the Mirroring Session

With the servers prepared for database mirroring, you next need to create some database activities in the AdventureWorks database before you establish the mirroring session so that you can better understand the previous section. Perform the following steps to do so:

1. Connect to the principal server, and execute the ModifyData.sql script (code file: ModifyData.sql). This script updates data in the AdventureWorks.person.address table.

2. Connect to the principal server and execute BackupLogPrincipal.sql (code file: BackupLogPrincipal.sql):

    ```
    USE MASTER
      GO
      BACKUP LOG AdventureWorks TO DISK = '<your folder>\AdventureWorks.trn'
    ```

    That backs up the transaction log of AdventureWorks. Now the AdventureWorks databases on the principal and the mirror are *not* in sync. See what happens if you try to establish the mirroring session between these two databases.

3. Connect to the mirror server, and execute the SetupMirrorServer.sql script (code file: SetupMirrorServer.sql): (This runs successfully.)

    ```
    USE MASTER
    GO
    ALTER DATABASE AdventureWorks
    SET PARTNER = 'TCP://YourPrincipalServer:5022'
    ```

4. Now, connect to the principal server, and execute the SetupPrincipalServer.sql script (code file: SetupPrincipalServer.sql):

    ```
    USE MASTER
    GO
    ALTER DATABASE AdventureWorks
    SET PARTNER = 'TCP://YourMirrorServer:5023'
    ```

    You can either keep track of the port numbers used for data mirroring, or you can query sys.tcp_endpoints to identify the port used by data mirroring.

    This script fails on the principal with the following message:

    ```
    Msg 1412, Level 16, State 0, Line 3
    The remote copy of database "AdventureWorks" has not been rolled forward to
    a point
    in time that is encompassed in the local copy of the database log.
    ```

5. This shows that the database on the mirror server is not rolled forward enough to establish the mirroring session, so now you must restore the transaction log that you backed up on the principal server to the mirror server with NORECOVERY mode to synchronize the mirror with

the principal. Connect to the mirror server, and execute the `RestoreLogOnMirror.sql` script (code file: `RestoreLogOnMirror.sql`):

```
USE MASTER
GO
RESTORE LOG AdventureWorks
FROM DISK = '<your folder>\AdventureWorks.trn'
WITH NORECOVERY
```

This script assumes that you have copied the transaction log in the drive on the mirror server. If you put the transaction log somewhere else, substitute that folder location, and then run the script. Now the principal and mirror databases are in sync.

6. Connect to the mirror server and execute the `SetupMirrorServer.sql` script again.

7. Then connect to the principal server, and execute the `SetupPrincipalServer.sql` script. It should succeed now because the transaction log has been restored, and you have just established the mirroring session.

When you execute the `SetupPrincipalServer.sql` or `SetupMirrorServer.sql` scripts, you may get the following type of error:

```
Database mirroring connection error 4 'An error occurred
while receiving data: '64(The specified network name
is no longer available.)'.' for TCP://YourMirrorServer:5022'.
Error: 1443, Severity: 16, State: 2.
```

It's possible that the firewall on the mirror or principal server is blocking the connection on the port specified. Go to Windows Firewall and Advanced Security to verify that the port numbers chosen for database mirroring are not blocked.

High-Safety Operating Mode Without Automatic Failover

When you establish the mirroring session, the transaction safety is set to FULL by default, so the mirroring session is always established in high-safety operating mode *without* automatic failover. In this operating mode, a witness is not set up, so automatic failover is not possible. Because the witness server is not present in this operating mode, the principal doesn't need to form a quorum to serve the database. If the principal loses its quorum with the mirror, it still keeps serving the principal database, and the mirror transactions are queued on the principal and sent once the mirror becomes available.

Next you learn how to change this to automatic failover.

High-Safety Operating Mode with Automatic Failover

Automatic failover means that if the principal database (or the server hosting it) fails, the database mirroring will fail over to the mirror server, and the mirror server will assume the principal role and serve the database. However, you need a third server, the witness, for automatic failover to the mirror. The witness just sits there as a third party, and is used by the mirror to verify that the principal is really down, providing a "2 out of 3" condition for automatic failover. No user action is necessary to fail over to the mirror if a witness server is present.

Witness Server

If you choose the `SAFETY FULL` option, you have an option to set up a witness server (refer to Figure 19-1). The presence of the witness server in high-safety mode determines whether or not you can perform automatic failover when the principal database fails. Automatic failover happens when the following conditions are met:

➤ Witness and mirror are both connected to the principal when the principal is failing (going away).

➤ Safety is set to `FULL`.

➤ Mirroring state is synchronized.

You must have a separate instance of SQL Server other than the principal and mirror servers to take full advantage of database mirroring with automatic failover. You can use the same witness server to participate in multiple, concurrent database mirroring sessions.

Returning to the example, you establish the witness server by following these steps:

1. Connect to the principal, and execute the `SetupWitnessServer.sql` script (code file: `SetupWitnessServer.sql`):

    ```
    USE MASTER
      GO
      ALTER DATABASE AdventureWorks
      SET WITNESS = 'TCP://YourWitnessServer:5024'
    ```

You must connect to the principal to execute this script. When you execute the script, both the principal and the mirror servers must be up and running. You have now established a witness server, which provides automatic failover support. Any SQL Server edition from SQL Express to Enterprise Edition can act as a witness. A witness can be a SQL Server instance that is used by other database operations; it does not have to be exclusively a witness server.

> **NOTE** *The witness server is optional in database mirroring, though it is required if you want automatic failover.*

The Quorum

When you set up the witness server, it becomes the *quorum* in the database mirroring session for automatic failover. A quorum is a relationship between two or more connected server instances in a database mirroring session, which acts as a tiebreaker to determine which server instance should be the principal.

Quorums can be in three mode types during database mirroring:

➤ **Full**—Both partners and the witness are connected.

➤ **Partner-to-partner**—Both partners are connected, but not the witness.

➤ **Witness-to-partner**—A witness and one of the partners are connected.

A database in its data mirroring session must be in one of these three quorum event types to serve as the principal database.

High-Performance Operating Mode

By default, the SAFETY is ON when you establish the mirroring session, so to activate the high-performance operating mode, you must turn the safety OFF, like so:

```
USE Master
ALTER DATABASE AdventureWorks SET PARTNER SAFETY OFF
```

There is minimal impact on transaction throughput and response time in this mode. The log transfer to the mirror works the same way as in high-safety mode, but because the principal doesn't wait for hardening the log to disk on the mirror, it's possible that if the principal goes down unexpectedly, you may lose data.

You can configure the witness server in high-performance mode, but because you cannot do automatic failover in this mode, the witness will not provide any benefits. Therefore, don't define a witness when you configure database mirroring in high-performance mode. You can remove the witness server by running the following command if you want to change the operating mode to high performance with no witness:

```
USE Master
ALTER DATABASE AdventureWorks SET WITNESS OFF
```

If you configure the witness server in a high-performance mode session, the enforcement of quorum means the following:

➤ If the mirror server is lost, the principal must be connected to the witness. Otherwise, the principal server takes its database offline until either the witness server or the mirror server rejoins the session.

➤ If the principal server is lost, forcing failover to the mirror requires that the mirror server be connected to the witness.

The only way you can fail over to the mirror in this mode is by running the following command on the mirror when the principal server is disconnected from the mirroring session. This is called *forced failover*. (Refer back to Table 19-1 for a description of the different failover types.)

```
USE MASTER
ALTER DATABASE AdventureWorks SET PARTNER FORCE_SERVICE_ALLOW_DATA_LOSS
```

The forced failover causes an immediate recovery of the mirror database, which may cause data loss. This mode is best used for transferring data over long distances (such as for disaster recovery to a remote site) or for mirroring an active database for which some potential data loss is acceptable. For example, you can use high-performance mode for mirroring your warehouse. Then, you can use a database snapshot (as discussed in the "Database Snapshots" section later in this chapter) to create a snapshot on the mirror server to enable a reporting environment from the mirrored warehouse.

DATABASE MIRRORING AND SQL SERVER 2014 EDITIONS

Now that you understand the operating modes of database mirroring, it is a good idea to keep in mind which of these operating modes is available on your edition of SQL Server. Table 19-2 summarizes which features of database mirroring are available in which SQL Server 2014 editions.

TABLE 19-2: SQL Server 2014 Features Supported by Edition

DATABASE MIRRORING FEATURE	ENTERPRISE EDITION	DEVELOPER EDITION	STANDARD EDITION	BUSINESS INTELLIGENCE EDITION	SQL EXPRESS EDITION
Partner (principal or mirror)	√	√	√	√	
Witness	√	√	√	√	√
Safety = FULL	√	√	√	√	
Safety = OFF	√	√			
Available during UNDO after failover	√	√	√	√	
Parallel REDO	√	√			

The SQL Express edition can be used only as a witness server in a mirroring session. For some other features such as high-performance operating mode, you need the Enterprise or Developer edition.

SQL Server 2014 may use multiple threads to roll forward the log in the redo queue on the mirror database. This is called *parallel redo*. If the mirror server has fewer than five CPUs, SQL Server uses only a single thread for redo. Parallel redo is optimized by using one thread per four CPUs. This feature is available only in the Enterprise or Developer editions.

DATABASE MIRRORING ROLE CHANGE

You have likely noticed that if you try to query the AdventureWorks database on your mirror server, you get an error like the following:

```
Msg 954, Level 14, State 1, Line 1
The database "AdventureWorks" cannot be opened. It is acting as a mirror database.
```

You cannot access the mirrored database, so how do you switch the roles of the mirroring partners? You can fail over to the mirror server in three ways (also described earlier):

➤ Automatic failover

➤ Manual failover

➤ Forced failover

The failover types depend on which transaction safety is used (FULL or OFF) and whether a witness server is present.

Automatic Failover

Automatic failover is a database mirroring feature in high-availability mode (SAFETY FULL when a witness server is present). When a failure occurs on the principal, automatic failover is initiated. Because you have set up database mirroring in high-availability mode with a witness server, you are ready to do automatic failover. The following events occur in an automatic failover scenario:

1. **The failure occurs**—The principal database becomes unavailable. This could be the result of a power failure, a hardware failure, a storage failure, or some other reason.

2. **The failure is detected**—The failure is detected by the mirror and the witness. Both partners and witness continually ping each other to identify their presence. Of course, it is more than just a simple ping, detecting things such as whether the SQL Server is available, whether the principal database is available, and so on. A timeout is specified for the ping, which is set to 10 seconds by default when you set up the database mirroring session. You can change the timeout using ALTER DATABASE as described earlier.

   If the principal does not respond to the ping message within the timeout period, it is considered to be down, and failure is detected. You should leave the default setting for timeout at 10 seconds, or at least do not change it to less than 10 seconds, because under heavy load and sporadic network conditions, false failures may occur, and your database will start failing over back and forth.

3. **A complete redo is performed on the mirror**—The mirror database has been in the restoring state until now, continuously redoing the log (rolling it forward onto the database). When failure is detected, the mirror needs to recover the database. To do that, the mirror needs to redo the remaining log entries in the redo queue.

4. **The failover decision is made**—The mirror now contacts the witness server to form a quorum and determines whether the database should failover to the mirror. In the high-safety mode with automatic failover, the witness must be present for automatic failover. The decision takes about 1 second, so if the principal comes back up before step 3 is complete, that failover is terminated.

5. **The mirror becomes the principal**—The redo continues while the failover decision is being made. After both the witness and the mirror have formed a quorum on the failover decision, the database is recovered completely. The mirror's role is switched to principal. Recovery is run (this involves setting up various database states, rolling back any in-flight system transactions, and starting up rollback of user transactions). Then the database is available to the clients, and normal operations can be performed.

6. **Undo**—There may be uncommitted transactions (that is, the transactions sent to the mirror while the principal was available, but not committed before the principal went down in the transaction log of the new principal), which are rolled back.

Normally, the time taken to fail over in this operating mode is short, usually seconds, but that mostly depends on the redo phase. If the mirror is already caught up with the principal before the principal has gone down, the redo phase will not introduce time lag. The time to apply the redo records depends on the redo queue length and the redo rate on the mirror. The failover will not happen if the `mirroring_state` is not synchronized. Some performance counters are available that you can use to estimate the time it will take to apply the transaction log for the redo queue on the mirror server.

To measure the actual time, you can use the SQL Profiler to trace the event. See Chapter 13, "Performance Tuning T-SQL," to learn more about running traces with SQL Profiler, which you use here to measure the actual time it takes to fail over:

1. Open SQL Profiler.
2. Connect to the mirror server.
3. Choose the Database Mirroring State Change event under the Database events group.
4. Choose the `TextData` and `StartTime` columns.
5. Start the trace.
6. Stop the SQL Server service on the principal server. Soon, automatic failover happens.

Two columns in the trace are of interest. `TextData` provides the description of the database mirroring state change event. `StartTime` represents the timestamp at which time the event took place. Figure 19-5 shows the SQL Profiler trace of the events.

In the event "Synchronized Mirror with Witness," the mirror informs the witness server that the connection to the principal is lost, as shown in the step 4 event in Figure 19-2. Then the mirror fails over to become the principal. This means that the principal will be running without a partner, and, if it were to fail, the database will be offline. You also see a message similar to the following in the mirror server SQL error log:

```
The mirrored database "AdventureWorks" is changing roles from "MIRROR" to
"PRINCIPAL" due to Auto Failover.
```

In the `StartTime` column, the actual failover time for this automatic failover was approximately 7 seconds.

The duration of the failover depends on the type of failure and the load on the database. Under load, it takes longer to fail over than in a no-load situation. You see messages similar to the following in the SQL error log:

```
The mirrored database "AdventureWorks" is changing roles from "MIRROR" to
"PRINCIPAL" due to Failover from partner.
Starting up database 'AdventureWorks'.
```

```
Analysis of database 'AdventureWorks' (9) is 81% complete (approximately 0
seconds
remain).
Analysis of database 'AdventureWorks' (9) is 100% complete (approximately 0
seconds
remain).
Recovery of database 'AdventureWorks' (9) is 0% complete (approximately 30
seconds
remain). Phase 2 of 3.
Recovery of database 'AdventureWorks' (9) is 16% complete (approximately 17
seconds
remain). Phase 2 of 3.
13 transactions rolled forward in database 'AdventureWorks' (9).
Recovery of database 'AdventureWorks' (9) is 16% complete (approximately 17
seconds
remain). Phase 3 of 3.
Recovery of database 'AdventureWorks' (9) is 100% complete (approximately 0
seconds
remain). Phase 3 of 3.
```

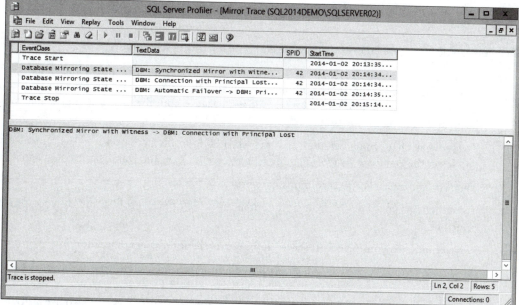

FIGURE 19-5

The additional steps during analysis and recovery of the database cause the manual failover to take longer.

When the failover happens, the clients must be redirected to the new principal server. The later section, "Preparing the Mirror Server for Failover," discusses that, along with other tasks you must do on the mirror server to prepare it for failover and take on the database workload.

Manual Failover

In a manual failover, you make a decision to switch the roles of the partners. The current mirror server becomes the new principal, and the current principal becomes the new mirror. You can use the following command for manual failover:

```
ALTER DATABASE AdventureWorks SET PARTNER FAILOVER
```

> **NOTE** *For manual failover, the* SAFETY *must be set to* FULL. *It doesn't matter whether you have a witness server set up.*

You must run this command on the principal server to successfully fail over. In addition, the `mirroring_state` must be synchronized for failover to succeed. If it is not synchronized, you get the following message when you try to execute the failover command on the principal:

```
Msg 1422, Level 16, State 2, Line 1
The mirror server instance is not caught up to the recent changes to database
"AdventureWorks". Unable to fail over.
```

Now you can do a manual failover using your database mirroring servers:

1. Open the `DatabaseMirroringCommands.sql` script. When you performed automatic failover earlier, you stopped the original principal SQL Server service. Ensure that you start that service back up before the manual failover, because both the mirror and principal must be up and running for this step.

2. To see what's happening behind the scenes, start SQL Profiler, connect it to the mirror server, and select the Database Mirroring State Change event under the Database event group.

3. Then run the trace. The two columns in the trace of interest are `TextData` and `StartTime`.

4. To see activities on the principal, start another instance of SQL Profiler and connect it to the principal.

5. Now, connect to your principal server and execute the following command:

```
ALTER DATABASE AdventureWorks SET PARTNER FAILOVER
```

You have just forced a manual failover from the principal to the mirror. You can also use SQL Server 2014 Management Studio to execute a manual failover as follows:

1. Right-click the principal database, and select Tasks ➪ Mirror to access the dialog box shown in Figure 19-6.

2. Click the Failover button to get a failover confirmation dialog box.

3. Click OK.

You can use manual failover for planned downtime, migrations, and upgrading, as discussed in the later section, "Preparing the Mirror Server for Failover."

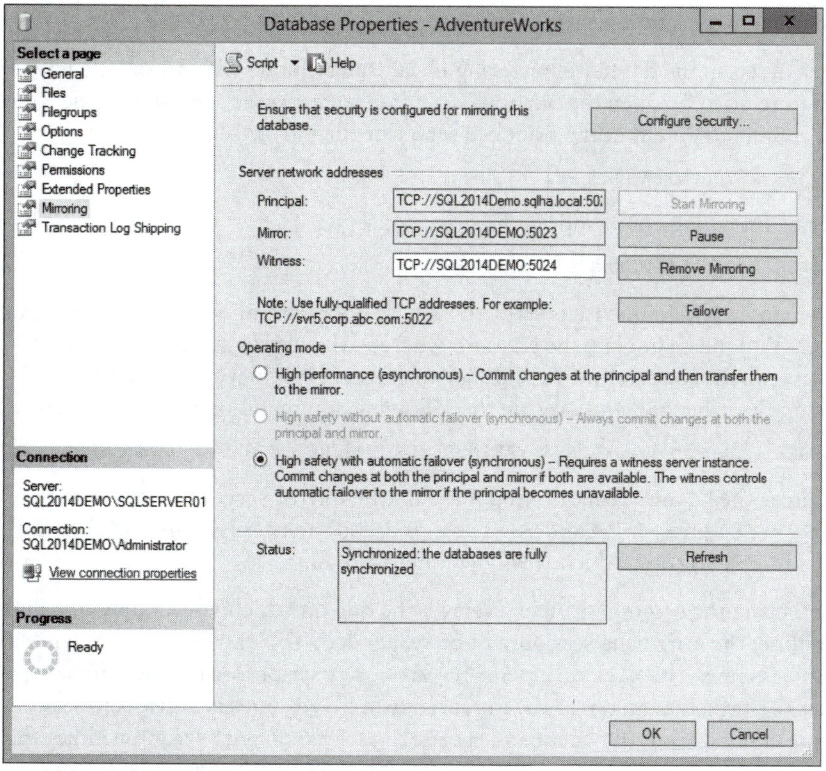

FIGURE 19-6

Forced Failover

For forced failover, you must execute the following command on the mirror server.

```
ALTER DATABASE AdventureWorks SET PARTNER FORCE_SERVICE_ALLOW_DATA_LOSS
```

> **WARNING** *Be cautious about using this command because you risk data loss by running it.*

When you run this command, the mirror should not be able to connect to the principal; otherwise, you cannot failover. If your principal is up and running and the mirror can connect to it when you try to run the command, you get the following error message:

```
Msg 1455, Level 16, State 2, Line 1
The database mirroring service cannot be forced for database "AdventureWorks"
because the database is not in the correct state to become the principal database.
```

Now try this exercise using your data mirroring servers:

1. Because you have set up the database mirroring in full-safety mode with automatic failover, you first need to remove it. Open the `DatabaseMirroringCommands.sql` script, and execute the following command on either the principal server or the mirror server:

   ```
   ALTER DATABASE AdventureWorks SET WITNESS OFF
   ```

2. Then execute the following command on the principal server:

   ```
   ALTER DATABASE AdventureWorks SET SAFETY OFF
   ```

3. Now the `AdventureWorks` database is set with `SAFETY OFF` with no witness, and you can force a failover. You must simulate the scenario whereby the mirror server cannot form a quorum (that is, cannot connect) with the principal server. To achieve that, stop the SQL Server service on the principal, and execute the following command on the mirror server:

   ```
   ALTER DATABASE AdventureWorks SET PARTNER FORCE_SERVICE_ALLOW_DATA_LOSS
   ```

This command now forces the `AdventureWorks` database on the mirror server to recover and come online. The `mirroring_state` (`sys.database_mirroring`) doesn't matter (synchronized or not) in this case because it is a forced failover, which is why you may lose data.

Now, notice that if you bring the original principal server (the one on which you stopped the SQL Server service) back online, the mirroring session will be suspended. You can execute the `sys.data-base_mirroring` catalog view in the `MirroringCatalogView.sql` script to view the mirroring state by connecting to either the principal server or the mirror server. To resume the mirroring session, execute the following command from the `DatabaseMirroringCommands.sql` script on either the principal or the mirror:

```
ALTER DATABASE AdventureWorks SET PARTNER RESUME
```

MONITORING USING DATABASE MIRRORING MONITOR

The SQL Server 2014 Database Mirroring Monitor will monitor the database mirroring activities. This makes the DBA's life easier. You can access this tool by right-clicking any user database in Object Explorer in SQL Management Studio on any registered SQL Server 2014 server and select Tasks ➪ Launch Database Mirroring Monitor. You can monitor all your mirroring sessions from it.

You must register the mirrored database in the Database Mirroring Monitor before you can use it. To do so, click Action ➪ Register Mirrored Database, and follow the wizard. You can give the wizard either the principal server name or the mirror server name; it will figure out the other partner. Figure 19-7 shows the Database Mirroring Monitor with a registered mirrored database.

You can monitor the key counters mentioned in the previous section using this GUI. You can also set alerts for these counters to receive an e-mail or take an action if any counter exceeds a set threshold, as covered later.

If you set up mirroring using the SQL Server 2014 Management Studio, it creates the SQL job called the Database Mirroring Monitor job, which runs every minute by default to refresh these counters. This data is stored in the `msdb.dbo.dbm_monitor_data` table. You can change the job schedule if you want. If you set up database mirroring using the scripts provided here, you can create the SQL job using the following command to refresh the counters:

```
sp_dbmmonitoraddmonitoring [ update_period ]
```

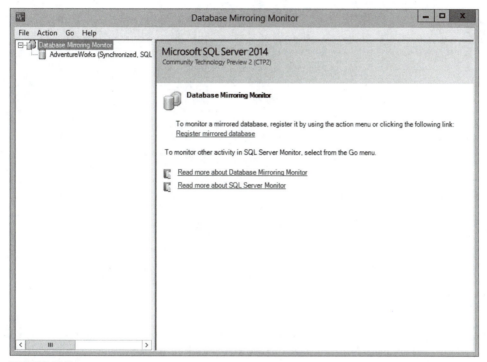

FIGURE 19-7

By default, the [`update_period`] is 1 minute. You can specify a value between 1 and 120 (in minutes). If you don't create this job, just press F5 when you are at the Database Mirroring Monitor screen. It calls the `sp_dbmmonitorresults` stored procedure to refresh the data (adding a row for new readings) in the `msdb.dbo.dbm_monitor_data` table. Actually, `sp_dbmmonitorresults` calls another stored procedure in the `msdb` database called `sp_dbmmonitorupdate` to update the status table and calculate the performance matrix displayed in the GUI. If you press F5 more than once in 15 seconds, it won't refresh the data again in the table.

Look at the Status tab details in Figure 19-8. The Status area is where the server instance names, their current role, mirroring state, and witness connection status (if there is a witness) comes from the `sys.database_mirroring` catalog view. If you click the History button, you get a history of the mirroring status and other performance counters. The mirroring status and performance history is kept for 7 days (168 hours) by default in the `msdb.dbo.dbm_monitor_data` table. If you want to change the retention period, you can use the `sp_dbmmonitorchangealert` stored procedure, like this:

```
EXEC sp_dbmmonitorchangealert AdventureWorks, 5, 8, 1
```

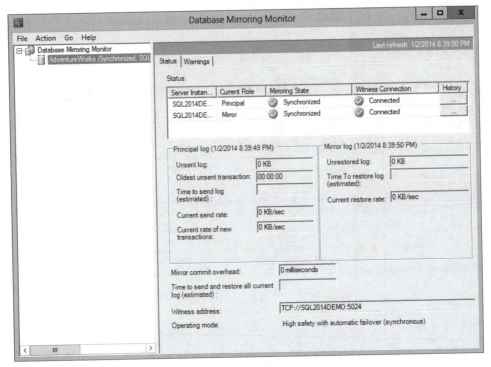

FIGURE 19-8

This example changes the retention period to 8 hours for the AdventureWorks database where 5 is the alter_id and 1 is enabled. You can refer to SQL 2014 Books Online for a description of this stored procedure.

Following are detailed explanations of the different counters that are available in the Status tab:

➤ **Principal Log:**

➤ **Unsent log**—This counter provides the same value as the Log Send Queue KB counter on the principal. Unsent Log reads the last value, so if you want to compare the Performance Monitor and this counter, look at its last value. You can run the ModifyData.sql script from earlier in the chapter into a loop after suspending the mirroring session using the following command:

```
ALTER DATABASE AdventureWorks SET PARTNER SUSPEND
```

You will see this counter value start to go up as work is accumulating in the unsent log.

➤ **Oldest unsent transaction**—This counter gives you the age (in hh:mm:ss format) of the oldest unsent transaction waiting in the send queue. It indicates that the mirror is behind the principal by that amount of time.

➤ **Time to send log (estimated)**—This indicates the estimated time the principal instance requires to send the log currently in the send queue to the mirror server. Because the rate of the incoming transaction can change, this counter can provide an estimate only. This counter also provides a rough estimate of the time required to manually fail over. If you suspend the mirroring, you notice that this counter shows a value of `Infinite`, which means that because you are not sending any transaction logs to the mirror, the mirror never catches up.

➤ **Current send rate**—This counter provides the rate at which the transaction log is sent to the mirror, in kilobytes per second. This is the same as the Performance Monitor counter Log Bytes Sent/Sec. The counter Current send rate provides the value in kilobytes, whereas the counter Log Bytes Sent/Sec provides the value in bytes. When Time to Send Log is Infinite, this counter shows a value of 0KB/Sec because no log is being sent to the mirror server.

➤ **Current rate of new transaction**—This is the rate at which new transactions are coming in per second. This is the same as the Transaction/sec counter in the `Database` object.

➤ **Mirror Log:**

➤ **Unrestored log**—This counter is for the mirror server. It provides the amount of logs in kilobytes waiting in the redo queue yet to be restored. This is the same as the Redo Queue KB counter for the mirror server. If this counter is `0`, the mirror is keeping up with the principal and can fail over immediately if required.

➤ **Time to restore log**—This counter provides an estimate (in minutes) of how long the mirror will take to replay the transactions waiting in the redo queue. You saw this calculation earlier. This is the estimated time that the mirror requires before failover can occur.

➤ **Current restore rate**—This is the rate at which the transaction log is restored into the mirror database, in kilobytes per second.

➤ **Mirror committed overhead**—This counter measures the delay (in milliseconds) spent waiting for a commit acknowledgment from the mirror. This counter is the same as the Transaction Delay on the principal. It is relevant only in high-safety mode. For high-performance mode, this counter is zero because the principal does not wait for the mirror to harden the transaction log to disk.

➤ **Time to send and restore all current log (estimated)**—This counter measures the time needed to send and restore all of the log that has been committed at the principal at the current time. This time may be less than the sum of the values of the Time to Send Log (Estimated) and Time to Restore Log (Estimated) fields, because sending and restoring can operate in parallel. This estimate does predict the time required to send and restore new transactions committed at the principal while working through backlogs in the send queue.

➤ **Witness address**—This is the fully qualified domain name of the witness, with the port number assigned for that endpoint.

➤ **Operating mode**—This is the operating mode of the database mirroring session. It can be one of the following:

➤ High performance (asynchronous)

➤ High safety without automatic failover (synchronous)

➤ High safety with automatic failover (synchronous)

Setting Thresholds on Counters and Sending Alerts

You can set warnings for different mirroring thresholds so that you receive alerts based on the threshold you have set. Figure 19-9 shows the Warnings tab of the Database Mirroring Monitor.

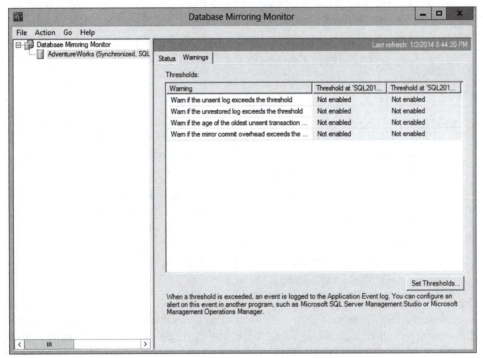

FIGURE 19-9

Following are instructions on how to set thresholds for the different warnings:

1. Start by clicking the Set Thresholds button on the Warnings tab, which opens the dialog box shown in Figure 19-10. Here, you can set the threshold for counters on both the principal and mirror servers individually so that you can either keep the thresholds the same, or vary them based on your requirements.

2. For this example, select the check box for the first warning, "Warn if the unsent log exceeds the threshold," and set the threshold value to 100KB, just for the principal server.

3. Next, under the Alert folder in SQL Server Agent in SQL Server 2014 Management Studio, add a new alert. You see a dialog box similar to the one shown in Figure 19-11. Type the alert name, and select the database name for which you need this alert—in this case, AdventureWorks.

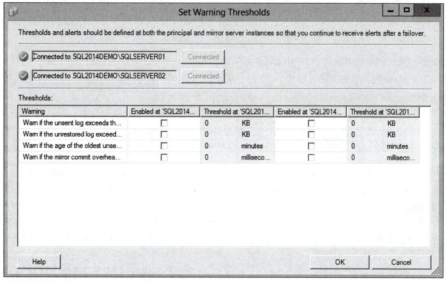

FIGURE 19-10

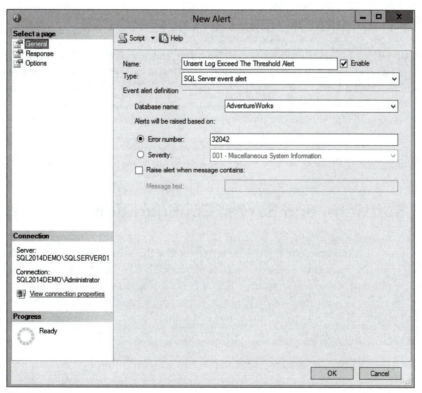

FIGURE 19-11

4. SQL Server raises the error when the threshold you set is exceeded. Enter **32042** for the error number. Refer to the section "Using Warning Thresholds and Alerts on Mirroring Performance Metrics" in SQL 2014 Books Online to get the error numbers for other events.

5. Now, click Response on the left pane and fill out the operator information to specify who will receive the alert when the threshold is exceeded.

On the principal, you can test this alert by suspending database mirroring using the following command:

```
ALTER DATABASE AdventureWorks SET PARTNER SUSPEND
```

The log will not be sent to the mirror, and the Unsent Log counter will start increasing. When it reaches the threshold of 100KB, you should get the alert.

> **NOTE** *You can monitor database mirroring with SQL Profiler using the Database Mirroring State Change event under the Database event class of SQL Profiler in SQL Server. This event records all the database mirroring state changes (suspended, synchronizing, synchronized, and so on) that occur on the server.*

PREPARING THE MIRROR SERVER FOR FAILOVER

When you set up mirroring, your intentions are clear that, in the event of failover, the mirror takes on the full load. For the mirror to be fully functional as a principal, you must do some configurations on the mirror server. Database mirroring is a database-to-database failover solution only; the entire SQL Server instance is not mirrored. If you want to implement full SQL Server instance failover, you should consider Windows failover clustering, discussed in Chapter 16, "Clustering SQL Server 2014."

When preparing your mirror server for failover, the first place to start is with your hardware and software.

Hardware, Software, and Server Configuration

Your mirror server hardware should be identical (CPU, memory, storage, and network capacity) to that of the principal if you want your mirror server to handle the same load as your principal. You may argue that if your principal is a 32-core, 64-bit server with 256GB of RAM, having identical mirror hardware is a costly solution if your principal is not going down often and such expensive hardware is sitting idle. If your application is not critical, you may want to have a smaller server just for failover and taking the load for some time, but it is arguable that if the application is not that critical, you do not need to have such extensive hardware on the primary either.

Moreover, with such hardware, the process on the server must be heavy, so if you fail over, your mirror should handle that load even if it is for a short time. In addition, you must consider the business cost versus the hardware cost, and then make the decision. You can also use your mirror server for noncritical work so that even though it is a mirror, it can be used for some other work. Of course, you must plan that out properly to make good use of your mirror server. Provided that your database server performance characteristics can be supported within the virtual server maximum performance capacity, data mirroring can be deployed on virtual servers.

Ensure that you have the same operating system version, service packs, and patches on both servers. During a rolling upgrade (as discussed in the later section, "Database Availability During Planned Downtime"), service packs and patch levels can be temporarily different.

You must have the same edition of SQL Server on both partners. If you use a witness, you don't need the same edition on it. You can use a smaller server for the witness because it doesn't carry any actual load—it is used only to form a quorum. Of course, the availability of the witness server is critical for automatic failover. Refer to Table 19-2 earlier in the section, "Database Mirroring and SQL Server 2014 Editions," for more details on which editions support which database mirroring features.

Ensure that you have an identical directory structure for the SQL Server install and database files on both the partners. If you add a database file to a volume/directory and that volume/directory does not exist on the mirror, the mirroring session will be suspended immediately.

On both principal and mirror, ensure that all the SQL Server configurations are identical (for example, `tempdb` size, trace flags, startup parameters, memory settings, and degree of parallelism).

All SQL Server logins on the principal must also be present on the mirror server; otherwise, your application cannot connect if a failover occurs. You can use SQL Server 2014 Integration Services with the Transfer Logins Task to copy logins and passwords from one server to another. (Refer to Chapter 18, "SQL Server 2014 Log Shipping," for more information.) Moreover, you still must set the database permission for these logins. If you transfer these logins to a different domain, you have to match the security identifier (SID)—that is, the unique name that Windows uses to identify a specific username or group.

On the principal, many other objects may exist and be needed for that application (for example, SQL jobs, SQL Server Integration Services packages, linked server definitions, maintenance plans, supported databases, SQL Mail or Database Mail settings, and DTC settings). You must also transfer all these objects to the mirror server.

If you use SQL Server authentication, you must resolve the logins on the new principal server after failover. You can use the `sp_change_users_login` stored procedure to resolve these logins.

Be sure to have a process in place so that when you make any changes to any configuration on the principal server, you repeat or transfer the changes on the mirror server.

Additionally, SQL Server 2014 can resolve the login dependency by using the `Contained Database` property in the database property where user authentication can then be stored directly in the database, and authentication can be made directly to the database removing the login dependency. For new deployments, you should consider using the `Contained Database` property and removing the login dependency.

After you set up your mirror, fail over the database and let your application run for some time on the new principal because that is the best way to ensure that all the settings are correct. Try to schedule this task during a slow time of the day, and deliver the proper communication procedures prior to testing failover.

Database Availability During Planned Downtime

This section describes the steps required to use a *rolling upgrade* technique to perform a software and hardware upgrade while keeping the database online for applications. The steps to perform a rolling upgrade vary based on database mirroring session transaction safety configuration (that is, `SAFETY FULL` or `SAFETY OFF`).

Safety Full Rolling Upgrade

Assuming that you have configured the mirroring session with `SAFETY FULL`, if you must perform software and hardware upgrades, perform the following steps in order:

1. Perform the hardware and software changes on the mirror server first. If you must restart the SQL Server 2014 or the server itself, you can do so. As soon as the server comes back up again, the mirroring session will be established automatically, and the mirror will start synchronizing with the principal. The principal is exposed while the mirror database is down, so if you have a witness configured, make sure that it is available during this time. Otherwise, the principal will be running in isolation and cannot serve the database because it cannot form a quorum.

2. After the mirror is synchronized with the principal, you can fail over using the following command:

    ```
    ALTER DATABASE <database_name> SET PARTNER FAILOVER
    ```

    The application now connects to the new principal. The later section, "Client Redirection to the Mirror," covers application redirection when the database is mirrored. Open and in-flight transactions during failover will be rolled back at this point. If that is not tolerable for your application, you can stop the application for the brief failover moment, and restart the application after failover completes.

3. Now, perform the hardware or software upgrade on your old principal server. When you finish with upgrades and the database becomes available on the old principal, it assumes the mirror role, the database mirroring session is automatically established, and it starts synchronizing.

4. If you have a witness set up, perform the hardware or software upgrade on that server.

5. At this point, your old principal acts as a mirror. You can fail back to your old principal now that all your upgrades are done. If you have identical hardware on the new principal, you may leave it as-is so that you don't have to stop the application momentarily. But if your hardware is not identical, consider switching back to your original principal.

Safety Off Rolling Upgrade

If you have configured the database mirroring with SAFETY OFF, you can still use the rolling upgrade technique by following these steps:

1. Perform the hardware and software changes on the mirror first. See the preceding section for more details.

2. On the principal server, change the SAFETY to FULL using this command:

   ```
   ALTER DATABASE <database_name> SET SAFETY FULL
   ```

> **NOTE** *Plan this activity during off-peak hours to reduce the mirror server synchronization time.*

3. After the mirror is synchronized, you can perform the failover to the mirror.

4. Perform the hardware and software upgrade on the old principal. After the old principal comes back up, it assumes the mirror role and starts synchronizing with the new principal.

5. When synchronized, you can fail back to your original principal.

If you use mirroring just to make a redundant copy of your database, you may not want to fail over for planned downtime because you may not have properly configured all the other settings on the mirror, as described earlier in the section "Hardware, Software, and Server Configuration." In that case, you must take the principal down for upgrade, and the database will not be available.

SQL Job Configuration on the Mirror

For identical configuration on both the principal server and the mirror server, you must also synchronize SQL jobs on your mirror server as mentioned earlier. When the database is the mirror, you do not want these SQL jobs to run. Following are the recommended options regarding how to do that:

➤ Have some logic in the SQL job steps that checks for the database mirroring state and runs the next step only if the database mirroring state is the principal.

➤ Listen for the database mirroring change event when the database becomes the principal, and execute a SQL job that enables all the SQL jobs you want to run. Stop or disable these jobs again when the event is fired, indicating that the database state has changed to mirror.

> **NOTE** *Technically, you could also disable the jobs and enable them manually when the database becomes the principal. However, as a DBA, you do not want to manage these jobs manually, so this is not a good option.*

Client Redirection to the Mirror

In SQL Server 2014, if you connect to a database that is being mirrored with ADO.NET or the SQL Native Client, your application can take advantage of the drivers' capability to automatically redirect connections when a database mirroring failover occurs. You must specify the initial principal server and database in the connection string and optionally the failover partner server.

You can write the connection string in several ways, but here is one example, specifying `ServerA` as the principal, `ServerB` as the mirror, and `AdventureWorks` as the database name:

```
"Data Source=ServerA;Failover Partner=ServerB;Initial Catalog=AdventureWorks;
Integrated Security=True;"
```

The failover partner in the connection string is used as an alternative server name if the connection to the initial principal server fails. If the connection to the initial principal server succeeds, the failover partner name is not used, but the driver stores the failover partner name that it retrieves from the principal server in the client-side cache.

Assume a client is successfully connected to the principal, and a database mirroring failover (automatic, manual, or forced) occurs. The next time the application attempts to use the connection, the ADO.NET or SQL Native Client driver detects that the connection to the old principal has failed, and automatically retries connecting to the new principal as specified in the failover partner name. If successful, and a new mirror server is specified for the database mirroring session by the new principal, the driver retrieves the new partner failover server name and places it in its client cache. If the client cannot connect to the alternative server, the driver tries each server alternatively until the login timeout period is reached.

The advantage of using the database mirroring client support built into ADO.NET and the SQL Native Client driver is that you do not need to recode the application, or place special codes in the application, to handle a database mirroring failover.

If you do not use the ADO.NET or SQL Native Client automatic redirection, you can use other techniques that enable your application to failover. For example, you could use network load balancing (NLB) to redirect connections from one server to another while remaining transparent to the client application that is using the NLB virtual server name. On failover, you can reconfigure NLB to divert all client applications using the database to the new principal by tracking the mirroring state change event from the Windows Management Instrumentation (WMI). Then change the NLB configuration to divert the client applications to the new principal server.

Additionally, you could consider writing your own redirection code and retry logic. Moreover, the Domain Name System (DNS) service provides a name-to-IP resolution that can be used to redirect clients to the new principal server. Provided that the administrator has access to the DNS server either by script or by using the Windows DNS management tool to modify the IP address to redirect client applications during a failover, DNS acts as the cross-reference for the client applications, because they will continue to connect to the same name. After the DNS modification, it redirects the database request to the new principal server.

DATABASE MIRRORING AND OTHER HIGH-AVAILABILITY SOLUTIONS

Database mirroring is just one feature in the arsenal of SQL Server high-availability solutions. SQL Server 2014 provides at least five high-availability solutions. Of course, each solution has some overlap with the others, and each has some advantages and disadvantages:

➤ **Database mirroring**—For this discussion, consider the high-safety mode with a witness.

➤ **Failover clustering instances**—This is a typical solution for high availability with a two or more node Windows failover clusters running SQL Server instances. Clustering is discussed in more detail in Chapter 16, "Clustering SQL Server 2014."

➤ **Transactional replication**—For comparison purposes, consider a separate distribution server with a single subscriber server as a standby if the publisher fails.

➤ **Log shipping**—SQL Server 2014 has built-in log shipping. Log shipping is discussed in detail in Chapter 18, "SQL Server 2014 Log Shipping."

➤ **Availability Groups**—Server 2014 has Availability Groups in SQL Server 2014. Availability Groups is discussed in detail in Chapter 25, "AlwaysOn Availability Groups."

Now, let's see how database mirroring compares with these other technologies.

Database Mirroring versus Clustering

Obviously, the biggest difference between database mirroring and a Windows failover cluster solution is the level at which each provides redundancy. Database mirroring provides protection at the database level, as you have seen, whereas a cluster solution provides protection at the SQL Server instance level.

If your application requires multiple database dependencies, clustering is probably a better solution than mirroring. If you need to provide availability for one database at a time, mirroring is a good solution, and has many advantages compared to clustering (for example, ease of configuration).

Unlike clustering, database mirroring does not require shared storage hardware and does not have a single failure point with the shared storage. Database mirroring brings the standby database online faster than clustering, and works well in ADO.NET and SQL Native Access Client for client-side redirect.

Another important difference is that, in database mirroring, the principal and mirror servers are separate SQL Server instances with distinct names, whereas a SQL Server instance on a cluster gets one virtual server name and IP address that remains the same no matter which node of the cluster hosts that SQL Server instance.

You can use database mirroring within a cluster to create a hot standby for a cluster SQL Server 2014 database. If you do, be aware that because a cluster failover is longer than the timeout value on database mirroring, a high-availability mode mirroring session will react to a cluster failover as a failure of the principal server. It would then put the cluster node into a mirroring state. You can increase the database mirroring timeout value by using the following command:

```
ALTER DATABASE <database_name> SET PARTNER TIMEOUT <integer_value_in_seconds>
```

Database Mirroring versus Transactional Replication

The common process between database mirroring and transactional replication is reading the transaction log on the originating server. Although the synchronization mechanism is different, database mirroring directly initiates I/O to the transaction log file to transfer the log records.

Transactional replication can be used with more than one subscriber, whereas database mirroring is a one-partner-to-another solution. You can read nearly real-time data on the subscriber database, whereas you cannot read data on the mirrored database unless you create a database snapshot, which is a static, point-in-time snapshot of the database.

Database Mirroring versus Log Shipping

Database mirroring and log shipping both rely on moving the transaction log records and restoring them. In database mirroring, the mirror database is constantly in a recovering state, which is why you cannot query the mirrored database. In log shipping, the database is in standby mode, so you can query the database if the log is not being restored at the same time. In addition, log shipping supports the bulk-logged recovery model, whereas mirroring supports only the full recovery model.

In the high-performance mode, there is a potential for data loss if the principal fails and the mirror is recovered using a forced failover recovery. If you are log shipping the old principal, and the transaction log file of the old principal is undamaged, you can create a "tail of the log" backup from the principal to get the last set of log records from the transaction log. If the standby log-shipping database has had every other transaction log backup applied to it, you can then apply the "tail of the log" backup to the standby server and not lose any of the old principal's data. You can then compare the data in the log-shipping standby server with the remote database and potentially copy missing data to the remote server.

You can use log shipping and mirroring together if you like. You can use log shipping to ship the log to a remote site for disaster recovery, and have a database-mirroring, high-availability configuration within the data center.

Database Mirroring versus Availability Groups

Database mirroring and Availability Groups both rely on moving the transaction log records and restoring them. Availability Groups is a high-availability feature first made available with SQL Server 2012 with similar functionality to data mirroring, but has the following additional capabilities:

➤   Availability Groups relies on Windows failover clustering for a virtual IP/virtual name for client connection. But unlike Windows failover clustering, it doesn't require a shared disk resource, but instead uses nonshared disks such as data mirroring.

➤ Availability Groups implementations can contain one or more databases to fail over as a single failover group; data mirroring failover is a single database.

➤ Availability Groups can support up to eight failover partners in a combination of synchronous or asynchronous modes. Data mirroring supports two partners.

➤ Availability Groups supports read-only replica databases kept in sync that can be used for reporting or database backup. With data mirroring, the mirrored database is only accessible using a database snapshot.

DATABASE SNAPSHOTS

As you have probably figured out by now, the mirror database is in NORECOVERY mode, so you cannot query it. If you want to read data from the mirror database to be used for reporting, SQL Server 2014 (Enterprise Edition and Developer Edition) has a feature called *database snapshots*, first introduced in SQL Server 2005. A database snapshot is a point-in-time, read-only, static view of a database (the source database). This feature comes in handy for reading the mirror database. Multiple database snapshots can exist, but they always reside on the same SQL Server instance as the database. Each database snapshot is transactionally consistent with the source database at the point in time of the snapshot's creation. A snapshot persists until it is explicitly dropped by the database owner.

Using this feature, you can create a snapshot on the mirror database. Then, you can read the database snapshot as you would read any other database. The database snapshot operates at a data-page level. Before a page of the source database is modified for the first time after the database snapshot, the original page is copied from the source database to the snapshot file. This process is called a *copy-on-write* operation. The snapshot stores the original page, preserving the data records as they existed when the snapshot was created. Subsequent updates to records in a modified page on the source database do not affect the data contents of the snapshot. In this way, the snapshot preserves the original pages for all data records that have ever been modified since the snapshot was taken. Even if you modify the source data, the snapshot will still have the same data from the time when it was created. (See the topic "Database Mirroring and Database Snapshots" in SQL Server 2014 Books Online for more information.)

The following example shows how to create a snapshot on the AdventureWorks database:

```
CREATE DATABASE AdventureWorks_Snapshot ON
(NAME = AdventureWorks, FILENAME = '<your folder>\ADW_Mirroring_
snapshot_Data1.SS')
AS SNAPSHOT OF AdventureWorks
```

Because new data changes will be continuous on the mirrored database, if you want to read more recent data not in the database snapshot after you have created it, you must drop the database snapshot and re-create it. You can drop the snapshot in the same manner as you would drop a database:

```
DROP DATABASE AdventureWorks_Snapshot
```

Generating a database snapshot has some performance impact on the mirror server, so evaluate the impact if you want to create many snapshots on multiple databases on a server. Most importantly, from a database mirroring perspective, having too many snapshots on a mirror database can slow down the redo and cause the database to fall more and more behind the principal, potentially resulting in longer failover times.

In addition, prepare an area of disk space as big as the size of the source database, because as data changes on the source database, the snapshot will start copying the original pages to the snapshot file, and it will start growing. Additionally, you may want to evaluate SQL Server replication as an alternative reporting solution.

SUMMARY

Database mirroring provides a database redundancy solution using the log-transfer mechanism. The transaction log records are sent to the mirror transaction log as soon as the log buffer is written to the disk on the principal.

You can configure mirroring in either high-performance mode or high-safety mode. In high-safety mode with a witness, if the principal fails, the mirror server automatically becomes a new principal and recovers its database.

Understanding application behavior in terms of log-generation rate, number of concurrent connections, and size of transactions is important to achieve the best performance.

Network bandwidth plays an important role in a database mirroring environment. When used with a high-bandwidth and low-latency network, database mirroring can provide a reliable, high-availability solution against planned and unplanned downtime.

In Chapter 20, you learn about the many and varied administrative tasks involved with managing SQL Server Integration Services (SSIS).

20

Integration Services Administration and Performance Tuning

WHAT'S IN THIS CHAPTER?

➤ Getting to know SSIS

➤ Deploying and configuring SSIS Packages

➤ Securing and administering SSIS

➤ Understanding common pitfalls with SSIS performance

In keeping with the theme of focusing on how SQL Server 2014 changes the role of the DBA, in this chapter you learn how you can be better equipped as a DBA to maintain SQL Server's Business Intelligence (BI) components. The SQL Server 2014 Business Intelligence stack includes Integration Services (SSIS), Analysis Services (SSAS), and Reporting Services (SSRS).

This chapter looks at the many and varied administrative tasks required for managing Integration Services. First, an overview of the Integration Services service is provided so that you will have a better understanding of the moveable parts that require the attention of an administrator. After becoming comfortable with the architecture of Integration Services, you can focus on the administration of Integration Services, including configuration, event logs, and monitoring activity. Next, you gain an understanding of the various administrative tasks required of Integration Services packages, the functional component within SSIS, including creation, management, execution, and deployment. Last, you learn how to secure all the Integration Services components.

> **NOTE** *For more in-depth information about Integration Services, see* Professional Microsoft SQL Server 2014 Integration Services, *by Brian Knight et al. (Indianapolis: Wrox, 2014).*

A TOUR OF INTEGRATION SERVICES

Certainly the most important Business Intelligence (BI) component to Microsoft's arsenal is SSIS. Its core responsibility is the movement and cleansing of data. Without this cleansing and movement, every other component would not exist or, at a minimum, would report bad data.

Integration Services is a solution that provides enterprise-level data integration and workflow solutions that have as their goal the extraction, transformation, and loading (ETL) of data from various sources to various destinations. SSIS includes a wide range of tools and wizards to assist in the creation of the workflow and data flow activities that you need to manage in these complex data-movement solutions.

Integration Services Uses

Before diving into the detailed components within Integration Services, you should understand some of the more common business scenarios that involve creating SSIS solutions. Following are some common uses for SSIS:

- ➤ Archival of data (export)
- ➤ Loading of new data (import)
- ➤ Transferring data from one data source to another
- ➤ Data cleansing or transformation of dirty data
- ➤ DBA tasks like purging old files or indexing a database

One common scenario is combining data from different sources stored in different storage systems. In this scenario, SSIS is responsible for connecting to each data source, extracting the data, and merging it into a single data set. For example, in today's information systems topology, this is becoming increasingly common because businesses archive information that is not needed for regular operations, but is invaluable to analyze business trends or meet compliance requirements. You can also find this scenario when different parts of a business use different storage technologies or different schemas to represent the same data. In these cases, SSIS performs the homogenization of the information. SSIS seamlessly handles multiple divergent data sources and the transformations that can alter data types, split or merge columns, and look up descriptive information that becomes a powerful asset for these situations.

Another common scenario is the population and maintenance of data warehouses and data marts. In these business uses, the data volumes tend to be exceptionally large, and the window of time in which to perform the extraction, transformation, and loading of the data tends to be rather short. SSIS includes the capability to bulk-load data directly from flat files in SQL Server, and has a destination component that can perform a bulk load into SQL Server. A key feature for large data volume and complex enrichment and transformation situations such as these is restartability. SSIS includes checkpoints to handle rerunning a package from a task or container within the control flow so that you can elegantly handle various types of errors that may occur during these complex data-loading scenarios.

A denormalized database structure is common in data warehouses. Therefore, in data warehouse loads, the ability to source a particular destination from many different tables or files is important. SSIS packages can easily merge data into a single data set and load the destination table in a single process without the need to stage or land the data at each step of the process.

You often require the management or partitioning of history within your data warehouses to review the state of activity at a certain point in time. This history management creates complex updating scenarios, and SSIS handles this with the assistance of the Slowly Changing Dimension Wizard. This wizard dynamically creates and configures a set of data transformation tasks used to manage inserting and updating records, updating related records, and adding new columns to tables to support this history management.

Often, businesses receive data from outside of their systems and need to perform data-quality routines to standardize and clean the data before loading it into their systems. SSIS can handle most data situations from heterogeneous databases or flat files. This is commonly the case when different areas of the business use different standards and formats for the information or when the data is being purchased (such as with address data). Sometimes the data formats are different because the platforms from which they originate differ from the intended destination. In these cases, SSIS includes a rich set of data-transformation tasks to perform a wide range of data-cleaning, converting, and enriching functions. You can replace values or get descriptions from code values by using exact or fuzzy lookups within SSIS. Identifying records that may be duplicates by using SSIS grouping transformations helps to successfully remove them before loading the destination.

The ability to dynamically adjust the data transformations being performed is a common scenario within businesses. Often, data must be handled differently based on certain values it may contain, or even based upon the summary or count of values in a given set of records. SSIS includes a rich set of transformations that are useful for splitting or merging data based upon data values, applying different aggregations or calculations based on different parts of a data set, and loading different parts of the data into different locations. SSIS containers specifically support evaluating expressions, enumerating across a set of information, and performing workflow tasks based on results of the data values.

Lastly, you commonly have operational administrative functions that require automation. SSIS includes an entire set of tasks devoted to these administrative functions. You can use tasks specifically designed to copy SQL Server objects or facilitate the bulk loading of data. You also have access in SSIS to a SQL Management Objects (SMO) enumerator to perform looping across your servers to perform administrative operations on each server in your environment. When complete, you can also schedule all your SSIS packages and solutions using SQL Server Agent jobs.

The Main Parts of Integration Services

SQL Server 2014 has two models that can impact your team's development and you as an administrator: a package deployment model and a project deployment model. The decision on which model to use is made when you first create the project, and can always be changed later, but should not be changed lightly. While you can use both models in your environment interchangeably, you should try to guide your development toward the project deployment model since it turns on all the features of 2014.

The package deployment model was the only model a DBA and developer had prior to SQL Server 2012. This model has you deploy a package by itself, and the package's project is just an arbitrary container that doesn't do a lot. Packages run in this model can be deployed to the msdb database or the server's filesystem. There is also an SSIS service in this model that monitors the execution of packages. Packages can be configured externally at runtime with configuration files or entries in a configuration table.

The project deployment model, introduced in SQL Server 2012, is a model in which the project that contains the packages is more important in previous SQL Server editions. In this model, parameters can be passed into the project or package to reconfigure the package at runtime. Projects take a more vital role in this model because you deploy the entire project at a time, and you cannot deploy individual packages. When you deploy packages, they are added to the SSIS catalog database, and can be executed in T-SQL or through Windows PowerShell.

Moving forward in SQL Server 2014, you should use the new project deployment model because it offers a more robust configuration, logging, and management infrastructure. The package deployment model remains available for backward compatibility, but should not be used as your first choice.

The package deployment model contains many important components, including the service, runtime engine and components, object model, and dataflow engine and components. The following sections cover each of these components. In the package deployment model, the components have not changed in SQL Server 2014.

Integration Services Service

The SSIS service is the component of architecture within SSIS that is responsible for managing the storage of packages and monitoring them as they execute. Its primary job is to cache the data providers, monitor which packages are being executed, and monitor which packages are stored in the package store. This service is used only in the package deployment model.

Integration Services Runtime Engine and Runtime Components

The SSIS runtime engine works across both deployment models. It is responsible for saving the layout and design of the packages, running the packages, and providing support for all additional package functionality (such as transactions, breakpoints, configuration, connections, event handling, and logging). The specific executables that make up this engine include packages, containers, and tasks. You can find three default constraints within SSIS: success, completion, and failure.

Integration Services Object Model

The managed application programming interface (API) is used to access SSIS tools, command-line utilities, and custom applications in the SSIS object model. Although this object model isn't discussed in detail, it is a major component of Integration Services.

Integration Services Data Flow Engine and Data Flow Components

Within an SSIS package's control flow, a Data Flow Task creates instances of the data flow engine. This engine is responsible for providing the in-memory data movement from sources to destinations. In addition, this engine performs the requested transformations to enrich the data for the purposes you specify. Three primary components make up the data flow engine:

➤ *Sources* provide connectivity to, and extract data from, a wide range of sources (such as database tables or views, files, spreadsheets, and even XML files).

➤ *Destinations* permit the insertion of information on a similar wide range of destinations.

➤ *Transformations* enable you to modify the source data before loading it into a destination using capabilities such as lookups, merging, pivoting, splitting, converting, and deriving information.

Project Management and Change Control

In BI, the line between development and DBA has blurred, and the two roles must now work closer together. The shared view of development by administrators and developers alike is enacted through the SQL Server Data Tools (SSDT), previously named Business Intelligence Development Studio (BIDS). SSDT was previously a Visual Studio shell that optionally installed when you install SQL Server. With the SQL Server 2014 release, SSDT is no longer included with the SQL Server media, and you must now download and install SSDT separately. For Integration Services, SSIS solutions and projects are created in the SSDT environment.

Generally, the configuration of the SSDT solutions and projects is handled by the developers; however, administrators are called upon to help configure various aspects of these solutions. The administration and management of Integration Services is primarily performed within SQL Server Management Studio. Often, moving the Integration Services solutions from environment to environment means changing dynamic information within the package, and setting up any information referenced by the packages. Examples of these elements include Package Configuration settings, referenced XML or configuration files, and solution data sources, which are all covered later in this chapter.

When a developer clicks Save or executes the package in SSDT, the old version of the package is immediately overwritten in the filesystem. To remedy this, you should integrate the SSIS development environment into a source control system—such as Team Foundation Server (TFS), for example. After such integration, when a package is saved, you can always roll back to an earlier release of the package. You can use any type of source control system that integrates with Visual Studio.

ADMINISTRATION OF THE INTEGRATION SERVICES SERVICE

Now that you have a better understanding of the parts of Integration Services, let's take a look at the various administrative aspects of Integration Services, including the details you need to become comfortable working with the components. Let's start with a review of the Integration Services service, and then look at various configuration elements of the service. Next, you learn how you can adjust properties of the SSIS service using either the Windows Services Snap-In or the SQL Server Configuration Manager. Understanding how you can modify Windows Firewall follows, and then you learn about the management and configuration of event logs and performance monitoring.

An Overview of the Integration Services Service

The Integration Services service is a Windows service used to manage SSIS packages deployed in the package deployment model. Accessed through SQL Server Management Studio, it provides the following management capabilities:

➤ Starting and stopping local and remote packages

➤ Monitoring local and remote packages

➤ Importing and exporting packages from different sources

➤ Managing the package store

➤ Customizing storage folders

➤ Stopping running packages when service stops

➤ Viewing the Windows Event Log

➤ Connecting to multiple SSIS server instances

To be clear, you don't need this service for designing or executing packages. The primary purpose of this service is to manage packages within Management Studio. One side benefit to having the service running is that the SSIS Designer in SSDT can use the service to cache the objects used in the designer, thus enhancing the designer's performance.

Configuration

The configuration of the Integration Services service includes viewing and possibly modifying the XML file responsible for the runtime configuration of the service, setting service properties using either the Windows Services Snap-In or SQL Server Configuration Manager, and, potentially, configuring Windows Firewall to permit access by Integration Services.

XML Configuration File

The MsDtsSrvr.ini.xml file responsible for the configuration of the Integration Services service is located in <SQL Server Drive>\Program Files\Microsoft SQL Server\120\DTS\Binn by default. You can also move this file to a new location by changing the HKEY_LOCAL_MACHINE\ SOFTWARE\Microsoft\Microsoft SQL Server\120\SSIS\ServiceConfigFile Registry key. This file includes settings for specifying whether running packages stop when the service stops, a listing of root folders to display in the Object Explorer of Management Studio, and settings for specifying which folders in the filesystem are managed by the service.

One example of a configuration change that must be made is when you connect to a named instance of SQL Server. The following example shows the modification for handling a named instance

(MyServerName\MyInstanceName). This is because the default configuration for the SSIS service always points to ". " and must be configured for a clustered or named instance.

```xml
<?xml version="1.0" encoding="utf-8"?>
<DtsServiceConfiguration xmlns:xsd="http://www.w3.org/2001/XMLSchema"
xmlns:xsi="http://www.w3.org/2001/XMLSchema-instance">
  <StopExecutingPackagesOnShutdown>true</StopExecutingPackagesOnShutdown>
  <TopLevelFolders>
    <Folder xsi:type="SqlServerFolder">
      <Name>MSDB</Name>
      <ServerName>MyServerName\MyInstanceName</ServerName>
    </Folder>
    <Folder xsi:type="FileSystemFolder">
      <Name>FileSystem</Name>
      <StorePath>..\Packages</StorePath>
    </Folder>
  </TopLevelFolders>
</DtsServiceConfiguration>
```

Other common configuration file change scenarios include adding additional paths from which to display packages other than the default SSIS package store path of C:\Program Files\Microsoft SQL Server\120\DTS\Packages and creating a centralized folder structure for multiple servers by storing the service configuration file in a central file share.

Creating a Central SSIS Server

Many enterprise companies have so many packages that they decide to separate the service from SQL Server and place it on its own server. When you do this, you must still license the server just as if it were running SQL Server. The advantages of this are that your SSIS packages do not suffocate the SQL Server's memory during a large load, and you have a central spot to manage. The disadvantages are that now you must license the server separately, and you add another layer of complexity when you debug packages. When you create a dedicated server, you create a fantastic way to easily scale packages by adding more memory to your central server, but you also create an added performance hit, because all remote data must be copied over the network before entering the data flow buffer.

To create a centralized SSIS hub, you need to modify only the MsDtsSrvr.ini.xml file and restart the service. The service can read a UNC path such as \\ServerName\Share and can point to multiple remote servers. Mapped drives are not recommended because the account that starts the SSIS service would need to be aware of the drive and could create an unnecessary dependency on that account. To add additional storage locations, simply duplicate the <Folder> node in the XML, replacing the Name and ServerName values with new server locations.

You can schedule your packages through SQL Server Agent, or through a scheduling system such as Task Scheduler from Windows. You already pay for a license of SQL Server, so it's better to install SQL Server on your server and use SQL Server Agent because it gives you much more flexibility. You can also store configuration tables and logging tables on this SQL Server to centralize its processing as well.

Each time you make a change to the configuration file, you must stop and start the SSIS service, as described in the following sections. Now that you know how to configure the MsDtsSrvr.ini.xml file responsible for the configuration of the Integration Services service, you need to know how to set the service's properties.

Setting Service Properties Using the Windows Services Snap-In

As with any other Windows service, the Integration Services service has properties that dictate how it is to be started. Specifically, you can manage the following from the Windows Services Snap-In:

➤ Configure the startup type as Manual, Automatic, or Disabled.

➤ Request that the service is started, stopped, or restarted.

➤ Establish how the computer reacts to service failures.

➤ View or modify a listing of dependent services (none are set up by default).

To view and modify SSIS services properties using the Windows Services Snap-in, follow these steps:

1. Open the Services Snap-In from Control Panel ⇨ Administrative Tools (or using the Category view from Performance and Maintenance ⇨ Administrative Tools).

2. Locate and right-click SQL Server Integration Services 12.0 in the list of services.

3. Select Properties to view the currently applied settings.

4. On the General tab, you can view or change the Startup type (Automatic, Manual, or Disabled). When set to either Manual or Automatic, you can change the Service status to Start, Stop, or Resume.

5. On the Log On tab (see Figure 20-1), you can view or alter the account used to start and run the service. By default, this runs under the NT Service\MsDtsServer120 account, but most people use a domain service account.

FIGURE 20-1

6. On the Recovery tab, you can configure how the server responds to failures of the service by setting the First, Second, and Subsequent failures options to either Take No Action (the default), Restart the Service, Run a Program, or Restart the Computer. You can also instruct the service to reset the failure count after a certain number of days.

7. You can modify the list of services on which the SSIS service depends (none by default) and view the list of services dependent on the SSIS service (none by default) on the Dependencies tab.

Setting Service Properties Using SQL Server Configuration Manager

As with using the Windows Services Snap-In, you can also configure a limited set of Integration Services service properties using the SQL Server Configuration Manager. Specifically, you can both configure the logon information used by the service and establish the startup model of the service.

Follow these steps to view and modify SSIS Services properties using the SQL Server Configuration Manager:

1. Open the SQL Server Configuration Manager from All Programs ⇨ Microsoft SQL Server 2014 ⇨ Configuration Tools.

2. On the list of services on the right side, right-click SQL Server Integration Services and select Properties.

3. On the Log On tab, you can view or alter the account used to start and run the service. By default, this runs under the NT Service\MsDtsServer120 account. This resembles Figure 20-1.

4. On the Service tab, you can view or change the Startup type (Automatic, Manual, or Disabled).

Now that you are comfortable setting up the service properties for the Integration Services service using either the Windows Services Snap-In or the SQL Server Configuration Manager, you next learn how you can modify Windows Firewall to permit access to Integration Services.

Event Logs

Integration Services records events raised by packages during their execution in logs. The SSIS log providers can write log entries to text files, SQL Server Profiler, SQL Server, Windows Event Log, or XML files. To perform logging, SSIS packages and tasks must have logging enabled. Logging can occur at the package, container, and task level, and you can specify different logs for packages, containers, and tasks.

To record the events raised, a log provider must be selected and a log added for the package. You can create these logs only at the package level, and a task or container must use one of the logs created for the package. After you configure the logs within packages, you can view them either using Windows Event Viewer or within SQL Server Management Studio.

To view SSIS event logs using the Windows Event Viewer, follow these steps:

1. Open the Event Viewer from Control Panel ⇨ Administrative Tools (or use the Category view from Performance and Maintenance ⇨ Administrative Tools).

2. Within the Event Viewer dialog, click Application.

3. After the Application snap-in displays, locate an entry in the Source column valued at SQLISService120 or SQLISPackage120. The SQLISPackage120 source logs would be generated from the package logs, and the SQLISService120 source logs would be simple messages from the SSIS service.

4. Right-click the entry, and select Event Properties to display descriptive information about the entry.

To view these events in SQL Server Management Studio, follow these steps:

1. Open Management Studio, and connect to the target Integration Services server.

2. In Object Explorer, right-click Integration Services (the topmost node) and click View Logs.

3. Select SQL Server Integration Services from the Select Logs section.

4. You can see the details for an event displayed in the lower pane by clicking an event in the upper pane.

Monitoring Activity

Part of the performance monitoring of the Integration Services service includes configuring the logging of performance counters. These counters enable you to view and understand the use of resources consumed during the execution of SSIS packages. Specifically, the logging encompasses event-resource usage, whereas packages perform the Data Flow Tasks.

Begin by focusing on some of the more insightful counters, including the following (at a server-level under SQLServer:SSIS Pipeline 12.0):

➤ **Rows Read**—Provides the number of rows read from all data sources during package execution

➤ **Buffers in Use**—Details the number of pipeline buffers (memory pools) in use throughout the package pipeline

➤ **Buffers Spooled**—Specifies the number of buffers used to handle the data flow processes

The Buffers Spooled counter is important because it is a good indicator of when your machine runs out of physical memory or runs out of virtual memory during data flow processing. The importance of using buffers rather than spooling to disk is the difference between a package with an execution time of 20 minutes versus 20 hours in some cases. Each time you see a buffer spooled, a 10MB buffer has been written to disk.

One example of how these performance counters can be used includes ensuring that your server running the SSIS packages has enough memory. One of the bottlenecks in any transformation process includes input/output operations, whereby data is staged to disk during the transformations. Integration Services was designed to optimize system resources when transforming data between a source and destination, including attempting to perform these transformations in memory, rather than having to stage data to disk and incur I/O performance penalties. You should expect to see the value of the Buffers Spooled counter remain at zero (0) when only memory is being used during the transformation processes being performed by the SSIS packages. When you observe that the Buffers Spooled counter is normally valued higher than zero (0), it's a good indication that more memory is needed on the server processing the SSIS packages.

SQL Server Profiler enables you to analyze the data operations and query plans generated for various data flow pipeline activities. You can use this information to refine indexes or apply other optimization techniques to the data sources your SSIS solution uses.

ADMINISTRATION OF INTEGRATION SERVICES PACKAGES IN PACKAGE DEPLOYMENT MODEL

Now that you've learned about the various aspects of Integration Services service administration, this section provides an overview of SSIS package elements and administration, and then you look at various ways to create packages. Next, you look at the management of the developed SSIS packages. When you understand how to create and manage packages, you can move on to the deployment, execution, and scheduling of SSIS packages and solutions.

Using Management Studio for Package Management

As discussed earlier in the "Administration of the Integration Services Service" section, packages are managed primarily via Management Studio and its connection to the Integration Services service. Upon connecting to the service, you see two main folders: Running Packages and Stored Packages. The packages displayed are stored in either the msdb database sysssispackages table, or the filesystem folders specified in the Integration Services service configuration file.

The main uses of Management Studio include monitoring running packages and managing the packages stored within the Integration Services environment.

You can see information regarding currently executing packages within the Running Packages folder. Information about these packages displays on the Summary page, whereas you can obtain information about a particular executing package by clicking the package under the Running Packages folder and viewing the Summary page. You can stop the execution of a package listed within this folder by right-clicking the package and selecting Stop.

You can make changes to the storage of packages by adding custom folders and by copying packages from one type of storage to another using the Import and Export utilities. You can configure the logical folders displayed within the MSDB folder in Management Studio by right-clicking on a given folder, or by altering the sysssispackagefolders table within the msdb database. The root folders in this table are those in which the parentfolderid column contains null values. You can add values to this table to add logical folders, bearing in mind that the folderid and parentfolderid columns are the key values used to specify the folder hierarchy. In addition, you can configure the default folders in the filesystem that Management Studio displays. This is discussed in the "XML Configuration File" section earlier in this chapter. Importing and exporting packages are discussed in the "Deployment" section later in this chapter.

The main management tasks you can perform on packages within Management Studio include the following:

➤ Creating new Object Explorer folders to display packages saved in either the filesystem or SQL Server (msdb database sysssispackages table)

➤ Importing and exporting packages

➤ Running packages

➤ Deleting packages

➤ Renaming packages

Using the DTUtil Package Management Utility

Other than using Management Studio to manage packages, you also have the assistance of a command prompt utility named DTUtil. The primary reason you need to understand DTUtil is that this utility permits you to manage packages using schedulers or batch files. As with using Management Studio, DTUtil enables you to copy, delete, move, sign, and even verify whether the server contains specified packages.

Using this utility, you include either the /SQL, /FILE, or /DTS options to specify where the packages that you want to manage are located. You use options (parameters) to specify particular behavior you want to use when running the utility. The options start with either a slash (/) or a minus sign (-), and can be added to the command line in any sequence.

You receive exit codes that let you know when something is wrong with your syntax or arguments, or you simply have an invalid combination of options. When everything is correct, DTUtil returns exit code 0 and displays the message "The Operation Completed Successfully." The following other exit codes may be returned:

➤ 1: Failed

➤ 4: Cannot locate package

➤ 5: Cannot load package

➤ 6: Cannot resolve the command

You must observe the following syntactical rules when you create the commands:

➤ Values for options must be strings, and must be enclosed in quotation marks or contain no whitespace.

➤ Escaping single quotation marks in strings is done by enclosing the double-quoted string inside single quotation marks.

➤ Other than passwords, there is no case-sensitivity.

One way you can use DTUtil is to regenerate package IDs for packages copied from other packages. Recall that when a copy of an existing package is made, the name and ID of the new package matches that of the copied package. You can use DTUtil along with the /I [D Regenerate] switch to regenerate the package IDs, and, in some cases, to correct corruption issues within your package.

> **NOTE** *To update multiple packages with just a single execution of* DTUtil, *you can create a batch file that can iterate through a given folder looking for all* .dtsx *(package) files and have* DTUtil *regenerate the package IDs. If you want to execute this command from within a batch file, use the following syntax from the directory containing the SSIS project:*
>
> ```
> for %%f in (<FilePath>\*.dtsx) do dtutil.exe /i /File %%f
> ```

By understanding the DTUtil utility, you have a powerful weapon to add to your package management arsenal.

Importing and Exporting Packages

Another common activity you must understand as an administrator involves the ways in which you can move packages among the various storage locations and formats. The import and export functionality enables you to add or copy packages from one storage location and format to another storage location and format. Thus, not only can you add or copy the packages, but also change storage formats (for example, from filesystem folders to the SQL Server msdb database).

To import a package using Integration Services from within Management Studio, follow these steps:

1. Open Management Studio, and connect to an Integration Services server.

2. In Object Explorer, expand the Stored Packages folder and any subfolders to locate the folder into which you want to import a package.

3. Right-click the target folder, and select Import Package.

4. On the Import Package dialog, select the package location from SQL Server, FileSystem, or SSIS Package Store.

5. On the Import Package dialog, when the package location is SQL Server, specify the server, authentication type, username, and password. When the package location is SSIS Package Store, specify the server.

6. Also on the Import Package dialog, click the Browse button next to Package path, and select the package to import. From this screen, you can also change the package name to how it should appear in the new location, and specify the protection level of the package.

Using similar steps, you can export packages. The one notable difference is that you right-click the package to be exported and select Export, rather than right-click the target folder and select Import. You can also perform these import and export operations using the DTUtil command-line utility.

Deployment

When Integration Services packages and solutions have been developed either on local computers or on development servers, they need to be deployed to test on production servers. Usually, you start the deployment process after you ensure that the packages run successfully within SSDT.

You deploy your packages or solutions via one of the following methods:

➤ Creating a package deployment utility and using the Package Installer Wizard

➤ Using import or export package utilities in Management Studio

➤ Saving or moving copies of packages in the filesystem

➤ Executing the DTUtil Package Management Utility

Often, the modifications made to your Integration Services solution dictate which deployment method and tools to use. For example, if you modify only a single package out of a 30-package solution, using the import package utility within Management Studio or saving or moving copies of packages in the filesystem might be simpler than deploying the entire solution using the Package deployment utility and Package Installer Wizard.

You can further categorize these four options for deployment into either automated and manual. Using a Package deployment utility with the Package Installer Wizard would be best categorized as an automated deployment method, whereas the other options represent manual deployment methods. The following sections take a detailed look at each of these deployment methods.

Automated Package Deployment

A common way to deploy packages involves using the Package deployment utility. This utility is only available in the package deployment model. It builds your SSIS packages, package configurations, and any supporting files into a special deployment folder located within the bin directory for the Integration Services project. In addition, this utility creates a special executable file named ProjectName.SSISDeploymentManifest and places it within this deployment folder. After creating the deployment utility, you then execute the manifest file to install the packages.

This deployment method relies upon two separate steps. First, you create a deployment utility that contains all the files needed for deployment. Second, you use the Package Installer Wizard to perform the deployment of these files to a target deployment server.

Using the Package Deployment Utility

The following steps walk you through using the Package deployment utility to deploy your Integration Services solution:

1. Open SQL Server Data Tools and an Integration Services solution.

2. Right-click your solution or project (the topmost node) in Solution Explorer, and select Properties.

3. On the [Solution/Project Name] Property Pages dialog, select the Deployment Utility section.

4. Within the Deployment Utility section of the Property Pages dialog, set the value of the CreateDeploymentUtility to True, as shown in Figure 20-2.

5. Optionally, you can configure the deployment to enable configuration changes by setting the AllowConfigurationChanges value to True. This option enables updating the configuration

of key elements of your packages that would be machine or environment dependent, such as server names or database initial catalogs that are both properties of database connection managers.

6. Build your project as normal. The build process creates the `ProjectName` `.SSISDeploymentManifest` file, and copies the packages to the `bin/Deployment` folder or whatever folder was specified for the `DeploymentOutputPath` on the project's Property Page in the Deployment Utility section.

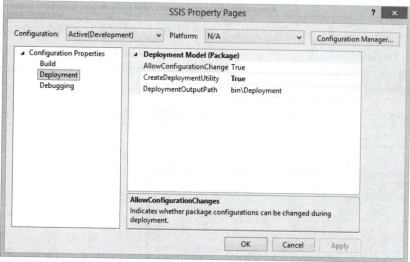

FIGURE 20-2

Because this utility copies all solution files as part of the process, you can deploy additional files (such as a `Readme` file) with the project by simply placing these files in the `Miscellaneous` folder of the Integration Services project.

Using the Package Installer Wizard

After you create an `SSISDeploymentManifest` file using the Package deployment utility, you can install the packages by using the Package Installer Wizard, which can be started by clicking the `SSISDeploymentMainfest` file. This wizard runs the `DTSInstall.exe` program, and copies the packages and any configuration to a designated location.

Using the Package Installer Wizard provides you with some useful functionality that you either can't find or is difficult to achieve using the manual deployment methods. For example, you may choose either a file-based or SQL-based deployment. Your file-based dependencies will always be installed to the filesystem. Another important (as well as useful) capability of this deployment process includes the ability to modify configurations for use on the target deployment server. This enables you to update the values of the configuration properties (such as server name) as part of the wizard.

Following are the steps you must take to ensure a successful deployment of your packages using the Package Installer Wizard:

1. Use Windows Explorer to browse to the file path location in which the SSISDeploymentManifest file was created (usually the solution or project location /bin/ Deployment).

2. After creating the files within the Deployment folder, copy the Deployment folder and all its files to a target deployment server.

3. On the target deployment server, open the Deployment folder, and double-click the SSISDeploymentManifest file to launch the Package Installer Wizard (DTSInstall.exe).

4. On the Deploy SSIS Packages page, select whether you want to deploy your packages to the filesystem or to SQL Server, as shown in Figure 20-3. Optionally, you can also have the packages validated after they have been installed.

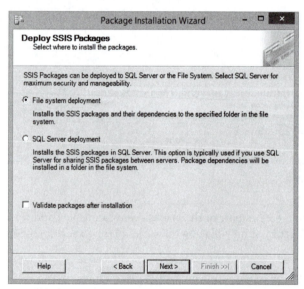

FIGURE 20-3

5. On the Select Installation Folder page, either provide a folder path for a filesystem deployment, or provide a server name and the appropriate server credentials for a SQL Server deployment.

6. For a SQL Server deployment, on the Select Installation Folder page, provide a folder path for the package dependencies that require storing within the filesystem. If you accept the default property here, you could be moving the location of your package configuration files.

7. Optionally, if the package includes configurations and you set the AllowConfigurationChanges value to True when the deployment manifest was created, the Configure Packages page displays so that you can update the values for the configurations.

8. Optionally, if you requested validation of the packages, the Packages Validation page displays so that you can review the validation results.

Import or Export Package Deployment

Earlier in this chapter, you learned about using the import and export functionality, which enables you to add or copy packages from one storage location and format to another storage location and format. One obvious use of this functionality is to deploy packages after development and testing have been completed.

An interesting benefit this approach may yield involves the capability of the import or export to change storage formats (for example, from filesystem folders to the SQL server msdb database). This alteration of storage formats may be useful for disaster recovery (as a further safeguard for your Integration Services solutions) by saving them in various storage formats and locations.

File Save/Move Package Deployment

Probably the simplest way to get packages deployed involves copying them out of the Visual Studio project bin directory and copying it to the target server. This method does not have any of the more useful capabilities, but it can work quite well for smaller-scale Integration Services solutions. One distinct capability missing from this deployment method is the ability to deploy to SQL Server.

DTUtil Package Deployment

As with using Management Studio, DTUtil enables you to copy or move packages. As previously stressed in this chapter, the benefit of using DTUtil is that the commands created can be scheduled or run later. Therefore, using these capabilities, you could schedule the deployment of your packages to another server simply by using DTUtil COPY or MOVE commands to move the modified packages to a target server.

The following example demonstrates how you can use a DTUtil copy command for deployment:

```
dtutil /DTS srcPackage.dtsx /COPY SQL;destPackage
```

ADMINISTRATION OF INTEGRATION SERVICES PACKAGES IN PROJECT DEPLOYMENT MODEL

Much of this chapter to this point has focused on the package deployment model, which was the only way to operate in SQL Server 2005 and 2008. In SQL Server 2012 and 2014, you can now administer and deploy packages as a project, which is a group of packages and how most developers operate. This section shows how to configure the SSIS catalog and then deploy packages to it.

Configuring the SSIS Catalog

In the package deployment model, you can deploy to the msdb database or the filesystem of the server. With the project deployment model, you can deploy only to the SSIS catalog, which exists inside the database instance. This means that you also no longer need the Integration Services Windows service. The packages execute in the context of the database instance, and if the database engine were to fail, SSIS also fails or fails over in a cluster.

Before you can deploy your project, you need an SSIS catalog to deploy to. To do this, open Management Studio and follow these steps:

1. Connect to the database engine in Management Studio.

2. Right-click on Integration Services Catalogs, and select Create Catalog. This opens the Create Catalog dialog box shown in Figure 20-4. In the dialog box, you must type a password that generates a key for encryption. Common Language Runtime (CLR) is also turned on here to execute packages via T-SQL. Click OK to create the catalog.

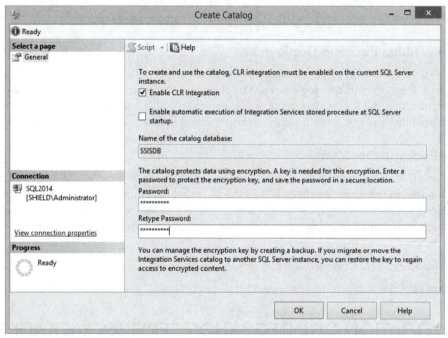

FIGURE 20-4

Creating the catalog also creates a database called `SSISDB`. There is only one catalog per database instance, and you can use this database to query to find some metadata about your packages. You can also read some of the tables in this database to gather operational data about which packages have failed recently from some of the logs.

With the catalog now created, it is time to configure it. To do so, right-click the previously created catalog and select Properties. This opens the Catalog Properties dialog box shown in Figure 20-5. In this dialog box, you can choose the level of logging and the number of days you're retaining the logs. You can set the level of logging to be basic (default), verbose, performance, or none. If you choose verbose or performance, you will see SSIS performance issues with SSIS packages. Those two options are only for temporary debugging of the package.

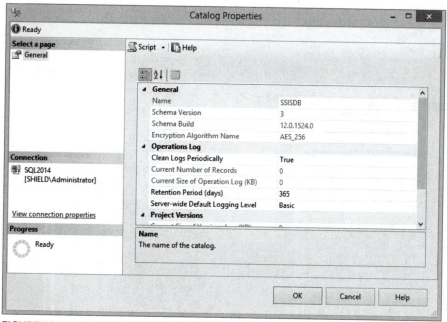

FIGURE 20-5

You can also select how many versions of the project will be kept as you deploy. This enables you to roll back to a previous release of the project. By default, ten versions of packages are kept.

Deploying Packages

The simplest way to deploy packages is with the project deployment model with the Integration Services Deployment Wizard. You can launch it from SSDT by right-clicking the project and selecting Deploy, or by selecting the wizard in the SQL Server 2014 ⇨ Integration Services program group. The wizard asks you a few questions to complete the deployment. The first screen (shown in Figure 20-6) asks to which server you want to deploy and which path.

If the folder does not exist on the server you want to deploy, click Browse and you can create it. To deploy, you must have a folder. The folder acts as a container for one or more projects, and helps control the configuration of your environment later.

After you select a valid path, select Next to deploy the package. You can also now find an .ispac file in your project's Deployment folder in Windows Explorer. If you send this one file to the administrator, he or she can double-click it to reopen this same wizard. The file contains all package and configuration information necessary for the entire project.

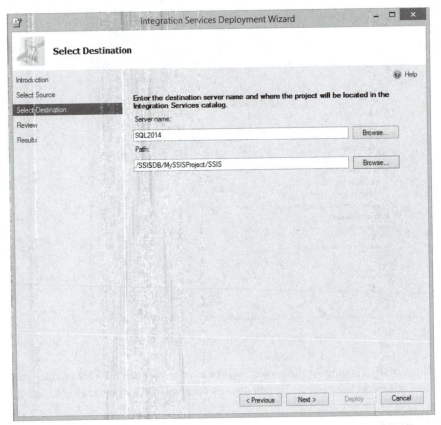

FIGURE 20-6

ROLLING PROJECT CHANGES

Imagine the developer accidentally sends the DBA the wrong project file to deploy, and, at 3 A.M., the DBA can't seem to get the environment rolled back. In SQL Server 2014, you can easily roll the project back by right-clicking the project in Management Studio and selecting Versions. In the Project Versions dialog box (shown in Figure 20-7), simply select the older version and click Restore to Selected Version to roll back the entire project to an earlier release. Do not use this as your core source control system. This is only a mechanism to roll back changes on your server and does not fix developer errors during development prior to the deployment.

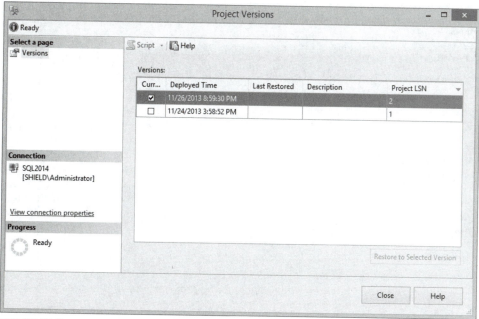

FIGURE 20-7

Configuring Packages

The next step after deployment is to configure the package to run in your environment. For example, the developer may have left the packages using the development server's name and passwords. In the package deployment model, you would use configuration files, but in the project deployment model, parameters are used. The developer's responsibility is to create parameters and configure the packages to use those parameters. When the developer creates those, the DBA can then change the values of those parameters to reconfigure the package.

Environments

Environments are ways to do a large reconfiguration of packages to point to new variables for different clients on the same server, or perhaps to reconfigure the packages to use development variables versus production variables. Environments contain a collection of variables that you can create that hold the configuration for the project or package. To do so, perform the following steps:

1. Open Management Studio, and expand the `Integration Services Catalogs` node.

2. Under the node expand your folder, right-click the `Environments` node, and select Create Environment.

3. For this example, create one environment called Client A and another called Client B. After each environment is created, right-click the environment and select Properties, which opens the Environment Properties dialog box, as shown in Figure 20-8.

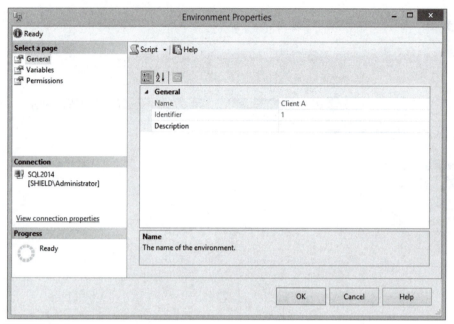

FIGURE 20-8

4. Go to the Variables tab and create a new string variable called `ServerName` with the value of `ServerA`. Repeat this step for the Client B environment but use `ServerB` for its value. You can also click Sensitive if you want to encrypt the value.

Using Environments

To use the environments, you must first allow the project to see the environments and then follow these steps:

1. Right-click the project in the folder and select Configure.

2. Then, go to the References page, and add a reference to any environment you want to be used by this project by clicking the Add button, as shown in Figure 20-9.

3. With the references now created, you can reconfigure the package to use them. In the Configure Project screen, go to the Parameters page, as shown in Figure 20-10. Here, you see a list of parameters and connection managers that you can easily configure outside the package. In Figure 20-10, the `ServerName` parameter is underlined. This means that it actually references the environment variable you created in the last section.

4. To change the value of any parameter, select the ellipsis button next to the parameter. This opens the Set Parameter Value dialog box shown in Figure 20-11. In this screen, you can change the parameter's value to any value you want by selecting the Edit Value radio box, or change it to an environment's value by selecting the environment's variable in the drop-down box.

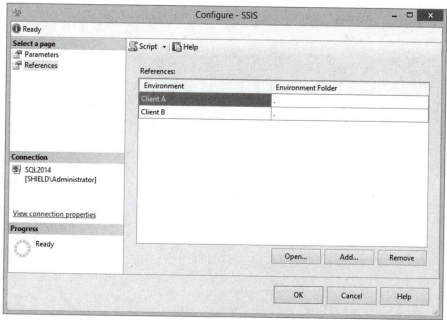

FIGURE 20-9

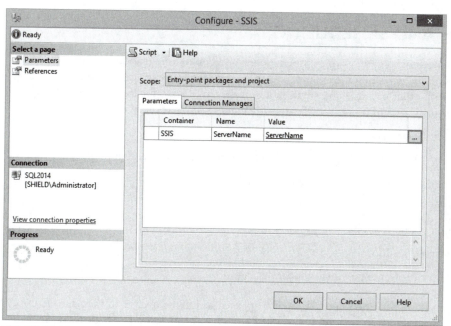

FIGURE 20-10

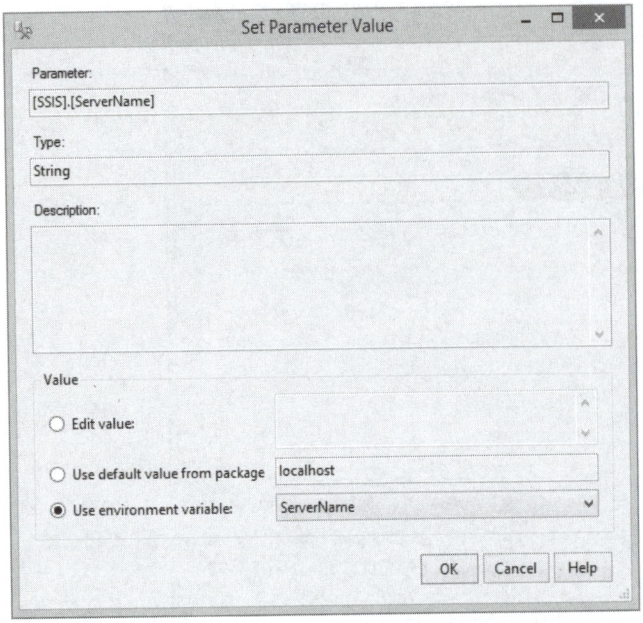

FIGURE 20-11

EXECUTION AND SCHEDULING

Thus far, you have looked at ways to create, manage, and deploy Integration Services solutions. This section focuses on the ways in which you can execute and schedule execution of these solutions. As you have seen with other package and solution administrative tasks, the execution of packages can be performed using different tools. Specifically, you can execute packages from the following:

➤ SQL Server Data Tools

➤ SQL Server Import and Export Wizard (when run from Management Studio)

➤ DTExec package execution command-line utility

➤ DTExecUI package execution utility

➤ Execute Package Tool

➤ SQL Server Agent jobs

➤ T-SQL (for project deployment model packages)

Which tool you should use often depends on factors such as in which stage of the package life cycle you are presently working. For example, the SSIS Designer within SSDT is a logical choice for package execution during development because of the features designed to assist in development (such as visually displaying package execution progress by changing the background color of tasks).

Running Packages in SQL Server Data Tools

Probably the first executions of packages will occur within SSDT because this is the development environment used to create your Integration Services solutions. Within SSDT, you simply either right-click the package and then select Execute Package, or press the F5 function key (or the Start button on the menu bar). The best way to execute packages from SSDT is by right-clicking the package and selecting Execute Package. Executing this way can prevent other packages from executing in case of misconfiguration.

Running Packages with the SQL Server Import and Export Wizard

The Import and Export Wizard is a utility for copying data between two locations. This can be between SQL Servers, or even between SQL Server and flat files. In the background, the Import and Export Wizard creates a very basic SSIS package.

When you use the Import and Export Wizard from Management Studio, you have an option to execute the package immediately. This provides an opportunity to both relocate and execute packages in one administrative step.

Running Packages with DTExec

The primary use of DTExec is to enable you to run packages either from the command line, from a script, or using a scheduling utility. All configuration and execution features are available using this command. You can also load and run packages from SQL Server, the SSIS service, and the filesystem.

The following additional syntactical rules must be followed when you create these commands:

➤ All command options start with a slash (/) or a minus sign (–).

➤ Arguments are enclosed in quotation marks when they contain any whitespace.

➤ Values that contain single quotation marks are escaped by using double quotation marks within quoted strings.

The general syntax for the DTExec commands is as follows:

```
Dtexec /option value
```

Following is an example that shows how to run a sample package called CaptureDataLineage .dtsx. The /FILE is pointing to a package stored on the filesystem in the package deployment model. The /CONNECTION switch is changing a connection manager at runtime.

```
Dtexec /FILE "C:\Program Files\Microsoft SQL Server\120\Samples\Integration
Services\Package Samples\CaptureDataLineage
Sample\CaptureDataLineage\CaptureDataLineage.dtsx " /CONNECTION
" (local).AdventureWorks "; "\ "Data Source=(local);Initial
Catalog=AdventureWorks;Provider=SQLNCLI.1;Integrated Security=SSPI;Auto
Translate=False;\ " "  /REPORTING
E
```

Whenever you execute a package using DTExec, one of the following exit codes may be returned:

➤   `0: Successful execution`

➤   `1: Failed`

➤   `3: Canceled by User`

➤   `4: Unable to Find Package`

➤   `5: Unable to Load Package`

➤   `6: Syntax Not Correct`

There are numerous options you can use to alter how the package execution is run. Some examples include /Decrypt, which sets the package password used to secure information within the package, and /Set, which you use to assign values to SSIS variables at runtime. The options are processed in the order in which they are specified. When using the /Set and /ConfigFile commands, the values are also processed in the order in which they are specified. Neither options nor arguments (except passwords) are case-sensitive.

Running Packages with DTExecUI (Package Deployment Model)

You can configure the various options you need to run packages using the graphical equivalent to the DTExec utility: the DTExecUI utility. With the wizard that this utility uses to gather details regarding the package execution, you can better understand many of the options and see the syntax required to run the package execution. To use this wizard, complete the following steps:

1. Launch the DTExecUI utility by double-clicking a file with a .dtsx extension, or, from inside Management Studio, by right-clicking a package and selecting Run.

2. Select the options that you need to run the package along the left side of the utility pages, and configure the options in the main part of the page. When you finish, you can view the last page, which shows you the command line needed to execute the package with the options you selected.

3. After you complete the various pages and review the command line that will be submitted, click the Execute button. This submits the command line to the Integration Services engine by using the DTExecUI utility. Be careful when you use this utility in a 64-bit environment because this utility runs in Windows on Win32, not on Win64. Thus, for 64-bit environments, you should use the 64-bit version of the DTExec utility at the command prompt, or use SQL Server Agent.

The main reason you should become more familiar with both the DTExec and DTExecUI utilities is that they are useful for testing your packages and ultimately validating the proper command line that you may schedule using the SQL Server Agent.

Running Packages with the Execute Package Tool (Project Deployment Model)

In the project deployment model, package execution and configuration are even easier. To execute packages in this model, complete the following steps:

1. Right-click the package in Management Studio, and select Execute. This opens the Execute Package dialog box shown in Figure 20-12.

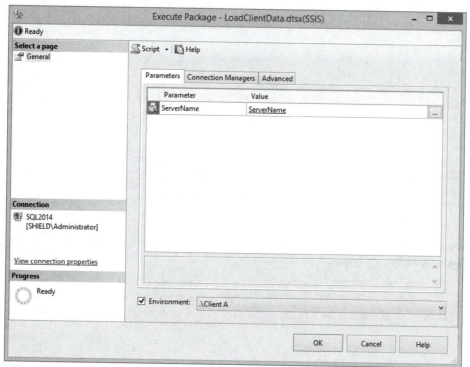

FIGURE 20-12

2. If your package requires an environment variable, check the box, and select your environment under which you want to execute. Doing this reconfigures the package to run under the collection of environment variables you created earlier.

3. If you need to change the connection managers, use the Connection Managers tab. This changes only the connection for one execution. In the Advanced tab, you can configure the package to run in 32-bit mode and the logging levels.

4. Click OK and the package executes asynchronously, meaning that the package execution runs in T-SQL in the background.

5. To view the status of the package execution, open the operational reports by right-clicking the SSIS catalog and selecting Reports ⇨ Standard Reports ⇨ Integration Services Dashboard. When opened, you can drill into the package execution by viewing the Overview report. This report (shown in Figure 20-13) enables you to see what parameters were passed to the package, as well as performance-related information.

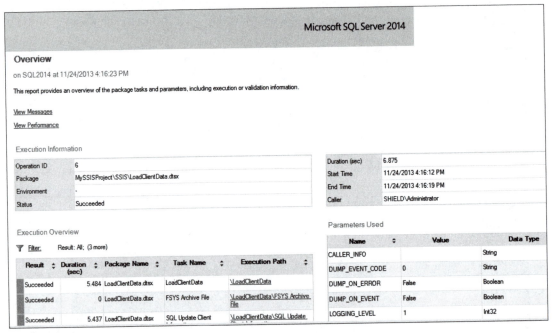

FIGURE 20-13

Scheduling Execution with SQL Server Agent

You need the ability to automate the execution of your Integration Services packages. Although many popular scheduling tools are available to accomplish this automation, here you learn how SQL Server Agent can assist in automating execution.

You start by creating a job and then including at least one step of the SQL Server Integration Services Packages type. You can also configure other job options. One option you may configure includes job notifications to send e-mail messages when the job completes, succeeds, or fails. Another job option you may configure includes job alerts to send notifications for SQL Server event alerts, performance condition alerts, or Windows Management Instrumentation (WMI) event alerts. Much of this configuration can be done through environments set up by the DBA.

To set up SQL Server Agent to execute a package, follow these steps:

1. Open Management Studio, and connect to a SQL Server.

2. In Object Explorer, expand the SQL Server Agent.

3. Within the SQL Server Agent section of Object Explorer, right-click the `Jobs` folder, and select New Job.

4. On the General page of the New Job dialog, provide a name, owner, category, and description for the job.

5. On the Steps page of the New Job dialog, click the New button along the bottom.

6. On the New Job Step dialog (shown in Figure 20-14), provide a step name, and select SQL Server Integration Services Packages type. In addition, configure the SSIS-specific tabbed sections with the information required to run your package. This SSIS section is almost identical to the options you provided when using the `DTExecUI` utility or the Package Execution dialog box. You have a package source that you set to SSIS Catalog for the project deployment model, or for the package deployment model you have SQL Server, filesystem, or SSIS package store. Next, you provide the package you want to schedule. When you select the Command Line tab, you can review the detailed command line that will be submitted by the SQL Server Agent to execute the package. You may want to compare this to the command-line values generated by the `DTExecUI` utility while you were testing package execution.

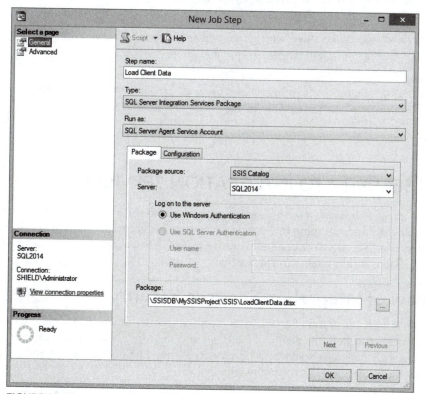

FIGURE 20-14

7. On the Advanced page of the New Job Step dialog, you can specify actions to perform when the step completes successfully, the number of retry attempts, the retry interval, and actions to perform should the step fail. After accepting the step configuration by clicking OK, the

Step page of the New Job dialog shows your new step. After adding multiple steps, you can reorder the steps on this page.

8. After accepting the step configuration, from the New Job dialog, you can optionally configure execution schedules, alerts, notifications, and target servers.

Running Packages with T-SQL

To execute a package in T-SQL, you can use the stored procedures in the catalog schema. First, you must create an execution using the `catalog.create_execution` stored procedure. This creates a unique identifier (GUID) that you then call and execute using the `catalog.start_execution` stored procedure. You can also set parameters of the package using the `catalog.set_execution_parameter_value` stored procedure. A complete execution can be seen in the following code snippet:

```
Declare @execution_id bigint
EXEC [SSISDB].[catalog].[create_execution] @package_name=N'2-OtherFeature.dtsx',
    @execution_id=@execution_id OUTPUT,
@folder_name=N'EDW', @project_name=N'ExpeditionDenali',
@use32bitruntime=False, @reference_id=Null
Select @execution_id
DECLARE @var0 sql_variant = N'localhost'
EXEC [SSISDB].[catalog].[set_execution_parameter_value] @execution_id,
    @object_type=30, @parameter_name=N'ServerName',
@parameter_value=@var0
DECLARE @var1 smallint = 1
EXEC [SSISDB].[catalog].[set_execution_parameter_value] @execution_id,
    @object_type=50, @parameter_name=N'LOGGING_LEVEL',
@parameter_value=@var1
EXEC [SSISDB].[catalog].[start_execution] @execution_id
GO
```

APPLYING SECURITY TO INTEGRATION SERVICES

You have now learned about most of the important package administrative tasks, including creating, managing, deploying, and executing Integration Services solutions. In addition, you have reviewed the major Integration Services service administrative tasks. This section describes the detailed security options available within Integration Services.

An Overview of Integration Services Security

Like all of SQL Server, Integration Services uses layers of security that rely on different mechanisms to ensure the integrity of both the design of packages and the administration and execution of packages. For the package deployment model, SSIS security is found on both the client and the server, implemented with features such as the following:

➤ Package protection levels to encrypt or remove sensitive information from the package

➤ Package protection levels with passwords to protect all or just sensitive information

➤ Restricting access to packages with roles

➤ Locking down file locations where packages may be stored

➤ Signing packages with certificates

Within packages, Integration Services generally defines sensitive data as information such as passwords and connection strings. You cannot define what should and should not be considered sensitive by SSIS unless you do so within a custom-developed task.

Integration Services defines sensitive information as the following:

➤ Connection string password (Sensitive) or Whole connection string (All)

➤ Task-generated XML nodes tagged as sensitive by SSIS

➤ Variables marked as sensitive by SSIS

For the project deployment model, much of this complexity goes away. As you deploy the package to the catalog database, the database handles the encryption, and then you secure the package with roles.

Securing Packages in Package Deployment Model

The two primary ways in which you secure packages within Integration Services include setting package protection levels and configuring appropriate database SSIS roles. The following sections look at these two security implementations.

Package Protection Levels

Many organizations have sensitive information in the SSIS package and want to control where that information resides within the organization. Your packages may contain passwords from your environment that, if executed by the wrong individual, may produce data files that could be sensitive.

These security concerns are addressed in Integration Services through the use of package protection levels. First, you can ensure that sensitive information that would provide details about where your information resides (such as connection strings) can be controlled by using `EncryptSensitive` package protection levels. Second, you can control who can open or execute a package by using `EncryptAll` package passwords.

The following package protection levels are at your disposal within Integration Services:

➤ Do not save sensitive.

➤ Encrypt (all/sensitive) with User Key.

➤ Encrypt (all/sensitive) with Password.

➤ Rely on server storage for encryption (SQL storage only).

The package protection levels are first assigned using SSDT. You can update these levels after deployment or during import or export of the package using Management Studio. In addition, you can alter the package protection levels when packages are copied from SSDT to any other location in which packages are stored. This is a nice compromise between development and administration because developers can configure these levels to suit their rapid development requirements, and administrators can follow up and revise these levels to meet production security standards.

Database Integration Services Roles for Package Deployment Model

If you deploy your packages to SQL Server (msdb database), you need to protect these packages within the database. Like traditional databases, this security is handled by using database roles. Three fixed database-level roles can be applied to the msdb database to control access to packages: db_dtsadmin, db_dtsltduser, and db_dtsoperator.

You apply these roles to packages within Management Studio, and these assignments are saved within the msdb database, in the sysssispackages table within the readerrole, writerrole, and ownersid columns. As the column names imply, you can view the roles that have read access to a particular package by looking at the value of the readerrole column, the roles that have write access to a particular package by looking at the value of the writterrole column, and the role that created the package by looking at the value of the ownersid column.

Follow these steps to assign a reader and writer role to packages for packages in the package deployment model:

1. Open Management Studio, and connect to an Integration Services server.

2. In Object Explorer, expand the Stored Packages folder, and expand the subfolder to assign roles.

3. Right-click the package within the subfolder to assign roles.

4. In the Packages Roles dialog, select a reader role in the Reader Role list and a writer role in the Writer Role list.

For packages in the project deployment model, the configuration steps are almost identical. The only difference is you configure the project, not the packages. You can right-click the project and select Properties and then go to the Permissions tab. Because packages in this model are all stored in the database instance, you can also run them with SQL authenticated logins.

You may also create user-defined roles if the default execute and update actions for existing roles do not meet your security needs. To define these roles, you connect to a SQL Server instance and open the Roles node within the msdb database. In the Roles node, right-click the database roles, and select New Database Role. After a new role has been added to the msdb database, you must restart the SSIS service before you can use the role.

These database Integration Services roles help to configure your msdb database sysssispackages table with package security options for reading and writing to specific packages. By applying this level of security, you provide security at the server, database, and table levels. Again, the security discussed within this section applies only when you save your packages within SQL Server (msdb database).

Database Integration Services Roles for Project Deployment Model

If you deploy packages using the project deployment model to the SSIS catalog, you can secure the packages at a project level. To do so, perform the following steps:

1. To configure permissions, right-click on the project in Management Studio and select Properties.

2. Go to the Permissions page (shown in Figure 20-15) and click Browse to grant rights to a new role or SQL Server user that's in the catalog database called SSISDB. One important note is that, by default, any user in the DBO role of the SSISDB database will automatically have full rights to your project unless you revoke those rights.

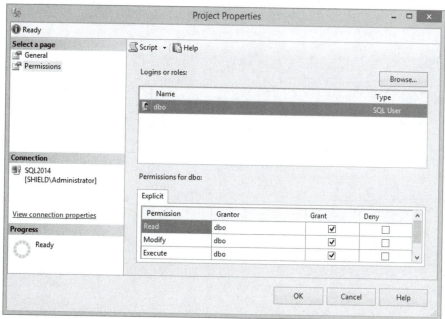

FIGURE 20-15

You can grant a user read rights if you just want them to be able to see the package and perhaps scan the metadata from the packages in the project. "Execute rights" enables the user or role to run a package in the project, and "Modify rights" enables the user to overwrite the project or configure it.

SUMMARY

You are now familiar with many of the various administrative functions related to Integration Services. There are two modes for deployment in SSIS: the package and project deployment models. The project deployment model only enables you to deploy the entire project and has most of the new

SSIS features (such as parameters) associated with it. The package deployment model is similar to what you've had in SQL Server 2005 and 2008. Packages in the project deployment model can be configured with environments easily so you can run the package with a set of variables for a given customer.

In Chapter 21, "Analysis Services Administration and Performance Tuning," you learn about similar administrative functions related to Analysis Services.

21

Analysis Services Administration and Performance Tuning

WHAT'S IN THIS CHAPTER?

➤ Understanding the two types of Analysis Services instances

➤ Administering the SSAS server properties

➤ Performance-tuning SSAS

Now that you've learned how to administer SQL Server Integration Services (SSIS), you will now continue your exploration of business intelligence (BI) administration by looking at how the DBA can perform SQL Server Analysis Services (SSAS) administrative tasks. The focus of this chapter is on the regular activities that a DBA may be called upon to perform, rather than the various details that developers might perform.

This chapter first takes a quick tour of Analysis Services so that you have some common frame of reference for both the covered administrative and optimization aspects. Next, you look at the administration of the Analysis Server, including reviewing server settings and required services. You also learn how to script various administrative activities (such as moving an Analysis Services database from development to production, and backing up an Analysis Services database). With that covered, you can learn about the management of the Analysis Services databases (including deployment, backup, restore, and synchronization), and then look at how you can monitor the performance of Analysis Services.

Next is an examination of the administration of storage (including storage modes and configuring partitions), as well as the design of aggregations. With storage concepts in mind, you next learn about the administration of processing tasks used to connect your designs with the data.

> **NOTE** *A discussion of how to use Analysis Services from a developer's perspective is beyond the scope of this book, so you do not examine that issue here. If you want to learn more, read* Professional Microsoft SQL Server Analysis Services 2012 with MDX and DAX *by Sivakumar Harinath, et al. (Indianapolis: Wiley, 2012).*

TOUR OF ANALYSIS SERVICES

To better understand the various touch points that you must manage as a DBA, let's begin with a quick tour of SSAS. The primary value that Analysis Services brings to businesses is useful, important, and timely information that can be difficult or even impossible to obtain from other sources (enterprise resource planning systems, accounting systems, customer relationship management systems, supply chain management systems, and so on). If you hear the term *self-service reporting*, the person is likely using an Online Analytical Processing (OLAP) system, which is the type of server that SSAS provides its users.

Analysis Services has two modes: Multidimensional OLAP (MOLAP) and the Tabular model. When you install an instance of Analysis Services you must decide which type of model to use. Each has its strengths and weaknesses, which are covered in this section.

The MOLAP model starts with a full star-schema data model that has data in it, and then builds a cube from this. The MOLAP model also gives you access to data mining and the highest possible scalability. Refreshing the data is much more flexible in this model, giving you options such as incremental loads.

> **NOTE** *For more information about data models, see* The Data Warehousing Toolkit: The Definitive Guide to Dimensional Modeling *by Ralph Kimball (Indianapolis: Wiley, 2013).*

The Tabular model has a lower learning curve and development cost by starting with data (with or without a data warehouse) and then building the cube from that data. It's extremely simple to build, enabling users to build the cube from within Excel or Visual Studio.

Whichever model you go with, you produce a cube behind the scenes with the Analysis Services engine. The decision for most depends on data refresh. With the Tabular model, the entire cube or partition is wiped and loaded when you refresh the cube. With the MOLAP model, you can refresh individual partitions through a full or incremental refresh of the data.

In both models, it is important to note that the OLAP engine must be optimized for lightning-quick data retrieval, but it also offers the following strategic benefits:

➤   Consolidated shared data access across multiple data sources that includes security at the most granular level, and the ability to write back data

➤ Rapid, unencumbered storage and aggregation of vast amounts of data

➤ Multidimensional views of data that go beyond the traditional row and column two-dimensional views

➤ Advanced calculations that offer better support and performance than relational database management system (RDBMS) engine capabilities

➤ Advanced data mining techniques to predict future activities based on the historical data in your database

So, what is the DBA role within SSAS? If you consider a traditional DBA skill set, Table 21-1 shows some of what a DBA does in SSAS.

TABLE 21-1: Mapping your DBA to SSAS

SQL SERVER DBA SKILL	SSAS SKILL COMPARISON
Creating logins	Creating roles
Creating indexes	Configuring aggregations
Partitioning tables	Partitioning measure groups
Backing up a database	Backing up an SSAS database

Now that you have basic understanding of the MOLAP and Tabular models, the next section focuses on a deeper dive into each of the models.

MOLAP Components

In Analysis Services, the Multidimensional OLAP model (or MOLAP model) is the cube. The MOLAP model cube combines dimensions and fact tables into a single navigable view for users to perform self-service analytics. Following is a look at the composition of the MOLAP model:

➤ **Data source view**—At the heart of the MOLAP model is the logical data schema that represents the data from the source in a familiar and standard manner. This schema is known as the data source view (DSV), and it isolates the cube from changes made to the underlying sources of data.

➤ **Dimensional model**—This model provides the framework from which the cube is designed. Included are the measures (facts) that users need to gain measurable insight into their business, and the dimensions that users employ to constrain or limit the measurements to useful combinations of factors.

➤ **Calculations (expressions)**—Often, a cube must be enhanced with additional calculations to add the necessary business value that it is expected to achieve. The calculations within the MOLAP model are implemented by writing Multi Dimensional Expression (MDX) language code snippets. MDX is to the cube what SQL is to the database. In other words, MDX is what you use to get information from a cube to respond to various user requests.

➤ **Familiar and abstracted model**—Many additional features enhance the analysis experience of end users by making their reporting and navigation through the cube more natural.

Again, like calculations, the model is often enhanced to include features not found in the data sources from which the cube was sourced. Features that are part of the MOLAP model include language translations, aliasing of database names, perspectives to reduce information overload, and Key Performance Indicators (KPIs) to quickly summarize data into meaningful measurements.

➤ **Administrative configuration**—With the cube designed and developed, the administrative aspects of the MOLAP model come to the forefront. Often, administrative tasks such as configuring the security to be applied to the cube, or devising a partitioning scheme to enhance both query and processing performance, are applied to the MOLAP model.

Tabular Model Components

A Tabular model has very similar components to the MOLAP model, except simplified. Instead of starting with a model and working backward, the user creates a Tabular model by first importing data. Then, the user creates the model with the data he or she imported. The data can be imported from a variety of sources, such as Excel, flat files, or nearly any data source that is compliant with OLE DB or ODBC. Following are some of the elements you'll find in a Tabular model:

➤ **Connections**—A list of data connections required to make the cube

➤ **Tables**—The actual data on which the cube is built

➤ **Roles**—The DBA mechanism to secure the cube or data in the cube

Analysis Services Architectural Components

Now that you understand the basics about the MOLAP and the Tabular models, it's time to turn to the components that make up SSAS. The Analysis Services server (msmdsvr.exe application) is implemented as a Microsoft Windows service, and consists of a query processor (for MDX queries and Data Mining Extensions (DMX) data-mining queries), an XMLA listener, and XML for Analysis (XLMA). The following list describes these components in greater detail:

➤ **Query processor**—The query processor parses and processes statements similarly to the query processing engine within SQL Server. This processor is also responsible for the caching of objects, storage of MOLAP model objects and their data, processing calculations, handling server resources, and managing transactions.

➤ **XML for Analysis**—XLMA is a SOAP-based protocol used as the native protocol for communicating with SSAS. All client application interactions use XMLA to communicate with SSAS. This protocol is significant in that clients who must communicate with SSAS do not need to install a client component, as past versions of Analysis Services required (such as PivotTable Services). As a SOAP-based protocol, XMLA is optimized for disconnected and stateless environments that require time- and resource-efficient access. In addition to the defined protocol, Analysis Services also added extensions to support metadata management, session management, and locking capabilities. You have two different methods to send XMLA messages to Analysis Services: The default method uses TCP/IP, and an alternative is HTTP.

➤ **XMLA listener**—This listener component facilitates and manages communications between various clients and the Analysis Services server. The port configuration for this listener is located in the `msmdsrv.ini` file, which is located in the `C:/Program Files/Microsoft SQL Server/MSAS12.MSSQLSERVER/OLAP/Config` folder by default. A value of `0` in this file under the `<Port>` tag simply indicates that SSAS is configured to listen on the default TCP/IP port of 2383 for the default instance of SSAS, and 2382 for other instances of SSAS.

SSAS named instances can use a non-default port. The SQL Server Browser keeps track of the ports on which each named instance listens, and performs any redirection required when a client does not specify the port number along with the named instance. You should use a firewall to restrict user access to Analysis Services ports from the Internet.

> **NOTE** *Analysis Services can be quite RAM and I/O hungry, and can suffocate your other resources (such as SQL Server) if not configured correctly. As your implementation crosses over into a larger implementation (for example, a hundred gigabytes of data), consider creating an isolated instance of Analysis Services on its own physical machine. Watch memory pressure to determine if you've reached this threshold.*

ADMINISTERING ANALYSIS SERVICES SERVER

This section looks at some of the important administrative activities for the server instance of SSAS. You can use two tools with SSAS: SQL Server Data Tools (SSDT) for development and SQL Server Management Studio for administration. This discussion first reviews the configuration settings for the server in Management Studio, followed by details of the services needed for SSAS to run. Finally, it ends with an introduction to the Analysis Services Scripting Language (ASSL) and its use in performing administrative tasks.

Notice that when you connect to SSAS inside of Management Studio, the icons for SSAS appear different based on the type of instance. You must connect to SSAS using Windows authentication only.

The dialog box shown in Figure 21-1 shows you two instances of SSAS. The first (`localhost`) is configured to run in traditional MOLAP model mode. The second (`localhost\tabular`) is a Tabular model instance. A third type that is out of scope for this book is used to support PowerPivot spreadsheets in SharePoint. This final type must be named `POWERPIVOT` and is essentially the same as the Tabular model instance.

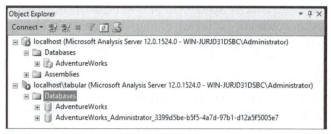

FIGURE 21-1

One thing you might notice in Figure 21-1 is the two similar databases in the `localhost\tabular` Tabular instance. This is because as you open the development tools, a temporary workspace is created while you modify the cube in the SSDT. The database name for this temporary workspace ends with the user's name and a GUID. This applies only to the Tabular models, because the MOLAP model is developed offline and then deployed to the server.

Server Properties

The server properties covered in this section are important for configuring the behavior of the SSAS server instance. To review and adjust the server properties, perform the following steps:

1. Open SQL Server Management Studio.

2. Connect to the Analysis Services server using the Object Explorer.

3. Right-click the server (the topmost node) and choose Properties.

By going to the Properties window, you can see dozens of properties that can help you tune your SSAS instance. You can see more properties by checking Show Advanced Properties check box. This section covers some of the important properties for SSAS.

Log Properties

If you're trying to diagnose why a query is taking longer than anticipated, this set of properties will help you troubleshoot performance. The log properties control how and where logging takes place. This property group includes details related to error logging, exception logging, the Flight Recorder (discussed later in this chapter), query logging, and tracing.

Some examples include the `QueryLog/QueryLogConnectionString` and `QueryLog/QueryLogTableName` properties, which direct the server to where the query logging is persisted (database and table). The `QueryLog/QueryLogConnectionString` property specifies the SQL Server instance and database that hold the Analysis Services query log. By default, after you specify this and set the `CreateQueryLog Table` property to `True`, SQL Server begins to log every tenth query to the table. If you have an active Analysis Services instance, you may want to decrease this setting to every hundredth query.

You can use this query log later to tune your SQL Server by using a Usage Based Optimization tool, whereby you tune the Analysis Services cube based on queries used in the past.

Memory Properties

The memory properties dictate how the server utilizes system memory resources. The `LowMemoryLimit` represents a threshold percentage of total physical memory, at which point the server attempts to perform garbage collection for unused resources to free more resources. The default value is configured at 65 percent of total physical memory. The `TotalMemoryLimit` tells the server how much of the total physical memory of the server hardware should be made available for use by Analysis Services. This limit is configured to 80 percent of all server memory by default.

Essentially, this means that Analysis Services can take between 65 and 80 percent of your server's memory resource and not give it back after it crosses 65 percent.

In the Tabular model, the `VertipaqMemoryLimit` property identifies at what point the SSAS will start allowing paging. This paging occurs only if the `VertipaqPagingPolicy` property is set to 1 (an advanced property only available if you check the Show Advanced Properties check box). Paging is turned on by default.

Network Properties

The network properties are a group of properties that control the network communication resources used by the server. Most notable are the settings that dictate whether the listener uses IPv4 or IPv6 protocols, and whether the server permits the use of Binary XML for requests or responses. In Windows Server 2008 R2 or later and Windows 7 or later, IPv6 is enabled by default.

OLAP Properties

The OLAP properties control how the server performs processing of the server objects (cubes, dimensions, and aggregations). Along with the processing properties, this section includes configuration properties for the way the server processes queries. Some of these query-processing properties are useful for simulating many testing scenarios. For example, you could adjust the `IndexUseEnabled`, `UseDataSlice`, and `AggregationUseEnabled` properties to benchmark different query-handling scenarios to determine whether some of these optimizations can provide the wanted performance enhancement.

Security Properties

The security properties are responsible for controlling how the server handles permissions. An example of these properties is `RequireClientAuthentication`, which configures whether clients connecting to the server require authentication. By setting `BuiltInAdminsAreServerAdmins` to `False`, local server administrators are not implicitly given administrator rights to your SSAS instance. Both the local administrators and the service account are given escalated rights to Analysis Services by default because of this property.

Required Services

The Windows services required by Analysis Services include SQL Server Analysis Services, SQL Server Agent (only if you want to schedule processing of jobs), and SQL Server Browser. The SQL Server Browser service supports the Analysis Services redirector used when clients connect to named instances.

Commonly, the logon account used by any service should be one that has the least number of privileges required to function properly. More often than not, an account that has network rights is required, and this account would need to be granted access rights on the remote resources in addition to configuring the account to be used by the service.

Analysis Services Scripting Language

Now, as a DBA, consider how many of your administrative tasks can be automated by using the built-in scripting language. The Analysis Services Scripting Language (ASSL) is a language that will automate administrative tasks for Analysis Services. This language is based on XML, and is what client applications use to get information from Analysis Services.

The scripting language has two distinct parts. The first part defines the objects and server properties that are part of the server, including the objects used to develop solutions (measures and dimensions). The other part requests that the server perform actions, such as processing objects or performing batch operations.

It is important to focus on the scripting language components that help you manage the Analysis Services server. Start by looking at some examples of how you can use the language to process objects. Processing enables you to fill objects with data so that they can be used by end users for business analyses. Some of the objects you can process include cubes, databases, dimensions, and partitions. To perform this processing using the scripting language, you use the language's `Process` command.

Following is an example of a script that would process the `AdventureWorks Employee` dimension:

```
<Batch xmlns="http://schemas.microsoft.com/analysisservices/2003/engine">
  <Parallel>
    <Process xmlns:xsd="http://www.w3.org/2001/XMLSchema"
xmlns:xsi="http://www.w3.org/2001/XMLSchema-instance"
xmlns:ddl2="http://schemas.microsoft.com/analysisservices/2003/engine/2"
xmlns:ddl2_2="http://schemas.microsoft.com/analysisservices/2003/engine/2/2"
xmlns:ddl100_100="http://schemas.microsoft.com/analysisservices/2008/engine/
      100/100"
xmlns:ddl200="http://schemas.microsoft.com/analysisservices/2010/engine/200"
xmlns:ddl200_200="http://schemas.microsoft.com/analysisservices/2010/engine/
      200/200"
xmlns:ddl300="http://schemas.microsoft.com/analysisservices/2011/engine/300"
xmlns:ddl300_300="http://schemas.microsoft.com/analysisservices/2011/engine/
      300/300"
xmlns:ddl400="http://schemas.microsoft.com/analysisservices/2012/engine/400"
xmlns:ddl400_400="http://schemas.microsoft.com/analysisservices/2012/engine/400/
      400">
      <Object>
        <DatabaseID>AdventureWorks</DatabaseID>
        <DimensionID>Dim Employee</DimensionID>
      </Object>
      <Type>ProcessUpdate</Type>
      <WriteBackTableCreation>UseExisting</WriteBackTableCreation>
    </Process>
  </Parallel>
</Batch>
```

You can script many of the actions that you can configure in SQL Management Studio. For example, you can generate the example script shown here by right-clicking the `AdventureWorks` cube and selecting the Process menu option. This displays the Process Cube dialog box shown in Figure 21-2. From this dialog box, click the Script button located along the top under the title bar, and then select the location in which you want to generate the script.

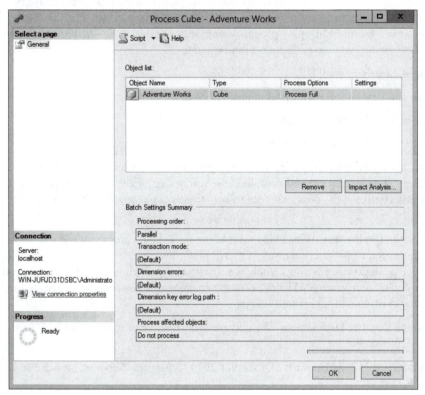

FIGURE 21-2

Don't worry about the options in this screen yet; the "Processing Analysis Services Objects" section later in this chapter discusses them.

ADMINISTERING ANALYSIS SERVICES DATABASES

Now that you understand more about the Analysis Services server, let's look at the administrative tasks needed for the databases that are ultimately deployed and run on the Analysis Services server. The primary tasks associated with managing the Analysis Services databases include deployment to the server, processing Analysis Services objects, performing disaster-recovery activities (such as backup and restore operations), and synchronizing databases to copy entire databases.

Deploying Analysis Services Databases

Obviously, without deploying databases, there is no value to running Analysis Services. When you deploy Analysis Services databases to the server, changes to the design of the database are applied to the server.

When performing administrative tasks, you can either use Management Studio to effect changes directly in a database in what is commonly referred to as *online mode,* or you can work within SSDT to effect changes via a Build and Deploy process commonly referred to as *offline mode.* More specific to database deployment, you have the following options:

➤ Deploy changes directly from SSDT

➤ Script changes and deploy from within Management Studio

➤ Make incremental deployments using the Deployment Wizard

➤ Process changes using the Synchronize Database Wizard

Many of these options are useful only in specific circumstances and, as such, are not given much attention in this chapter. The most useful and complete method to deploy the databases is to use the Deployment Wizard. Alternatively, the next best tool to assist with deployment is the Synchronize Database Wizard.

The main advantage of the Deployment Wizard is that it is the only deployment method that applies the database project definition to production or any environment, and enables you to keep many of the production database configuration settings (such as security and partitioning). This is important because neither direct deployment from SSDT nor scripting from Management Studio permits the deployment to maintain existing configuration settings.

The following steps show how the Deployment Wizard operates so you can understand how valuable it is for handling deployment:

1. From the Start menu, under Microsoft SQL Server 2014 ➪ Analysis Services, launch the Deployment Wizard.

2. On the Specify Source Analysis Services Database page, enter a full path to an Analysis Services database. This file, with the extension of .asdatabase, should be provided to you by the SSAS developer, or you can find it under the SSAS project folder. This one file contains all the metadata for the cube, security, and partitions. It does not contain any data.

3. On the Installation Target page shown in Figure 21-3, indicate the server to which the database should be deployed, along with the wanted database name. (It defaults to the filename of the database.) If you don't like the default database name, you can type over it.

4. On the Specify Options for Partitions and Roles page shown in Figure 21-4, indicate which configuration options ("Partitions" or "Roles and members") should be maintained on the deployment target database and, thus, not overwritten by this deployment. This screen is especially useful if you make changes in Management Studio to roles or partitions, and do not want the developer's files to overwrite your own configuration.

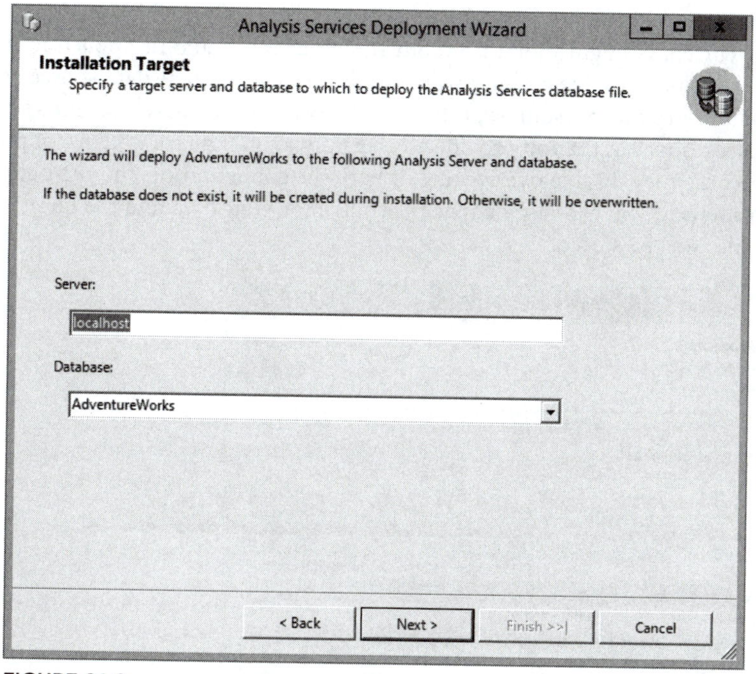

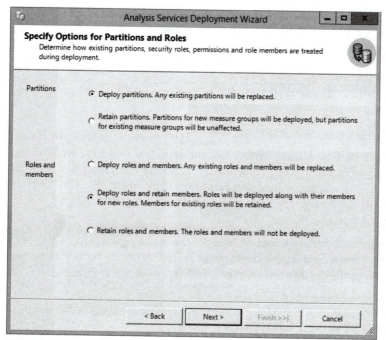

FIGURE 21-3

FIGURE 21-4

5. On the Specify Configuration Properties page shown in Figure 21-5, select which configuration settings from the current configuration file (`.configsettings`) should be applied to the target database. These settings provide a useful way to redirect items such as data source connection strings to point to production sources, rather than those used for development and testing. The Retain check boxes at the top provide an elegant way to manage updates of previous deployments because they disable overwriting of both the configuration and the optimization setting. On this screen, you can also change the source for your data and the target of where your physical files will be stored.

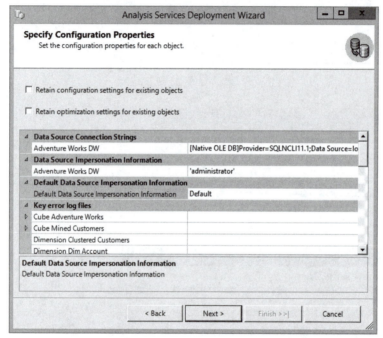

FIGURE 21-5

6. On the Select Processing Options page shown in Figure 21-6, enter the desired processing method and change any writeback table options that the developer may have set. To support a robust deployment, you can also select the option to include all processing in a single transaction that can roll back all changes should any part of the deployment fail. The "Default processing" method enables Analysis Services to review the modifications to be applied and determine the optimal processing needed.

7. On the Confirm Deployment page is an option to script the entire deployment. This option is useful when either the person running the Deployment Wizard is not authorized to perform the actual deployment, or the deployment must be scheduled so as not to interfere with other activities.

Processing Analysis Services Objects

Now that you understand how to deploy Analysis Services databases, you must add data to these objects by processing them. In addition, if the cubes must be updated to reflect development changes made after the initial deployment, you must reprocess them. Lastly, when data sources have changes made to their information, you must perform (minimally) an incremental reprocessing of the cube to ensure that you have up-to-date data within the Analysis Services solution. Developers often build and test designs locally; the local schema from SSDT must first be deployed to the server before performing any processing.

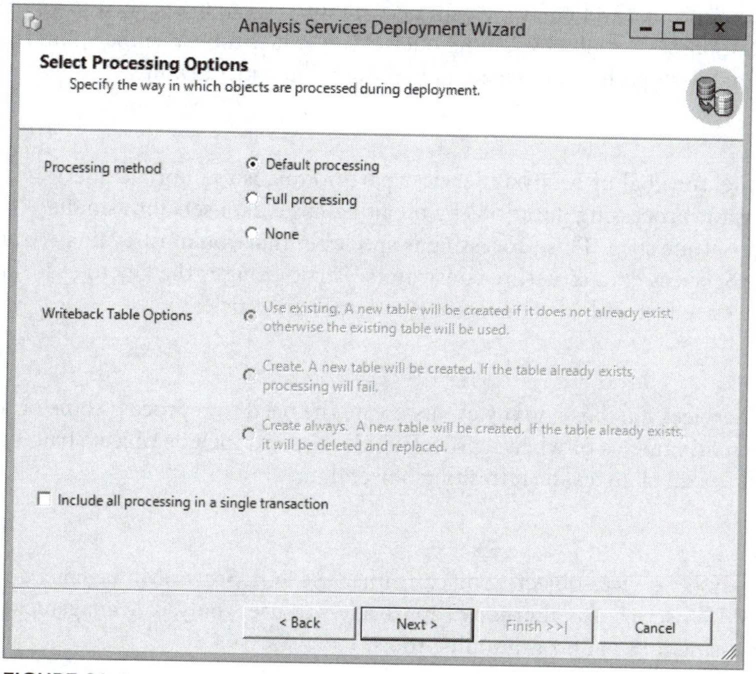

FIGURE 21-6

Processing a MOLAP Model

The Analysis Services MOLAP model objects that require processing include measure groups, partitions, dimensions, cubes, mining models, mining structures, and databases. The processing is hierarchical—that is, processing an object that contains any other objects also processes those objects.

For example, consider a database that includes one or more cubes, and these cubes contain one or more dimensions. So, processing the database would also process all the cubes contained within that database, and all the dimensions contained in or referenced by each of the cubes. For the Tabular model, you simply reprocess the tables fully (not incrementally).

The following sections cover how to process individual objects. If your SSAS database is smaller (roughly less than 20GB), you could potentially process the entire database and still be online prior to your users needing the data. You could then do this by fully processing the database (essentially a wipe and load) with much less complexity to you.

Processing Dimensions

Analysis Services processes dimensions by simply running queries that return data from the data source tables for the dimensions. This data is then organized into the hierarchies and ultimately into map files that list all the unique hierarchical paths for each dimension. Processing dimensions can be optimized primarily through strategic indexes on the primary key and other key attributes. Prior to processing your cube or partition, you must first process the dimension if you are processing items selectively.

Processing Cubes

The cube contains both measure groups and partitions, and is combined with dimensions to give the cube a data definition. You can process a cube by issuing queries to get fact-table members and the related measure values such that each path of dimensional hierarchies includes a value.

Processing Partitions

Just as in database partitioning, the goal of Analysis Services partitioning is to improve query response times and administrator processing durations by breaking large data sets into smaller files—typically, by some sort of time slice. This processing is special in that you must evaluate your hardware space and Analysis Services data structure constraints. Partitioning is the key to ensuring that your query response times are fast and your processing activities are efficient.

Reprocessing

After deploying an Analysis Services database, many events create the need to reprocess some or all the objects within the database. Examples of when reprocessing is required include object structural/schema changes, aggregation design changes, or refreshing object data.

Performing Processing

To perform processing of Analysis Services objects, you can either use SQL Server Management Studio or SSDT, or run an XMLA script. An alternative approach is to use Analysis Management Objects (AMO) to start processing jobs via programming tools.

> **NOTE** *When using these methods to process manually, as Analysis Services objects are being committed, the object is not available to process user requests. That's because the processing commit phase requires an exclusive lock on the Analysis Services objects being committed. User requests are not denied during this commit process, but rather are queued until the commit successfully completes. One alternative to processing your cube manually is called proactive caching. This is a more advanced option that incrementally gathers new data, and loads the data into a new cached cube while queries are still happening in the original cube. As soon as the processing finishes, the new cube is opened to users and the old one is disposed. Once configured, your cube remains online during processing, and changes automatically move online and become available to your users a few moments after being inserted into the warehouse.*

To perform processing for an Analysis Services database from within SQL Server Management Studio, follow these steps:

1.   Open Management Studio, and connect to an Analysis Services server.

2. Right-click an Analysis Services database and select Process. The Process Database dialog box appears, where you can configure the details of the processing (refer to Figure 21-2).

3. Click the Impact Analysis button to get an idea of the effect that performing the specified process can have on related objects. For example, by fully processing a dimension, all measure groups pointing to that dimension also must be processed.

4. Configure processing options such as the processing order by clicking Change Settings. You should see the screen shown in Figure 21-7. Available options for the order include processing in parallel within a single transaction, or processing sequentially within one or separate transactions. An important option is "Process affected objects." This option controls whether all the other objects that have dependencies on the database can also be processed. A common architectural design employed in data warehousing involves the use of shared dimensions. These dimensions can be shared across the organization and allow for low maintenance and uniformity. Therefore, the "Process affected objects" setting can have a profound impact when you use an architecture involving shared dimensions, because it may force reprocessing of many other databases in which the shared dimensions are used.

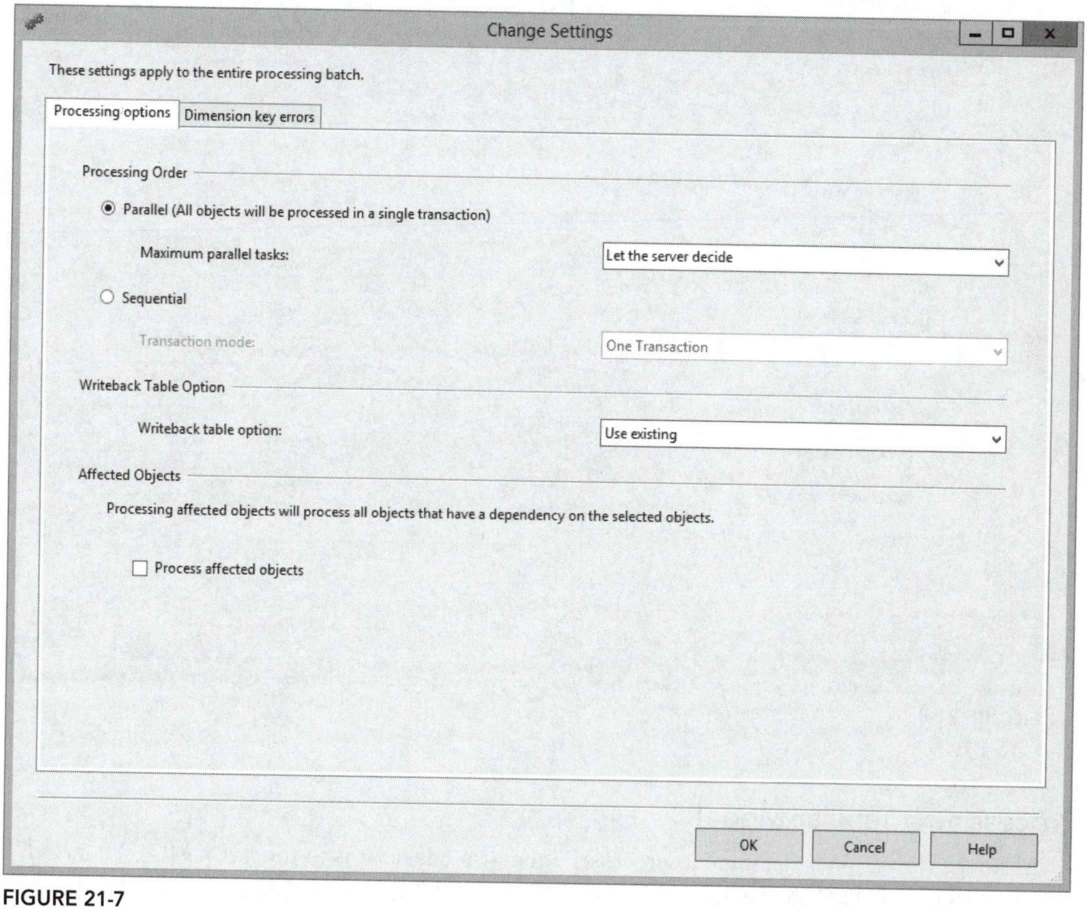

FIGURE 21-7

5. You can also configure sophisticated dimension key error handling by clicking the "Dimension key errors" tab, as shown in Figure 21-8. For example, you can configure the options to use a custom error configuration, which converts key errors to an unknown record, rather than terminating the processing. In addition, you can specify error limits and what action to take when those limits have been exceeded. Lastly, you can choose to handle specific error conditions such as "Key not found" or duplicate keys by reporting and continuing to process, by ignoring the error and continuing to process, and by reporting and stopping the processing. Using these settings typically means you have data issues and you should go back to the extract, transfer, and load (ETL) to fix such issues, because you're simply masking the issues.

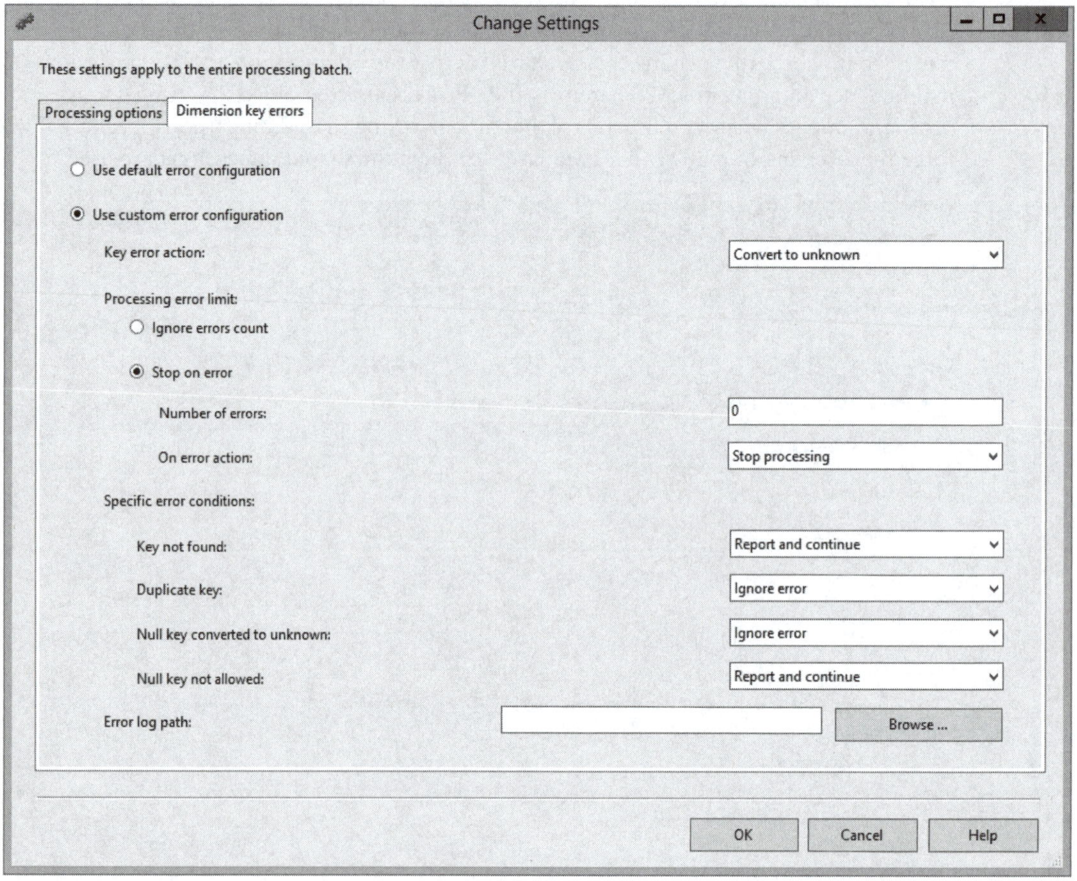

FIGURE 21-8

Processing a Tabular Model

Although the action is the same to process a Tabular model as it is to process a MOLAP model, what happens behind the scenes is different. To process a Tabular model, right-click the object you want to process, and select Process in Management Studio to produce the screen shown in Figure 21-9. Doing this goes back to the original data sources (SQL Server, Access, Excel, and so on) and wipes and loads the SSAS tables.

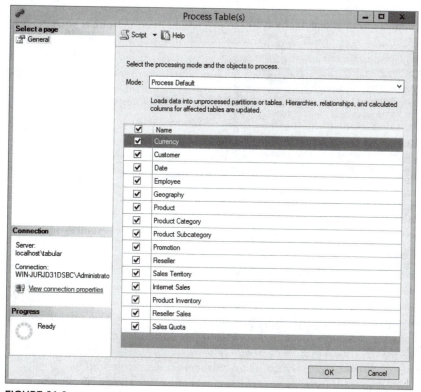

FIGURE 21-9

When you click OK, the tables begin to refresh. Figure 21-10 shows the number of rows that were refreshed per table. If the data sources have moved (such as an Access database moving to a new directory), you can change its path in the Connections node of Management Studio.

Backing Up and Restoring Analysis Services Databases

Without question, performing backup and restore tasks are common functions within the domain of any DBA. A backup of the Analysis Services database captures the state of the database and its objects at a particular point in time to a file on the filesystem (named with an .abf file extension), whereas recovery restores a particular state of the database and its objects to the server from a backup file on the filesystem. Backup and recovery, therefore, are useful for data recovery if problems occur with the database on the server in the future, or simply to provide an audit of the state of the database. Although you have ways to back up just the physical files in SSAS, using the backup steps in this section will produce one reliable file that's encrypted and compressed.

FIGURE 21-10

> **WARNING** *The backups back up only the Analysis Services database contents, not the underlying data sources used to populate the database. Therefore, you must perform a backup of the data sources using a regular database or filesystem backup with the Analysis Services backup to capture a true state of both the Analysis Services objects and their sources at or about the same point in time.*

The information that the backup includes varies depending on the storage type configured for the database. A detailed message displayed at the bottom of the Backup Database dialog box clearly communicates the various objects included in a backup based on the type of storage. Following are the available options to be included in the backup:

➤ Metadata that defines all the objects

➤ Aggregations calculated

➤ Source data used to populate the objects

Now, let's examine how to perform these backup functions for Analysis Services databases. Again, you can use Management Studio to assist with the setup and configuration of these tasks and script the results to permit scheduling. Perform the following steps:

1. Open Management Studio, and connect to an Analysis Services server.

2. Right-click an Analysis Services database and select Backup. The Backup Database dialog box shown in Figure 21-11 appears. Here you can configure the details of the backup, such

as applying compression, where the backup file should be located, or whether the file should be encrypted. Storage types are covered later, but you get a clear statement of what information is part of the backup at the bottom of this dialog box. Basically, the backup is backing up only the Analysis Services information (partitions, metadata, source data, and aggregations) available to a database based on the storage type.

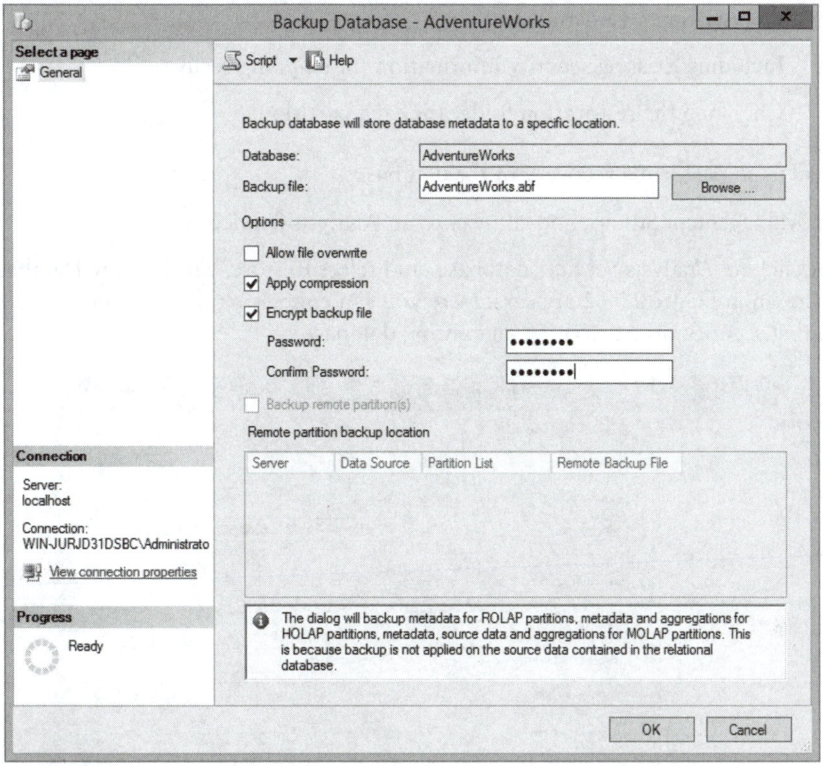

FIGURE 21-11

3. Optionally, you can script the backup by clicking the Script button along the top of the dialog box. The resulting script looks like the following example (including the password not shown here):

```
<Backup xmlns="http://schemas.microsoft.com/analysisservices/2003/engine">
  <Object>
    <DatabaseID>AdventureWorks</DatabaseID>
  </Object>
  <File>AdventureWorks.abf</File>
  <Password>password</Password>
</Backup>
```

4. The script will be opened automatically in a new XMLA query window in SQL Server Management Studio. You can choose to execute the script here as you would with MDX and T-SQL, copy it to another server, or save it for later use. Now that you have a backup

of an Analysis Services database, it's time to turn your attention to the recovery of Analysis Services databases. Recovery takes a previously created backup file (named with an .abf file extension) and restores it to an Analysis Services database. Several options are available during this process:

➤ Using the original database name (or specifying a new database name)

➤ Overwriting an existing database

➤ Including existing security information (or skipping security)

➤ Changing the restoration folder for each partition

Follow these steps to perform a recovery of the database:

1. Open Management Studio, and connect to an Analysis Services server.

2. Right-click an Analysis Services database, and select Restore. The Restore Database dialog box shown in Figure 21-12 appears. Here you can configure the restoration details, such as including security or overwriting an existing database.

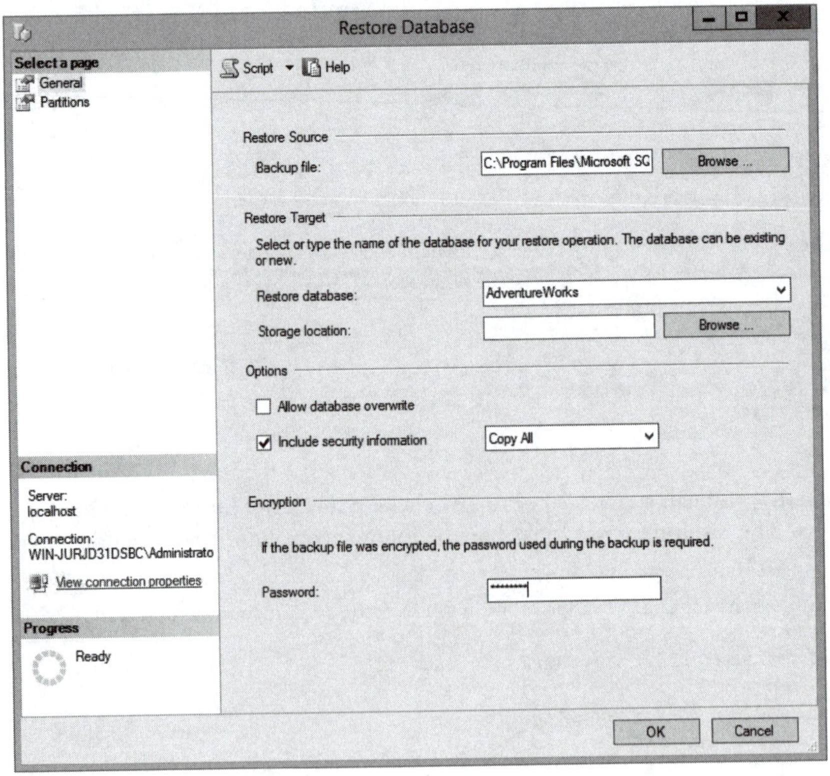

FIGURE 21-12

3. Optionally, you can script the restore by clicking the Script button along the top of the dialog box. The resulting script would look like the following example (including, again, a poor practice of including the password):

```
<Restore xmlns="http://schemas.microsoft.com/analysisservices/2003/engine">
  <File>C:\Program Files\Microsoft SQL Server\MSAS12.MSSQLSERVER\OLAP\Backup\
    AdventureWorks.abf</File>
  <DatabaseName>AdventureWorks</DatabaseName>
  <Password>password</Password>
</Restore>
```

4. The script will be opened automatically in a new XMLA query window in SQL Server Management Studio. You can choose to execute the script here as you would MDX or T-SQL, copy it to another server, or save it for later use.

You can also click the Partitions tab along the left side of the dialog box to change the storage location of each of the partitions.

Synchronizing Analysis Services Databases

Another important activity to perform involves synchronizing Analysis Services databases from one server to another. This is usually done as a mechanism for deploying from a test or quality assurance (QA) server to a production server. This feature is attractive for this purpose because users can continue to browse the production cubes while the synchronization takes place. When the synchronization and processing completes, a user is automatically redirected to the newly synchronized copy of the database, and the older version is removed from the server.

This differs greatly from what happens when you perform a deployment because part of the deployment usually involves processing of dimensions and cubes. As you may recall, certain types of processing of Analysis Services objects require that the cube be taken offline, making it unavailable to users until the processing completes.

As with many other database tasks, you can run the synchronization immediately from the Synchronize Database Wizard, or you can save the results of the selections to a script file for later execution or scheduling.

To synchronize an Analysis Services database between servers, follow these steps:

1. Open Management Studio, and connect to the target Analysis Services server.

2. On this target server, right-click the databases folder, and select Synchronize.

3. On the Select Databases to Synchronize page, specify the source server and database. The destination server is hard-coded to the server from which you launched the synchronization.

4. If applicable, on the Specify Locations for Local Partitions page, the source folder displays the folder name on the server that contains the local partition, whereas you can change the destination folder to reflect the folder into which you want the database to be synchronized.

5. If applicable, on the Specify Locations for Remote Partitions page, you can modify both the destination folder and server to reflect where you want the database to be synchronized. In addition, if the location has remote partitions contained in that location that must be included in the synchronization, you must place a check beside the Sync option.

6. On the Specify Query Criteria page, enter a value for the security definitions and indicate whether compression should be used. The security options include copying all definitions and membership information, skipping membership information but including the security definitions, and ignoring all security and membership details.

7. On the Select Synchronization Method page, you can either run the synchronization immediately, or script to a file for later use in scheduling the synchronization.

Processing is one of those topics where the lines between development and production DBAs blur. The same line becomes blurred with performance-tuning a cube. The developer will likely perform the base performance tuning, but will rely on the DBA to create long-term performance-tuning through aggregations.

ANALYSIS SERVICES PERFORMANCE MONITORING AND TUNING

Successful use of Analysis Services requires continual monitoring of how user queries and other processes perform, and making the required adjustments to improve their performance. The main tools for performing these tasks include the SQL Profiler, performance counters, and the Flight Recorder.

Monitoring Analysis Services Events

You now have two ways to monitor SQL Server and Analysis Services: SQL Server Profiler and xEvents. Profiler will eventually be removed from SQL Server in a future release, making xEvents the future. The events you trap are the same whether you use xEvents or Profiler.

Chapter 12 provides detailed coverage of how to use SQL Profiler, so here you learn what is important about using this tool for monitoring your Analysis Services events. With SQL Server Profiler, you can review what the server does during processing and query resolution. Especially important is the ability to record the data generated by profiling to either a database table or file to review or replay it later to get a better understanding of what happened. Lastly, you can place the events side by side with any machine or SSAS performance counters to spot trends affecting performance.

The main focus here is tracing the Analysis Services server activity and investigating the performance of the MDX queries submitted to the server to process user requests for information. The useful event categories include the following:

➤ Command events that provide insight into the actual types of statements issued to perform actions

➤ Discovery events that detail requests for metadata about server objects, including the Discovery Server State events (such as open connections)

➤ Error and Warning events that show any errors or warnings being thrown by the instance of SSAS

➤ Query events that trap queries being passed into SSAS

Because of all the detail that a trace returns, use the Column Filter button to display only the activities sent to a specific Analysis Services database. You can also use these traces to replay against other servers to see how your server will scale.

Using Flight Recorder for After-the-Fact Analysis

As an administrator, you are often disappointed when you cannot find the cause of a particular problem. Mostly, you are stymied when you cannot reproduce reported problems. These situations arise as you attempt to re-create what happened to determine how things could have been handled differently to avoid the reported problem.

Using the Flight Recorder, you may be able to replay the problem conditions that led to the reported problems. The Flight Recorder operates similarly to a tape recorder. It captures the Analysis Services server activity during run time without requiring a trace. Each time the server restarts, a new trace file automatically starts. In addition, the recorder is automatically enabled and can be configured using the Analysis Services Server Properties.

To use the trace file created by the Flight Recorder to replay server activity, follow these steps:

1. Open SQL Server Profiler, and open the trace file created by the Flight Recorder, located by default at `C:/Program Files/Microsoft SQL Server/MSAS12.MSSQLSERVER/OLAP/Log` and named `FlightRecorderCurrent.trc`.

2. On the toolbar select Replay ⇨ Start.

3. On the Connect to Server dialog box, enter the server name and authentication information.

4. On the Replay Configuration dialog box, set up the playback features you desire, such as replaying only statements issued to the server within a given timeframe.

This replay is rather useful because Analysis Services will begin to run the statements captured in the trace. Obviously, factors such as number of open connections and even the number of sessions that existed at the time of the original problem are important to consider when troubleshooting problems. When you replay the traces made by the Flight Recorder, these factors are simulated on your behalf.

> **NOTE** *You can also capture the MDX out of this trace file to run as a SQL Server Agent job. Doing so warms the SSAS cache in MOLAP model mode, and brings the data off the disk and into memory (memory permitting).*

SUMMARY

You covered a lot of ground in this chapter while learning about the various administrative functions related to Analysis Services. You can use two types of models in SSAS: MOLAP and Tabular.

Administration for the Tabular model is similar to the MOLAP model, but the processing involves refreshing the entire table. You are now equipped to deploy new databases, as well as changes to existing databases, using the Analysis Services Deployment Wizard. You have also learned how to perform backups and restores of Analysis Services databases through the GUI and scripting.

Now that you've learned about administering Analysis Services, you can move on to Chapter 22, which discusses how to administer the Reporting Services (SSRS) in SQL Server 2014.

22

SQL Server Reporting Services Administration

WHAT'S IN THIS CHAPTER?

➤ Using SQL Server Configuration Manager to set up your newly installed SQL Server Reporting Services server

➤ Navigating and understanding the properties associated with an installed Reporting Services server

➤ Managing and executing reports with Report Manager

WROX.COM CODE DOWNLOADS FOR THIS CHAPTER

The wrox.com code downloads for this chapter are found at www.wiley.com/go/prosql2014admin on the Download Code tab. The code is in the Chapter 22 download and individually named according to the names throughout the chapter.

After reading this chapter, you'll understand why SQL Server Reporting Services (SSRS) is one of the simplest tools in the Microsoft stack to configure. This is because of the easy-to-use SQL Server Configuration Manager and the complete (yet understandable) properties of an SSRS server, accessed through SQL Server Management Studio.

To understand how SSRS works, you must understand how a report is built and executed. Thus, a brief overview of Report Builder (which is a useful way for DBAs to create reports) is in order. Then the real fun begins as you see SSRS in action through the use of Report Manager. Report Manager is a suite of web pages that ships with SSRS. These pages enable users to easily execute their reports and give administrators methods to manage, schedule, and maximize server resources.

SQL SERVER REPORTING SERVICES CONFIGURATION MANAGER

SSRS is configured using its own tool, separate from the SQL Server Configuration Manager. In most cases, you'll have already configured your instance of SSRS during the install of SQL Server. Following are reasons why you might need to alter the configuration:

➤ You need to change a value, such as the service account that SSRS runs under.

➤ During install, you chose not to configure SSRS.

➤ You set up additional instances of SSRS.

➤ You need to configure a scale-out implementation of SSRS.

➤ You install SSRS after the initial database engine install.

You can accomplish any of these tasks (and more) using the Reporting Services Configuration Manager. Complete the following steps to start using this tool:

1. To launch the Configuration Manager, go to Start ➪ Microsoft SQL Server 2014 ➪ Configuration Tools ➪ Reporting Services Configuration Manager.

> **NOTE** *The Reporting Services Configuration Manager is version-specific. The configuration tool that came with SQL Server 2014 may be used only to manage a SQL Server Reporting Services 2014 server. To manage the SSRS server for previous versions of SQL Server, use the Configuration Manager specific to that product.*

2. When the tool launches, select the SSRS server to configure, as well as the instance of SSRS, as shown in Figure 22-1.

   Typically, you configure the computer on which the Reporting Services Connection Manager is working, but you can also manage multiple SQL Server 2014 Reporting Services servers using the same Configuration Manager.

3. After you select the server to manage, simply click Connect to open the main tool.

The opening screen shown in Figure 22-2 displays some basic information about the server you are configuring. You can see the specific instance name and ID, along with the specific edition and version number. The name of the database containing the reporting items is also shown. In the example shown in Figure 22-2, the default of ReportServer was taken.

You can see the service runs in Native mode. SSRS can also run in SharePoint Integrated mode. Starting with 2012, configuration of SSRS running in SharePoint Integrated mode should be done through the SharePoint console, not the SSRS Configuration Manager.

In SharePoint Integrated mode, SharePoint manages all aspects of reporting. Reports are uploaded to and stored in SharePoint. Security and subscriptions are controlled within SharePoint. A feature that is only available in SharePoint Integrated mode is Data Alerts. These are similar to subscriptions in that they send out information to users but only get sent when certain conditions are met, thus alerting the recipient of an event. Also, features of SharePoint libraries such as version control and alerts are supported with reports.

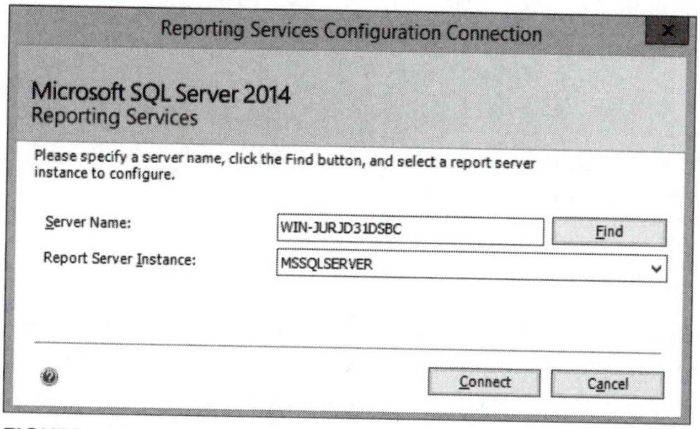

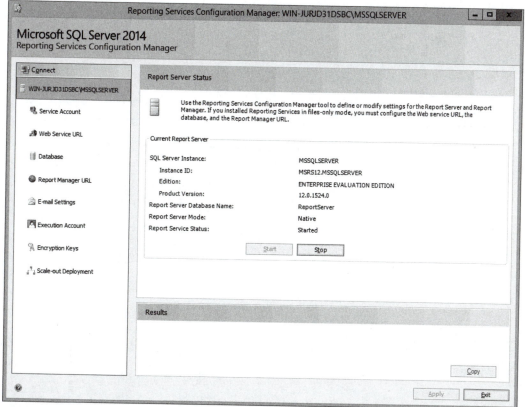

FIGURE 22-1

FIGURE 22-2

However, there are some disadvantages to running SSRS in Integrated mode. Not supported when running in SharePoint Integrated mode are items such as custom security extensions, the capability to manage reports within Report Manager, and the capability to use the Reporting Services Configuration Manager.

> **NOTE** *A discussion about how to configure with SharePoint console is outside the scope of this chapter, but you can fine more information on this topic at* `http://msdn.microsoft.com/en-us/library/bb326356.aspx`.

Finally, you might occasionally have changes that prompt you to recycle SSRS. You can do so by starting and stopping the service, as shown in Figure 22-2.

The Service Account

The Report Server service account is the user account under which SSRS runs. Although initially configured during the installation of SQL Server, it can be updated or modified on the Service Account screen shown in Figure 22-3. It is under the service account that the Report Server web service, Report Manager, and background process tasks all run.

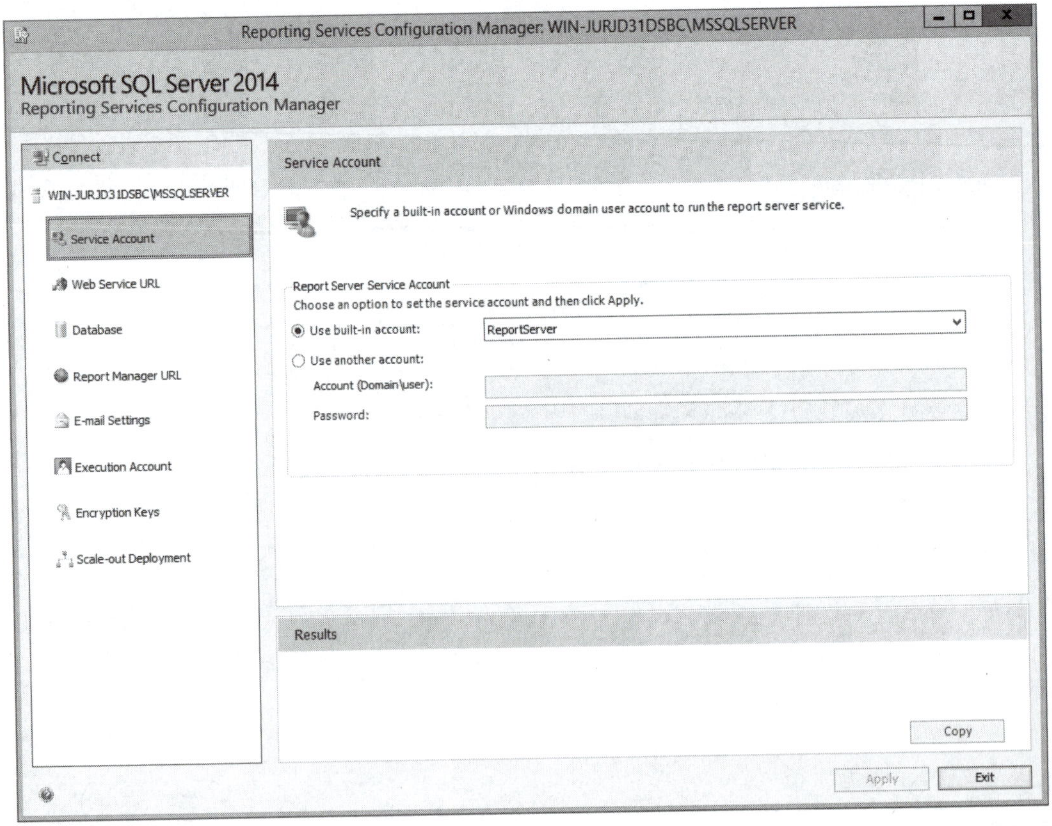

FIGURE 22-3

Should you decide to change the account, you have two options:

➤ **Built-in account**—With Windows Server 2008 and previous versions, you may opt to use one of the built-in accounts, such as Network Service, Local System, or Local Service. Of these, Microsoft recommends the use of the Network Service account.

Beginning with Windows Server 2008 R2, SQL Server now installs all of its services (including SSRS) to run using virtual accounts. A *virtual account* is a local account on the server running under the NT Service account. SQL Server manages all this for you, and as you can see in Figure 22-3, the installer has been configured to run with the ReportServer virtual account. When you have more than one instance of SSRS installed, their virtual accounts have the name of the instance integrated into the virtual account name.

➤ **Specific account**—As an alternative to the built-in account, you can instead choose a specific Windows user account. This could be an account specific to a computer and entered in the format *<computer name>\<user name>*, or a domain account in the *<domain>\<user>* format. Avoid using the account of the domain administrator. This account has a greater set of permissions than are needed to run SSRS and could present a vector for a security breach. The account you select must already exist. Reporting Services Configuration Manager cannot create a new account for you. It does, however, handle the duty of granting the needed permissions to the account you select.

Before you set up a specific account, however, you must be aware of a few limitations.

➤ The account name cannot exceed 20 characters.

➤ If you specify a domain user account and run in a Kerberos environment, you must register a Service Principal Name for the ID you use on your Report Server.

> **WARNING** *Running SQL Server on the same server that is the domain controller is not advised. It sometimes occurs, however, especially in cases of a small development machine where a single server hosts everything. When you have that specific situation, be aware that built-in service accounts (such as Local Service or Network Service) are not supported as service accounts for SSRS.*

After changing the service account, you are prompted to back up your encryption keys. You should be ready to do so, because it is imperative these keys are properly backed up. Encryption keys are discussed later in this chapter, but for now, be ready to back them up when prompted.

The Web Service URL

One of the great things about SSRS is its capability to integrate with other applications. Reports may be called as a hyperlink in a web page. They may be embedded in Report Viewer control in an ASP.NET or Windows application. All of this is possible because SSRS exposes its capabilities through a web service.

A *web service* is a program that uses a Uniform Resource Locator (URL)—a fancy way of saying an HTTP address—as its interface. When a formatted http command is passed to the web service address, the web service processes that request and returns data, typically formatted as an HTML page.

Web services can do more than just return data, though. Using the SSRS web service, you can upload reports, execute them, run the report and export the data to a file, validate parameters, and more.

All these actions require you to use an application to interface to the web service. Some of the applications from Microsoft that can interact with the web service are Report Builder, SQL Server Data Tools (SSDT), and Report Manager. You may also write your own application that interacts with the web service using one of the many .NET languages available.

To customize the web service URL for this instance of SSRS, use the Web Service URL page, as shown in Figure 22-4. The default URL is the name of the server, followed by the port number, and then the virtual directory `ReportServer`, all of which are configurable.

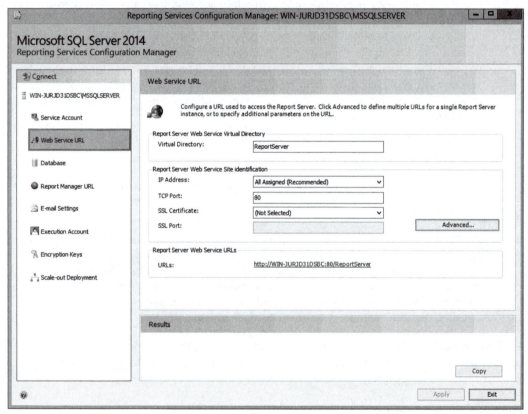

FIGURE 22-4

You can have more than one web service URL exposed by SSRS. To do so, click the Advanced button and add additional URLs to this server. SSRS also supports secure connections via Secure Socket Layer (SSL). Simply specify the SSL certificate and port number.

One of the first places you'll likely use the web service URL is within SQL SSDT. From within SSDT, you can deploy your reports to the report server. To do so, you first must go to the Properties page for the report project. One of the properties is the target server; it is the web service URL you use for this property.

Figure 22-5 shows an example of what you see if you try to navigate to the web service URL from within your web browser. It is a simple listing of the reports, with links that enable you to open or drill down into folders. This can be a good way to validate the web service URLs you use in your applications, but it is a terrible interface for the average user. Fortunately, Microsoft provides a complete solution for users to interface with SSRS in the form of Report Manager, which is covered in-depth in the "Report Manager" section later in this chapter.

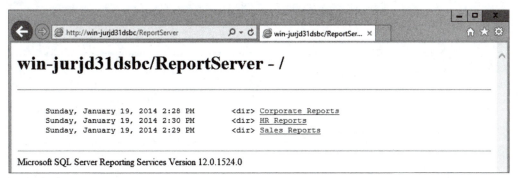

FIGURE 22-5

Reporting Services Databases

SSRS requires two databases to do its work. You can create these during the installation of SSRS, or afterward using the Reporting Services Configuration Manager. By default, these databases are named `ReportServer` and `ReportServerTempDB`, although these may be renamed during their creation. Figure 22-6 shows the configuration screen for setting up these databases.

These databases are visible inside SQL Server Management Studio alongside any other user databases.

The `ReportServer` database stores all the reports, as well as data source information, logins, subscriptions, and more. All sensitive data is encrypted using the encryption keys, a topic covered in the "Encryption Keys" section later in this chapter.

As its name implies, `ReportServerTempDB` holds temporary information for SSRS. Cached reports are one example of an entity that is stored. If you had a report that was used by many users—perhaps a morning status report—you could have that report generated and cached so that the report accesses only the source database once. Users executing the report would see the cached report, instead of having to completely regenerate it on each execution. When the cache time expires, the report is flushed from the `ReportServerTempDB` cache.

You should be aware that important distinctions exist between the two databases. It's vital that the `ReportServer` database be backed up, because it contains all your information about the reports hosted on this instance of SSRS. If a restore is needed, you can restore this database much as you would any other. After restoring it, you must restore the encryption keys for the encrypted information to be decipherable by SSRS.

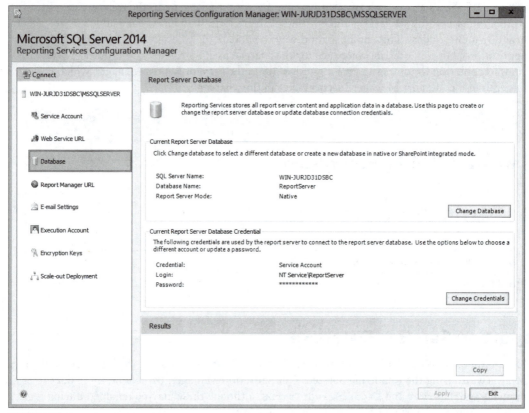

FIGURE 22-6

The `ReportServerTempDB` is quite the opposite. All data within the temporary database can be deleted without permanent damage to your SSRS installation. However, that would require all reports with caching enabled to be rerun and cached because the cache would be lost if `ReportServerTempDB` goes away.

For disaster-recovery purposes, you have two options. First, you can choose to back up `ReportServerTempDB` along with `ReportServer`. However, the temporary database typically grows fairly large, and can consume a lot of time and disk space in backups. For that reason, you may want to generate a script to create `ReportServerTempDB`. If a recovery occurs, then the script is run, and, if necessary, any reports that need to be cached can be executed. To create a script, simply right-click the `ReportServerTempDB` database name, select Script Database As ⇨ Create To ⇨ File, and save the output.

The names `ReportServer` and `ReportServerTempDB` are the default names for these databases. If multiple instances of SSRS are installed on the same server, the default names are appended with an underscore and then the instance name. As a best practice, you should retain these names because that is what most SQL IT Professionals are accustomed to. However, you can change these if the need arises.

To change the database, simply click the Change Database button. This brings up a wizard that provides two options: connect to an existing database or create a new database. After you select your option, the wizard walks you through a series of questions common to both choices. You select the server for the databases, the name of the database, the credentials to use, and so forth. When you are finished, SSRS now uses the database you indicated in the wizard.

Although it's not uncommon to have the `ReportServer` and `ReportServerTempDB` databases on the same SQL Server that SSRS runs on, it is not required. You can elect to put the reporting databases on a separate server and have only SSRS run on the report server.

This flexibility is commonly used with a scale-out deployment. You can implement two topologies in this scenario. In the first, the `ReportServer` and `ReportServerTempDB` databases reside on a server containing a SQL Server database engine. Then, two servers are created that run only SSRS. Both point to the `ReportServer` and `ReportServerTempDB` databases on the database's first server.

The second topology is a slight variation that has only two servers. The first server holds both the databases and SSRS; the second runs only SSRS and points back to the first server for the `ReportServer` and `ReportServerTempDB` databases.

Although these are the most common setups, you are not limited to only two SSRS servers in a scale-out situation. You could simply configure the additional servers to point to the central `ReportServer` and `ReportServerTempDB` databases. See the "Scale-Out Deployment" section later in this chapter for more information.

In a single-server environment, if you chose to install and configure SSRS during the install of SQL Server, you generally won't need to alter the information in Figure 22-6. You should understand how the reporting databases are used, though, and how they can be configured within your server environment.

The Report Manager URL

SSRS ships with an interface called Report Manager, which enables users to upload, configure, and run reports. Through Report Manager, you can apply security to a specific user or to a group. Permissions can vary from as basic as having only the capability to run certain reports, to having full administrative control over the report server.

By default, the URL is the name of the server, followed by the default port of 80, followed by the virtual directory name of `Reports`. This URL is configurable, and may be changed on the Report Manager URL page, as shown in Figure 22-7.

As with the web service URL, you can specify multiple URLs by clicking the Advanced button of the Report Services Configuration Manager. For example, you may want to have one standard HTTP-style URL for internal use and an SSL version of the address (HTTPS) for external use.

Report Manager is a big topic, and is covered in-depth in the "Report Manager" section later in this chapter.

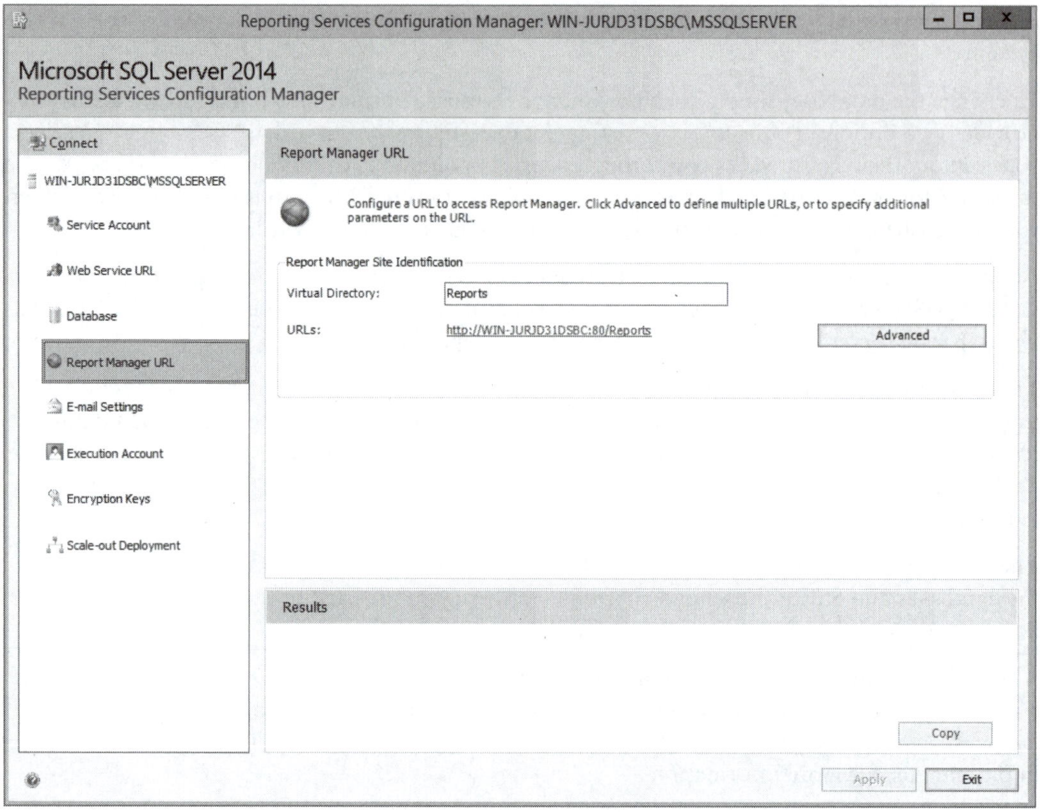

FIGURE 22-7

E-mail Settings

One of the options SSRS provides is the capability to set up e-mail-based subscriptions for reports. Users may elect to have reports automatically generated and e-mailed to them. To support this, SSRS must have access to an e-mail account. Figure 22-8 shows the E-Mail Settings page where you enter your e-mail information.

As with most accounts used with servers, you must ensure the account has a non-expiring password and that it has rights to e-mail the various attachment types supported by SSRS. You must be careful with this capability, however. Some reports can become quite large and flood your e-mail servers with attachments. Consider having reports generated and stored in a central repository, and instead e-mail links to the reports.

Execution Account

There are times when a report requires data, but the credentials to get to that data haven't been stored with the report. SSRS needs a set of credentials it can use to try to retrieve the source data. Through the Execution Account page of the Configuration Manager shown in Figure 22-9, you can select a specific domain account to use. This account then becomes the execution account. The domain account used for the execution account should have the least amount of required permissions for doing its job. For example, it should have read-only permissions to any source data used by the reports.

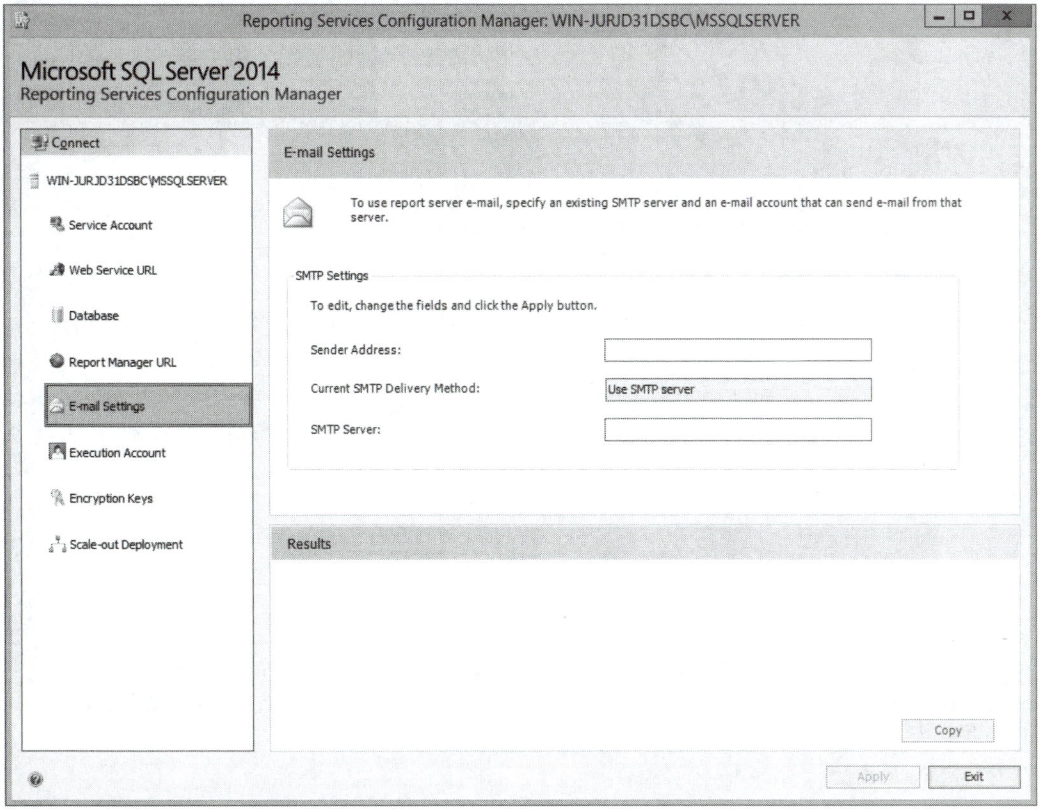

FIGURE 22-8

Reports also have the capability to display images stored externally to the report. The execution account credentials access the location of these images.

> **NOTE** *Don't confuse the execution account with the service account. The service account is the account under which all SSRS is actually running. The execution account is used strictly for accessing data or stored images when no other credentials have been supplied.*

The domain account used for the execution account should be different from the service account. The execution account needs different and typically less permissions from the service account. By using different accounts, you minimize your security risks.

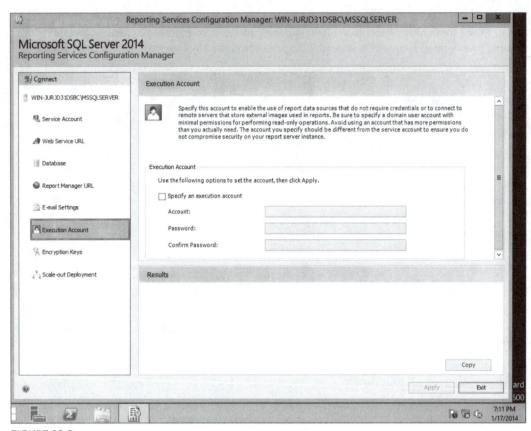

FIGURE 22-9

Encryption Keys

SSRS requires a good deal of confidential information to do its job. Credentials, connection strings, and the like must be stored in a secure manner. This kind of sensitive data is stored in the SSRS report database. But before it is stored, it is encrypted using an encryption key. Encryption keys are managed using the Encryption Keys screen shown in Figure 22-10.

It is vital that this encryption key be backed up. If the SSRS database must be restored (either because of a crash, or to facilitate moving the instance to a new server), you must restore the encryption keys. If you don't restore the encryption keys, all the confidential information stored is unusable, and you are faced with the laborious task of re-creating all the credentials manually.

After you restore the report database, you can restore the encryption keys through the dialog shown in Figure 22-10. Once the keys are restored, SSRS again has the capability to properly decrypt the stored credentials, thus restoring the server to full functionality.

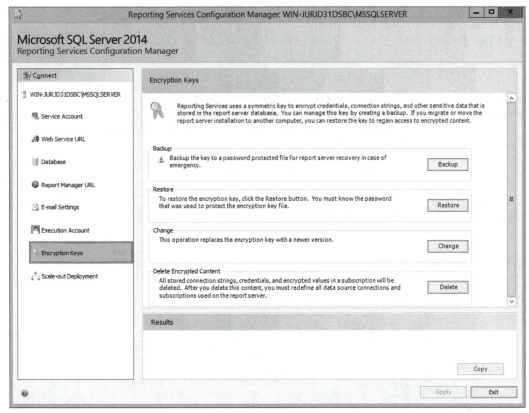

FIGURE 22-10

There may be occasions in which you want to change the security credentials. For example, you might have lost the backup of the encryption key, which would present a potential security issue. Or, you may have corporate rules requiring periodic refreshes of all your encryption keys. By clicking the Change button shown in Figure 22-10, you can create a new security key. Of course, after changing the key, be sure to back it up.

You may also have the need to remove any sensitive data stored in the report database. You can click the Delete button to remove any confidential information stored by SSRS.

Scale-Out Deployment

At some point, the demands on your SSRS server may grow too large for a single server to handle effectively. Microsoft has provided for that situation through the use of Scale-out Deployment. In a Scale-out Deployment scenario, multiple servers can process reports. All the servers share a common SSRS database.

Before you start planning your scale-out environment, you must be aware of some prerequisites. First, Scale-out Deployment is an Enterprise edition-only feature. Although you can also set it up in the Developer or Evaluation versions, this is meant strictly for learning, development, and evaluation, and not a production situation. The Standard, Workgroup, and Express versions of SQL Server do not support Scale-out Deployment for SSRS.

Next, all servers in the scale-out farm must run the same major version number and have the same updates and service packs applied. They must also be on the same domain or in a trusted domain. Finally, the servers must use the same authentication modes. If you have created any custom authorization extensions, the same extension must exist on the servers.

> **NOTE** *Although not a strict requirement, it is best if both servers have an identical physical configuration, or as close as is possible.*

Now that you have met the basic requirements, it's time to configure your servers. This example uses the most common scenario. The first server has both SSRS and the `ReportServer/ReportServerTempDBs` installed on it. The second server runs only SSRS.

Follow these steps:

1. Set up your first SSRS server, as has been described throughout this chapter.

2. Next, install SSRS on a second server. (Although you can install multiple instances of SSRS on the same server and configure them for scale-out, there is no benefit to doing so.) When you get to the installation step for SSRS, select the "Install but do not configure server" option.

3. After installation completes, open the SQL Server Reporting Services Configuration Manager, and, on the opening dialog, select your new server. Begin by going to the Database page, and point the database to the SSRS database on the original server.

4. Next, go to the Report Server Web Service URL and Report Manager URL pages and configure their URLs. Don't test them yet, however, because they won't be available until you join this server to the Scale-out Deployment, which is the next step.

5. Close out your connection to the second SSRS server, re-open the configuration tool, and point it to the original server. Return to the Scale-out Deployment page; you should now see both servers listed. The original server should already show its status as Joined. Your new server should be listed; however, its status should read Waiting to Join.

6. Simply select the new server, and then click the Add Server button. After it has joined, you can verify it by going to the Report Services or Report Manager URLs specified when you configured the new server.

SSRS also supports being installed on a network load-balanced cluster. If you do so, you must configure a few additional items. For more information, see the Books Online article, "Configure a Report Server on a Network Load Balancing Cluster."

THE REPORT EXECUTION LOG

In this section, you see what is in the report execution log. To get started, follow these steps:

1. Open SQL Server Management Studio, and connect to the Database Engine where the ReportServer database is stored. By default, the database has the name ReportServer, and that's how you can refer to it here. However, if you changed the name during the install or using the Reporting Services Configuration Manager, select the database you named.

2. Within the Views branch, are three views directly related to logging: ExecutionLog, ExecutionLog2, and ExecutionLog3. Each contains the same basic information—the ID of the report, the server instance the report ran on, how long it took to run the report, who ran the report, and so forth. The second and third versions of the view extend the amount of information returned.

   You can create a SQL statement to extract data from the view. This statement is the basis for a report you create in the next section. The view contains most of the information you need; the only missing element is the name of the reports, which you can find in the dbo.Catalog table. Listing 22-1 (code file: Listing22-1.sql) shows the query that provides the information you need.

LISTING 22-1: SQL Script to Display Basic Error Log Information

```
SELECT [InstanceName]
    , C.[Path] AS [ReportFolder]
    , C.[Name] AS [ReportName]
    , [UserName]
    , CASE [RequestType]
        WHEN 0 THEN 'Interactive Report'
        ELSE 'Subscription Report'
        END AS [ReportType]
    , [TimeStart]
    , [TimeEnd]
    , [TimeDataRetrieval] AS [TimeDataRetrievalMilliseconds]
    , [TimeProcessing] AS [TimeProcessingMilliseconds]
    , [TimeRendering] AS [TimeRenderingMilliseconds]
    , CASE [Source]
        WHEN 1 THEN 'Live'
        WHEN 2 THEN 'Cache'
        WHEN 3 THEN 'Snapshot'
        WHEN 4 THEN 'History'
        WHEN 5 THEN 'Ad Hoc'
        WHEN 6 THEN 'Session'
        WHEN 7 THEN 'RDCE'
        ELSE 'Other'
        END AS [ReportSource]
    , [Status]
    , [ByteCount]
    , [RowCount]
    FROM [ReportServer].[dbo].[ExecutionLog] E
    JOIN [ReportServer].[dbo].[Catalog] C ON E.ReportID = C.ItemID
```

You can explore to see what further information is available.

REPORT MANAGER

After a report generates, it is ready to be passed to SSRS so it can be managed. You need to use the Report Manager tool to do this.

The Report Manager tool is a web interface that both IT professionals and end users can use to manage and execute their collection of reports. You get to the Report Manager by opening Internet Explorer (or similar web browser) and going to the URL specified on the Report Manager URL page of the Reporting Services Configuration Manager. From here, you can do a lot, but specifically you can perform three main types of tasks:

➤   From within SSDT, you can organize reports into report projects. You can then deploy these reports from within SSDT to the SSRS server via the web services URL designated in the Reporting Services Configuration Manager.

➤   You can save reports from Report Builder directly to the SSRS server via the Web Service URL.

➤   Report Manager has the capability to upload a report to it from a disk drive.

Managing Report Manager

Report Manager has a quirk—for all the features to work correctly, you must run it in administrator mode. Find the Internet Explorer (IE) icon on your Start menu, right-click it, and select Run as Administrator.

When IE is open, navigate to the Report Manager URL. Your screen should be similar to the one shown in Figure 22-11 (although, don't be alarmed if it doesn't match exactly).

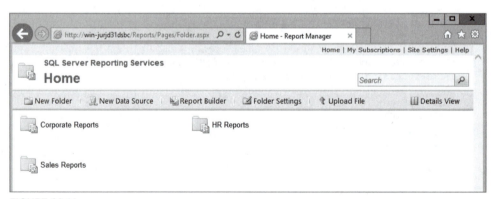

FIGURE 22-11

The Navigation Menu

In the upper-right corner of Figure 22-11 is a navigation menu. The Home option takes you back to the home page, as shown in Figure 22-11. My Subscriptions takes users to their private report storage area. If My Subscriptions is turned off, this does not appear to the users.

The Site Settings menu option is for SSRS administrators only, and is not visible to anyone but designated administrators. As shown in Figure 22-12, the available settings are a subset of the properties you can set from within SQL Server Management Studio. The Help option provides some basic help for the Report Manager.

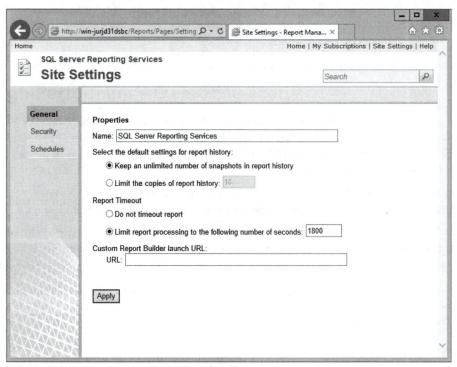

FIGURE 22-12

On the Site Settings page, you should change the server name to something appropriate for your environment, if you have not done so already. Typically, this is the name of your company, but it may also be a departmental name. For test or development servers, it's a good practice to show that in the name of the server.

After you change the name of your server (or any of the other properties), you must click the Apply button, as shown in Figure 22-12. This is true not only for this page, but also for all the pages in Report Manager. Anywhere you make a change, you must click the Apply button, or your changes will be lost.

So far, you've been looking at the General page of Site Settings, as indicated by the page menu on the left. Under it is another important page, Security. Through it you can add or edit users (or groups of users). In the screen shown in Figure 22-13, you can see the two users listed for this server and the roles they have.

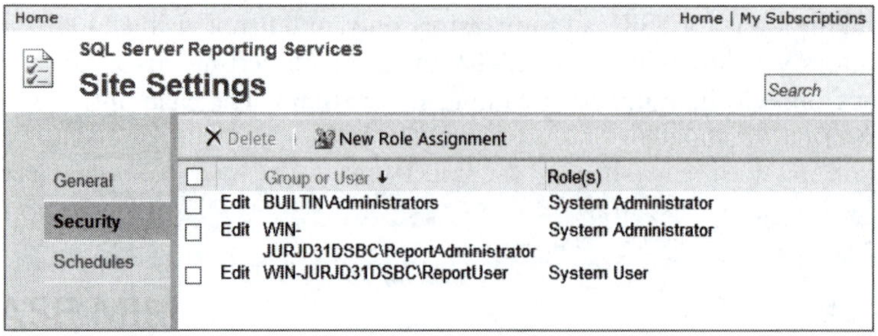

FIGURE 22-13

To add a new user, simply click the New Role Assignment button (not shown in the portion of the screen shown in Figure 22-13). A New System Role Assignment page displays, as shown in Figure 22-14. Start by entering the Active Directory user or group name, and then check the desired role. Choose from the two following User options:

➤ **System Administrator**—This should be given out only with careful thought. System administrators can change any of the properties, add/remove users, reports, and so on. This role should be reserved for DBAs or similar IT professionals.

➤ **System User role**—This is fairly straightforward. It allows the designated users to see (but not alter) system properties and shared schedules. They are also allowed to launch Report Builder.

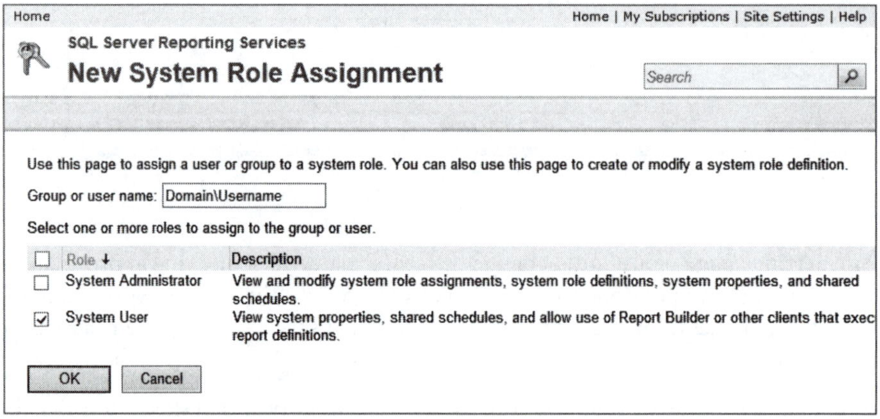

FIGURE 22-14

The Schedules page (accessed by clicking the Schedules option on the left of the Site Settings page, as shown in Figure 22-13) is used to establish a shared schedule for capturing snapshots of reports. Say you have three reports that have important financial information about the company. These reports may run several times a day, independent of each other.

For auditing purposes, you need to run all three reports at the same time every day and store a snapshot of these. To accomplish this, you can first set up a shared schedule. Simply click the New Schedule menu option, fill out what time of day to run, what days to run, and when to start and optionally stop running the report and save it. Figure 22-15 shows one schedule named Daily Corporate Snapshot. Remember this as you see where to use this later in the chapter.

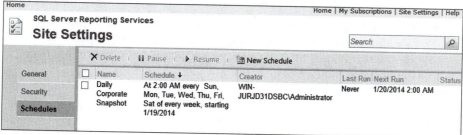

FIGURE 22-15

The Task Menu

Returning to the Home screen (refer to Figure 22-11), there is a more prominent task menu across the top of the screen. Starting from the left is the New Folder option. Report Manager enables reports to be organized into logical folders, similar to the way folders are used on a hard drive. When you move into a folder, the second line in the title will be updated to show the current folder name.

Figure 22-16 reflects the new name of your SSRS server, and shows that you have moved into the `Sales Reports` folder. This example also lets the user know there are no reports in the folder, a much better option than showing nothing and making the user wonder.

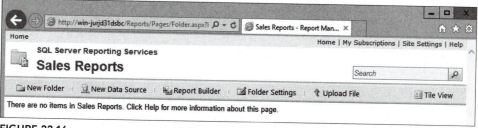

FIGURE 22-16

Next to the New Folder menu option on the Home page is New Data Source. When you create a report in Report Builder, you start by building a data set. In creating that data set, the first thing you are asked for is the data source.

You have the option to use a shared data source. You can create a shared data source through the New Data Source option in Report Manager. Then you simply point to it from Report Builder.

Shared data sources make management much easier. If you have a group of reports that all connect to the same database, and that database is moved to a new server, the connection must be updated only once, rather than for each report. Shared data sources also facilitate report development. You can set up a testing SSRS server, on which the data source points to a test database. When the report has passed all its tests, it can be uploaded to the production server that has a shared data source with the same name, but pointing to the production database. No update to the report would be required.

Although straightforward, setting up a data source, does require some knowledge about how SSRS works, as well as how your reports will be used. As the New Data Source page shown in Figure 22-17 indicates, you should start things by giving your data source a descriptive name. You can provide an optional description to add clarity.

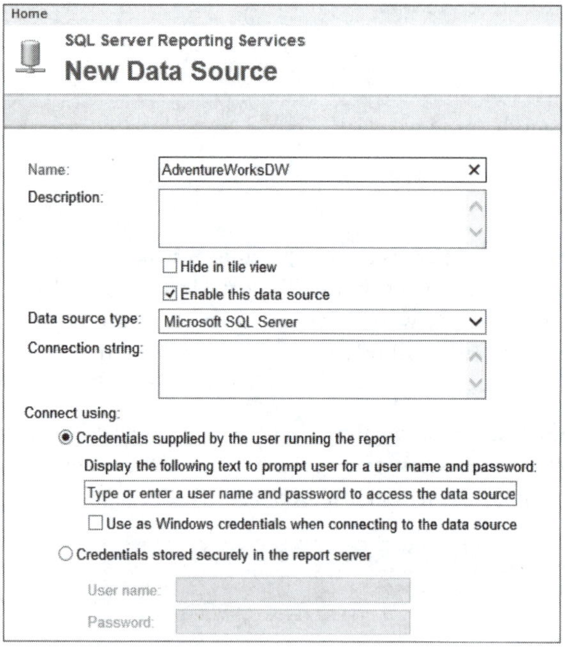

FIGURE 22-17

The Home screen (refer to Figure 22-11) is displayed in Tile Mode. This is the mode most users use to interact with Report Manager. (There is a second mode, Details View, which is covered later.) You can suppress the display of a data source by checking "Hide in tile view" check box shown in Figure 22-17, and it is common to do so. This reduces the number of items in Report Manager, therefore increasing simplicity for the users.

Moving down the page shown in Figure 22-17, you next see the "Enable this data source" option. As its name implies, you can use this check box to disable and re-enable this data source from use.

The data source type is the next option. SSRS can access a rich set of data sources beyond SQL Server. SQL Server Analysis Services, SQL Azure, OLE DB, and Oracle are just a few of the many sources available to SSRS.

The connection string can vary by the data source type. For SQL Server, it takes the form of Data Source= followed by the name of the server. If the instance is not the default one, you must also add the name of the SQL Server instance. That will be followed by a semicolon, Initial Catalog=, and the name of the database to get data from. Note the spaces between the words Data Source and Initial Catalog, which need to be there.

Thus, to connect to the reporting execution log for your demo test server, the connection string looks as follows:

```
Data Source=WIN-JURJD31DSBC;Initial Catalog=ReportServer
```

The next section, "Connect using," has four options. These have a big impact on how the report can be used on the server.

➤ **Credentials supplied by the user running the report**—With this option, users are prompted to enter their credentials each time they run the report. The text of the prompt may be specified, and there is an option to use the supplied credentials as Windows credentials. Most users find it annoying to have to enter their credentials each time a report is run, at the very least. Thus, this option is rarely used.

A good example of where it might be useful, though, is in a facility where large numbers of temporary workers are brought in for short time periods. Setting up Active Directory accounts for all those users is not practical. This option becomes even more beneficial when the workers share a common PC (for example, on a manufacturing production floor where maintenance is done). A handful of IDs could be created and shared among a group of workers. When maintenance people run the report, they enter a generic credential for all maintenance people, and the report displays only the data that job role is allowed to see. Likewise, shift supervisors would see only data they are allowed, and so on.

When this method of authentication is used, the report cannot be set up for unattended execution. You learn more about unattended execution in a moment.

➤ **Credentials stored securely in the report server**—With this option, you must enter a specific set of credentials with which to run the report. This may be a SQL Server ID or an Active Directory ID. If an Active Directory ID is used, you should also check the "Use as Windows credentials when connecting to the data source" option.

By default, the data source cannot see the Windows user as the person making the request, but rather the ID supplied here. This is good when you don't need user-specific security around the data being accessed. However, if you do require the data source to know who the Windows user is, you can check the final option, "Impersonate the authenticated user after a connection has been made to the data source" (not shown in Figure 22-17). SSRS passes the Windows user ID through to the data source, allowing it to return data based on the user's ID (or Active Directory group membership).

This is one of the two options, which enables you to run a report in unattended execution mode.

➤ **Windows integrated security**—With the "Windows integrated security" option (not shown in Figure 22-17), SSRS can automatically detect the Windows credentials of the user accessing SSRS, and pass them along to the data source. This option cannot allow a report to be run in unattended execution mode.

➤ **Credentials are not required**—(This option is not shown in Figure 22-17.) There are some situations in which credentials are not required, or not even usable. A good example is a report generated from an XML file. XML has no concept of authentication. This mode enables unattended execution.

There are two basic methods for executing a report. With the first method, the report is executed on demand by a user. Commonly, it is done via Report Manager, but it may also occur with reports launched from an application (such as an ASP.NET website). In this situation, SSRS knows who the user is, and can pass the user's credentials to the data source. Refer to this mode as *attended execution.*

In the second method, it is SSRS that launches the report. This occurs when a report is scheduled to be run, or a snapshot is due to be created on a specific schedule. Thus, this is known as *unattended execution* mode.

In this light, the connection methods make sense. To run unattended, the credentials for the data source must be stored on the server, or must not be required.

After you fill out all the information in the New Data Source screen, be sure to click OK to save the shared data source.

You can set these same options for an individual report. You see where to do that in the next section. However, the connection options are identical for both shared and report-specific data sources.

The third item in the task menu shown at the top of Figure 22-11 is Report Builder. This launches Report Builder for the user, and if Report Builder has not yet been installed, it installs it as well.

The Folder Settings task enables you to set security for the current folder. The operation is similar to the site settings you saw in Figure 22-13 and Figure 22-14, but specific to the current folder and, by default, any subfolders. The security options are slightly different, though, as shown in Figure 22-18.

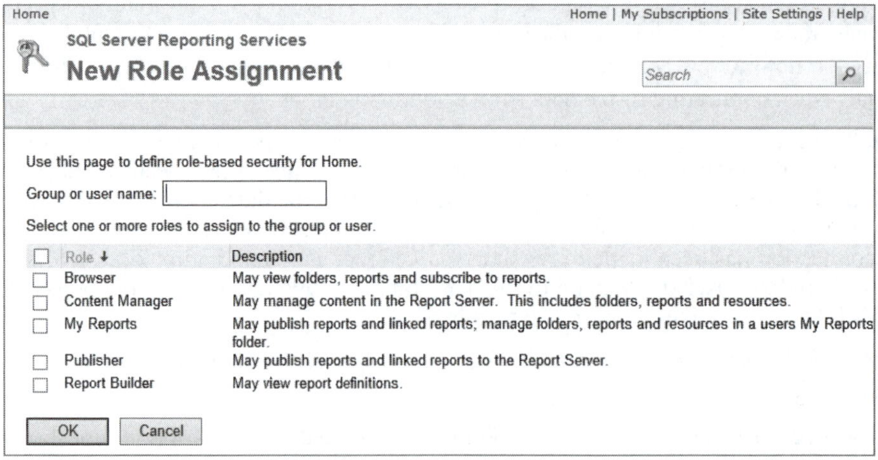

FIGURE 22-18

Microsoft did a great job with the screen shown in Figure 22-18, spelling out what rights each role has; thus they don't need much more explanation. A user may have more than one role, as needed. As with most security, it's best to start out with the most minimal right (Browser), and increase privileges as needed.

In addition to saving reports directly to the server, Report Builder also enables you to save reports to a hard drive. This is a great option for reports that were built to run once and then discarded.

Some companies have tight security settings around their report servers. Users who want to develop reports must save them locally, and then send the completed report (in the form of an RDL file) to IT where it can be validated.

To get the file into Report Manager, you utilize the Upload File task at the top of the Home page. This brings up a simple web page where a user can upload a report. When updating an existing report, the uploader must also check the Overwrite check box. This is a safety mechanism so that existing reports won't be overwritten accidentally.

In the earlier discussion on defining a data source, you saw an option called "Hide in tile view" (refer to Figure 22-17). Although Tile View is the most common way to look at reports, there is another option, Details View, which can be accessed by picking the last option in the task menu, appropriately named Details View.

Details View provides additional information, such as the last run date for the report, the last modified date, and who did the modification. It also lists all objects in this folder, which might be hidden. This is how you can get to an item you may have hidden previously.

In addition, two more menu options appear in the task bar on the left: Delete and Move. When you check one or more of the objects, these buttons will be enabled, allowing you to permanently delete the selected items, or move them to another folder within the same Report Manager site.

So far, you've seen how to manage the Report Manager, as well as manage the folders, data sources, and reports that reside in Report Manager. In the next section, you see how to manage a report.

Managing Reports

Whether you are in Tile View or Detail View, you begin by hovering over any report. A yellow border surrounds the report, and a yellow drop-down button appears on the right. Clicking that button opens up the report management menu, as shown in Figure 22-19.

Some of the options are self-explanatory. Move and Delete behave like they do in Detail View. Download enables you to save the report or data source to your hard drive. "Edit in Report Builder" launches Report Builder, and loads the selected report for you, ready to edit.

The main way to manage a report is through the "Manage" (web pages) option, which you see in a moment. Subscribe, View Report History, and Security are shortcuts to pages contained in the Manage web pages; you look at those in the context of the Manage pages.

And, finally, is the Create Linked Report option. This is analogous to a shortcut within Windows. It creates a clone of the entry for the report, but not the report itself. You can then change all the properties (which you'll see momentarily) in the Manage web pages. Thus you run the same report with two different sets of parameters, schedules, snapshots, and the like.

Creating a linked report is easy. After clicking the menu option, all you need to tell it is what you want the link to be named, and what folder you want to put it in. It defaults to the current folder, but you can change it if you want. From there you can alter any of the properties in the Manage area, as you see next.

FIGURE 22-19

Properties

When you click Manage, you are greeted with the Properties page, as shown in Figure 22-20. By now, you should be familiar with most of these commands shown in the task menu and properties, having seen them in other places. The only new command here is Replace, which is just a shortcut to the Upload command. The only difference is Upload lacks the "Overwrite if exists" check box. SSRS assumes if you are at this point, it's a safe assumption you want to overwrite, so it doesn't bother to ask.

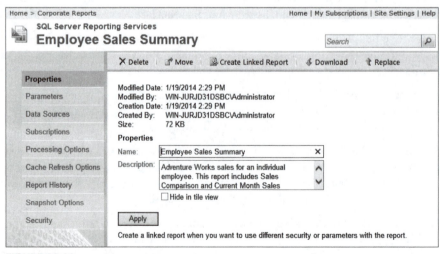

FIGURE 22-20

> **NOTE** *With all the pages in the Manage area, be sure to click the Apply button when you finish. If you move to another page within Manage web pages without clicking Apply first, you will lose your changes.*

In addition to the Properties page, the list on the left-hand side of this screen also provides links to the following pages:

➤ Parameters

➤ Data Sources

➤ Subscriptions

➤ Processing Options

➤ Cache Refresh Options

➤ Report History

➤ Snapshot Options

➤ Security

Each of these is worth taking a closer look at.

Parameters

The second page in the Manage area allows you to see all the Parameters in a report. Here you will find both hidden and visible parameters. The first time this screen is opened, it will show the defaults that were assigned during design time in SQL Server Data Tools or Report Builder. Making changes on this screen will modify the defaults. Here you can also show or hide parameters from the user, change the Display Text that appears before the parameter, and see the data type for each parameter. However, you cannot change the data set that feed a parameter, create parameters, or delete parameters. All of these functions must be done in SSDT or Report Builder.

Data Sources

Moving down the list of pages on the left side of the Manage area, you come to the Data Sources, as shown in Figure 22-21. At the top, you can select "A shared data source." (See the previous section for more information on setting up a shared data source.) When you pick that option, it enables the Browse button. It is then a simple matter to navigate the folder structure and pick the data source you previously set up.

Alternatively, as shown in Figure 22-21, you can establish a "Custom data source" specific to this report. When you do, the options behave identically to the shared data source.

The Connect Using section of Figure 22-21 tells the data source how the execution credentials are to be supplied. To schedule a report, you need to use credentials that allowed for unattended execution. This would require selecting Credentials stored securely in the server. When selecting this option, credentials can be passed with SQL Authentication or Windows Authentication.

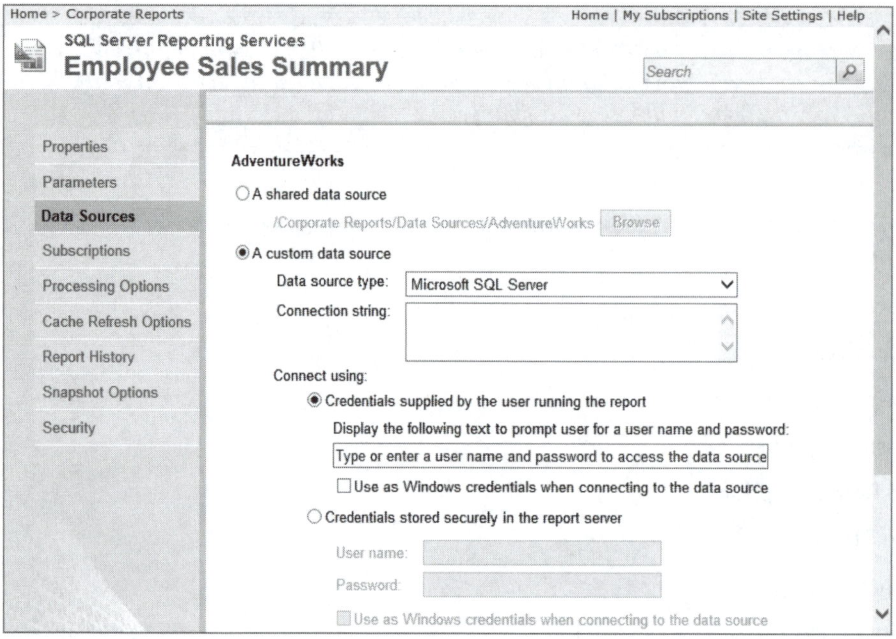

FIGURE 22-21

> **NOTE** *Whenever you make changes it is always a good idea to test, so be sure to take advantage of the Test Connection button.*

Subscriptions

Subscriptions are a useful tool in SSRS. They enable reports to be generated and delivered to the users without their intervention. This is an ideal solution for long-running reports, or when a report will be run on a regular basis (such as daily).

When entering the Subscriptions page for the first time, there won't be any subscriptions listed. You have two choices to create a subscription: New Subscription and New Data-Driven Subscription.

New Subscription

New subscriptions are run on a timed basis. When you select this option, you will be asked what delivery method you want, and when you want it to run, as shown in Figure 22-22.

Assuming you set up an e-mail address in the Reporting Services Configuration Manager's E-mail page, you can choose between two delivery methods: E-Mail and Windows File Share. You are given the chance to set basic details about the report delivery: what format should the report be in, who should it go to, and more. The Windows File Share is similar. With it, you set the path to save to, the format of the report, and the credentials used to access the file share.

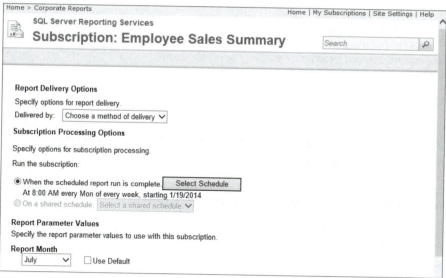

FIGURE 22-22

On the lower half of the New Subscription page, you specify when you want the report to run. The first option enables you to set a custom schedule for this specific report. The second option enables you to use a shared schedule. Shared schedules are set up in the Site Settings area, as discussed earlier in this chapter in the "The Navigation Menu" section.

New Data-Driven Subscription

The second option is data-driven subscriptions. This is a bit misleading, because the data referred to is not the source data. Rather, it is data used to set options around the report at the time it is run. Who gets the report, how should it be delivered, and what format should it be in are examples of report execution options that can be pulled from data.

Before you can create a data-driven subscription, you must first create a table to hold the data you need. There is no set format for the table. The number of columns, column names, and sizes are all up to you.

Perform the following steps to create a table:

1. First create a simple table to hold data that could be used to drive either e-mail or output to a Windows file path. Listing 22-2 (code file: `Listing22-2.sql`) lists the T-SQL for the table. Where you store the table is up to you. In this example a new database was created called `ReportSubscriptions`.

LISTING 22-2: Create a Table to Hold Subscription Information

```
CREATE TABLE [dbo].[SubscriptionInfo] (
      [SubscriptionInfoID] [int] NOT NULL PRIMARY KEY
    , [SubscriberName] [nvarchar] (50) NOT NULL
    , [EmailAddress] [nvarchar] (256) NOT NULL
    , [Path] [nvarchar] (256) NOT NULL
```

continues

LISTING 22-2 *(continued)*

```
        , [FileName] [nvarchar] (256) NOT NULL
        , [Format] [nvarchar] (20) NOT NULL
        , [Comment] [nvarchar] (256) NOT NULL
        , [ReportNameFilter] [nvarchar] (200) NOT NULL
    ) ON [PRIMARY]
    GO
```

2.   Next, put some data in the table. That's what the code in Listing 22-3 (code file:
     `Listing22-3.sql`) accomplishes.

LISTING 22-3: Load Subscriptions to the SubscriptionInfo Table

```
INSERT INTO [dbo].[SubscriptionInfo]
        ( [SubscriptionInfoID]
        , [SubscriberName]
        , [EmailAddress]
        , [Path]
        , [FileName]
        , [Format]
        , [Comment]
        , [ReportNameFilter]
        )
VALUES (   '1'
        , 'Bradley Schacht'
        , 'bogusaddress@somedomain.com'
        , '\\JURJD31DSBC\FileShare'
        , 'Bradleys File'
        , 'IMAGE'
        , 'Hi Bradley, here is your report.'
        , 'Employee Sales Summary')
    , (   '2'
        , 'Collin Knight'
        , 'bogusaddress@somedomain.com'
        , '\\JURJD31DSBC\FileShare'
        , 'Collins Data'
        , 'MHTML'
        , 'Hey Collin, here is your report.'
        , 'Employee Sales Summary'
        )
    , (   '3'
        , 'Captain America'
        , 'arcanecode@gmail.com'
        , '\\JURJD31DSBC\FileShare'
        , 'Captain Americas Stuff'
        , 'PDF'
        , 'The Hulk stole my shield again.'
        , 'Employee Sales Summary'
        );
```

Now that you have data to work with, you can set up a data-driven subscription. On the
subscriptions page, select the New Data-Driven Subscription option. Now walk through the
following series of steps needed to set up the subscription:

1. The first step is illustrated in Figure 22-23. After giving your subscription a name, you are asked about your delivery option. You can pick from E-mail or a Windows File Share. In the previous section, on regular nondata-driven subscriptions, you used e-mail, so for this example, use Windows File Share. The final option is to indicate the data source.

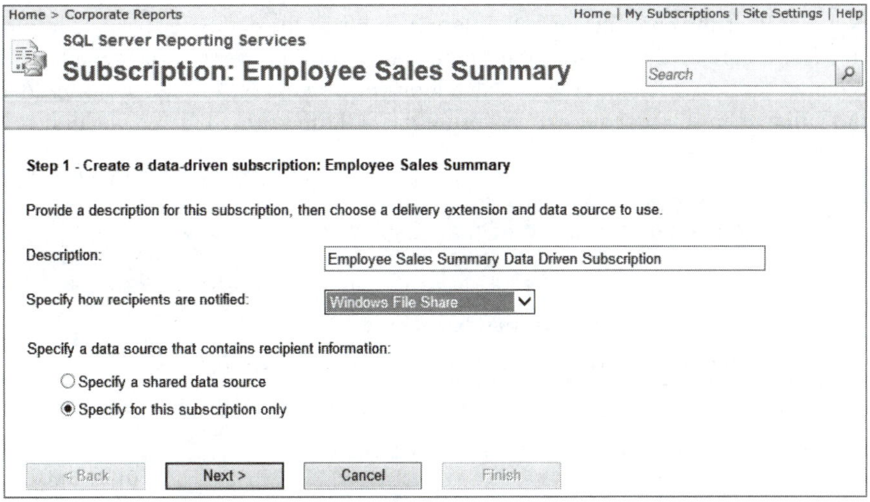

FIGURE 22-23

2. Because, in the previous step, the data source selected was for this subscription only, you are now prompted for connection information, as shown in Figure 22-24. If you select a shared data source, this step would instead give you the chance to select an existing shared data source.

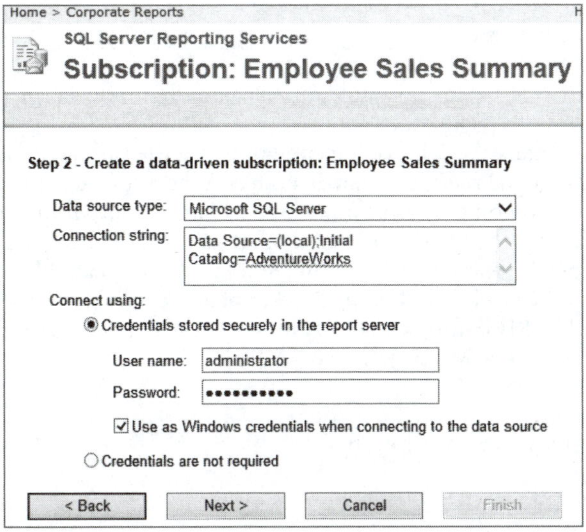

FIGURE 22-24

> **NOTE** *One annoyance here is that each time you perform this step, you must fill out the password. It won't retain it, so if you return to edit this subscription later, be sure to have the password.*

3. Now, provide the appropriate SQL query to apply to the database specified in the previous step (see Figure 22-25). In addition to the query, you can override the default by entering a different timeout duration if you have a long-running query. Finally, you should always use the Validate button (not shown) to ensure the SQL query you entered is valid.

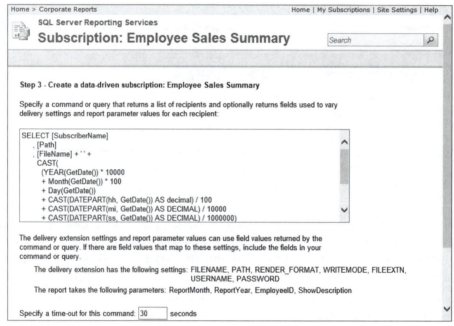

FIGURE 22-25

Because the screen shown in Figure 22-5 is not big enough to see the full query, it is displayed here in Listing 22-4 (code file: `Listing22-4.sql`). When you run this query, it returns the following information on the file share: where to put the output file, which filename to use, and what format the file should be in. Some date math is appended to the end of the filename. You typically want some mechanism to avoid duplicate files trying to be created in the target file share. The code in Listing 22-4 appends a number to the end of the filename in YYYYMMDD.HHMISS format. For example, 20140131.011221 would be 12 minutes and 21 seconds after 1 A.M. on January, 31, 2014.

LISTING 22-4: Query for a Data-Driven Subscription

```
SELECT [SubscriberName]
     , [Path]
```

```
    , [FileName] + ' ' +
      CAST(
        (YEAR(GetDate()) * 10000
        + Month(GetDate()) * 100
        + Day(GetDate())
        + CAST(DATEPART(hh, GetDate()) AS decimal) / 100
        + CAST(DATEPART(mi, GetDate()) AS DECIMAL) / 10000
        + CAST(DATEPART(ss, GetDate()) AS DECIMAL) / 1000000)
      AS nvarchar(20)) AS [FileName]
    , [Format]
    , [Comment]
  FROM [dbo].SubscriptionInfo
WHERE [ReportNameFilter] = 'Employee Sales Summary'
```

Incorporating the date into the filename is just one method of creating unique filenames. You might also use a GUID, or have another process update the subscription table to have a new filename each time. Finally, you might have a separate process that removes all files in the share prior to the time the report is scheduled to run.

4. Next, you must supply information specific to the output method you selected. Figure 22-26 shows the screen for your selected Windows File Share output. Values can be supplied from static text, as you can see with the file username and password. They may also be mapped from the query you ran in step 3. The filename, path, and render format have all been mapped from the query (refer to Figure 22-26). Finally, you can decide to supply no value at all, as done with the write mode and file extension.

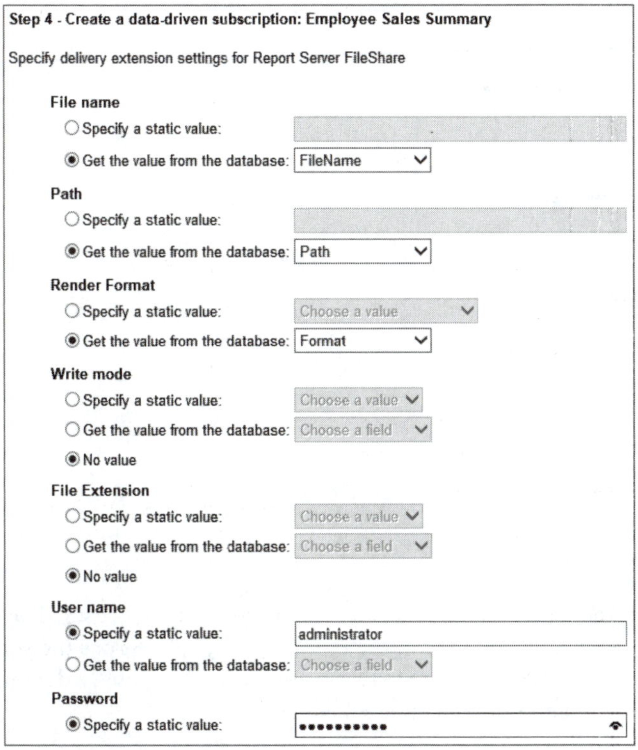

FIGURE 22-26

The path must be in UNC naming format: \\SERVERNAME\\FILESHARENAME. In this example, the UNC path to your file share (stored in the table, refer to Listing 22-3) was \\WIN-JURJD31DSBC\FileShare. If you had picked E-mail as your delivery option, then this step would have fields oriented toward sending e-mails. It would map the same way as you did with the Windows File Share in Figure 22-26.

5. If you had put any parameters on your report, now is the time to map values from your SQL query to the report parameters. This can be an effective manner in which to reuse reports multiple ways.

   For example, for each manager, a report could be created that would list the employees and total number of hours worked for the week. In the subscription table for that report, the manager's name, e-mail address, and department name could be stored. The data-driven subscription could map the department name to a parameter in the report, so only people in that department would be on the instance of the report being e-mailed to the associated manager.

   Figure 22-27 shows the parameter mapping screen. You can specify static values as shown, accept the report defaults, or use data stored in the database, as you saw on the subscription configuration in Figure 22-26.

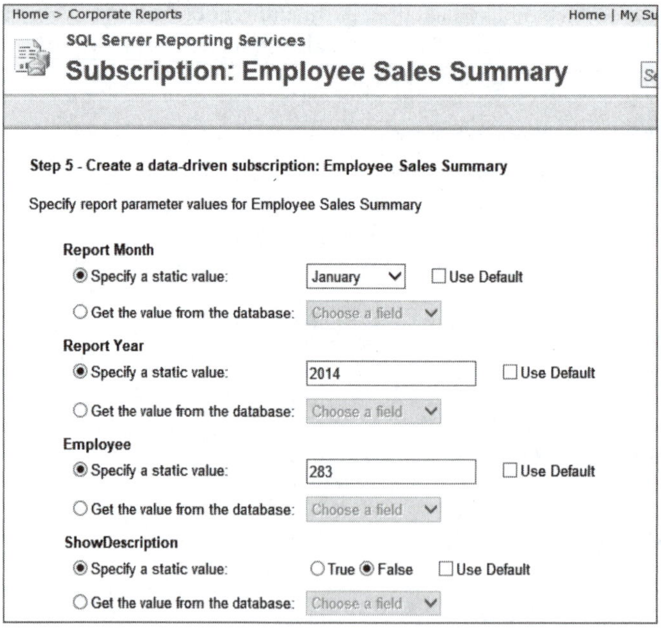

FIGURE 22-27

6. Next, you specify when the report should execute, as shown in Figure 22-28. The first option, "When the report data is updated on the report server," SSRS runs the subscription when a report execution snapshot is updated. This is useful when you have data updated on a limited, infrequent basis on an unpredictable schedule.

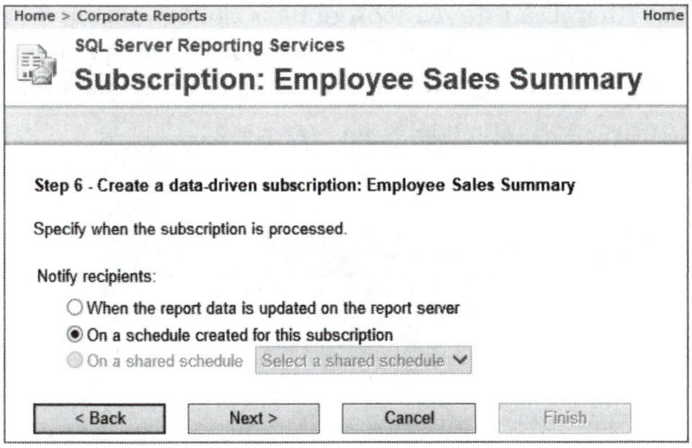

FIGURE 22-28

The other two options set the report to run on a time schedule. The lower option enables you to reuse an existing schedule (see the information on Site Settings in the "Navigation Menu" section earlier in this chapter). When either the first or last option is selected, the Finish button is enabled, and you are done.

If you select the middle option, you have one more step where you must set up the schedule for this subscription.

7. In the final step of setting up a data-driven subscription, you simply need to supply the information on when and how often the report should execute. Figure 22-29 shows there is a lot of flexibility when configuring the schedule.

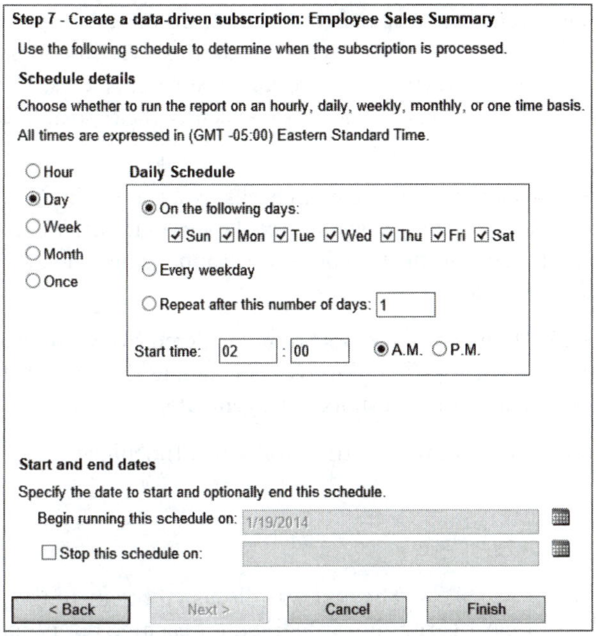

FIGURE 22-29

That was a lot of effort, but well worth it. Data-driven subscriptions can be valuable when you need to run the same report many times, each time with different values for the parameters and processing options. Figure 22-30 shows the listing of existing subscriptions created in this section.

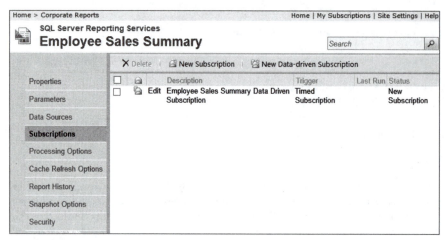

FIGURE 22-30

Processing Options

Figure 22-31 shows you a lot of different processing options, but they can be summarized as a choice between caching and snapshots. The report cache is for storing temporary copies of the report, whereas the snapshots can be retained for a specified duration. Users can see previous snapshots of reports, whereas cached reports are lost forever when they expire. Of course, you can elect not to cache or snapshot reports at all, as the first option in Figure 22-31 shows. When you choose to neither cache nor snapshot the report, each time a user executes the report, SSRS makes a call to the database to get the report data.

With the cache options, when a user runs a report, SSRS first checks to see if it is in the cache. If so, it returns the report from the cache instead of going to the source database. If not, it executes the report and adds it to the cache. The difference in the two options is simply when the cache expires: either after a set time or on a specific schedule.

The second option shown in Figure 22-31 enables the report to be rendered from a snapshot. As mentioned earlier, snapshots are copies of the report and its associated data that is stored long term. With this option, you may also set a schedule for snapshots to be generated.

The final option enables you to override the standard settings for report timeouts for this specific report.

Cache Refresh Options

A report can get into the report cache in two ways. The first was discussed briefly in the previous section, "Processing Options." When a report is run, if it is marked for caching but is not in the cache, it is executed and then added to the cache.

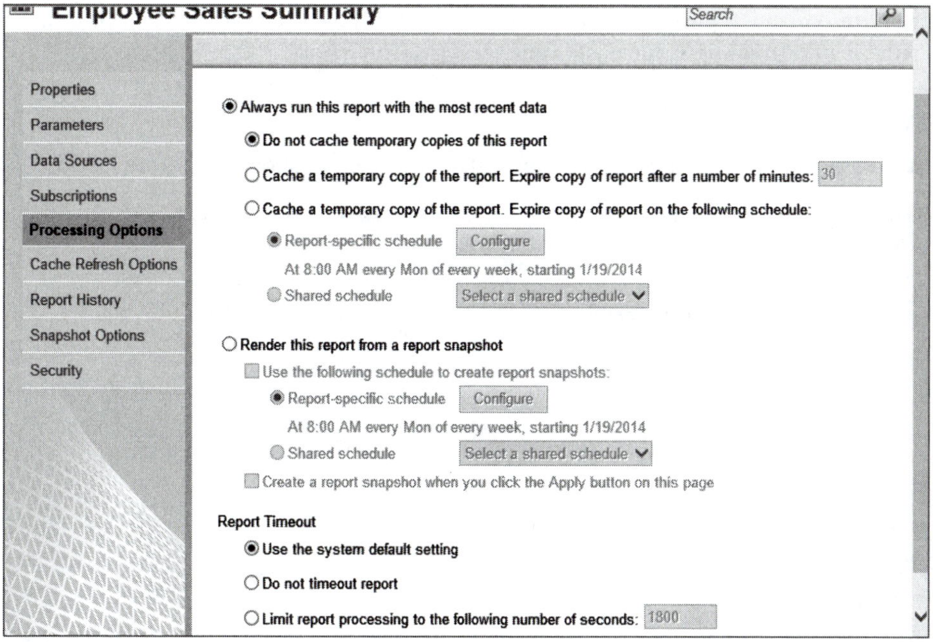

FIGURE 22-31

The second way is to set up a cache refresh plan, as shown in Figure 22-32. When you set up a new refresh plan, you are taken to a simple web page where you are asked if you want to create a specific schedule or reuse an existing one.

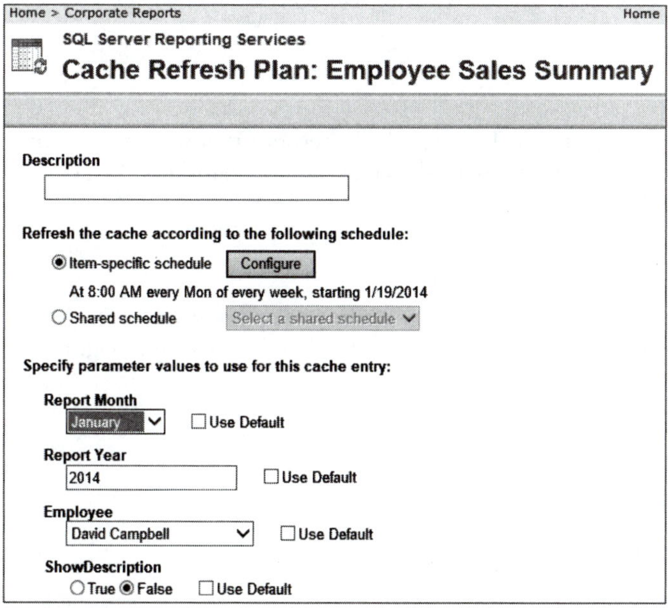

FIGURE 22-32

Using a cache refresh plan is a good way to ensure the reports in the cache stay fresh, while, at the same time, reducing the amount of time users must wait for the report.

Report History

To view past snapshots of a report, use the Report History screen, as shown in Figure 22-33.

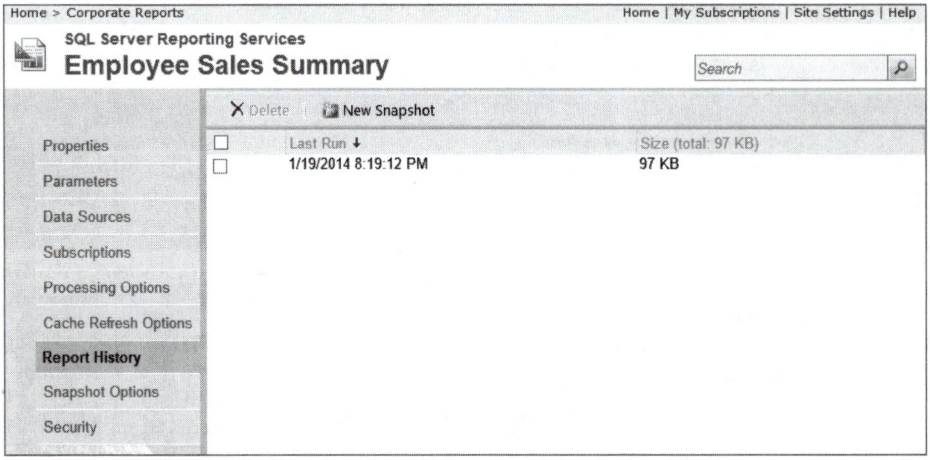

FIGURE 22-33

The Report History page provides a listing of every snapshot of the report. To view one, simply click the last run date/time (refer to Figure 22-33). You also have the option to generate a new snapshot by clicking the New Snapshot button. This causes the report to execute immediately and be stored as a snapshot.

Snapshot Options

When you use snapshots, you must manage them. Through the Snapshot Options page shown in Figure 22-34, you can establish a schedule for automatically creating new snapshots. You can also determine how many snapshots should be retained.

Security

Security is the final section of the Manage web pages. This enables you to fine-tune access for this specific report. The dialog and actions are identical to those for the folders, as seen in Figure 22-18.

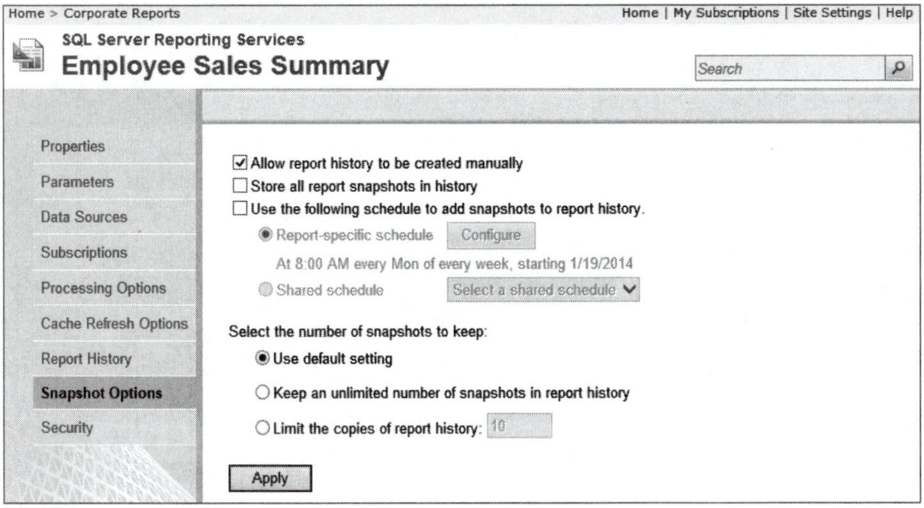

FIGURE 22-34

SUMMARY

SQL Server Reporting Services offers a rich toolset you can use to manage both the server and the reports it contains. The Reporting Services Configuration Manager enables you to configure critical options such as the databases SSRS needs to do its job, encryption keys, URLs, and more.

Using the Properties settings in SQL Server Management Studio, you can fine-tune your instance of SSRS. Properties such as execution timeouts, logging, history, and security are set via SQL Server Management Studio.

Report Manager is the tool of choice for managing and executing your reports. You can configure reports to run on schedules, and to be placed into a cache for reuse. You can also store and track them as snapshots.

With the understanding acquired here, the DBA will be well equipped to manage SSRS.

Now that you have learned about Business Intelligence in SQL Server 2014, you are ready to move on to Chapter 23, which discusses SQL Server integration with SharePoint.

23

SQL Server 2014 SharePoint 2013 Integration

WHAT'S IN THIS CHAPTER?

➤   Advanced reporting and self-service BI capabilities

➤   Supporting SharePoint as a DBA

➤   Managing data in a SharePoint environment

With the advent of all the new features discussed in preceding chapters, Microsoft is leveraging previous improvements to SharePoint to enable increased SQL Server 2014 capabilities around business intelligence (BI), performance, and office integration. Users demand faster access to changing data, and the BI stack in SQL Server 2014 delivers that with some exciting new enhancements focused specifically at integrating with users' experience in SharePoint 2013.

SharePoint 2013 leverages the power and scalability of SQL Server to drive servicing content, configuration data, and metadata about users and security. The major area of integration for SharePoint 2013 is databases that support the service applications. This chapter dives deeper into the BI features of SQL Server that interact with and require SharePoint to experience their full functionality.

COMPONENTS OF INTEGRATION

When you think about integration in the SQL Server and SharePoint world, you are looking at service applications inside of SharePoint that interact with products or features in the SQL Server ecosystem. This integration has many components, including service applications, SQL Server features, and Reporting Services features such as Power View. The following sections cover each component in greater detail.

PowerPivot

PowerPivot is a free, versatile self-service add-in for Excel. This add-in is used for working with large amounts of data within Excel and is great for BI professionals and also for DBAs working with performance data and other counters. The PowerPivot add-in in for Excel provides a lot of the capabilities of Analysis Services tabular models within Excel from a data sorting and manipulation perspective. The functionality of PowerPivot is greatly extended when used with SharePoint to provide an extension of *personal BI*, sometimes referred to as *team BI*. In either scenario use case, PowerPivot provides users a simple, familiar interface for slicing data without the need for consolidating data into a data warehouse. Even with collaboration in SharePoint being the end goal, PowerPivot documents will be created inside Excel. In this PowerPivot environment, data will be imported, compressed by the xVelocity engine, relationships will be built, and key performance indicators (KPIs), charts, and graphs will be created.

When the initial creation of the PowerPivot document has been completed, it is saved as an Excel 2010 or 2013 file just like any other Excel workbook. At this point, the workbook will be uploaded to a SharePoint site for consumption by others inside the organization.

Using Excel with SharePoint

Setting up PowerPivot for SharePoint has several requirements. This includes an Excel Services application to render the workbook in the browser for the user to consume. Additionally, you need an Analysis Services instance for PowerPivot workbooks to run interactive queries. The Analysis Services instance is the main difference between the client and SharePoint versions of PowerPivot. On a client workstation, Analysis Services runs within the context of the Excel application. In SharePoint, Analysis Services requires its own instance.

Installation

Before installing PowerPivot, the SQL Server Analysis Services (SSAS) instance name "PowerPivot" must be available. The easiest way to get PowerPivot up and running is on a new SharePoint farm installation, although you can add it after by doing the SharePoint installation and indicating you are doing the setup for an existing farm.

> **NOTE** *PowerPivot for SharePoint is an Enterprise feature that requires the server to join to a domain. SharePoint 2010 Service Pack 1 or SharePoint 2013 is also required.*

To install PowerPivot for SharePoint, follow these steps:

1. Run the SharePoint 2010 with Service Pack 1 or SharePoint 2013 installation wizard, using either the Enterprise or Enterprise Evaluation edition.

2. At the end of the installation wizard, choose the option to configure the farm later, by unchecking the box indicating that the Product Configuration Wizard will be run after the setup finishes. This allows for PowerPivot and all the relevant database objects to be installed, and then the Configuration Wizard is started by the SQL Server install.

3. Run the SQL Server 2014 Installation Wizard.

4. On the initial setup screen, choose the "SQL Server PowerPivot for SharePoint" option. Optionally, you can choose the setting to include a relational database engine in the installation. When you check this option, the database engine installs under the instance name of PowerPivot. You can choose this to consolidate the databases, or if you don't have an existing database engine. If a database engine is already set up, you don't need to select this option. Remember where the databases will be stored for SharePoint, another instance, or the PowerPivot instance. You need this information during the farm setup.

5. *For SharePoint 2013 only*, download and install `spPowerPivot.msi` to provide server-side data refresh and management support. `spPowerPivot.msi` is not supported by SharePoint 2010 and, therefore, is not required.

SharePoint Configuration

After you complete all the necessary SQL Server installation steps to create the PowerPivot instance (as described in the previous section), and after the farm configuration has been run, you must create a new service application. Before creating the service application, you must run one more configuration wizard.

1. On the server where the SQL Server PowerPivot for SharePoint installation was run, click the Start menu and navigate to Microsoft SQL Server 2014 ➪ Configuration Tools.

2. Select the appropriate PowerPivot for SharePoint Configuration for the version of SharePoint you are running. For SharePoint 2010, select "PowerPivot for SharePoint Configuration," and for SharePoint 2013 select "PowerPivot for SharePoint 2013 Configuration."

3. The configuration wizard will scan your system and determine which configuration steps must be completed based on the current installation. Click through all the actions in the left pane and fill in all required fields in the right pane.

4. Click the Validate button in the bottom-right corner of the screen.

5. Fix any validation errors that appear and rerun the validation.

6. Click the Run button next to Validate. A series of Windows PowerShell commands will be executed to configure the Secure Store Service, deploy solution files, and create the first PowerPivot Service application.

Follow these steps to create additional PowerPivot Service applications in Central Administration:

1. In Central Administration, click Manage Service Applications to bring up a list of the service applications.

2. From the New menu in the top-left of the screen, select SQL Server PowerPivot Service Application.

3. Activate PowerPivot inside the site collection by browsing to it. Under the Site Collection Features section of the site settings, select Activate next to "PowerPivot Feature Integration for Site Collection."

You must also set up an unattended service account to handle things such as data refresh. The security for this application account is very specific for the environment of your organization. Treat this as a regular application account that needs access to read data from your data source. The data source will likely be the `SQL Server Analysis Services\PowerPivot Instance`. To get started, set aside a location on the site to store the PowerPivot workbooks, which is known as a *PowerPivot Gallery*. To create a new one in SharePoint 2010, create a site, then click Site Actions ⇨ More Options, and search for the PowerPivot Gallery. In SharePoint 2013, you can find the PowerPivot Gallery on the "Add an App" screen.

From this point, you can schedule and restrict PowerPivot data refresh in SharePoint, set the history retention settings, and monitor workbook performance and use right from inside Central Administration.

> **NOTE** *When you first visit a PowerPivot Gallery, you may be prompted to install Silverlight. This should be acceptable, as long as your corporate policies allow it.*

Reporting Services

Reporting Services continues to be an integral part of the Microsoft BI stack. With SQL Server 2014, Reporting Services integration is accomplished through a SharePoint service application for Reporting Services.

SQL Server 2014 Architecture

While Reporting Services native mode is still available, SharePoint integration is consolidated with the rest of the SharePoint services. The biggest requirement for setting up Reporting Services 2014 in SharePoint integrated mode is SharePoint 2010 Service Pack 1 or SharePoint 2013. Two options must be selected on the Feature Selection page of the SQL Server installation: Reporting Services— SharePoint and Reporting Services Add-In for SharePoint Products. Following the completion of the installation, all further setup is handled within SharePoint.

Much like configuring other service applications such as Excel Services, in SharePoint Central Administration, click Manage Service Applications, click New in the top-left corner, and select SQL Server Reporting Services Service Application. All settings for the Reporting Services configuration are handled in Central Administration. This includes specifying an application pool, a corresponding security account, and the location of the Reporting Services database.

This approach provides many benefits. As mentioned previously, the reporting databases have their locations specified inside SharePoint Central Administration. This is advantageous because they can easily be placed on any server (including on the same instance as the SharePoint content databases) without the need to go outside the SharePoint environment. A service application is the name of an application that runs inside SharePoint. It is easy to set up multiple service applications for Reporting Services for use in the farm. When this happens, each gets its own set of databases on the back end; they are not shared.

With all the Reporting Services pieces for SharePoint integrated mode contained inside SharePoint, the maintenance model is simplified. Scale-out can also be handled on the SharePoint side, rather than worrying about scaling Reporting Services and SharePoint.

Installation

Starting with the 2012 release of SQL Server, the installation and configuration of Reporting Services in SharePoint is streamlined. This change holds true in SQL Server 2014. All configuration and management of SQL Server Reporting Services (SSRS) is now handled inside of SharePoint Central Administration. However, you will need to run the SQL Server installation and add two shared features, "Reporting Services - SharePoint" and "Reporting Services Add-in for SharePoint Products."

To install and configure SSRS in SharePoint, follow these steps:

1. Run the SQL Server installation and choose SQL Server Feature Installation on the Setup Role screen.

2. On the next screen, Feature Selection, check the box next to "Reporting Services - SharePoint" and "Reporting Services Add-in for SharePoint Products" in the Shared Features section, as shown in Figure 23-1.

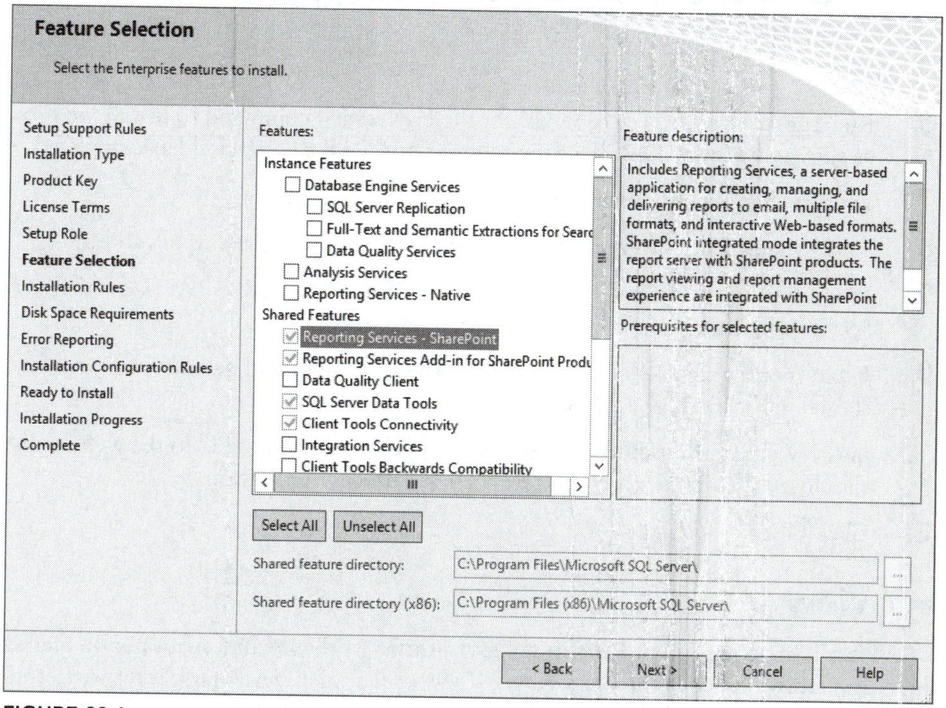

FIGURE 23-1

3. Accept the remaining default selections and click Install on the last page of the wizard.

4. After the installation completes launch the SharePoint 2013 Management Shell from the Start menu.

5. Run `Install-SPRSService` at the PowerShell command to install the SharePoint service, as shown in Figure 23-2. If no message is returned, the command has completed successfully.

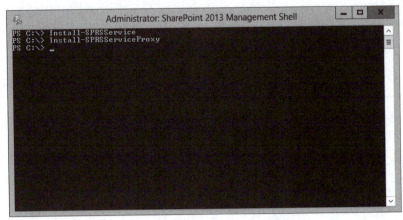

FIGURE 23-2

6. Run `Install-SPRSServiceProxy` at the PowerShell command to install the proxy service, as shown in Figure 23-2. If no message is returned the command has completed successfully.

7. Launch SharePoint Central Administration.

8. Click Manage Service Applications to bring up a list of service applications.

9. From the New menu in the top-left of the screen, select SQL Server Reporting Services Service Application, as shown in Figure 23-3.

10. Fill in the resulting page with the appropriate app pool and database server information, as shown in Figure 23-4.

11. In the Web Application Association section, check the box next to the web applications that should be allowed to access this Reporting Services application.

12. Click OK.

Power View

Power View is an extension of Reporting Services that works in combination with SharePoint to provide interactive ad-hoc reporting. Power View works with Developer, Enterprise, and Business Intelligence versions of SQL Server 2014. It also requires an Enterprise edition of SharePoint 2010 or SharePoint 2013, and the Reporting Services add-in for SharePoint to be enabled. Power View reports can be developed against both tabular models and multidimensional cubes.

FIGURE 23-3

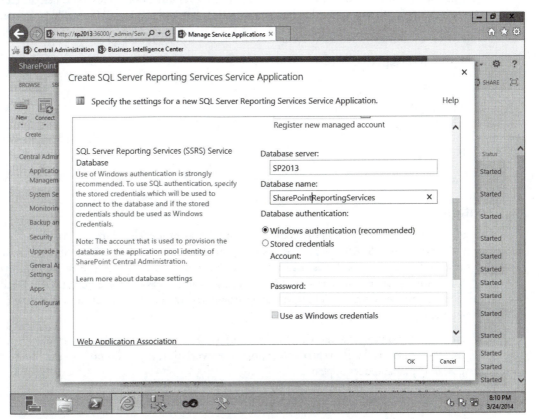

FIGURE 23-4

What Is Power View?

Power View provides an innovative way to interact with your data by way of Silverlight renderings. These reports are developed and fed from PowerPivot workbooks deployed to a SharePoint PowerPivot Gallery, or connections to multidimensional cubes and tabular models deployed to SSAS 2014.

This is not meant to be a replacement for traditional Reporting Services reports or Report Builder. Power View is meant for ad-hoc data exploration, which is to say moving through your data and looking at how it relates across your business. The traditional file created by the current Reporting Services tools is a *report definition file (RDL)* and cannot be edited or viewed in Power View. Because Power View is also used only inside SharePoint, it is not applicable for use in every situation, depending on the reporting needs. Each of these technologies has its place in the reporting environment.

Presentation Layer

Unlike a traditional Reporting Services report, Power View is an "always on" presentation type that doesn't require you to preview reports. The data is always live. There is also the added advantage of exporting Power View reports to PowerPoint where each individual report becomes its own slide. The full-screen viewing and PowerPoint slides work in the same way. Both enable interaction with data such as applying filters that the builder added, or using visualizations. However, neither enables further development. In this state, the data is interactive, but you cannot add new filters or visualizations.

Following are some of the visualizations available in Power View:

- ➤ Table/Matrix
- ➤ Chart
- ➤ Bubble Chart
- ➤ Scatter Chart
- ➤ Cards
- ➤ Tiles

Creation

You initiate all Power View report creation from tabular model elements, `.xlsx` files, or connection files pointing to SSAS tabular models or multidimensional cubes, within SharePoint document libraries or PowerPivot Galleries. Clicking the arrow next to an applicable element can reveal an option for Create Power View Report. Selecting this option opens the Power View Designer. You can edit existing reports by clicking the drop-down arrow next to a report and selecting Edit in Power View.

When you save Power View reports, they are in RDLX format. The option to save corresponding images is also available. When you export to PowerPoint, if you do not use the option to save images, only placeholders appear.

DATA REFRESH

As a SQL professional, your job focuses on the ability to get data in and out quickly and efficiently. This is important for the performance of your data environment and the applications serviced by it. You've already seen a significant amount of DBA-related items such as PowerPivot and Power View earlier in this chapter, but more is added here. This section focuses on managing and controlling data refresh with your reports and data in SharePoint. Many possible data sources exist, so it is best to focus on those that typically come out of SQL Server, such as the following:

➤ Excel Services

➤ PerformancePoint Services

➤ Visio Services

➤ PowerPivot

Using Data Connections in Excel

Every Excel workbook that uses external data contains a connection to a data source. Connections consist of everything required to establish communications with and retrieve data from an external data source. These requirements include the following:

➤ A *connection string*, which specifies to which server to connect and how to connect to it

➤ A *query*, which is a string that specifies what data to retrieve

➤ Any other specifics required to get the data (such as impersonation, proxy mode, and so on)

➤ Embedded and linked connections

Excel workbooks can contain embedded connections and can link to external connections. Embedded connections are stored internally as part of the workbook. External connections are stored in the form of Office Data Connection (ODC) files that can be referenced by a workbook.

Excel embedded connections and external connections function the same way. Both correctly specify all the required parameters to connect to data successfully. External connection files can be centrally stored, secured, managed, and re-used. They are a good choice when planning an overall approach to getting a large group of users connected to external data. For more information, see http://technet.microsoft.com/en-us/library/ff604007.aspx#section4.

For a single connection, a workbook can have both an embedded copy of the connection information and a link to an external connection file. The connection can be configured to always use an external connection file to refresh data from an external data source. In this case, if the external connection file cannot be retrieved, or if it does not establish a connection to the data source, the workbook cannot retrieve data to refresh what is there. The results of this vary based on the data connection settings. If the connection is not configured to use only an external connection file, Excel attempts to use the embedded copy of a connection. If that fails, Excel attempts to use the connection file to connect to the external data source.

For security purposes, Excel Services can be configured to enable only connections from connection files. In this configuration, all embedded connections are ignored for workbooks loaded on the SharePoint server, and connections are tried only when there is a link to a valid connection file that is trusted by the server administrator. For more information, see `http://technet.microsoft.com/en-us/library/ff604007.aspx#section4`.

> **WARNING** *Excel Services is not available in SharePoint by default. You must turn it on and configure it.*

Data Providers

Data providers are drivers that applications (such as Excel and Excel Services) use to connect to specific data sources. For example, a special MSOLAP data provider can connect to Microsoft SQL Server 2008 Analysis Services (SSAS). The data provider is specified as part of the connection string when you connect to a data source.

Data providers handle queries, parsing connection strings, and other connection-specific logic. This functionality is not part of Excel Services. Excel Services cannot control how data providers behave.

Any data provider used by Excel Services must be explicitly trusted by Excel Services. For information about how to add a new data provider to the trusted providers list, see `http://technet.microsoft.com/en-us/library/ff191200.aspx`.

By default, Excel Services trusts many well-known data providers. In most cases, you do not have to add a new data provider. Data providers are typically added for custom solutions.

Authentication to External Data

Database servers require a user to be *authenticated* (that is, identify oneself to the server). The next step is *authorization* (that is, communicating to the server the permitted actions associated with the user).

Authentication is required for the data server to perform authorization, or to enforce security restrictions that prevent data from being exposed to anyone other than authorized users.

Excel Services supports the following authentication options:

➤ **Windows Authentication**—Excel Services uses Integrated Windows authentication and attempts to connect to the data source by using the Windows identity of the user who displays the workbook.

➤ **Secure Store Service (SSS)**—Excel Services uses the credentials associated with the specified Secure Store target application.

➤ **None**—Excel Services impersonates the unattended service account and passes the connection string to the data source.

The authentication option is configured in Microsoft Excel and is a property of the external data connection. The default value is Windows Authentication.

Integrated Windows Authentication

If you choose the Windows Authentication option, Excel Services attempts to pass the Windows identity of the user viewing the Excel workbook to the external data source. Kerberos delegation is required for any data source located on a different server than the server where Excel Calculation Services runs, if that data source uses Integrated Windows authentication.

In most enterprise environments, Excel Calculation Services runs on a different computer than the data source. This means that Kerberos delegation (constrained delegation is recommended) is required to enable data connections that use Windows authentication. For more information about how to configure Kerberos constrained delegation for Excel Services, see http://technet .microsoft.com/en-us/library/ff829837.aspx.

Secure Store Service

Secure Store is a SharePoint Server 2010 service application used to store encrypted credentials in a database for use by applications to authenticate to other applications. In this case, Excel Services uses Secure Store to store and retrieve credentials for use in authenticating to external data sources.

If you choose the SSS option, you must then specify the application ID of a Secure Store target application. The specified target application serves as a lookup used to retrieve the appropriate set of credentials. Each target application can have permissions set so that only specific users or groups can use the stored credentials.

When provided with an application ID, Excel Services retrieves the credentials from the Secure Store database for the user who accesses the workbook (either through the browser or using Excel Web Services). Excel Services then uses those credentials to authenticate to the data source and retrieve data.

For information about how to use Secure Store with Excel Services, see http://technet .microsoft.com/en-us/library/ff191191.aspx.

None

When you select the None option, no credential retrieval occurs, and no special action is taken for authentication for the connection. Excel Services does not try to delegate credentials, and does not try to retrieve credentials stored for the user from the Secure Store database. Instead, Excel Services impersonates the unattended service account and passes the connection string to the data provider that handles authentication.

The connection string may specify a username and password to connect to the data source, or may specify that the Windows identity of the user or computer issuing the request be used to connect to the data source. In either case, the unattended account is impersonated first, and then the data source connection is made. The connection string and the provider determine the authorization method. Additionally, authorization can be based on either the credentials found in the connection string, or the impersonated unattended account's Windows identity.

Excel Services Security and External Data

Excel Services manages workbooks and external data connections by using the following:

➤ **Trusted file locations**—Locations designated by an administrator from which Excel Services can load workbooks

➤ **Trusted data connection libraries**—SharePoint Server data connection libraries that have been explicitly trusted by an administrator from which Excel Services can load data connection files

➤ **Trusted data providers**—Data providers that have been explicitly trusted by an administrator

➤ **Unattended service account**—A low-privileged account that Excel Services can impersonate when it makes data connections

Trusted File Locations

Excel Services loads workbooks only from trusted file locations. A *trusted file location* is a SharePoint Server location, network file share, or web folder address from which the administrator has explicitly enabled workbooks to be loaded. These directories are added to a list that is internal to Excel Services. This list is known as the *trusted file locations list*.

Trusted locations can specify a set of restrictions for workbooks loaded from them. All workbooks loaded from a trusted location adhere to the settings for that trusted location. Following is a short list of the trusted location settings that affect external data:

➤ **Allow External Data**—Defines how external data can be accessed.

➤ **No Data Access Allowed (Default)**—Only connection files in a trusted SharePoint Server data connection library are allowed.

➤ **Warn on Refresh**—Defines whether to show the query refresh warnings.

➤ **Stop When Refresh on Open Fails**—Defines whether to fail the workbook load if external data does not refresh when the workbook opens. This is used in scenarios in which the workbook has cached data results that will change depending on the identity of the user viewing the workbook. The objective is to hide these cached results and make sure that any user who views the workbook can see only the data specific to that user. In this case, if the workbook is set to refresh on open and the refresh fails, the workbook does not display.

➤ **External Data Cache Lifetime**—Defines external data cache expiration times. Data is shared among many users on the server to improve scale and performance, and these cache lifetimes are adjustable. This accommodates scenarios in which query execution should be kept to a minimum because the query might take a long time to execute. In these scenarios, the data often changes only daily, weekly, or monthly, instead of by the minute or every hour.

Trusted Data Connection Libraries and Managed Connections

A *data connection library* is a SharePoint Server library designed to store connection files, which can then be referenced by Office applications (such as Excel and Microsoft Visio). Excel Services loads only connection files from trusted SharePoint Server data connection libraries. A *trusted data connection library* is a library that the server administrator has explicitly added to an internal trusted list. Data connection libraries enable you to centrally manage, secure, store, and reuse data connections.

➤ **Managing connections**—Because workbooks contain a link to the file in a data connection library, if something about the connection changes (such as a server name or a Secure Store application ID), only a single connection file must be updated instead of potentially many workbooks. The workbooks can obtain the connection changes automatically the next time they use that connection file to refresh data from Excel or Excel Services.

➤ **Securing connections**—The data connection library in a SharePoint library supports all the permissions that SharePoint Server does, including per-folder and per-item permissions. The advantage that this provides on the server is that a data connection library can become a locked-down data connection store that is highly controlled. Many users may have read-only access to it. This enables them to use the data connections, but they can be prevented from adding new connections. By using access control lists (ACLs) with the data connection library, and letting only trusted authors upload connections, the data connection library becomes a store of trusted connections.

You can configure Excel Services to load connection files only from data connection libraries explicitly trusted by the server administrator, and block the loading of any embedded connections. In this configuration, Excel Services uses the data connection library to apply another layer of security around data connections.

You can use data connection libraries together with the new Viewer role in SharePoint Server that enables those connections to refresh workbooks rendered in a browser by Excel Services. If the Viewer role is applied, users cannot access the connection file contents from a client application (such as Excel). Therefore, the connection file contents are protected, but still can be used for workbooks refreshed on the server.

➤ **Storing connections**—Storing data connections is another important role for document libraries. These data connections are stored as objects like documents or images in a library, and can be accessed by services and reports throughout the farm depending on permissions.

➤ **Reusing connections**—Users can reuse connections created by other users and create different reports that use the same data source. You can have the IT department or a BI expert create connections, and other users can reuse them without understanding the details about data providers, server names, or authentication. The location of the data connection library can even be published to Office clients so that the data connections display in Excel or in any other client application that uses the data connection library.

Trusted Data Providers

Excel Services uses only external data providers on the Excel Services trusted data providers list. This is a security mechanism that prevents the server from using providers that the administrator does not trust.

Unattended Service Account

Excel Services runs under a highly privileged account. Because Excel Services has no control over the data provider and does not directly parse provider-specific connection strings, using this account for the purposes of data access would be a security risk. To lessen this risk, Excel Services uses an *unattended service account*. This is a low-privileged account that is impersonated by Excel Services under the following circumstances:

➤ Any time that it tries a connection where the None authentication option is selected.

➤ Whenever the Secure Store Service (SSS) option is selected and the stored credentials are not Windows credentials.

➤ If the None option is selected and the unattended account does not have access to the data source, Excel Services impersonates the unattended service account and uses information stored in the connection string to connect to the data source.

➤ If the None option is selected and the unattended account has access to the data source, a connection is successfully established using the credentials of the unattended service account. Use caution when you design solutions that intentionally use this account to connect to data. This is a single account that potentially can be used by every workbook on the server. Any user can open a workbook with an authentication setting of None using Excel Services to view that data by using the server. In some scenarios, this might be needed. However, Secure Store is the preferred solution for managing passwords on a per-user or per-group basis.

➤ If the SSS option is selected and the stored credentials are not Windows credentials, Excel Services impersonates the unattended service account, and then attempts to connect to the data source by using the stored credentials.

➤ If the Windows Authentication option is selected, or if the SSS option is selected and the stored credentials are Windows credentials, then the unattended service account is not used. Instead, Excel Services impersonates the Windows identity and attempts to connect to the data source.

PerformancePoint Data Connections

PerformancePoint is a scorecard and dashboard creation tool built into SharePoint. Although PerformancePoint doesn't require any special SQL Server components to be installed (like PowerPivot and Reporting Services do), it frequently interacts with SQL Server as a data source. These data sources can be SQL Server databases, Analysis Services Multidimensional cubes, or Tabular models.

In PerformancePoint Services, you must create a connection to the data source or sources you want to use in your dashboard. All data used in PerformancePoint Services is external data, living in data repositories outside of PerformancePoint. After you establish a data connection, you can use the data in the various PerformancePoint feature areas.

PerformancePoint supports both tabular data sources (including SharePoint Lists, Excel Services, SQL Server tables, and Excel workbooks) and Analysis Services data sources. It also supports PowerPivot for Excel.

Tabular Data Sources

A user can create a data connection to SharePoint Lists, Excel Services, SQL Server tables, or Excel workbooks. For these kinds of data sources, you can view a sample of the data from the Dashboard Designer tool, and set specific properties for the data depending how you want it to be interpreted within PerformancePoint. For example, you can indicate which data sets should be treated as a dimension; you can specify if a data set is to be treated as a dimension or a fact; or, if you do not want the data to be included, you can select Ignore. If you decide to set the value as a fact, you can indicate how those numbers should be aggregated in PerformancePoint Services. You can also use data sets that have time values within PerformancePoint Services, and use the PerformancePoint Services Time Intelligence features to set time parameters and create dashboard filters.

SharePoint Lists

You can use data contained in a SharePoint List on a SharePoint Site in PerformancePoint Services by creating a SharePoint List data source in Dashboard Designer. Data from SharePoint Lists can only be read, not modified. Modification to SharePoint List data must be done from SharePoint. Users may connect to any kind of SharePoint List.

Excel Services

Data in Excel files published to Excel Services on a SharePoint Site can be used in PerformancePoint Services by creating an Excel Services data source. Supported published data can be read only in PerformancePoint Services. Published parameter values can be modified from the Dashboard Designer. If you use an Excel Services parameter in calculating a KPI, it is easy to make additional changes. PerformancePoint Services supports the following Excel Services components: Named Ranges, Tables, and Parameters.

SQL Server Tables

You can create a data source connection to a SQL Server database and use the data within PerformancePoint Services. Tables and views are supported data sources within PerformancePoint Services.

Excel Workbooks

You can use the content of an actual Excel file stored in PerformancePoint as a data source in PerformancePoint Services by creating an Excel Workbook data source connection, and selecting only the data to be used. The original Excel file will be independent from the PerformancePoint copy. PerformancePoint Services 2010 supports Excel 2007 and Excel 2010 workbooks as data sources.

Analysis Services

Use data residing in a SQL Server Analysis Services multidimensional cubes or tabular models in PerformancePoint Services by creating a data connection to the source. PerformancePoint Services enables you to map the wanted time dimension and the required level of detail for its hierarchies to the internal PerformancePoint Services Time Intelligence.

PowerPivot for Excel

In PerformancePoint Services you can use a PowerPivot model as a data source to build your PerformancePoint Services dashboards. To use PowerPivot as a data source within a PerformancePoint Services dashboard, you must have PerformancePoint Services activated on a SharePoint Server farm, and have PowerPivot for SharePoint installed. After you have created a PowerPivot model by using the PowerPivot add-in for Excel, you must upload or publish this Excel file to a SharePoint site that has PowerPivot Services enabled. Create the data source connection in Dashboard Designer using the Analysis Services data source template.

Visio Services Data Refresh

The Visio Graphics Service can connect to data sources. These include SharePoint Lists, Excel workbooks hosted on the farm, databases such as Microsoft SQL Server, and custom data sources. You can control access to specific data sources by explicitly defining the trusted data providers, and configuring them in the list of trusted data providers.

When Visio Services loads a data-connected Web Drawing, the service checks the connection information that is stored in the Web drawing to determine whether the specified data provider is a trusted data provider. If the provider is specified on the Visio Services trusted data provider list, a connection is tried; otherwise, the connection request is ignored.

After an administrator configures Visio Services to enable connections to a particular data source, additional security configurations must be made, depending on the kind of data source. The following data sources are supported by Visio Services:

- ➤ Excel workbooks stored on SharePoint Server with Excel Services enabled
- ➤ SharePoint Lists
- ➤ Databases such as SQL Server databases
- ➤ Custom data providers
- ➤ Visio Web drawings connected to SharePoint Lists

> **NOTE** *Published Visio Drawings can be connected to SharePoint Lists on the same farm on which the drawing is hosted. The user viewing the Web drawing must have access to both the drawing and the SharePoint List to which the drawing connects. SharePoint Server manages these permissions and credentials.*

Visio content in SharePoint can be refreshed in a number of ways. Two of the most common ways are discussed in the following sections. They include Excel Services and SQL Server data.

Visio Web Drawings Connected to Excel Services

Published Visio drawings can connect to Excel workbooks hosted on the same farm as the Web Drawing with Excel Services running and configured correctly. To view the Web Drawing, the user must have access to both the drawing and the Excel workbook to which the drawing connects. These permissions and credentials are managed by SharePoint Server.

Visio Web Drawings Connected to SQL Server Databases

When a published Visio Web Drawing is connected to a SQL Server database, Visio Services uses additional security configuration options to establish a connection between the Visio Graphics Service and the database.

Visio Services Authentication Methods

Visio supports the following authentication types:

➤ **Integrated Windows Authentication**—In this security model the Visio Graphics Service uses the drawing viewer's identity to authenticate with the database. Integrated Windows Authentication with constrained Kerberos delegation is more helpful for increasing security than the other authentication methods shown in this list. This configuration requires constrained Kerberos delegation to be enabled between the application server running the Visio Graphics Service and the database server. The database might require additional configuration to enable Kerberos-based authentication.

➤ **Secure Store Service**—In this security model, the Visio Graphics Service uses the Secure Store Service to map the user's credentials to a different credential that has access to the database. The Secure Store Service supports individual and group mappings for both Integrated Windows authentication and other forms of authentication such as SQL Server authentication. This gives administrators more flexibility in defining one-to-one, many-to-one, or many-to-many relationships. This authentication model can be used only by drawings that use an Office Data Connection (ODC) file to specify the connection. The ODC file specifies the Secure Store target application that can be used for credential mapping. The ODC files must be created with Microsoft Excel.

➤ **Unattended service account**—For ease of configuration the Visio Graphics Service provides a special configuration where an administrator can create a unique mapping associating all users to a single account by using a Secure Store target application. This mapped account (known as the *unattended service account*) must be a low-privilege Windows domain account that is given access to databases. The Visio Graphics Service impersonates this account when it connects to the database if no other authentication method is specified. This approach does not enable personalized queries against a database, and does not provide auditing of database calls. This authentication method is the default authentication method used when you connect to SQL Server databases. If no ODC file is used in the Visio Web drawing that specifies a different authentication method, then Visio Services uses the credentials specified by the unattended account to connect to the SQL Server database.

In a SharePoint farm with many Visio drawings, it is likely a mix of the authentication methods described here. Consider the following authentication behaviors when setting up Visio security and plan accordingly:

➤ Visio Services supports the use of both ODC files and the unattended service account in the same farm. In Web Drawings connected to SQL Server data that do not use ODC files, the unattended account is required and always used.

➤ If Integrated Windows authentication is selected, and authentication to the data source fails, Visio Services does not attempt to render the drawing using the unattended service account.

➤ Integrated Windows authentication can be used together with the Secure Store by configuring drawings to use an ODC file that specifies a Secure Store target application for those drawings that require specific credentials.

PowerPivot Data Refresh

PowerPivot data refresh is a scheduled server-side operation that queries external data sources to update embedded PowerPivot data in an Excel workbook stored in a content library.

Data refresh is a built-in feature of PowerPivot for SharePoint, but using it requires that you run specific services and timer jobs in your SharePoint farm. Additional administrative steps (such as installing data providers and checking database permissions) are often required for data refresh to succeed.

After you ensure that the server environment and permissions are configured, data refresh is ready to use. To use data refresh, a SharePoint user creates a schedule on a PowerPivot workbook that specifies how often data refresh occurs. Creating the schedule is typically done by the workbook owner or author who published the file to SharePoint. This person creates and manages the data refresh schedules for the workbooks that he or she owns. The following sections provide a list of steps you should follow to perform a successful PowerPivot data refresh.

Step 1: Enable Secure Store Service and Generate a Master Key

PowerPivot data refresh depends on Secure Store Service to provide credentials used to run data refresh jobs and to connect to external data sources that use stored credentials.

If you installed PowerPivot for SharePoint using the New Server option, the Secure Store Service is configured for you. For all other installation scenarios, you must create and configure a service application manually and generate a master encryption key for Secure Store Service. You complete this by performing the following steps:

1. In Central Administration, under Application Management, click "Manage service applications."

2. In the Service Applications Ribbon, under Create, click New.

3. Select Secure Store Service.

4. In the Create Secure Store Application page, enter a name for the application.

5. Under Database, specify the SQL Server instance that will host the database for this service application. The default value is the SQL Server Database Engine instance that hosts the farm configuration databases.

6. Under Database Name, enter the name of the service application database. The default value is `Secure_Store_Service_DB_<guid>`. The default name corresponds to the default name of the service application. If you entered a unique service application name, follow a similar naming convention for your database name so that you can manage them together.

7. Under Database Authentication, the default is Windows Authentication. If you choose SQL Authentication, refer to the SharePoint administrator guide for guidance on how to use the authentication type in your farm.

8. Under Application Pool, select "Create new application pool." Specify a descriptive name that can help other server administrators identify how the application pool is used.

9. Select a security account for the application pool. Specify a managed account to use. This should be a domain user account.

10. Accept the remaining default values, and then click OK. The service application appears alongside other managed services in the farm's service application list.

11. Click the Secure Store Service application from the list.

12. In the Service Applications Ribbon, click Manage.

13. Under Key Management, click Generate New Key.

14. Enter and then confirm a pass phrase. The pass phrase will be used to add additional Secure Store shared service applications.

15. Click OK.

> **NOTE** *Audit logging of Store Service operations, which is useful for trouble-shooting purposes, must be enabled before it is available.*

Step 2: Turn Off Credential Options That You Do Not Want to Support

PowerPivot data refresh provides three credential options in a data refresh schedule. When workbook owners schedule data refresh, they choose one of these options, thereby determining the account under which the data refresh job runs. As an administrator, you can determine which of the following credential options are available to schedule owners:

➤ **Option 1**—Use the data refresh account configured by the administrator, which always appears on the schedule definition page, but works only if you configure the unattended data refresh account.

➤ **Option 2**—Connect using the credentials shown in Figure 23-5, which always appear on the page, but work only when you enable the "Allow Users to Enter the Custom Windows Credentials" option in the service application configuration page. This option is enabled by default, but you can disable it if the disadvantages of using it outweigh the advantages.

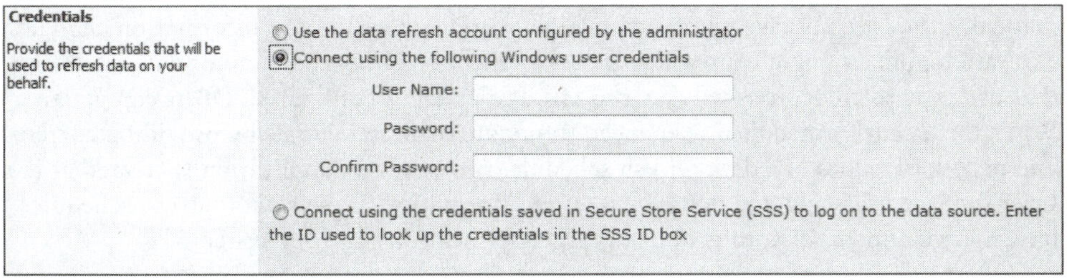

Credentials

Provide the credentials that will be used to refresh data on your behalf.

○ Use the data refresh account configured by the administrator
◉ Connect using the following Windows user credentials

User Name:
Password:
Confirm Password:

○ Connect using the credentials saved in Secure Store Service (SSS) to log on to the data source. Enter the ID used to look up the credentials in the SSS ID box

FIGURE 23-5

➤ **Option 3**—Connect using the credentials saved in Secure Store Service, which always appear on the page, but work only when a schedule owner provides a valid target application. An administrator must create these target applications in advance, and then provide the application name to those who create the data refresh schedules. This option only works if this service is configured and prevents other credentials such as option 2.

A PowerPivot service application includes a credential option that allows schedule owners to enter an arbitrary Windows username and password to run a data refresh job. This is the credential option shown in Figure 23-1 (and also referred to previously in option 2).

This credential option shown in Figure 23-5 is enabled by default. When this credential option is enabled, PowerPivot System Service generates a target application in Secure Store Service to store the username and password entered by the schedule owner. A generated target application is created using this naming convention: `PowerPivotDataRefresh_<guid>`. This can be seen in Figure 23-6. One target application is created for each set of Windows credentials.

	Target Application ID↑	Type	Target Application Name
Central Administration	☐		
Application Management	☐ Excel	Group	Excel
System Settings	☐ Excel Services Application Unattended Service Account	Group	Excel Services Application Unattended Service Account
Monitoring	☐ PerformancePoint	Group	PerformancePoint
Backup and Restore	☐ PowerPivot	Individual	PowerPivot
Security	☐ PowerPivotDataRefresh_d47f802a-25ef-4f48-91a4-a973919b7564	Individual	PowerPivotDataRefresh_d47f802a-25ef-4f48-91a4-a973919b7564
Upgrade and Migration			

FIGURE 23-6

The primary advantage to using this credential option is ease of use and simplicity. Advance work is minimal because target applications are created for you. Also, running data refresh under the credentials of the schedule owner simplifies permission requirements downstream. Most likely, this user already has permissions on the target database since they are likely the person who created the workbook. When data refresh runs under this person's Windows user identity, any data connections that specify "current user" work automatically.

The disadvantage is limited management capability. Although target applications are created automatically, they are not deleted automatically or updated as account information changes. Password expiration policies might cause these target applications to become out of date. Data refresh jobs that use expired credentials will start to fail. If alerting is configured, DBAs can get an e-mail alert. When this occurs, schedule owners need to update their credentials by providing current username and password values in a data refresh schedule. A new target application is created at that point. Over time, as users add and revise credential information in their data refresh schedules, you might have a large number of auto-generated target applications on your system.

Currently, there is no way to determine which of these target applications are active or inactive, nor is there a way to trace a specific target application back to the data refresh schedules that use it. In general, you should leave the target applications alone because deleting them might break existing data refresh schedules. Deleting a target application still in use causes data refresh to fail, with the message "Target Application Not Found" appearing in the data refresh history page of the workbook.

If you choose to disable this credential option, you can safely delete all of the target applications that were generated for PowerPivot data refresh.

Step 3: Create Target Applications to Store Credentials Used in Data Refresh

When Secure Store Service is configured, SharePoint administrators can create target applications to make stored credentials available for data refresh purposes, including the PowerPivot unattended data refresh account or any other account used to either run the job or connect to external data sources.

Recall from the previous section that you must create target applications in order for certain credential options to be usable. Specifically, you must create target applications for the PowerPivot unattended data refresh account, plus any additional stored credentials that you expect would be used in data refresh operations.

Step 4: Install Data Providers Used to Import PowerPivot Data

A data refresh operation is essentially a repeat of an import operation that retrieved the original data. This means that the same data providers used to import the data in the PowerPivot client application must also be installed on the PowerPivot application server.

You must be a local administrator to install data providers on a Windows server. If you install additional drivers, be sure to install them on each computer in the SharePoint farm that has an installation of PowerPivot for SharePoint. If you have multiple PowerPivot application servers in the farm, you must install the providers on each server.

> **NOTE** *Remember that SharePoint servers are 64-bit applications. Be sure to install the 64-bit version of the data providers you use to support data refresh operations.*

Step 5: Grant Permissions to Create Schedules and Access External Data Sources

Workbook owners or authors must have Contribute permission to schedule data refresh on a workbook. Given this permission level, they can open and edit the workbook's data refresh configuration page to specify the credentials and schedule information used to refresh the data.

In addition to SharePoint permissions, database permissions on external data sources must also be reviewed to ensure that accounts used during data refresh have sufficient access rights to the data. Determining permission requirements requires careful evaluation on your part because the permissions that you need to grant can vary depending on the connection string in the workbook and the user identity under which the data refresh job runs. When making this determination, it is important to consider the following questions:

➤ **Why do existing connection strings in a PowerPivot workbook matter to PowerPivot data refresh operations?** When data refresh runs, the server sends a connection request to the external data source using the connection string created when the data was originally imported. The server location, database name, and authentication parameters specified in that connection string are now re-used during data refresh to access the same data sources. The connection string and its overall construction cannot be modified for data refresh purposes. It is simply re-used as-is during data refresh. In some cases, if you use non-Windows authentication to connect to a data source, you can override the username and password in the connection string.

For most workbooks, the default authentication option on the connection is to use trusted connections or Windows integrated security, resulting in connection strings that include `SSPI=IntegratedSecurity` or `SSPI=TrustedConnection`. When this connection string is used during data refresh, the account used to run the data refresh job becomes the current user. As such, this account needs read permissions on any external data source accessed via a trusted connection.

➤ **Did you enable the PowerPivot unattended data refresh account?** If yes, then you should grant that account read permissions on data sources accessed during data refresh. The reason why this account needs read permissions is because, in a workbook that uses the default authentication options, the unattended account will be the current user during data refresh. Unless the schedule owner overrides the credentials in the connection string, this account needs read permissions on any number of data sources actively used in your organization.

➤ **Are you using credential option 2, allowing the schedule owner to enter a Windows username and password?** Typically, users who create PowerPivot workbooks already have sufficient permissions because they have already imported the data. If these users subsequently configure data refresh to run under their own Windows user identity, their Windows user account (which already has rights on the database) will be used to retrieve data during data refresh. Existing permissions should be sufficient.

➤ **Are you using credential option 3, using a Secure Store Service target application to provide a user identity for running data refresh jobs?** Any account used to run a data refresh job needs read permissions, for the same reasons as those described for the PowerPivot unattended data refresh account.

Step 6: Enable Workbook Upgrade for Data Refresh

By default, workbooks created using the SQL Server 2008 R2 version of PowerPivot for Excel cannot be configured for scheduled data refresh on a Microsoft SQL Server 2014 version of PowerPivot for SharePoint. If you host newer and older versions of PowerPivot workbooks in your SharePoint environment, you must upgrade SQL Server 2008 R2 workbooks first before they can be scheduled for automatic data refresh on the server.

Step 7: Verify Data Refresh Configuration

To verify data refresh, you must have a PowerPivot workbook published to a SharePoint site. You must have Contribute permissions on the workbook and permissions to access any data sources included in the data refresh schedule.

To schedule data refresh on a workbook, follow these steps:

1. On SharePoint, open a library that contains a PowerPivot workbook.

2. Select the workbook and click the down arrow to display a list of commands. Note that you may need to switch from the Gallery view to the All Documents view.

3. Click Manage PowerPivot Data Refresh.

4. In the first section, labeled Data Refresh, check the box next to Enable.

5. In the Schedule Details section, set a frequency for data refresh, as shown in Figure 23-7. If there are multiple data sources in the workbook, this will control the default schedule. Individual schedules can be modified later.

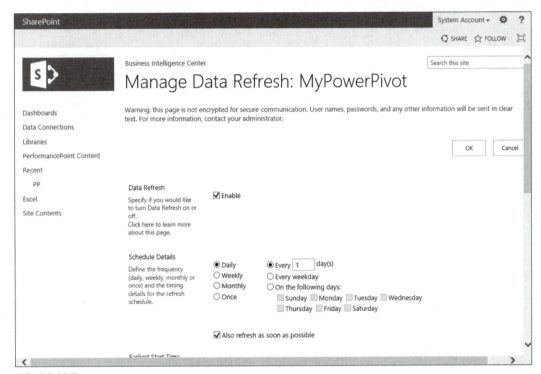

FIGURE 23-7

6. You have the option to send email when data refresh fails. To do so enter the users to be notified in the box labeled Email Notifications.

7. Using the information you learned earlier in the section, "Step 2: Turn Off Credential Options That You Do Not Want to Support," choose the credential options for data refresh.

8. If you wish to specify a custom schedule for any data source inside the workbook, do so in the Data Sources section shown in Figure 23-8.

9. Click OK.

When you create the schedule, select the "Also refresh as soon as possible" check box seen in Figure 23-7 to run data refresh immediately. You can then check the data refresh history page of that workbook to verify that it ran successfully. The PowerPivot Data Refresh timer job runs every minute. It can take at least that long to get confirmation that data refresh succeeded.

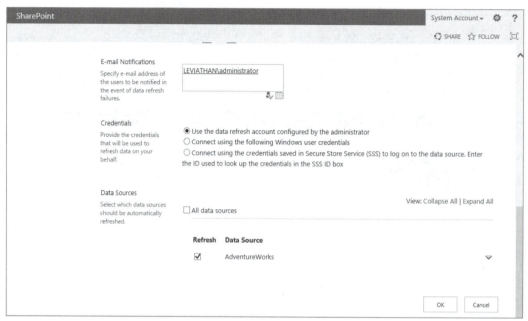

FIGURE 23-8

Be sure to try all the credential options you plan to support. For example, if you configured the PowerPivot unattended data refresh account, verify that data refresh succeeds using that option.

If data refresh fails, refer to the Troubleshooting PowerPivot Data Refresh page on the TechNet wiki for possible solutions. You can find this at http://technet.microsoft.com.

Modify Configuration Settings for Data Refresh

Each PowerPivot service application has configuration settings that affect data refresh operations. This section explains the two major ways to modify those settings.

Reschedule the PowerPivot Data Refresh Timer Job

Scheduled data refresh is triggered by a PowerPivot Data Refresh timer job that scans schedule information in the PowerPivot service application database at 1-minute intervals. When data refresh is scheduled to begin, the timer job adds the request to a processing queue on an available PowerPivot server.

You can increase the length of time between scans and disable the timer job to temporarily stop data refresh operations while you troubleshoot problems.

The default setting is 1 minute, which is the lowest value you can specify. This value is recommended because it provides the most predictable outcome for schedules that run at arbitrary times throughout the day. For example, if a user schedules data refresh for 4:15 P.M., and the timer job scans for schedules every minute, the scheduled data refresh request will be detected at 4:15 P.M. and processing will occur within a few minutes of 4:15 P.M.

If you raise the scan interval so that it runs infrequently (for example, once a day at midnight), all the data refresh operations scheduled to run during that interval are added to the processing queue all at once, potentially overwhelming the server and starving other applications of system resources. Depending on the number of scheduled refreshes, the processing queue for data refresh operations might build up to such an extent that not all jobs can complete. Data refresh requests at the end of the queue might be dropped if they run into the next processing interval.

To adjust the timer job schedule, perform the following steps:

1. In Central Administration, click Monitoring.

2. Click Review Job Definitions.

3. Select the PowerPivot Data Refresh Timer Job.

4. Modify the schedule frequency to change the interval on which the timer job scans for data refresh schedule information. The options include on a defined interval of minutes or hours, as well as a specific time each day, week, or month. The default settings are shown in Figure 23-9.

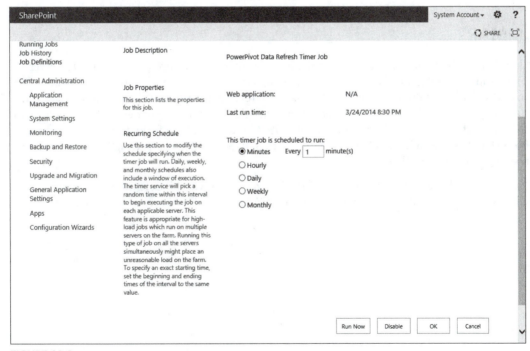

FIGURE 23-9

Disable the Data Refresh Timer Job

The PowerPivot Data Refresh timer job is a farm-level timer job that is either enabled or disabled for all PowerPivot server instances in the farm. It is not tied to a specific web application or PowerPivot service application. You cannot disable it on some servers to force data refresh processing to other servers in the farm.

If you disable the PowerPivot Data Refresh timer job, requests that were already in the queue will be processed, but no new requests will be added until you re-enable the job. Requests that were scheduled to occur in the past are not processed.

Disabling the timer job has no effect on feature availability in application pages. There is no way to remove or hide the data refresh feature in web applications. Users who have Contribute permissions or above can still create new schedules for data refresh operations, even if the timer job is permanently disabled.

To disable the timer job, perform the following steps:

1. In Central Administration, click Monitoring.

2. Click Review Job Definitions.

3. Select the PowerPivot Data Refresh Timer Job.

4. Scroll to the bottom of the screen and click the Disable button shown in Figure 23-9.

SUMMARY

SharePoint will continue to be an integral part of business intelligence (BI) within SQL Server 2014. The setup and configuration of PowerPivot, along with Reporting Services being consolidated to a shared service, lead the way in helping to make SharePoint a better tool. The addition of new features such as Power View will undoubtedly enhance the SharePoint experience for everyone who will begin using the new BI Semantic Model (BISM) analysis service format and continue using PowerPivot. In the end, SharePoint, together with SQL Server 2014, is getting better, more user-friendly, and more intelligent.

Now that you have gotten an overview of the BI integration with SharePoint, you can move on to Chapter 24. There you will get an introduction to Azure SQL Databases and administrative tasks.

24

SQL Database Administration and Configuration

WHAT'S IN THIS CHAPTER?

➤ Understanding Windows Azure SQL Database configuration

➤ Understanding server and database management

➤ Understanding administration tasks

This chapter provides a look at administering and configuring Windows Azure SQL Database. This discussion assumes that you already have a Windows Azure account, and that you have some familiarity with the Azure platform. SQL Database is a platform as a service (PaaS) offering provided as part of the Windows Azure Platform. Based on Microsoft SQL Server, it is a transactional database that includes many of the same SQL Server features that you know and love. Unlike SQL Server, though, you don't need to worry about installing and maintaining the hardware and software in which SQL Database runs. SQL Database is provided as a service, hosted in a Microsoft data center. As such, Microsoft not only takes care of the physical maintenance of the hardware and software layer, but it also offers built-in high availability, enabling you to focus on the important aspects such as database design and development.

GETTING TO KNOW WINDOWS AZURE SQL DATABASE

SQL Database is Microsoft's transactional and relational database offering for cloud computing based on Microsoft SQL Server 2012. It supports many of the features of SQL Server, including tables, primary keys, stored procedures, views, and much more.

SQL Database exposes the tabular data stream interface for T-SQL just like SQL Server. Therefore, your database applications can use SQL Database databases in the same way they use SQL Server. The only difference is that SQL Database is a database delivered as a service, meaning administration is slightly different.

SQL Database abstracts the logical administration from the physical administration. For example, you continue to administer databases, logins, and users, but Microsoft handles the administration of the physical aspects such as drives and storage, as well as the physical server.

Even with the separation of logical and physical administration, the SQL functionality has not changed. SQL Database is not a NoSQL database. It is a relational and transactional database that contains most of the objects and functionality found in SQL Server. Yet, SQL Database offers more great features than its on-premises cousin, SQL Server. SQL Database provides built-in high availability and disaster recovery—features that would be fairly expensive to add in an on-premises architecture—without any additional cost.

SQL DATABASE ARCHITECTURE

The SQL Database architecture consists of the following four distinct layers of abstraction that work together to provide a cloud-based relational database:

➤ Client

➤ Services

➤ Platform

➤ Infrastructure

As shown in Figure 24-1, these four layers of architecture enable SQL Database to work with open-source, third-party applications, as well as many of the familiar Microsoft technologies.

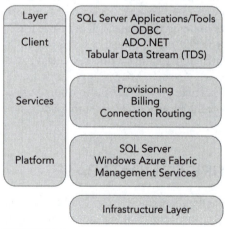

FIGURE 24-1

This layered architecture is quite similar to an on-premises architecture, except for the Services layer. The Services layer is a special SQL Database layer that provides much of the database platform functionality specific to SQL Database, as described in the following sections.

Client Layer

The Client layer is the layer that exists and resides closest to your application. Your application uses this layer to communicate with SQL Database. This layer can reside on-premises or be hosted in Windows Azure. SQL Database uses the same tabular data stream (TDS) interface as SQL Server, which enables developers to use familiar tools and libraries to develop cloud-based client applications. This layer provides data access through ADO.NET and other providers, giving you the flexibility to manipulate the data using standard T-SQL statements and familiar technologies.

Services Layer

The Services layer is the gateway between the Client layer and the Platform Layer, and is responsible for the following:

➤ **Provisioning**—Creates and provisions the databases you specify either through the Azure platform portal or SQL Server Management Studio.

➤ **Billing and metering**—Handles the usage-based metering and billing on individual Azure platform accounts.

➤ **Connection routing**—Handles all the connections routed between applications and the physical servers where the data resides.

Platform Layer

This layer includes the physical servers and services that support the Services layer. It is the Platform layer that contains the many SQL instances of SQL Server.

The key part of this layer is the *SQL Database fabric*, a distributed computing system that is installed on each SQL Server, and is made up of tightly integrated networks, servers, and storage. The SQL Database fabric provides the automatic failover, load balancing, and automatic replication between servers.

Infrastructure Layer

The Infrastructure layer represents the physical IT administration of the actual hardware and operating systems that support the Services layer.

Understanding the Differences

The key to understanding the SQL Database architecture is to remember the responsibilities of the Service layer—connections aren't connecting directly to the physical SQL Server. When connecting to SQL Server, connections are made to a physical server. In SQL Database, connections are made through a TDS endpoint via the Services layer, which routes the connection to the physical server behind the Services layer. Figure 24-2 shows the differences between on-premises and SQL Database connections.

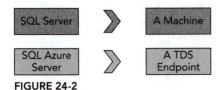

FIGURE 24-2

You can see an example of this in the differences between server names of an on-premises SQL Server and SQL Database. For example, when connecting to an on-premises SQL Server, the server name typically is the name of the physical server. In SQL Database, the server name is a Fully Qualified DNS Name (FQDN), which follows the format of `server.database.windows.net`.

The server portion of the FQDN is a unique 10-digit, randomly generated set of characters. The entire string must be used when making a connection to SQL Database.

CONFIGURING SQL DATABASE

After you create your Azure account, you are ready to start working with SQL Database. First, you must create your SQL Azure server and database, and learn the different ways to work with SQL Database. One of these is the Azure Management Portal, a web-based Azure management tool that enables you to manage all aspects of the Azure platform. This platform includes the following:

➤ **Compute Services**—Virtual machines, cloud services, websites, mobile services

➤ **Data Services**—Storage, SQL Database, Backup, Cache, HDInsight, Hyper-V Recovery Manager

➤ **App Services**—Media Services, Active Directory, Multi-Factor Authentication, Service Bus, Notification Hubs, BizTalk Services, Scheduler, Visual Studio Online

➤ **Network Services**—Virtual Network, Traffic Manager

The following sections walk you through the process of creating and configuring your SQL Database database.

Server and Database Provisioning

The simplest way to provision (create) a new server is through the Azure Management Portal. You can access the Azure Management Portal (shown in Figure 24-3) at `http://manage .windowsazure.com`.

Within the Azure Management Portal, you have the capability to manage all aspects of your SQL Database subscription. Notice in Figure 24-3 that each account can have multiple subscriptions, each subscription can have multiple servers, and each server can contain multiple databases.

Creating a new SQL Database is as simple as clicking the New button on the toolbar at the bottom of the page from the main portal page. From the New menu that pops up, select Data Services, SQL Database, and the Quick Create option to quickly create a database, database server, and login while leaving other configuration options (for example, database sizes, editions, and so on) for later. Alternatively, you can the select Custom Create option, which guides you through a wizard to create your SQL Database.

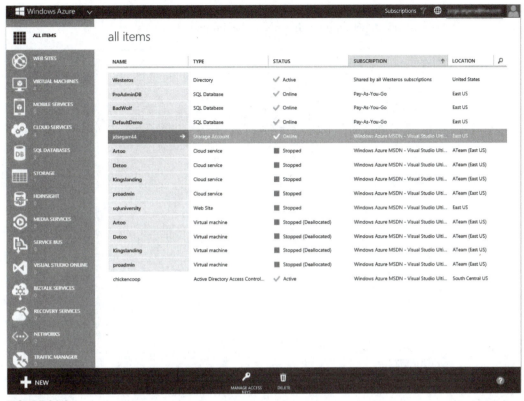

FIGURE 24-3

Let's walk through the Custom Create by clicking New in the bottom toolbar. From the New menu, navigate to Data Services, SQL Database, and the Custom Create option:

1. The first step in the wizard is to provide some basic information with which to create your database and server, as shown in Figure 24-4. From this screen, you will specify the name of your database, the edition (Web, Business, or Premium), database size, database collation, and SQL Database server to deploy this database to. Here is a quick rundown of the differences between editions:

   ➤ **Web**—Supports databases of either 1GB or 5GB in size. Runs on shared resources and has built-in replicas within a data center.

   ➤ **Business**—Supports database sizes of 10GB, 20GB, 30GB, 40GB, 50GB, 100GB, or 150GB in size. Also runs on shared resources, and has built-in replicas within a data center.

   ➤ **Premium**—Built on the foundation of Web and Business editions. However, resources are a fixed capacity and not shared with any other database. You can upgrade your existing databases to Premium to achieve better performance predictability than Web or Business. The upgrade process for a database may take from a few minutes to a few hours, depending on the size of the database.

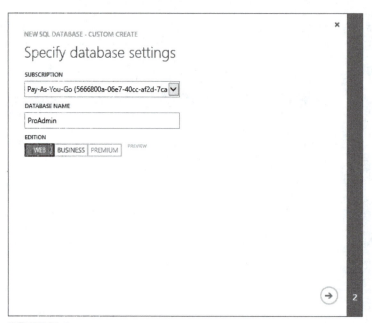

FIGURE 24-4

For this example, create a database called `ProAdminDB`. After you've made your selections, click the arrow in the lower-right corner of the screen to continue.

2. Next, select the size of your database. The sizes available are dependent on the edition you chose in the previous step. You can also change your database collation options here. The default is `SQL_Latin1_General_CP1_CI_AS`. However, you can change it to any of the supported collation options presented in the drop-down menu. Finally, choose a server to which to deploy your database. If you created a server previously, you'll see the option available to you.

You can also choose an option to create a new SQL Database server, as shown in Figure 24-5. Creating a new server will allow you to select which data center the server will reside in, but the name is generated for you. Select the option to create New SQL Database server and click the right arrow icon to continue.

3. On the "SQL database server settings" screen shown in Figure 24-6, configure your SQL Database server, which is the logical container that houses your SQL Database. First, create a new SQL login name and password. This account is the server-level principal for the SQL Database you create. This login is equivalent to the SQL Server Administrator (`sa`) account in an on-premises server.

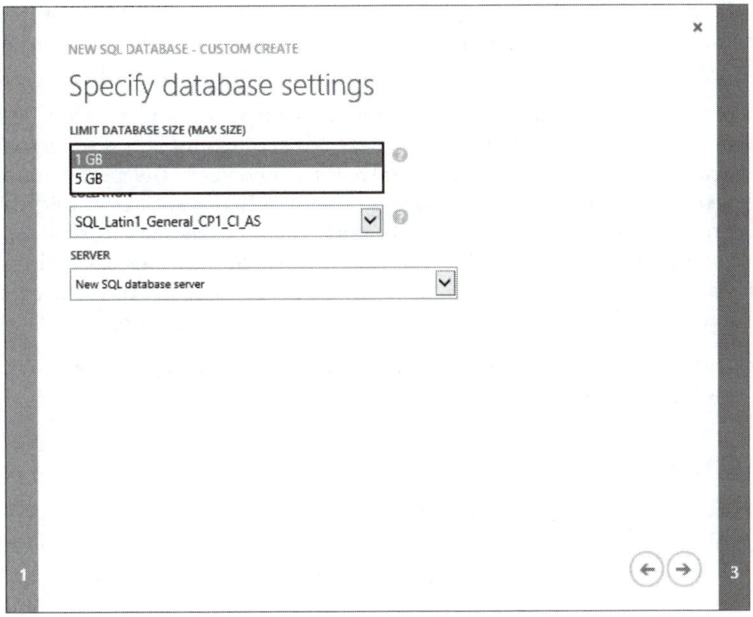

FIGURE 24-5

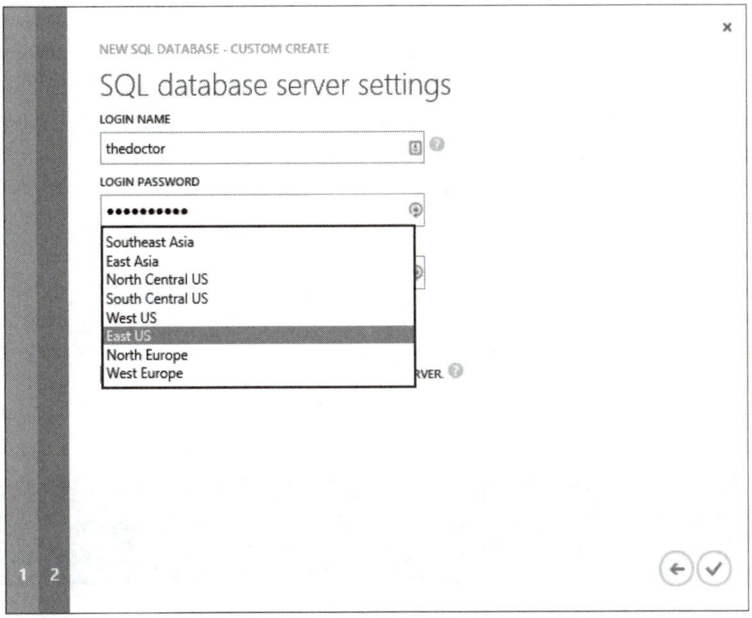

FIGURE 24-6

Finally, select a region to deploy your SQL Database server. Ideally, you'll want to deploy your server and database in the region closest to where your users and application will reside. Select a region from the drop-down menu, as shown in Figure 24-6.

However, in some cases you may not want to deploy your server and database in the region closest to where your users and application will reside. For example, say a company in Australia picked an Asia data center thinking that it would get better performance by selecting a data center closest to it. It soon discovered that it actually got better performance by selecting the South Central U.S. data center because the pipe between Australia and the United States was much bigger than the pipe between Australia and Asia. Although it is important to take into consideration things such as this, most of the time the best way to choose is to start with the data center closest to you, and test it thoroughly.

You have now successfully created your SQL Database server and database. But before you begin learning how to work with it, let's review some important information.

Server Name and Databases

After your server has been created, in the center of the "sql databases" section of the portal, the DATABASES section displays the list of all the SQL Database databases in your Azure subscription (including the one you just created), along with what SQL Database server it's located on, as shown in Figure 24-7.

FIGURE 24-7

Just in case there is any confusion, click the subscription name in the navigation toolbar at the top right of the screen. If you have multiple subscriptions, the center of the portal window lists all the

SQL Database databases that pertain to your selected subscription. The DATABASES list shown when you click the DATABASES tab contains the following columns:

➤ **Name**—Database name

➤ **Status**—Online status

➤ **Location**—Data center location

➤ **Subscription**—Subscription name database is contained on

➤ **Server**—SQL Database server name

➤ **Edition**—Edition of the SQL Database (and also indicates if database is transitioning to or from a Premium edition database)

➤ **Max Size**—Maximum database size

Let's take a closer look at your newly created SQL database. Click the arrow next to the database name to view more details for this database. When you click this link for the first time, you're greeted with a Quick Start menu, as shown in Figure 24-8. Here you'll be given easy access to links to download SQL Server Data Tools, download a starter project for your SQL Database, set up firewall rules for your current IP address, links to help you connect to your SQL database with development tools and programming languages, as well as the FQDN for your SQL Database server.

FIGURE 24-8

Notice that the first part of the FQDN is the same as the Server Name. When you hear people refer to the SQL Database server, they are referring to the value in the server column on the SQL Databases page, as shown in Figure 24-7. In fact, when specifying the "server name" for an application connection string, it is the value of the FQDN that needs to be used, like so:

```
servername.database.windows.net
```

You need to know this server name (FQDN) when the topic of connecting to SQL Database is discussed later in this chapter. So, highlight the entire SQL Database server name and copy it to the clipboard. You can also find the FQDN under the Quick Glance section of the DASHBOARD view, as shown in Figure 24-9. You can get to a dashboard view for a specific database by clicking on the database's name from the SQL Databases page (as shown in Figure 24-7), and then clicking the Dashboard link from the Quick Start page.

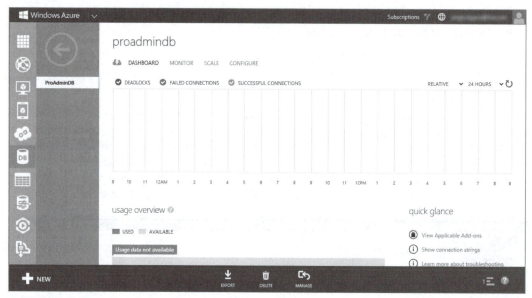

FIGURE 24-9

You are also able to view details on the SQL Database server itself by clicking the Servers tab (see Figure 24-7) and clicking the arrow next to the server name. Like the Quick Start screen of the database section, you're presented with quick links to common tasks such as creating a new database or managing the server itself.

Even though you are not connecting to a physical computer, your SQL Database server still behaves similarly to that of an on-premises SQL Server, meaning that a SQL Database server contains a logical group of databases and acts as the central administrative point for multiple databases. As such, you can create many of the same objects that you can with on-premises databases (such as tables, views, stored procedures, and indexes). Again, use the mouse to highlight the complete server name and copy that to the clipboard (Ctrl+C), because this will be used shortly.

When the SQL Database server is created, the master database is automatically provisioned. This database contains configuration and security information for your databases. To access and manage the master database, you can click the Manage icon in the bottom navigation bar of the SQL Database server DETAILS tab shown in Figure 24-7.

> **NOTE** *Windows Azure is fairly intelligent with regard to firewall configuration. If you're accessing a portion of the portal, or configuring something that requires firewall access, the portal will automatically prompt you with a pop-up from the bottom of the screen asking if you'd like your current IP to have access. This allows you to quickly configure a security setting for yourself so that you can continue with any other configurations you may need to complete, as shown in Figure 24-10.*

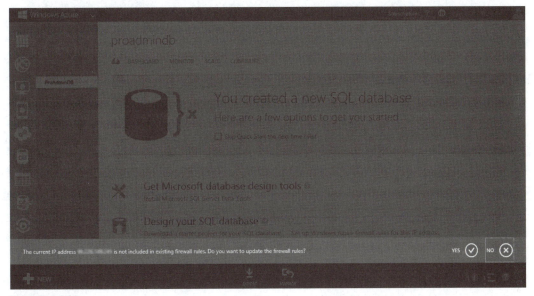

FIGURE 24-10

On the Quick Start page for the SQL Database (see Figure 24-8), you also have the capability to manage your firewall rules by clicking the link to "Set up Windows Azure firewalls rules for this IP address" option under "Design your SQL database." Using this link, you can quickly grant firewall access for your existing IP address/network. Clicking the link prompts you to add your current IP address to the firewall rules and continue configuring more advanced firewall options.

For a more detailed configuration of firewall rules, click the DASHBOARD tab in the Quick Glance page. Click the link to "Manage allowed IP addresses," as shown earlier in Figure 24-9. One of the advantages of this option is the capability to create, modify, or delete a range of IP addresses, rather than just a single IP address. This configuration option is ideal if you'll be configuring your database for an organization where you'll have machines from many different IP addresses accessing the SQL Database. Firewall rules are the first level of security for SQL Database, and are critical in protecting your data. You learn more about configuring SQL Azure firewall rules later in this chapter.

Premium Edition Option

As of this writing, SQL Azure supports three database "editions" and several database sizes based on the edition. As described earlier, SQL Database includes the *Web* and *Business* database editions. There really is no difference in the databases between these editions, except for size. In other words, the functionality of the database is the same regardless of the edition you choose.

The third edition, *Premium* edition, is really an extension of the first two. As mentioned previously, Premium edition is an upgrade step for an existing Web or Business edition database. In upgrading a database to Premium edition, you get more powerful and predictable performance. Premium edition databases are ideal for applications that require sustained demands on resources, high concurrency, and require predictable latency. You are able to upgrade and downgrade SQL Databases to and from Premium edition based on your needs. However, there is a delay ranging from a few minutes to a few hours, depending on the size of the database.

Throttling and Load Balancing

Throttling is SQL Database's mechanism for ensuring that one subscriber's application or code (stored procedure or T-SQL) does not seize all the resources. Because SQL Database works behind the scenes to provide a high-performing database, it uses a *load balancer* mechanism to help ensure that a server is not in a continuous state of throttling. To fully understand throttling and load balancing, let's first take a step back and look at how (and where) SQL Database creates new databases.

The goal for Microsoft SQL Database is to maintain (currently) 99.9 percent availability for the subscriber's database. This high availability is achieved through several methods.

First, Microsoft uses commodity hardware that can be quickly and easily replaced in the case of hardware failure. Second, and more importantly, Microsoft implements the automatic management of database replicas. When you create a database, you actually get three databases—one primary and two secondary replicas—within the same data center. These databases are always in sync, automatically, without any interaction from the end user.

You, your application, or anyone else cannot access the secondary databases directly, but they are there and for an important purpose. If, for any reason, your primary database should become unavailable, SQL Database will take it offline, select one of the secondary databases, promote it to primary, and then spin up another secondary database and bring that up to date. All this happens behind the scenes automatically. Any connections to the database that is now unavailable still need to be taken care of, though. In this scenario, best practice states that you add a connection and statement execution retry functionality to your application. This way, if the primary database goes down, your application can pick it up, and by the time your application retries, a new primary should be ready to accept the incoming request.

> **NOTE** *In reality, you should be implementing a connection and statement execution retry functionality in your applications anyway. The last thing end users need to see is an error that the work they just did can't be completed. Every application should have logic that can automatically retry based on certain errors returned from SQL Server. The same applies to Windows Azure and SQL Database.*

The Azure platform is a *shared environment* platform, meaning that you share server resources with other Azure subscribers. On top of that, other processes running on each server along with your databases are crucial to the steady and fluent running and execution of SQL Database. To ensure that one database doesn't consume critical resources from another database, or from the SQL Database server itself, Microsoft has implemented the Engine Throttling component, whose job it is to ensure that the health of the machine is not jeopardized. The Engine Throttling component ensures that all the appropriate processes have all the resources they need to operate smoothly and efficiently, that no one uses more resources than needed, and that resource limits are not exceeded.

If limits are exceeded (such as CPU usage or log size), the Engine Throttling component steps in and applies the necessary measures to correct the situation. These measures could include dropping connections, rejecting reads or writes for a period of time (10 seconds or so), or even permanently rejecting reads and writes if the source of the problem is deemed to continue to cause problems. Other catalysts that could initiate throttling are I/O-intensive operations such as index maintenance.

As new databases are added, the load balancer determines the locations of the new primary and secondary replica databases based on the current load of the machines in the data center.

The location of these databases may be fine for a while, but it is impossible to foresee the workload of other subscribers. Therefore, the load balancer has the responsibility of ensuring proper performance of the databases. If one machine becomes too loaded, the load balancer may automatically move a database to a server that is less loaded. This move is seamless, and has no impact on the application.

A way to minimize throttling issues is by upgrading a database to Premium edition. Premium edition databases provide more consistent performance by offering reserved capacities and isolated resources. It is worth noting that upgrading a database to Premium edition incurs higher costs. You can manage that by only upgrading databases to Premium for the periods of time that your application/database requires predictable performance. During non-peak times, you can downgrade your database back to a lower edition to save on costs.

> **NOTE** *You can find more detailed information on avoiding connectivity issues with your applications at* `http://social.technet.microsoft.com/wiki/contents/articles/1541.windows-azure-sql-database-connection-management.aspx`

Configuring SQL Database Firewalls

You now know how to create your server and databases and what happens behind the scenes of SQL Database to ensure high availability and great database performance. Yet, it won't do any good if you can't connect to the databases. This is where the SQL Database Firewall comes in.

You could have developed a great application, designed a great database, set the proper connection string, and so on, but unless you define the appropriate firewall rules, it will have been all for naught. The SQL Database Firewall is the first level of security to help protect your data and prevent unwanted access to your SQL Database server. All access to your SQL Database server is rejected and blocked until you specify which computers have permission. Connection attempts coming from the Internet, and even within Azure itself, cannot reach your SQL Database server until you specify who has access.

Firewall rules are IP address-based, and only acceptable addresses or ranges can be defined. Firewall rules are defined under the Configure section for the database server. You can reach this page by clicking "Set up Windows Azure firewall rules for this IP address," as shown in Figure 24-8.

To configure a firewall rule, click the "Manage allowed IP addresses" link under the Quick Glance section in the DASHBOARD view of the database you're configuring. On the ensuing screen shown in Figure 24-11, underneath the "allowed ip addresses" section, you see three inputs: RULE NAME, START IP ADDRESS, and END IP ADDRESS.

FIGURE 24-11

To quickly add a new firewall rule for your current IP address, simply click the "add the allowed ip addresses" link, which will be listed next to your current IP, as shown in Figure 24-11. Alternatively, you can provide an IP address range to allow multiple IP addresses access. Once you've added your desired rules, click the Save button at the bottom of the screen to confirm your changes.

You'll also notice in Figure 24-11 that there's a section for "allowed services" that lets you control whether other Windows Azure services are allowed to connect to your SQL Database. By default, this is set to YES, but you can change it to NO and use custom rules to allow services to connect.

Connecting to SQL Database

Now that you have created your databases and defined the firewall rules, you are ready to connect to your SQL Database server. To start your SQL Database connection journey, follow these steps:

1. Open up SQL Server Management Studio. Connecting to SQL Database requires SQL Server 2008 or later versions of SQL Server Management Studio. When the "Connect to Server" dialog box shown in Figure 24-12 opens, you must enter the FQDN server name. This should still be on your clipboard. If not, go back to the Azure Management portal, recopy it, and then paste it into the "Server name" box.

FIGURE 24-12

2. SQL Database only supports SQL Authentication, so select SQL Server Authentication and then enter the login name and password you created in Figure 24-6. If you have configured your SQL Database firewall with the appropriate IP address, you should successfully connect. If, for some reason, the firewall rules are not configured correctly, you should see an error message stating so, as shown in Figure 24-13.

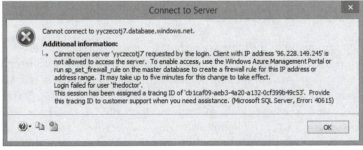

FIGURE 24-13

3. As a quick exercise, open a new query window (using Ctrl+N, or right-clicking the server in Object Explorer and selecting New Query from context menu) and make sure you connect to the `master` database. In the query window, execute the following command:

    `SELECT @@VERSION`

    Figure 24-14 shows the Results window displaying the SQL Database version currently running as of this writing.

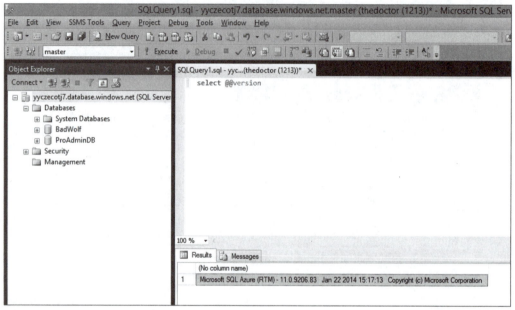

FIGURE 24-14

Now you are connected to your SQL Database server via SQL Server Management Studio. You are now ready to learn about the logical administration aspect of working with SQL Database, including creating logins and users.

ADMINISTERING SQL DATABASE

One of the big misconceptions about SQL Database is that it is nothing like SQL Server. The truth is that both SQL Server and SQL Database use the same authorization model, with users and roles created in each database and associated to the user logins. SQL Server has fixed server-wide roles such as `serveradmin`, `securityadmin`, and `dbcreated`, which do not exist in SQL Database. They don't need to, though, because of the logical administration aspect of SQL Database. Instead, SQL Database has a `loginmanager` role to create logins and a `dbmanager` role to create and manage databases. These roles can be assigned to users only in the `master` database.

Creating Logins and Users

SQL Database provides the same set of security principals available in SQL Server authentication, which you can use to authorize and secure your data. In SQL Database, logins are used to authenticate access to SQL Database at the server level. Database users are used to grant access to SQL Database at the database level, and database roles are used to group users and grant access to SQL Database at the database level.

Creating a New Login

Creating a login is nearly identical to SQL Server, except that you cannot create a login based on Windows credentials. Thus, all logins are SQL logins for SQL Authentication. The following steps outline how to do this:

1. In SQL Server Management Studio, open a new query window and connect to the `master` database using an administrator account. In the query window, type and run the following command:

   ```
   CREATE LOGIN AzureTest WITH PASSWORD = 'T3stPwd001'
   ```

   This creates a new login called `AzureTest`, as shown in Figure 24-15.

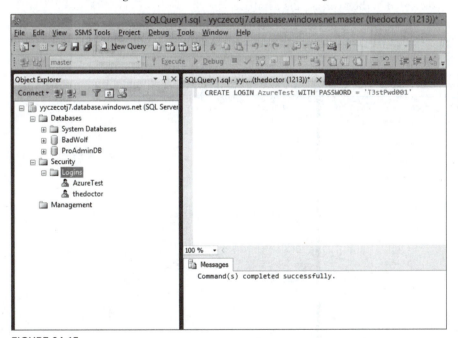

FIGURE 24-15

2. Although Figure 24-15 shows the login created in SQL Server Management Studio, you can also query the `sys.sql_logins` table to view all logins for the server like so:

   ```
   SELECT * FROM sys.sql_logins
   ```

Even though your logins are created, you cannot log in until a user has been created, which the next section discusses.

> **WARNING** *If you attempt to create the login account in a user database, you receive an error stating that the login must be created in the* master *database. Likewise, if your password is not complex enough, you receive an error message stating the password validation failed, and that the password does not meet Windows policy requirements. These policies include Latin uppercase and lowercase letters (A through Z), base-10 digits (0 through 9), and non-alphanumeric characters. In SQL Database, the password policy cannot be disabled.*

Creating a New User

After your login is created, you must create a user account for it. To create the user account, connect to the specific user database using an administrator account and run the following command:

```
CREATE USER AzureTest FROM LOGIN AzureTest
```

Figure 24-16 shows the command executed and the corresponding results. You can see that the user was indeed created in the ProAdminDB database.

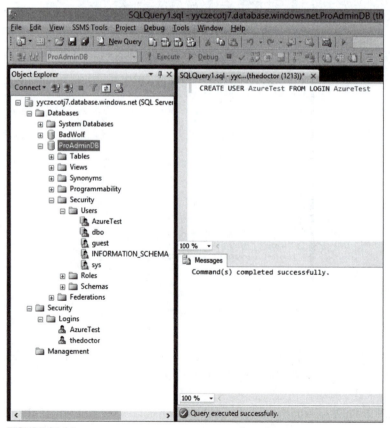

FIGURE 24-16

If you attempt to create a user without first creating the login account, you receive a message stating that the user is not a valid login. Login-less users are not allowed in SQL Database.

Assigning Access Rights

The next step in the administration process is to assign access rights to the newly created user account. To allow the AzureTest account to have unlimited access to the selected user database, you must assign the user to the db_owner group, as shown here:

```
EXEC sp_addrolemember 'db_owner', 'AzureTest'
```

At this point, the AzureTest user can create tables, views, stored procedures, and more. But just like SQL Server, you can get granular with your permissions. You can grant and revoke permissions and grant insert, update, create, and delete privileges just like you can with SQL Server. In SQL Server, user accounts are automatically assigned to the public role. This is not the case in SQL Database, because the public role cannot be assigned to user accounts for enhanced security. As a result, specific access rights must be granted to use a user account.

WORKING WITH SQL DATABASE

Working in SQL Server Management Studio has provided a nice and easy way to create databases and tables, and to do a lot of the management and maintenance of SQL Server through a great user interface. However, some of the better user interface features aren't automatically available. There is still a way to enjoy them, though, if you are up for writing some code. To do so, perform the following steps:

1. Right-click the Database node in Object Explorer and select New Database from the context menu. A query window appears with a template to create a new database.

2. In the Query Editor window, you'll notice that, instead of a dialog to create a new database, you'll see the DDL template code to create a new database. In Figure 24-17, there are a couple examples of syntax you can use to create databases with different options. Specify the name of the database, the edition, and the size. If you leave out the edition and size, you'll get a 1GB Web edition database by default.

Similarly, you can write code to create tables and views, and when working with permissions. Figure 24-18 shows the result of right-clicking the Tables node in Object Explorer and selecting New Table from the context menu.

Even though the user-interface features aren't quite there yet, that doesn't mean that the functionality isn't there. You just need to write code (with the same T-SQL syntax you are used to) to accomplish most of the things you need to do.

Backups with SQL Database

Some of the most prevalent questions potential Azure customers have concern backups. Currently, backups with the on-premises SQL Server do not exist in SQL Database. Instead, a feature called

Database Copy enables you to make a transactionally consistent copy of your primary SQL Database database into another SQL database. The syntax for this is simple:

```
CREATE DATABASE DB2 AS COPY OF DB1
```

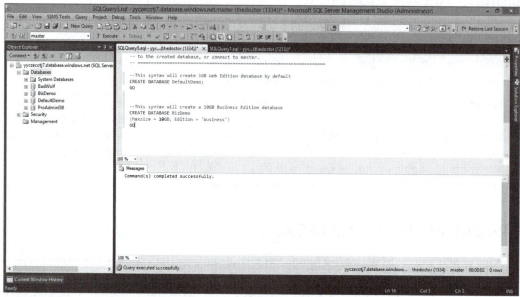

FIGURE 24-17

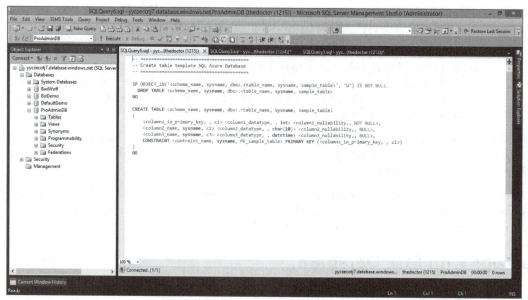

FIGURE 24-18

You can also copy databases between servers using the same syntax; you just need to be an administrator on both servers. However, administering two servers does entail paying for two databases, and more importantly, this makes it difficult to do daily backups and keep a history.

Object Explorer for SQL Database

When you connect to SQL Database in Azure in SQL Server Management Studio, you notice that a few nodes are missing—specifically the `Server Objects`, `Replication`, and `SQL Server Agent` nodes. The following sections explain why these aren't there (yet), and what you might expect down the road.

Server Objects

Looking at the subnodes in `Server Objects`, you see the following:

- ➤ Backup Devices
- ➤ SOAP Endpoints
- ➤ Linked Servers
- ➤ Triggers

Here are a few specific reasons why these items are not included in SQL Database:

- ➤ Backup Devices—First, because you don't have access to the physical hardware that SQL Database runs on, you don't need to create a backup device and won't have access to it anyway. Second, except for the current backup solutions discussed earlier, there isn't any other way to back up your databases. Until Microsoft provides more functional backup capabilities, the Backup Devices node doesn't need to be there.

- ➤ SOAP Endpoints—SOAP endpoints go back to SQL Server 2005 and enable you to essentially create web services that expose database access over HTTP. Microsoft has let it be known that this feature will be deprecated in future releases of SQL Server. SQL Database has a better solution for SOAP endpoints—OData. With just a few clicks, you can expose your SQL Database data via the OData protocol. The OData Service for SQL Database provides a simple, no-code solution for providing an OData endpoint through an open HTTP protocol.

- ➤ Linked Servers—These are typically used to handle distributed queries. Distributed queries aren't supported in SQL Database, but something even better will appear that makes the distributed queries a thing of the past. Microsoft announced in late 2010 a technology called SQL Database Federation—the capability to partition, or shard, your data to improve the scalability and throughput of your database.

> **NOTE** *Sharding is the process of breaking an application's logical database into smaller chunks of data and then distributing those chunks of data across multiple physical databases to achieve application scalability. In sharding, one or more tables within a database are split by row and portioned out across multiple databases. This partitioning can be done with no downtime, and client applications can continue accessing data during sharding operations with no interruption in service.*

Quite a few blog posts and articles are available on MSDN that drill into detail about this, but with SQL Database Federation, linked servers aren't needed.

➤ `Triggers`—Enabling these in a shared environment creates a whole new level of complexity, such as potential security risks and possible performance issues.

Replication

Because of SQL Database Data Sync Services, replication just isn't needed in SQL Database. As mentioned earlier, you have three copies of every database you create: the primary and two replicas. SQL Database keeps these in sync for you, and automatically provides the high availability and redundancy you need.

SQL Database Data Sync Services works far better and is far easier to configure and use than replication. Data Sync Services is built entirely on top of the Sync Framework and, therefore, includes a much richer data synchronization platform for moving data, including conflict handling and status reporting.

If you need to "replicate" data from one database to another database, SQL Database Data Sync Services provides an easy-to-use, wizard-driven interface that provides multi-direction data synchronization between two SQL Database databases (primary to primary), or between SQL Database and an on-premise SQL Server database.

SQL Server Agent

SQL Server Agent doesn't exist for SQL Database, but many articles on the web that explain how to use a Windows Azure Worker Role to mimic the functionality of the SQL Server Agent.

SQL Server Agent is a Microsoft Windows Service that executes scheduled administrator tasks called *jobs* and provides alerting capabilities. A good look at a Windows Azure Worker Role reveals that it is basically a Windows Service in the cloud. *Worker Roles* are roles used to perform background tasks and long-running/intermittent tasks.

What makes Worker Roles great is that their structure is close to that of a Windows Service, including the starting, stopping, and configuration concepts that you see in a Windows Service. You can find a great blog post about this at `http://blogs.msdn.com/b/sqlazure/archive/2010/07/30/10044271.aspx`.

Another potential solution is using an on-premises SQL Server and its SQL Server Agent to schedule Windows PowerShell scripts and tasks to manage your SQL Databases using Windows Azure cmdlets. You can read more about Azure cmdlets at `http://msdn.microsoft.com/en-us/library/windowsazure/jj554332.aspx`.

WHAT'S MISSING IN SQL DATABASE

As you start working with SQL Database, or, if you are already familiar with SQL Database, you will, at some point, wonder why it doesn't have a specific feature or functionality you are looking for (such as Full-Text Search). For example, if you were to do a feature-to-feature comparison, you would quickly see that a few features are not present in SQL Database.

The reason for the lack of certain features and functionality in SQL Database is not publicly known. However, this section can at least provide information on a couple of features that appear to be missing.

SQL Common Language Runtime (SQLCLR) is, in fact, "partially" supported. For example, the XML and Spatial data types are actually CLR data types, and you will certainly find these data types in SQL Database. What SQL Database doesn't support for SQLCLR is the capability to create assemblies in managed code (see Chapter 7, "SQL Server CLR Integration") and deploy those to SQL Database. It is unknown if and when that will be supported.

Microsoft is working hard to include encryption, but it must solve certain problems before you will see it included. The big issue really is how to support multiple levels of encryption in a shared environment. Remember that SQL Database is a shared environment, and as such, databases are spread out over multiple instances. For example, your database and your co-worker's database could potentially be located on the same server. In this scenario, the problem arises when you use one level of encryption and your co-worker uses another.

These are just a couple of examples of missing features and, depending on the feature, it will elicit a different response. For example, you may notice that there are no BI-specific components in Azure yet (for example, Reporting Services, Analysis Services, Integration Services). Microsoft is working on them, but when and how they will be included is yet to be seen.

The moral of this story is that you just won't see some features because it doesn't make sense to include them. With other features, you should just be patient.

SUMMARY

The goal of this chapter was to provide a solid overview of how to configure and administer SQL Database, including creating your SQL Database server, creating databases, and discussing what happens behind the scenes to provide the great high availability and failover needed in a cloud-based solution.

The logical administration of SQL Database plays an important role in understanding topics such as creating a SQL Database Server and associated databases. Although differences between on-premises SQL Server and SQL Database do exist, SQL Database still maintains power and flexibility as SQL Server "in the cloud."

Chapter 25 discusses another exciting feature of SQL Server that is great for both reporting and high-availability scenarios: AlwaysOn Availability Groups.

25

AlwaysOn Availability Groups

WHAT'S IN THIS CHAPTER?

➤ Identifying all aspects of Availability Groups and mastering all their intricacies

➤ Researching hardware and software configurations to identify what works best for your organization

➤ Configuring hardware and then clustering the operating system

➤ Configuring SQL Server 2014 Availability Groups

➤ Administering and troubleshooting the production SQL Server 2014 Availability Group

➤ Testing, monitoring, and tuning for performance

An Availability Group is a feature of AlwaysOn in SQL Server 2014 delivering robust, high-availability enhancements that greatly improve the data mirroring capabilities that shipped starting with SQL Server 2005. With AlwaysOn, SQL Server 2014 implements Availability Groups that deliver similar capabilities to database mirroring. In addition to these key enhancements, it can support up to nine replica partners, multiple databases in a single group, and readable replica secondary servers. The primary and replica servers can be mixed in asynchronous/synchronous modes and do not require shared disks. As a result, they can deploy across different geographical locations.

When these databases have dependencies, you can group them in a single Availability Group to failover together as a single failover unit. For example, by supporting readable replica servers, you can offload a reporting or read-only workload to a secondary replica, reducing the load on the primary replica and thus enabling it to scale and support its production workload better and respond to requests faster. You can also perform database backups on a secondary replica to reduce the backup load on the primary server. Availability Groups supports built-in transport compression/encryption; Automatic, Manual, and Forced Failover; flexible failover policy; and automatic application redirection using the Availability Group Listener network name.

AlwaysOn Availability Groups support the following features or components of SQL Server:

➤ Change data capture

➤ Change tracking

➤ Contained databases

➤ Database encryption

➤ Database snapshots

➤ FileStream and FileTable

➤ Full-text search

➤ Remote Blob Storage (RBS)

➤ Replication

➤ Service Broker

➤ SQL Server Agent

This chapter takes a detailed look at AlwaysOn Availability Groups.

ARCHITECTURE

An Availability Group is a set of up to nine SQL servers configured into a failover for a discrete set of user databases, known as *availability databases*. Each set of availability database(s) is hosted by an *availability replica*, and every availability replica is assigned a role. Each availability replica also has associated with it an *availability mode*. Figure 25-1 shows an Availability Group architecture in detail, and the following sections elaborate on these various components.

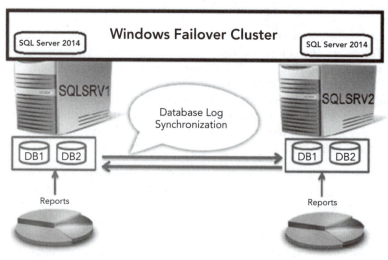

FIGURE 25-1

Availability Group Replicas and Roles

As stated previously, an availability database is hosted by an availability replica. Two types of availability replicas exist:

➤ A single primary replica makes the primary databases available for read-write connections from clients, and also sends transaction log records for each primary database to every secondary replica.

➤ One to eight secondary replicas maintain a set of secondary databases. Every secondary replica applies transaction log records to its own set of secondary databases, and serves as a potential failover target for the Availability Group.

Optionally, you can configure one or more secondary replicas to support read-only access to secondary databases, and you can configure any secondary replica to permit backups on secondary databases.

Every availability replica is assigned an initial role—either the *primary role* or the *secondary role*, which is inherited by the availability databases of that replica. The role of a given replica determines whether it hosts read-write databases or read-only databases. The primary replica is assigned the primary role and hosts read-write databases, which are known as *primary databases*. At least one secondary replica is assigned the secondary role. A secondary replica hosts read-only databases, known as *secondary databases*.

For the replicas to participate in Availability Groups, they must be deployed as a Windows Failover Cluster (WFC). Therefore, to implement an Availability Group, you must first enable WFC in each server participating in the Availability Group. Inside of a WFC, an Availability Group is a cluster resource with its own network name and cluster IP address used for application clients to connect to the Availability Group. However, the major difference from a SQL Server cluster installation is that an Availability Group does not require a shared disk—that is, in this configuration, each server does not share its disks with the other server.

Availability Modes

Each availability replica contains a property that determines its availability mode in relationship to the transaction record data movement that it receives, which determines how current its data is in relationship to the primary replica that is moving the data to all the other replicas. Two modes of availability are supported:

➤ **Asynchronous-commit mode**—The primary replica commits transactions without waiting for acknowledgment from the asynchronous-commit secondary replica that has hardened the transaction log. Asynchronous-commit mode minimizes transaction latency on the secondary replica databases, but enables them to lag behind the primary replica databases, increasing the probability of a failure or possible data loss.

➤ **Synchronous-commit mode**—The primary replica waits for a synchronous-commit from each secondary replica to acknowledge that it has finished hardening the log. Synchronous-commit mode ensures that when a given secondary replica database is synchronized with the primary replica database, committed transactions are fully protected. This protection comes at the cost of increased request latency, and increases the user transaction times because the latency is included in the overall database response time.

Types of Failover Supported

During failover, the primary and secondary replicas are interchangeable, where one of the secondary replicas becomes the primary and the former primary becomes the secondary replica. The new primary brings its Availability Group databases online and makes its databases available for read/write operations. The former primary that is now the secondary replica then begins to receive transactional data from the new primary replica after the failover. If the failover is caused by a failure to the former primary such that it becomes unavailable for a time, when the former primary returns online, it automatically joins in its Availability Group and takes a secondary replica role.

Three modes of failover exist: automatic, manual, and forced (with possible data loss). Support is based on the availability mode configured, as shown in Table 25-1.

TABLE 25-1: Supported Failover Modes

AVAILABILITY MODE	FAILOVER MODE SETTING	SECONDARY REPLICA FAILOVER SUPPORTED
Synchronous	Manual	Manual (without data loss)
Synchronous	Automatic	Automatic/Manual (without data loss)
Asynchronous	Manual	Manual (possible data loss)

The following list explains each supported failover mode from Table 25-1 in greater detail:

➤ **Manual failover (without data loss)**—A manual failover occurs after a DBA issues a manual-failover command. It causes a synchronized secondary replica to transition to be the primary replica role (with guaranteed data protection) and the primary replica to transition as the secondary replica role. The DBA can specify to which secondary replica to failover. A manual failover requires that both the primary replica and the target secondary replica run under synchronous-commit mode, and the secondary replica must already be synchronized.

➤ **Automatic failover (without data loss)**—An automatic failover occurs in response to a failure that causes a synchronized secondary replica to transition to the primary role (with guaranteed data protection). When the former primary replica becomes available, it transitions to the secondary role. Automatic failover requires that both the primary replica and the target secondary replica run under synchronous-commit mode with the failover mode set to Automatic. In addition, the secondary replica must already be synchronized.

➤ **Manual failover (possible data loss)**—Under asynchronous-commit mode, the only form of failover is manual forced failover (with possible data loss). A forced failover should only be used for disaster recovery because there is a good risk of data loss. Manual is the only form of failover possible when the target secondary replica is not synchronized with the primary replica, even for synchronous-commit mode.

Allowing Read-Only Access to Secondary Replicas

The main purpose of the Availability Group is to deliver high availability and disaster recovery, but in addition, a secondary replica can be configured for read-only database access. In such a scenario, read-only workloads are offloaded on the secondary replica databases, optimizing the primary replica to support read/write mission-critical workloads.

For example, if you want to run reports, rather than running them on the primary replica and over-burdening it, you can select one of the secondary replicas to run the reports. You can also execute database backups from the secondary replica. Full database, file, and filegroup backups are supported, but differential backup is not supported. Transaction log backup is supported in the secondary replica. These are copy-only backups. (For a more detailed explanation, see the "Backup on the Secondary Replica" section later in this chapter.)

Consider the following capabilities of read-only secondary replicas:

➤ The secondary replica's data is maintained to near real time with the primary replica. Real time depends on the network latency between the primary and secondary, the redo operation, locking on the secondary databases, and activities running on the secondary server.

➤ Read-only on the secondary replica applies to all the Availability Group databases.

➤ To greatly reduce locking in the secondary read-only replica, the secondary replica databases are configured by default in snapshot isolation to keep read activities from blocking the redo log that is updating the data. Snapshot isolation adds a 14-byte row identifier to maintain row version, and maintains last committed row(s) in tempdb as the redo operation updates the replica databases.

➤ For the optimizing of the read-only workload, any index required by the secondary replica or database statistics must be created in the primary replica database and transferred to all replicas by the transactional log data movement because the secondary is read-only. However, to support read-only workload, SQL Server 2014 does have the capability to create temporary database statistics that are stored in tempdb. These temporary statistics will be lost when the SQL Server instance is restarted, or when the secondary replica is promoted to the primary during a failover.

➤ Similar to data mirroring, Availability Groups support automatic page repair. Each availability replica tries to automatically recover from corrupted pages on a local database by resolving certain types of errors that prevent reading a data page. If a secondary replica cannot read a page, the replica requests a fresh copy of the page from the primary replica. If the primary replica cannot read a page, the replica broadcasts a request for a fresh copy to all the secondary replicas, and gets the page from the first to respond. If this request succeeds, the unreadable page is replaced by the copy, which usually resolves the error.

➤ A client application can connect to a read-only replica. You can connect to a secondary replica that supports read-only access in one of two ways: either directly by specifying the SQL Server instance name in the connection string, or by using the Availability Group Listener name and leveraging read-only routing to reconnect to the next available secondary read-only replica. For more detailed information, see the section, "Secondary Replica Client Connectivity," later in this chapter. Access to the secondary replica is based on the Availability Group property, as shown in Table 25-2.

TABLE 25-2: Setting for the Secondary Replicas to Support Read Operations

READABLE SECONDARY	DESCRIPTION
No	The secondary replica does not allow read operations. Any connections to the secondary replica will be denied.
Read-intent only	The secondary replica allows read operations, but it accepts only connections with the application intent READONLY. This READONLY intent is a new connection property available as part of new Tabular Data Stream (TDS) protocol. Older client applications or client applications that do not specify a READONLY property for application intent cannot connect to the read-only secondary replica. To connect to the secondary replica, you must provide the following in the connection string: **ApplicationIntent = ReadOnly**.
Yes	The secondary replica enables read operations. It accepts all connections, including the ones that don't specify the READONLY application intent property in the connection string. This option enables legacy client applications to connect to the secondary replica for read workload because only read-only commands succeed. Commands that try to create or modify data will fail with this error message: Msg 3906, Level 16, State 1, Server SQLHA2, Line 1 Failed to update database "AdventureWorks" because the database is read-only.

> **NOTE** *You cannot include* master, msdb, tempdb, *or* model *databases in an Availability Group; only user databases are supported.*

AVAILABILITY GROUP EXAMPLE

To learn about Availability Groups, it is beneficial to go through a step-by-step example that shows how to set up and configure them. First you will configure a new Availability Group, and then add a new replica. Next, you create a new availability database, and finally connect to the Availability Group. Once your Availability Group has been deployed, you can perform failover testing.

> **NOTE** *You can find all the example scripts for this chapter in the Chapter 25 download on this book's website at* www.wrox.com, *but you need to make a few modifications before running the scripts.*

Configure a New Availability Group

As stated previously, a prerequisite to deploying an Availability Group is a Windows Failover Cluster. The following steps begin with creating a Windows 2012 R2 Failover Cluster and continue through the whole process of configuring a new Availability Group:

1. Start with installing a Windows 2012 R2 Failover Cluster on each server that will participate in the Availability Group. To install, see Chapter 16, "Clustering SQL Server 2014."

2. Install SQL Server 2014 as a standalone instance on each server that will participate in the Availability Group. To install, see Chapter 2, "SQL Server 2014 Installation Best Practices."

3. Next, on each SQL Server that will be participating in the Availability Group, open SQL Server Configuration Manager, choose SQL Server Services, and then select the SQL Server properties. Under AlwaysOn High Availability, check the Enable AlwaysOn Availability Groups check box, as shown in Figure 25-2. Then you must restart the SQL Server for the setting to take effect.

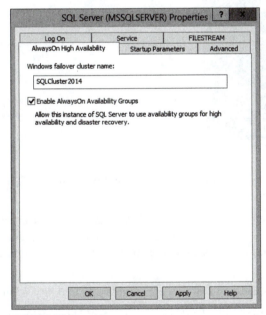

FIGURE 25-2

Now you are ready to create the Availability Group. Follow these steps:

1. Choose one of the SQL Servers as the primary replica. This SQL Server must have the database(s) that will be included in the Availability Group. In this example, it is SQLHA1 and the AdventureWorks database.

2. In the Microsoft SQL Server Management Studio, click the SQL Server (in this example, SQLHA1), then right-click and choose New Availability Group Wizard, as shown in Figure 25-3.

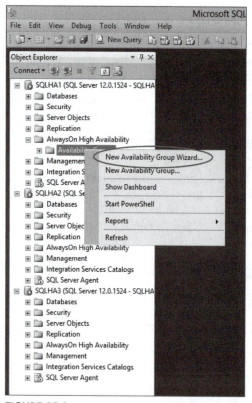

FIGURE 25-3

3. In the Introduction, click Next. On the ensuing Specify Availability Group Name page, choose a name (for example AG1, as shown in Figure 25-4).

4. Click Next. On the next Select Databases page shown in Figure 25-5, click the check box for the databases (for example, AdventureWorks). If more than one database meets prerequisites, it will appear in the list for you to choose. For a database to be eligible, it must meet the following prerequisites:

    ➤ Be a user database. System databases cannot belong to an Availability Group.

    ➤ Be a read-write database. Read-only databases cannot be added to an Availability Group.

    ➤ Be a multiuser database.

    ➤ Not use AUTO_CLOSE.

➤ Use the full recovery model.

➤ Possess a full database backup.

➤ Reside on the SQL Server instance where you are creating the Availability Group and be accessible to the server instance.

➤ Not belong to another Availability Group.

➤ Not be configured for Database Mirroring.

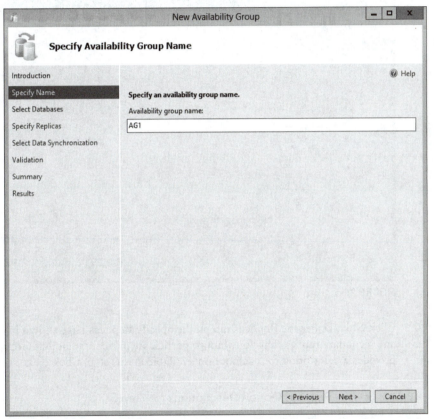

FIGURE 25-4

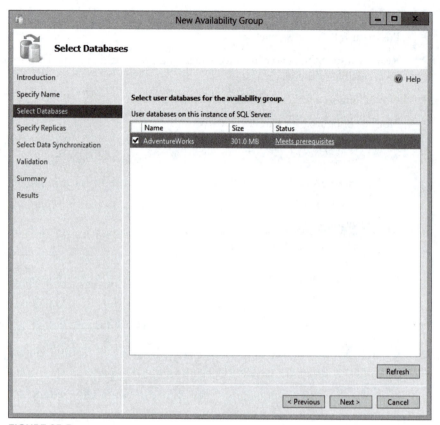

FIGURE 25-5

5. Click Next. Under the Replicas tab on the Specify Replicas page shown in Figure 25-6, choose any secondary replica that you want to participate in the Availability Group. Table 25-3 also provides a description for each option available in this step. Click Next again.

TABLE 25-3: Specify Replicas Option Descriptions for Step 5

INITIAL ROLE	IDENTIFY THE INITIAL PRIMARY OR SECONDARY REPLICAS
Automatic Failover (Up to 2)	If you want to configure automatic failover, choose up to two availability replicas to be automatic failover partners, where one of the partners chosen must be the initial primary replica. Both of these replicas use the synchronous-commit availability mode, and only two replicas are supported in automatic failover.
Synchronous Commit (Up to 3)	Here you have the option to choose additional replicas to use synchronous-commit mode with only planned manual failover. Only three replicas are supported in synchronous-commit mode. Leave the check box blank if you want the replica to use asynchronous-commit availability mode. Then this replica will support only forced manual failover (with possible data loss).

Readable Secondary	**No:** No direct connections are allowed to the secondary databases of this replica. They are not available for read access. This is the default setting.
	Read-intent only: Only direct read-only connections are allowed to secondary databases of this replica. The secondary database(s) are all available for read access.
	Yes: All connections are allowed to secondary databases of this replica, but only for read access. The secondary database(s) are all available for read access.

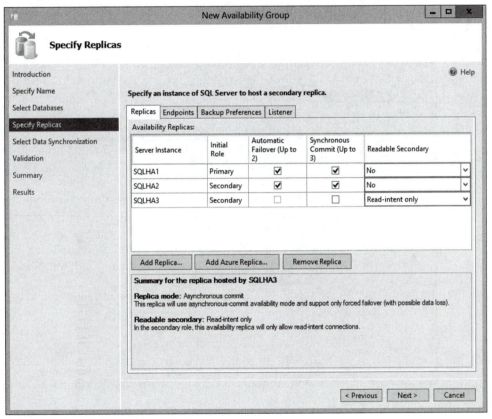

FIGURE 25-6

6. Under the Backup Preferences tab on the Specify Replicas page shown in Figure 25-7, specify where backups should occur from the following options:

   ➤ **Prefer Secondary**—Specifies that backups should occur on a secondary replica except when the primary replica is the only replica online. In that case, the backup should occur on the primary replica. This is the default option.

   ➤ **Secondary only**—Specifies that backups should never be performed on the primary replica. If the primary replica is the only replica online, the backup should not occur.

➤ **Primary**—Specifies that the backups should always occur on the primary replica. This option supports creating differential backups, which are not supported when backup is run on a secondary replica.

➤ **Any Replica**—Specifies that you prefer for backup jobs to ignore the role of the availability replicas when choosing the replica to perform backups. Backup jobs might evaluate other factors such as backup priority of each availability replica in combination with its operational state and connected state.

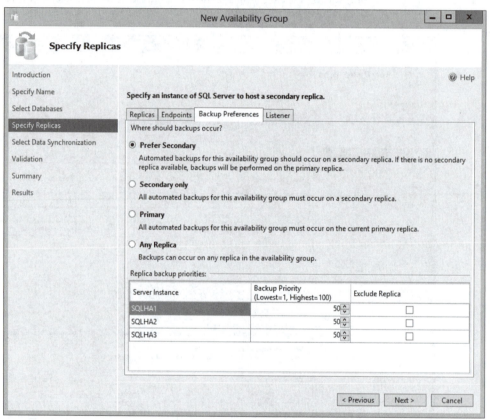

FIGURE 25-7

7. Under the Listener tab on the Specify Replicas page shown in Figure 25-8, choose "Create an availability group listener." Provide a Listener DNS name, which is the network name that client applications use to connect to this Availability Group.

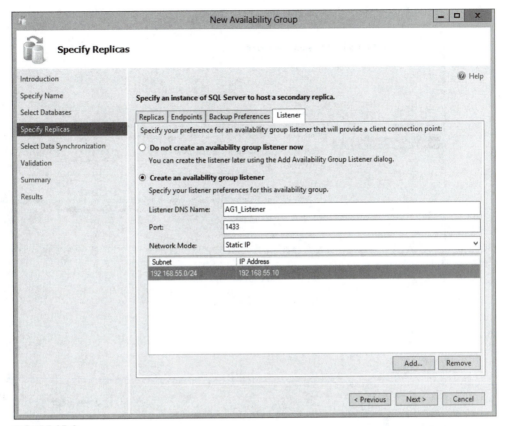

FIGURE 25-8

By default, SQL Server listens on port 1433. If you changed the port number to a non-default value, provide that port number value.

Then choose either a DHCP or Static IP for the Availability Group Listener. In this example, a Static IP was given to the Availability Group Listener.

If you want, you can skip and create the Availability Group Listener later. For this example, the Listener is AG1_Listener with port number 1433. Click Next.

8. On the Select Initial Data Synchronization page shown in Figure 25-9, choose Full. For "Specify a shared network location accessible by all replicas," choose a shared folder accessible by all participating replicas—for this example, \\SQLHA1\DBBackups. Also, you can choose "Skip initial data synchronization" and manually restore to each secondary replica.

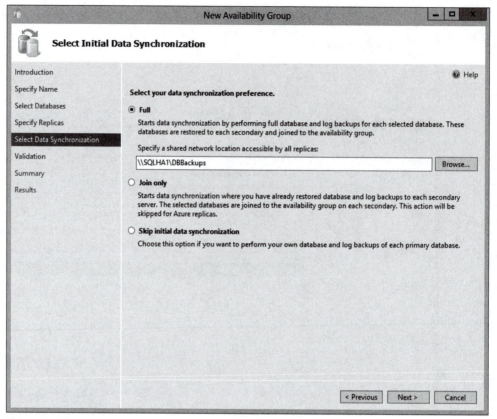

FIGURE 25-9

9. Click Next to run the validation, as shown in Figure 25-10. Then click Next. On the next Summary page, click Finish to create the AG1 Availability Group.

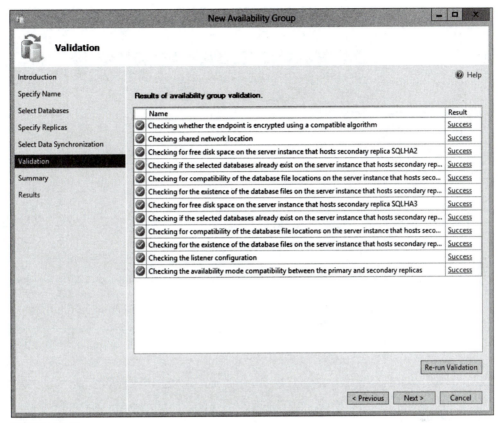

FIGURE 25-10

10. When you finish, you should be able to go to the Windows Failover Cluster Manager to see that the Availability Group has been created, as shown in Figure 25-11.

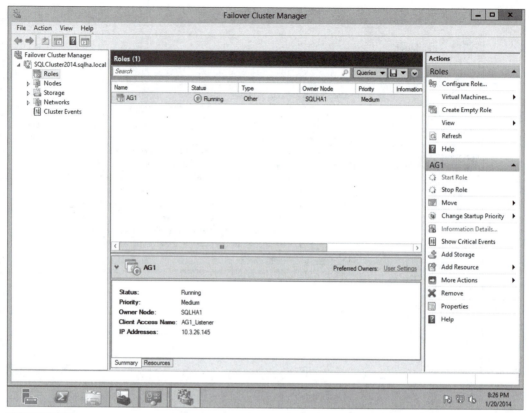

FIGURE 25-11

When a SQL Server login is added to the primary replica, the same login must be synchronized to exist on each secondary replica so that, in a failover, that login will be available to authenticate. An Availability Group is not supported for System databases where the logins exists. However, with SQL Server 2014, login data can be stored in the user database with the Contained Database feature, which means that any logins created will be synchronized as data by the Availability Group. If the database has been configured with Containment Type set to Partial, as shown in Figure 25-12, the user-login relationship can be configured and authenticated at the database level rather than on the SQL Server's System database.

> **NOTE** *You can find more detailed information on contained databases in Chapter 4, "Managing and Troubleshooting the Database Engine."*

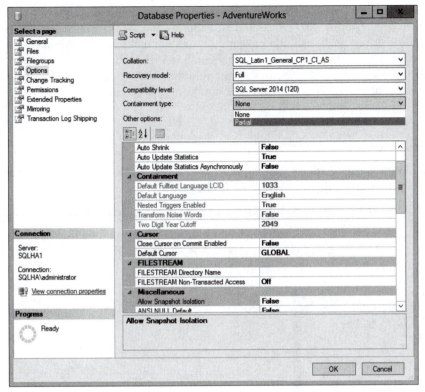

FIGURE 25-12

Configure an Existing Availability Group

Now you have an Availability Group deployed and are relying on it for your high-availability, disaster-recovery, and reporting needs. At some point, a new requirement may arise if one of the following situations occurs:

➤ The application is upgraded and an additional, new database is created that has dependencies to the other availability databases inside the Availability Group.

➤ The company has increased reporting requirements and needs to deploy another read-only database to offload the work on the primary replica.

➤ A disaster-recovery site is identified and you are asked to deploy a replica there.

➤ Backups are running on the primary replica and are impacting its performance. You have been asked to deploy a replica to perform backups.

➤ You have consolidated several databases from the Availability Group and must remove one of them.

➤ You want to remove a replica because it is no longer needed, or it has been replaced with another replica running on faster hardware.

For situations like these, Availability Groups deliver the flexibility to start with at least a two-replica Availability Group, then deploy additional replicas and availability databases as your needs change. This section covers how to deploy additional replicas (up to a maximum of nine) or additional availability databases. You can remove replicas and availability databases when they are no longer needed as part of the Availability Group. When performing these operations in a production environment, consider doing so during your maintenance window, and not during normal production time.

Add/Remove Replica

Any time you want to add a replica, follow these steps:

1. Join the new replica to the Windows Cluster group from Windows Failover Cluster Manager. See Chapter 16, "Clustering SQL Server 2014," for help on doing so.

2. Enable AlwaysOn Availability Group for that SQL Server instance (refer to Figure 25-2).

3. On the `Availability Groups` node in SQL Server Management Studio, right-click the Availability Group (for example, AG1), and choose Add Replica, as shown in Figure 25-13. Then follow the wizard to add a new replica.

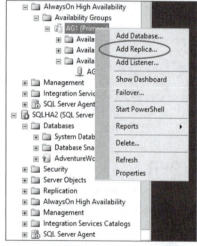

FIGURE 25-13

To remove a replica, simply choose the replica, right-click, and select Delete.

To remove an Availability Group, choose the Availability Group, right-click, and select Delete.

Add Azure Replica

In SQL Server 2014, an Add Azure Replica Wizard enables you to add or create a new Availability Group replica as a Windows Azure Infrastructure as a Service (IaaS) virtual machine (VM), which is automatically created by the wizard in SQL Server 2014 Management Studio as part of the hybrid IT environment. This feature enables you to extend a replica to Azure for read-only workloads, database backups, and for disaster recovery without allocating local hardware. The following pre-requisites must be met to add the Azure replica VM:

➤ You must execute the wizard from the server instance that hosts the current primary replica.

➤ The Availability Group must contain on-premise availability replicas, and the network environment must contain an on-premise subnet that has a site-to-site virtual private network (VPN) with Windows Azure.

➤ Clients to the Availability Group Listener must have connectivity to the Internet if they want to maintain connectivity with the Listener when the Availability Group is failed over to a Windows Azure replica.

Once these prerequisites are met, you can launch the Add Azure Replica Wizard from inside the SQL Server 2014 Management Studio with the Specify Replicas Page. You can do this from either the Use the Availability Group Wizard or the Add Replica to Availability Group Wizard. Once you have launched the Add Azure Replica Wizard, follow these steps:

1. Click Download button to download a management certificate for your Windows Azure subscription to use for the Azure VM Replica.

2. Then you must sign in to your Windows Azure subscription where you want to create the Windows SQL Server VM, where the wizard installs a management certificate onto your local server. Note that if you download multiple management certificates, you can click the ... button and then choose the management certificate you want to use.

3. To then connect to your subscription, click the Connect button. After the connection has been made, the drop-down lists of the wizard are populated with Windows Azure parameters (such as Image, VM Size, Virtual Network, and Virtual Network Subnet), as shown in Table 25-4.

TABLE 25-4: Windows Azure Parameter Descriptions

PARAMETER	DESCRIPTION
Image	Choose from the list of Windows Azure SQL Server images.
VM Size	Choose the Windows Azure VM size.
VM Name	Choose the DNS name for your Windows Azure VM for SQL Server.
VM Username	Choose the default administrator username for the Windows Azure VM.
VM Administrator Password (and Confirm Password)	Choose the default administrator password for the Windows Azure VM.

continues

TABLE 25-4 *(continued)*

PARAMETER	DESCRIPTION
Virtual Network	Choose the virtual network that has been configured to allow the Windows Azure VM to access the on-premise replicas.
Virtual Network Subnet	Choose the virtual network subnet that has been configured to allow the Windows Azure VM to access the on-premise replicas.
Domain	Join the Windows Azure VM to the Active Directory (AD) domain with the other members of the Availability Group.
Domain Username	Provide the AD username that has permissions to join the Windows Azure VM to the domain.
Password	Provide the AD password that has permissions to join the Windows Azure VM to the domain.

4. Choose the settings for your Windows Azure VM to host the new Windows Azure secondary replica.

5. Then click OK to commit the settings and to exit the Add Azure Replica Wizard.

6. Then, back on the Specify Replicas page, continue to configure and complete the new replica.

After the Availability Group Wizard or the Add Replica to Availability Group Wizard completes, the configuration process will have performed all necessary Windows Azure operations to create the new Windows Azure VM, join it to the AD domain, add it to the Windows Failover Cluster, enable AlwaysOn High Availability, and add the new Windows Azure replica to the Availability Group.

Add/Remove a Database

Any time you want to add an availability database, follow these steps:

1. In SQL Server Management Studio, select the `Availability Groups` folder, right-click the Availability Group (for example AG1), and choose Add Database, as shown in Figure 25-14.

2. Follow the wizard to add a new database.

> **NOTE** *Doing a large database backup and file copy can adversely impact the production environment, so you may want to perform it during a maintenance window.*

To remove a database from the Availability Group, simply choose the database, right-click, and select Delete.

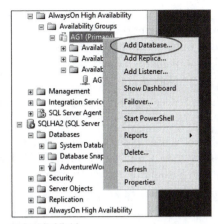

FIGURE 25-14

Availability Group Failover Operation

Two failover modes are available: automatic and manual. Failover of the Availability Group depends on which of these two modes the replica is configured with.

In automatic failover mode (synchronous mode), when the primary replica goes down, the secondary replica takes over without any user intervention. The client applications that are connected using the Availability Group Listener (for example, AG1_Listener) automatically reconnect to the new primary replica, provided that the application is configured to reconnect when it loses the connection.

In manual failover mode (synchronous mode), in a failover, the secondary replica failover requires manual failover action. From within SQL Server Management Studio, follow these steps to manually fail over:

1. Connect to a SQL Server instance that hosts a secondary replica of the Availability Group that needs to be failed over, and expand the server tree.

2. Expand the AlwaysOn High Availability and Availability Groups folders.

3. Right-click the Availability Group to be failed over, and select Failover.

You can also perform failover by using T-SQL. The following code snippet forces the AG1 Availability Group to fail over to the local secondary replica:

```
ALTER AVAILABILITY GROUP AG1 FAILOVER;
```

To force a failover with data loss, use this T-SQL command:

```
ALTER AVAILABILITY GROUP AG1 FORCE_FAILOVER_ALLOW_DATA_LOSS;
```

Additionally, you can perform failover using Windows PowerShell. The following example performs a forced failover (with possible data loss) of the Availability Group AG1 to the secondary replica of the SQL Server instance:

```
Switch-SqlAvailabilityGroup `-Path
    SQLSERVER:\Sql\SecondaryServer\InstanceName\AvailabilityGroups\
    AG1 `-AllowDataLoss
```

After a forced failover, the secondary replica to which you failed over becomes the new primary replica, and all secondary databases are suspended. Before you resume any of the suspended databases, however, you might need to reconfigure the Windows Failover Cluster's quorum and adjust the availability-mode configuration of the Availability Group. Consider these two scenarios:

➤ If you failed over outside of the automatic failover set of the Availability Group, adjust the quorum votes of the Windows Failover Cluster nodes to reflect your new Availability Group configuration (see "Chapter 16, "Clustering SQL Server 2014," for quorum settings).

➤ If you failed over outside of the synchronous-commit failover set, consider adjusting the availability mode and failover mode on the new primary replica, and on remaining secondary replicas, to reflect your desired synchronous-commit and automatic failover configuration.

For each scenario, you must manually resume each suspended database individually. On resuming, a secondary database initiates data synchronization with the corresponding primary database. When the former primary replica becomes available, it switches to the secondary replica role, becoming a secondary replica, and immediately suspends its now-secondary databases. Under the asynchronous-commit mode, the accumulated unsent log is a possibility on any of the new secondary databases. Resuming a new secondary database causes it to discard unsent log records and to roll back any changes that were never received by the now-primary replica.

If an availability replica that failed will not be returning to the availability replica, or will return too late for you to delay transaction log truncation on the new primary database, consider removing the failed replica from the Availability Group.

Suspend an Availability Database

During a performance bottleneck, you may decide to suspend a secondary availability database. An availability database that is suspended means no transaction record data movement occurs, and that the transaction log on the primary replica keeps growing and cannot be truncated. If you suspend a secondary database on a secondary availability replica, only the local secondary database is suspended. If the suspended database is on the primary replica, transaction record data movement is suspended to all secondary databases on every secondary replica. When a secondary database is suspended, its database state is changed to SUSPENDED, and it begins to fall behind the primary database. The primary database remains available, and if you have only one secondary replica, the primary database runs exposed.

To suspend a database using SQL Server Management Studio, follow these steps:

1. In SQL Server Management Studio, connect to the SQL Server instance that hosts the availability replica on which you want to suspend a database.

2. Expand the AlwaysOn High Availability and Availability Groups folders.

3. Expand the Availability Databases folder, right-click the database, and click Suspend Data Movement, as shown in Figure 25-15.

4. In the Suspend Data Movement dialog box, click OK.

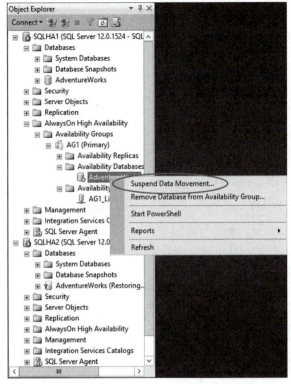

FIGURE 25-15

To suspend a database using T-SQL, follow these steps:

1. Connect to the SQL Server instance that hosts the replica whose database you want to suspend.

2. Suspend the secondary database by using the following ALTER DATABASE statement:

```
ALTER DATABASE database_name SET HADR SUSPEND;
```

Additionally, you can suspend an availability database by using the following Windows PowerShell commands.

1. Change directory (cd) to the server instance that hosts the replica whose database you want to suspend.

2. Use the Suspend-SqlAvailabilityDatabase cmdlet to suspend the Availability Group.

Resume an Availability Database

After a database has been suspended, when the replica is resumed, the initial state is SYNCHRONIZING until it catches up. The primary database eventually resumes all its secondary databases that were suspended as the result of suspending the primary database.

To resume a database using SQL Server Management Studio, follow these steps:

1. In SQL Server Management Studio, connect to the server instance that hosts the availability replica on which you want to resume a database.

2. Expand the `AlwaysOn High Availability` and `Availability Groups` folders.

3. Expand the `Availability Databases` folder, right-click the database, and click Resume Data Movement.

4. In the Resume Data Movement dialog box, click OK.

To resume a database using T-SQL, follow these steps:

1. Connect to the server instance that hosts the database you want to resume.

2. Resume the secondary database by using the following `ALTER DATABASE` statement like so:

   ```
   ALTER DATABASE database_name SET HADR RESUME;
   ```

Additionally, you can resume an availability database by using the following Windows PowerShell commands:

1. Change directory (`cd`) to the server instance that hosts the replica whose database you want to resume.

2. Use the `Resume-SqlAvailabilityDatabase` cmdlet to resume the Availability Group.

Client Application Connections

To support failover, two options are available for client applications to connect to the primary replica: using the network name assigned to the Availability Group Listener, or using the database-mirroring connection strings.

When you create and configure an Availability Group, you create the Availability Group Listener, which creates a network name and IP address in the Windows Server Failover Cluster (refer to Figure 25-8). Then, when a failure occurs and the primary replica becomes unavailable, the secondary replica becomes the new primary replica with the network name in connection strings. The network name automatically redirects client applications to the new primary replica.

You can provide client connectivity to the primary replica of a given Availability Group by using one of the two aforementioned methods, described in greater detail in the following two sections.

Availability Group Listener Network Name

When the Availability Group fails over and the client applications have the network name in the connection strings, the network name directs connections to the new primary replica. You must create a network name that is unique in the domain for each Availability Group. As you create a network name, the IP address is assigned to the network name. Only the TCP protocol is supported for using a network name and, optionally, an IP address to connect to an Availability Group. In the connection strings that your client applications use to connect to the databases in the Availability Group, specify the Availability Group network name rather than the server name; then applications can connect directly to the current primary replica. Following are examples of client application connection strings:

```
Server=tcp:MynetworkName;Database=AdventureWorks;IntegratedSecurity=SSPI
Server=tcp:MynetworkName,1433;Database=AdventureWorks;IntegratedSecurity=SSPI
```

Database-Mirroring Connection Strings

While performing a migration from database mirroring to an Availability Group, if an Availability Group contains only two availability replicas and is not configured to allow read access to the secondary replica, client applications can connect to the primary replica by using database mirroring connection strings.

This approach can be useful while migrating an existing client application from database mirroring to an Availability Group, as long as you limit the Availability Group to two availability replicas. However, before you add additional availability replicas, you must create an Availability Group Listener network name for the Availability Group, and update your client application to use it.

When using database mirroring connection strings, the client can use either SQL Server Native Client or .NET Framework Data Provider for SQL Server. The connection string provided by a client application must minimally supply the name of one server instance, the *initial partner name*, to identify the server instance that initially hosts the availability primary replica to which you intend to connect. Optionally, the connection string can also supply the name of the secondary replica (which is the failover partner name) to identify the server instance that initially hosts the secondary replica as the failover partner name. Following is an example:

```
"Data Source=ServerA;Failover Partner=ServerB;Initial Catalog=AdventureWorks;
 Integrated Security=True;"
```

ACTIVE SECONDARY FOR SECONDARY READ-ONLY

This section covers the secondary replica capabilities offered by Availability Groups in relation to running reports and read-only queries on the secondary replicas. Availability Groups enable read-only secondary replicas. The primary purpose of secondary replicas is for high availability and disaster recovery, but secondary replicas can be configured to offload read-only queries for running reports from the primary replica. Then, the primary replica can better deliver the mission-critical data activity while read-only reporting is executed on a secondary replica.

New in SQL Server 2014, when disconnected from the primary replica or during cluster quorum loss, readable secondary replicas now remain available for read workloads. When configured in read-only mode, the secondary replica is in near real time, just seconds behind data changes from the primary replica because the latency of transaction log synchronization impacts data freshness and the redo thread to update the data in each secondary replica before it is available to a query.

Read-Only Access Behavior

When you configure read-only access for a secondary replica, all databases in the Availability Group allow read-only access. The behavior that determines the type of access allowed when a replica is in a secondary role is shown in Figure 25-6 under the Readable Secondary column. Read-only access does not mean that the secondary databases are set to read-only. It means that user connections to the secondary databases have read-only access to the data. Even though you cannot write any data to the secondary databases, you can write to individual databases that do not belong to the Availability Group, including System databases such as tempdb. An instance of SQL Server can concurrently host multiple availability replicas along with databases that do not belong to an Availability Group.

> **NOTE** *For an explanation of the descriptive option settings for the Readable Secondary for the replica when it is configured as a secondary replica, refer to Table 25-3.*

As shown in Table 25-5, the initial primary replica, SQLHA1, enables read-write connections, and the secondary replica, SQLHA2, enables all direct connections, including connections that do not include the Application Intent property. When a failover occurs, the replicas switch roles; SQLHA2 (which now runs under the primary role) enables read-write connections, whereas SQLHA1 (which now runs under the secondary role) disallows all direct connections.

TABLE 25-5: Readable Secondary Behavior

REPLICA NAME	INITIAL ROLE	READABLE SECONDARY
SQLHA1	Primary	No
SQLHA2	Secondary	Yes

Secondary Replica Client Connectivity

When an Availability Group failover occurs, existing persistent connections to the Availability Group are terminated and the client applications must re-establish a new connection. On failover, the replicas switch roles, where the secondary replica becomes the primary. When this occurs, you want another secondary replica to take over the read-only reporting. To do so, the client applications executing read-only reporting need to know how to connect to the next available read-only secondary replicas. You can connect to a secondary replica that supports read-only access in one of two ways: either directly by specifying the SQL Server instance name in the connection string, or by using the Availability Group Listener name and leveraging read-only routing to reconnect to the next available secondary read-only replica.

Read-only routing route connections that come into an Availability Group Listener change over to a secondary replica that is configured to enable read-only workloads. Read-only routing works only if the connection string references an Availability Group Listener. An incoming connection referencing an Availability Group Listener name can automatically be routed to a read-only replica if the following are true:

➤ The application intent of the incoming connection is set to read-only.

➤ The connection access supported on the secondary replica is set to read-only.

➤ The READ_ONLY_ROUTING_URL for each replica is set by the CREATE or ALTER AVAILABILILTY GROUP T-SQL command, as part of the SECONDARY_ROLE replica options. You must set this option before configuring the read-only routing list.

➤ The READ_ONLY_ROUTING_LIST is set for each replica in the CREATE AVAILABILITY GROUP or ALTER AVAILABILITY GROUP T-SQL command, as part of the PRIMARY_ROLE replica options.

➤ The READ_ONLY_ROUTING_LIST can contain one or more routing targets. You can configure multiple routing targets, and routing will take place in the order in which targets are specified in the routing list.

The following example demonstrates modifying an existing Availability Group for read-only routing support:

```
ALTER AVAILABILITY GROUP [AG1]
 MODIFY REPLICA ON
N'SQLHA1' WITH
(SECONDARY_ROLE (READ_ONLY_ROUTING_URL = N'TCP://SQLHA1. contoso.com:1433'));
ALTER AVAILABILITY GROUP [AG1]
 MODIFY REPLICA ON
N'SQLHA2' WITH
(SECONDARY_ROLE (READ_ONLY_ROUTING_URL = N'TCP://SQLHA2. contoso.com:1433'));
ALTER AVAILABILITY GROUP [AG1]
MODIFY REPLICA ON
N'SQLHA1' WITH
(PRIMARY_ROLE (READ_ONLY_ROUTING_LIST=('SQLHA2','SQLHA1')));
```

Then, based on the application intent specified in the connection string (read-write or read-only property), the client application will be directed to either the read-write or read-only replica. In this example, the application intent connection string property is read-only and the connection will be routed to the read-only secondary replica:

```
Server=tcp:AGListener,1433;Database=AdventureWorks;
    IntegratedSecurity=SSPI;ApplicationIntent=ReadOnly
```

Performance

To support concurrency, and to prevent readers and writers from blocking each other, snapshot isolation is enabled by default on the databases of the secondary replicas. When read-only secondary replicas are enabled, the primary databases add 14 bytes of overhead on deleted, modified, or inserted data rows to store pointers to row versions on the secondary replica database(s). The row versioning structure is copied to the secondary databases, which generate row versions as needed by read-only workloads. Row versioning increases data storage in both the primary and secondary replicas. Also, as the 14-byte overhead is added to data rows, page splits may occur.

For running a read-only workload, often indexes may need to be created to support these read-only queries. Because the read-only secondary databases cannot create a new index, any indexes must be created in the primary replica, and have the data movement apply them to the secondary replicas.

Statistics on columns of tables and index views are transferred from the primary replica to the secondary replicas through the transaction record data movement, but the read-only workload in the secondary replica may require additional statistics. This is addressed where temporary statistics are allowed to be created by SQL Server on the `tempdb` of each secondary replica. If you need to create statistics yourself, you must create them in the primary replica. Keep the following actions in mind when creating these statistics:

➤ To delete temporary statistics, use the `DROP STATISTICS` T-SQL statement.

➤ Monitor statistics using the `sys.stats` and `sys.stats_columns` catalog views where `sys.stats` contains a column named `is_temporary`, to indicate which statistics are permanent and which are temporary.

➤ Temporary statistics will be automatically dropped if the secondary replica is restarted as `tempdb` is re-created or a failover event occurs and the replicas roles are switched.

The read-only secondary replicas are usually behind the primary replica (in most cases, by seconds) because secondary replicas are impacted by the following:

➤ The length of the database transaction.

➤ The workload on the secondary replica. The timely transaction record data movement processing may be reduced if the replica is busy running a read-only workload.

➤ The network latency between the primary and secondary replicas.

➤ When the workload is I/O-intensive (for example, when data is transferred to the secondary replicas), it can create index or bulk copy operations.

In addition, a query in the secondary replica will see data from the primary replica after the redo thread in the secondary replica has applied that data. The steps for data to arrive to a query on the secondary replica require the following operations (see Figure 25-16):

1. Data arrives to the secondary replica, and it is applied and hardened to the transaction log.

2. An acknowledgment is sent to the primary replica.

3. The redo thread applies the transaction log changes to the data page.

4. Then the query in the secondary replica can see the new data.

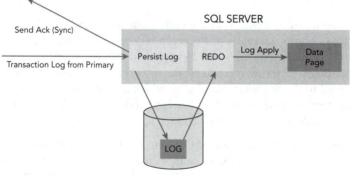

FIGURE 25-16

BACKUP ON THE SECONDARY REPLICA

One of the features of Availability Groups in SQL Server 2014 is that you can run backups from any availability primary or secondary replicas. Therefore, you can offload a backup that is a high I/O and CPU operation from the primary replica to a secondary replica. (See the earlier section, "Allowing Read-Only Access to Secondary Replicas," for more information.) By offloading the backup operations to a secondary replica, you can use the primary replica to run uninterrupted, mission-critical workloads that run the business. In addition, backups can be performed on either synchronous or asynchronous replicas, and transaction log backups across the replicas can be combined to form a single transaction log chain.

As shown in Figure 25-17, a copy-only full backup is supported on the secondary replicas for full database, files, and filegroups backups. This has the following characteristics:

➤ A *copy-only full backup* is a SQL Server backup that is independent of the sequence of conventional SQL Server backups. It doesn't affect the overall backup or restore procedures for the database.

➤ Copy-only full backups are supported in all recovery models.

➤ A copy-only full backup cannot serve as a differential base or differential backup, and does not affect the differential base. Differential backups are not supported on the secondary replicas.

➤ The secondary replica backup can be performed only when that secondary replica can communicate with the primary replica, and it is synchronized or in the process of synchronizing.

You can configure where the database backup jobs will be permitted to run in the primary or secondary replicas using the following settings during the CREATE AVAILABILITY GROUP and ALTER AVAILABILITY GROUP T-SQL statements:

➤ Configure the AUTOMATED_BACKUP_PREFERENCE option to determine whether the backups run as described in Figure 25-7.

➤ AUTOMATED_BACKUP_PREFERENCE is not enforced by SQL Server. You need to evaluate the AUTOMATED_BACKUP_PREFERENCE returned value and take it into account in your backup job logic to enforce it.

➤ If you don't want one of the availability replicas to run the backups, you can set the BACKUP_PRIORITY = 0, which means no backup will run on it.

➤ At the replica level, you can specify an ordered preference among secondary replicas for running database backup jobs by setting the BACKUP_PRIORITY to a value from 1 to 100, where 100 is the highest priority.

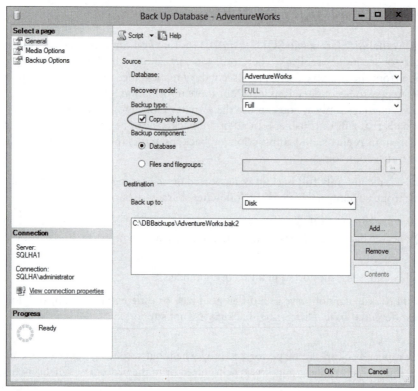

FIGURE 25-17

Evaluate Backup Replicas Metadata

You may want to know where the database backups are running to ensure that there is free storage available, and that the secondary replica has the performance capacity to execute the database backups. If you want to identiffy the preferred location of where your database backup would run, you can easily determine this by running this query:

```
SELECT automated_backup_preference, automated_backup_preference_desc
    FROM sys.availability_groups;
```

To interpret the returned values from the query, see Table-25-6 for a description of the `automated_backup_preference` and `automated_backup_preference_desc` columns.

TABLE 25-6: Values for the automated_backup_preference and automated_backup_preference_desc

COLUMN	VALUE
automated_backup_preference	0 = Performing backups on the primary replica is preferable.
	1 = Performing backups on a secondary replica is preferable.
	2 = Performing backups on a secondary replica is preferable, but performing backups on the primary replica is acceptable if no secondary replica is available for backup operations.
	3 = No preference about whether backups are performed on the primary replica or on a secondary replica.
automated_backup_preference_desc	PRIMARY
	SECONDARY_ONLY
	SECONDARY
	NONE

You can easily determine the priority of a given availability replica to run the database backup relative to the other replicas by running the following query, where `backup_priority` represents the priority for performing backups on this replica relative to the other replicas in the same Availability Group. The value is an integer in the range of 0–100.

```
SELECT backup_priority FROM sys.availability_replicas;
```

ALWAYSON GROUP DASHBOARD

To monitor AlwaysOn Availability Groups, availability replicas, and availability databases in Microsoft SQL Server 2014, you can use the dashboard or Data Management Views (DMVs). From the dashboard, you can determine the health and performance of each Availability Group. To access the Availability Group Dashboard, follow these steps:

1. In SQL Server Management Studio, connect to the instance of SQL Server on which you want to run Availability Group Dashboard (which is either the primary or a secondary replica).

2. Expand the `AlwaysOn High Availability` and `Availability Groups` folders.

3. Right-click your Availability Group name (in this example, AG1), and then click Show Dashboard. Figure 25-18 shows the resulting dashboard.

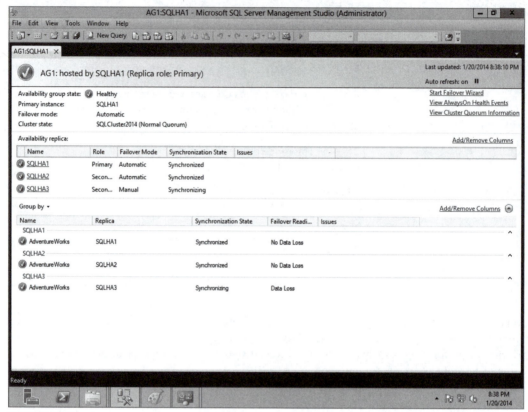

FIGURE 25-18

Table 25-7 gives an explanation of the key parameters that the dashboard displays.

TABLE 25-7: Important Dashboard Values

VALUE	DESCRIPTION
Availability Group State	Displays the state of health for the Availability Group.
Primary Instance	Name of the server instance that is hosting the primary replica of the Availability Group.

VALUE	DESCRIPTION
Failover Mode	Displays the failover mode for which the replica is configured. Following are the possible failover mode values: **Automatic:** Indicates that two replicas are in automatic-failover mode **Manual:** Indicates that no replica is in automatic-failover mode
Role	The current role of the availability replica values is Primary or Secondary.
Synchronization State	Indicates whether a secondary replica is currently synchronized with the primary replica. Following are the possible values: **Not Synchronized:** The database is not synchronized, or has not yet been joined to the Availability Group. **Synchronized:** The database is synchronized, with the primary database on the current primary replica (if any), or on the last primary replica. **NULL (Unknown):** This value occurs when the local server instance cannot communicate with the Windows Server Failover Clustering (WSFC) failover cluster (that is, the local node is not part of WSFC quorum). **Synchronizing:** The database is synchronizing with the primary database on the current primary replica (if any), or on the last primary replica.

Additionally, instead of using the AlwaysOn Group Dashboard, you can choose to use the `sys.dm_hadr_availability_replica_states` DMV to query for the preceding information.

MONITORING AND TROUBLESHOOTING

Like any solution, you must monitor an Availability Group as part of regular operations to identify any issues with the Availability Group that may prevent the data from being synchronized with the secondary replicas, or if failover to a secondary replica fails. To monitor Availability Groups, availability replicas, and availability databases using SQL Server Management Studio, follow these steps:

1. In SQL Server Management Studio, connect to the instance of SQL Server on which you want to monitor an Availability Group, and click the server name.

2. Expand the `AlwaysOn High Availability` and `Availability Groups` folders.

3. The Object Explorer Details pane displays every Availability Group for which the connected server instance hosts a replica. For each Availability Group, the Server Instance (Primary) column displays the name of the server instance currently hosting the primary replica. To display more information about a given Availability Group, select it in Object Explorer. The Object Explorer Details pane then displays the availability replicas and availability databases for the Availability Group.

To perform detailed monitoring and troubleshooting, use the DMVs provided in Table 25-8 to identify, verify, and to then troubleshoot an Availability Group.

TABLE 25-8: Monitoring and Troubleshooting for Availability Groups

DMV	DESCRIPTION
sys.availability_groups	Returns a row for each Availability Group for which the local instance of SQL Server hosts an availability replica.
sys.dm_hadr_availability_group_states	Returns a row for each Availability Group that possesses an availability replica on the local instance of SQL Server.
sys.availability_replicas	Returns a row for every availability replica in each Availability Group for which the local instance of SQL Server hosts an availability replica.
sys.dm_hadr_availability_replica_states	Returns a row showing the state of each local availability replica, and a row for each remote availability replica in the same Availability Group.
sys.dm_hadr_database_replica_states	Returns a row for each database that is participating in any Availability Group for which the local instance of SQL Server is hosting an availability replica.
sys.dm_hadr_database_replica_cluster_states	Returns a row containing information to provide detail into the health of the availability databases in each Availability Group on the Windows Server Failover Clustering (WSFC) cluster.
sys.availability_group_listener_ip_addresses	Returns a row for every IP address that is currently online for an Availability Group Listener.
sys.availability_group_listeners	For a given Availability Group, returns either zero rows indicating that no network name is associated with the Availability Group, or returns a row for each Availability Group Listener configuration in the WSFC cluster.
sys.dm_tcp_listener_states	Returns a row containing dynamic-state information for each TCP listener.
sys.fn_hadr_is_primary_replica	Returns a 1 when the current database is running on the primary replica; otherwise, returns a 0.

SUMMARY

AlwaysOn Availability Groups provide a robust high-availability solution that supports up to nine partners. You can configure this solution for synchronization and asynchronization modes with no shared disk infrastructure using a network name to seamlessly fail over client applications across the replicas. You can also use the secondary replicas to perform backup and to run read-only operations, therefore offloading the primary replica. The Availability Group functionality leverages the best of breeds between Windows Failover Clustering and SQL Server Data Mirroring and more to deliver a feature set to support mission-critical applications throughout the enterprise.

INDEX

O

P

Try Safari Books Online FRE
for 15 days and take 15% of
for up to 6 Months*

Gain unlimited subscription access to thousands of books and videos.

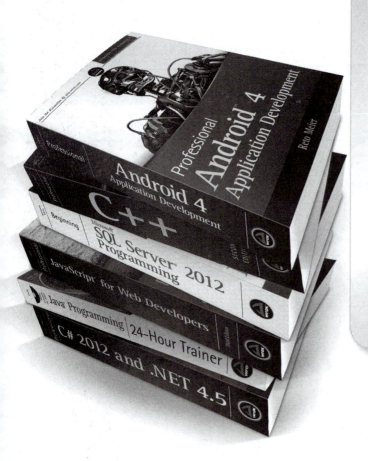

With Safari Books Online, learn without limits from thousands of technology, digital media and professional development books and videos from hundreds of leading publishers. With a monthly or annual unlimited access subscription, you get:

- Anytime, anywhere mobile access with Safari To Go apps for iPad, iPhone and Android

- Hundreds of expert-led instructional videos on today's hottest topics

- Sample code to help accelerate a wide variety of software projects

- Robust organizing features including favorites, highlights, tags, notes, mash-ups and more

- Rough Cuts pre-published manuscripts

START YOUR FREE TRIAL TODAY!

Visit: www.safaribooksonline.com/wrox

Safari
Books Online

wrox

An Imprint of W
Now you know